TECHNIQUES OF GUIDANCE

EDUCATION FOR LIVING SERIES
Under the Editorship of H H. REMMERS

TECHNIQUES OF GUIDANCE

ARTHUR E. TRAXLER

LECTURER IN EDUCATION, UNIVERSITY OF MIAMI
FORMERLY PRESIDENT AND EXECUTIVE DIRECTOR, EDUCATIONAL RECORDS BUREAU

ROBERT D. NORTH

ASSOCIATE DIRECTOR, PROFESSIONAL EXAMINATIONS DIVISION,
THE PSYCHOLOGICAL CORPORATION
FORMERLY VICE PRESIDENT AND ASSOCIATE DIRECTOR, EDUCATIONAL RECORDS BUREAU

 3rd EDITION

HARPER & ROW, PUBLISHERS, NEW YORK AND LONDON

To
The Member Schools
and the Staff
of
The Educational Records Bureau

Contents

Foreword

When the first edition of this book was published in the spring of 1945, I had been associated for some nine years with the Educational Records Bureau, the main function of which is to assist its member institutions in the use of objective techniques in guidance and instruction. The Bureau helps the schools to plan two testing programs annually; fills orders for the tests recommended for these programs; provides scoring, statistical, and reporting services; maintains a cumulative record service; carries on research with the test results; and makes suggestions concerning the uses and the limitations of the results by means of personal interviews, correspondence, and publications.

In that edition, I attempted, in an objective, straightforward way, to present for a larger audience the Bureau's point of view and procedures with regard to testing and guidance. The central idea was to gather as much relevant information as possible about each pupil, organize it so that it would show both status at any given time and growth over a period of years, and use these data to understand pupils, to help them understand themselves, and to help them in choosing among educational and vocational opportunities and in adjustment.

Since questions received from those who performed guidance functions showed that specific information and concrete suggestions were especially needed and desired, the book included much detailed explanation concerning tests and other instruments of evaluation, as well as a large number of illustrative record forms. The book appeared just at the end of World War II when the development of instruments and techniques of educational measurement was practically at a standstill, and when most school guidance programs were either frozen at their prewar level or had retrogressed.

Twelve years later, when the second edition was published in the spring of 1957, test development activities had gone into high gear once more, and guidance programs were being undertaken in a variety of forms by numerous schools which had had no such activities previously. Also, several professional groups, such as clinical psychologists, psychotherapists, and proponents of sociometry, had become much more active in guidance than they were formerly.

Some of their points of view that were impinging on the guidance area tended to vary widely. Hence, the guidance scene at that time was changing rapidly and somewhat indistinct. However, the most notable changes were still in the future.

It will be recalled that the year 1957 was the year of Sputnik I and that during the following year the National Defense Education Act of 1958 was passed. Under Title V of that Act, for the first time in our history, rather ample federal funds became available to encourage the development of testing and guidance programs, and the training of counselors.

The ensuing years have seen a release of energy and a revision and renewal of the total educational effort unlike anything in previous history. Greatly enlarged guidance efforts and, concomitantly, expanded testing programs have become a part of this new development.

At the same time, there has come from within the guidance field itself a strong drive toward higher professionalization of guidance and counseling. Standards with regard to the training of counselors have become accepted, and most states now have laws pertaining to the certification of counselors.

Counselors speak fluently of the need for the development of a self-concept on the part of each counselee, while, at the same time, counseling as a profession has been seeking a self-concept for itself.

The guidance field is today, even more than it was a dozen years ago, both a meeting ground and a battleground of theoretical viewpoints. What is the counselor's role? Is it primarily to work hand in hand with the school administration? Is it to serve as therapist, or even on occasion as psychiatrist without portfolio? Or is it to be the counselee's advocate in his ceaseless striving with the home and with the school for independence and maturity?

Theorists may ultimately decide these crucial questions within their own ranks, but in the meantime the total guidance program in thousands of schools must go on, and there is evidence that it *is* going on without much preoccupation with theory, but with far more understanding than was true of the guidance programs of the past. Surveys also indicate that while many laymen and some authorities in the guidance field deplore the wide use of tests with students at all educational levels, the schools themselves believe that tests and other evaluative devices *are* important in carrying on their guidance services. In fact, they are using more tests than ever before and are searching eagerly for ways to use more effectively the great wealth of test data that the new computers and data-processing equipment have placed within their reach.

As it has been since the first edition, the approach of this book to guidance services tends to be scientific rather than intuitive. For, while it is imperative that everyone recognize that there is an element of error in all measurement and observation, it is believed that objective data treated cumulatively and studied with understanding by both the counselor and counselee will help to provide a better basis for decisions than will intuition and subjective judgment alone, however sophisticated the latter may be. So, this edition of the book, like the preceding ones, is written from that viewpoint. But it is recognized, too, that clinical psychology, psychotherapy, projective techniques, and group dynamics all have important contributions to make to the total job of guiding students and making it possible for them to guide themselves. Counseling is, most of all, a *learning* process, and who can say, a priori, which learning process is best suited to an individual young person?

The present book is a rather thorough revision of the 1957 edition. The general organization and chapter headings have been retained, and one new chapter has been added. Many of the chapters have been fairly extensively rewritten, and hundreds of recent references have been consulted and cited.

It is an especial pleasure to welcome as coauthor of the new edition Dr. Robert D. North of The Psychological Corporation, and formerly of the staff of the Educational Records Bureau. For about eleven years he and I worked together very closely on all matters pertaining to the program of the Bureau. Dr. North took almost complete responsibility for Chapters V, VI, and VII, jointly with me wrote the final chapter, and has been an invaluable adviser and contributor to the other chapters. The revision of the book has taken much of our time for more than a year.

As was true of the preceding revision, my own part in preparing this revision would have been completely impossible without the intelligent and devoted collaboration of my secretary, Marguerite McCarthy Vecchione. She not only typed and helped organize the manuscript, but she checked innumerable details and references and read the whole thing critically. Dr. North's secretary, Mary Crowe Kraljic, likewise, rendered splendid service in the preparation of the manuscript.

As indicated at the beginning of this foreword, this book, in a sense, grows out of the testing and guidance programs of the institutional members of the Educational Records Bureau. Many of these have carried on annual fall and spring schoolwide testing programs for thirty-five years or more. During the period spanned by the three editions, the number of Bureau member schools has almost tripled—from about 380 schools in 1945, to approximately 675 in 1957, to more than 950 in 1965—and most of the newer members are likewise carrying on regular measurement programs as one of the main bases of their guidance services. Dr. North joins with me in acknowledging our debt of gratitude to the member schools of the Bureau for continuing to demonstrate that pupil guidance and the individualization of instruction should have a factual and scientific basis.

Dr. North and I also owe a great debt of gratitude to Dr. and Mrs. Ben D. Wood, who more than any others have been responsible for building and maintaining the Educational Records Bureau. We are likewise deeply in the debt of Dr. H. H. Remmers, editor emeritus of this series, who persuaded the senior author to write the book in the first place and who gave extremely helpful editorial counsel on the subsequent editions.

Finally, the understanding attitudes and sympathetic interest of our wives, Bobbi Traxler and Janet North, made it possible for us to find the time and energy to complete this job.

Arthur E. Traxler

New York City

TECHNIQUES OF GUIDANCE

CHAPTER I

Background and Orientation

THE TERMS "GUIDANCE SERVICES," "COUNSELING," and "personnel work" were rarely, if ever, used in a school setting until the twentieth century. Since about 1910, however, these terms have gradually found their way into common usage until they have become part of the basic vocabulary of education, although their meanings have varied.

The rapid development of guidance in the schools of the United States has been due mainly to new social conditions and needs, to a new psychology which has emphasized individual differences and the development of a self-concept by each person, to new techniques for studying individuals, and to an expanded idea of the function of the school as a social institution.

Psychologically, a need for guidance is found wherever the environment is sufficiently complex to permit a variety of responses and whenever individuals are not equipped to react instinctively or habitually to the stimuli of the environment. Among animals and in primitive social orders, the guidance of youth is taken care of by the parents. Even in an advanced but fairly homogeneous civilization, the home can continue to be the chief guidance agency. Thus, in the largely agrarian society which obtained in the United States until the early 1900s, there was no keenly felt need for organized guidance other than that provided by the family.

It is unnecessary to point out that within the last half century our environment has become more and more complex and that we can anticipate an ever-growing complexity in the future. The astonishing development of pure and applied science and the mechanization and electronization of industry have led to minute vocational specialization and to an infinite number of vocational choices, many of which are new and require an ever-higher degree of basic education and training.

The growth of huge industries and the pyramiding of the financial structure have led to dense concentrations of the population in certain areas; the attendant sociological problems are pertinent to all age levels, but particularly to youth. The proximity in which people dwell, the speed of travel, the incredible speed of machine computation, the impact of new means of communication, the greatly increased amount of leisure time which new inventions and modern living have brought—all these have contributed to the confusion of millions of our youth and to an alarming rise in juvenile delinquency, a major concern of the entire nation. We seek to meet the situation, which often assumes the character of a crisis, by enlisting the help of all our social institutions, especially our schools.

The attempt of the schools to keep pace with the ever-growing need for social and industrial education and, at the same time, to promote that kind of liberal education conducive to the development of creative minds and stable personal qualities has so expanded the curriculum that the pupil is presented with a bewildering array of subject choices; frequently he has little or no information concerning those for which he is best fitted. The needs for guidance created by these comparatively new conditions have been greatly intensified by the circumstances attendant upon three shooting wars and a cold war of indeterminate duration that seems to go through endless cycles of tension and uneasy relaxation.

At the same time, changing environmental conditions have placed a much greater responsibility upon young people for making wise choices, and have allowed them less margin for error. Educational and psychological agencies have become aware of large differences among individuals in their potential for success in different areas. The application of measurement techniques and statistical methods has indicated that individuals tend to distribute themselves widely on almost every measurable characteristic, and that, in many instances, although not in all, the distributions assume the appearance of the normal, or bell-shaped, curve. It should not be inferred, of course, that the position of an individual on this curve is fixed and unchangeable, but at any given time it is important for the individual to have as much information available as possible concerning his current level of ability.

Our increasingly complex environment and awareness of individual differences make an attempt at guidance in the schools inevitable. Regardless of differences in theoretical concepts concerning the function of counseling, such an attempt would be largely characterized by trial and error were it not that techniques of measuring and recording observations have laid the basis for an applied science of guidance. A main purpose of this book is to provide a description and illustration of the application of this modern science to the problems of youth.

It is true, of course, that schools have always provided some guidance for their pupils, even though they may not have used the word guidance. The very routine of enrolling pupils, holding classes, forming personal relationships, and carrying on the work of instruction makes it inevitable that pupils will, to some extent, be guided. In the past, however, schools have rarely taken full advantage of their opportunities for guidance because they have not clearly recognized their responsibility in this respect; and, too, they have often been more concerned over the details of the curriculum and the maintenance of academic standards than over the adjustment of young people to the school environment and to the broader and far more complicated environment of postschool life. Until fairly recently, the guidance afforded by most schools had not been organized and well planned, but had been left largely to the individual initiative of the principal and the several teachers.

Systems of planned, organized guidance began to appear in the schools of the United States about 1910. So rapidly has the guidance movement grown that at present nearly all the more forward-looking high schools and many of the elementary schools provide some kind of individual guidance for their pupils. Of necessity, schools attempt to reduce the counseling load by means of group guidance procedures where such procedures are applicable.

MEANING OF GUIDANCE

Guidance is one of the most difficult of all educational subjects to discuss because of the past and continuing confusion and uncertainty concerning its nature and function. Many persons feel that guidance is as broad as all education and that the whole program of the school should be organized for guidance purposes, whereas others would restrict it to some relatively narrow aspects such as vocational or personal and moral guidance. Some guidance programs consist largely of courses in occupational information. The main emphasis in other guidance programs is on the placement of pupils in courses in such manner as to eliminate or reduce failure, or to allow those with special abilities to proceed at a more rapid rate. Still other programs stress therapy and the treatment of adjustment difficulties as the main purpose of the counseling relationship. Not infrequently, character building is stressed in guidance. Too often, one fears, the guidance program consists of little more than approval of a nebulous concept, useful in the public relations of the school but having little influence on the lives of the individual pupils. Fortunately, this is less true than it was 25 years ago or even 10 years ago, but it is still characteristic of the practice of guidance in too many schools.

Not only is there lack of agreement concerning guidance in its totality, but there is also misapprehension in regard to the main divisions of the guidance field. Notwithstanding the critical attitude maintained for years by various authorities on guidance, there continue to flourish the popular misconceptions that there is a logical cleavage between educational guidance and vocational guidance, and another cleavage between these two and guidance concerned with adjustment problems. It should be clearly understood that all three are inextricably interwoven. While there may be differences in emphasis on one or another aspect at various age levels and with different individuals, no realist will try to separate them. The division of guidance into adjustment and distribution, as advised many years ago by Koos and Kefauver (23)[1] and others, is a much more pertinent distinction, but even this division is for convenience in thinking rather than functional. In working with individual cases, counselors often find that the key to adjustment is better distribution of the pupils to the offerings of the school. Or, conversely, they find that the resolution of adjustment problems removes blocks to learning and facilitates placement of "problem" pupils in regular class groups.

The practice of guidance is a whole process, as unitary as the lives of the individuals with which it deals. No school can successfully engage in a few selected aspects of guidance, because the personalities of individuals cannot be divided into compartments. Hence, no school

[1] The numbers in parentheses refer to numbered items in the list of references at the end of the chapter. Item numbers are in italics and page numbers in roman.

should attempt a guidance program unless it is willing ultimately to undertake all phases of it. This is not to say that a school unable to launch a full-scale guidance program at the outset should hesitate to begin in a small way, if it has plans for gradually broadening and improving its services.

Ideally conceived, guidance enables each individual to know his abilities, interests, and personality traits, to develop them as well as possible, to keep them flexible in order to meet the demands of a fluid environment, to relate them to his life goals and to clarify these goals, and finally to reach a state of complete and mature self-guidance as a desirable citizen of our democratic social order and of the world. Guidance is thus vitally related to every aspect of the school: the curriculum, the methods of instruction, the supervision of instruction, disciplinary procedures, attendance, problems of scheduling, the extracurriculum, the health and physical fitness program, and home and community relations. This, of course, implies the closest kind of cooperation between guidance functionaries and all the other members of the staff, because those charged with responsibility for the guidance program cannot be specialists in all these fields. Their functions are to collect and to synthesize accurate information about pupils, to provide an individual counseling service coordinated with group guidance relative to certain areas such as vocational exploration, and to carry on a dynamic educational program among their colleagues and the parents—one that will lead to intelligent use of the information that the guidance department is able to provide.

INFLUENCES THAT HAVE CREATED GUIDANCE PROGRAMS

The varied status of guidance in American schools may be traced in part to the diversified nature of the factors which have been influential in the conception and development of guidance programs. Historically, the guidance movement stems mainly from five divergent and highly dissimilar sources. One of the oldest of these is *philanthropy,* or *humanitarianism,* which stresses benevolent regard for the welfare of mankind. The philanthropists or humanitarians look on life about them and, seeing the many misfits, particularly in the vocations, they say, "People should be guided when they are young so that these maladjustments will be reduced or eliminated. This is a job for the schools." Here was the impelling force which led Frank Parsons, often called the "father of the vocational guidance movement," to launch his Vocational Bureau of Boston. Similar motivation was

back of the efforts of the High School Teachers Association under the leadership of Eli W. Weaver in New York City, the Consumers' League of Philadelphia, the Schmidlapp Fund in Cincinnati, the Civic Club of Chicago, and many others, as attempts at guidance multiplied in cities across the nation during the second decade of this century.

Another old and strong source of the guidance movement is *religion.* The religious man looks upon the world, and sees what he interprets as a constant struggle between the forces of righteousness and those of evil. In turn, he says, "We must get hold of people when they are very young and train them for the good life. We must build character in our youth." And so he has customarily looked to the educational system to help him with this task, and rightly so, because it is the school which has the inside track. Nearly every school administrator has, on occasion, felt the relentless pressure of religious guidance groups.

A third, and more recent, but in some respects similar, guidance source is *mental hygiene,* with its present-day counterparts in *counseling psychology, clinical psychology,* and *psychiatry.* This school of thought sees in adjustment problems a need for mental and emotional therapy. According to this point of view, people should, when they are young, be taught a realistic perspective of their abilities in relation to life goals; be taught to prefer overt, frank, open behavior to retiring, secretive behavior; to understand the significance of sex and to take a rational attitude toward it; to meet problems squarely rather than to retire into fantasy and other forms of escapism; to avoid infantile fixations detrimental to the development of a set of maturing interests; to develop a clear and sensible concept of self; to evolve gradually from a state of parental dependence to one of self-dependence through demonstrated achievement in fields within their own capacity; and to assume other qualities which characterize a healthy, adult mental and emotional state. Anyone who has ever had the privilege of observing as a competent psychiatrist struggles through an hour interview with a shy, introverted child, and seeks to draw him out and to understand the organization of his tight little personality, knows that here is an intricate and sometimes extremely difficult aspect of guidance. There are clinics that handle this kind of guidance for markedly neurotic children, but even individuals within the normal range occasionally need guidance in mental hygiene. For the great mass of children, this function must be performed by the school; so still another guidance force impinges upon the school, one that inevitably implies the employment of specialists to cooperate in meeting this need.

A fourth source of interest in guidance manifests itself

so notably through the administrative aspect of the school that we are sometimes misled into thinking that it originates with administrators, when, as a rule, it stems from *social change*. In brief, during the period between the two world wars technological unemployment, a world-wide depression, rising ethical standards with respect to child labor, compulsory school attendance laws, and similar forces drove into the secondary school thousands of young people who had no marked desire to be there, had no clear idea why they were there or what they expected to get from their secondary school training, and did not know where they were going when they were to leave school. Pressure of numbers and the essentially nonacademic character of these pupils created a whole set of new problems for administrators.

As a natural first step, they greatly broadened the curriculum to provide for this horde of young people, but they soon saw clearly that this was not enough. They found that the outstanding need was for individual attention and counseling to help each pupil marshal his assets of aptitude and previous training in order to find his way through the complex school environment, and the still more complex environment outside the school, to a personal and economic self-dependence and security. The administrator, realizing his inability to cope with the situation singlehanded, naturally tried to utilize the counseling resources of his staff, notwithstanding that the staff often had no previous training for this work and no real knowledge of the pupils as individuals. From this source many guidance programs were introduced. Some turned out to be highly successful, but many could not function effectively because the teachers were almost as bewildered by the situation as the pupils, and neither teachers nor pupils had any tangible basis on which to begin the personnel work.

After the conditions of the mid-1930s had led numerous school administrators to take a cordial and very practical interest in the development of guidance services, our country went through the greatest war in history, followed after a brief interval by a war of limited scope —both of which created temporarily abnormal demands for the services of young people, either in the Armed Forces or in war-related industries, and gave them an unparalleled breadth of experience. Upon our return to an uneasy normalcy, the schools once more bulged with pupils, with the crest of the tidal wave created by a markedly increased birth rate moving steadily upward through the schools. The need for guidance, both extensively and intensively, became greater than it had ever been.

In the late 1950s and the early 1960s, all the civilized world, and particularly the schools, were shaken by two additional forces of awesome power. One of these broke upon us suddenly in 1957 when the Russians launched Sputnik I and ushered in the "space age." The other, less dramatic, was the development of electronic computers and data processing equipment, and its immediate acceptance and use by government, business, industry, the professions, and other walks of life. These forces have changed and are still changing our social and economic structure in ways and in directions that we do not yet see clearly. The problems of educating and guiding young people to live in, and contribute usefully to, the new and changing environment are still too stupendous for anyone to grasp fully.

But, on the whole, our schools are far better prepared to meet guidance needs now than they were during the first mass attempts at guidance programs prior to World War II, for they have acquired three decades of experience, and they have at their disposal many special services not available 30 years ago. The schools with more advanced personnel programs now exhibit an erudition concerning guidance problems formerly confined mainly to university departments of psychology, and it appears that the schools which have made only average progress with guidance services are now at a stage equal to that of the best schools a quarter of a century ago.

The fifth of the major sources of the guidance movement is one that has usually been identified in our thinking with the measurement movement in education, but which, when it is analyzed, is seen to involve a much broader concept. That is, the simple yet fundamental thesis that the first duty of the school is *to know its pupils as individuals and to enable each individual to understand himself*. It involves, first, a recognition of the essential dignity and worth of the individual and, second, a willingness to study him and help him study himself by every means which the resources of the school can command. Those who take this approach to guidance point out that in any large school it is virtually impossible for any one person to know more than a few of the pupils well enough to attempt to provide guidance on the basis of personal acquaintance alone. The solution for this seeming impasse, they insist, is for each school to make a systematic collection of information about each individual and then to pool its essential knowledge year after year. The physical manifestation of this pooling of information is the cumulative record, a device which is itself undergoing metamorphosis because of the development of data processing equipment. For the collection of data for the cumulative record, objective tests are the most useful instrument yet devised, but they are by no means the only instrument. Social history records, health records, rating scales, anecdotal records, marks and similar records of school progress, and other procedures can contribute pertinent information to this record.

Beginning in the early 1940s, an additional, a sixth, influence strongly affected guidance work, both in schools and outside. This influence can hardly be regarded as a source of the guidance movement, but it has tended to revamp guidance philosophy and reshape counseling procedures in many ways. This is the school of *nondirective therapy,* or *client-centered counseling,* initiated by Carl Rogers and long under his leadership. More will be said about the Rogerian influence upon guidance and counseling later. Suffice it here to point out that, while it may be questioned whether the guidance program at the school level can or should be strictly nondirective, Rogers and his associates performed a distinct service in helping to neutralize the highly directive, paternal, authoritarian methods which too often characterized the clumsy efforts at counseling in the earlier stages of guidance in the schools of the United States.

With its beginnings in 1958, a seventh influence has had a great effect on the initiation, growth, and development of guidance programs, particularly in public secondary schools. This is Title V of the National Defense Education Act, which was enacted in 1958 and revised and strengthened in 1963 (*11, 30*). This legislation, through making greatly needed federal funds available to the schools, has probably done more than anything else to turn dreams and theoretical concepts into actuality.

This 1963 legislation was embodied in Public Law 88-210 which consists of three parts, of which Parts A and B are of particular interest to guidance personnel. Part A is the Vocational Education Act of 1963, and Part B amends NDEA and extends the coverage downward to include Grades 7 and 8 in addition to Grades 9–12. In 1963, the Manpower Development and Training Act was likewise amended in order to attack the most difficult problems of training for employment. The amendments are contained in Public Law 88-214.

When the guidance movement is seen as resulting from so many influences, there can be little wonder that there has been a good deal of confusion and uncertainty in and about the guidance field. The concept of the cumulative record, and of the systematic collection of information for it by means of regular testing and other procedures, was one of the last to develop. This has been unfortunate, for it is believed that this aspect of guidance is basic to the successful functioning of all other aspects. The development of dynamic guidance programs throughout the schools of this country depends, in large measure, upon a realization that we must first of all make personnel work a science, that we must assemble the facts, so far as we can determine them, about our students, and merge these facts with those overtones of personal relationship and those inspirational qualities which can contribute a great deal, provided they are founded on understanding on the part of counselors and counselees alike.

Many schools, when planning a guidance program, begin by giving detailed attention to the kind of guidance structure that should be developed and to who should coordinate the guidance work. These are important, but not the matters of first importance. The first duty of schools charged with the development of a guidance program is to build a plan that will enable the school to *know its pupils.* As Dr. Ben D. Wood began urging upon educators many years ago, this is "the major strategy of guidance." Without it, no type of guidance organization can have any important effect upon the lives of the pupils. With it, a school can achieve considerable success with almost any kind of guidance setup, provided the data are interpreted by trained and experienced professionals. It will be desirable, however, to consider briefly the general types of guidance organizations that have been developed in our secondary schools.

STAFF ORGANIZATION FOR GUIDANCE

The guidance organization and its functionaries vary greatly from school to school. In a good many small schools that have no clearly defined counseling program, the principal is still the chief guidance officer. In some fairly large schools, the work of guidance is carried on by the assistant principals or by the "dean of boys" or "dean of girls," although the latter terms are used less frequently now than they formerly were. In others, homeroom teachers, under the leadership of the principal or director of guidance, conduct such guidance functions as can be carried on in an essentially classroom setting. However, in recent years, some have found the homeroom inadequate and have come to regard it with disfavor. In many small schools and some larger ones, an attempt is made to use the majority of the teachers as guidance functionaries. Many of the larger school systems employ a professionally trained guidance director and a staff of trained counselors, quite apart from the staff of teachers, to carry on the personnel work. There is a steadily growing trend in this direction. Visiting teachers are an important guidance agency in a number of school systems. Finally, in a considerable proportion of the large and medium-size schools, committees on guidance services, whose members have been specially selected from the teaching staff and trained in NDEA guidance institutes, carry on guidance functions.

Because of differences in local situations, it would not be advisable to recommend the adoption of any one type of guidance structure to the exclusion of all others. Two rather definite trends, however, may be noted. One is the tendency to separate as much as possible the functions of guidance from those of administration. Good administrative officers who perform their tasks with imagination will, of course, always do important guidance work, but experience indicates that the relationships between the pupils and those charged with the special responsibility of counseling are likely to be more natural and cordial if the counselors perform no administrative or disciplinary functions. In the small proportion of

fill this position it may be necessary to go outside the local school system. But counselors frequently may be recruited from the regular teaching staff and given opportunities for special study and training to fit them for their new tasks. Teachers have always of necessity performed many of the functions of guidance; consequently, every experienced teacher has already had some experience in this field, though he may never have considered his work in that light. Not every teacher has the potential to make a good guidance officer. Some authorities, in fact, go so far as to say that a school is fortunate

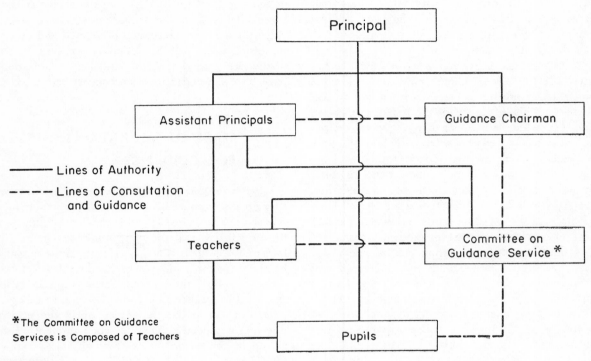

FIGURE 1.

schools where a major share of the counseling is done by assistant principals or deans, emphasis should be placed upon the guidance functions of these principals or deans, and discipline should be a minor part of their work. The well-qualified dean usually considers his most important function that of working with and through teacher-counselors, guidance personnel, or by means of whatever type of organization is used to provide a counselor for every student.

The other trend in guidance organization is toward the establishment of a closer relationship between guidance and teaching. It is essential that the guidance director be a person with special training in psychology, personnel work, and educational measurement, and to

if one fourth of its teachers can be trained for guidance work, but nearly all agree that a school's own staff can be an important source of counselors. Even those teachers who do not have direct responsibility for counseling can contribute a great deal to the guidance program of a school. All the teachers should be instructed in the guidance philosophy of the school and in the legitimate use of guidance records.

If a school adopts a policy of drawing all or nearly all its counselors from its teaching staff, one important question still remains to be decided. Shall the counselors be withdrawn from teaching entirely—except, perhaps, for giving orientation courses in occupations—and their places on the teaching staff filled by new appointees?

Or shall the guidance work be spread as widely as possible and each counselor retain perhaps four fifths of his former teaching load? There are advantages to both plans, and successful programs of both types are in operation. If the counselors give all or nearly all their time to personnel work, their interests will center in it, their professional growth as counselors will probably be greater, and they will not have their loyalty and efforts divided

stages of both individual guidance and the individualization of instruction are almost identical, and it may be economical and efficient to have the same functionaries engage in both types of activity.

A graphic representation of lines of relationship in a guidance program which was organized on the basis of a committee on guidance services consisting of 25 classroom teachers under the chairmanship of a specialist in

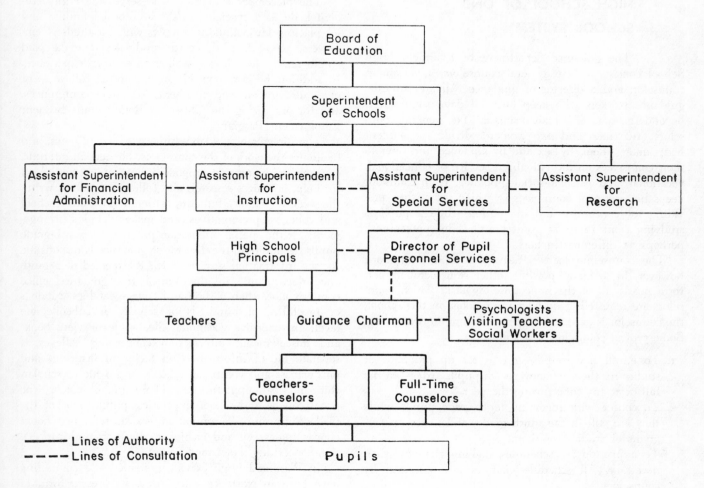

FIGURE 2.

between guidance and teaching. On the other hand, if they continue to teach it is possible to arrange the pupils' programs so that the counselors have in class those pupils who are in their own guidance group; in this way, close acquaintance and mutual confidence between pupils and counselors may be fostered.

Perhaps the strongest argument favoring a close relationship between counseling and teaching is that in both it is necessary first of all to know each individual pupil, before their objectives can be realized. Thus, the initial

guidance and testing is shown in Figure 1. It will be observed that in this plan the lines of consultation and guidance are carefully differentiated from those of administration (authority).

The foregoing plan is suitable for small and medium-size high schools. A more complex plan of organization is, of course, required for the guidance services of an entire city school system. One such organization is shown in Figure 2.

For those who prefer information in verbal rather than

graphic form, a description of a guidance department in a high school of a small eastern city is given in the next section.

A BRIEF DESCRIPTION OF THE GUIDANCE DEPARTMENT OF THE HIGH SCHOOL OF ONE SCHOOL SYSTEM[2]

"The guidance department of Plainfield High School consists of four general counselors, a placement counselor, and a director of guidance. All are full-time guidance workers who keep busy all day, usually well beyond the time of school dismissal. The general counselors (two men and two women) divide the student body among them, by sex and by alphabet, and offer to their counselees an individualized service of educational, vocational, and personal-social guidance. Each counselor keeps his group of counselees for three years, thus providing for continuity and integration while a pupil is studying from 12 to 15 courses and is in contact with perhaps 25 different teachers.

"The counseling load is heavy for these counselors; however, in so far as possible, other staff members perform nearly all of the noncounseling tasks which counselors are required to do in many schools; in this school, the counselor is expected to spend his time in *counseling*. Some typical counselor duties are:

1. To enroll new pupils and to set up programs of studies for them whenever such pupils arrive—in the fall or at any time during the year.
2. To confer with incoming tenth-grade pupils while they are still in the ninth grade, and to set up programs of studies for them.
3. To adjust pupils' schedules, making changes when necessary. All schedule changes are processed by counselors.
4. To confer with pupils concerning subjects for the following year and/or post-high-school plans.
5. To interpret results of standardized tests to pupils, parents, and teachers.
6. To confer with pupils who are in academic difficulties.
7. To confer and cooperate with parents who are concerned about their children.
8. To prepare descriptive comments and to make recommendations on the transcripts which go to colleges and other post-high schools.

[2] Provided through the courtesy of Mr. William V. Sette, Director of Guidance, Plainfield High School, Plainfield, N.J.

9. To counsel pupils who have difficulties in interpersonal relationships, who show signs of emotional disturbance, who need more than casual support and encouragement, who have personal problems of one sort or another.
10. To recognize and refer to proper channels those cases which require more psychological training, more time, or better facilities than the counselor possesses.

"The placement counselor, who serves the entire student body, is a specialist in the area of job-finding and job-placing. He maintains contacts with hundreds of employers, keeps detailed records, and tries to make paid employment a *learning*, as well as an *earning*, experience. In addition, he is responsible for the initial follow-up of graduates, for an extensive series of career conferences, and for organizing the Christmas Retail Trade Student Employment Program.

"The director of guidance supervises, coordinates, and facilitates the work of the counselors. He acts on referrals, counsels graduates and dropouts who come to the school for help, organizes research and follow-up studies, writes the weekly guidance bulletin, confers with visiting school and college representatives, and makes detailed arrangements for the special orientation program for ninth-grade pupils. In addition, the director of guidance is responsible for the information service which is expected of a guidance department; in this school the guidance office contains more than a thousand college catalogs, catalogs or brochures of hundreds of schools of subcollegiate level, an extensive vocational file, a file of view books and miscellaneous information concerning colleges, a separate file of information on technical institutes and on business and vocational schools, and a file of scholarship and loan opportunities. There are, of course, the usual college and school directories, publications of the College Entrance Examination Board, reference books concerning careers and/or higher education, and information concerning the Armed Forces.

"In Plainfield High School, guidance and counseling have been in existence since 1936. Its present form in structure and procedure is the result of continuous study, evaluation, and evolution. We are still *evolving*, still trying to improve our services."

COSTS OF GUIDANCE

Most school administrators will agree that the essentials of guidance—a staff trained in counseling and in the interpretation and use of guidance data, a comprehensive testing program, a cumulative record system, and a library containing information on educational and vocational opportunities—are fine in theory, but sometimes they will feel that these are not possible for their own school because of the expense involved. This reluctance to enter into guidance commitments because of the costs has lessened, however, since the advent, in 1958, of the National Defense Education Act, which provides for federal aid to states in promoting guidance programs.

Various studies of the costs of guidance services have been made—such as one by Emery (13) in the early 1950s. Such studies are very useful in furnishing information on the level of guidance costs at any given time and in specific geographical areas, but steadily rising expenses of all kinds tend, after a few years, to make the reported costs too low. The percentage of the budget spent for guidance is probably a more stable figure. Emery found in the metropolitan Boston area that the percentage of the total school budget which went for guidance services ranged from 0.31 to 3.40, with an average of 1.64. These percentages seem very small for a service that is coming to be regarded as essential for a complete school program. More recent information is available from a study by Palm (32) among six high schools in the Minneapolis area. He found that the mean expenditure for guidance services was $24.98 per student, or 5.3 percent of the mean total high school expenditure.

The costs of guidance may be grouped under four main headings: personnel, clerical services for the maintenance of records, testing programs, and information materials. There is a fifth kind of cost that results from the physical requirements for counseling and other aspects of the guidance program, but frequently these requirements can be met through more efficient use of available space without actual additional financial outlay.

The cost of *guidance personnel* is likely to be much the largest item of expense. However, this cost varies greatly in different schools, depending on the plan adopted. At one extreme, there are schools in which the salary of a counselor for every 200 or 300 pupils and that of a director of guidance are added to the budget. At the other extreme, there are schools in which nothing is added for personnel because the work of guidance is absorbed by the existing staff. In the first group, the cost of guidance may be greater than it needs to be. In the second group, guidance usually suffers because of the rigorous economy: the guidance program is likely to start without the full approval of the staff and to be conducted in a desultory manner because it represents an added burden for which the teachers are not adequately prepared.

For many years, the guidance program in the Providence Public Schools seems to have met the problem of cost of personnel with unusual success. In 1938, the late Richard D. Allen, who was assistant superintendent in charge of guidance at Providence, published an article on the costs of guidance based on the experience of his school system (1). Although the detailed costs have increased greatly since that article was written, the essentials of the plan have stood the test of time and are still in use. In that school system, the group guidance instruction—including occupational information—has a recognized standing in the curriculum. Each counselor gives three fifths of his time to group guidance instruction, one fifth to other subject instruction, and one fifth to individual interviews with pupils. Since the four fifths of his time that is devoted to instruction would have to be taken over by the teaching staff even if the guidance program were discontinued, it is felt at Providence that the only cost for guidance personnel is the one fifth of each counselor's time that is given to interviews—the interviews being so scheduled that the counselor regularly has one conference of approximately 15 minutes' duration each term with each pupil in his group. At Providence, the annual cost of replacing, through the employment of new teachers, the time that is taken from instruction and given to individual interviews, is approximately $3.90 per pupil; that is, it is necessary to add one beginning teacher at a salary of $4600 a year for approximately every 1200 pupils interviewed by the counselors. If it were impossible to afford new teachers, it is estimated that the cost of interviewing could be absorbed by adding one pupil to each class in the school.

Admitting that this plan may involve some costs which do not appear on the surface, one must still be impressed by the relatively small cost of counseling personnel in a school system which has long maintained one of the foremost guidance programs in the United States. It should also be pointed out that the apparent cost may be more than balanced by the effect of the guidance program, not alone in values to pupils but in actual dollars and cents. Dr. Allen stated that when the guidance program was introduced into the Technical High School and Commercial High School in Providence, the savings resulting from reduction in failure and from elimination of small elective courses—which it had been necessary to maintain when the pupils did not have adequate guidance—were "equal to approximately five times the additional cost of the guidance department in these schools." Recent information received from the Providence schools indicates that this statement is currently applicable.

The cost of *services* for the maintenance of cumulative records depends upon the nature of the records, the care with which they are kept up to date, the degree of detail in the entries, the prevailing rates for clerical work, the degree to which the records are adapted to data processing, and various other factors. Published data on the cost of maintaining cumulative records are almost nonexistent. Some unpublished figures on this point were made available by the Plainfield, New Jersey, High School in the mid-1950s. This high school has long maintained a vigorous guidance program in which much use is made of the cumulative record, all parts of which are kept up to date. At the time the cost figures were released, the per-pupil cost for the record itself was about ten cents, and it was estimated that the yearly per-pupil cost of servicing the record was approximately fifty cents, making a total of $1.60 for the three senior-high-school years. Recent information indicates that the cost has risen at least 50 percent since the mid-1950s. Even so, it is doubtful that the amount spent for cumulative records could in any other way be invested in the education of the pupil so as to yield such high returns in increased educational efficiency.

The *testing program* is one of the main elements in the cost of guidance. As will be indicated in greater detail later, the basic program should consist of at least six tests annually: tests of academic aptitude and reading ability, and achievement tests in English, mathematics, and at least two of several other fields—science, social studies, foreign language, commercial subjects, fine arts, practical arts—depending on what the pupil is studying. The annual cost of six test booklets and six answer sheets for each pupil would be about $1.50, but this cost can be reduced materially through the repeated use of the same test booklets when the pupils record their responses on separate answer sheets. The cost of answer sheets varies from about four to eight cents each.

The cost of test material is usually the smallest part of the expense of a testing program. Under most conditions, the scoring and concomitant statistical work are more important items of cost. Teachers and counselors are frequently subjected to the drudgery of local scoring, but, if the average teacher's or counselor's time is worth more than that of the average scoring clerk or scoring machine, this is one of the most expensive ways of getting the scoring done.

If the tests in the guidance program are to be scored locally by hand, or if outside manual scoring services are utilized, probably the minimum amount that should be allowed for a testing program is $3.00 per pupil annually. However, many schools are able to reduce their testing costs materially through the use of machine scoring, either in the local school system or through a service agency.

The first test-scoring machine produced by the International Business Machines Corporation, the IBM 805, has been available since 1935. This machine greatly stimulated the development of large-scale testing programs, since it made possible the scoring of several hundred tests in an hour's time. When the responses were recorded with special pencils on separate answer sheets, either standardized tests or teacher-made tests could be scored in this way.

The IBM 805 contributed greatly to educational and psychological measurement, and, indirectly, to guidance services. However, it is now outdated. High-speed test-scoring machines—each of which is coordinated with other machines that will perform many other operations needed in the treatment of test data before they are ready for use in guidance—were produced by Dr. E. F. Lindquist of the State University of Iowa, by the Educational Testing Service, Princeton, New Jersey, by the National Computer Systems in Minneapolis, Minnesota, and by The Psychological Corporation, New York City. Special answer sheets are designed for each of these machines except that of the Psychological Corporation, which processes IBM 805 answer sheets. Schools and other organizations may arrange for test processing by means of this equipment.

Still more recent developments in machine scoring are the production by the International Business Machines Corporation of its 1230 scoring machine—which is much faster than the 805 and free from some of its limitations—and of the Digitek optical scoring machine by The Digitek Corporation, Fairless Hills, Pennsylvania. The 1230 scoring machine is available for local installation on a rental basis, just as the 805 was. The purchase price and the rental of the new IBM machine vary according to the special features desired, but the costs without the special features are: purchase price, $15,400; monthly rental, $220. The Digitek 100A Basic Machine sells for $17,985 or rents for $297 a month. A more extensive discussion of developments in machine scoring will be found in Chapter X.

It is obvious, of course, that only a fairly large school system can afford to maintain a test-scoring machine, such as the IBM, for its own exclusive use, but it may be feasible for a number of medium-size school systems in the same locality to cooperate in the use of a scoring machine in connection with their guidance programs. The possibilities of solving some of the problems of testing and guidance by cooperative effort deserve special consideration.

SOLVING GUIDANCE NEEDS THROUGH COOPERATION

Needless to say, measurement and cumulative records will not in themselves insure a worthwhile guidance program. The most important elements in guidance, as in instruction, are the quality and training of the personnel involved and their understanding of the psychology of the individual pupil.

At the same time, the thesis is widely accepted that a vitally important instrument for implementing guidance is the individual cumulative record, and that an indispensable source of data for the cumulative record is a well-organized testing program. Numerous schools that are otherwise fairly well prepared to carry on guidance services are notably weak in obtaining objective information on their pupils through measurement. Inertia, unfavorable attitudes toward objective procedures, lack of understanding of what is involved and how to proceed, and reluctance to pay for the minimum testing program that any specialist in guidance is willing to recommend seem almost insurmountable obstacles in many schools. A way of overcoming these obstacles is through the cooperation of the schools in each locality, working under the leadership of those who are conversant with both measurement and personnel work.

The first essential is to place a testing program within the reach of all schools. For this purpose, the state seems to be the logical unit for the public schools. According to replies to a questionnaire submitted in 1954, 26 states had statewide testing programs,[3] and the number has increased since that date. These range in scope from elaborate programs—such as the one in Iowa, which includes the construction of an extensive battery of tests, as well as the scoring of the tests and the reporting of results—to programs that consist of little more than the recommendation of a uniform set of tests throughout the state which may be used in establishing statewide norms. Among the largest and most thoroughly planned programs, in addition to the one in Iowa, are those in Connecticut, Florida, Illinois, Michigan, Minnesota, New York, Ohio, Tennessee, Virginia, and Wisconsin.

It is highly desirable for all public schools located in regions where a state testing program is available to take advantage of the testing services of their own state. For schools that do not have access to a state testing program, certain service agencies, such as Lindquist's Measurement Research Center at the University of Iowa and the Educational Records Bureau in New York, make scoring services available at nominal costs. Various test publishers, including the Educational Testing Service, The Psychological Corporation, Harcourt, Brace, and World, and the California Test Bureau, among others, specialize in scoring the tests which they publish.

States which have testing programs need to go beyond

providing the best possible machinery for the administration and scoring of tests. They need to conduct a program for educating the schools in the use of the results for guidance purposes. The lack of information about the proper use of tests in instruction and guidance is probably the greatest weakness in the average testing and guidance program. Gradually, however, materials on the use of tests prepared especially for teachers and counselors who are not highly trained in statistics, and even for parents, are being made available from various sources (2, 12, 33, 38). It is beleved that the use of such materials, in preparing the staff to carry on the functions of guidance, should be as much a part of the testing program as the administration of the tests themselves.

THE RELATION OF GUIDANCE TO EDUCATION IN A DEMOCRACY

It has been pointed out many times that individuals cannot be trained for life in a democratic state merely by rules and indoctrination, or simply by the establishment of emotional loyalty. The only effective training for citizenship in a democracy is practice in democratic living. The facts concerning each individual's potentialities, his interests, the things to which he responds with emotional satisfaction, his skills, his rate of development, and his major points of strength and weakness must be accurately ascertained and assembled as objectively and dispassionately as possible, and using this whole picture he must be led to evolve for himself a satisfactory level of living, and at the same time maintain a balance between his own welfare and that of the group. Thus, training for living in a democracy and guidance as exemplified by carefully organized personnel programs are one and the same process.

The point will bear repeating that guidance, as defined by those who approach the problem rationally, implies recognition and understanding of the individual, and creation of conditions that will enable each individual to develop his fullest capacities, and ultimately to achieve the maximum possible self-guidance and security, both economically and socially. This concept of guidance epitomizes our democratic philosophy. It is as enduring as democracy itself, for basically it is democracy applied to the life of the school.

REFERENCES

1. Allen, Richard D. "The Costs of Guidance in Secondary School," *Clearing House*, XIII (October 1938), 73–77.

[3] Arthur E. Traxler, "The Status of Statewide Testing Programs," *1954 Achievement Testing Program in Independent Schools and Supplementary Studies*, pp. 86-92. Educational Records Bulletin No. 63 (New York: Educational Records Bureau, July 1954). Pp. xii + 96.

2. Anderson, Scarvia, Katz, Martin, and Shimberg, Benjamin. *Meeting the Test.* New York: Four Winds Press, 1965. Pp. vi + 184.

3. Berdie, Ralph F.; Swanson, Edward O.; Hagenah, Theda; and Layton, Wilbur L. *Testing in Guidance and Counseling.* New York: McGraw-Hill Book Company, Inc., 1963. Pp. 286.

4. Brickman, Leonard. "Project Able—An Experiment in Guidance," *High Points,* XLVI (April 1963), 24–27.

5. Clare, Sister Mary Julia. "Teacher-Counselor in the Small High School," *Catholic School Journal,* LXIII (October 1963), 45–46.

6. Conant, James Bryant. *A Memorandum to School Boards: Recommendations for Education in the Junior High School Years.* Princeton, N.J.: Educational Testing Service, 1960. Pp. 46.

7. Cottingham, Harold F. "Changing Perspectives in Vocational Guidance," *Vocational Guidance Quarterly,* XI (Summer 1963), 282–285.

8. Cribbin, James J. "Essentials and Incidentals in Guidance," *Catholic Educational Review,* LIX (December 1961), 609–619.

9. Crow, Lester D., and Crow, Alice. *Organization and Conduct of Guidance Services.* New York: David McKay Company, Inc., 1965. Pp. 735.

10. Diebold, John. "Automation: Its Implications for Counseling," *Vocational Guidance Quarterly,* XI (Autumn 1962), 11–14.

11. Dugan, Willis E. "The Impact of NDEA Upon Counselor Preparation," *Personnel and Guidance Journal,* XXXIX (September 1960), 37–40.

12. Durost, Walter, and Prescott, George A. *Essentials of Measurement for Teachers.* New York: Harcourt, Brace & World, Inc., 1962. Pp. viii + 167.

13. Emery, Clifton. "The Cost of Guidance," *Personnel and Guidance Journal,* XXX (April 1962), 525–526.

14. Farwell, Gail F., and Peters, Herman J. (eds.). *Guidance Readings for Counselors.* Chicago: Rand McNally & Company, 1960. Pp. x + 691.

15. Fossett, Katherine. "Guidance Institutes, NDEA," *Personnel and Guidance Journal,* XXXIX (November 1960), 207–209.

16. Glanz, Edward C. "Emerging Concepts and Patterns of Guidance in American Education," *Personnel and Guidance Journal,* XL (November 1961), 259–265.

17. Goldman, Leo. "Cooperative Plan for Guidance and Admission," *Personnel and Guidance Journal,* XLII (September 1963), 64–68.

18. Hatch, Raymond N., and Stefflre, Buford. *The Administration of Guidance Services: Organization, Supervision, Evaluation.* Englewood Cliffs, N.J.: Prentice-Hall, Inc., 1958. Pp. vi + 449.

19. Hill, Warren G. "The Professional Practice of Vocational Guidance—the State of the Field," *Vocational Guidance Quarterly,* XI (Spring 1963), 151–157.

20. Humphreys, J. Anthony, Traxler, Arthur E., and North, Robert D. *Guidance Services,* rev. ed. Part I. Chicago: Science Research Associates, Inc., 1960. Pp. xv + 414.

21. Johnson, Walter F., Stefflre, Buford, and Edelfelt, Roy A. *Pupil Personnel and Guidance Services.* New York: McGraw-Hill Book Company, Inc., 1961. Pp. 407.

22. Koile, Earl A. "Counseling Policies and Programs," *The School Review,* LXIX (Summer 1961), 181–190.

23. Koos, Leonard V., and Kefauver, Grayson N. *Guidance in Secondary Schools,* pp. 15–22. New York: The Macmillan Company, 1932. Pp. vi + 640.

24. Kowitz, Gerald T., and Kowitz, Norma G. *Guidance in the Elementary Classroom.* New York: McGraw-Hill Book Company, Inc., 1959. Pp. v + 314.

25. Lloyd-Jones, Esther, and Westervelt, Esther M. (eds.). *Behavioral Science and Guidance: Proposals and Perspectives.* New York: Bureau of Publications, Teachers College, Columbia University, 1963. Pp. 128.

26. Lowe, R. N. *A Rationale and Models for Organizing and Administering Programs of Pupil Personnel Services.* Eugene, Ore.: Bureau of Educational Research, School of Education, University of Oregon, 1962. Pp. 35.

27. Mortensen, Donald G., and Schmuller, Allen M. *Guidance in Today's Schools.* New York: John Wiley & Sons, Inc., 1959. Pp. 436.

28. Moser, Leslie E., and Moser, Ruth S. *Counseling and Guidance: An Exploration.* Englewood Cliffs, N.J.: Prentice-Hall, Inc., 1963. Pp. xviii + 432.

29. Mueller, Kate H. *Student Personnel Work in Higher Education.* Boston: Houghton Mifflin Company, 1960. Pp. xiv + 570.

30. "1964–65 NDEA Counseling and Guidance Institutes," *School Life,* XLVI (January–February 1964), 10, 13.

31. Oliver, Gary L. "Cooperative Guidance Research Among Smaller Schools," *Vocational Guidance Quarterly,* VIII (Summer 1960), 202–204.

32. Palm, Harold J. "High School Guidance: What Does It Cost Today?" *Vocational Guidance Quarterly,* IX (Spring 1961), 169–172.

33. *Parents' Guide to Understanding Tests.* New York: Educational Records Bureau, 1964. Pp. vii + 43.

34. *Personnel Services in Education,* Part II of 1959 Yearbook of the National Society for the Study of Education (Nelson B. Henry, ed.). Chicago: The University of Chicago Press, 1959. Pp. iv + 304.

35. Peters, Herman J., and Farwell, Gail F. "Junior High School Vocational Guidance: A New Frontier," *Vocational Guidance Quarterly,* VII (Winter 1958–1959), 99–101.

36. Samler, Joseph. "The Professional Practice of Guidance—Commentary," *Vocational Guidance Quarterly,* XI (Spring 1963), 157–161.

37. Stoops, Emery (ed.). *Guidance Services: Organization and Administration.* New York: McGraw-Hill Book Company, Inc., 1959. Pp. 302.

38. *Testing Guide for Teachers.* New York: Educational Records Bureau, 1961. Pp. 43.

39. Weitz, Henry. "The Role of the Guidance Worker in the Schools," *Personnel and Guidance Journal,* XXXVII (December 1958), 226–267.

40. Wesman, Alexander G. "NDEA—Opportunities and Re-

sponsibilities in Test Development and Test Use," *Personnel and Guidance Journal,* XXXIX (September 1960), 41–44.

41. Wilkins, William D., and Perlmutter, Barbara J. "The Philosophical Foundations of Guidance and Personnel Services," *Review of Educational Research,* XXX (April 1960), 97–104.

42. Williamson, E. G. "An Outsider's View of Junior College Guidance Programs," *Junior College Journal,* XXX (May 1960), 489–501.

43. Williamson, E. G. *Student Personnel Services in Colleges and Universities.* New York: McGraw-Hill Book Company, Inc., 1961. Pp. xiv + 474.

44. Wolfle, Dael. "Guidance and Educational Strategy," *Personnel and Guidance Journal,* XXXVII (September 1958), 17–25.

45. Zeran, Franklin R., and Riccio, Anthony C. *Organization and Administration of Guidance Services.* Chicago: Rand McNally & Company, 1962. Pp. 302.

CHAPTER II

Essentials in Launching
a Guidance Program

CAREFUL PLANNING IN THE INITIAL STAGES CAN do much to insure the success of a guidance program. The following questions are some of those which members of a school faculty may ask themselves in order to determine whether or not they are laying a sound foundation for their guidance services.

1. *Is the guidance program appropriate to the objectives and functions of the local school?* The broad objectives of education in the particular school and community must be identified, and must be stated in definite terms rather than based on vague generalizations. This is the only sound starting point for the formulation of a guidance program. For example, there will inevitably be noteworthy differences among the guidance services offered by high schools in a suburban community where the majority of the pupils are college preparatory, in an industrial section of a large city, and in a small rural community.

2. *Does the guidance program have administrative support?* Not infrequently, members of a school staff, who have a friendly interest in their pupils and are conscious of their needs for counseling, will become imbued with enthusiasm for a program of guidance services. In their impatience to see some constructive steps undertaken, they may rush into a hastily conceived plan that is attempted with administrative consent, but without the wholehearted approval and strong support of the administration. Greater eventual progress may be made by concentrating in the beginning upon the enlistment of unquestioned administrative support. Among the reasons why there must be full administrative interest in the program from its early stages is the very practical one that new guidance services involve a new financial commitment. The program requires complete support

from the school head in budgetary planning if it is ever to be more than a paper program and an expression of good intentions.

3. *Is faculty attitude favorable to a guidance program?* The converse of the previous situation is to be observed in some schools. The head of the school is strongly in favor of undertaking guidance services, but his faculty is not ready for this step. At this point, we are concerned with attitudes, not techniques. It is not to be expected that a school faculty will be well acquainted with guidance procedures, at the outset. While the question is one of attitude, it is to be noted that it is not a question of *attitude toward guidance.* The central question has to do with the attitudes of staff members *toward their job* and *toward young people.* Are they even more interested in their students than in the subjects they teach? Do they understand, and have they accepted, the concept of individualized education—so far as it is possible to individualize instruction under the group conditions of the classroom which still obtain in nearly all schools? If not, it is going to be difficult to lead them to an understanding of the purposes of a guidance program. If so, they are already engaged in some aspects of guidance—a guidance program is, in a sense, already under way in the school —and the main problem is one of the organization and development of skills and techniques.

4. *Does the school have on its staff specialized guidance personnel; if not, does it have qualified staff members who are able and willing to acquire the necessary special training?* In a large proportion of our schools, even today, such guidance as is offered to students is provided by personnel with rather limited training for this work. It should be emphasized that it is seldom feasible to concentrate a school's guidance functions entirely in the

hands of special personnel. Schools in general cannot meet the guidance needs of their pupils simply by employing one or two counselors who are expected to handle all the guidance services, while the instructional staff continues its traditional role of teaching subject matter. On the other hand, it is not possible to carry on a modern guidance program simply by using the classroom teachers, and without the leadership of one or more specially trained persons. Procedures of appraising individuals and providing counseling appropriate to the individual situation call for a broad background of training in psychology and the use of special skills and techniques. Standards for guidance workers have been widely adopted in the various states (3). Information concerning financial assistance available to students in guidance and personnel graduate study programs in a wide variety of institutions is published annually by the American Personnel and Guidance Association (25). As for institutions where graduate courses in guidance and personnel work are available, a list of 310 such institutions was published in *Lovejoy's Guidance Digest* in 1965 (23).

The most desirable guidance situation in a school is one in which the entire faculty participates, or at least lends its wholehearted support, under the leadership of trained personnel—which would vary with the size of the school from a single psychologist or guidance chairman to a corps of trained specialists. In this connection, it should be kept in mind that the field of guidance services is undergoing growth and rapid improvement, and that it is very sensitive to new developments in psychology. The training of specialized guidance personnel should therefore be a continuous process, with frequent periods of further study even for staff members who have had a great deal of graduate training.

5. *Has provision been made for the physical equipment needed to carry on a guidance program?* Is there adequate provision for privacy in counseling interviews under reasonably pleasant surroundings? Are offices provided for the use of persons engaged in counseling? Is there a large, suitably equipped office for records, and are the counselors' offices adjacent to it? Is there a convenient filing system for the records? Are tests provided in sufficient quantity and variety for regular testing programs?

If the school building was constructed years ago, when no thought was given to guidance services, an attempt should be made to adapt certain rooms for guidance use. A large classroom, for example, can be divided by means of temporary partitions into a number of small offices for counseling purposes. A portion of the room can be fashioned into an outer office for records, or an adjoining room can be used for this procedure.

When a new school building is constructed, careful attention should be given to plans for the guidance services. A desirable plan is to have a series of rooms arranged so that the records office is between the principal's office and the small offices used for counseling, with each of these units readily accessible from the corridor. Through careful planning and detailed attention to the physical setup, much can be done to promote the efficient functioning of the guidance program.

6. *Does the school have a comprehensive, well-organized cumulative record, and are these records kept up to date by trained clerical workers, assisted where feasible by data-processing equipment?* A cumulative record will not insure a successful guidance program, but it is next to impossible to provide dependable guidance services without this kind of record for each pupil in the school. The topic of cumulative records is dealt with extensively and in detail in Chapter XIII.

7. *Has the school developed systematic procedures for the objective appraisal of individual pupils?* There is almost universal recognition of the need for appraisal of individuals in connection with programs of guidance. But the way to get a program of evaluation started is often unclear. It is common experience for a test-service organization to receive a request from a school worded somewhat as follows: "We have decided to start a guidance program. Please send us some guidance tests." Needless to say, this is not the way to begin.

Tests are indispensable instruments in guidance, but they are not the point from which one begins thinking about the appraisal aspects of guidance. One begins by determining the kinds of objective information that are needed about individuals, and then one attempts to decide what kinds of techniques will yield this information.

An analysis will ordinarily show a need for at least the ten kinds of information discussed in Chapter IV. Tests will yield helpful data with regard to all these areas, but it is highly desirable to supplement tests with other approaches, such as school marks, anecdotal records, behavior descriptions, projective techniques, and sociometric devices. The need for these less highly structured techniques is especially apparent in connection with the appraisal of interests, personal qualities, and mental health.

It is definitely recommended that after the program is well launched, some experimental work be done with anecdotal records or with some similar system, such as the Personal and Social Development Program, prepared by John C. Flanagan (10). The writing of anecdotes by members of the faculty, and their subsequent summarization, is very time-consuming, and this plan will not work out in every school. But it should be given a trial, for if ways can be found to implement even a modified and simplified anecdotal plan in a school, this plan will constitute a marked step ahead in the potential of the guidance services the school can provide.

The details of the testing program are covered in later chapters. Among the essentials are comprehensiveness, careful planning and regularity of administration, and comparability of the results from year to year.

8. *Does the school use systematic procedures for collecting information concerning educational and vocational opportunities?* Are there well-defined ways of making this information available to students? All students can profit from the availability of guidance services in orienting themselves toward occupations. A proportion of the students—varying from 20 percent or less in some high schools in industrial areas, to 95 percent or more in high schools in residential areas and in private secondary schools—need guidance in deciding on attendance at higher institutions. The next chapter is concerned with these questions.

9. *Do the staff members participating in the counseling of individual pupils agree on certain principles of counseling, and do they carefully prepare for their counseling activities with these principles in mind?* Counseling is a professional activity calling for the use of special skills and techniques. The main purposes of counseling are to improve the individual adjustment and self-reliance of the counselee. The interview is the central process of counseling.

Some years ago, there were sharp differences of opinion between the proponents of the directive and nondirective approaches to counseling. The present tendency at the school level, and to a considerable extent at the college level as well, is toward "eclectic" counseling; that is, the selection of those aspects of either directive or nondirective counseling that seem appropriate to the specific situation. It is generally agreed that the counselee should take the lead, to the limit of his ability, and should assume the final responsibility for making decisions. It is recognized, on the other hand, that school pupils lack the maturity and experience to enable them to reach decisions concerning the techniques to be applied—such as tests—or independently to think through an involved problem frequently having several psychological connotations. The young counselee needs help in assembling and interpreting information about himself, in reaching decisions consistent with his life situation, and in carrying out the decisions made.

Constant care should be used to avoid allowing assistance to become domination. The counselee's personal integrity and self-esteem should be protected at all times, and he should be allowed as much responsibility for reaching his own decisions as he is able to assume.

The counseling relationship is, thus, a constantly changing one, depending on the nature of the problem and the maturity, self-reliance, and personality of the counselee. The basis of effective counseling is an understanding on the part of both counselor and counselee of the individual and his problem. The counselor cannot depend alone upon intuition and flashes of insight to acquire this understanding. Detailed study of the individual's cumulative record and of the circumstances surrounding his immediate problem and careful preparation for each individual interview are essential.

It should be kept in mind that not all counseling deals with problems. The great majority of counselees in the school guidance program are "normal" young people, and many of them may never bring a problem to their counselor. Nevertheless, regularly scheduled interviews with each pupil in the counselor's group, perhaps once a semester, will provide an opportunity for clearing up minor difficulties, and will enable the counselor to keep a check on the development of each individual.

10. *Are referral agencies available, and have the services which these agencies can render to the school been explored?* Although the guidance services of the school should be able to handle the majority of the questions and problems of most pupils, occasionally counselors and teachers are likely to get beyond their depth in their attempt to diagnose and provide treatment for cases of severe maladjustment or retardation. Some schools will have the special personnel on their own staff or will be able to afford to hire such persons, but many must depend upon outside services. Public-supported and non-profit mental-health bureaus, psychological service centers, vocational counseling services, and remedial clinics will usually be the main sources of assistance, although the services of reputable psychologists and psychiatrists in private practice may also be utilized.

11. *In establishing a guidance program, is a special effort being made to build up mutually helpful relations with other agencies in the community that are particularly concerned with the problems of young people?* A continuous program should be undertaken to keep parents informed about the nature and purposes of the school guidance services and their value to their own children, and to enlist the parents' help in providing information for the individual inventory or cumulative record. Other guidance agencies with which the school may cooperate are to be found in local civic and religious organizations, youth organizations, and social welfare groups. It is also very desirable for the school's guidance officers to develop cordial relations with personnel officers in local industries.

12. *Is there a well-organized plan for following up individuals after they leave the school?* This question is directed toward one of the most vulnerable spots in the entire structure of the guidance services. There is an in-

consistency in the fact that many schools are undertaking guidance programs at considerable expense, without doing the follow-up needed to appraise the worth of these programs and to obtain information that may indicate needed improvements. Also, failure to provide follow-up services is shortsighted in that it suggests that a school believes that its responsibility to the individual ceases as soon as his enrollment is terminated.

A follow-up plan should include not only graduates, but all school leavers. In fact, so far as the individual is concerned, it is frequently the nongraduate who especially needs to be followed up and assisted in postschool adjustment.

Studies of school leavers should be carried on at regular intervals. The purposes of these studies are to obtain facts about the postschool adjustment of graduates and other former pupils, to learn the opinions of former students with regard to the school organization, curriculum, and guidance program, and to identify school leavers who need further services from the school.

Pupils still in the school should be followed up, particularly if they have recently been through a period of remedial work or other intensive training. The follow-up is dealt with at greater length in Chapter XVII.

13. *Is the school undertaking a continuous program of education of faculty members in guidance philosophy, principles, and techniques?* This is the most important matter of all. The guidance program is likely to be successful in direct proportion to the extent to which the entire staff is able to cooperate intelligently with it.

Among the procedures that may be used in promoting faculty understanding and participation are a cooperative effort in the preparation or revision of cumulative record forms, case conferences concerning individual pupils, discussions of test results made definite and practical through the use of various devices—film strips and opaque projectors, etc.—and lectures by outside experts in the special areas related to guidance services, such as psychiatry, social case work, projective techniques, and vocational education. Guidance services, as suggested in an earlier section, should be an all-faculty function under trained leadership, provided the faculty members have sufficient understanding of the elementary principles and techniques of guidance to enable them to take an intelligent and effective part in this work. This is not to say that teachers should attempt to perform kinds of service for which they are not prepared, but all should give full cooperation to the counselors and other specialists.

One final question may be raised: *Do the foregoing questions apply to the elementary school, as well as to the secondary school?* The answer is yes; nearly all these questions can be applied to the elementary school, but with less force than they apply to the secondary school.

The natural organization of the elementary school is more conducive to effective individualized guidance services than is the secondary school organization. Since, in the typical elementary school organization, each class group is in the charge of one teacher, there are a close acquaintance and a personal relationship between teacher and individual pupil, which readily create an understanding and an atmosphere favorable to informal counseling.

Moreover, elementary school teachers seem, on the whole, to be somewhat more "guidance minded" than secondary school and college teachers. It seems that as one goes further and further downward through the grade levels, he finds greater and greater interest in the development of the child as a person, and less and less interest in the teaching of a specific subject matter. Finally arriving at the kindergarten and preschool level, one finds teachers spending practically all their school time on the all-around development of individual children.

Elementary school teachers do comparatively little talking about guidance service, but they probably enter into guidance activities in connection with their daily teaching more extensively than do teachers at any other level. Nevertheless, they may be expected to do an appreciably better job if they are acquainted with the uses of cumulative records, test results, anecdotal procedures, the psychology of counseling, and the other techniques of a modern guidance program, and if they, too, have the leadership of specially trained guidance and counseling personnel.

REFERENCES

1. Andrew, Dean C., and Willey, Roy DeVerl. *Administration and Organization of the Guidance Program.* New York: Harper & Row, Publishers, 1958. Pp. 330.
2. Bechtold, Mary Lee. "Guidance for Elementary Grades," *School and Community*, L (November 1963), 30.
3. Brewster, Royce E. *Guidance Workers' Certification Requirements.* Washington, D.C.: Superintendent of Documents, 1960. Pp. 98.
4. Byrn, Delmont K. "A Glossary of Guidance Terms," *Vocational Guidance Quarterly*, X (Summer 1962), 244.
5. Cottingham, Harold F., and Hopke, William E. *Guidance in Junior High Schools.* Bloomington, Ill.: McKnight & McKnight Publishing Company, 1961. Pp. 390.
6. Derthick, Lawrence G. "Guidance and the Nation's Needs," *Personnel and Guidance Journal*, XXXVII (October 1958), 107–113.
7. Diffenbaugh, Donald J., and Bowman, Douglas J. "Guidance Services at the Intermediate Level," *Personnel and Guidance Journal*, XLI (September 1962), 25–28.
8. Dyer, Henry S. "The Need for Do-it-Yourself Prediction

Research in High School Guidance," *Personnel and Guidance Journal*, XXXVI (November 1957), 162–167.

9. Eckerson, Louise O., and Smith, Hyrum M. "Successful Guidance in the Elementary Schools," *Education Digest*, XXVIII (November 1962), 20–22.

10. Flanagan, John C. *Personal and Social Development Program*. Chicago: Science Research Associates, Inc., 1956. (Temporarily out of print.)

11. Froehlich, Clifford P. *Guidance Services in Schools*, 2nd ed. New York: McGraw-Hill Book Company, Inc., 1958. Pp. 383.

12. Gowen, J. C. "Organization of Guidance for Gifted Children," *Personnel and Guidance Journal*, XXXIX (December 1960), 275–279.

13. Gowin, D. B. "Prospects for Philosophic Inquiry in Guidance," *The School Review*, LXIX (Summer 1961), 191–205.

14. "Guidance Trends in High Schools," *California Education*, I (November 1963), 11.

15. *Guiding Today's Youth*. Division of Research and Guidance, Office of Los Angeles County Superintendent. Monterey: California Test Bureau, 1962. Pp. xiv + 411.

16. Hatch, Raymond N., and Costar, James W. *Guidance Services in the Elementary School*. Dubuque, Iowa: William C. Brown Co., 1961. Pp. 194.

17. Hill, George E. "Guidance in Elementary Schools," *Clearing House*, XXXVIII (October 1963), 111–116.

18. Hill, George E., and Nitzschke, Dale F. "Preparation Programs in Elementary School Guidance," *Personnel and Guidance Journal*, XL (October 1961), 155–159.

19. Hulslander, Stewart C., and Scholl, Charles E. "U.S. School Principals Report Their Counselor Needs," *Vocational Guidance Quarterly*, VI (Autumn 1957), 3–4.

20. Humphreys, J. Anthony, Traxler, Arthur E., and North, Robert D. *Guidance Services*, rev. ed., Part IV. Chicago: Science Research Associates, Inc., 1960. Pp. xv + 414.

21. Kinane, M. "Evolving Role of Dean of Students," *Catholic Education Review*, LXI (September 1963), 403–407.

22. Lifton, Walter M. "Social Forces and Guidance in the Elementary School," *Vocational Guidance Quarterly*, XII (Winter 1963–1964), 89–92.

23. *Lovejoy's Guidance Digest*, XVII, No. 7 (March 1965), 5.

24. McCully, C. Harold. "A Rationale for Counselor Certification," *Counselor Education and Supervision*, I (Fall 1961), 3–9.

25. McDaniels, Carl. "Financial Aid for Guidance and Personnel Graduate Study," *Personnel and Guidance Journal*, XLIII (January 1965), 492–507.

26. McDougall, William P., and Reitan, Henry M. "The Elementary Counselor as Perceived by Elementary Principals," *Personnel and Guidance Journal*, XLII (December 1963), 348–354.

27. Malcolm, David D. "The Image of the Future Secondary School Guidance Program," *California Journal of Secondary Education*, XXXVI (February 1961), 72–78.

28. Martinson, Ruth A., and Smallenburg, Harry. *Guidance in Elementary Schools*. Englewood Cliffs, N.J.: Prentice-Hall, Inc., 1958. Pp. xiii + 322.

29. Metzler, John H. "Evaluating Counseling and Guidance Programs: A Review of the Literature," *Vocational Guidance Quarterly*, XII (Summer 1964), 285–289.

30. Munger, Paul F. "Guidance for Rural Schools," *Education*, LXXX (April 1960), 488–490.

31. Munger, Paul F., and Mathisen, James D. "Title Five Has Helped North Dakota," *Personnel and Guidance Journal*, XLI (March 1963), 629–630.

32. National Defense Education Act (NDEA): Title V: Guidance, Counseling and Testing: Identification and Encouragement of Able Students. Public Law 85–864, 1958.

33. Polmantier, Paul C., and Schmidt, Lyle D. "Areas of Preparation for School Guidance Workers," *Personnel and Guidance Journal*, XXXIX (September 1960), 45–46.

34. Rapaport, A. "Some Guidance Activities for the Elementary School," *Chicago Schools Journal*, XLV (October 1963), 32–33.

35. Rothney, John W. M. "The Evaluation of Guidance and Personnel Services," *Review of Educational Research*, XXX (April 1960), 168–175.

36. Shertzer, Bruce, and Stone, Shelly. "Administrative Deterrents to Effective Guidance Programs," *Education Digest*, XXIX (October 1963), 40–43.

37. Silverman, Hirsch L. "Psychological and Guidance Services in the Public Schools," *Vocational Guidance Quarterly*, VIII (Winter 1959–1960), 107–110.

38. Steel, C. "Emerging Programs of Counseling and Guidance," *Bulletin of the National Association of Secondary-School Principals*, LXVII (September 1963), 10–18.

39. Thelen, Herbert A. "Education and the Human Quest: What's to Become of Johnny?" *School Review*, LXVIII (Summer 1960), 136–151.

40. Twiford, Don D. "Physical Facilities for Guidance," *Vocational Guidance Quarterly*, VI (Autumn 1957), 5–6.

41. Utter, Lou. "Filing Career Information," *Vocational Guidance Quarterly*, VI (Winter 1957–1958), 76–77.

42. Wise, W. M. "Student Personnel Work—Future Trends," *Personnel and Guidance Journal*, XXXIX (May 1961), 704–709.

43. Zimmerman, W. D. "The Changing Nature of the Personal Dimension of Education," *Liberal Education*, XLIX (December 1963), 520–527.

CHAPTER III

Opportunities for Young People

ONE OF THE MOST IMPORTANT FUNCTIONS OF guidance is to help bring about better distribution of young people to the offerings of the school, to the opportunities for higher education, and to vocations. In this area, the main responsibilities of counselors are, first, to become familiar with the current and probable future opportunities for young people and to acquaint them with these opportunities; second, to know the aptitudes, interests, achievements, and personal qualities of individual pupils, and to help the pupils understand the significance of test data and other information concerning themselves; and third, to develop a continuous program of individual counseling and group instruction which will lead young people to discover and recognize the opportunities best suited to their potentialities.

At the upper elementary and the secondary school levels, a main responsibility of the counselor is not so much to help young people choose specific occupations, as it is to help them learn how to prepare and to choose in a world where employment opportunities are changing and developing with great rapidity.

As Venn (145) has pointed out, under the new conditions faced by modern youth, high school dropouts, and even graduates who do not go on to college, are entering a technological world where they are not prepared to survive.

THE NATURE OF OPPORTUNITIES FOR YOUTH

The counselor's program should include provision for the intelligent guidance of individual boys and girls toward the immediate opportunities provided by the school and the community, and toward long-time educational and vocational opportunities available after secondary school is finished. The opportunities for any given individual are dependent both upon his environment and upon his aptitudes and personal qualities.

CURRENT OPPORTUNITIES OF THE SCHOOL

When new pupils enter the secondary school from the elementary grades, either at the end of Grade 6 or the end of Grade 8, or enter senior high school from junior high school, a first responsibility of the guidance services is to orient them to the opportunities provided by the high school. This orientation is preferably begun in the last grade of the sending school, through group meetings between the pupils and the counselor to whom they will be assigned in high school. The organization of even a medium-size high school is complex in comparison with that of an elementary school. It saves a good deal of confusion on the part of many pupils if they can be informed in a general way about what to expect before they actually enter high school. It is also very helpful for the counselor to become acquainted with the parents of the prospective secondary school pupils while the pupils are still in the elementary school. Printed booklets containing information about the high school, its organization, customs, and traditions may well be distributed to pupils and their parents at this time.

Group meetings with new pupils at the beginning of the fall term can be used to give them more information concerning the curriculum, the extracurriculum, and the school plant and its equipment. The library facilities, including the card catalog and modern information retrieval devices, as well as other helps to the ready location of study materials, should be carefully explained with the cooperation of the librarian. Group meetings in which study habits and procedures are discussed should be followed by opportunities for individual conferences. The counselor should prepare himself for each pupil conference through a study of the available information about each new pupil. In many places, this information will be comparatively meager, but in school systems where individual cumulative record cards are maintained in the elementary school, as well as at the high school level, the essentials of which move along with the pupil from one school level to the next, the counselor will have ready access to a variety of pertinent and very helpful information.

THE SECONDARY SCHOOL CURRICULUM

One of the main areas of opportunity within the school is, of course, the curriculum. Throughout the elementary school, pupils are concerned to a large extent with acquisition of a common set of basic skills. Opportunities for choice among subjects are necessarily restricted.

Guidance is needed at the point where choices are presented to a pupil and his parents and where decisions must be made. High schools, of course, vary widely in the opportunities for choice which they allow. When there is only a single curriculum consisting of constants which all pupils are expected to take, as was true of many schools a half century ago and is virtually true of some small high schools even today, the possibilities of guidance in relation to the curriculum are decidedly limited. But with the many curricula offered in modern metropolitan high schools, or under conditions where there is a curriculum consisting of constants supplemented by a wide choice of variables, there must be a program of careful individual guidance of pupils toward the offerings best suited to them as individuals. Otherwise there will inevitably be a great waste of teacher and pupil effort, which will eventuate in many cases of failure and maladjustment and increased costs for school support.

It is true, of course, that even in the most progressive of secondary schools there is not complete freedom of choice. Virtually all high schools require at least three years of English and a year or more each of social studies, science, and mathematics, and in many high schools the amount of prescription is considerably greater than that. For college preparatory pupils, in particular, choices are likely to be more limited, since these pupils are still bound to a considerable degree by the requirements of the colleges. Similar circumstances are true of a large borderline group of pupils who are uncertain about ultimate college attendance. Nevertheless, in middle-size and large high schools, all pupils have opportunities for a number of electives. And their decisions with regard to these

electives often have much influence upon their future, both educationally and vocationally.

Classroom teachers cooperating in the guidance program are likely to be well prepared to help counselors provide guidance in the area of the curriculum. It is sometimes difficult, however, for them to be completely objective in this guidance and to resist a natural tendency to point up the advantages of their own field of study to the pupil. This is not always unfortunate, for the enthusiasm of a thoroughly dedicated teacher frequently transfers itself to his students. Teacher-counselors need to keep in mind, however, that they have an obligation to assure themselves that the pupil has the necessary aptitudes for a field of study before suggesting that he give serious consideration to it.

It should be remembered, too, that the modern trend is not for counselors to decide *for* the individual just how he may use the available information concerning the opportunities open to him and about his own abilities and interests. It is, rather, to place a large amount of responsibility upon the *individual himself* for understanding the information made available to him, and for using it in reaching his own decisions so that he may gradually grow into a mature, self-reliant person who finally has little or no need for the services of counselors. Obviously, the application of these procedures must be a reasonable process, adjusted to the maturity of the student, placing responsibility upon the individual no more rapidly than he is able to assume it.

THE EXTRACURRICULUM OR CO-CURRICULUM

The extracurriculum affords a second area of opportunity for boys and girls of school age. The extracurriculum, which in the early history of the secondary school was very limited in scope, has expanded tremendously during the present century. In all but the smaller schools, there is now such a variety of sports, clubs, and hobbies included in the extracurricular activities that some aspects of it should appeal to the interests of every normal pupil. School administrators recognizing its educational value are tending, to an increasing extent, to accord the extracurriculum a place closely parallel to the curriculum itself.

Boys and girls vary greatly in the degree to which they take advantage of the opportunities provided by the extracurriculum. The average pupil takes part in three or four of these activities. At one extreme, there are individuals to whom the extracurriculum is by far the most important aspect of school life, and who participate so extensively in extracurricular activities that there is great interference with the learning process fostered by their regular curriculum. At the other extreme, there are timid, backward, solitary, retiring individuals who do not take part in a single extracurricular activity unless participation in at least one such activity is a requirement laid down by the school. The pupils at both extremes are greatly in need of guidance leading to the choice of a moderate number of activities best suited to them.

It is through the extracurriculum that many personal problems and difficulties of social adjustment are resolved. The therapeutic values of assimilation with one's peers in relatively free activity should never be overlooked. As Krugman (71) pointed out, the social group can often serve as a most effective preventive and therapeutic agent in reaching and helping pupils who may not be reached by even the most skillful psychologist or psychiatrist.

OPPORTUNITIES IN THE COMMUNITY

The community provides a third area of immediate opportunities for young people. Many of the opportunities afforded by the community are educational, and they may be used to supplement and reinforce the program of the school. In fact, in many places, it would be entirely possible to replace many elements of the school curriculum by a program based on a study of the resources of the community or through a thoroughly planned, long-range project in community living.

In metropolitan areas, contacts with the business life and civic organization of the community, and with the civilizing influences provided by the agencies of literature and art, will do much to infuse with real content and meaning the curriculum which the pupil pursues in school. It is known, for example, that pupils read with much better comprehension when they have had first-hand experience with the concepts dealt with in the reading material.

In a rural or small town environment, the young people may be so well acquainted with the community educational resources that little guidance in this area is needed—although even in such an environment the counselors have some functions of this kind to perform, and field trips under the auspices of the guidance services to nearby cities or industrial centers can be handled in a way to provide worthwhile educational experience for pupils in the local school. In a complex metropolitan environment, boys and girls are likely to be acquainted with only those community resources which are along the line of their special interests or which are in their own neighborhood, and they need guidance in getting a balanced sampling of the community opportunities.

Part-time and summer work opportunities are also available for a considerable number of pupils of secondary school age—particularly during the periods of recurrent severe manpower shortage occasioned by unstable international conditions—and guidance into these openings is a function of counseling. From a long-term guidance point of view, the chief objective in this type of vocational counseling is not so much to help the student economically as it is to provide him with a background of work experience which will be useful when he is ready to choose a lifetime vocation.

For the placement of pupils in suitable part-time and summer employment, the guidance functionaries of the school may advisedly develop close working relations with personnel managers in the local business and industrial concerns and with community guidance agencies, even though the major concern of the latter is likely to be the guidance of out-of-school youths and adults.

OPPORTUNITIES FOR HIGHER EDUCATION AND GUIDANCE TOWARD COLLEGE

Opportunities for young people at the end of secondary school may be classified broadly into those of higher education and those of the vocations, although it is becoming increasingly apparent that education through college will be more and more necessary for a larger number of vocations (146). The process of transition from school to college is often thought of as an act or event of considerable abruptness, and is frequently treated in the same manner. It is perhaps more properly viewed as a long-term guidance process, one which begins in the elementary school and continues throughout the junior and senior high schools and into the junior college. The thinking of the individual himself, his home and family, and many staff members in his school and his college should be brought to bear cooperatively upon the process.

One of the most important areas of guidance for the college-bound student is *guidance in the choice of possible colleges*. The guidance services have two main functions in this regard—first, providing information concerning colleges, and, second, relating information about the abilities and interests of individual pupils to information about the offerings of the colleges.

The replies of college freshmen to a questionnaire distributed in the mid-1950s by the Committee on School and College Relations of the Educational Records Bureau to a total of nearly 500 freshmen in 27 colleges indicated that a fairly large proportion of these students had experienced difficulty in deciding to which college application should be made. Twenty-two percent, a little more than one student in five, indicated that insufficient secondary school guidance was a reason for difficulty in choice of college. Approximately one student in six checked lack of sufficient information about colleges as a problem. More than a fourth of the students felt that difficulty in deciding which college to attend was due at least in part to a lack of clearly defined vocational objectives. About one student in seven checked lack of clearly defined educational objectives. Financial needs were mentioned by approximately one student in three, which suggested a need for a broader scholarship program in the colleges and better information concerning the availability of scholarships (137).

Fortunately, college guidance services of high schools have improved in the last dozen years; but, even so, anxiety about college admission is one of the most acute problems that plague college-bound students, according to a study sponsored by the same committee and published in 1962 (82).

In providing pupils with information concerning colleges, the counselor needs to make frequent reference to the pattern of abilities of each student, as revealed by his cumulative record. Oftentimes students, and more frequently their parents, set their sights too high or aim in the wrong direction. Judicious use of the objective data on the cumulative record in conference with the person concerned can often bring about a gradual change in aim, and the setting of goals consonant with aptitude, long before the student reaches his senior year, where final decisions must be made.

In order to discharge adequately the function of guidance in choice of college and college admission, counselors need information on a wide variety of colleges enrolling students of varying ability levels. It is true, of course, that the student and his family may often reject the kind of college in which he could be well-adjusted and successful. However, an understanding of the student's cumulative record, and acquaintance with the offerings of many colleges, may help in the setting of goals more realistic than those sometimes adhered to in the beginning. Counselors in secondary schools in the more densely populated areas, such as the New England and Middle Atlantic states, may advisedly guide some of their students toward small liberal arts colleges in the Midwest and South. Certain studies have indicated that a sizeable number of graduates of some of these colleges achieve distinction in later life (138, 139).

Guidance concerning choice of college is a relatively straightforward, uncomplicated area of counseling, and, it would seem, one in which secondary schools could considerably improve their services.

Another important area of counseling of college preparatory pupils, as well as those not intending to go to college, is *guidance in self-dependence, responsibility, and long-term planning*. One fact which loomed up very clearly in the replies of the college freshmen to the questionnaire distributed by the Educational Records Bureau is that these students felt a vast difference in the degree of freedom accorded students in secondary schools and colleges. Many of them stated that they had difficulty in adjusting to the much greater amount of freedom they had in planning their activities in college. One-third of the freshmen said they had difficulties in academic adjustment because of inability to organize work and study. Many students attributed this lack of ability to the failure of their high schools to train them to be on their own and to take major responsibility for their own activities.

Among the many statements made by the freshmen on this point, the following quotations are typical: "In high school you can do well if you pay attention in class; in college it is the work you do outside that counts;" "My secondary school could have given me more experience in being independent and in using my own initiative;" "One of the greatest problems of college life has been learning to get along on my own;" "The biggest difference between high school and college is the emphasis on responsibility;" "I have never had to budget my time before and find it hard to do so now;" "The high school has too much control over the individual; the problems are solved for him; he should be set free and allowed to run, at least for the most part, his own life;" "I think the high school should start us thinking for ourselves, seeing the problem, analyzing it, and solving it."

Without question, the change is so abrupt that many students are confused and have difficulty in finding themselves for at least a semester after they enter college. A large proportion of the high school work is in terms of daily assignments, and pupils are given close supervision and held accountable by their teachers for the completion of these assignments. In the typical college course, on the other hand, a large proportion of class time is given over to lectures by the instructors, and assignments are given in large blocks, or perhaps for an entire semester, so that ability to plan and organize is a basic factor in success. High school counselors need to inform pupils preparing for college concerning this difference and help prepare them to make the changeover.

This, however, is only a minor part of the need. The entire staff of the high school ought to cooperate in helping students make the gradual transition from the psychology of daily preparation to the psychology of the more mature preparation situation encountered in college. This means that, beginning somewhere in the junior year of high school and developing much more in the senior year, there should be a gradual departure from the daily assignments in favor of the setting up of long-term projects, which would help to develop initiative, independence, and organizational ability on the part of the students. In a questionnaire sent by the Committee on School and College Relations to colleges in 1963, one of the questions asked about weaknesses of entering freshmen. Deficiencies in study habits and skills, presumably meaning inability to do independent study, were mentioned very frequently by the colleges replying to the questionnaire (2).

At the same time, there is a need for college instructors to recognize that the students from many high schools have had no preparation for the freer study situation and the absence of definite daily assignments in the usual college course (advanced placement courses at the high school level are an exception to this), and they ought to take time to help students new in the college over this very difficult hurdle.

Responsibility for managing their own finances also gives some students trouble when they go on from high school to college. In the words of one freshman, "The most disturbing problem has been one of learning to really live on an allowance and budgeting one's own money." Another student suggested that "Proper orientation in budgeting of money should be given." This is a practical problem to which guidance services in secondary schools could well give some attention.

Transition from school to college could be made much smoother through closer cooperation between secondary school and college personnel services. Guidance is a continuous process, or it ought to be, for the development of the individual is a continuous growth process. Counselors at each higher educational level should always be able to build upon what is known about the student—his aptitudes and achievements, his strengths and weaknesses—at the lower levels. Information should also be made available to college admission offers concerning the nature and quality of the educational environment from which the applicant comes. A good illustration of a way of meeting this need is a leaflet entitled "Information for Colleges about Glen Ridge High School, Glen Ridge, New Jersey," which furnishes a kind of profile concerning that high school and the community in which it is located.

Communication between guidance personnel at the school and college levels needs to be greatly improved. At present, there is communication of sorts, but usually it is by way of the administrative office of the high school through the admission office of the college, and it is too often a one-way street, with practically all the information going from the high school to the college, and very little flowing back from the college to the high school regarding the adjustment and success of its graduates. This communication needs to be supplemented and

strengthened by direct lines of communication between school and college guidance functionaries.

This is easy to suggest, but difficult to carry out. A college typically draws its students from many different high schools, and the high school usually sends its graduates to many different colleges. These may be widely separated geographically. Still, much could be done through brief, simple leaflets distributed by high schools to let colleges know the nature of the high school guidance program, and through communications from colleges to high schools informing them about the kind and quality of students who are admitted and who are successful, and concerning the personnel services available to the students that the high schools may send them. A prototype of the kinds of information secondary schools need from colleges is the College Board's *Manual of Freshmen Class Profiles,* mentioned later in this chapter (84).

A greater degree of uniformity in records and in admissions blanks would also be helpful. If a uniform admission blank were to be adopted by schools and colleges throughout the country, it might be possible to include as a part of such a form a sheet which would contain guidance data and which would automatically be separated from the rest of the blank and passed along to the college guidance personnel for all students admitted to the college. An important step toward greater uniformity and toward the use of data processing equipment in guidance records has been taken by the Cooperative Plan for Guidance and Admission, to which reference is made in Chapter XIII (150).

These general suggestions can be considerably improved upon by schools and colleges in certain regions. Some secondary schools send the majority of their college preparatory graduates to a single college, and some colleges draw most of their students from a small number of high schools. This is especially true in rural areas of the country where a college may be the only one in a certain geographical area, and in large cities such as New York City where the municipal college may be the only public college in a particular borough. The guidance officers in these schools and colleges have a favorable opportunity for developing close relationships and for increasing the information of secondary school students concerning the opportunities the college affords, by means of talks by college personnel officers to high school pupil groups and through visits of groups of high school juniors and seniors to the college campus. Under the leadership of the local college, an association of guidance functionaries could well be formed for the exchange of information and for mutual assistance.

As guidance workers, we like to see individuals well-adjusted and imbued with a sense of accomplishment. We try to help individuals think their plans through and adjust to their environment. Where individuals cannot meet the requirements of the environment they desire, then, sometimes, we would like to modify the environment. With regard to college entrance, this means that we may tend to favor the broadening of standards for entrance to college and provision for students to pursue a greater variety of objectives after they are admitted.

But the needs and desires of the individual must be balanced against the welfare of the social group. In view of the development of more meaningful criteria of admission, colleges might well abandon narrow standards of time served in high school classes expressed in terms of units. But colleges prepared to provide high quality education are limited in the degree to which they can and should water down their basic standards of admission. The identification, the guidance, and the liberal education of the gifted are inescapable responsibilities of secondary and higher education, for it is from this group that most of our leaders come, and it is through the contributions of individuals in this group that most of the social and material progress of our civilization is accomplished.

In fact, the future of our whole civilization may depend upon how well this task is accomplished by the educational institutions of the nations of the free world. The identification and training of the best minds of the nation may be decisive in the long struggle with communism. The need for improved selection and guidance is great in the natural sciences, but it is even greater in the social sciences, since progress in this area lags greatly behind that in the other sciences.

As the birth rate rises and the number of children increases, the rising tide of students threatens to overwhelm the services of the elementary and secondary schools and to engulf many of the colleges. Even though colleges expand their facilities to the maximum, it is doubtful whether they will be able to continue over a long period to provide a four-year liberal education followed by professional training for the greatly increased number who will desire such advanced training. Intelligent, informed guidance and selection procedures that are high in validity are imperative. The personnel services of secondary schools and colleges must develop plans and procedures to assure that the most able young people will be given an opportunity for the most advanced and rigorous training of which they are capable. This is a civic, as well as a professional, duty.

Our duty is equally great to provide less demanding education and training, up to the limit of their ability, for the students who are not at the top of their group in aptitude or achievement. This means much greater opportunity for study beyond secondary school than has been available in the past and improved methods of guiding students into these opportunities.

LONG-TERM VOCATIONAL OPPORTUNITIES

Guidance services should, so far as possible, be oriented toward current and future economic and social conditions and trends. During periods that are relatively stable politically and economically, this is not an extremely difficult requirement, although, even under those conditions, schools too often continue to prepare boys and girls for kinds of adult work and service that fast become obsolete. There are, of course, great basic human needs, which in the long view, make for considerable institutional and occupational stability. But, for any generation of young people going through our schools and colleges, the opportunities for satisfactory placement and adjustment in the adult world are considerably determined by worldwide political and economic conditions. In recent years, increased tensions among nations, along with a vast technological revolution, have made the task of predicting future industrial and social progress particularly baffling. There probably has never been a time in our history when young people needed educational and vocational guidance so much as they do now, or when it has been so difficult to provide any kind of intelligent, long-term guidance for them. But one thing seems clear: the world of the future will need, to an ever-increasing degree, young people who are able to think and plan constructively, to utilize to its limit modern labor-saving equipment, and to work together harmoniously for the common good. These needs call for broad cultural and vocational education, not training in narrow vocational skills.

In a world of political and social ferment, and in an increasingly complex vocational setting, what can counselors do to keep informed of developments that have implications for guidance and of the changing opportunities for young people, and how may they make this information available to their counselees?

In the first place, guidance officers should, in a sense, be students of world affairs. On the national scene, particularly, they need to be informed and to help their counselees become informed, not only concerning existing conditions and laws as they affect education and industry, but also about proposed and pending legislation. Full information is also needed on opportunities for vocational placement through local employment agencies and personnel departments of industrial organizations in the community, and particularly through state employment services.

In the second place, much information may be obtained concerning both educational and vocational opportunities through the maintenance of an up-to-date library of books, handbooks, and periodical literature in these fields. Detailed suggestions concerning such reference materials will be found in the next section of this chapter.

In the third place, counselors should be informed about the major occupational groups and the changing demands for workers in these groups. The United States Employment Service has developed a standard classification of occupations based on the kinds of work involved. These occupational groups, as listed in the revised *Dictionary of Occupational Titles* (27), which is described in a later section (Sources of Information Concerning Vocational Opportunities) of the chapter, are as follows:

professional, technical, and managerial occupations
clerical and related occupations
sales and related occupations
service occupations
farming, fishery, forestry, and related occupations
industrial occupations

The influence of labor and trade unions upon entry into and work in the industrial occupations is an area about which both counselors and counselees should be informed.

Eleven major occupational groups were listed in connection with the 1960 census, and information on employment in these occupations was given (143). These occupational groups are as follows: (1) professional, technical, and kindred workers; (2) farmers and farm managers; (3) managers, officials, and proprietors, except farm; (4) clerical and kindred workers; (5) sales workers; (6) craftsmen, foremen, and kindred workers (7) operatives and kindred workers; (8) private household workers; (9) service workers, except private household; (10) farm laborers and foremen; (11) laborers, except farm and mine. The largest group consists of operatives and kindred workers (more than 18 percent), and the smallest groups are composed of private household workers and farm laborers and foremen (each less than 3 percent).

When one is considering a specific occupation, he naturally desires information concerning both the nature and conditions of the work in the occupation. In addition, the counselor should assist him in obtaining a number of other kinds of information, among which the following are important: (1) the mental abilities required in the occupation as compared with the measured abilities of the individual; (2) the extent and kind of general and special education required for entrance into the occupation; (3) requirements for certification to work in the occupation, such as examinations; (4) the long-term trend of employment in the occupation and the extent to which it is sensitive to changes in general economic conditions; (5) average income, range of income, and security afforded by the occupation; (6) possible restrictions on or

difficulties of entering the occupation as related to the sex, background, and personal qualities of the individual; and (7) the status and value of the occupation in the social order.

In addition to the provision of pertinent information concerning vocational opportunities, it is a function of guidance services to assess the aptitudes and interests of each pupil, and to attempt to see that each pupil develops some fairly broad ability while he is still in school. Various groupings of aptitudes are inherent in several of the aptitude test batteries, some of which are based on factorial analysis and others of which are derived from logical classifications of aptitude. The Differential Aptitude Tests, a widely used aptitude test battery in junior and senior high schools, use the following grouping of aptitudes: verbal reasoning, numerical ability, abstract reasoning, spatial relations, mechanical reasoning, clerical speed and accuracy, and language usage (28). A classification of occupational interests into broad groups, as indicated by the Kuder Preference Record—Vocational, is as follows: outdoor, mechanical, computational, scientific, persuasive, artistic, literary, musical, social service, and clerical (72). It will be observed that, although these classifications are not identical, they are similar in that both sets are pertinent to broad areas instead of being narrowly vocational. This distinction is important at the school level. The development of pupil aptitudes should be in the nature of a set of abilities basic to work in a large field, not merely an occupational trick. The broader the basis of preparation, the better one's chances of vocational adjustment in a changing world. The abilities to be especially stressed in the education of each individual depend upon an inventory of the potentialities of the individual himself.

Individual counseling with regard to vocations may be supplemented in a very helpful way by various group activities.[1] Such activities are commonly carried on through vocational exploratory courses and sometimes by means of carefully planned discussions in homerooms. In recent years, a considerable number of schools have adopted the plan of holding an annual career conference. This kind of conference ought to be planned by the faculty and pupils as a group project, and may well be centered around the major occupational interests of the pupils and pertinent questions raised by them. Outside speakers, including guidance specialists and representatives of different professional and vocational groups, are usually invited to participate in the career conference.

That a course in job finding and job orientation for high school students pays off in better placement and better satisfaction with jobs was indicated in a report of research carried on by Cuony and Hoppock (25).

[1] Group activities are discussed at greater length in Chapter XX.

SOURCES OF INFORMATION
ABOUT OPPORTUNITIES

Counselors, as well as pupils, need to be instructed concerning the opportunities available to young people. The counselor's information about opportunities afforded by the school will be obtained mainly through reading school catalogs, detailed study of course outlines, conferences with faculty members, and a careful survey of the entire school plant. The counselor should not only become thoroughly informed about all aspects of the opportunities which the school provides, but also should be alert to inadequacies in the total school program, and should use his influence to improve and broaden the opportunities.

INFORMATION CONCERNING OPPORTUNITIES
AFFORDED BY COLLEGES

A common and frequently used source of information concerning the postschool opportunities of college preparatory pupils is, of course, college catalogs. There should be available for use by both counselors and pupils a complete and up-to-date file of the catalogs of all colleges to which the school customarily sends students. Each counselor should try to become familiar with the pertinent guidance information in these catalogs. In particular, counselors should be alert to new and helpful statements that appear from time to time in college catalogs. These reflect changes in concepts of what the requirements for entrance to college ought to be and of what constitutes the characteristics of a well-prepared applicant. For instance, among the items in the questionnaire which the Committee on School and College Relations of the Educational Records Bureau submitted to colleges in 1963 (2), the following question appeared:

In order to help the schools to give better preparation, do you state in the catalog that certain habits, skills, and other qualities are of great importance to successful college work? Examples: ability to use a library effectively, to write a well-organized report, to profit from a lecture, and the like.

Thirty-six percent, or a little more than one third, answered this question affirmatively. Although it was found earlier that the majority of the colleges are favorable to a statement of this kind, only a sizeable minority actually include such a statement in their catalogs.

As the number of applicants to college increases and as the difficulties of entrance to highly selective colleges increase, those secondary schools which formerly considered sending their graduates to only a small list of colleges ought to extend their contacts and become ac-

quainted with the opportunities afforded by a much wider variety of colleges. Students who show interest in colleges other than those to which the graduates of the local secondary school traditionally go should be encouraged to write to these other colleges for catalogs and other information, and the counselor should help them obtain and study this information. This suggestion applies especially to eastern private schools and suburban public schools which long tended to be rather insular in their contacts with, and understanding of, colleges, but many of which are now broadening their contacts to include colleges throughout the United States.

Books and handbooks providing general information and descriptive listings of colleges and universities constitute a second kind of source of information about opportunities in higher education. Among these are *The College Handbook* (131) and the *Manual of Freshman Class Profiles* (84), both issued by the College Entrance Examination Board; *American Universities and Colleges* (9th edition), edited by Cartter (17); *American Junior Colleges* (6th edition), edited by Gleazer (44); and *Lovejoy's College Guide* (78). *The College Handbook* contains extensive information concerning the member institutions of the College Board, including descriptions of the colleges, accreditation, programs of study, expenses, and financial aid, including scholarships. The *Manual of Freshman Class Profiles* is designed to provide detailed information concerning the most recent freshman class in each of a large number of colleges, thus making it possible for a counselor to compare the qualities of a prospective applicant with the general characteristics of the students enrolled in the different colleges. *American Universities and Colleges* and *American Junior Colleges*, both published by the American Council on Education, make available thorough information on nearly all colleges and junior colleges in the United States up to 1962-1963. Sections such as the following appear in the description of each college listed: calendar, requirements, fees, departments and staffs, degrees conferred, ROTC units, recent developments, enrollment, foreign students, special devices, library, publications, student aid, finances, buildings and grounds, and administrative officers.

Lovejoy's College Guide is a popular handbook for pupils, parents, counselors, and teachers. The revised edition lists by state and briefly describes more than 2000 colleges and universities in this country. A monthly supplementary service, known as *Lovejoy's College Guide Digest* (79), supplies current information about colleges and furnishes up-to-date corrections of the information given in the *College Guide*. A newer book in the Lovejoy series, *Lovejoy's Vocational School Guide: A Handbook of Job Training Opportunities* (80) is a directory of more than 6500 public and private vocational schools throughout the United States.

Among other useful reference materials is the handy paperback guide by Brownstein (10), in which colleges throughout the country are listed by state, and pertinent information concerning each one is given concisely in tabular form. The Student Admission Center (G. James Hechtman, Director) in New York City issues up-to-date information about colleges and assists students in finding colleges suited to their capabilities.

A third kind of helpful information pertinent to the opportunities available to college-bound secondary school students is to be found in various studies of these problems of transition from school to college. In addition to the many studies issued over the years by individuals, various organizations have been active in this field. The College Entrance Examination Board has issued such studies throughout its history of more than 60 years. Reports of the Committee on School and College Relations of the Educational Records Bureau were referred to earlier. Ever since it was formed, about 1930, this committee has carried on periodic studies of college admission practices and has on occasion made recommendations which have had a strong guidance orientation.

In recent years, there has been a tendency for individual and committee research efforts in this field to be supplemented by, or perhaps somewhat replaced by, cooperative studies with foundation financial support. The Fund for the Advancement of Education has been particularly active in this area. Such studies inevitably imply well-planned and coordinated guidance throughout the secondary school and college years.

SOURCES OF INFORMATION CONCERNING VOCATIONAL OPPORTUNITIES

Among the many sources of information about vocational opportunities, several are indispensable for the counselor. One of these sources is the *Dictionary of Occupational Titles,* prepared by the United States Employment Service, and first published in four separate books in 1939. A revised edition was published in 1949, and a second revision in 1965. The new edition consists of two volumes. Volume I contains definitions of thousands of jobs arranged alphabetically, just as the corresponding volume in the preceding edition did. The new Volume I is based on recent observations and analysis of jobs throughout all industries. Some 6000 new jobs are listed. The functions required of the worker are given and the more important requirements are outlined.

The new Volume II, which takes the place of the older Volume II and Part IV, covers occupational classification structure. The individual classifications are identified by means of 6-digit code numbers. In the first classification, jobs are grouped into 6 broad categories, which are then subdivided into a total of some 90 divisions. In the second classification, all jobs are regrouped into 7 categories to show whether the worker is mainly involved with data, things, or people. These categories are also subdivided into about 90 subgroups.

There are cross references between Volumes I and II so that a counselor may more easily locate information, regardless of whether he begins with a job or with an individual counselee (27, 31).

Books and monographs about occupations provide a second indispensable source of information for the library of the school counselor. Among books of this kind published in recent years are Baer and Roeber's *Occupational Information,* one of the volumes in the SRA Professional Guidance Series (4); Forrester's *Methods of Vocational Guidance* (38); Greenleaf's *Occupations and Careers* (46); and Shartle's *Occupational Information* (119).

A third valuable source of vocational information is the *Occupational Outlook Handbook* (96), the *Occupational Outlook Quarterly* (97), and the *Occupational Outlook Report Series* (98), which are available from the Superintendent of Documents, Washington, D.C. The *Handbook* explores probable employment trends and economic conditions for the next several years, and presents concise profiles of almost 700 occupations and 30 major industries. The *Quarterly* expands and updates occupational information between editions of the *Handbook.* The *Outlook Report Series* consists of reprints from the *Handbook* which provide helpful career information to students, parents, counselors, teachers, and others.

Booklets and pamphlets prepared by various occupational groups concerning their own fields furnish an ever growing source of information relative to vocational opportunities. This source of information is particularly pertinent to the professions. These publications tend to be simply and clearly written, for they are usually aimed directly at promising young persons who are potential candidates for the profession in question, and their parents. For instance, the American Institute of Certified Public Accountants published a small illustrated booklet, *Accounting May Be the Right Field for You* (1), which provides an objective appraisal of the opportunities, requirements, work, returns, and professional growth afforded by a career as a CPA. Similarly, the General Motors Corporation issued a simple, illustrated booklet called *Can I Be An Engineer?* (12); the American Institute of Mining and Metallurgical Engineers published a monograph on *Careers in the Mineral Industries* (6); and the American Association of Advertising Agencies made available *Career Opportunities in Advertising* (14). Many other free or inexpensive pamphlets on occupations may be collected by alert counselors and made available to pupils in the guidance library. For instance, the Committee of Presidents of Statistical Societies has prepared a booklet, *Careers in Statistics,* which is available free to counselors from the American Statistical Association, Washington, D.C. (*15*).

A series of articles prepared by representatives of various professions and high-level occupations and run as a series of advertisements in lay magazines contains helpful information for parents and their children on a variety of careers. Among these articles, which are available in reprint form, are the following: "Should Your Child be an Accountant?" "Should Your Child be a Chemist?" "Should Your Child be a Public Servant?" "Should Your Child be a Teacher?" "Should Your Child be a Lawyer?" "Should Your Child be a Doctor?" "Should Your Child be a Farmer?" "Should Your Child be a Newspaper Man?" "Should Your Child be an Architect?" "The Cost of Four Years at College" (*94*).

A bibliography of occupational literature prepared by the Career Information Services of the New York Life Insurance Company is also available (*50*).

Still another source of information with regard to vocational opportunities is a coordinated series of pamphlets, such as the *SRA Career Information Kit* (*127*), published by Science Research Associates, and the *Counselor's Information Service* (*23*), issued by B'nai B'rith Vocational Service.

For a good, brief list of occupational materials and suggestions concerning choice of occupation, see the *Kiplinger Washington Letter* for June, 1964.

Books and monographs on occupations tend to become out of date unless they are revised rather frequently. Counselors and counselees may be helped in keeping abreast of new developments by reading current magazines and professional journals, such as the *Personnel and Guidance Journal* (*99*), which is published monthly from September through May by the American Personnel and Guidance Association, Washington, D.C., and the *Vocational Guidance Quarterly* (*148*), which is issued four times a year by the National Vocational Guidance Association, Washington, D.C.

Practically all these occupational materials are suitable for use either individually and informally or with organized groups, although the use of certain ones, such as the *Dictionary of Occupational Titles* (*27*), calls for explanation and assistance from the counselor. Vocational orientation courses are probably the most generally used means of informing pupils in a systematic way about occupational opportunities. The success of such courses is largely dependent upon the initiative, industry, imagination, and enthusiasm of the instructor. Much work

and planning is required to render such courses thoroughly dynamic and strictly up-to-date.

Exploratory courses form another means of disseminating information about occupational opportunities among young people. These courses allow pupils at the junior high school level to sample the work experience of various kinds of occupations within a relatively brief period of time. This type of direct experience should be supplemented by visitation and observation in local business and industrial plants. Visitation trips need to be carefully selected and planned, for they are time-consuming. But with young people these no doubt leave more lasting impressions concerning occupations than any which may be secured through the reading of occupational materials alone. Classes in vocations are also found in the senior high school and even at the college level (*55*). Exploratory courses in occupations may be supplemented by well-planned career conferences (*11*).

A book by Norris (*95*) is a pioneer effort in the provision of occupational information for teachers and guidance workers at the elementary school level.

INFORMATION ABOUT THE PUPIL HIMSELF AND HIS SCHOOL AND LIFE OPPORTUNITIES

The last kind of informational material to be mentioned here includes books, pamphlets, and films prepared to help the pupil understand himself and appreciate the current and future opportunities which his school makes available to him. While these materials are informational in character, they frequently have inspirational elements as well. There is now a large number of books addressed directly to the pupil himself and written from the standpoint of adolescent psychology.

Among these books are the following: *You: Today and Tomorrow,* by Katz (*66*); *Stairway to College,* by Ruby and Ruby (*114*); *College Orientation: A Study-Skills Manual,* by Weigand and Blake (*151*); *College Ahead,* by Wilson and Bucher (*153*); and *How to Visit College,* published by the National Vocational Guidance Association (*60*).

The SRA Activity Texts and Guidance Booklets for elementary and high school pupils make available a long series of comparatively inexpensive books and booklets designed for planning their educational and vocational future. These materials are classified according to grade level from the primary grades through the junior college. Some of the titles for the different levels are: K-1, *A Book About Me;* Grades 4-7, *Learn How to Study;* Grades 9-12, *Charting Your Job Future;* Grades 7-9, *Looking Toward High School;* Grades 10-12, *Handbook of Job Facts;* Grades 7-9, *Planning My Future;* Grades 10-12, *How to*

Get Into College and Stay There; Grades 10-12, *Handbook of Job Facts* (127).

Films, such as *Finding Your Life Work* (36), *Planning Your Career* (102), *Discussion Problems in Group Living* (29), *College: Your Challenge* (22), and *Thinking Collegewise* (132), can be used to supplement reading materials and promote worthwhile group discussions. A set of five guidance film strips, developed by the Society for Visual Education and made available by Science Research Associates, may be used to introduce junior high school pupils to the world of work. There is some research evidence, such as that in a study by Miller (86), which indicates that films are almost as effective as visits to industries in furnishing occupational information to students.

REFERENCES

1. *Accounting May Be the Right Field for You,* rev. ed. New York: American Institute of Certified Public Accountants, 1961. Pp. 25.
2. *Admission to American Colleges.* New York: Educational Records Bureau, 1964. Pp. 28.
3. Arbuckle, Dugald S. "Occupational Information in the Elementary School," *Vocational Guidance Quarterly,* XII (Winter 1963–1964), 77–84.
4. Baer, Max F., and Roeber, Edward C. *Occupational Information: The Dynamics of Its Nature and Use.* Chicago: Science Research Associates, Inc., 1964. Pp. 494.
5. Banks, Waldo R. "College Day—Boon or Ban," *Personnel and Guidance Journal,* XLII (February 1964), 613–615.
6. Beall, John V., and Lutzjin, George P. *Careers in the Mineral Industries.* New York: American Institute of Mining and Metallurgical Engineers (not dated). Pp. 32.
7. Beals, Lester, and Simmons, Patricia. "Counseling Needs of Gifted High School Students," *Personnel and Guidance Journal,* XL (April 1962), 712–716.
8. Bell, Hugh M. "Ego-Involvement in Vocational Decisions," *Personnel and Guidance Journal,* XXXVIII (May 1960), 732–736.
9. Berdie, Ralph F., and Hood, Albert B. "Changing Plans of High School Graduates," *Personnel and Guidance Journal,* XLII (September 1963), 43–46.
10. Brownstein, Samuel C. *College Bound.* Woodbury, N.Y.: Barron's Educational Series, 1963. Pp. 320.
11. Brundage, Erven, and Frank, Stanley D. "The Career Conference Concept in San Diego County," *Personnel and Guidance Journal,* XL (October 1961), 174–175.
12. *Can I Be an Engineer?* Detroit: Department of Public Relations, General Motors Corporation (not dated).
13. Caplan, Stanley W., Ruble, Ronald A., and Segel, David. "A Theory of Educational and Vocational Choice in Junior High School," *Personnel and Guidance Journal,* XLII (October 1963), 129–135.
14. *Career Opportunities in Advertising,* 5th ed. New York: American Association of Advertising Agencies, 1964. Pp. 22.
15. *Careers in Statistics,* 2nd ed. Washington, D.C.: American Statistical Association, 1963. Pp. 24.
16. Carey, Walter F. *The Development of Our Manpower Resources.* Washington, D.C.: Chamber of Commerce of the United States, 1965. Pp. 23.
17. Cartter, Allan M. (ed.). *American Universities and Colleges,* 9th ed. Washington, D.C.: American Council on Education, 1964. Pp. xv + 1339.
18. Cass, James, and Birnbaum, Max. *Comparative Guide to American Colleges.* New York: Harper & Row, Publishers, 1965. Pp. 576.
19. Cassel, Russell N. "Space Age Critical Problem Areas," *Vocational Guidance Quarterly,* VIII (Spring 1960), 126–128.
20. Chapin, Arthur B., and others. "Career Counseling Builds Good Will," *Bulletin of the National Association of Secondary-School Principals,* XLIV (September 1960), 63–67.
21. Cohn, G. "Reorganization of College Advising," *High Points,* XLIV (May 1962), 70–75.
22. *College: Your Challenge.* Chicago: Coronet Films, 1953.
23. *Counselor's Information Service.* Washington, D.C.: B'nai B'rith Vocational Service.
24. Cox, Rachel D. "New Emphases in Vocational Guidance," *Vocational Guidance Quarterly,* X (Autumn 1961), 11–15.
25. Cuony, Edward R., and Hoppock, Robert. "Job Course Pays Off," *Personnel and Guidance Journal,* XXXII (March 1954), 389–391.
26. Dettre, J. R. "High School Record and the Employer," *Ohio School,* XXXIX (April 1961), 23ff.
27. *Dictionary of Occupational Titles.* Washington, D.C.: Superintendent of Documents, 1965.
28. *Differential Aptitude Tests,* by George K. Bennett, Harold Seashore, and Alexander G. Wesman. New York: The Psychological Corporation, 1947–1951.
29. *Discussion Problems in Group Living.* New York: Young America Films, Inc., 1951–1954.
30. Eckerson, Andrew B. "The New Dictionary of Occupational Titles: Its Implications for Guidance," *Vocational Guidance Quarterly,* X (Summer 1962), 202–205.
31. Eckerson, Andrew B. "The New Dictionary of Occupational Titles," *Vocational Guidance Quarterly,* XII (Autumn 1963), 40–42.
32. *Education and Training: The Bridge between Man and His Work.* Washington, D.C.: Superintendent of Documents, 1965. Pp. 61.
33. *Electronic Business Data Processing Peripheral Equip-*

ment Occupations. Washington, D.C.: Superintendent of Documents, 1964. Pp. ii + 114.

34. Endicott, Frank S. *Guiding Superior and Talented High School Students.* Chicago: North Central Association of Colleges and Secondary Schools, 1961. Pp. 84.

35. Ferrer, Terry. "The College Panic," *New York Herald Tribune* (April 9, 1964), 23, 25.

36. *Finding Your Life Work.* New York: Association Films, Inc.

37. Flanagan, John C. "The Effective Use of Manpower Resources," *Personnel and Guidance Journal,* XLII (October 1963), 114–118.

38. Forrester, Gertrude. *Methods of Vocational Guidance,* rev. ed. Boston: D. C. Heath and Company, 1951. Pp. x + 464.

39. Forrester, Gertrude. *Occupational Literature: An Annotated Bibliography,* 1964 ed. New York: The H. W. Wilson Company, 1964. Pp. 675.

40. Forte, James J. "What Business Expects of the High School Graduate," *Vocational Guidance Quarterly,* VI (Winter 1957–1958), 103–105.

41. *From High School to College: Readings for Counselors.* Papers Presented at the Work Conference on Guidance for School-College Transition, August 17–28, 1964, at Teachers College, Columbia University. New York: College Entrance Examination Board, 1965. Pp. vi + 86.

42. Gamble, Glenn. "Liberal Arts College Admission Requirements Today," *Vocational Guidance Quarterly,* IX (Spring 1961), 164–167.

43. Getzels, Jacob W., and Jackson, Philip W. *Creativity and Intelligence: Explorations with Gifted Students.* New York: John Wiley & Sons, Inc., 1962. Pp. xvii + 293.

44. Gleazer, Edmund J., Jr. *American Junior Colleges,* 6th ed. Washington, D.C.: American Council on Education, 1963. Pp. xii + 551.

45. Greenberg, Sylvia B. "Job Placement of the Emotionally Handicapped," *Vocational Guidance Quarterly,* VIII (Summer 1960), 247–249.

46. Greenleaf, Walter J. *Occupations and Careers.* New York: McGraw-Hill Book Company, Inc., 1955. Pp. iv + 580.

47. Guidance Information Review Service (William E. Hopke, chairman). "Current Occupational Literature," *Vocational Guidance Quarterly,* XIII (Winter 1964–1965), 148–151.

48. Guidance Information Review Service (William E. Hopke, chairman). "Current Occupational Literature," *Vocational Guidance Quarterly,* XIII (Spring 1965), 222–227.

49. "Guidance Services," *Annual Report 1962–63: 60th Report of the College Entrance Examination Board,* (Douglas D. Dillenbeck, director), pp. 17–20. New York: The College Entrance Examination Board, 1964. Pp. 97.

50. *Guide to Career Information: A Bibliography of Occu-pational Literature.* Career Information Service, New York Life Insurance Co. New York: Harper & Row, Publishers, 1957. Pp. 203.

51. Harbison, Frederick, and Myers, Charles A. *Education, Manpower, and Economic Growth: Strategies of Human Resource Development.* New York: McGraw-Hill Book Company, Inc., 1964. Pp. 229.

52. Hart, Dale J., and Lifton, Walter M. "Of Things to Come—Automation and Counseling," pp. 282–286; Paterson, Donald G. "Comments," p. 287, *Personnel and Guidance Journal,* XXXVII (December 1958).

53. Harwood, Michael. *The Student's Guide to Military Service,* rev. ed. Manhasset, N.Y.: Channel Press, 1964. Pp. 293.

54. Hawes, Gene R. *The New American Guide to Colleges.* New York: Signet Books, New American Library of World Literature, Inc., 1962. Pp. 272.

55. Hewer, Vivian H. "Group Counseling, Individual Counseling, and a College Class in Vocations," *Personnel and Guidance Journal,* XXXVII (May 1959), 660–665.

56. Hewer, Vivian H. "What Do Theories of Vocational Choice Mean to a Counselor?" *Journal of Counseling Psychology,* X (Summer 1963), 118–125.

57. Hoedt, Kenneth C., and Rothney, John W. M. "Guidance for Superior Students," *Vocational Guidance Quarterly,* XI (Spring 1963), 199–201.

58. Holland, John L. "A Theory of Vocational Choice: Vocational Images," *Vocational Guidance Quarterly,* XI (Summer 1963), 232–239.

59. Holland, John L. "A Theory of Vocational Choice: Self-Descriptions, Coping Behavior, Competencies, and Vocational Preferences," *Vocational Guidance Quarterly,* XII (Autumn 1963), 17–21.

60. *How to Visit College.* Washington, D.C.: National Vocational Guidance Association, 1964. Pp. 32.

61. Hunt, J. T. "Guidance and Exceptional Children," *Education,* LXXX (February 1960), 344–348.

62. Hunter, William F. "Occupational Information for Rural Youth," *Vocational Guidance Quarterly,* VIII (Autumn 1958), 51–54.

63. Hutson, P. W. "Vocational Choices, 1930 to 1961," *Vocational Guidance Quarterly,* X (Summer 1962), 218–222.

64. Jones, Vernon. "Attitude Changes in an NDEA Institute," *Personnel and Guidance Journal,* XLII (December 1963), 387–392.

65. Kalist, Richard A. *Making the Most of College.* San Francisco: Wadsworth Publishing Co., 1959. Pp. vii + 248.

66. Katz, Martin R. *You: Today and Tomorrow,* 3rd ed. Princeton, N.J.: Educational Testing Service, 1959. Pp. 102.

67. Keppel, Francis. *Education and Employability in a Technological Society.* Washington, D.C.: Department of Health, Education and Welfare, 1963. Pp. 8 (mimeographed).

68. Kohler, Mary C., and Freedman, Marcia K. *Youth in*

the World of Work. New York: Taconic Foundation, 1962. Pp. 59.

69. Komisar, David D. "Squandering Creative Talent," *Vocational Guidance Quarterly*, IX (Summer 1961), 230–232.

70. Krippner, Stanley. "Junior High School Students' Vocational Preferences and Their Parents' Occupational Levels," *Personnel and Guidance Journal*, LXI (March 1963), 590–595.

71. Krugman, Morris. "Appraisal and Treatment of Personality Problems in a Guidance Program," *Education in a Free World* (ed. by Arthur E. Traxler), pp. 114–121. Report of Twentieth Educational Conference Sponsored by the Educational Records Bureau and the American Council on Education. Washington, D.C.: American Council on Education, 1955. Pp. viii + 164.

72. Kuder, G. Frederic. *Kuder Preference Record—Vocational*. Chicago: Science Research Associates, Inc., 1934–1951.

73. Laime, Barbara F., and Zytowski, Donald G. "Women's Scores on the M and F Forms of the SVIB," *Vocational Guidance Quarterly*, XII (Winter 1963–1964), 116–118.

74. Landis, Paul H. *So This Is College*. New York: McGraw-Hill Book Company, Inc., 1954. Pp. 205 (out of print).

75. Lifton, Walter M. "Vocational Guidance in the Elementary School," *Vocational Guidance Quarterly*, VIII (Winter 1959–1960), 79–81.

76. Lifton, Walter M. "The Non-college Bound," *NEA Journal*, LI (December 1962), 27–28.

77. Lopez, Jacqueline. "Cases in Vocational Counseling Career Planning Five Years After High School," *Vocational Guidance Quarterly*, X (Spring 1962), 175–178.

78. Lovejoy, Clarence E. *Lovejoy's College Guide*. New York: Simon and Schuster, Inc. Published biennially.

79. Lovejoy, Clarence E. *Lovejoy's College Guide Digest*. New York: Simon and Schuster, Inc. Published monthly.

80. Lovejoy, Clarence E. *Lovejoy's Vocational School Guide: A Handbook of Job Training Opportunities*. New York: Simon and Schuster, Inc., 1955. Pp. 215.

81. Lovejoy, Clarence E. *Lovejoy's Preparatory School Guide*, rev. ed. New York: Harper & Row, Publishers, 1963. Pp. 136.

82. Mallery, David. *High School Students Speak Out*. New York: Harper & Row, Publishers, 1962. Pp. xv + 171.

83. *Making of the Future: Report for 1963*. New York: Vocational Advisory Service, 1964.

84. *Manual of Freshman Class Profiles*, 1964 ed. New York: College Entrance Examination Board, 1964. Pp. xiv + 584.

85. Menninger, William C. *All About You*. Chicago: Science Research Associates, Inc., 1955. Pp. 48.

86. Miller, Ray A. "Teaching Operations Using Films and Field Trips," *Personnel and Guidance Journal*, XXXI (March 1953), 373–375.

87. Moore, Gilbert D. "Counseling the Gifted Child," *School Review*, LXVIII (Spring 1960), 63–70.

88. Morman, Robert R. "Automation and Counseling," *Personnel and Guidance Journal*, XL (March 1962), 594–599.

89. Munger, Paul F., and Johnson, Carleton A. "Changes in Attitudes Associated with an NDEA Counseling and Guidance Institute," *Personnel and Guidance Journal*, XXXVIII (May 1960), 751–753.

90. Murray, Evelyn. "Work: A Neglected Resource for Students," *Personnel and Guidance Journal*, XLI (November 1962), 229–233.

91. Musselman, D. L., and Willig, L. A. "The Science Fair: A Vocational Guidance Opportunity," *Vocational Guidance Quarterly*, IX (Spring 1961), 153–157.

92. Nason, Leslie J. *Keys to Success in School*. Washington, D.C.: Public Affairs Press, 1963. Pp. 129.

93. "NDEA Adds 300 Guidance Personnel to California High Schools," *California Education*, I (October 1963), 23.

94. New York Life Insurance Company Series of Advertisements Presented to Help Guide America's Children to a Better Future. Reprints available from the New York Life Insurance Company, New York, N.Y.

95. Norris, Willa. *Occupational Information in the Elementary School*. Chicago: Science Research Associates, Inc., 1963. Pp. xi + 243.

96. *Occupational Outlook Handbook*. Washington, D.C.: Superintendent of Documents, 1964. Pp. 792.

97. *Occupational Outlook Quarterly*. Washington, D.C.: Superintendent of Documents. Published in September, December, February, and May.

98. *Occupational Outlook Report Series*. Washington, D.C.: Superintendent of Documents.

99. *Personnel and Guidance Journal*. Washington, D.C.: American Personnel and Guidance Association.

100. Peters, Herman J. "The Riddle of Occupational Information," *Vocational Guidance Quarterly*, XI (Summer 1963), 253–258.

101. Piel, Gerard. "The Future of Work," *Vocational Guidance Quarterly*, X (Autumn 1961), 4–10.

102. *Planning Your Career*. Wilmette, Ill.: Encyclopaedia Britannica Films, Inc.

103. Poppel, Norman. "Vocational Planning Sessions: A Suggested Approach," *Vocational Guidance Quarterly*, XII (Autumn 1963), 57–60.

104. Poppel, Norman. "College Planning Sessions: A Suggested Approach with Parents," *Vocational Guidance Quarterly*, XII (Spring 1964), 182–186.

105. *Prep Club Members Guide and Handbook*. Everett, Mass.: National Prep Club Foundation, Inc., 1964. Pp. 77.

106. Prince, Richard. "Values, Achievements, and Career Choice of High School Students," *Elementary School Journal*, IX (April 1960), 376–384.

107. Pritchard, David H. "The Occupational Exploration

Process: Some Operational Implications," *Personnel and Guidance Journal*, XL (April 1962), 674–680.

108. Rauner, Therese M. "Occupational Information and Occupational Choice," *Personnel and Guidance Journal*, XLI (December 1962), 311–317.

109. Riccio, Anthony C., and Peters, Herman J. "Vocational Guidance and Familial Influences," *Vocational Guidance Quarterly*, VIII (Winter 1959–1960), 70–71.

110. Ritzman, Elmer R. "Subject Career Day," *Vocational Guidance Quarterly*, VIII (Spring 1960), 155–156.

111. Roman, John C. "Will Engineers and Scientists Become Clerks of the Future?" *Balance Sheet*, XLII (November 1960), 129.

112. Roskins, Ronald W. "Informal Observations in Guidance: Career Day," *Personnel and Guidance Journal*, XXXVI (March 1958), 501–502.

113. Rubenfeld, William A., and Hoppock, Robert. "Occupational Courses Evaluated Eight Years Later," *Vocational Guidance Quarterly*, X (Autumn 1961), 45–48.

114. Ruby, Normie, and Ruby, Harold. *Stairway to College: A Guidebook for the Prospective College Student*. Boston: Porter Sargent, 1955. Pp. 80.

115. Rundquist, Richard M., and Apostal, Robert. "Occupational and Educational Information," *Review of Educational Research*, XXX (April 1960), 148–157.

116. Sanford, Nevitt. *The American College*. New York: John Wiley & Sons, Inc., 1962. Pp. vi + 1084.

117. Seashore, Harold G. "Women Are More Predictable Than Men," *Journal of Counseling Psychology*, X (Summer 1963), 261–270.

118. Selden, William. "Guidance for Business Education," *Vocational Guidance Quarterly*, XI (Winter 1963–1964), 107–112.

119. Shartle, Carroll L. *Occupational Information: Its Development and Application*, 3rd ed. New York: Prentice-Hall, Inc., 1959. Pp. 384.

120. Shulim, Joseph I. "Experimenting with a Career-Curricular Conference," *Personnel and Guidance Journal*, XXXVIII (November 1959), 222–225.

121. Sifferd, Calvin S. *College and You*. Bloomington, Ill.: McKnight & McKnight Publishing Company, 1952. Pp. 104.

122. Simpson, Richard L., and Simpson, Ida Harper. "Values, Personal Influences, and Occupational Choice," *Social Forces*, XXXIX (December 1960), 116–125.

123. Sinick, Daniel, and Hoppock, Robert. "Research by States on the Teaching of Occupations," *Personnel and Guidance Journal*, XXXIX (November 1960), 218–219.

124. Smith, David Wayne. "Vocational Planning for the Mentally Limited," *Vocational Guidance Quarterly*, VI (Spring 1958), 142–146.

125. Spiegler, Charles, and Hamburger, Martin. *If You're Not Going to College*. Chicago: Science Research Associates, Inc., 1959. Pp. 80.

126. *SRA Better Living Booklets*. Chicago: Science Research Associates, Inc.

127. *SRA Career Information Kit*. Chicago: Science Research Associates, Inc., 1965.

128. Strom, Merl T. (ed.). *Needs of Adolescent Youth*. Danville, Ill.: Interstate Printers and Publishers, Inc., 1963. Pp. 145.

129. Sulkin, Sidney. *Complete Planning for College*. New York: McGraw-Hill Book Company, Inc., 1962. Pp. 320.

130. Super, Donald E., and Crites, John O. *Appraising Vocational Fitness*, rev. ed. New York: Harper & Row, Publishers, 1962. Pp. xv + 688.

131. *The College Handbook, 1963–1965*. New York: College Entrance Examination Board, 1963. XXIII + 614.

132. *Thinking Collegewise*. Saxtons River, Vt.: Guidance Information Center, 1961.

133. Thistlethwaite, Donald L. "Counseling High-Aptitude Students on Scholarship Opportunities," *Personnel and Guidance Journal*, XXXVII (April 1959), 574–577.

134. Thompson, Albert S. "Personality Dynamics and Vocational Counseling," *Personnel and Guidance Journal*, XXXVIII (January 1960), 350–357.

135. Thorndike, Robert L. "The Prediction of Vocational Success," *Vocational Guidance Quarterly*, XI (Spring 1963), 179–187.

136. Torrance, E. Paul. *Guiding Creative Talent*. Englewood Cliffs, N.J.: Prentice-Hall, Inc., 1962. Pp. xi + 278.

137. Townsend, Agatha. *College Freshmen Speak Out*. New York: Harper & Row, Publishers, 1956. Pp. x + 136.

138. Traxler, Arthur E. "Many Colleges Lead in Successful Graduates," *College Board Review*, XXXV (Spring 1958), 18–20.

139. Traxler, Arthur E. "Where Are the Leading Colleges for Women?" *College Board Review*, L (Spring, 1963), 22–25.

140. Traxler, Arthur E., and Townsend, Agatha (eds.). *Improving Transition from School to College*. New York: Harper & Row, Publishers, 1953. Pp. xiv + 166.

141. Treires, James J. "The New Occupational Outlook Handbook," *Vocational Guidance Quarterly*, X (Autumn 1961). 24–27.

142. Trumpe, Richard M., and Isaacson, Lee E. "The Student Handbook—A Bridge to Better Understanding," *Vocational Guidance Quarterly*, VII (Summer 1959), 231–235.

143. U.S. Bureau of Census. *U.S. Census of Population: 1960*, "Occupations by Industry," Part I, United States Summary. Washington, D.C.: Government Printing Office, 1963. Pp. xvii + 146.

144. Uzzell, Odell. "Influences of Occupational Choice," *Personnel and Guidance Journal*, XXXIX (April 1961), 666–669.

145. Venn, Grant. *Man, Education, and Work: Postsecondary Vocational and Technical Education*. Washington, D.C.: American Council on Education, 1964. Pp. 184.

146. *Vocational and Technical Education: A Review of Activities in Federally Aided Programs*. Washington,

D.C.: Department of Health, Education, and Welfare, 1963. Pp. 68.

147. *Vocational Education Act of 1963.* Washington, D.C.: Superintendent of Documents, 1965. Pp. 29.

148. *Vocational Guidance Quarterly.* Washington, D.C.: National Vocational Guidance Association.

149. Walther, Regis H. "The Functional Occupational Classification Project: A Critical Appraisal," *Personnel and Guidance Journal,* XXXVIII (May 1960), 698–706.

150. Walton, Wesley W. "The Electronic Age Comes to the Schoolhouse," *Systems for Educators* (January–February 1962).

151. Weigand, George, and Blake, Walter S., Jr. *College Orientation: A Study-Skills Manual.* Englewood Cliffs, N.J.: Prentice-Hall, Inc., 1955. Pp. 149.

152. Williams, Elsa H., and Cantoni, Louis J. "Vocational Rehabilitation of the Severely Disabled," *Vocational Guidance Quarterly,* VIII (Winter 1959–1960), 68–70.

153. Wilson, Eugene S., and Bucher, Charles A. *College Ahead,* rev. ed. New York: Harcourt, Brace & World, Inc., 1961. Pp. vi + 168 + Appendix.

154. Winthrop, Henry. "Automation and the Future of Personnel and Industrial Psychology," *Personnel and Guidance Journal,* XXXVII (January 1959), 326–333.

155. Wolfbein, Seymour L. "Transition from School to Work," *Personnel and Guidance Journal,* XXXVIII (October 1959), 98–105.

156. Wolfbein, Seymour L. "The Outlook for the Skilled Worker in the United States: Implications for Guidance and Counseling," *Personnel and Guidance Journal,* XL (December 1961), 334–339.

157. Wolfman, Earl F., Jr. "A Medical Careers' Day Conference," *Vocational Guidance Quarterly,* IX (Summer 1961), 217–219.

158. Wood, Helen. "New Edition of the *Occupational Outlook Handbook,*" *Vocational Guidance Quarterly,* VIII (Autumn 1959), 7–8.

159. Wrenn, C. Gilbert. *The Counselor in a Changing World.* Washington, D.C.: American Personnel and Guidance Association, 1962. Pp. 195.

CHAPTER IV

Kinds of Information Needed: Use of Interviews and Questionnaires in Collecting Information

NEEDED INFORMATION ABOUT INDIVIDUAL PUPILS

THERE ARE AT LEAST TEN AREAS OF THE HISTORY and development of the individual pupil within which we need information for guidance purposes. In this chapter these areas will be listed separately for purposes of definition and discussion. At first glance this approach may seem to be inconsistent with the suggestion that guidance is a unitary process; however, the interrelationship rather than the separation of definable areas is stressed in this chapter. Although the areas may seem to consist of separate bits of information, they contain factors which are closely interrelated. One of the primary functions of the counselor is to obtain from these related factors a picture of the student as a whole, and at the same time detect factors which may dominate the individual's whole adjustment.

One of the ten areas is *home background*. It is desirable to obtain facts concerning the parents, including type of occupation, education, health, birthplace, citizenship, and language spoken. Likewise, the names, sex, birth dates, education, and health of siblings should be listed. In addition, it is helpful to have information about the community in which the home is located, study conditions in the home, availability of books and magazines for home reading, and other factors—such as "broken home."

A second type of information has to do with *school history and record of classwork*. Information should be available concerning names and types of schools attended, achievement in subjects and activities, and school diffi-

culties encountered. There should, of course, be a complete record of the subjects studied by the pupil and of his progress in these subjects. This has, from the beginning, been the most common kind of information kept for individual pupils in schools, and it is probable that this is still true in the majority of schools in the United States. While all schools keep a record of the classwork of their pupils, not all of them make the record in identical terms. This situation is to be expected, for we are in a period of transition with respect to records of classwork. The conventional bases of reports of classwork—the unit of work and the school mark—have been under fire for some years. Many schools, colleges, and other groups, including the Carnegie Foundation for the Advancement of Teaching, have said that they favor abandonment of the "Carnegie Unit." Various individuals and groups have pointed to its limitations, including its tendency to cause the accumulation of credits to be the major objective of many students and its inapplicability to the curriculums of many modern secondary schools. It has been urged that, in view of the development of objective measurement techniques, it has become possible to assess the ability, knowledge, and proficiency of any individual more dependably through the use of these devices than by means of units of credits often based largely upon time spent in class.[1]

As for the other time-honored basis of reports of classwork, dissatisfaction with the indefinite and unreliable

[1] Arthur E. Traxler and Agatha Townsend (eds.) *Improving Transition from School to College,* pp. 62–65. New York: Harper & Row, Publishers, 1953.

nature of marks and with their tendency to vary widely from one institution to another has caused some schools to abandon them in favor of a verbal statement of success achieved in the different fields of study. The guidance value of records of school work will be greatly enhanced if the information is made available in meaningful, qualitative terms, instead of, or supplementary to, marks and credits expressed in units.

A third kind of information needed for guidance is an appraisal of the *mental ability* or *academic aptitude* of each pupil. It is generally recognized now that academic aptitude is not entirely, or even primarily, an innate characteristic, but is a combination of native capacity and training, in proportions that vary according to the individual and the environment. The appraisal of the intelligence or academic aptitude of each individual might be done by means of subjective rating procedures, but tests are so much more reliable than opinion that they have become the standard procedures for use in investigating aptitude.

Most secondary schools now administer one intelligence, or academic aptitude, test to their pupils at some time during their high school course, and a considerable number obtain the results of two or more such tests for each individual. Many schools administer different forms of the same test at intervals of a year, or perhaps every two or three years, in order to obtain a record which would indicate growth in mental ability. In the past, schools have commonly employed tests yielding just one mental age and IQ. While the results of tests of this kind are generally helpful, it is now widely recognized that tests yielding scores that have diagnostic values are more valuable in placement and guidance. Other things being equal, a school should give preference to an academic aptitude test that yields, in addition to a gross score, separate scores for at least linguistic aptitude and quantitative aptitude, or language and nonlanguage aptitude. There is a growing tendency to use academic aptitude tests that yield from two to eight, or even more, part scores.

Nearly all tests of academic aptitude call for much reading, and the results are highly correlated with reading test scores. It is desirable, nevertheless, for the school to obtain reading test results as further evidence of academic aptitude. Reading ability is so important in school and college that students with a special reading disability are almost certain to experience difficulty with courses in the humanities, social studies, and natural sciences.

A fourth kind of guidance information concerning the individual has to do with *achievement and growth in different fields of study.* The class record furnishes information concerning the achievement of a student, but it is determined partly by the subjective judgment of the various teachers and is inevitably influenced to some extent by the effort, interest, enthusiasm, and personality of the student. The school should, if possible, supplement the class record with objective evidence of achievement based on comparable tests. A comprehensive achievement testing program should include for each pupil four or five tests, which are usually administered near the end of the year. Tests commonly used for college preparatory pupils in such a program are an English test, a foreign language test, and either broad field tests or the appropriate subject tests in mathematics, science, and social studies. For pupils in other courses, tests in English and social studies, and achievement tests appropriate to the particular courses may be used. For example, in the commercial field, tests of shorthand, typewriting, bookkeeping, business law, and so forth may be employed. The results of all acheivement tests should be recorded cumulatively in either tabular or graphic form or both.

Information concerning achievement and growth obtained in the secondary school not only is valuable for guidance while the pupil is in school, but is also helpful in making reports for selection and guidance purposes to higher institutions and to business and industrial organizations. One of the recommendations that the Committee on School and College Relations of the Educational Records Bureau submitted in 1941 to colleges was that in considering a candidate for entrance, colleges should give full weight to the results of comparable tests which have been constructed, administered, and scored by competent persons. The colleges apparently agreed with this recommendation in principle. Of the 400 colleges that replied to the questionnaire, more than three-fourths favored the recommendation (7). However, in a study of actual practices in college admission, which the committee undertook in 1949–1950, it was found that only about 30 percent of the 607 colleges expressed willingness to accept test records from high schools (1). Doubt on the part of the colleges concerning the adequacy of the administration and scoring of tests used in many high schools and lack of comparability among the various tests employed were reasons given for reluctance to accept such records. In a study reported by the same committee in 1964, it was again found that most colleges were reluctant to accept test results from secondary schools *in lieu of* entrance tests, and it was inferred that their reluctance resulted from the difficulty of equating test records from different schools (2).

A fifth type of guidance information deals with the *health* of the individual pupil. This kind of information may be obtained from questionnaires, interviews with the pupil, tests, and records of examination by the home or school physician. Mental, as well as physical, health should be included.

In the cumulative folder or file for each pupil, there

should be a brief summary of the health and physical characteristics of the pupil, including vigor or lassitude, assets, and disabilities or limitations. In addition, there should be a more detailed record of health, including periodic physical examinations and a disease history record. This information will usually be filed in the physical education office or the office of the school physician.

A sixth type of information needed in guidance consists of notes on the *out-of-school experiences* of the pupil. This type of information will be secured mainly by questionnaires and personal interviews. Special attention should be given to summer experiences and work experiences. Information in regard to work experiences should cover such items as type, duration, hours per week, earnings, and the degree to which the individual liked and enjoyed the work.

A seventh type of guidance information is concerned with the *educational and vocational interests* of the individual pupil. Modern psychology emphasizes the dynamic role of interest in all aspects of mental and emotional development. Interests should invariably be one of the reference points in personnel work with individuals.

The school should secure two kinds of information about the interests of each pupil. In the first place, it should keep a record of his activities as an indication of functioning interests. In the second place, it should be able to make a summary statement concerning the interests of the pupil on the basis of observation and scores on standardized interest questionnaires.

In the interpretation of interest data, the counselor should keep in mind the fact that the interests of many individuals change markedly during the secondary school years. Trends in interest development may be fully as important as the pattern of interests at any given time.

At present, many secondary schools record information concerning the activities in which the pupil is engaged. They also attempt to summarize the pupil's interests, but the value of this report often depends almost entirely on the accuracy of the counselor's judgment. Not many schools have extensive objective data on interests, although the number that recognize the importance of this phase of the pupil's development and the need for adequate information concerning it is significantly larger than it was 25 years ago. An increasing number of schools administer an interest inventory, such as the Strong Vocational Interest Blank or the Kuder Preference Record—Vocational, at least once to each secondary school pupil.

Closely related to interests is an eighth aspect of pupil development about which the school should obtain information for guidance purposes. This type of information includes the student's *special aptitudes*—art, litera-

ture, music, mechanical skill, and so forth. In the case of many students, perhaps the majority of them, the secondary school cannot record anything very significant under this category, for a large proportion of the pupils have no unusually marked aptitude in any one field. But when a pupil has exceptionally high aptitude of a particular kind, the counselor should become informed of this fact as soon as possible. Awareness that the student possesses the aptitude will unquestionably influence the counselor's advice concerning courses and other relationships in the school, and plans for future education and vocational choice. Information in regard to a pupil's special aptitudes may be obtained from the record of his activities in the school, the comments of his teachers and others who know him well, and the results of various aptitude tests. Few schools use specific aptitude tests extensively, and the main reliance will usually be placed on more subjective criteria of evaluation.

A ninth, and very important, area in which the guidance department needs information about individual pupils is that of *personality*. The eight categories already considered are indirectly related to personality, but here we are concerned more directly with a complex of qualities which, acting together, tend to shape the personality of the individual.

There is close agreement among teachers and counselors at all levels of the school that much attention should be given to personality development. It would, however, be impossible to suggest a list of personal characteristics which would be satisfactory to all educators. Every group that has tried to formulate a comprehensive set of personality traits has come out with a somewhat different list, although all of them overlapped to some extent. The components of personality may ultimately be isolated by means of factor analysis, but meanwhile lists of personal characteristics formulated as a result of a subjective analysis must be used as the basis of appraisal. One list is included in the "Description of Behavior" section of the American Council on Education cumulative record form. It covers responsibility, creativeness, influence, adjustability, concern for others, seriousness of purpose, and emotional stability (14).

Many present-day schools are giving an increased amount of attention to the appraisal of the personal qualities of their students. Nevertheless, most schools are probably less well prepared to furnish valid information concerning this aspect of the status and growth of their pupils than about any of the other categories discussed in this chapter.

If schools in general are to be able to supply their guidance departments with really valid information in this area, they must devote much time and thought to the improvement of procedures for appraising personality. Ratings made hastily by one individual, perhaps the principal or the counselor, at the end of the pupil's high school course are subject to large error. Personality "tests" are of some value in a counseling program, if they are used cautiously along with other information about the pupil and if the school has on its staff someone competent to interpret the scores, but those measures have not reached the stage of development where they can be employed with a high degree of confidence. Anecdotal records have possibilities as a basis for personality appraisal, but few schools have as yet solved the problems of obtaining systematic records from all the teachers and of summarizing the anecdotes. Behavior descriptions of the type devised by the Reports and Records Committee during the Eight-Year Study of the Progressive Education Association and reproduced in modified form in the ACE cumulative record probably provide one of the most workable procedures for the evaluation of personal qualities thus far developed. Through this plan, behavior descriptions can be obtained at regular intervals from all staff members acquainted with the individual, and summarized when the pupil is graduated from the secondary school. Experience indicates that when a summary of behavior descriptions or of ratings of personal qualities is made, the school should not merely average them—for the average rating may not be the rating assigned by any one of the staff members—but it should also determine the most frequent rating and the spread of the ratings. Variability in behavior or in personal characteristics in different situations may be very significant from the personnel point of view.

The Personal and Social Development Program worked out in detail by Flanagan (6) on the basis of his critical incidents technique seems especially promising for use by teachers. Certain revisions in the Program originally published are contemplated.

The last area of guidance information which will be mentioned here is *plans for the future*. This area should include educational and occupational plans as indicated by the pupil, his parents, and his counselor. The information will be obtained chiefly from interviews and questionnaires.

It will be observed that in connection with the foregoing list of kinds of information needed, certain techniques for the collection of the information were mentioned repeatedly. These techniques included questionnaires, interviews, rating scales, behavior descriptions, objective tests, records in the form of anecdotal material, and cumulative records. These techniques will be discussed in considerable detail in the next section and in the following chapters.

PROCEDURES FOR COLLECTING INFORMATION

As indicated in the first part of this chapter, a considerable amount of the information about individuals which is needed for guidance may be obtained from tests and other objective techniques. For those areas in which they are applicable, objective techniques should be preferred, for they provide data whose reliability and impersonal quality are highly desirable as a starting point in counseling. It is obvious, however, that certain kinds of information must necessarily be collected directly from the parents or the pupil, not through objective procedures, but by means of interviews or questionnaires. These kinds of information include especially home background, social history, certain aspects of the school history, certain aspects of the health history, extracurricular activities, work and summer experiences, interests, school subjects preferred and those disliked, conditions for study outside the school, voluntary reading, and educational and vocational plans.

THE INTERVIEW AS A MEANS OF GATHERING INFORMATION[2]

If time were available for extensive conferences, there can be little doubt that the most satisfactory procedure for the collection of information in some of the areas listed would be a personal interview with each individual. The interview is a particularly fortunate medium because of its flexibility, the possibility of pursuing main questions through a series of more detailed questions, and the opportunity for drawing pupils out and getting them to express themselves freely concerning activities, interests, plans, and so forth. It is the most extensively used technique in personnel work. In independent schools,[3] which are well staffed in proportion to the number of pupils enrolled, and in some of the smaller public schools, it may be possible to dispense with questionnaires altogether and to handle the collection of social background information entirely by means of interviews. The interview, of course, has many other uses, some of them therapeutic, but we are here con-

[2] For an extensive and authoritative discussion of this topic, see Walter V. Bingham, Bruce V. Moore, and John W. Gustad, *How to Interview*, 4th ed. New York: Harper & Row, Publishers, 1959. Pp. viii + 277.

[3] Independent schools, as the term is used in this book, include college preparatory schools, church-supported schools, military schools, and all other schools not publicly maintained and controlled.

cerned with the value of the interview in gathering information.

When guidance information is to be derived from interviews, the counselor should, of course, plan carefully for each interview. He should formulate a definite series of questions, and he should have them so well in mind that the interview will take on a certain objective and

INTERVIEW RECORD

Name of Student:_____

Name of Counselor:_____

Date: _____

FORM 1.

scientific character notwithstanding its freedom and latitude.

Although the counselor should be prepared to ask certain important questions in a predetermined way, he should avoid allowing the interview to seem stereotyped and formal to the pupil. He should spend a few moments at the beginning of the interview in establishing rapport, and his questions should seem to arise naturally in the course of a pleasant conversation. The carrying out of a

definite line of questioning in an informal and cordial setting is a difficult achievement which calls for natural sympathy and diplomacy and considerable experience. Properly applied, however, it is the most satisfactory technique for obtaining information in the less tangible areas.

Care should be taken that the interview does not take on the character of an inquisition, or even that of an oral questionnaire. Too direct a line of questioning may defeat its purpose by arousing a feeling of antagonism and resentment. The pupil should be encouraged to talk freely and to volunteer information which he feels is important.

When the counselor is obtaining information for use in guidance later, he will, of course, need to make a written record of the pertinent facts. Nevertheless, he should do as little writing as possible during the interview. A counselor whose memory is good can probably avoid writing anything while the interview is in progress, while one who does not easily recall factual statements may need to make occasional notes, with the counselee's consent. In this event, the writing should be done so briefly and easily that the thread of the conversation is not broken. Immediately after each interview, the counselor should make a detailed written summary of the information secured. He cannot afford to depend for long upon his memory, nor should he, even if he could hold the facts in mind indefinitely, for a brief written record of the interviews which take place between pupil and counselor and also between the counselor and persons who know the pupil will be an important addition to the cumulative record.

The interview record may be set down in the form of notes or paragraph statements, or it may be made on a specially prepared blank. Some schools have devised their own blanks for this purpose. A very simple blank which may serve the counselor for everyday use in interviewing pupils is illustrated in Form 1.

While it is ordinarily desirable to keep a record of each interview, a counselor may sometimes receive information which is too confidential to be written down. Or, if it seems necessary to make a record of certain confidential information, it is advisable to keep it in a sealed envelope which is to be opened by a person other than the counselor only under very extraordinary circumstances. Not only does the counselor have a moral obligation to protect the privacy of the counselee, but he may lay himself open to civil suit if he does not (13). The general rule is that information given in confidence during interviews is "privileged communication," and ethical standards require that such confidences be guarded as a trust, not to be revealed except when they imply "clear and imminent danger to an individual or to society" (5). There may occur, however, circumstances in which a school counselor may be required by a court of law to release confidential records. The legal immunity to the revealing of information obtained in professional confidence is not so great for counselors as it is for members of more firmly established professions, such as medicine.

USE OF QUESTIONNAIRES IN COLLECTING INFORMATION

Notwithstanding the advantages of the interview as a means of gathering information, it is not practicable for counselors in a large school to try to interview every new pupil at the beginning of the school year in order to secure the information needed as a starting point for the guidance of the individual. In gathering the required data, most schools will necessarily resort to a printed or mimeographed information blank or questionnaire. Questionnaires have often been criticized for their unreliability, but their reliability can be greatly increased if they are used as standardized interview forms and are filled out under careful supervision.

It is preferable to have the information concerning social history and home background supplied by the parents rather than by the pupils themselves; in fact, this is the only reliable procedure if the children are young. In private schools and in public schools in small communities, it may be possible to have one of the parents, usually the mother, of each pupil come to the school and fill out the social history questionnaire. A plan of this kind was used for years in connection with the Records Office of the University of Chicago Laboratory Schools. Regardless of whether the child was entering the kindergarten, the elementary school, or the high school, one of the parents was asked to come to the Records Office and fill out an extensive social history blank. The questionnaire was based directly on the master record cards, and all information requested was needed in filling out the cards. A representative of the Records Office was always present to answer questions and assist the parent in providing the needed information.

In large public schools, it is seldom feasible to try to get the parents to fill out the questionnaire under supervision, and the school must either send it to the parents to be filled out and returned, or depend on getting the information from the pupils. In junior and senior high schools, the latter plan is probably preferable, for the pupils can readily be assembled and instructed to fill out, under supervision, a questionnaire specially prepared for them. Moreover, if the pupils are relatively mature, certain questions, such as those pertaining to interests and to educational and vocational plans, should be answered by the pupils themselves.

Experience has shown that if the questionnaire is carefully planned and if specific directions are given for answering the questions, it can be filled out in home-rooms or guidance rooms with satisfactory accuracy. There should be either an oral or a written introductory statement explaining the purpose of the questionnaire to the pupils and enlisting their cooperation. A clear and diplomatic statement of the purpose of the questionnaire is important, for some of the pupils may feel that certain questions tend to encroach upon their privacy. They will be more likely to answer the questions willingly and honestly if they know that the information will be treated confidentially by the counselors and will be used to help the pupils themselves as individuals.

The guidance department in each school should formulate its pupil questionnaire to fit its own situation. A questionnaire which was prepared by a guidance chairman to obtain background information from the pupils in one high school is shown in Form 2. It was filled out in the guidance groups under the supervision of the counselors and was filed in the pupil's cumulative folder, kept by his counselor.

Some high schools employ a still more extensive and detailed pupil questionnaire, particularly in the earlier years of high school. An excellent questionnaire of this kind was developed and used for years at the Plainfield High School, Plainfield, New Jersey, under the direction of Dr. Adria Galbraith, who was in charge of testing and records. This questionnaire was filled out in ninth and tenth grade homerooms and was kept as a part of the counselor's individual pupil file. More recently, that questionnaire was replaced by a shorter one which is used to provide information for the cumulative record. This questionnaire is shown in Form 3.[4]

If the school maintains individual cumulative record cards to which information from the pupil questionnaires is transferred, it is, of course, desirable to employ a questionnaire, the items of which will closely parallel certain items on the cumulative record. For example, the questionnaire shown as Form 4 is designed to be used with the Educational Records Bureau Cumulative Record for Independent Schools which appears as Form 9 in Chapter XIII.

Other illustrations of pupil questionnaires suitable for use in a guidance program can be found in educational journals. For example, Hoyt (10) presented a personal history blank, designed to be filled out in a group, and discussed its uses.

[4] Made available through the courtesy of Mr. William V. Sette, Director of Guidance.

QUESTIONNAIRE FOR HIGH SCHOOL PUPILS

<u>To the pupil.</u> Please fill out this questionnaire so that your counselor may have more information about you and thus be in a better position to help you with any problems that may arise. The information will be treated confidentially.

1. Name _____ 2. Date _____
                  Last   First   Middle

3. Address _____ 4. Tel. No. _____

5. Birthplace _____ 6. Citizenship _____

7. Age _____ 8. Date of Birth _____
                                                                Mo.   Day   Year

9. Father's name _____ 10. Father's occupation _____

11. Mother's name _____ 12. Mother's occupation _____

13. Do you live in a house or in an apartment? _____

14. Do you have a separate room? _____

15. Number of older brothers _____ Number of older sisters _____

    Number of younger brothers _____ Number of younger sisters _____

16. Names of brothers and sisters who have attended or are attending this school _____

    _____

17. What elementary school or schools did you attend? _____

    _____

18. Have you attended any high school other than this one? _____ If so, what one? _____

    _____ What high school years _____

19. Date of entrance to this school _____ Grade entered _____

20. What subject or subjects in school do you like best? _____

    _____ Why? _____

    _____

21. Are there any subjects that you dislike? _____ What ones? _____

    _____

FORM 2(a).

22. Do you study at home?_____ How many hours per day, on the average?_____

23. Have you ever repeated a school subject or grade?_____ If so state what subject or grade
_____

24. Do you play a musical instrument?_____ What one?_____

25. Do you take part in interscholastic sports?_____ What ones?_____
_____ In intramural sports?_____ What ones?_____
_____

26. Why do you prefer the kind of athletics in which you take part?_____
_____

27. Estimate the number of hours you spend in recreation outside school each day
_____

28. To what school clubs do you belong?_____
_____

29. What school offices are you holding now?_____
_____

30. What school offices have you held before this year?_____
_____

31. Do you expect to go to college?_____ To what college?_____

32. In what department do you expect to specialize?_____

33. Have you selected a vocation?_____ If so, what one?_____

34. Do you enjoy reading?_____ If so, what type of book do you prefer?_____
_____

35. Who are your favorite authors?_____

36. What magazines do you read?_____

37. How often do you attend the movies?_____

38. What kind of movies do you like best?_____

FORM 2(b).

39. Approximately how much time do you spend each week listening to the radio?_____

Listening to records played on your own record player?_____

Watching television?_____

40. How did you spend your past summer?_____

_____

41. Name any summer camps you have attended and give dates _____

_____

42. Have you traveled in this country or abroad?_____ If so, state the nature and extent of

travel _____

_____

43. Do you have any responsibilities or duties at home?_____ If so, describe briefly_____

_____

44. Do you participate in any church or club activities?_____ If so, what ones? _____

_____

45. What special interests do you carry on during your spare time and approximately how long have

you had each special interest? _____

_____

_____

_____

46. Remarks_____

_____

_____

_____

FORM 2(c).

REFERENCES

1. *A Brief Report on College Admission,* pp. 16–25. Fifth Report on Committee on School and College Relations of the Educational Records Bureau. New York: Educational Records Bureau, 1951. Pp. iv + 62.
2. *Admission to American Colleges.* Sixth Report of Committee on School and College Relations of the Educational Records Bureau. New York: Educational Records Bureau, 1964. Pp. iv + 28.
3. Bingham, Walter V., Moore, Bruce V., and Gustad, John W. *How to Interview,* 4th ed. New York: Harper & Row, Publishers, 1959. Pp. viii + 277.
4. Clark, Charles M. "Confidentiality and the School Coun-

selor," *Personnel and Guidance Journal,* XLIII (January 1965), 482–484.
5. *Ethical Standards for Psychologists,* pp. 53–56. Committee on Ethical Standards for Psychology, American Psychological Association. Washington, D.C.: American Psychological Association, 1953. Pp. xv + 172.
6. Flanagan, John C. *Personal and Social Development Program.* Chicago: Science Research Associates, Inc., 1956. (Temporarily out of print.)
7. *Fourth Report of Committee on School and College Relations of the Educational Records Bureau* (Eugene R. Smith, chairman), p. 8. New York: Educational Records Bureau, 1943. Pp. vi + 56.
8. Garner, Walton. "Problems Discussed During the Coun-

PLAINFIELD HIGH SCHOOL
PLAINFIELD, NEW JERSEY

The following information is needed to complete your permanent record. Please be accurate. This information will be considered *confidential* and will not be furnished to unauthorized persons.

NAME _____ M ___ F ___ Homeroom _____
       Last   First   Middle

1. Where were you born? _____
                          (City and State, or City and Foreign Country)

2. When is your birthday? _____
                          Month   Day   Year

3. Address _____ 4. Telephone No. _____

5. Is your health good? _____ If not, please explain _____

   _____

6. Are you living with both of your parents? _____ If not, please explain, if you care to

   _____

7. *Father's* name _____ Living? _____

   Birthplace? _____ Occupation _____
              (City and State; or City, Foreign Country)
   Education: (Highest Grade) _____ If College, give name: _____ Degree: _____

8. *Mother's* name _____ Living? _____

   Birthplace? _____ Occupation _____
              (City and State; or City, Foreign Country)
   Education: (Highest Grade) _____ If College, give name: _____ Degree: _____

9. To be answered only if #7 and #8 do not apply: _____

   Step-parent or *guardian's* name _____

   Birthplace? _____ Occupation _____
              (City and State; or City, Foreign Country)

10. Clubs, activities, sports: (give years)   11. School offices you have held: (give years)

12. Special interests or hobbies:

43

FORM 3.

WOODLAWN HIGH SCHOOL PUPIL QUESTIONNAIRE

Name _____ Date _____

Address _____

Age _____ Birthdate _____ Birthplace _____

General Health _____

Religion* _____ Race or Nationality* _____

Father's name _____ Birthdate _____

Birthplace _____ General Health _____

Religion _____ Race or Nationality* _____

Occupation _____ Business Address _____

Mother's name _____ Birthdate _____

Birthplace _____ General Health _____

Religion _____ Race or Nationality* _____

Occupation _____ Business Address _____

Language spoken in home before age 10 _____ after age 10 _____

Type of community lived in before age 10 _____ after age 10 _____

In case parents are separated, give year of separation, if known _____

Name of counselor _____

Do you enjoy physical education? _____ Do you take part in sports? _____

What ones? _____

Please list your out-of-school activities and interests _____

_____

FORM 4(a).

*It should be noted that the propriety of including questions about race or religion varies from one place to another. In some of the smaller, comparatively homogeneous communities or schools, these are not emotionally related questions, and it may be proper to ask them, if this procedure is in conformity with state laws. In other places, particularly some of the large metropolitan communities, these questions are likely to be objectionable to pupils and parents, and they should not be asked. In certain states, questions of this kind are forbidden by law.

44

What noteworthy experiences have you had, such as living or travel in foreign countries, summer jobs, and so forth _____

_____

What plans do you have for future education? _____

_____

Have you chosen the kind of vocation you expect to enter as a life work? _____

If so, what one? _____

_____

Remarks _____

_____

_____

_____

_____

_____

_____

_____

_____

_____

_____

FORM 4(b).

seling Interviews," *Vocational Guidance Quarterly*, VI (Winter 1957–1958), 69–72.

9. Hays, Donald G., and Rothney, John W. M. "Educational Decision-Making by Superior Secondary School Students and Their Parents," *Personnel and Guidance Journal*, XL (September 1961), 26–30.

10. Hoyt, Kenneth B. "How Well Can Classroom Teachers Know Their Pupils?" *School Review*, LXIII (April 1955), 228–235.

11. Jackson, Robert M., and Rothney, John W. M. "A Comparative Study of the Mailed Questionnaire and the Interview in Follow-up Studies," *Personnel and Guidance Journal*, XXXIX (March 1961), 569–571.

12. Kinling, William J. "Dissemination of Guidance Information Using Data Processing Equipment," *Personnel and Guidance Journal*, XXXIX (November 1960), 220–222.

13. Livingston, Inez B. "Is the Personnel Worker Liable?" *Personnel and Guidance Journal*, XLIII (January 1965), 471–474.

14. *1941 Revision of American Council on Education Cumulative Record Card for Junior and Senior High Schools.* Prepared by Committee on the Revision of Cumulative Records, (Eugene R. Smith, chairman). Washington, D.C.: American Council on Education, 1941.

15. Traxler, Arthur E., and Townsend, Agatha (eds.). *Improving Transition from School to College.* New York: Harper & Row, Publishers, 1953. Pp. xviii + 166.

CHAPTER V

Appraisal of Aptitudes for Guidance Purposes

LET US TURN FROM QUESTIONNAIRES AND INterviews to more objective procedures for collecting information for guidance. These procedures include tests, rating scales, and other devices for measurement and evaluation. Tests may be divided into three broad classes: aptitude tests, achievement tests, and tests of personal qualities, including interests. The present chapter will deal with the first group—tests of aptitude. No attempt will be made in this chapter to provide a complete coverage of all aptitude tests in the manner of a book on tests and measurements, but it will present a point of view concerning the measurement of aptitudes, and a discussion of certain selected instruments which experience and observation have shown to be useful in a guidance program.[1]

WHAT IS APTITUDE?

Aptitude is a present condition which is indicative of a person's potential for developing proficiency in a certain area. The realization of this potential is usually dependent not only on the individual's learning ability in that area, but also on his motivation and opportunities for utilizing this ability. Among the numerous aptitudes commonly assessed for educational and vocational guidance are those for language (verbal aptitude), arithmetic and higher mathematics, abstract reasoning, art, music, clerical work, and mechanics.

[1] For a thorough, and not too technical treatment of all aspects of testing discussed in this and subsequent chapters, see H. H. Remmers, N. L. Gage, and J. F. Rummel, *A Practical Introduction to Measurement and Evaluation.* New York: Harper & Row, Publishers, 1960.

Laymen, and sometimes teachers and counselors, may mistakenly regard aptitudes as characteristics that are almost entirely inborn, and aptitude tests as measures of innate characteristics. It should be clearly understood that aptitude tests measure a complex of innate tendencies and results of training, and that there is no way of separating the influences of heredity and environment in the test results.

In guidance work, it is often necessary to estimate the effects of environmental limitations or opportunities on measured aptitudes, especially when these environmental conditions vary widely for different individuals. For example, the scores of two individuals on tests for mechanical aptitude might be radically different, principally because one of them had considerable experience with motors, levers, gears, and other mechanical contrivances, while the other did not. It is possible that the other individual, who scored low on this aptitude test, might have scored just as high as the first one if the mechanical experience of the two individuals had been similar.

When opportunities for learning are nearly equal for all the members of a group, the differences among their aptitude scores are likely to reflect variations in aptitude, or a combination of aptitude, interest, and motivation. Since home and neighborhood influences play an important role in presenting opportunities for learning, environmental factors from these sources can account for wide ranges of differences in aptitude test scores (6). This is particularly true for culturally oriented aptitudes, such as those involving language or mathematics. Individuals who come from culturally impoverished neighborhoods are likely to be handicapped when they are tested for aptitudes of this nature. Remedial work in vocabulary development and reading might help a pupil to improve his verbal aptitude. Similarly, special help in arithmetic might strengthen a child's aptitude for mathematics. Courses in engineering drawing apparently have a tendency to raise a student's aptitude for spatial visualization (5).

On the other hand, some aptitudes are not readily influenced by environment and experience. For example, musical and artistic aptitudes seem to include important hereditary components. It is doubtful that instruction in music can have much effect on the musical aptitude of an individual who lacks a sense of pitch, time, rhythm, timbre, or other fundamental musical qualities.

For the practical purposes of diagnosis and short-range prediction, the counselor usually needs information about the individual's present aptitude pattern, regardless of the influences that lie behind those aptitudes. For long-range prediction, it is important for the counselor to recognize that most aptitudes are subject to continuous modification by day-to-day experiences. Major changes in the student's opportunities for learning, or in his interests and motivation, may result in substantial changes in his aptitude pattern. Nevertheless, the aptitudes of most individuals tend to be fairly stable. A child who is definitely superior in a certain aptitude will, as a rule, be above average in that aptitude at age 16 or 26. If it were not for the relatively persistent nature of most aptitudes, a long-term guidance program would hardly be worthwhile.

INDIVIDUAL DIFFERENCES IN APTITUDES

No individual is uniformly weak or uniformly strong in all aptitudes. If it were possible to make perfectly valid and reliable measurements of a person's numerous aptitudes, a graph of the results would show an array of peaks and valleys. Almost every normal individual learns some activities easily, others with moderate effort, and still others only with extremely long and arduous application, if at all. The variations in a person's strengths and weaknesses from one area to another are termed *intra-individual differences*.

Also, people differ greatly from one another in their aptitudes (*inter-individual differences*). A certain type of curve expresses the distributions of these differences, as well as those of practically all other characteristics that can be measured on a continuum. This curve is bell-shaped and is called the *normal* curve. It represents the distribution that occurs whenever a large number of independent factors influence a trait or event. In the case of aptitudes, the basic factors are the person's genes and the environmental conditions that influence his development.

The type of distribution depicted by the normal curve is called a normal distribution. In this distribution, the scores (or other measures) of the individuals are heavily concentrated in the region surrounding the median or average, and thin out rapidly as the distance from the average increases on each side. The symmetrical, normal distribution and its related curve are the basis for many of the statistical techniques that are used in educational and psychological measurement and research.

The apparently normal distribution of measures of some characteristics may, in some instances, result from the way the measurement instrument was constructed or the level at which it was employed. For example, if a test of word meaning is carefully prepared through the usual test construction procedures for use with the usual public school population at the eighth grade level, it is highly probable that henceforth, whenever the test is employed with a large group of eighth grade pupils in the usual public school, the resulting scores will approximate a normal distribution. If, however, the test were to be given to a population very different from that for which it was designed—for example, pupils in Grade 3, college freshmen, eighth grade pupils in a very "underprivileged" community, or extremely superior eighth graders, the distributions of scores thus obtained would be far from normal.

Counselors need not be highly conversant with sampling and error theory, in which the normal curve hypothesis finds extensive application, but they should be aware that the normal curve and the standard deviation along the baseline under the normal curve are the bases of nearly all systems of converted, derived, or standard scores that are used for expressing the results of standardized tests (32). Figure 3 may be helpful in visualizing the normal curve, in seeing the relationship between the normal curve and the standard deviation (sigma) scale, and in understanding the relationships of both the normal curve and the sigma scale to several kinds of derived scores.

EXPLANATION OF NORMAL CURVE AND SCORES DERIVED FROM IT

The following paragraphs, which constitute a detailed explanation of the graph reproduced in Figure 3, are reprinted from *Test Service Bulletin* No. 48 (January 1955), pp. 1–4, with the permission of the late Dr. Harold G. Seashore, former editor of the *Test Service Bulletin* and director of the Test Division of The Psychological Corporation:[2]

arbitrary and call the average score zero. In technical terms we "equate" the mean raw score to zero. Similarly we can choose any convenient number, say 1.00, to represent the scale distance of one standard deviation. (The mathematical symbol for the standard deviation is the lower case Greek

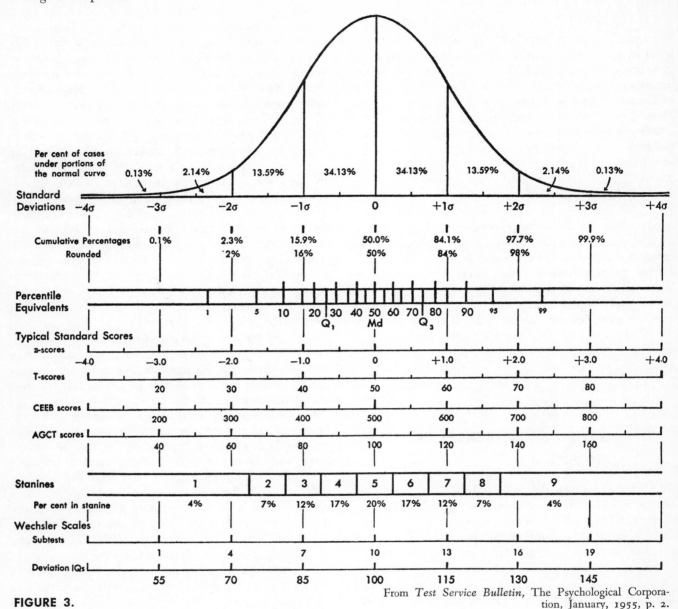

FIGURE 3.

From *Test Service Bulletin,* The Psychological Corporation, January, 1955, p. 2.

Let us look first at the curve itself. Notice that there are no raw scores printed along the baseline. The graph is generalized; it describes an idealized distribution of scores of any group on any test. We are free to use any numerical scale we like. For any particular set of scores, we can be

[2] Dr. Seashore's statement is quoted at length, not only because it provides an excellent explanation of the normal curve, but also because it discusses in simple language several kinds of widely used scores which are derived from this curve.

letter sigma, or σ. These terms are used interchangeably in this article.) Thus, if a distribution of scores on a particular test has a mean of 36 and a standard deviation of 4, the zero point on the baseline of our curve would be equivalent to an original score of 36; one unit to the right, $+1\sigma$, would be equivalent to 40, (36+4); and one unit to the left, -1σ, would be equivalent to 32, (36−4).

The total area under the curve represents the total number of scores in the distribution. Vertical lines have been drawn through the score scale (the baseline) at zero and at 1, 2, 3, and 4 sigma units to the right and left. These lines mark off subareas of the total area under the curve. The numbers printed in these subareas are per cents—*percentages of the total number of people.* Thus, 34.13 per cent of all cases in a normal distribution have scores falling between 0 and -1σ For practical purposes we rarely need to deal with standard deviation units below -3 or above $+3$; the percentage of cases with scores beyond $\pm 3\sigma$ is negligible.

The fact that 68.26 per cent fall between $\pm 1\sigma$ gives rise to the common statement that in a normal distribution roughly two-thirds of all cases lie between plus and minus one sigma. This is a rule of thumb every test user should keep in mind. It is very near to the theoretical value and is a useful approximation.

Below the row of deviations expressed in sigma units is a row of per cents; these show *cumulatively* the percentage of people which is included *to the left* of each of the sigma points. Thus, starting from the left, when we reach the line erected above -2σ, we have included the lowest 2.3 per cent of cases. These percentages have been rounded in the next row.

Note some other relationships: the area between the $\pm 1\sigma$ points includes the scores which lie above the 16th percentile (-1σ) and below the 84th percentile $(+1\sigma)$—two major reference points all test users should know. When we find that an individual has a score of 1σ above the mean, we conclude that his score ranks at the 84th percentile in the group of persons on whom the test was normed. (This conclusion is good provided we also add this clause, at least subvocally: *if this particular group reasonably approximates the ideal normal model.*)

The simplest facts to memorize about the normal distribution and the relation of the *percentile* system to deviations from the average in sigma units are seen in the chart. They are

Deviation from the mean	-2σ	-1σ	0	$+1\sigma$	$+2\sigma$
Percentile equivalent	2	16	50	84	98

To avoid cluttering the graph, reference lines have not been drawn, but we could mark off 10 per cent sections of area under the normal curve by drawing lines vertically from the indicated decile points (10, 20, . . . 80, 90) up through the graph. The reader might do this lightly with a colored pencil.

We can readily see that 10 per cent of the area (people) at the middle of the distribution embraces a smaller *distance* on the baseline of the curve than 10 per cent of the area (people) at the ends of the range of scores, for the simple reason that the curve is much higher at the middle. A person who is at the 95th percentile is farther away from a person at the 85th percentile in units of *test score* than a person at the 55th percentile is from one at the 45th percentile.

The remainder of the chart, that is, the several scoring scales drawn parallel to the baseline, illustrates variations of the *deviation score* principle. As a class these are called *standard scores.*

First, there are the z-scores. These are the same *numbers* as shown on the baseline of the graph; the only difference is that the expression, σ, has been omitted. These scores run, in practical terms, from -3.0 to $+3.0$. One can compute them to more decimal places if one wishes, although computing to a single decimal place is usually sufficient. One can compute z-scores by equating the mean to 0.00 and the standard deviation to 1.00 for a distribution of any shape, but the relationships shown in this figure between the z-score equivalents of raw scores and percentile equivalents of raw scores are correct only for normal distributions. The interpretation of standard score systems derives from the idea of using the normal curve as a model.

As can be seen, T-scores are directly related to z-scores. The mean of the raw scores is equated to 50, and the standard deviation of the raw scores is equated to 10. Thus a z-score of $+1.5$ means the same as a T-score of 65. T-scores are usually expressed in whole numbers from about 20 to 80. The T-score plan eliminates negative numbers and thus facilitates many computations.

The College Entrance Examination Board uses a plan in which both decimals and negative numbers are avoided by setting the arbitrary mean at 500 points and the arbitrary sigma at another convenient unit, namely, 100 points. The experienced tester or counselor who hears of a College Board SAT-V score of 550 at once thinks, "Half a sigma (50 points) above average (500 points) on the CEEB basic norms." And when he hears of a score of 725 on SAT-M, he can interpret, "plus $2\frac{1}{4}\sigma$. Therefore, better than the 98th percentile."

During World War II the Navy used the T-score plan of reporting test status. The Army used still another system with a mean of 100 and a standard deviation of 20 points.

Another derivative of the general standard score system is the *stanine* plan, developed by psychologists in the Air Force during the war. The plan divides the norm population into nine groups, hence, "standard nines." Except for stanine 9, the top, and stanine 1, the bottom, these groups are spaced in half-sigma units. Thus, stanine 5 is defined as including the people who are within $\pm 0.25\sigma$ of the mean. Stanine 6 is the group defined by the half sigma distance on the baseline between $+0.25\sigma$ and $+0.75\sigma$. Stanines 1 and 9 include all persons who are below -1.75σ and above $+1.75\sigma$, respectively. The result is a distribution in which the mean is 5.0 and the standard deviation is 2.0.

Just below the line showing the demarcation of the nine groups in the stanine system there is a row of percentages which indicates the per cent of the total population in each of the stanines. Thus 7 per cent of the population will be in stanine 2, and 20 per cent in the middle group, stanine 5.

Interpretation of the Wechsler scales (W-B I, W-B II, WISC, and WAIS) depends on a knowledge of standard scores. A subject's raw score *on each of the subtests* in these scales is converted, by appropriate norms tables, to a standard score, based on a mean of 10 and a standard deviation of 3. The sums of standard scores on the Verbal Scale, the Performance Scale, and the Full Scale are then converted into IQs. These IQs are based on a standard score mean of 100, the conventional number for representing the IQ of the average person in a given age group. The standard deviation of the IQs is set at 15 points. In practical terms, then, roughly two-thirds of the IQs are between 85 and 115, that is ±1σ. IQs of the type used in the Wechsler scales have come to be known as *deviation* IQs, as contrasted with the IQs developed from scales in which a derived mental age is divided by chronological age.[3]

Users of the Wechsler scales should establish clearly in their minds the relationship of subtest scaled scores and the deviation IQs to the other standard score systems, to the ordinary percentile rank interpretation, and to the deviation units on the baseline of the normal curve. For example, every Wechsler examiner should recognize that an IQ of 130 is a score equivalent to a deviation of +2σ, and that this IQ score delimits approximately the upper two per cent of the population. If a clinician wants to evaluate a Wechsler IQ of 85 along with percentile ranks on several other tests given in school, he can mentally convert the IQ of 85 to a percentile rank of about 16, this being the percentile equal to a deviation from the mean of −1σ. Of course, he should also consider the appropriateness and comparability of norms.

Efficiency in interpreting test scores in counseling, in clinical diagnosis, and in personnel selection depends, in part, on facility in thinking in terms of the major interrelated plans by which meaningful scores are derived from raw scores. It is hoped that this graphic presentation will be helpful to all who in their daily work must help others understand the information conveyed by numerical test scores.

KINDS OF APTITUDE TESTS

Aptitude tests may be divided into two broad classes, known as *tests of general aptitude* and *tests of aptitude in specific fields*. General aptitude tests are designed to measure a wide range of aptitudes, particularly those important in school work. Tests of aptitude in specific fields include tests of musical aptitude, art aptitude, mechanical aptitude, clerical aptitude, and so forth.

APTITUDE AND INTELLIGENCE

Tests of general scholastic aptitude have long been known as intelligence tests. There is now a tendency to favor the terms "academic aptitude test" or "scholastic apititude test" rather than "intelligence test," because to many people "intelligence test" implies a measure of native ability.

Intelligence is generally understood to be "ability to learn" or "ability to solve new problems." Tests of intel-

[3] Deviation IQs are also used with the Kuhlmann-Anderson Test, the Otis Quick-Scoring Mental Ability Tests, Form L-M of the Stanford-Binet Scale, and most other widely used intelligence tests.

ligence usually have not been composed wholly or even mainly of new problems, for it is very difficult to improvise problems or situations that will be new to everyone. The more common procedure in constructing intelligence tests has been to attempt to base the questions on materials which everyone for whom the test is designed has presumably had an opportunity to learn. The assumption is that under these conditions those who have learned more are more intelligent.

Some authorities have criticized the conventional verbal intelligence tests on the ground that they are partly culture-determined and that they contain items which individuals from certain social and economic levels had not had much opportunity to learn (15, 28). This point of view has led to the preparation of intelligence, or general aptitude, tests reputed to be "culture free," or at any rate "culture fair." These tests deserve careful consideration, although greater strength would be lent to the position of the proponents of culture-free tests if it could be shown that the factors making for success in higher education and in the higher level vocations were themselves culture free.

In earlier years, the results of most intelligence tests were reported in terms of the traditional IQ, which by definition is the mental age divided by the chronological age and multiplied by 100. There is a theoretical objection to the use of the traditional IQ and its related mental age (MA) for expressing the test results of persons who are mentally mature and brighter than average. This category would, of course, include many students in college, and even a considerable number in the last two years of secondary school. Mental ages begin to level off during adolescence, and show no significant increases with chronological age at the adult level, in so far as the mental ages are derived from tests of general intelligence.

The limitations to the use of mental ages and traditional intelligence quotients in connection with tests given to these students have been stated clearly by Thurstone and Thurstone, as follows:

The intelligence quotient is, by definition, the ratio of the mental age to the chronological age. The mental age of a test performance is the chronological age for which the test performance is the average. It follows from this definition that mental ages and intelligence quotients are indeterminate for the upper half of the adult population. If a person scores above the average for adults in a psychological examination, then there exists no age for which his score is the average. College students can be assumed to score above the average for the adult population of the country and, consequently, they cannot be assigned any mental ages or intelligence quotients. This is not a debatable question. It is a question of very simple and straightforward logic.

Intelligence quotients are assigned to the upper half of

the adult population by changing the definition of mental age. For example, a mental age of 15 or 18 does not mean the average test performance of people of that age. Such mental ages are arbitrary designations of what the test author may choose to call superior adult performance.[4]

Since the deviation IQs that are yielded by most of the newer editions of intelligence tests are not based on the MA-CA ratio, the Thurstones' argument does not apply to them. These deviation IQs should be regarded as indices of learning ability, somewhat comparable to the traditional IQs. As indications of brightness, they are often helpful to teachers and counselors in the differential instruction and guidance of pupils.

For a good many years, psychologists debated the constancy of the IQ, but this debate has subsided in recent years. Probably no reputable psychologist has ever believed that the IQ is entirely constant, although there has been some popular belief in its constancy. Numerous growth studies have refuted the hypothesis of complete stability of the IQ, and have shown that intelligence is influenced by schooling and other environmental factors. In addition, IQs obtained from different tests may not be directly comparable because of variations in item content, scaling, and norms. Furthermore, IQs involve errors of measurement, as do all scores that are derived from tests that are not perfectly reliable. The concept of the IQ continues to be useful nevertheless, provided these limitations are kept in mind.

TESTS OF GENERAL ACADEMIC APTITUDE

TESTS YIELDING ONE MENTAL AGE AND INTELLIGENCE QUOTIENT

As already indicated, the oldest and best known type of intelligence or scholastic aptitude test is the kind that provides a single IQ. An individually administered test, such as the Stanford-Binet scale,[5] is usually regarded as the best single measure of intelligence or academic aptitude, and it is highly desirable for a guidance department to have some member of its staff trained to administer, score, and interpret the scores of this kind of examination. However, few schools have the time and staff necessary for using individual tests with all pupils even initially, much less at the regular intervals that the measurement

[4] L. L. Thurstone and Thelma Gwinn Thurstone, *Psychological Examinations, 1941 Norms*. American Council on Education Studies, VI. Washington, D.C.: American Council on Education, May 1942.

[5] Detailed information concerning nearly all the tests listed in this section is given in the annotated list in the last part of this chapter.

of mental development warrants. In the usual school situation, such tests should be used with special or doubtful cases, and group tests—tests that can be administered to a number of individuals simultaneously—for the regular, coordinated school-wide testing program.

A group intelligence test that has been very widely used because of its ease of administering and scoring, coupled with satisfactory technical standards, is the Otis Quick-Scoring Mental Ability Test. This is a revision and extension of the earlier Otis Self-Administering Test of Mental Ability. The Otis Quick-Scoring Test Series covers the Grades 1–12 with its Alpha, Beta, and Gamma levels. The two upper levels yield only a single score and IQ, but the longer form of the Alpha level may be used to obtain nonverbal, verbal, and composite scores and IQs.

The Kuhlmann-Anderson Tests, Seventh Edition, which consist of a series of overlapping batteries extending from the kindergarten to the twelfth grade level, are in some respects preferable to the Otis tests. They represent a somewhat better balance of verbal, numerical, and spatial material, and the fact that there are eight batteries for successive grades probably results in better adjustment of the test items to the age level of the pupils. These tests must be carefully administered, however, because each booklet contains a number of subtests, each of which has a relatively short time limit. In the range from kindergarten through the sixth grade, each of the levels yields only a single score and IQ. Additional verbal and quantitative aptitude scores are obtained from the booklets designed for use in the Grade 7–12 range.

Other well-constructed and widely used tests of general scholastic ability are the Henmon-Nelson Tests of Mental Ability, the Ohio State University Psychological Test, and the Kuhlmann-Finch Intelligence Test. This last series of tests is of interest, since it was planned as an adaptation for group testing of the individual Kuhlmann-Binet Test.

In Great Britain, the Moray House Intelligence Tests are widely used with school children. These tests, which were originally prepared for use with pupils of ages 11 and 12 in order to help in deciding upon the kind of secondary education for which they were best suited, are largely verbal in nature. In general appearance and item type, the Moray House tests bear some resemblance to the Otis Self-Administering Tests of Mental Ability.

Another test of general mental ability has been in demand in recent years. This is the culture-free, or culture-fair, test, which was mentioned earlier and which represents an attempt to provide test items on which pupils with equivalent ability may be expected to perform equally well, regardless of the home background and general environment from which the pupil comes. The IPAT Culture-Free Test represents an approach to the problem of providing an intelligence test which is as fair to one social and economic group as it is to another. The idea behind the kind of test termed culture-free has wide appeal, but the rationale on which such a test is based should be carefully examined. Research needs to be conducted to determine whether the culture-free test does a better, or even a noticeably different, job of predicting success than is done by the more conventional measures of mental ability.

TWO-AXIS TESTS

While tests yielding one mental age and intelligence quotient continue to be used extensively, there is a growing tendency among guidance specialists to prefer scholastic aptitude tests which are to some extent diagnostic (88). For example, information concerning a pupil's aptitude in terms of language and nonlanguage factors is definitely helpful in both educational and vocational guidance, especially where reading difficulties or language handicaps are involved. The California Test of Mental Maturity represents an attempt to meet the need for this type of instrument. This test is available in a short form, requiring approximately one class period, and in a longer form, calling for two periods of working time. It provides mental ages and IQs for language and nonlanguage factors and total mental factors, as well as a more detailed profile which is intended to be diagnostic. The diagnostic sections, however, are not long enough to be very reliable.

Observation and research have indicated that two kinds of aptitude are related to success in a variety of school subjects and vocations. These are verbal or linguistic aptitude, and numerical or quantitative aptitude. One of the oldest and best known among the tests of academic aptitude, the American Council on Education Psychological Examination, yielded an L-score, or score for linguistic ability, a Q-score, or score for quantitative ability, and a total score, as well as scores on certain subtests within the linguistic and quantitative areas. Various forms of the high school edition and college freshman edition of this test were published up to 1954. This long-established examination was gradually replaced, beginning in 1955, by the Cooperative School and College Ability Tests, issued by the same publisher, the Cooperative Test Division of the Educational Testing Service. These tests, likewise, provide separate verbal and quantitative scores, as well as a total score. The successive levels of this series cover the range from the fourth grade through the college sophomore year. In 1964, the Educational Testing Service issued another two-axis test, called the Cooperative Academic Ability Test. This is designed for use with able secondary school pupils and college freshmen, and yields scores similar to those of the Cooperative School and College Ability Tests. It can be administered within one 40-minute class period.

The Junior Scholastic Aptitude Test, published by the National Association of Independent Schools, provides for the measurement of verbal aptitude and numerical aptitude in Grades 7, 8, and 9. It is used as a basis of entrance, placement, and guidance in a large number of independent schools. The Scholastic Aptitude Test of the College Entrance Examination Board, which has long been used as a college entrance test for high school seniors, also gives a verbal score and a mathematical score. A shorter version of this test, the Preliminary Scholastic Aptitude Test, is offered by the College Board for high school juniors.

Another series of tests of abstract intelligence, the Lorge-Thorndike Intelligence Tests, consists of five levels covering the range from kindergarten to college freshman. The three higher levels, which, taken together, extend from Grade 4 through Grade 13, are available in both a verbal battery and a nonverbal battery. The verbal and nonverbal series are published in separate booklets, but they may be used together to provide language and nonlanguage scores somewhat similar to those obtained with other so-called two-axis tests.

TESTS YIELDING SEVERAL APTITUDE SCORES

Since about 1935, the perfection of factor-analysis techniques and concomitant theoretical considerations have led to the development of several mental ability tests which are intended to be more highly diagnostic and which have important potential values for guidance. The Chicago Tests of Primary Mental Abilities, published in 1941, were a revised and shorter version of the Thurstone Tests for Primary Mental Abilities, which were first published in 1938 after several years of intensive work in factor analysis. They provided fairly independent measures of six mental factors. The 1963 edition of the SRA Primary Mental Abilities tests, a series of five overlapping batteries covering the range from kindergarten through the twelfth grade, is a still briefer version of the Thurstone tests. Each battery provides scores for four or five mental factors, along with a total battery intelligence score, and is intended for administration within an hour. As the length of the Primary Mental Abilities tests has been reduced to accord with the testing conditions of the classroom, the influence of rate of work on the results has naturally been increased.

Science Research Associates also publishes the SRA Tests of Educational Ability (TEA), which yield scores in the language, reasoning, and quantitative areas, in addition to a total score and IQ. These tests cover Grades 4 to 12 and require about an hour of testing time. Provisions are also made for obtaining a total nonreading score for the TEA at the 4-6 grade level.

Another battery of the diagnostic, or profile, kind is the Differential Aptitude Tests, or DAT, which consist of eight tests yielding a total of nine scores. The entire battery requires about four hours for administration, but the different tests may be used as units without reference to the others, if desired. There is an edition consisting of seven booklets, a two-booklet edition, and a combined booklet edition.

The Holzinger Crowder Uni-Factor Tests comprise a battery of nine tests yielding scores on four factors: verbal, spatial, numerical, and reasoning. They are useful for the measurement of the scholastic aptitude of junior and senior high school pupils when factor scores are wanted for counseling purposes.

There is need for research with all these test batteries that are designed to make diagnostic measurements of mental functions. Their guidance possibilities are great, but evidence concerning the meaning and value of the scores is still not extensive, except in the case of the Differential Aptitude Tests for which a large amount of research data has been reported by the test authors. In general, counselors and teachers may use the scores from these various test batteries experimentally, but until further studies are available, predictions based on them must be made with the understanding that such predictions grow out of logical assumptions concerning the relationship of the profile scores to criteria of success, rather than out of objective evidence that such relationships exist (78).

TESTS OF APTITUDE IN SPECIAL FIELDS

General academic aptitude tests have important implications for appraisal of aptitude in special fields. In fact, if we had extensive and detailed knowledge of the relationship of the various scores on the Differential Aptitude Tests, the SRA Primary Mental Abilities tests, or the Holzinger-Crowder Uni-Factor Tests to success in different special fields, we would have an excellent basis for differential prediction and guidance. It is not too much to expect that such tests will some day largely supersede the aptitude tests designed for individual fields, except perhaps in such a highly specialized area as music. For the present, however, aptitude tests designed for specific fields should have a place in a guidance program,

although, on the whole, such tests are less satisfactory for their purposes than general academic aptitude tests are for the purposes for which they are designed.

One reason why tests of aptitude in specific fields are not highly satisfactory is that usually they are designed according to different patterns and standardized on widely different populations, or, in the case of certain tests, hardly standardized at all. Thus there is no adequate basis of comparison between the results of tests in separate areas, and it is often difficult for a counselor to decide in which of several areas an individual possesses the greatest aptitude, even when a variety of test scores is available.

The appraisal of aptitude in special fields can be made on a fairly broad basis or it can be highly specific. One can, for example, test individuals for mechanical aptitude or for any one of the hundreds of occupations within the field of mechanics. For placement of workers in jobs, industrial establishments can well use tests of the latter type, but for purposes of a long-term guidance program, such tests would be almost worthless. Even if valid tests for all occupations were available, no guidance department could give more than a few of them to any individual, and the problem of selecting the most appropriate ones would involve a large element of subjective judgment concerning the aptitude of the individual concerned. Moreover, the occupations for which many of the tests were designed would include closely similar abilities, and thus the correlation would be too high for the tests to be of much use in differential guidance. Consequently, if a guidance department is going to employ tests of specific aptitudes, it needs to select and use a relatively small number of tests covering fairly broad functions. The guidance department should be acquainted with the administration, scoring, and interpretation of one or more tests in the fields of art, music, scientific aptitude, manual and mechanical aptitude, clerical aptitude, and perhaps aptitude for certain school subjects, such as algebra, geometry, and foreign languages.

Guidance officers should also be on the lookout for batteries of aptitude tests standardized on the same, or closely similar, populations. Few batteries of this kind have thus far been published. One such battery is the Flanagan Aptitude Classification Tests, or FACT. Another is the General Aptitude Test Battery prepared by the United States Employment Service. Still others are the Aptitude Tests for Occupations, devised by Wesley S. Roeder and Herbert B. Graham, and the Multiple Aptitude Tests prepared by David Segel and Evelyn Raskin. The last two series of tests are publications of the California Test Bureau. All these batteries are aimed primarily at vocational placement, but they also have potential values for educational guidance.

ART

Three of the better-known art tests are the Knauber Art Ability Test; the Meier Art Test, Test 1, Art Judgment; and the Lewerenz Tests in Fundamental Abilities of Visual Arts. The first test is, as the name implies, designed to measure ability in art, and it appears to be rather difficult for the beginning art student. The second test is planned to measure judgment of artistic production. Both these tests are planned for use from Grade 7 upward. The Lewerenz tests consist of a battery of nine brief tests and are potentially somewhat more diagnostic than the other two, although the part scores are probably not very reliable because of the brevity of the parts.

The three art tests named in the preceding paragraph have been available for 20 years or more. Another test in this field is the Graves Design Judgment Test, published in 1948. This test may be used from the junior high school through the college and adult levels.

MUSICAL APTITUDE

The Seashore Measures of Musical Talents have long been one of the standard procedures for the appraisal of aptitude for music. The revised edition was published in 1939 and the manual was revised again in 1956. The fact that a record player is required, and further that it is not practicable to test a large number of pupils simultaneously, has prevented the use of these measures in some schools. The Kwalwasser Test of Music Information and Appreciation and the Kwalwasser-Ruch Test of Musical Accomplishment are well-known paper-and-pencil tests of the group type.

The Wing Standardized Tests of Musical Intelligence, issued in England in 1948, are similar in some respects to the Seashore tests. These tests, which are on ten records, provide seven subscores and a total score. The Whistler-Thorpe Musical Aptitude Tests, Series A, are a comparatively recent set of measures of potential ability to learn music. A piano is required for administration.

SCIENTIFIC APTITUDE

Aptitude for scientific work may be inferred to some extent from aptitude batteries that provide a basis for diagnosis, such as the Differential Aptitude Tests or the SRA Primary Mental Abilities tests. The Aptitude Test for Occupations, published by the California Test Bureau, contains a scientific aptitude test. One of the first tests designed especially for the measurement of aptitude for science was the Stanford Scientific Aptitude Test. This test was published some thirty-five years ago, but it is still used in some high schools and colleges. A new test of this type is the Science Aptitude Test, published by the Science Service. This measure is designed for use with twelfth grade students, principally in connection with the Westinghouse annual Science Talent Search. An Engineering and Physical Science Aptitude Test is published by The Psychological Corporation.

TESTS OF MANUAL AND MECHANICAL APTITUDE

Some of the tests of manual and mechanical skill are administered through the use of special equipment. Among the tests of this type are the Pegboard and Finger Dexterity Board tests of the General Aptitude Test Battery, and the Minnesota Rate of Manipulation Test. Such tests are appropriate for use with special cases or small groups that are being studied intensively, but the general measurement program for guidance purposes will make more use of paper-and-pencil tests which can be administered to sizeable groups of pupils.

The MacQuarrie Test for Mechanical Ability is one of the oldest and most widely known group tests in this field. Three somewhat newer tests are the Revised Minnesota Paper Form Board Test, which is primarily a test of space perception; the SRA Mechanical Aptitude Test; and the Bennett Tests of Mechanical Comprehension. Data in the files of the Educational Records Bureau indicate that the Minnesota and Bennett tests measure aspects of mechanical aptitude which are fairly independent of one another (85). The correlation between the scores on these two tests was found to be about .40. It would seem, therefore, that the Revised Minnesota test and the Bennett test might be used to supplement one another in the same program.

The correspondence between scores on these tests, or any other tests of mechanical aptitude, and success in mechanical work probably varies considerably with the kind of job. It would seem desirable to administer more than one type of mechanical aptitude test and to keep a record of the value of the scores in predicting success in different employment situations.

CLERICAL APTITUDE

The Minnesota Clerical Test is probably the best known and most extensively used paper-and-pencil measure of clerical aptitude. This is a rather simple test based on number checking and name checking, but because of the extensive norms now available, it is one of the most useful tests in this area. Another test in the clerical field which has been available for many years is the Detroit Clerical Aptitude Examination, which has 8 brief parts and calls for 30 minutes of working time.

More recent tests of aptitude for clerical work are the General Clerical Test, issued by The Psychological Corporation, the SRA Clerical Aptitudes Test, and the Turse Clerical Aptitudes Test, published by Harcourt, Brace & World. These tests are considerably more elaborate than the Minnesota Clerical Test.

APTITUDE FOR PROFESSIONS

Aside from the multiple aptitude batteries, various tests have been devised to measure aptitude for different professions. Several of these tests are under the general control of professional associations in their respective fields and are administered by the Educational Testing Service in controlled programs of testing for admission to professional schools. Among these are the Law School Admission Test and the Pre-Engineering Ability Test. The National Teacher Examinations, another program administered by the Educational Testing Service, explore both the aptitudes and achievement of candidates for the teaching profession. Professional testing programs administered by other organizations include the medical and veterinarian aptitude testing programs carried on by The Psychological Corporation, and the various nursing aptitude and achievement examinations sponsored by that organization and by the National League for Nursing.

A testing program for the field of accounting was developed by the American Institute of Certified Public Accountants after many years of research; it is administered by The Psychological Corporation. This program consists of a college testing program and a professional testing program for employees or potential employees of accounting firms. An Orientation Test, two levels of Achievement Tests, and the Strong Vocational Interest Blank, for which special norms for accountants have been developed, are used in the college and professional testing program (58). A nonrestricted Accounting Orientation Test for high school pupils is also offered as a counseling instrument (38, 64).

APTITUDE FOR SPECIFIC SCHOOL SUBJECTS

More attention seems to have been given to the measurement of aptitude for mathematics than for any of the other school subjects. For the appraisal of aptitude for algebra and geometry, there are the Iowa Algebra Aptitude Test, the Iowa Plane Geometry Aptitude Test, the Lee Test of Geometric Aptitude, the Orleans Algebra Prognosis Test, the Orleans Geometry Prognosis Test, and the Survey Test of Algebraic Aptitude.

A noteworthy test of foreign language aptitude is the Modern Language Aptitude Test. The complete form is administered with a tape recording to evaluate the student's "ear for music" as well as his language learning ability. Three of the five parts may be used as a short form without the tape recording, however. The test is applicable for both classical and modern languages.

There are comparatively few aptitude tests in the field of the business subjects. The Turse Shorthand Aptitude Test is a rather well-known measure of the aptitude of prospective stenography students. Other tests in this field are the Stenographic Aptitude Test by Bennett and the E.R.C. Stenographic Aptitude Test.

While the small amount of research data available for the various tests of aptitude for school work indicates that the scores on these tests are significantly correlated with success in the subjects for which the tests are designed, a limiting factor in all these tests is that each is an independent unit. Thus, it is difficult to make valid comparisons from one test to another and to predict relative success in the different subjects which a pupil might choose to study. From this standpoint, tests of aptitude for school subjects are less satisfactory than achievement tests which are part of a comprehensive battery. The latter are normed on similar populations, which renders comparability among the different tests possible. Moreover, it has not yet been established by research that the results of tests designed to measure aptitude in some of the specific subjects or fields have significantly greater relationship to success in those areas than have the results of tests of general academic aptitude.

On the whole, tests designed to show aptitude for specific aspects of school work may play a useful role in a guidance program, but it is a less important role than that taken by tests of general academic aptitude and by achievement tests.

A point worth emphasis is that tests of general academic aptitude, tests of specific aptitude, and achievement tests have many elements in common, and that all three types have values for prediction in specific fields. As Coleman and Cureton (18) have shown, the overlap between the functions measured by a good school achievement test of reading and arithmetic, and a typical group intelligence test may be as high as 95 percent. In their use of all types of tests, counselors and other school staff members should constantly be on guard against the "jangle fallacy," or the tendency to apply different names to tests which in reality measure essentially the same abilities. The overlap in measurement is likely to be high when a school uses aptitude and achievement tests that fall near the middle of Cronbach's "educational loading spectrum" (22:235). Such would be the case for the School and College Ability Tests and the Sequential Tests of Educational Progress.

RELATION BETWEEN APTITUDE AND ACHIEVEMENT

The next chapter will be concerned with the measurement of achievement for guidance purposes. Well-defined thinking concerning the evaluation of aptitude and achievement requires an understanding of the relationship betwen these two terms. It is sometimes thought that aptitude and achievement have wholly separate origins. Aptitudes are naïvely assumed to be inborn characteristics, while achievements are regarded as the product of training; whereas the two simply represent different emphases upon ability and training. One's aptitudes are one's potentialities for success in given areas, but these depend on both inborn characteristics and experience. As indicated at the beginning of this chapter, it is not possible to separate the influences of heredity and environment upon aptitude, nor would this kind of separation necessarily be of practical importance in the prediction of success, even if it could be made. Similarly, one's achievement is the level of skill, knowledge, and understanding one has attained in a given field, and, as is true of aptitudes, this level depends upon a complex of inborn traits and experiences which do not yield themselves to precise analysis.

Both the difference and the similarity between aptitude and achievement may be clarified by noting the procedures we use in attempting to make evaluations in each field. When evaluating aptitude, we try to place the emphasis upon capacity by posing problems in which the individual has had no formal training. When evaluating achievement, we attempt to emphasize training by formulating tasks dealing with materials similar to those he has studied or with which he has had experience. For example, we often base the evaluation of numerical aptitude partly upon a test of number series, which, as a rule, is not specifically taught in the mathematics curriculum; in the evaluation of achievement in mathematics, on the other hand, one of the common tests is concerned with speed and accuracy in computation, which is taught in the mathematics curriculum.

Achievement tests are, however, sometimes used as indicators of aptitude. For instance, arithmetic test scores often serve as a useful basis for estimating aptitude for higher mathematics, and reading comprehension test scores have considerable value in predicting aptitude for the study of foreign languages.

It is to be noted further that when we are dealing with aptitudes for a certain field, or with achievement in a given area, we are concerned not only with a *combination* of aptitudes and achievement, but also with a *complex* of both aptitudes and achievements. So-called

mechanical aptitude, for instance, brings into play a number of discrete aptitudes—space perception, mechanical ingenuity, muscular coordination, and so forth—and a variety of achievements—familiarity with mechanical materials, skill in handling various tools, and other acquired reactions. It is true, as indicated in considerable detail elsewhere in this chapter, that instruments have been made available for the measurement of fairly pure "primary factors" and that further developments of that kind are to be expected, but in no field of human endeavor is success dependent upon just one of these factors. One always brings a combination of aptitudes and achievements to bear upon any major undertaking.

Supplementing aptitude tests and achievement tests, there is a kind of in-between category which includes so-called ability tests. In general, these tests have more elements in common with aptitude tests than with achievement tests, but they are likely to contain a larger proportion of items that may be directly influenced by classroom instruction than is true of the usual aptitude test. Since there is no clear dividing line between aptitude tests and ability tests, some tests which carry the word "ability" in their titles are included in this chapter.

ANNOTATED LIST OF APTITUDE TESTS

In the annotations of the tests in this list, an attempt is made to provide evidence concerning the reliability and validity of the tests, if such data are available. Correlation coefficients reported in this way should be regarded as indicative of the worth of the tests only in general terms. Space limitations render it inadvisable to try to report in detail the technique used in finding the correlations or the grade ranges involved, both of which are likely to have an important effect upon the magnitude of the correlation coefficients. In the case of certain widely used tests, it is possible to report here, even in very abbreviated summary fashion, only a small fraction of the extensive research data that have been reported for these tests. While an effort is made to utilize a wide range of studies reported in educational and psychological literature, frequent reference is made to data in the files of the Educational Records Bureau, partly because the Bureau has made a good many studies of particular tests, and partly because the writers are well acquainted with that series of reports.[6]

6 The majority of the tests annotated in this and the two following chapters are reviewed in Buros' *Fourth* and *Fifth Mental Measurements Yearbooks* (10, 11). For some of the tests listed, certain Buros reviews are specifically cited as references. In the case of many other tests, excellent reviews in the Buros book are

Academic Promise Tests by George K. Bennett, Marjorie G. Bennett, Dorothy M. Clendenen, Jerome E. Doppelt, James H. Ricks, Jr., Harold G. Seashore, and Alexander G. Wesman. New York: The Psychological Corporation, 1959–1961. $4.50 per 25 booklets; $3.75 per 50 IBM 805 answer sheets; $4.00 per 50 IBM 1230 or Digitek answer sheets; $1.10 per 50 student report forms; 50 cents for manual and scoring key for one form; 90 cents for specimen set of both forms, A and B.

Consists of four subtests, yielding seven scores as follows: Verbal—a verbal analogies test tapping word knowledge and reasoning; Numerical—arithmetic problems requiring understanding of concepts and processes; Abstract Reasoning—a nonlanguage test utilizing simple line drawings to evaluate abstract reasoning and concept formation; Language Usage—a test of the pupil's mastery of the essentials of acceptable verbal communication, requiring the identification of errors of grammar, punctuation, spelling, and proper usage in sentences. Yields scores on these four tests, plus a combined verbal and language usage score, and a combined abstract reasoning and numerical score, as well as a total on the complete battery. Percentile norms for each grade in the 6–9 range are provided, based on a norm group of more than 34,000 pupils in 37 states.

Overall time limit is less than two hours. Test-retest reliabilities reported in the manual range from .81 to .90 for the separate tests, from .88 to .92 for the two composite scores, and from .93 to .94 for the total score.

Aptitude-Intelligence Tests (formerly called Factored Aptitude Series), by Joseph E. King. Tucson, Ariz.: Industrial Psychology, Inc., 1947–1957. Copy of any one test, 20 cents; apparatus for motor test, $15.00; manual, $10.00.[7]

This series of tests is designed for adults, but might be considered for experimental use in schools. The 15 tests are: office terms, sales terms, tools, numbers, perception, judgment, precision, fluency, memory, parts, blocks, dimension, dexterity, motor, and factory terms. One form. Working time three minutes for dexterity, six minutes each for fluency

and motor, ten minutes for factory terms, and five minutes each for the other tests. Raw scores are converted to stanines. Caution seems advisable in using this test, since available reliability and validity data for the different parts are limited. The tone of the handbook seems to be somewhat more nearly that of sales promotion than of objective evaluation. The tests are attractively printed and the directions are written in a style that is easily understood. *References:* Super (78), Buros (11:667–669).

Army General Classification Test, First Civilian Edition. Chicago: Science Research Associates, Inc., 1940–1960. For hand scoring: reusable test booklets, Form AH, $10.80 per 20; self-scoring pin-punch answer pads, $2.40 per 20; review set, 75 cents. For machine scoring: reusable test booklets, Form AM, $10.80 per 20; answer sheets, $5.00 per 100; scoring stencils, $1.00 per set of two; review set, 75 cents.

Developed during World War II to classify service personnel according to ability to learn. Contains 150 items of three types: vocabulary (verbal), arithmetic (quantitative), and block counting (spatial). Suitable for use with high school pupils, college students, and adults. Working time, 40 minutes; total time, about 50 minutes. May be used to predict school and college success. Norms for Grades 9–12, adult males, and 125 civilian occupations. *Reference:* Buros (11:431–432).

California Test of Mental Maturity, 1963 Revision, by Elizabeth T. Sullivan, Willis W. Clark, and Ernest W. Tiegs. Monterey: California Test Bureau, 1936–1964. Booklets: regular edition, which requires approximately two class periods for administration, Levels 0 and 1, $6.30 per 35; other levels, $7.00 per 35; short form, which can be administered within one class period, Levels 0 and 1, $4.20 per 35; other levels, $4.90 per 35. IBM answer sheets, 5 cents each, specimen set, $1.00 each for one edition at any one level.

One of the widely used intelligence tests in which an attempt is made to provide diagnostic measurement of mental abilities. The regular edition has five main parts, designed to cover these factors: logical reasoning, spatial relationships, numerical reasoning, verbal concepts, and memory. Each part has either two or three subtests. The spatial relationships part is not included in the short form, which has one to three subtests in each of its four parts. IQs, MAs, percentile ranks, standard scores, and stanines may be obtained for the Language, Non-Language, and Total raw scores. Percentile ranks, standard scores, and stanines may be assigned to the factor raw scores. Regular edition, six levels: Level 0, kindergarten and Grade 1; Level 1, Grades 1–3; Level 2, Grades 4–6; Level 3, Grades 7–9; Level 4, Grades 9–12; Level 5, Grade 12, college, and adult. Short form, eight levels: Level 0, kindergarten–L1; Level 1, Grades H1–L3; Level 1H, Grades 3 and 4; Level 2, Grades 4–6; Level 2H, Grades 6 and 7;

---

not given as references in the annotations, since the present writers have had so much experience with the tests involved that they have not had occasion to refer to the Buros reviews of those particular tests. Hence, it is not to be inferred that comments by Buros reviewers which are specifically mentioned in the annotations are necessarily better than those not so mentioned.

[7] In the annotations of tests listed in this chapter and the next two chapters, prices are given. These are prices quoted in publishers' catalogs or obtained from publishers by telephone or correspondence during the year, 1965. These are not guaranteed to users of this book as the correct prices over a period of time. It is well known that prices of tests, like those of all other commodities, vary as the economy fluctuates upward or downward. Nevertheless, even though the exact prices may become out of date as time passes, it was felt that it would be helpful to users of this book if they could have available figures which would enable them to draw inferences about the *relative* costs of the tests listed.

Level 3, Grades 7 and 8; Level 4, Grades 9–12; Level 5, Grade 12, college, and adult.

Kuder-Richardson reliabilities of short form as reported by authors for Levels 2, 3, 4, and 5: total test, .90–.93; Language section, .88–.90; Non-Language section, .78–.84. The short form was used as the basis for scaling and norming the long form of the 1963 edition.

The 1963 revision is a major revision of the 1957 edition, scaled to the Revised Stanford-Binet Intelligence Scale, Third Revision. Deviation IQs replace the ratio IQs of the older edition. Coordination with the California Achievement Tests allows achievement expectancies to be computed. *Reference* (1957 edition): Buros (11:435–439).

Cattell Culture-Fair Intelligence Test, by Raymond B. Cattell and A. K. S. Cattell. Champaign, Ill.: Institute for Personality and Ability Testing, 1933–1960. (Scales 2 and 3 are also published by The Bobbs-Merrill Company, Inc.) Three scales: Scale 1, Ages 4–8, booklets, $3.50 per 25; scoring key, 50 cents; handbook, 75 cents; specimen set, $1.35; Scale 2, Ages 8–13 and average adults, booklets, $3.30 per 25; answer sheets, $1.90 per 50; handbook, $1.60; hand-scoring keys for test booklets, 50 cents; hand-scoring keys for answer sheets, 50 cents each; specimen set, $2.20; Scale 3, Grades 10–16 and superior adults, same prices for booklets, answer sheets and scoring keys as for Scale 2; handbook, $1.90, specimen set, $2.45.

Former names for this series were the IPAT Culture-Free Intelligence Tests and the Culture-Free Test. The current edition is briefer, and is available in three levels instead of one. The tests are intended to provide measures of intelligence which are not influenced by environmental factors, such as home background and previous training. The Cattell tests are based largely on perceptual and spatial materials, which are regarded as adequate samplings of "G," or general intelligence. These tests are considerably briefer than most tests of mental ability.

Scale 1, of which there is only 1 form, requires 21 minutes of working time; Scales 2 and 3, each of which exists in 2 forms, A and B, call for 14 minutes of working time, including time for directions. Any of the 3 scales may easily be given in less than an ordinary class period. Separate answer sheets are available for Scales 2 and 3 but these are not adapted for IBM machine scoring. Each level of the test yields an IQ, but the norms for all 3 levels are based on rather small populations. Available reliability and validity data are meager. According to handbook for Scale 2, test-retest reliabilities based on 2 groups are .82–.85 and split-half reliabilities for 4 groups are .70–.92. In another report, correlations of Cattell IQs with grade point averages for 10 different groups range from .37 to .91, with an average of .51, and correlations of the Cattell with Otis Self-Administering Test of Mental Ability for same groups range from .34 to .90, with an average of .73. *References:* Buros (11:473–474), Cattell (14), and Cattell, Feingold, and Sarason (15).

College Entrance Examination Board Scholastic Aptitude Test, prepared by College Entrance Examination Board, N.Y., and Educational Testing Service, Princeton, N.J. Various editions issued from 1926 to present. A carefully controlled test available only in CEEB testing program.

The Scholastic Aptitude Test is the most extensively used test in the CEEB program. It yields two scores, verbal and mathematical, resulting from five 30-minute subtests, three of which are verbal and two mathematical. The test is usually administered in a Saturday morning session, beginning at 8:30 A.M. and ending about 12:30 P.M. Items carefully constructed and validated. Much research has been done on the SAT, and the results have appeared in CEEB publications. The data indicate that the SAT compares favorably with the better tests commercially available, although it does not appear that this examination is superior, from the standpoint of reliability and validity, to the best of the scholastic aptitude tests that may be purchased directly from the publishers. *Reference:* Buros (11:441–442).

The *Preliminary Junior Scholastic Aptitude Test* is a two-hour version of the SAT, intended to be used principally for guidance purposes in secondary schools. Its standard score scale of 20 to 80 is approximately equivalent to the 200–800 scale of the SAT.

College Qualification Tests, by George K. Bennett, Marjorie G. Bennett, Wimburn L. Wallace, and Alexander G. Wesman. New York: The Psychological Corporation, 1955–1960. Combined booklet edition: booklets, $5.00 per 25; IBM 805 answer sheets, $3.50 per 50; hand scoring keys, 50 cents; machine scoring keys, 75 cents; IBM 1230 or Digitek answer sheets, $3.80 per 50; hand scoring keys, 60 cents; machine scoring keys, 80 cents. Separate booklet edition (CQT-V, CQT-N, or CQT-I): booklets, $2.50 per 25; IBM 805 answer sheets, $2.00 per 50; hand scoring keys, 25 cents; machine scoring keys, 30 cents; manual, 50 cents; specimen sets: combined booklet, 75 cents; separate booklets, 90 cents.

This battery of three tests may be used for high school guidance purposes or in college admission, placement, and scholarship programs. Form A is available to high schools; Forms B and C are restricted to college use. The component tests are: CQT-Verbal, a vocabulary test with synonym-antonym items, requiring 15 minutes of testing time; CQT-Numerical, a test of mathematical skills drawing on arithmetic, algebra, and geometry, with a 35-minute time limit; CQT-Information, a test of general information in science (physics, chemistry, and biology) and social studies (history, government, economics, and geography), yielding subscores in science and in social studies as well as a total information score, with a time limit of 30 minutes.

Percentile norms are given for Grades 11–13 for the five subscores and the total score. College freshman norms given separately for men and women, for four types of colleges and universities, and for six types of degree programs. Split-half reliabilities reported in the manual for college freshmen are .96–.97 for the total score and .78–.95 for the subscores. Correlations of total scores with first-semester grade-point averages in fourteen colleges range from .34 to .71. *References:* Kirk (43) and Buros (11:445–449).

Cooperative Academic Ability Test, prepared by the staff of the Cooperative Test Division of Educational Testing Service. Princeton, N.J.: Educational Testing Service, 1963. Booklets, $4.00 per 20; IBM 1230 answer sheets, $1.00 per 20; specimen set, $2.00. (*Note:* This test was initially entitled *Cooperative Academic Aptitude Test.*)

This test is one of the successors of the American Council on Education Psychological Examination, which is now out of print. It is designed for use with college preparatory students and college freshmen. Two forms, A and B, are currently available. Forty minutes of working time are required for the total test.

The CAAT has two parts—verbal ability and mathematical ability—with 50 four-choice items and 20 minutes of working time for each. The verbal ability items are word analogies. In the mathematical part, two quantities are given for comparison in each item, and the student is required to decide whether one of the two quantities is greater than the other, the two are equal, or the size relationship cannot be determined from the information presented.

Initial research evidence indicates that the part and total scores have satisfactory reliabilities, yield correlations in the range of .67 to .83 with the corresponding scores on the college freshman edition of the ACE, and are about on a par with the ACE scores with respect to correlations with English grades, mathematics grades, and College Board SAT scores (92). Kuder Richardson Formula 20 reliabilities reported in the manual range from .89 to .94 for the total score in Grades 10–12, and from .78 to .92 for the part scores. Correlations with the College Board SAT scores for a group of 244 public high school seniors are given in the manual as .83 for the Verbal part and .86 for the Mathematical part. *Reference:* (19), Traxler (91, 92).

Cooperative School and College Ability Tests, by the staff of Cooperative Test Division, Educational Testing Service. Princeton, N.J.: Educational Testing Service: 1955–1956. Test booklets, any level, $4.00 per 20; IBM 1230 answer sheets (accommodating one of the STEP tests on reverse side), $25.00 per 500; Digitek answer sheets, $25.00 per 500; Directions for Administering and Scoring, 25 cents; Manual for Interpreting Scores, $1.00; Technical Report, $1.00; specimen set, $2.00.

This test series has six levels: college juniors and seniors, Form UA; college freshmen, college sophomores, and superior, Grade 12, Forms 1A, 1B, 1C; Grades 10–12, Forms 2A and 2B; Grades 8–10, Forms 3A and 3B; Grades 6–8, Forms

4A and 4B; Grades 4–6, Forms 5A and 5B. Levels that will extend this series down to Grade 1 are being prepared. Forms UA and 1C are reserved for college use. Each test consists of four parts, two verbal and two quantitative. The total working time is 70 minutes. Verbal, Quantitative, and Total scores are obtained.

Reliability and validity data are presented in the comprehensive manuals and Technical Report, which appropriately stress the concept that a test score is not to be regarded as a precise point but rather as a fairly wide band. The reported reliabilities are about .95 for the total score and from .88 to .94 for the V and Q scores. Correlations with College Board SAT scores range from .78 to .86. *References:* North (57), Traxler (90, 91) and Buros (11:450–457).

Differential Aptitude Tests, by George K. Bennett, Harold G. Seashore, and Alexander G. Wesman. New York: The Psychological Corporation, 1947–1963. Seven test booklets for Form A or B, with prices as follows: package of 25—verbal reasoning, $3.00; numerical ability, $2.25; abstract reasoning, $3.00; space relations, $3.50; mechanical reasoning, $3.75; clerical speed and accuracy, $3.00; language usage, 3.00; answer sheets, $2.00 per package of 50; scoring stencils, $1.25 per set for hand scoring, $1.40 per set for machine scoring; individual report forms, $1.25 per package of 50; interpretative manual, $2.00; specimen set, including interpretative manual, $3.00; any one test, A or B, with directions only, 50 cents.

Also available in a two-booklet edition (1963), Forms L and M, at these prices: Booklet 1 (verbal, numerical, abstract, and space), $7.75 per 25; Booklet 2 (mechanical, clerical, and language), $7.75 per 25; answer sheets, $10.00 per 50 IBM 805, $10.50 per 50 IBM 1230 or Digitek; scoring stencils, 80 cents per set; individual report forms, $1.25 per package of 50; interpretative manual, $2.00; specimen set, including interpretative manual, $3.00; specimen set without manual, $1.50.

The Differential Aptitude Tests are a comprehensive, carefully prepared test battery. These tests are published in Forms A, B, L, and M. Forms L and M are adaptations of Form A and B, respectively, and are specially designed for processing by automatic scoring machines. Each of the L and M forms is published as a two-booklet edition, while the A and B forms are available in either a combined-booklet edition (three booklets) or a separate-booklet edition. Each form yields nine scores—one score for each of the first six booklets, two scores (spelling and grammar) for the language usage booklet, and a total score for the verbal reasoning and numerical ability tests for use as an indication of general scholastic aptitude.

This battery is not derived from factorial analysis studies, but rather represents an attempt to provide an integrated set of tests that will have practical usefulness in educational and vocational guidance. Designed for Grades 8 through 12.

Working time, 25 to 35 minutes per booklet, except clerical speed and accuracy, which calls for only 6 minutes of working time. Total time for the battery, including time for administration and directions, probably about four hours. The interpretative manuals are exceptionally thorough, particularly from the standpoint of the amount of statistical data included. The authors are to be commended for their care in reporting a wealth of data on reliabilities, intercorrelations, means, and standard deviations of these tests. Reliabilities (split-half), except for highly-speeded clerical tests, range from .86 to .93, based on data given in manual (24). The median of the reported intercorrelations of the parts of the battery is only about .42, which indicates, on the whole, a moderate degree of independence among the different tests. *References:* Doppelt and Bennett (26), Doppelt (27), Super (78), and Buros (11:669–676).

Factored Aptitude Series—see *Aptitude-Intelligence Tests.*

Flanagan Aptitude Classification Tests (FACT), by John C. Flanagan. Chicago: Science Research Associates, Inc., 1951–1956. Sixteen separate booklets. Cost of each booklet per package of 20, $2.55; review set, $3.00; examiner's manual, 30 cents; student booklet (for reporting scores to students), 35 cents each.

A well-constructed, comprehensive series of aptitude tests designed for use from the high school to the adult level. The 16 test booklets include: inspection, coding, memory, precision, assembly, scales (reading scales, graphs, and charts), coordination, judgment and comprehension, arithmetic, patterns, components, tables, mechanics, expression (English usage), reasoning, and ingenuity. Forms A and B for coding, memory, and mechanics; only Form A for the thirteen other booklets. Working time per test, about three to forty minutes; total time for entire battery, three half-day sessions (about ten hours). Hand or machine scoring. Results reported in terms of percentiles. Norms based on national sample of about 11,000 students in Grades 9–12, tested in spring of 1958. Student booklets help explain the relation of the scores in 19 skill areas to 37 occupational areas. *References:* (30), Super (78), and Buros (11:684–692).

General Aptitude Test Battery, B-1002: Separate Answer Sheet Form. Washington: U.S. Employment Service, Bureau of Employment Security, U.S. Department of Labor, 1952. The General Aptitude Test Battery is not for sale generally. Inquiries concerning its use should be addressed to the United States Employment Service.

The current edition is a revision of the GATB published in 1946–1947. A unified battery of aptitude tests intended primarily for use with job applicants who have not had much experience. Two forms, A and B. The battery consists of 12 tests selected to measure nine aptitudes important for success in a wide variety of occupations. Eight of the tests are paper-and-pencil tests, comprising three booklets. The other four are apparatus tests. The 12 tests are: name comparison, computation, three-dimensional space, vocabulary, tool matching, arithmetic reasoning, form matching, mark making, place (pegs), turn (pegs), assemble, and disassemble. The aptitudes measured are: G, intelligence; V, verbal aptitude; N, numerical aptitude; S, spatial aptitude; P, form perception; Q, clerical perception; K, motor coordination; F, finger dexterity; and M, manual dexterity. Total administration time, 2¼ hours. Raw scores are converted to standard scores. Percentile norms also available. Norms for adults and high school students. Standard scores may be recorded on individual profile cards, then matched against minimum scores for various occupations. The occupational pattern structure is based on the *Dictionary of Occupational Titles.* Numerous statistical data are given in an extensive loose-leaf *Guide to the Use of GATB.* Median test-retest reliability about .82; median reliability derived from correlations between comparable forms about .83; reliability coefficients range from .54 to .96. Median of intercorrelations among aptitude scores about .32; range −.13 to .81. Some evidence of test battery validity has been obtained through correlations of test scores with criteria of academic or vocational success.

This test battery is available for use in nonprofit institutions in counseling, as well as by employers. Testing services are available from USES state and local offices, and these services are free when the United States Employment Service handles the program. Orders must be cleared through the USES offices. A highly useful test battery in vocational guidance of youth and adults. *References:* Super (78), Wysong (101), and Buros (11:692–700).

Henmon-Nelson Tests of Mental Ability, Revised Edition, by Tom A. Lamke, and M. J. Nelson. Boston: Houghton Mifflin Company, 1931–1958. Consumable or reusable booklets, Grades 3–6, 6–9, or 9–12, $3.60 per 35; MRC answer cards, $2.55 per 100; IBM 805 answer sheets, $3.30 per 100; IBM 1230 answer sheets, $4.20 per 100; IBM 805 or 1230 scoring keys, 30 cents each; manual 45 cents; specimen kit, Grades 3–12, $2.25.

One of the well-established, dependable group tests of mental ability of the single-score type. The total score may be converted to a deviation IQ, mental age equivalent, grade equivalent, and grade percentile. Two forms, A and B. Each level contains 90 multiple-choice items including linguistic, quantitative, perceptual, and spatial material, with the linguistic area weighted somewhat heavier than the other areas. Working time, 30 minutes. Split-half reliabilities for single age or grade range cluster around .94, as indicated by data reported by test authors. Correlations with several well-known intelligence tests range from .50 to .84, with a median of .76, according to data in the manual. *References:* Buros (11:469–473).

Henmon-Nelson Tests of Mental Ability, College Level, Revised Edition, by M. J. Nelson, Tom A. Lamke, and Paul C. Kelso. Boston: Houghton Mifflin Company,

1931–1958. Consumable or reusable booklets, $3.60 per 35; self-marking answer sheets, $2.52 per 35; IBM 805 answer sheets, $3.32 per 100; IBM 1230 answer sheets, $4.20 per 100; IBM 805 scoring keys, 90 cents per set; IBM 1230 scoring keys, 60 cents per set; manual, 48 cents; specimen set, $1.00.

Suitable for use with college freshmen. Two forms, A and B. Each form has 100 items, with quantitative and verbal types arranged in omnibus-cycle form. Yields quantitative, verbal, and total scores, which are convertible to college freshman percentiles. Hand scoring is rapid, since this is one of the tests in the Clapp-Young Self-Marking Series.

Holzinger-Crowder Uni-Factor Tests, by Karl J. Holzinger and Norman A. Crowder. New York: Harcourt, Brace & World, Inc., 1952. Two forms, Am and Bm. Test booklets, $6.75 per 35; answer sheet 1, $2.45 per 35; answer sheet 2, $1.80 per 35; set of five right keys for hand scoring or machine scoring, 50 cents; set of three item-elimination keys for machine scoring, 30 cents; specimen set, 60 cents.

The late Professor Karl J. Holzinger and his associates carried on factor analysis studies for many years at the University of Chicago. The Uni-Factor Tests are an outgrowth of those studies. They are designed to measure four factors: verbal, spatial, numerical, and reasoning. The battery consists of nine tests. An extensive manual of interpretation accompanies the tests. Grade range, 7–12; working time, 40-½ minutes; overall time, two 45-minute periods. The tests yield grade-level percentile norms for each factor, an overall score, and an IQ. A useful battery for guidance purposes at the high school level. Much statistical information on this battery is given in an excellent manual. Experimental data indicate that Forms Am and Bm are virtually equivalent in difficulty. Alternate-form reliabilites range as follows: verbal, .80 to .93; spatial, .78 to .86; numerical, .87 to .95; reasoning, .76 to .90. Medians of split-half reliabilities for verbal and reasoning factors: verbal, .93; reasoning, .93. Multiple correlation coefficients for factor scores and intelligence on six tests range from .71 to .86. Medians of correlations between factor scores and tests of achievement: verbal, .62; spatial, .33; numerical, .44; reasoning, .52. Medians of correlations between factor scores and teachers' marks: V, .57; S, .22; N, .46; R, .48. *References:* (36), Super (78), and Buros (11:700–704).

Junior Scholastic Aptitude Test, Revised Edition, by Geraldine Spaulding. Boston: National Association of Independent Schools. Copyrighted by precursive organizations, Secondary Education Board, Milton, Mass., and Independent Schools Education Board, Milton Mass., 1959–1960. Earlier editions, dating back to 1939, copyrighted by Bureau of Research, Secondary Education Board. Distributed and scored by Educational Records Bureau, New York, N.Y. Restricted for central scoring. Fee is $1.00 per individual for test material and scoring services; specimen set not available; no charge for descriptive leaflet.

An especially valuable test for admission, placement, and guidance in Grades 7, 8, and 9, particularly in independent or private schools. Based on extensive experimentation carried on by S.E.B. Bureau of Research and Educational Records Bureau. Present forms are A, B, and C. Provides separate scores for verbal and numerical aptitude. No total score, mental age, or IQ. Results are reported in terms of three-digit converted scores and fall or spring percentiles derived from independent school population. Total administration time, about 80 minutes. Split-half reliabilities for single grade range: verbal score, .93–.95, numerical score, .91–.95, Re-test reliabilities one-year interval, Forms A and B, verbal score, .84–.88, numerical score, .80–.88. Correlations with College Board SAT scores over 2–3 year period, verbal, .76–.78, numerical-mathematical, .71–.76. Part of income from JSAT scoring goes to National Association of Independent Schools to maintain continuous program of research directed toward improvement of test. *References:* Spaulding (74, 75, 76) and Buros (11:475).

Kuhlmann-Anderson Tests, 7th Edition, by F. Kuhlmann and Rose G. Anderson. Princeton, N.J.: The Personnel Press, 1961–1964. Write-in booklets for K, A, B, and CD tests, $3.25 per 25; reusable booklets for D, EF, G and H tests, $3.40 per 25; IBM 805 answer sheets, $2.40 per 50; IBM 1230 or Digitek answer sheets, $6.00 per 100; IBM 805 scoring keys, 25 cents per set; IBM 1230 scoring keys, 25 cents per set for D or EF, 50 cents per set for G or H; Digitek scoring stencils, 50 cents per set; norms manual, 25 cents each; technical manual, 50 cents each; specimen set, $1.00. (Separate manuals and specimen sets for K-CD, D-EF, and G-H.)

The Kuhlmann-Anderson Tests are a long-standing, dependable series. Formerly called intelligence tests, they are now subtitled "Measures of Academic Potential." They consist of seven overlapping batteries (booklets), with eight tests in each, covering the K–12 grade range. Only one form. The 7th Edition yields a deviation IQ derived from the total score, while the older editions gave a ratio IQ based on the median mental age of the subtests. Booklets D–H for the 4–12 grade range also yield verbal and quantitative aptitude scores. Grade percentile ranks and stanines are provided for the total score and IQ for all batteries and for the verbal and quantitative aptitude scores for the D–H booklets. Administration time ranges from about 80 minutes in the lower grades (K–3) to about 60 minutes in the upper grades.

Reliabilities reported in technical manuals: booklets K–CD —Spearman-Brown coefficients for total scores, .93–.95, test-retest within two to six months, .85–.87 for IQs; coefficients for IQs and total scores derived from factor analyses, .85 for booklet D, .90 for EF, .91 for booklet G, .93 for booklet H. V and Q reliabilities based on factor analyses, .80–.89, except .62 for Q for booklet D. One year test-retest reliabilities for independent school groups, .55 for Grades 1 and 2, .79–.89

for other grades through 8. Correlations with other general aptitude measures mostly in range of .60–.89, according to data in technical manuals. *References*: Kuhlmann and Anderson (45), Merwin (54), and North (60, 61, 62, 63).

Kuhlmann-Finch Scholastic Aptitude Tests, by F. H. Finch, based on plans of F. H. Kuhlmann. Minneapolis: American Guidance Services, Inc., 1951–1960. Test booklets, $2.95 per 25; hand-scoring or machine-scoring answer sheets, $2.40 per 50; scoring keys—hand-scoring, 25 cents; machine-scoring, 25 cents (it is necessary to specify grade in each instance); manual, $1.25; specimen set, single grade, 50 cents, all grades, $1.50.

This series of tests is a group adaptation of the Kuhlmann-Binet Individual Test based on many years of research by Dr. Finch. Eight test booklets as follows: Test I, Grade 1; Test II, Grade 2; Test III, Grade 3; Test IV, Grade 4; Test V, Grade 5; Test VI, Grade 6; Junior High School Test, Grades 7–9; Senior High School Test, Grades 10–12. Separate answer sheets available for Grade 4 upward. The simple plan of the tests lends itself to ease of administration. Each test consists of several five-minute subtests; overall working time, about one class period. Results are expressed in terms of mental ages and deviation IQs. Norms derived from standardization testing in 30 states, but sampling is not well defined. Spearman-Brown reliabilities for the batteries in single year-age ranges are estimated to be about .90, or possibly slightly higher. Test-retest reliabilities over a six-month period are reported to range from .75 to .84. Statistical data are limited. *References*: Finch (29) and Buros (11:476–478).

Lorge-Thorndike Intelligence Tests, by Irving Lorge and Robert L. Thorndike. Boston: Houghton Mifflin Company, 1954–1964. Consumable booklets, Level 1 or 2, nonverbal battery, $3.45 per 35; Levels 3, 4, or 5, verbal or nonverbal batteries, $2.85 per 35; reusable booklets, Level 3, 4, or 5, verbal or nonverbal batteries, $3.15 per 35; reusable multilevel booklets, 66 cents each; IBM 805 answer sheets, $1.44 per 35; IBM 1230 answer sheets, $4.20 per 100; scoring key for one level, verbal or nonverbal, IBM 805 or IBM 1230, 30 cents each; technical manual, 45 cents; specimen set, 45 cents each; complete specimen kit, separate level edition, $2.25.

This series of tests of abstract intelligence was constructed by two well-known authorities in educational measurement. Five levels recommended for use in the average school as follows: Level 1, kindergarten and Grade 1; Level 2, Grades 2 and 3; Level 3, Grades 4–6; Level 4, Grades 7–9; Level 5, Grades 10–12. The two upper levels may also be used with adults. The two lowest levels require comprehension of oral language but do not call for reading; Levels 3, 4, and 5 are available in both verbal and nonverbal batteries. Forms A and B at each level are available. Time required for administration approximately as follows: Levels 1 and 2, untimed, recommended time, 30 minutes for each setting; Levels 3, 4, and 5, verbal series, working time, 34 minutes, total time, 45 minutes; nonverbal series, working time 27 minutes, total time, 35–40 minutes. The 1964 Multi-Level Edition includes the verbal and nonverbal batteries in a single, reusable booklet for grades 3–13, with two forms, 1 and 2. Working time, 35 minutes for verbal battery, 27 minutes for nonverbal battery. Subtests in verbal batteries are designed to measure word knowledge, sentence completion, verbal classification, verbal analogies, and arithmetic reasoning. Nonverbal batteries cover figure analogies, figure classification, and number series. The nonreading levels, 1 and 2, include oral vocabulary, cross out, and pairing. The median item-test correlation reported by authors in general manual range from .43 to .70, which are quite high. Reported reliabilities of different levels range from approximately .76 to about .90. It is to be noted that these are alternate-form reliabilities and that they provide a more rigorous appraisal than Spearman-Brown split-half reliabilities. Intercorrelations among subtests and correlations between verbal and nonverbal series center around .6 to .7, which are usual for these kinds of measures. Correlations with certain other intelligence tests range from .52 to .64, which seem on the low side, although it is to be observed that these correlations are based on pupils in lower grades, where such correlations do not as a rule run high. Separate tables of norms are available for each level. The norms for the multilevel edition are coordinated with those of the Tests of Academic Progress (Grades 9–12) and the Iowa Tests of Basic Skills (Grades 3–8). *References*: Lorge and Thorndike (49) and Buros (11:478–484).

Ohio State University Psychological Test, by Herbert A. Toops. Columbus: Ohio State University, 1919–1959. Test blanks with inserted answer pad, 10 cents each; additional answer pads, 5 cents each (Forms 18 through 26); IBM answer sheets, 5 cents each (Forms 21 through 26). Form 21 also published by Science Research Associates, Inc., Chicago, with prices as follows: Form AH (hand scoring), 54 cents per test with answer pad; $2.40 per 20 answer pads; Form AM (machine scoring), 54 cents per test, $5.00 per 100 IBM answer sheets; 50 cents per scoring stencil; 75 cents per review set of either hand-scoring or machine-scoring edition.

A group test of ability to think, requiring about two hours of working time. The available forms are not independent parallel forms but are successive revisions. The latest form, 26, is the result of experimentation carried on since 1919. Includes three subtests: same-opposites, analogies, and paragraph comprehension, with a total of 150 test items. Separate answer pads or answer sheets must be used. In answer-pad edition, hidden key between leaves of pad eliminates necessity of scoring test in usual way. The scorer merely counts the number of squares correctly punched out on the answer key. Designed for secondary schools, colleges, and adults. There are grade norms for public high school pupils in each grade from 9 through 12, and college norms; also independent school norms for an earlier edition, 15, for Grades 9–12. Reliability resulting from four separate studies in which one form was correlated with another are .90, .91, .88, and .91. Reliability of Form 21 based on 300 cases as reported in manual is .93. Validity coefficient of .68 is reported between scores on Form 21 and grades based on results for 1030 college freshmen. This is a high coefficient for correlation between test scores and grades used as a criterion. Validities of Form 24, resulting from correlations between test scores and first-year or first-semester scholarship, are reported as .54, .58, and .60 for different groups of college freshmen. Evidence of the potential value of the test in selecting graduate students is indicated by a correlation of .82 reported between the test and the carefully controlled Miller Analogies Test (55). Toops' work on this test illustrates what can be done through long-continued research to bring a test to a high degree of technical excellence. *References:* Toops (82) and Buros (11:494–495).

Otis Quick-Scoring Mental Ability Tests, by Arthur S. Otis. New York: Harcourt, Brace & World, Inc., 1936–1954. Grades 1–4, Alpha Test, Forms A and B, $3.80 per 35 booklets; Form AS (short form), $3.20 per 35 booklets; Grades 4–9, Beta Test, Forms A and B, $2.70 per 35 booklets; Forms CM, DM, EM, and FM (machine scorable), $3.10 per 35 booklets; Grades 9–12, college, and adult, Gamma Test, Forms C and D, $2.70 per 35 booklets; Forms AM, BM, EM, and FM (machine scorable), $3.10 per 35 booklets; machine scorable answer sheets, IBM 805, for Beta or Gamma Test, $1.80 per 35; IBM 1230, 2.25 per 35; keys for machine scorable answer sheets, 20 cents each; specimen set, any level, 40 cents each.

The simple design of these tests makes them easy to administer and score. Deviation IQs with standard deviations of about 12–13 for the national population are obtained. Grade percentile rank tables for the IQs are available. The AS, EM, and FM forms constitute the new edition. The Alpha Test of the older edition requires no reading but may be used to get nonverbal, verbal, and composite-score IQs. This level requires about 55 minutes of testing time for Form A or B, and about 35 minutes for Form AS. The latter form yields only a single IQ. The Beta and Gamma tests can be administered in about 35 minutes. Reliabilities, as reported in manual of directions: Alpha Test, correlation between Forms A and B, for single grade range, median of 12 reliability coefficients, .83; Spearman-Brown odd-even reliabilities, median of six correlations, .86; Gamma Test, median of three odd-even correlations corrected by Spearman-Brown formula, .90. The new forms of the Beta and Gamma Tests are constructed to be equivalent to the earlier ones. The author reports that the average correlations between the Gamma Test and the older Otis Self-Administering Higher Examination is .86. *Reference:* Buros (11:496–500).

SRA Primary Mental Abilities, by L. L. Thurstone and Thelma Gwinn Thurstone. Chicago: Science Research Associates, Inc., 1946–1963. Five batteries for five grade-range levels: K–1, 2–4, 4–6, 6–9, and 9–12. Hand scoring for the two lower levels, machine or hand scoring for the other three levels. Grades K–1 and 2–4: test booklets with profile sheets and examiner's manual, $3.00 per 20; examiner's manual separately, 25 cents each; review set for one level, 50 cents each; Grades 4–6, 6–9, and 9–12: test booklets with examiner's manual, $11.00 per 20; examiner's manual separately 25 cents each; answer sheets, $5.00 per 100, $23.50 per 500; set of scoring stencils for one level, $1.00; profile sheets 70 cents per 20; review set of one level, $1.00 each; complete review set for Grades K–12, $3.00 each.

These tests are an abbreviated edition based on the original tests that resulted from Thurstone's intensive work in factor analysis. The first tests to eventuate from his factorial studies of mental ability were the Tests for Primary Mental Abilities, a highly reliable four-hour battery prepared mainly for high school and college students and published by the American Council on Education and Science Research Associates, Inc. That battery has been out of print for many years. The next step was the preparation of the Chicago Tests of Primary Mental Abilities, a similar but easier two-hour battery designed for ages 11 to 17. Those tests are also out of print. The present 1963 edition of the SRA Primary Mental Abilities is a still briefer version designed to cover the K–12 grade range. There is one form for each of the five levels. The total administration time is 60 minutes for each of the three batteries in the K–6 range, and 55 minutes for each of the two batteries in the 6–12 range. Each level is intended to measure mental factors as follows: Grades K–1, verbal meaning, spatial ability, perception, and number facility; Grades 2–4, verbal meaning, quantitative ability, spatial ability, and perception; Grades 4–6, verbal meaning, quantitative ability, spatial ability, perceptual speed, and reasoning; Grades 6–9 and Grades 9–12, verbal meaning, number sense, reasoning, and spatial ability. Each level yields a quotient score for each factor and an intelligence score for the test as a whole. *References:* Super (78), Thurstone (81), and Buros (11:708–717).

SRA Tests of Educational Ability (TEA) by L. L. Thurstone and Thelma Gwinn Thurstone. Chicago: Science Research Associates, Inc., 1957–1962. Booklets, $7.00 per 20; answer sheets, $7.00 per 100; scoring stencil, 50 cents each; examiner's manual, 35 cents each; Technical Supplement, $1.00 each; review set, Grades 4–12, $1.00 each.

Consists of Language, Reasoning, and Quantitative subtests for elementary and junior and senior high school pupils. Age-based quotients and grade percentiles are obtained for the three subtests and total score. Three levels: Grades 4–6 (52 minutes), Grades 6–9 (67 minutes), and Grades 9–12 (49 minutes). Restandardized on a national sample of 20,338 students in the spring of 1962. Data reported in the manual indicate that the Kuder-Richardson and Spearman-Brown reliabilities are in the range of .58 to .92 for the subtests, and .83 to .95 for the total scores. Correlations of the total score with the SRA Achievement Series composite score are reported to range from .66 to .89. *Reference:* Buros (11:510–513).

Stanford-Binet Intelligence Scale, Third Revision, by Lewis M. Terman and Maud A. Merrill. Boston: Houghton Mifflin Company, 1919–1960. Form L-M. Examiner's kit, including manual, $33.20. Record booklets, $4.40 per 35; record forms, $2.40 per 35; manual (book), $4.48.

A revision of the widely used individual intelligence scale first issued by Terman in 1916. May be used from age 2 to superior adult level. Should be administered, scored, and interpreted only by persons trained in the use of this particular scale. Many of the main concepts in Binet's original scale and of the two earlier Stanford revisions were conserved in this revision, but important innovations were made. The present revision incorporates the best subtests of Forms L and M of the Second Revision and shows improvement in standardization. An important feature of the Third Revision is the use of a deviation IQ scale to replace the quotient scale of the previous revisions. The deviation scale was adopted to improve the constancy of IQs from one age level to another by making the standard deviation of the IQs very nearly 16 at each age level. The test yields a mental age, which is converted to an IQ by means of a table in the manual. The older L and M forms are still available, and tables for converting the quotient IQs to deviation IQs are provided in the Third Revision Manual.

Reliability and validity data are based mainly on studies of the results of the Second Revision. The authors report that the reliabilities range from .98 for subjects whose IQs are below 70 to approximately .90 for subjects whose IQs are above 130. The authors also found reliability coefficients for 21 age groups, using subjects who were within four weeks of a birthday or half birthday. The coefficients ranged from .85 to .95, with a median of .91. Terman and Merrill's book, *Stanford-Binet Intelligence Scale* (80) includes a very complete manual for the test. Numerous correlations with other criteria, particularly with academic achievement, have been reported in extensive research literature concerning the test. In general, correlations with achievement are substantial, although not higher than those between achievement and the better group tests of intelligence. See Buros' *Mental Measurements Yearbooks* for bibliography of some 620 studies. *References:* Buros (8:242–244; 9:375–379; 10:461–464; 11:543–548); McNemar (50), and Terman and Merrill (80).

Tests of General Ability (TOGA), by John C. Flanagan. Chicago: Science Research Associates, Inc., 1960. Booklets for Grades K–2 or 2–4, $3.20 per 20; Grades 4–6, 6–9, or 9–12, $4.25 per 20; answer sheets for Grades 4–6, 6–9, or 9–12, $5.00 per 100; scoring stencils, 50 cents each; additional examiner's manual or Spanish manual, 25 cents; Technical Report, $1.00; complete review set with Technical Report, $2.00.

These nonverbal measures of mental ability are intended for use with children who have handicaps in language, reading, or cultural background. The directions may be given in either English or Spanish. One form, five levels: K–2, 2–4, 4–6, 6–9, 9–12. Grade expectancy and IQ scores may be obtained. Testing time is 35–45 minutes.

The reliabilities of these tests tend to be lower than those of most group intelligence tests. In the Technical Report, Spearman-Brown reliabilities are reported to range from .80 to .90, with a median of .87, and Kuder Richardson reliabilities range from .78 to .86, with a median of .82. For independent school groups. Kuder-Richardson reliabilities were found to range from .71 in Grade 6 to .83 in kindergarten, with a median of .79, and correlations with Kuhlmann-Anderson IQs ranged from .25 in Grade 2 to .72 in Grade 7 (59). The publisher reports correlations of .42 with Kuhlmann-Anderson mental ages in Grade, 4, .57 with Otis Beta IQs in Grade 6, and .74 with Kuhlmann-Anderson mental ages in Grade 9. *Reference:* Flanagan (31).

Wechsler Adult Intelligence Scale (WAIS), by David Wechsler. New York: The Psychological Corporation, 1939–1955. Examiner's set, with manual and 25 record forms, $24.00; record forms separately, $2.10 per 25; manual separately, $3.00

A revision and restandardization of Form I of the Wechsler-Bellevue Intelligence Scale, designed for use with adolescents and adults from age 16 to over 75. It consists of six verbal and five performance tests, yielding scores that are converted to standard scores and are then translated into deviation IQs from tables in the manual. A Verbal IQ, Performance IQ, and a Full-Scale IQ are obtained. The test can be administered to only one individual at a time, and the services of a specially trained examiner are required. It is one of the most widely used clinical instruments and undoubtedly the best measure of adult intelligence. Testing time, about 40–60 minutes. Standardized on 2175 subjects of both sexes, ages 16–75 and older. Author reports split-half reliabilities for 200 subjects in 18–19 year age range of .96 for Verbal IQ, .93 for Performance IQ, and .97 for Full-Scale IQ; correlations with Stanford-Binet Second Revision IQs for three different types of groups, .62 to .89 (99). *Reference:* Buros (11:548–551).

Wechsler Bellevue Intelligence Scale, by David Wechsler. New York: The Psychological Corporation, 1939–1947. Form II, $21.00 per set of test materials, including 25 record blanks and manual; $2.10 per package of 25 record blanks for Form I or Form II; manual alone for Form II, $2.25.

This scale was issued in 1939 to meet the need for more adequate sampling of adult intelligence than was provided by the Stanford-Binet Scale, which was more satisfactory for children than for adults. Individual administration by a trained examiner is required. Form I has been superseded by Wechsler Adult Intelligence Scale, but record blanks are still available for users equipped with this form. Form II is the retest form for either the WAIS or Form I. Suitable for ages 10 to adult. Testing time, about 40 to 60 minutes. Contains 11 tests of which 6 are verbal (vocabulary test need not be used) and 5 are nonverbal performance tests. Raw scores on each test are converted to standard scores, which are then added and converted to IQ equivalents through a procedure that makes adjustments for the ages of adults. Verbal, Performance, and Full-Scale IQs are obtained. Test-retest reliability reported as .94 for the full scale. Reported test-retest reliability coefficients for subtests range from .62 to .88. *References:* Buros (8:264–267; 9:384–387; 10:469–476), and Guertin, Frank, and Rabin (34).

Wechsler Intelligence Scale for Children (WISC), by David Wechsler. New York: The Psychological Corporation, 1949. $25.00 per complete set of test materials, including 25 record forms and manual; manual alone, $3.00; record forms, $2.50 per 25.

A downward extension of the Wechsler-Bellevue Intelligence Scale with content overlapping that of Form II. One form, ages 5–15. Twelve subtests, of which six are verbal and six are performance. One verbal test and one performance test are optional. Standardized on 2200 white American children. Testing time, 40–60 minutes. Individually administered by trained examiner. Raw scores are converted to standard scores, then to Verbal, Performance, and Full-Scale IQs. Spearman-Brown reliability coefficients reported in the manual range from .88 to .96 for the Verbal Scale, from .86 to .90 for the Performance Scale, and from .92 to .95 for the full scale. Correlations between WISC and Stanford-Binet IQs reported in several research studies for children in the 7–15 age range are between .70 and .90. For a list of 133 research references, see Buros (10:476–477; 11:555–561). Also, Seashore, Wesman, and Doppelt (72).

ACCOUNTING

Accounting Orientation Test—High School Level, by the staff of the Testing Project Office of the American Institute of Certified Public Accountants. New York: American Institute of Certified Public Accountants, 1953–1965. Test booklets, 20 cents each; answer sheets, 5 cents; scoring stencil, 25 cents; specimen set, $1.00.

An accounting aptitude test for students in Grades 10–12. Yields scores in business vocabulary, arithmetic reasoning, accounting problems, and for the test as a whole, with percentile norms for each of two forms, S and T. No knowledge of accounting is necessary for answering the items. Spearman-Brown reliabilities of part scores, .76–.87; total score, .91. Correlation of total scores with final grades in elementary accounting course for first-year college students, .41; with accounting achievement test scores .49 (64). *Reference:* North (58).

ART

Graves Design Judgment Test, by Maitland Graves. New York: The Psychological Corporation, 1948. Test booklets, reusable spiral-bound, 1–9 copies, $1.50 each; 10–99 copies, $1.30 each; 100 or more copies, $1.20 each; answer sheets for hand or machine scoring, $2.00 per package of 50, $16.50 per package of 500; manual and scoring key, if ordered separately, 35 cents per set; specimen set, complete, $1.85.

Devised as a measure of appreciation or production of art or of readiness to learn in this field. Subject is required to appraise 90 sets of designs represented in two or three dimensions. One form, 90 items. Grades 7–16 and adults. No time limit, but about 20 to 30 minutes required for administration. Spearman-Brown odd-even reliability reported as .81 to .93 with a median of .86. Information is given concerning differences between scores of art students and those in other curricula at both high school and college levels, but statistical data on validity of this test are lacking. *Reference:* Buros (10:335–337).

Knauber Art Ability Test, by Alma Jordan Knauber. Cincinnati: the author, 6988 Warder Drive, 1932–1935. 12 cents per test; $1.25 per manual; $1.30 per specimen set.

A production test using semiobjective scoring. One form, Grades 7–16 and adults. The test is not timed but requires about three hours. Author reports reliability of .95 by split-half technique, but this correlation is based on the scores of only 83 students. Some information is given relative to differences between scores of art majors and nonart majors. *Reference:* Knauber (44).

Meier Art Test: Test I: Art Judgment, by Norman C. Meier. Iowa City, Iowa: State University of Iowa, Bureau of Educational Research and Service, 1929–1942. $1.40 per book of test pictures; 80 cents for examiner's manual and scoring keys; $2.70 per 50 IBM 805 answer sheets; $1.50 per specimen set.

This test is a revision of the Meier-Seashore Art Judgment Test. It consists of 100 plates selected from 125 in the earlier test. Each plate presents a pair of pictures consisting of a picture created by a great artist and the same picture altered to reduce its artistic merit. The score is based on the number of unaltered masterpieces chosen by the subject as the better. One form suitable for use in Grade 7 and above and with adults. No time limit; administration may be expected to require about 40 minutes. The reliability of this test is given as .70 to .84. Percentile norms are available for the junior high school, the senior high school, and the college-adult level. *References:* Meier (53), Prothro and Perry (66).

MUSIC

Seashore Measures of Musical Talents, Revised Edition, by Carl E. Seashore, Don Lewis, and Joseph G. Saetveit. New York: The Psychological Corporation, 1919–1960. $12.00 per album of three unbreakable records, including manual, scoring key, and 50 answer sheets; $2.30 per 50 IBM 805 machine- or hand-scoring answer sheets; manual and scoring key, 60 cents.

One of the best known of all aptitude tests. Consists of two series of three double-faced phonograph records. Designed to measure sense of pitch, sense of intensity, sense of time, tonal memory, sense of rhythm, and sense of timbre. Records are played to the subjects, who enter their answers on special blanks. Grades 5–14 and adults. Series A is for the testing of unselected groups and for use in selection and guidance; Series B, a more difficult set of tests for use with musicians and prospective or actual students of music, is no longer available.

Percentile norms given for Series A in 1956 revision of manual for each of six scores at three levels: Grade 4–5, Grades 6–8, and Grades 9–16. Reliability of individual tests reported as follows: Grades 4–5, .55 to .85; Grades 6–8, .63 to .84; Grades 9–16, .68 to .84. Validity data for revised series have seldom been reported, notwithstanding the long period these tests have been in existence. This is due partly to the difficulty of obtaining suitable criteria. Music teachers tend not to be objective-minded·and often do not keep records on their students. *References:* Saetveit, Lewis, and Seashore (70); also bibliography in Buros (11:385).

Wing Standardized Tests of Musical Intelligence: A Test of Musical Ability on 10 Records, by H. D. Wing and Cecilia Wing. Sheffield City Training College, Sheffield, England, 1939–1960. $20.00 per set of ten records, manual, scoring key, and 50 answer sheets; $2.00 per single record; $2.00 per 100 answer sheets (prices as given may not be up to date).

Yields eight scores: chord analysis, pitch change, memory, rhythmic accent, harmony, intensity, phrasing, and a total score. Designed for ages 10 and over. One form. Testing time, 60 minutes. Similar in some respects to the Seashore tests, but the availability of a total score indicates an "omnibus" theory of musical ability as contrasted with Seashore's theory of specific abilities. Spearman-brown split-half reliability of subtests reported as .65 to .86 and that of total score as .90 to .91. The recording has been criticized as somewhat inferior from a technical standpoint, but the tests are, nevertheless, regarded as a valuable contribution to measurement in the musical field. *References:* Wing (100) and Buros (10:344–346).

Kwalwasser Test of Music Information and Appreciation, by Jacob Kwalwasser. Iowa City: State University of Iowa, Bureau of Educational Research and Service, 1927. $5.00 per 100 tests; 5½ cents a copy; specimen set, 25 cents.

A group test dealing with knowledge of composers—their nationality, compositions, types of composition—of artists, instruments and production of tones on them, and of musical structure and form in general. Testing time is 40 minutes. Percentile norms based on scores of high school and college students in music appreciation courses are given. Reliability,

.70 to .72. *Reference:* Semeonoff (73). Both this test and the following one by Kwalwasser are still used to a considerable extent, notwithstanding the early dates of publication.

Kwalwasser-Ruch Test of Musical Accomplishment, by Jacob Kwalwasser and G. M. Ruch. Iowa City: State University of Iowa, Bureau of Educational Research and Service, 1924–1927. $6.50 per 100 tests; 7 cents a copy, specimen set, 25 cents.

A group test designed to measure achievement of pupils in a typical public school music course in the elementary and high school grades. It includes knowledge of musical symbols and terms, recognition of syllable names, detection of pitch errors and time errors in a familiar melody, recognition of pitch names, time and key signature, note and rest values, and recognition of familiar melodies from notation. Testing time is 40 minutes. The split-half reliability of the total score is quoted as .97; reliability of subtests, .70 to .97. Norms are based on scores of 5414 pupils in Grades 4 to 12 and are given by deciles. *Reference:* Kwalwasser (46).

Musical Aptitude Test, Series A, by Harvey S. Whistler and Louis P. Thorpe. Monterey: California Test Bureau, 1950. $3.00 per set of test materials used by examiner; separate IBM 805 answer sheets, which must be used, 5 cents each; scoring stencils, hand or machine, 50 cents each.

A test of potential ability for learning music, consisting of five parts and yielding four scores: rhythm, pitch, melody, and a total score. A piano is used in administering the test. One form. Grades 4–10. Requires working time of about 40 minutes. Well-prepared manual of directions. Decile norms for each grade from 4 through 8 and for Grades 9 and 10 combined. Kuder-Richardson reliability of total score reported as .87; reliabilities of subscores, .64 to .77. A correlation of .78 corrected for attenuation has been obtained between total score and teachers' estimate of vocal talent. *Reference:* Buros (11:384–385).

SCIENCE

Stanford Scientific Aptitude Test, by David L. Zyve. Palo Alto, Calif.: Consulting Psychologists Press, 1929–1930. Test booklets, $5.50 per 25; manual and stencil, $1.00; specimen set, $1.25.

Developed to measure 11 components of scientific aptitude. One form which requires 60 to 120 minutes of working time. Suitable for senior high school and college students. Used for entrance to schools of engineering and science. An interesting and well-printed test, but one that is now quite old and not representative of the most advanced procedures of test construction. Norms based on scores of 323 college students. Reliability of .93 reported by author at time test was constructed. Benton and Perry reported correlations of .30 to .37 between aptitude scores and scholarship covering four years of work. Few other studies of the validity of this test have been made. The test suffers by comparison with modern tests in other fields, but it remains almost the only generally available test designed specifically to measure aptitude for the study of science. *References:* Zyve (102), Benton and Perry (4), Cooprider and Laslett (20), Marshall (52).

MECHANICAL APTITUDE

MacQuarrie Test for Mechanical Ability, by T. W. MacQuarrie. Monterey: California Test Bureau, 1925–1943. $4.20 per 35 booklets; manual and scoring key, 15 cents; scoring template, 10 cents each; specimen set, 50 cents.

One form which yields eight scores: tracing, tapping, dotting, copying, location, blocks, pursuit, and total. A group test for ages 7 and over. Testing time, 20 minutes. Norms based on results for 2000 adults. Retest reliability of the whole test reported by the author .90; reliabilities for subtests range from .72 for location to .96 for copying. Some data on predictive validity reported in manual. One of the oldest and most widely used of the mechanical ability tests. *References:* Buros (9:688–691, 10:759).

Mechanical Comprehension Tests, by George K. Bennett and others. New York: The Psychological Corporation, 1940–1951. Booklets, $4.75 for 1–9 packages including 25 tests; 10 or more packages, $4.30; single copies, 25 cents each; IBM 805 answer sheets (specify form), $2.00 per package of 50; specimen set, 50 cents.

Four forms: Form AA for general population, Form BB more difficult than Form AA; Form CC more difficult than Form BB; Form W1 for women. Form AA is suitable for use with boys in Grade 9 and above; Form BB with men in Grade 13 and over; Form CC with men in engineering schools; and Form W1 with girls and women in Grade 9 and over. Designed to measure understanding of the operation of physical principles. Not timed; usually requires about 30 minutes. Machine scorable. Each form contains 60 items. Split-half reliability corrected by the Spearman-Brown formula is reported at about .80 to .84, which is satisfactory for an unspeeded test of 60 items. Correlations of test scores with job performance of groups in various occupations have been reported. These are of the order of .3 to .6, which are as high as those usually obtained between predictive measures and success on the job. *Reference:* Buros (10:765–766).

Minnesota Paper Form Board Test, Revised, by Donald G. Paterson, Richard M. Elliott, L. Dewey Anderson, Herbert A. Toops, and Edna Heidbreder; revision by Rensis Likert and William H. Quasha. New York: The Psychological Corporation, 1930–1948. Forms AA and BB (hand scoring), $2.50 per 25; Forms MA and MB (machine scoring), $3.50 per 25; IBM 805 answer sheets, $2.00 per 50; specimen set (includes four forms) 75 cents.

Designed to measure ability to visualize and mentally manipulate geometric forms and objects in space, which is one aspect of success in mechanical and engineering occupations. Two comparable forms each for hand and machine scoring. Working time, 20 minutes. Norms are available for educational groups in elementary school, high school, and college, and for several occupational groups. On basis of scores of 290 high school seniors, reliability of one form reported as .85 and that of both forms as .92. Correlation with Otis Self-Administering Test of Mental Ability, .40; American Council Psychological Examination, 1940 High School Edition, .42; Bennett Mechanical Comprehension Test, .39. *References:* Quasha and Likert (67) and Buros (11:911–912).

SRA Mechanical Aptitudes, by Richardson, Bellows, Henry, & Co., Inc. Chicago: Science Research Associates, Inc., 1947–1950. Reusable booklets with manual, $12.00 per 20; answer pads, $3.00 per 20; profile sheets, $1.00 per 20; specimen set, $1.00.

Yields scores for three parts—tool usage, space visualization, and shop arithmetic—and a total score. Administration time, 40 minutes. Some rather inadequate norms based on scores of 444 high school graduates attending trade school are available. The test is well printed and interesting, and the items seem well chosen. Kuder-Richardson reliability of .83 reported in manual. Further research is needed. *Reference:* Buros (10:764–765).

CLERICAL APTITUDE

Detroit Clerical Aptitudes Examination, by Harry J. Baker and Paul H. Voelker. Indianapolis: The Bobbs-Merrill Company, Inc., 1937–1944. Test booklets, $3.85 per 35; single copy, 15 cents; specimen set, 50 cents. Ayres Handwriting Scale must be ordered separately at 50 cents a copy.

One form containing eight parts: rate and quality of handwriting, rate and accuracy in checking, knowledge of simple arithmetic, motor speed and accuracy, knowledge of simple commercial terms, visual imagery, rate and accuracy in classification, and alphabetical filing. Working time, 30 minutes. Designed for high school use and standardized on high school population. Reliability of .85 is reported by authors. Validities based on correlations of the test with marks in commercial courses are reported as .56 in bookkeeping, .37 in shorthand, and .32 in typewriting. *Reference:* Buros (9:634).

General Clerical Test, by The Psychological Corporation staff. New York: The Psychological Corporation, 1944–1950. Test booklets, $5.00 per 25; specimen set, 50 cents.

A test for use in selecting and upgrading clerical personnel. Grades 9–16 and applicants for clerical positions. Nine parts arranged to yield scores for clerical speed and accuracy, number facility and verbal facility, and a total score. Working time, 50 minutes. Test-retest reliabilites reported for part scores are .87, .82, and .91. Reliability of total, .94. Validity data based on correlations of test scores with performance ratings and instructors' ratings have been given. Most of these correlations are within the range .4 to .5. *Reference:* Buros (*10:720–723*).

Minnesota Clerical Test, by Dorothy M. Andrew, under the direction of Donald G. Paterson and Howard P. Longstaff. New York: The Psychological Corporation, 1933–1959. Tests booklets, $2.15 per 25; specimen set, 50 cents.

Formerly known as Minnesota Vocational Test for Clerical Workers. One form contains two parts. The first part consists of 200 pairs of numbers; the second part contains 200 pairs of names. Each pair is separated by a line; a check mark is to be made on the line if the two numbers or two names of a pair are exactly the same; no mark is made if they are different. High school level and above. Working time, 15 minutes. Norms by sexes, by age and by grade through high school and for clerical workers in the adult population. Split-half odd-even reliabilities reported in the manual are .86 for number checking, .93 for name checking, and .90 for the two combined. These are probably spuriously high because of the speed factor. Test-retest reliabilities reported in the manual range from .76 to .93 for number checking, from .77 to .86 for name checking, and from .85 to .91 for the entire test. Contingency coefficients between test scores and ratings of various groups of clerical employees fall within the range .28 to .66. *References:* Andrew (*2*) and Buros (*11:871–874*).

SRA Clerical Aptitudes, by Richardson, Bellows, Henry & Co., Inc. Chicago: Science Research Associates, Inc., 1947–1960. Reusable test booklets with manual, $12.00 per 20; answer pads, $3.00 per 20; profile sheets, $1.00 per 20; specimen set, $1.00 each.

Consists of three tests: office vocabulary, office arithmetic, and office checking. Suitable for high school pupils and applicants for clerical jobs. One form. Grades 9–12 and adult. Administration time, 35 minutes. Percentile norms for high school pupils and for applicants for clerical jobs. Reliabilities of total scores estimated by Kuder-Richardson Formula 21 reported in manual range from .85 to .90. Intercorrelations between parts, .30 to .50. Validity data lacking. *Reference:* Buros (*10:724–725*).

MATHEMATICS

Iowa Algebra Aptitude Test, rev. ed., by Harry A. Greene and Alva H. Piper. Iowa City: State University of Iowa, Bureau of Educational Research and Service, 1929–1942. Test booklets, $2.25 per 25; IBM answer sheets, 5 cents each; set of stencils for machine scoring, 25 cents; manual, 35 cents; specimen set, 65 cents.

Composed of four parts: arithmetic, abstract computation, numerical series, and dependence and variation. Yields four subscores and total score. Parts separately timed; total working time, 35 minutes. One form, suitable for hand or machine scoring. Grade range, high school. Percentile norms for end

of eighth grade and beginning of high school. Manual gives Kuder-Richardson reliability of .87 for revised edition, based on unselected end-of-year eighth-grade pupils. Correlation of total scores with algebra grades, .66; with an algebra achievement test, .76. These are rather high as validity coefficients go. *Reference:* Buros (*10:500–502*).

Orleans Algebra Prognosis Test, rev. ed., by Joseph B. Orleans. New York: Harcourt, Brace & World, Inc., 1928–1951. Booklets, $3.60 per 35; specimen set, 40 cents each.

Consists of 11 subtests, of which one is an arithmetic test, one is a summary test, and nine are tests which follow simple lessons which the pupil must study in order to work the problems. Total testing time is 39 minutes, of which 17 minutes are spent on study and 22 minutes on working the problems. Speed apparently an important factor in these brief subtests. One form. As is true of practically all prognostic tests for the study of high school subjects, the norms are not very adequate. Spearman-Brown split-half reliability of .92 as given in the manual may be spuriously high because of speed factor. Manual reports correlations of .59 and .60 between prognostic test score and scores on a standardized achievement test of beginning algebra students. *References:* Orleans (*65*) and Buros (*10:503–504*).

Survey Test of Algebraic Aptitude: California Survey Series, by Robert E. Dinkel. Monterey: California Test Bureau, 1959. Test booklets, $2.80 per 35; manual, 25 cents; scoring key for test booklets, 5 cents; IBM 1230 answer sheets, 5 cents each; IBM 1230 hand scoring stencil, 50 cents each; specimen set, 50 cents.

Designed to be a prognostic survey test for screening and counseling students before their enrollment in their first course in algebra. Taps reasoning powers in mathematics, knowledge of terms, recognition of relationships, flexibility in analyzing, and use of arithmetic fundamentals. Percentile and normalized standard score norms are provided, based upon results of more than 2000 eighth-grade students. Testing time, 40 minutes.

Iowa Plane Geometry Aptitude Test, rev. ed., by Harry A. Greene and Harold W. Bruce. Iowa City: State University of Iowa, Bureau of Educational Research and Service, 1935–1942. $2.25 per 25 tests; machine-scorable answer sheets, 5 cents each; manual, 30 cents; specimen set, 60 cents.

A prognostic test for high school pupils who have studied no geometry. One form. Total working time, 44 minutes. Authors report Kuder-Richardson reliability of .887 for revised edition based on 260 ninth-grade pupils. The authors also report a correlation of .705 with a test of achievement in geometry and one of .592 with first- and second-semester grades. Percentile norms are available, based on 1754 pupils tested in September before the beginning of instruction in plane geometry. *Reference:* Buros (*9:441*).

Lee Test of Geometric Aptitude, 1963 revision, by Dorris May Lee and J. Murray Lee. Monterey: California Test Bureau, 1963. Test booklets, $4.20 per 35; manual, 25 cents; scoring key for test booklets, 5 cents each; IBM 1230 answer sheets, 5 cents each; IBM 1230 hand scoring stencil, 50 cents each; specimen set, 50 cents.

Designed to measure aptitude for geometry of high school pupils who have not studied the subject. Four parts, including a total of 50 items of the recall type. One form requiring 26 minutes of working time. Corrected split-half reliability of .91 reported. Percentile norms are available. There is an illustrated procedure for preparing local expectancy tables that may have some guidance value. *Reference:* Lee and Lee (47).

Orleans Geometry Prognosis Test: Revised Edition, by Joseph B. Orleans. New York: Harcourt, Brace & World, Inc. $4.80 per 35 tests; specimen set, 40 cents.

A test for the prediction of geometry ability of pupils who have not studied the subject. Similar in purposes and general form to Orleans Algebra Prognosis Test. Contains several brief lessons, each followed by a short test. One form requires 39 minutes of working time; overall administration time about 45 minutes. Not much data on reliability and validity available, but would seem to be one of the better tests of its kind. *Reference:* Orleans (65).

FOREIGN LANGUAGES

Foreign Language Prognosis Test, by Percival M. Symonds. New York: Bureau of Publications, Teachers College, Columbia University, 1930–1959. $4.00 per 35 booklets; specimen set, 50 cents.

A test designed to predict success in learning a foreign language. Prediction may be better for classes taught by grammar-translation method than by less formal procedures. Two forms, A and B, for use in Grade 8 or 9. Working time, 44 minutes. Reliability .73–.78, based on correlation between total scores on Forms A and B. Correlations of .60 and .61 are reported between prognosis test scores and achievement test scores: *References:* Symonds (79) and Buros (10:348–349).

Modern Language Aptitude Test, by John B. Carroll and Stanley M. Sapon. New York: The Psychological Corporation, 1958–1959. Tape recording, $7.50; reusable booklets, $3.50 per 25; IBM 805 answer sheets, $3.60 per 50; manual and scoring keys, 60 cents; specimen set (without tape), 75 cents.

Uses samples of learning exercises to test aptitude for learning foreign languages. A tape recording is employed to appraise the student's "ear for language." One form with five parts: (1) Number Learning (aural); (2) Phonetic Script (audio-visual); (3) Spelling Clues; (4) Words and Sentences; (5) Paired Associates. Parts 3, 4, and 5 may be ad-

ministered as a short form when tape playback equipment is not available or when time is limited. Testing time is one hour for the complete test, 30 minutes for the short form. Percentile norms for Grades 9–11, college freshmen, and adults are given in the manual.

Validity coefficients based on correlations with course marks in Latin, Spanish, French, German, and Russian in various schools are reported in the manual. These correlations range from .13 to .78 for the total test and from .21 to .75 for the short form. In general, these correlations tend to be higher than those yielded by academic aptitude tests in the area of prediction of success in foreign languages. Spearman-Brown reliabilities reported in the manual range from .90 to .97 for the total test and from .83 to .96 for the short form. *Reference:* Carroll (13).

STENOGRAPHY

Stenographic Aptitude Test, by George K. Bennett. New York: The Psychological Corporation, 1939–1946. $2.40 per 25 booklets; specimen set, 50 cents.

Planned to measure ability to learn shorthand and typewriting. Consists of a transcription test and a spelling test. One form, calling for 15 minutes of working time; overall time, about 25 minutes. Range, high school and college. Norms for high school and private secretarial school students. Reliability of transcription test based on scores made in odd minutes with those made in even minutes reported in manual as .975, which may be inflated by the influence of speed. Reliability of spelling test obtained by correlating first half with second half given as .913. Point biserial correlation of transcription score with success or failure of students in a private secretarial school reported as about .27; correlation of spelling score with success approximately .48. *Reference:* Barrett (3).

Turse Shorthand Aptitude Test, by Paul L. Turse. New York: Harcourt, Brace & World, Inc., 1940. $3.90 per 35 booklets; specimen set, 40 cents.

Designed to measure the abilities related to success in stenography. Contains seven subtests: stroking, spelling, phonetic association, symbol transcription, word discrimination, dictation, and word sense. Time limits for parts rather brief. Total working time, 40 minutes; overall time, about 55 minutes. Answers are recorded in the booklet, and scoring is done with a strip key.

Percentile norms for total score based on results for 780 pupils about to begin the study of shorthand. Manual reports odd-even reliability coefficients for subtests ranging from .86 to .95, and total score reliability of .98. These reliabilities are exceptionally high for a test of this length; probably spuriously high due to influence of speed factor. Correlations between total aptitude scores obtained before study of shorthand and measures of stenographic achievement after one or two years of shorthand range from .49 to .68. As validity coefficients go, these correlations are substantial. No validation data available for actual success in the employment situation. *References:* Turse (94) and Tuckman (93).

REFERENCES

1. Anderson, Roy N. "Review of Clerical Tests (1929–1942)," *Occupations*, XXI (May 1943), 654–660.

2. Andrew, Dorothy M. *An Analysis of the Minnesota Vocational Test for Clerical Workers.* Unpublished Doctor's thesis, University of Minnesota, 1935.

3. Barrett, Dorothy M. "Prediction of Achievement in Typewriting and Stenography in a Liberal Arts College," *Journal of Applied Psychology*, XXX (December 1946), 624–630.

4. Benton, Arthur L., and Perry, James D. "A Study of the Predictive Value of the Stanford Scientific Aptitude Test (Zyve)," *Journal of Psychology*, X (October 1940), 309–312.

5. Blade, Mary F., and Watson, Walter S. "Increase in Spatial Visualization Test Scores During Engineering Study," *Psychological Monographs: General and Applied*, LXIX, No. 12 (Whole No. 397), 1955.

6. Bloom, Benjamin S. *Stability and Change in Human Characteristics.* New York: John Wiley & Sons, Inc., 1964. Pp. xiv + 237.

7. Buros, Oscar K. (ed.) *The Nineteen Thirty-Eight Mental Measurements Yearbook.* New Brunswick, N.J.: Rutgers University Press, 1938. Pp. xxii + 416

8. Buros, Oscar K. (ed.). *The Nineteen Forty Mental Measurements Yearbook.* Highland Park, N.J.: The Mental Measurements Yearbook, 1941. Pp. xxii + 674.

9. Buros, Oscar K. (ed.). *The Third Mental Measurements Yearbook.* New Brunswick, N.J.: Rutgers University Press, 1949. Pp. xvi + 1048.

10. Buros, Oscar K. (ed.). *The Fourth Mental Measurements Yearbook.* Highland Park, N.J.: The Gryphon Press, 1953. Pp. xvii + 1164.

11. Buros, Oscar K. (ed.) *The Fifth Mental Measurements Yearbook.* Highland Park, N.J.: The Gryphon Press, 1959. Pp. xxviii + 1292.

12. Buros, Oscar K. (ed.) *Tests in Print.* Highland Park, N.J.: The Gryphon Press, 1961. Pp. xxx + 480.

13. Carroll, J. B. "A Factor Analysis of Two Foreign Language Aptitude Batteries," *Journal of Genetic Psychology*, LIX (1958), 3–19.

14. Cattell, R. B. "Classical and Standard Score IQ Standardization of the IPAT Culture-Free Intelligence Scale 2," *Journal of Consulting Psychology*, XV (June 1951), 154–159.

15. Cattell, R. B., Feingold, S. N., and Sarason, S. B., "A Culture-Free Intelligence Test II. Evaluation of Cultural Influence on Test Performance," *Journal of Educational Psychology*, XXXII (January 1941), 81–100.

16. Chauncey, Henry and Dobbin, John E. *Testing: Its Place In Education Today.* New York: Harper & Row, Publishers, 1964. Pp. 240.

17. Clark, Willis W. "The Differentiation of Mental Abilities at Various Grade Levels," *Growing Points in Educational Research*, pp. 39–43. Official Report, American Educational Research Association, 1949. Pp. 340.

18. Coleman, William, and Cureton, Edward E. "Intelligence and Achievement: the 'Jangle Fallacy' Again," *Educational and Psychological Measurement*, XIV (Summer 1954), 347–351.

19. *Cooperative Academic Ability Test Handbook.* Princeton, N.J.: Educational Testing Service, 1964. Pp. 16.

20. Cooprider, H. A., and Laslett, H. R. "Predictive Values of the Stanford Scientific and the Engineering and Physical Science Aptitude Tests," *Educational and Psychological Measurement*, VIII (Winter 1948), 683–687.

21. Crawford, Albert B., and Burnham, Paul S. *Forecasting College Achievement: A Survey of Aptitude Tests for Higher Education. Part I: General Considerations in the Measurement of Academic Promise.* New Haven, Conn.: Yale University Press, 1946. Pp. 291.

22. Cronbach, Lee J. *Essentials of Psychological Testing*, 2nd ed. New York: Harper & Row, Publishers, 1960. Pp. xxii + 650.

23. Cureton, Edward E. "Service Tests of Multiple Aptitudes," *Proceedings of the 1955 Invitational Conference on Testing Problems*, pp. 22–39. Princeton, N.J.: Educational Testing Service, 1956. Pp. 152.

24. *Differential Aptitude Tests Manual (Third Edition).* New York: The Psychological Corporation, 1963. Pp. 36.

25. Division of Professional Services, California Test Bureau, with the assistance of James C. Coleman. *California Test of Mental Maturity: Summary of Investigations No. 3.* Monterey: California Test Bureau, 1956. Pp. 30.

26. Doppelt, Jerome E., and Bennett, George K. "A Longitudinal Study of the Differential Aptitude Tests," *Educational and Psychological Measurement*, XI (Summer 1951), 228–237.

27. Doppelt, Jerome E. "Progress in the Measurement of Mental Abilities," *Educational and Psychological Measurement*, XIV (Summer 1954), 261–264.

28. Eells, Kenneth; Davis, Allison; Havighurst, R. J.; and Tyler, Ralph W. *Intelligence and Cultural Differences: A Study of Cultural Learning and Problem Solving.* Chicago: The University of Chicago Press, 1951. Pp. 388.

29. Finch, F. H. *Kuhlman-Finch Intelligence Tests for Elementary and High School Levels: Manual.* Minneapolis: Educational Test Bureau, 1953.

30. *Flanagan Aptitude Classification Tests: Counselor's Booklet.* Chicago: Science Research Associates, Inc., 1953. Pp. 36.

31. Flanagan, John C. *Tests of General Ability Technical Report.* Chicago: Science Research Associates, Inc., 1960. Pp. 40.

32. Garrett, Henry E. *Statistics in Psychology and Education*, 5th ed. New York: David McKay Co., Inc., 1958. Pp. xii + 478.

33. Garrett, Henry E. *Elementary Statistics*, 2nd ed. New York: David McKay Company, Inc., 1962. Pp. vii + 203.

34. Guertin, Wilson H., Frank, George H., and Rabin,

Albert I. "Research with the Wechsler-Bellevue Intelligence Scale, 1950–1955," *Psychological Bulletin*, LIII (May 1956), 235–257.

35. Harding, F. D. "Tests As Selectors of Language Students," *Modern Language Journal*, XLII (1958), 120–122.

36. Holzinger, Karl J., and Crowder, Norman A. *Holzinger-Crowder Uni-Factor Tests: Manual*. New York: Harcourt, Brace & World, Inc., 1955. Pp. 30.

37. Jacobs, Robert. "The Reliability and Validity of the Scores on the SRA Primary Mental Abilities Test," *1947 Fall Testing Program in Independent Schools and Supplementary Studies*, pp. 49–58. Educational Records Bulletin 49. New York: Educational Records Bureau, February 1948. Pp. xii + 66.

38. Jacobs, Robert, and Traxler, Arthur E. "A Professional Aptitude Test for High School," *Clearing House*, XXVIII (January 1954), 266–268.

39. Johnson, Granville B. "Factors to be Considered in the Interpretation of Intelligence Test Scores," *Elementary School Journal*, LIV (November 1953), 145–150.

40. Jungeblut, Ann. "Stability of Results on the Junior Scholastic Aptitude Test," *1962 Fall Testing Program in Independent Schools and Supplementary Studies*, pp. 61–66. Educational Records Bulletin 83. New York: Educational Records Bureau, February 1963. Pp. xii + 84.

41. Jungeblut, Ann. "Some Further Data on the Lorge-Thorndike Intelligence Tests," *1963 Fall Testing Program in Independent Schools and Supplementary Studies*, pp. 69–71. Educational Records Bulletin 85. New York: Educational Records Bureau, February 1964. Pp. xii + 71.

42. King, Joseph E. "The Perception Factor in Industrial Testing," *American Psychologist, V* (July 1950), 331. (Abstract.)

43. Kirk, Barbara A., Cummings, Roger W., and Goodstein, Leonard D. "The College Qualification Tests and Differential Guidance With University Freshmen," *Personnel and Guidance Journal*, XLII (September 1963), 47–51.

44. Knauber, Alma Jordan. "The Construction and Standardization of the Knauber Art Tests," *Education*, LVI (November 1935), 165–170.

45. Kuhlmann, F., and Anderson, Rose G. *Kuhlmann-Anderson Test: Technical Manuals*, 7th ed. Princeton, N.J.: The Personnel Press 1960–1963. Booklets K–CD, pp. 30; booklets D–EF, pp. 24; booklets G and H, pp. 34.

46. Kwalwasser, Jacob. *Tests and Measurements in Music*, pp. 65–73, 107–135. Boston: C. C. Birchard and Company, 1927. Pp. xiv + 146.

47. Lee, J. Murray, and Lee, Dorris May, "The Construction of a Test of Geometric Aptitude," *Mathematics Teacher*, XXV (April 1932), 193–203.

48. Lewerenz, Alfred S. "Predicting Ability in Art," *Journal of Educational Psychology*, XX (December 1929), 702–704.

49. Lorge, Irving, and Thorndike, Robert L. *Lorge-Thorndike Intelligence Tests: General Manual*. Boston: Houghton Mifflin Company, 1954. Pp. 10.

50. McNemar, Quinn. *The Revision of the Stanford-Binet Scale*. Boston: Houghton Mifflin Company, 1942. Pp. 185.

51. McNemar, Quinn, "Lost: Our Intelligence? Why?" *American Psychologist*, 19 (December 1964), 871–882.

52. Marshall, Mortimer V. "A Study of the Stanford Scientific Aptitude Test," *Occupations*, XX (March 1942), 433–434.

53. Meier, Norman C. *Aesthetic Judgment as a Measure of Art Talent*. University of Iowa Studies, Vol. I, No. 19. Series on Aims and Progress of Research. Iowa City, Iowa: State University of Iowa, August 1936. Pp. 30.

54. Merwin, Jack C. "The Kuhlmann-Anderson Measure of Academic Potential (Seventh Edition)," *Journal of Counseling Psychology*, 12 (January 1965), 103–104.

55. Miller, W. S. *Manual for the Miller Analogies Test, Form G*. New York: The Psychological Corporation, 1947. Pp. 6.

56. Murphy, Harold D., and McQuary, John P. "A Look At the Flanagan Aptitude Classification Tests," *Personnel and Guidance Journal*, XLIII, No. 6 (February 1965), 607–611.

57. North, Robert D. "A Comparison of the Cooperative School and College Ability Tests: College Ability Test, and the American Council Psychological Examination: Reliabilities, Intercorrelations, and Correlations with the Diagnostic Reading Tests," *1955 Fall Testing Program in Independent Schools and Supplementary Studies*, pp. 65–72. Educational Records Bulletin 67. New York: Educational Records Bureau, February 1956. Pp. xii + 84.

58. North, Robert D. "Tests for the Accounting Profession," *Educational and Psychological Measurement*, XVIII (Winter 1958), 691–713.

59. North, Robert D. "An Appraisal of the SRA Tests of General Ability Based on Independent School Results," *1960 Fall Testing Program in Independent Schools and Supplementary Studies*, pp. 68–76. Educational Records Bulletin 78. New York: Educational Records Bureau, February 1961. Pp. xii + 76.

60. North, Robert D. "Results of the Seventh Edition Kuhlmann-Anderson Test for Independent School Pupils in Grades 7–12." *1961 Fall Testing Program in Independent Schools and Supplementary Studies*, pp. 56–65. Educational Records Bulletin 80. New York: Educational Records Bureau, February 1962. Pp. xii + 69.

61. North, Robert D. "A Further Analysis of the Kuhlmann-Anderson Seventh Edition Test," *1962 Fall Testing Program in Independent Schools and Supplementary Studies*, pp. 53–60. Educational Records Bulletin 83. New York: Educational Records Bureau, February 1963. Pp. xii + 84.

62. North, Robert D. "An Appraisal of the Kuhlmann-Anderson Seventh Edition Test for Grades K–3 in

Independent Schools," *1963 Fall Testing Program in Independent Schools and Supplementary Studies*, pp. 48–54. Educational Records Bulletin 85. New York: Educational Records Bureau, February 1964. Pp. xii + 71.

63. North, Robert D. "Kuhlmann-Anderson Seventh Edition IQs of Pupils in Independent Elementary Schools," *1964 Fall Testing Program in Independent Schools and Supplementary Studies*, pp. 50–56. Educational Records Bulletin 87. New York: Educational Records Bureau, February 1965. Pp. xii + 59.

64. North, Robert D. "Predicting Success in the Study of Elementary Accounting From Scores on the Accounting Orientation Test—High School Level," *College Accounting Testing Program Bulletin*, 49. New York: American Institute of Certified Public Accountants, October 1965. Pp. 32.

65. Orleans, Joseph B. "A Study of Prognosis of Probable Success in Algebra and in Geometry," *Mathematics Teacher*, XXVII (April–May 1934), 165–180, 225–246.

66. Prothro, E. Terry, and Perry, Harold T. "Group Differences in Performance on the Meier Art Test," *Journal of Applied Psychology*, XXXIV (April 1950), 96–97.

67. Quasha, W. H., and Likert, R. "The Revised Minnesota Paper Form Board Test," *Journal of Educational Psychology*, XXVIII (March 1937), 197–204.

68. Remmers, H. H., Gage, N. L., and Rummel, J. F. *A Practical Introduction to Measurement and Evaluation*. New York: Harper & Row, Publishers, 1960. Pp. xiii + 370.

69. Ryans, David G. "The Professional Examination of Teaching Candidates: A Report of the First Annual Administration of the National Teacher Examinations," *School and Society*, LII (October 5, 1940), 273–284.

70. Saetveit, Joseph G., Lewis, Don, and Seashore, Carl E. *Revision of the Seashore Measures of Musical Talent*, University of Iowa Studies, Series on Aims and Progress of Research, No. 65. Iowa City, Iowa: State University of Iowa, 1941. Pp. 62.

71. Seashore, Harold G. "Tenth Grade Tests as Predictors of Twelfth Grade Scholarship and College Entrance Status," *Journal of Counseling Psychology*, I (Summer 1954), 106–115.

72. Seashore, Harold G., Wesman, Alexander G., and Doppelt, Jerome. "The Standardization of the Wechsler Intelligence Scale for Children," *Journal of Consulting Psychology*, XIV (April 1950), 99–110.

73. Semeonoff, Boris. "A New Approach to the Testing of Musical Ability," *British Journal of Psychology*, XXX (April 1940), 326–340.

74. Spaulding, Geraldine. "Reliability and Other Data on the Revised Edition of the Junior Scholastic Aptitude Test, Forms A, B, and C," *1958 Achievement Testing Program in Independent Schools and Supplementary Studies*, pp. 75–79. Educational Records Bulletin 72. New York: Educational Records Bureau, July 1958. Pp. xii + 80.

75. Spaulding, Geraldine. "Some Observations on the Results of the Revised Junior Scholastic Aptitude Test," *1959 Fall Testing Program in Independent Schools and Supplementary Studies*, pp. 53–56. Educational Records Bulletin 76. New York: Educational Records Bureau, February 1960. Pp. xii + 68.

76. Spaulding, Geraldine. "Relations Between the NAIS Junior Scholastic Aptitude Test and the CEEB Scholastic Aptitude Tests," *1963 Achievement Testing Program in Independent Schools and Supplementary Studies*, pp. 55–62. Educational Records Bulletin 84. New York: Educational Records Bureau, July 1963. Pp. xii + 84.

77. Stenquist, John L. "The Case for the Low IQ," *Journal of Educational Research*, IV (November 1921), 241–254.

78. Super, Donald E. (commentator). *The Use of Multifactor Tests in Guidance*. (A reprint series from the *Personnel and Guidance Journal*.) Washington, D.C.: American Personnel and Guidance Association, 1958. Pp. ii + 91.

79. Symonds, Percival M. "A Foreign Language Prognosis Test," *Teachers College Record*, XXXI (March 1930), 540–556.

80. Terman, Lewis M., and Merrill, Maud A. *Stanford-Binet Intelligence Scale, Manual for the Third Revision, Form L-M*. Boston: Houghton Mifflin Company, 1960. Pp. xii + 364.

81. Thurstone, L. L. *Primary Mental Abilities*. Psychometric Monographs No. 1, Psychometric Society. Chicago: The University of Chicago Press, 1938. Pp. x + 122.

82. Toops, Herbert A. *The Ohio State Psychological Test: Manual of Directions*. Chicago: Science Research Associates, Inc., 1958.

83. Townsend, Agatha. "The Differential Aptitude Tests—Some Data on the Reliability and Intercorrelation of the Parts," *1949 Fall Testing Program in Independent Schools and Supplementary Studies*, pp. 39–47. Educational Records Bulletin 53. New York: Educational Records Bureau, January 1950. Pp. vi + 70.

84. Townsend, Agatha, and Spaulding, Geraldine. "The SRA Primary Mental Abilities in the Independent School Testing Program," *1951 Fall Testing Program in Independent Schools and Supplementary Studies*, pp. 58–70. Educational Records Bulletin 58. New York: Educational Records Bureau, February 1952. Pp. xii + 86.

85. Traxler, Arthur E. "Correlations between 'Mechanical Aptitude' and 'Mechanical Comprehension' Scores," *Occupations*, XXII (October 1943), 42–43.

86. Traxler, Arthur E., and Jacobs, Robert. "Validity of Professional Aptitude Batteries: Tests for Accounting," *Proceedings of the 1950 Invitational Conference on Testing Problems*, pp. 13–29. Princeton, N.J.: Educational Testing Service, 1951. Pp. x + 118.

87. Traxler, Arthur E. "Twelve Years of Experience with the Junior Scholastic Aptitude Test," *1952 Achievement Testing Program in Independent Schools and*

Supplementary Studies, pp. 79–92. Educational Records Bulletin 59. New York: Educational Records Bureau, July 1952. Pp. xiv + 106.

88. Traxler, Arthur E. "The Status of Measurement and Appraisal Programs in Large City School Systems—A Questionnaire Survey," *1953 Achievement Testing Program in Independent Schools and Supplementary Studies*, pp. 75–86. Educational Records Bulletin 61. New York: Educational Records Bureau, July 1953. Pp. xii + 86.

89. Traxler, Arthur E. "Comparative Value of Certain Mental Ability Tests for Predicting School Marks in Two Independent Schools," *1954 Fall Testing Program in Independent Schools and Supplementary Studies*, pp. 65–75. Educational Records Bulletin 65. New York: Educational Records Bureau, February 1955. Pp. xii + 84.

90. Traxler, Arthur E. "Should SCAT Scat ACE? A Comparison between the Cooperative School and College Ability Tests, Form 1A, and the American Council on Education Psychological Examination, 1948 College Freshman Edition, as to Difficulty and Value for Predicting School Marks," *1955 Fall Testing Program in Independent Schools and Supplementary Studies*, pp. 51–63. Educational Records Bulletin 67. New York: Educational Records Bureau, February 1956. Pp. xii + 84.

91. Traxler, Arthur E. "Some Independent School Results on the Cooperative School and College Ability Tests, Levels 2–5," *1959 Fall Testing Program in Independent Schools and Supplementary Studies*, pp. 57–64. Educational Records Bulletin 76. New York: Educational Records Bureau, February 1960. Pp. xii + 68.

92. Traxler, Arthur E. "The New Cooperative Academic Aptitude Test Compared With the American Council Psychological Examination," *1963 Fall Testing Program in Independent Schools and Supplementary Studies*, pp. 55–64. Educational Records Bulletin 85. New York: Educational Records Bureau, February 1964. Pp. xii + 72.

93. Tuckman, Jacob. "Study of the Turse Shorthand Aptitude Test," *Journal of Business Education*, XIX (November 1943), 17–18.

94. Turse, Paul L. "Problems in Shorthand Prognosis," *Journal of Business Education*, XIII (May 1938), 17–18.

95. Vaughn, K. W. "The Measurement and Guidance Project in Engineering Education," *Journal of Engineering Education*, XXXIV (March 1944), 516–520.

96. Vaughn, K. W. "The Pre-Engineering Inventory," *Journal of Engineering Education*, XXXIV (April 1944), 615–625.

97. Wechsler, David. *Manual for the Wechsler Intelligence Scale for Children.* New York: The Psychological Corporation, 1949. Pp. vi + 114.

98. Wechsler, David. *Manual for the Wechsler Adult Intelligence Scale.* New York: The Psychological Corporation, 1955. Pp. vi + 110.

99. Wechsler, David. *The Measurement and Appraisal of Adult Intelligence*, 4th ed. Baltimore: The Williams & Wilkins Company, 1958. Pp. x + 298.

100. Wing, Herbert D. "Tests of Musical Ability and Appreciation: An Investigation into the Measurement, Distribution, and Development of Musical Capacity," *British Journal of Psychology Monograph Supplements*, VIII. London: Cambridge University Press, 1948. Pp. viii + 88.

101. Wysong, H. Eugene. "The Use of the General Aptitude Test Battery in Grades Nine and Ten," *Personnel and Guidance Journal*, XLIII, No. 5 (January 1965), 509–512.

102. Zyve, D. L. "A Test of Scientific Aptitude," *Journal of Educational Psychology*, XVIII (November 1927), 525–546.

CHAPTER VI

Evaluation of Achievement in a Guidance Program

ACHIEVEMENT IS PROBABLY, WITH THE EXCEPTION of general scholastic aptitude, the most important area of appraisal for a guidance program. Scores on achievement tests are excellent bases for evaluating academic accomplishments and for predicting the educational progress of individuals in the subjects covered by the tests. They also provide very helpful clues for vocational guidance, since they are usually correlated with aptitudes and interests. Thus, tests of achievement should form the core of the systematic testing program of every school that hopes to do a thorough and objective job of guidance.

Although the appraisal of achievement has always been one aspect of the process of educating and advising young people, it is well known that this type of evaluation was almost entirely subjective until about 60 years ago. The first objective measures of achievement were applied to facts and skills. Various other kinds of achievement were gradually attacked objectively. At present, we still depend to some extent upon subjective methods, particularly in the appraisal of processes such as ability to do creative writing, but objective procedures are being applied successfully to several areas for which they were formerly thought to be unsuited. For instance, by means of a series of questions all centered around a problem stated in paragraph form, it is possible to evaluate a pupil's ability to draw logical inferences from a set of data or to generalize from specific facts.

STEPS IN CONSTRUCTION OF AN ACHIEVEMENT TEST

The breadth of measurement provided by modern objective tests and their potential worth as counseling instruments may perhaps best be shown by indicating the steps taken in the construction of one of these instruments.

The usual standardized achievement test consists mainly of multiple-choice items. At first glance, it looks like the sort of thing that almost any teacher could make up without special training, since there is little surface evidence of the careful work that goes into the construction of a good standardized achievement test. The construction process actually involves at least 13 steps as follows:

1. A survey of the aims or objectives in the subject or subject field for which the test is to be made, through the use of textbooks, courses of study, and questionnaires to schools.
2. Selection of those purposes which are widely accepted and which can be measured objectively.
3. A decision concerning the weight to be assigned to the different objectives; that is, the proportion of the test to be devoted to each objective.
4. Preparation of test items bearing upon the various objectives.
5. The setting up of a trial form of the test, including at least 50 percent more items than will be used in the final form.
6. Submission of the trial form to specialists for criticism.
7. Administration of the experimental form to several groups of pupils who are at the level or levels for which the test is being planned.
8. A statistical analysis of the items in terms of difficulty and validity as measured by a suitable criterion.
9. Selection of the best items for the final form of the test on the basis of the item analysis and the comments of critics who are preferably specialists in the field for which the test is prepared.
10. The scaling of the test, on the basis of the performance of a defined criterion group, so that it may be compared

with other forms of the test and with tests in other fields.

11. The finding of norms for various ages, grades, or years of study.

12. The formulating of precise directions for administering and scoring, so that it will be possible for all persons giving the test and scoring it to obtain comparable results.

13. The collection and reporting of thorough statistical information on the reliability and validity of the test, and the interpretation of these data in terms that persons who are not statisticians can understand.

Thus the construction of a valid achievement test is a painstaking and detailed process calling for the cooperation of many persons. When all these steps are carefully followed by test makers, and when the reliability and validity data are favorable, counselors may regard the resulting test with considerable confidence.

ACHIEVEMENT TEST BATTERIES AND SERIES

Most of the achievement tests used in elementary and secondary schools are published as either batteries or series that afford coordinated measurement in the major skill and subject areas. The general achievement batteries for elementary and secondary schools may be classified into these three types: (1) single-level, designed to serve a range of grades, with different starting and stopping points for each grade; (2) multi-level, with consecutive batteries for specified grade spans; and (3) multi-level, with consecutive batteries for each single grade level.

The Iowa Tests of Basic Skills, designed for Grades 3–9, illustrate the first type. The second type is represented by the California Achievement Tests, the Metropolitan Achievement Tests, the SRA Achievement Tests, and the Stanford Achievement Test. The Coordinated Scales of Attainment form the third type.

The Iowa Tests of Basic Skills are published in a single spiral-bound booklet with a designated grade range of 3 to 9. There are four alternate forms—1, 2, 3, and 4. The five major areas covered are, vocabulary, reading comprehension, language skills, work-study skills, and arithmetic skills.

In general, the one-battery type tends not to be well suited to the lowest and highest grades that it is designed to serve. On the other hand, there is evidence that the equating between the batteries of some of the existing tests of the overlapping or separate battery type is not very precise, and that caution needs to be exercised in drawing conclusions concerning growth of individual pupils on the bases of results from successive batteries.

The California, Metropolitan, and Stanford achievement series not only cover the elementary schools grades, but also include a battery for the secondary grades. The California tests provide for more detailed diagnosis than do most of the other achievement tests, but they do not include so broad a range of subjects as is found in the Stanford and Metropolitan Achievement Tests. The tests in the California batteries are confined to reading, arithmetic, and language usage, while those in the Metropolitan and Stanford batteries cover practically all elementary-school subjects. The SRA Achievement Tests, with a grade coverage of 2–9, comprise tests in reading, language, and arithmetic for the full grade span and an additional test in work study skills for the 4–9 range. Areas covered by the Coordinated Scales of Attainment at the various grade levels include reading, language, arithmetic, history, geography, science, and literature.

Two well-known achievement test batteries are designed expressly for the secondary school grades. One of these batteries is the Iowa Tests of Educational Development. There are two editions of this battery, each containing nine tests. One of these editions is issued in a single booklet of 56 pages and is distributed for central scoring only; the other is published in nine separate booklets and is available for local scoring. The ITED measures educational development of a broad nature, including reasoning, reading comprehension, and the application of knowledge rather than factual knowledge per se.

Another widely used secondary school achievement test battery is the Essential High School Content Battery, devised by David P. Harry and Walter N. Durost. This battery has two forms, each consisting of four tests: mathematics, science, social studies, and languages and literature.

Houghton Mifflin Company recently published a new secondary school achievement test battery entitled Tests of Academic Progress. The six component tests are in the areas of social studies, composition, science, reading, mathematics, and literature. Each of the two forms is published as a single spiral-bound booklet with four different overlapping tests, one for each grade, in each of the six areas.

In addition to these batteries, several series of coordinated tests are available for achievement measurement. These series consist of separate tests for the various subject fields. Typically, each of these subject tests is published in a separate booklet. It is important for a school to choose tests within a single series, if possible, so that the results may be interpreted in terms of a common normative scale. In other words, provision should be made for comparing students' achievement and progress in different fields of study. It is also advisable to use academic aptitude tests or intelligence tests that have a normative linkage with the achievement tests. Guidance can then be planned in accordance with the indicated strengths and weaknesses.

During the 1930s one set of tests virtually took command of objective achievement testing in secondary schools and colleges. That was the extensive series of Cooperative tests produced by the Cooperative Test Service of the American Council on Education under a grant from the General Education Board. Under the direction of Ben D. Wood and with the assistance of many subject matter and testing specialists, the Cooperative Test Service issued new forms of tests annually from 1932 to 1941 in nearly all academic subjects. World War II necessitated curtailment in the construction of tests for school use. The Cooperative tests are now published by the Cooperative Test Division of Educational Testing Service.[1] A major revision of the series was begun in 1960, and most of the tests have been revamped since that date.

The earlier forms of nearly all the Cooperative tests were 90 minutes long. After five 90-minute forms had been made for most subjects, the Cooperative Test Service changed in 1937 to the production of a series of 40-minute tests that could be administered within the ordinary class period. Several forms of 40-minute tests were made available for nearly all the secondary school subjects. As a result of careful selection of the items, the total scores of these shorter tests proved to be almost as reliable as those of the earlier 90-minute tests.

An important innovation of the Cooperative tests was the development of a procedure for translating the raw scores into uniform Scaled Scores. This Scaled Score system, which was devised by John C. Flanagan, incorporated the concept of the norm in each individual score and made possible the comparison of scores in different fields, as well as direct comparability among scores of different forms of the same test. The Scaled Score concept was explained in a bulletin published by the Cooperative Test Service (16) and in a bulletin of the Educational Records Bureau (15).

In the editions of the Cooperative tests published since 1960, the Scaled Scores have been replaced by another type of converted score. These three-digit scores do not have the normative meaning that was associated with the Scaled Scores, but they serve to make the scores of different forms of a given test directly comparable. The majority of the tests in the current editions can be administered in one class period, but some require two periods,

[1] The Educational Testing Service was founded in 1948 through a merger of the testing activities of the American Council on Education, the College Entrance Examination Board, and the Carnegie Foundation for the Advancement of Teaching.

and the complete language tests (MLA-Cooperative) take three periods. The latter tests were produced with the assistance of the Modern Language Association.

The Cooperative Test Division of ETS also publishes a series of achievement tests for the 4–14 grade range in which application of skills and knowledge is tested, rather than specific course mastery. This series, called the Sequential Tests of Educational Progress, includes 70-minute tests in reading, writing, listening, mathematics, science, and social studies, and a 35-minute essay test. There are four levels of these separate-booklet tests. The series is coordinated with the Cooperative School and College Ability Tests (SCAT).

The Evaluation and Adjustment Series, published by Harcourt, Brace & World, Inc., is another set of separate tests of subject matter taught in high school and college. In general, the difficulty levels of these tests are lower than those of similar tests in the Cooperative series. The series covers various areas of English language knowledge and skills, mathematics, science, and social studies. Most of the tests can be administered in a single class period. A uniform standard score conversion system is used to facilitate comparison of the scores of different forms and in the various subject areas. In the manual for many of these tests, expectancy charts indicate the scores to be expected from students at each Otis IQ level.

READING TESTS

Achievement in the various subject areas is usually measured by the tests included in the batteries and series discussed in the preceding section. Separate tests are often used, however, for measurement and diagnosis in the important basic-skills area of reading. Some of the widely used reading tests have several levels to cover a wide range, while others have just a single level for a restricted range of grades.

The eminent specialist in the field of reading, Dr. Arthur I. Gates, is the author of a variety of reading tests published by the Bureau of Publications of Teachers College, Columbia University. The Gates Reading Survey Test is available in a hand-scorable booklet for Grades 3 through 10, and in a machine-scorable edition for Grades 4 through 10. It yields scores in vocabulary, comprehension, and speed and accuracy of reading. The test is probably more suitable for children in the lower part of the designated grade range than for those in the upper grades. Broader and more intensive coverage of reading skills in the 3–8 grade range is provided by the Gates Basic Reading Tests. For measurement of word recognition, sentence reading, and paragraph reading skills of children in the first grade or the first half of the second grade, the Gates Primary Reading Tests are available. The Gates Advanced Primary Reading Tests, designed for use in the second half of Grade 2 and in Grade 3, consist of tests in word recognition and paragraph reading.

A series of reading tests that was developed for both evaluative and diagnostic purposes is published by the Committee on Diagnostic Reading Tests, Inc., a nonprofit educational service corporation. The Survey Section of these Diagnostic Reading Tests is published in three levels: kindergarten through the fourth grade, Lower Level for Grades 4–8, and Upper Level for Grade 7 through the college freshman year. The Diagnostic Battery of this series consists of separate tests (sections) in vocabulary, comprehension (auditory and silent), rates of reading (general, social studies, and science), and word attack (oral and silent) for the Grade 7–college freshman range. Word attack tests are also available for the kindergarten–Grade 4 range and for the Grades 4–8 range.

Among the other well-known reading measures are the Iowa Silent Reading Tests, the Traxler Silent Reading Tests, the Nelson-Denny Reading Test, and the Gilmore Oral Reading Test. Achievement batteries and series that offer reading tests as separate booklets include the California, Iowa Tests of Basic Skills, Metropolitan, Stanford, Cooperatives, and Evaluation and Adjustment Series.

READINESS TESTS

A few tests have been designed specifically for measuring the readiness for school learning of children in the age range of 5 to 8 years. The Metropolitan Readiness Test includes both reading readiness and arithmetic readiness. Kindergarten and first-grade percentile norms are given for the part and total scores. The Harrison-Stroud Reading Readiness Profiles contain subtests covering these six abilities: using symbols, making visual discriminations, using the context, making auditory discriminations, using context and auditory clues, and giving the names of the letters. The authors recommend the use of this test for detecting areas where a child needs further training before the initial period of reading instruction, for grouping children, and for determining when a child is ready to profit from reading instruction. Public school norms are provided for the part scores, but not for an average or a total score. The norms are based on the scores of first-grade pupils, tested at the end of the reading readiness training programs. The Lee-Clark Reading Readiness Test has parts that test

visual discrimination, vocabulary and concept formation, and letter and word identification. Norms are available for the part and total scores at both the kindergarten and beginning first-grade levels.

In the New York Test of Arithmetical Meanings, pictorial items are used to measure a child's mastery of numerical and premeasurement concepts. Level One of the test is appropriate for pupils who are near the end of the first grade, and Level Two is suitable for use near the end of the second grade. Percentile norms are available for both levels.

The annotated list of achievement tests in this chapter is necessarily selected from a much larger possible list. A considerable proportion of the tests listed and briefly discussed are used, or have been used at times, in the fall and spring testing programs of the member schools of the Educational Records Bureau. Thus, the comments on many of the tests are based on actual experience and observation of the functioning of the tests in action. The list of secondary school tests is rather heavily weighted with the Cooperative tests, although a number of other tests are included, especially in fields such as reading.

No school should be satisfied to depend entirely upon the tests in this annotated list or any other list of standardized tests. Each school needs to supplement objective tests with essay tests, laboratory tests, and other types of tests of its own construction, specifically in line with its objectives. All schools, too, should be alert to the possibilities for the measurement of some of the less tangible objectives of secondary education through the use of tests similar to those which were developed during the 1930s and early 1940s in the Eight-Year Study of the Progressive Education Association (31), or by means of essay examinations and short-answer tests, such as those exemplified in some of the work of John M. Stalnaker (33, 34), the earlier work of the College Entrance Examination Board, and the examinations of the National Association of Independent Schools. The NAIS tests are especially useful as diagnostic and placement examinations in connection with secondary school admissions. Needless to say, teacher-made essay examinations and semi-objective tests are an indispensable supplement to standardized achievement tests.

The achievement tests prepared under the auspices of the United States Armed Forces Institute have played an important part in the educational evaluation and guidance of men returning to college from the armed services. There are high school and college levels of these tests.[2]

[2] Inquiries concerning the USAFI Tests of General Educational Development, High School and College Levels, Form B, should be addressed to Veterans Testing Service, American Council on Education, Washington, D.C.

As explained in the annotation later in this chapter, several forms of the General Educational Development Tests are available for use by the Armed Forces.

ANNOTATED LIST OF ACHIEVEMENT TEST BATTERIES

American College Testing Program tests, prepared by E. F. Lindquist and Ted McCarrel for the American College Testing (ACT) Program under the auspices of Measurement Research Center, Inc., Iowa City, Iowa. The tests are restricted for use in this controlled national program.

The ACT battery consists of tests in English, mathematics, social studies, and science, with an average working time of 45 minutes for each. Half-day testing sessions are scheduled about four times a year at national testing centers. The tests are similar to those in the Iowa Tests of Educational Development series, tapping reasoning and understanding more than specific subject knowledge. The program services include validation and prediction studies for each participating college, based on data for enrolled students (*1*). *References:* Brown and Wolins (6) and Foster and Danskin (*17*).

American School Achievement Tests, by Willis E. Pratt, Robert V. Young, Miriam E. Wilt, Clara E. Cockerille, and Carroll A. Whitmer. Indianapolis: The Bobbs-Merrill Company, Inc., 1941–1958. Restandardized 1960. Prices per 35 booklets: Primary Battery I, $4.00; Primary Battery II, $5.75; Intermediate Battery, $8.50; Advanced Battery, $8.50. Specimen set: 50 cents for Primary I or Primary II Battery; 75 cents for Intermediate or Advanced Battery.

A series of four levels designed to measure progress in terms of grade and age norms. Two forms, D and E, of Primary Battery I, and four forms, D, E, F, and G, of the other three batteries. Primary Battery I, for Grade 1, is planned to measure word recognition, word meaning, and numbers. Total time, about 35 minutes. Primary II, for Grades 2 and 3, tests sentence and word meaning, paragraph meaning, arithmetic computation, arithmetic problems, language, and spelling. Working time, 65 minutes. Intermediate Battery, for Grades 4–6, measures sentence and word meaning, paragraph meaning, arithmetic computation, arithmetic problems, language, and spelling. Working time, 107 minutes. Advanced Battery contains same tests as Intermediate Battery, but more difficult materials. Working time, 127 minutes.

Range of Spearman-Brown reliabilities of subtests in achievement batteries, as reported by the publisher, is as follows: Primary Battery I, .76 to .96; Primary Battery II, .77 to .96; Intermediate Battery (parallel-forms method),

.86 to .94; Advanced Battery (parallel-forms method), .73 to .86. Since these reliabilities are for subtests, and since they are based on intercorrelations of different forms (Intermediate and Advanced Batteries), the reliabilities may be regarded as fairly high. The items for the tests seem to have been well chosen, but the norms do not appear to be as adequate or as representative as those for some of the other test batteries. *Reference:* Buros (8:1–6).

California Achievement Tests, by Ernest W. Tiegs and Willis W. Clark. Monterey: California Test Bureau, 1933–1957. Norms revised 1963. Prices per 35 booklets: Lower Primary battery, Grades 1–2, $5.60; Upper Primary battery, Grades 2.5–4, $5.95; Elementary battery, Grades 4–6, $6.65. IBM 1230 answer sheets, 15 cents per set for Elementary, Junior High, or Advanced batteries; hand-scoring stencils, $1.50 per set. Specimen set: Lower Primary or Upper Primary, 75 cents; Elementary, Junior High, or Advanced, $1.00.

The Lower Primary and Upper Primary batteries are available in Forms W and X; the Elementary and Junior High batteries in Forms W, X, Y, and Z; the Advanced battery in Forms W, X, and Y. There are six main subtests in each battery: reading vocabulary, reading comprehension, arithmetic (mathematics) reasoning, arithmetic (mathematics) fundamentals, mechanics of English and grammar, and spelling. The first and second tests are combined to provide a total reading score; the third and fourth tests form a total arithmetic score (mathematics score for the Advanced battery); and the fifth and sixth tests furnish a total language score. There is also a total score on the battery. At each level there are from two to five subtests in all tests except the sixth, spelling. Grade placement norms and grade and age percentile norms are provided. Time limits are approximately as follows: Lower Primary battery, 110 minutes; Upper Primary battery, 145 minutes; Elementary battery, 165 minutes; Junior High battery, 190 minutes; Advanced battery, 180 minutes. Reliabilities at single grade level as reported by publisher: Lower Primary battery, total score, .97; range for 6 tests and 3 subtotals, .78 to .93; Upper Primary battery, total score, .96 to .97; range for 6 subtests and 3 subtotals, .57 to .95; Elementary battery, total score, .97 to .98; range for 6 subtests and 3 subtotals, .72 to .95; Junior High battery, total score, .98; range for 6 tests and 3 subtotals, .75 to .95; Advanced battery, total score, .98; range for 6 tests and 3 subtotals, .74 to .96. The reading, arithmetic, and language tests are available in separate booklets, as well as in a single booklet covering the entire battery. The California Achievement Tests are a revision of the Progressive Achievement Tests. *Reference:* Buros (8:6–8).

Cooperative General Achievement Tests: Test I, A Test of General Proficiency in the Field of Social Studies, by Jeanne M. Bradford and Elaine Forsyth Cook; Test II, A Test of General Proficiency in the Field of Natural Sciences, by Paul J. Burke, Carl A. Pearson, and John G.

Zimmerman; Test III, A Test of General Proficiency in the Field of Mathematics, by Paul J. Burke and Bernice Orshansky. Princeton, N.J.: Cooperative Test Division, Educational Testing Service, 1937–1956. Booklets, $4.00 per 25; IBM 805 answer sheets, $1.00 per 25; IBM 1230 answer sheets, $25.00 per 500; scoring stencils, 10 cents each; specimen set, $1.00. Same prices apply to each of the three tests.

A continuation of the general achievement tests formerly published by the Cooperative Test Service. Three separate booklets, each requiring 40 minutes of working time. Present forms are XX and YZ. Each test contains two parts. The first measures knowledge of terms and concepts needed for an understanding of the field for which the test is designed; the second tests the student's ability to read, comprehend, and interpret typical materials in the field. These tests do not measure knowledge of facts and topical content in the three fields. Grades 9–12 and college freshmen. Scaled Scores and percentile norms for high school pupils and entering college freshmen on total scores only are available. No data on validity are available. Publisher reports standard errors of measurement at a Scaled Score of 60 as follows: social studies, three Scaled Score units; science, about 1.7 Scaled Score units; mathematics, about 1.6 Scaled Score units.

Coordinated Scales of Attainment, by M. E. Branom, L. J. Brueckner, August Dvorak, James A. Fitzgerald, Ellen Grogner, U. W. Leavell, Victor L. Lohmann, Ethel V. Nelson, Dora V. Smith, Victor C. Smith, and Edgar B. Wesley. Minneapolis: American Guidance Service, 1946–1954. Eight batteries covering Grades 1–8. $2.65 per 25 booklets for Grades 1, 2, and 3; $3.60 per 25 booklets for Grades 4–8; $2.00 per 25 IBM answer sheets for Grades 4–8; 75 cents for 25 Normal Progress Charts, Grades 4–8; $1.00 per set of scoring keys, Grades 4–8; Master Manual for Grades 1–3 or Grades 4–8, $1.50 each; Guide to Remedial Work, 25 cents; specimen set, $2.00.

Battery I, Grade 1, eight scores: picture-word association, word-picture association, vocabulary recognition, reading comprehension, arithmetic experience, number skills, problem reasoning, and computation. Forms A and B. Estimated working time, 90 minutes. Battery II, Grade 2, nine scores: spelling, in addition to those yielded by Battery I. Forms A and B. Estimated working time, 110 minutes. Battery III, Grade 3, seven scores: picture-word association, word-picture association, vocabulary recognition, reading comprehension, problem reasoning, arithmetic computation, and spelling. Forms A and B. Estimated working time, 100 minutes. Batteries IV–VIII, 11 scores: punctuation, usage, capitalization, reading, history, geography, science, literature, computation, problem reasoning, and spelling. Forms A and B. Estimated working time, 256 minutes.

It is recommended that these tests be administered in several sittings. They are reputed to be power tests, since

directions for administration indicate that pupils should work on each part of each battery until approximately 90 percent are through. Results may be interpreted in terms of grade equivalent, age equivalent, and percentile rank. Standardization based on schools in 40 states, presumably distributed according to population. Validity claimed on basis of analysis of state and city courses of study. Reliability coefficients not reported, but following statement appears in supervisor's manual: "The probable error of measurement of each of the attained scores profiled on the Coordinated Scales of Attainment is less than two score units."

Essential High School Content Battery, by David P. Harry and Walter N. Durost. New York: Harcourt, Brace & World, Inc., 1950–1952. $9.90 per 35 tests; $2.45 per 35 answer sheets; specimen set, 60 cents; cumulative individual profile chart, 70 cents per 35.

A revision of the Sones-Harry Achievement Test Battery. Consists of four tests printed in one booklet: mathematics, science, social studies, and language and literature. Based on analysis of textbooks and courses of study and opinions of specialists in the different fields. Forms Am and Bm. Designed for Grades 10–12 and college freshmen. Working time, four periods of 40 minutes each and one period of 45 minutes, or total of 205 minutes. Scoring by either hand or machine. End-of-year percentile norms for subtests and battery median; midyear percentile norms available on request. Results may be graphed on individual profile chart. Manual of directions reports split-half and alternate form reliability coefficients. Split-half reliabilities of parts computed by separate grade levels range from .76 to .95; alternate form reliabilities range from .67 to .92; total score reliabilities of .95 and .96 were obtained by split-half method. Form Bm slightly easier than Form Am, except in science.

Iowa Every-Pupil Tests of Basic Skills, by Ernest Horn, Maude McBroom, H. A. Greene, E. F. Lindquist, and H. F. Spitzer. Boston: Houghton Mifflin Company, 1940–1947.

Separate Booklet edition, two levels, Grades 3–5 and 5–9. Four tests at each level, printed in separate booklets. Single test, Elementary battery, $3.60 per 35; single test, Advanced battery, $3.75 per 35; IBM answer sheets, Advanced battery, $1.44 per 35 per test; IBM 805 rights key, 30 cents each for Test A, 60 cents per set for Test B, C, or D; examiner's manual, 45 cents per test; manual of general information, 75 cents; cumulative record forms, $1.05 per 35.

A well-constructed set of achievement tests. Forms L, M, N, and O. The skills measured by these tests, which are published in separate booklets, are as follows:
Test A: Elementary battery: reading comprehension and vocabulary; Advanced battery: paragraph comprehension, details, organization, total meaning, total reading comprehension, and vocabulary.
Test B: Elementary battery: map reading, use of refer-

ences, use of index, use of dictionary, and alphabetization; Advanced battery: comprehension of maps, references, use of index, use of dictionary, and reading graphs, charts, and tables.

Test C: Elementary battery: punctuation, capitalization, usage, spelling, and sentence sense; Advanced battery, similar to the Elementary battery with omission of test of sentence sense.

Test D: Elementary battery, Part I, vocabulary and fundamental knowledge; Part II, computational skill in whole numbers, fractions, and decimals; Part III, solution of problems. Advanced battery similar to Elementary battery except for Part II, which includes whole numbers, fractions, percentage, decimals, and denominate numbers.

Working time: Elementary battery: Test A, 46 minutes; Test B, 47 minutes; Test C, 46 minutes; Test D, 57 minutes; Advanced battery, Test A, 67 minutes; Test B, 77 minutes; Test C, 55 or 58 minutes; Test D, 63 or 68 minutes.

Scores may be expressed in grade equivalents, age equivalents, or percentiles. Results may be graphed to show profile of strengths and weaknesses. Norms based on about 197,000 pupils in approximately 350 schools. There is an extensive manual for administration and interpretation. No statistical data on reliability given in manual, but length of these tests and the care with which they were constructed should assure reliability which compares favorably with that of other achievement test batteries. Likewise, the face validity seems favorable. *Reference:* Buros (7:32–42).

Iowa Tests of Basic Skills, multi-level edition for Grades 3–9, by E. F. Lindquist and A. N. Hieronymus (with assistance of Julia Peterson, Rolland Ray, Leonard Feldt, Miriam M. Bryan, Geraldine Spaulding, Gunnar Sausjord, Betty Humphry, Ruth Miller, and Janet Afflerbach). Boston: Houghton Mifflin Company, 1956. Test booklets (96 pages, all tests in one booklet), 84 cents each; IBM 805 answer sheets, $1.44 per 35 for each of four main divisions of test; IBM 1230 answer sheets, $4.20 per 35 for each of four divisions; IBM 805 or 1230 rights keys, 30 cents each for Test A, 60 cents per set for other three divisions; teacher's manual, 45 cents; pupil report folders, 90 cents per 35; class record sheets, 90 cents per 35; profile chart for averages, 90 cents per 35; pupil profile charts, 90 cents per 35; manual for administrators, supervisors, and counselors, 90 cents; specimen kit, $2.25.

A new edition of these well-known tests. New test items are used. All tests for all grades from 3 through 9 are in one 96-page booklet. Separate answer sheets must be used. Battery measures vocabulary; reading comprehension; language skills, including spelling, capitalization, punctuation, and usage; work study skills, covering map reading, reading graphs and tables, and knowledge and use of reference materials; and arithmetic, including arithmetic concepts and arithmetic problem solving. Total working time, 279 minutes. Each grade works only on those portions of battery which are

of suitable difficulty. Results shown on grade equivalent or percentile profile graph. Forms 1, 2, 3, and 4. A very impressive test battery showing excellent technical competence and splendid test format. Face validity seems high, although no statistical data on validity are in Teacher's Manual or Manual for Administrators, Supervisors, and Counselors. Reported reliability coefficients range from .70 to .96. Reliability of composite is .97 or .98 for single grade range. *Reference:* Buros (8:30–37).

Iowa Tests of Educational Development, by E. F. Lindquist and Leonard S. Feldt. Chicago: Science Research Associates, Inc., 1942–1962. Available in both a single-booklet edition (nine tests in 56-page booklet) and a separate-booklet edition. For the single-booklet edition (Forms X-4 and Y-4) the prices are: booklets, $1.00 each; IBM 1230 or Digitek answer sheets, $7.00 per 100 (for testing 20 students on complete battery); hand-scoring stencils for IBM 1230 answer sheets, $2.25 per set. For the separate-booklet edition (Forms X-3S and Y-3S) the prices are: booklets, $2.40 per 20; IBM 805 answer sheets, $5.00 per 100; IBM 805 scoring stencils, 50 cents each. Examiner's manual, 25 cents for IBM 805 scoring, 50 cents for IBM 1230 or Digitek scoring; general manual, 50 cents; norms booklet, 25 cents; pupil profile leaflets, 90 cents per 20; review set, $3.00.

Both single-booklet and separate-booklet editions cover the same nine areas: understanding of basic social concepts, general background in the natural sciences, correctness and appropriateness of expression, ability to think quantitatively, interpretation of reading materials in the social sciences, interpretation of reading materials in the natural sciences, interpretation of literary materials, general vocabulary, and use of sources of information. Battery yields separate scores for these nine tests plus a composite score on Tests 1–8 inclusive. Results expressed in standard scores that may be graphed on profile form. Range, Grades 9–13. A well-planned, carefully constructed test battery. Norms based on approximately 50,000 high scoool pupils. Spearman-Brown odd-even reliability coefficients for subtests in single grade range from .81 to .94. All forms may be administered by either the "full-length" or "class-period" method. Full-length method requires 22 to 65 minutes per test, or approximately two full school days. The "class-period" method takes from 22 to 40 minutes per test, or nine classroom periods. *Reference:* Buros (8:37–40).

Metropolitan Achievement Tests, by Harold H. Bixler, Walter N. Durost, Gertrude H. Hildreth, Kenneth W. Lund, and J. Wayne Wrightstone. New York: Harcourt, Brace & World, Inc., 1958–1962. Primary I battery, for second half of Grade 1, $6.25 per 35 booklets; Primary II battery, for Grade 2, $8.00 per 35 booklets; Elementary battery, for Grades 3–4, $8.00 per 35 booklets; Intermediate battery, for Grades 5–6, $11.00 per 35 Complete battery booklets, $9.00 per 35 Partial battery booklets; Advanced battery, for Grades 7–9, $11.00 per 35 Complete battery booklets, $9.00 per 35 Partial battery booklets. Intermediate and Advanced batteries are also available in reusable booklets for use with machine scorable answer sheets at $12.00 per 35 Complete battery booklets and $9.80 per 35 Partial battery booklets. IBM 805 answer sheets for Intermediate and Advanced batteries: Arithmetic, $1.80 per 35; Reading and Spelling, $2.00 per 35; Language and Study Skills, $2.00 per 35; Social Studies and Science, $2.00 per 35. IBM 805 machine scoring keys, $1.00 per set of 5. IBM 1230 answer sheets, $2.50 per 35; IBM 1230 stencil key, 20 cents each. Examiner's kit, any one battery, 80 cents.

The component subtests and the total testing time requirements for the various batteries are: Primary I battery—word knowledge, word discrimination, reading, arithmetic concepts and skills—1 hour and 45 minutes; Primary II battery—word knowledge, word discrimination, reading, spelling, arithmetic—2 hours; Elementary battery—word knowledge, word discrimination, reading, spelling, language, arithmetic computation, arithmetic problem solving and concepts—2 hours and 45 minutes; Intermediate and Advanced batteries—word knowledge, reading, spelling, language, language study skills, arithmetic computation, arithmetic problem solving and concepts, social studies information, social studies study skills, science—4 hours for Intermediate battery, 4 hours and 15 minutes for Advanced battery. The social studies information and science subtests are not included in the Intermediate and Advanced Partial batteries, which take 30 minutes less working time than the Complete batteries. In the hand-scoring edition, Forms A, B, and C are available for Primary I and Primary II batteries, Forms A, B, C, and D for the other three batteries. Machine scoring forms are AM, BM, CM, and DM for Intermediate and Advanced batteries.

Results may be expressed in terms of standard scores, stanines, grade equivalent scores, or percentiles. The stanines may be shown graphically on an individual pupil profile chart to show strengths and weaknesses in achievement. Public school norms based on wide sampling of schools throughout the country. Certain subtests may be obtained as separate booklets. *References:* North (25, 26).

Metropolitan Achievement Tests, High School Battery, by Walter N. Durost (gen. ed.), William H. Evans, James D. Leake, Howard A. Bowman, Clark Cosgrove, and John G. Reed. New York: Harcourt, Brace & World, Inc., 1962. Booklets, $10.50 per 35. IBM 805 answer sheets: reading, spelling, and language, $2.25 per 35; study skills and social studies, $2.00 per 35; mathematics and science, $2.00 per 35. IBM 805 scoring keys, $1.20 per set of 5. IBM 1230 answer sheets: reading, spelling, and language, $2.50 per 35; study skills and social studies, $2.25 per 35; mathematics and science, $2.25 per 35. In-

dividual student profile charts, 75 cents per 35; specimen set, $1.00.

This upward extension of the well-known Metropolitan Achievement Tests series is comprised of 11 subtests yielding comparable measures in reading, spelling, language, language study skills, social studies study skills, social studies vocabulary, social studies information, mathematical computation and concepts, mathematical analysis and problem solving, scientific concepts and understandings, and science information. Total time required is 5 hours and 15 minutes. Percentile and stanine norms by grade are available for each subtest.

Sequential Tests of Educational Progress (STEP), by the staff of the Cooperative Test Division, E.T.S. Princeton, N.J.: Cooperative Test Division, Educational Testing Service, 1956–1959. Seven separate tests: booklets for reading, writing, listening, mathematics, science, and social studies, $4.00 per 20; essay booklets, $1.00 per 20. Answer sheets for any one of the 6 objective tests, $1.00 per 20 IBM 805, $25.00 per 500 IBM 1230. Digitek answer sheets accommodating all 6 objective tests, $37.50 per 500. Directions for administering and scoring for all fields except listening and essay, 25 cents each; directions for administering and scoring listening test, $1.00; manual for interpreting scores, $1.00 per field; essay-examiner's handbook, $1.00; technical report, $1.00; teacher's guide, $1.00; student report form, $1.00 per 20; comprehensive specimen set with one form of each test at each level, $5.00.

This widely used series of achievement tests evaluates a student's application of skills and knowledge in reading, writing, listening, mathematics, science, and social studies. All the tests except essay writing are objectively scored, requiring separate answer sheets. The essay writing test is scored by comparing with samples included in the examiner's handbook. Time required, 70 minutes for objective tests, 35 minutes for essay. Four levels: 1 for college freshmen and sophomores; 2 for Grades 10–12; 3 for Grades 7–9; 4 for Grades 4–6. Four forms, A, B, C, and D, at each level for essay; two forms, A and B, at each level for the other tests. Percentile norms for converted scores for each grade, 4 through college sophomore. Kuder-Richardson median reliabilities reported in technical manual range from .84 to .92. *References:* Buros (8:62–75) and Traxler (44).

SRA Achievement Tests, by Louis P. Thorpe, D. Welty Lefever, and Robert A. Naslund. Chicago: Science Research Associates, Inc., 1954–1958. Grades 1–2, $3.50 per 20 reading booklets, $2.50 per 35 arithmetic booklets; Grades 2–4, separate booklets for reading, arithmetic, and language arts, $2.00 per 20 booklets; Grades 2–4, single booklet with all three tests, $5.50 per 20 booklets; Grades 4–9, multilevel edition, $16.00 per 20 booklets; work-study skills supplement, $6.00 per 20; Grades 4–6, separate booklet edition, $2.15 per 20 booklets (reading, arithmetic, language arts, or work-study skills); Grades 6–9, separate booklet edition, $2.00 per 20 booklets (same areas as tests for Grades 4–6). Answer sheets, Grades 4–9 multilevel edition, $18.00 per 100 sets of 3 for IBM 805 scoring, $14.00 per 100 sets of 2 for IBM 1230 scoring. IBM 805 scoring stencils, $3.50 per set of 7. IBM answer sheets for separate-booklet edition, $5.00 per 100 for Grades 4–6 or 6–9; hand scoring stencils, 50 cents each; machine scoring stencils, $1.00 per test, except reading and work-study skills in 6–9 level which are 50 cents per test. Pupil progress and profile charts, 90 cents per 20; review set, one level, $2.00.

A well-printed and carefully constructed achievement test series for Grades 1–9. Each of the batteries contains reading and arithmetic subtests. Language arts subtests are also included in all batteries except the lowest one, covering Grades 1–2. The multilevel battery for Grades 4–9 also has supplementary subtests in social studies and science. A unique feature is the availability of the multilevel booklet in three levels of difficulty: for below-average, average, and above-average pupils. Forms C and D for Grades 1–2, 2–4, and 4–9 (multilevel); Forms A and B for separate booklets in 4–6 and 6–9 levels. Total time required, 5½ hours for Grades 1–2, 125 minutes for Grades 2–4, 445 minutes for Grades 4–6, 370 minutes for Grades 6–9. Public school grade equivalent norms and percentile norms are available. Reliabilities (Kuder-Richardson) reported in examiner's manual for the series for Grades 4–6, based on 200 cases at each of the three grade levels, range from .73 to .92. These reliabilities seem moderately satisfactory for the separate tests within a battery, although not especially high in view of the amount of time required for administration. *Reference:* Buros (8:48–55).

Stanford Achievement Test, by Truman L. Kelley, Richard Madden, Eric F. Gardner, and Herbert C. Rudman. New York: Harcourt, Brace & World, Inc., 1964. Five complete batteries and three partial batteries as well as separate subject tests. Prices per 35 booklets: Primary I battery, Grades 1.5–2.4, $5.65; Primary II battery, Grades 2.5–3.9, $5.80; Intermediate I, Grades 4.0–5.4, $9.75 for Complete battery, $8.25 for Partial battery; Intermediate II, Grades 5.5–6.9, $9.75 for Complete battery, $8.25 for Partial battery; Advanced, Grades 7.0–9.9, $9.75 for Complete battery, $8.25 for Partial battery. IBM 805 answer sheets, 35 sets, $5.80 for Intermediate I Complete battery, $6.00 for Intermediate II or Advanced Complete battery; $4.00 for Intermediate I, Intermediate II, or Advanced Partial battery. Prices not yet available for IBM 1230 or Digitek answer sheets and keys. Specimen set, 80 cents each for Primary I or Primary II battery, $1.00 each for other batteries.

Primary I battery tests word reading, paragraph meaning, vocabulary, spelling, word study skills, and arithmetic; total administration time, about 2 hours and 40 minutes. Primary II battery tests word meaning, paragraph meaning, science and social studies concepts, spelling, word-study skills, language, arithmetic computation, and arithmetic concepts; total administration time, about 3 hours and 50 minutes. Intermediate I battery tests word meaning, paragraph meaning, spelling, word study skills, language, arithmetic computation, arithmetic concepts, arithmetic applications, social studies, and science; total administration time, about 3 hours and 50 minutes. Intermediate II battery has same coverage as Intermediate I battery, except that the word study skills subtest is omitted; total administration time, 3 hours and 40 minutes. Advanced battery has all tests in Intermediate I areas except word meaning and word study skills; total administration time, 3 hours and 20 minutes.

These tests are the fourth revision of the Stanford Achievement Tests first published in 1923. There are four forms of all batteries in this series, W, X, Y, and Z. Raw scores are translated into grade equivalents, percentiles, or stanines, and may be graphed in form of a profile. At each battery level a single booklet is used, regardless of the response medium or scoring method chosen. The national standardization group, including more than 850,000 pupils from 264 communities distributed throughout the United States, was one of the largest and most carefully chosen standardization populations ever used in a test-development program.

The Educational Records Bureau has fall and spring independent school percentile norms for the Stanford. An evaluation of the series based on independent school results has been reported by the Bureau (28). For the independent school groups and for the publisher's public school groups, the estimated Kuder-Richardson reliabilities of most of the subtests throughout the grade range fall between .85 and .95, but a few are below .80. *Reference:* Stake and Hastings (32).

United States Armed Forces Institute Tests of General Educational Development. Washington: Veterans Testing Service of the American Council on Education. Orders, inquiries concerning prices, and requests for additional information should be addressed to Veterans Testing Service.

USAFI Tests of General Educational Development, as well as USAFI subject tests, have had an important place in the history of educational measurement since 1943. Thousands of veterans who were not high school graduates have been admitted to colleges throughout the United States on the basis of these tests. USAFI test results have also been used as guides for placement within colleges. Likewise, in employment situations, many nongraduates of high school have demonstrated high school equivalency by taking these tests, and thus have qualified for jobs calling for high school education.

Two levels, high school and college. There are several equivalent forms of the high school level. Form B is the only one of these which may be purchased by educators for civilian use. Forms C, D, E, and F are administered by official agencies of the Veterans Testing Service. Forms T, V, W, X, Y, and Z are used exclusively within the Armed Services for men on active duty. High school level consists of five tests printed in separate booklets: correctness and effectiveness of expression, interpretation of reading materials in the social studies, interpretation of reading materials in the natural sciences, interpretation of literary materials, and general mathematical ability. College level includes first four kinds of tests but does not contain test of mathematics. Each test calls for two hours of working time. Separate answer sheets must be used. Results reported in standard scores and percentiles. Regional percentile norms for high school edition and percentiles for college edition arranged according to type of college are available. The USAFI series also includes subject tests and end-of-course tests. Reference is made to the subject tests in the appendix of this book. Extensive fact-finding study of results of these tests reported by Tyler (52); briefer report by a committee of American Council on Education published in 1956 (11). Detailed 1955 normative study by Bloom (4).

ANNOTATED LIST OF ACHIEVEMENT TESTS IN SEPARATE SUBJECTS

ENGLISH

Barrett-Ryan-Schrammel English Test, New Edition, by E. R. Barrett, Teresa M. Ryan, and H. E. Schrammel. New York: Harcourt, Brace & World, Inc., 1938–1954. Booklets, $4.30 per 35; IBM 805 answer sheets, $2.00 per 35; specimen set, 40 cents.

Five subtests designed to measure functional grammar, the sentence (including parts of speech and parts of a sentence), punctuation, vocabulary, and knowledge of correct pronunciation. Designed for Grades 9–13. Working time, 60 minutes. Scoring is completely objective; planned for use with either hand-scoring or machine-scoring answer sheets. Percentile norms are available for subtests and total scores for Grades 9–12 and college freshmen. Forms Dm and Em. Spearman-Brown split-half reliability coefficients for total score at single grade level range from .88 to .95; alternate form reliabilities, .85 to .88 according to the manual of directions.

Cooperative English Tests, 1960 edition, by the staff of the Cooperative Test Division, E.T.S. Princeton, N.J.: Cooperative Test Division, Educational Testing Service, 1960. Test booklets, Reading Comprehension or English Expression, $4.00 per 20; single-booklet edition containing both tests, $6.00 per 20. IBM 805 answer sheets, $1.00 per 20; IBM 1230 or Digitek answer sheets, $25.00 per 500. Directions for administering and scoring, 25 cents; manual for interpreting scores, $1.00; student report

profile, $1.00 per 20; technical report, $1.00; specimen set containing one form of test from each area, $2.00.

Published in two levels: Forms 1A, 1B, and 1C for Grade 12, college freshmen and sophomores; Forms 2A, 2B, and 2C for Grades 9–12. Form 1C reserved for use by colleges and universities. The two parts, Reading Comprehension and English Expression, are available separately or as a single booklet, but a single answer sheet accommodates both parts. Working time, 40 minutes for each part, or 80 minutes total. Public school and college percentile norms are available for the converted scores. The Educational Records Bureau has independent school norms for the Level 1 forms for Grades 10–12 and for the Level 2 forms for Grades 7–9. Widely used by schools and colleges throughout the country. Alternate-form reliabilities, as reported in the technical manual, range from .91 to .94 for the Reading Comprehension scores, and from .81 to .86 for the English Expression scores.

Cooperative Test of Usage, Spelling, Vocabulary, by the staff of the Cooperative Test Division, E.T.S. Princeton: N.J.: Cooperative Test Division, Educational Testing Service, 1937–1939. $4.00 per 25 booklets; $1.00 per 25 IBM 805 answer sheets; specimen set, $1.00.

This test consists of three parts and provides separate scores for usage, spelling, and vocabulary, as well as a total score. Two machine-scoring forms, OM and PM. Working time, 70 minutes. Public school norms are available for Grades 7 through 12. Most public schools, however, find it better suited for Grade 9 and upward than for Grades 7 and 8. In addition, there are norms for all college years. Scaled Scores corresponding to raw scores are shown on the scoring keys; also standard errors of measurement. Obtained reliability coefficients for Form O (hand-scoring edition of Form OM, which is no longer in print) reported as .98 for the total score; .95 for usage, .97 for spelling, and .95 for vocabulary. Correlation of English scores with marks of college freshmen reported as .48.

Brown-Carlsen Listening Comprehension Test, by James I. Brown and G. Robert Carlsen. New York: Harcourt, Brace & World, Inc., 1953. $2.20 per 35 IBM 805 answer sheets; scoring keys, 20 cents per set; manual of directions, 40 cents; specimen set, 60 cents.

One of the tests in the Evaluation and Adjustment Series. Since administration is entirely oral, test booklets are not required. Test may be given to groups of regular class size. Contains five parts designed to measure immediate recall, following directions, recognizing transitions, recognizing word meanings, and lecture comprehension. Grade range, 9–13. Administration time, 45 to 50 minutes. Percentile norms for total scores.

Durost-Center Word Mastery Test, by Walter N. Durost and Stella S. Center. New York: Harcourt, Brace & World, Inc., 1950. $5.00 per 35 tests; $2.00 per 35 IBM 805 answer sheets; specimen set, 40 cents.

This test purports to measure general vocabulary level and ability of student to learn meanings of unknown words from context. Same list of words is presented first in multiple-choice vocabulary test and then, in a second testing period, with the words used in meaningful sentences. Difference between scores on the two administrations is regarded as measure of pupil's ability to learn meanings from context. In Evaluation and Adjustment Series. Working time, 25 minutes, first testing period; 35 minutes, second testing period. Grade range, 9–12. All responses marked on separate answer sheets. Scoring may be done with perforated stencil key by hand or machine. Public school percentile norms arranged by grade are available.

Inglis Tests of English Vocabulary, by Alexander Inglis. Boston: Ginn and Company, 1923–1951. $3.00 per 30 tests (lower extension, $2.00 per 30).

One of the older tests but still among the more useful measures of vocabulary power. Consists of 150 multiple-choice items. No time limit. Forms A, B, and C. Based on a sampling of the field covered by the intelligent reader's general vocabulary. Norms for Grades 9–12 and college freshmen and college graduates. Reliability resulting from correlations between the different forms, .90. *Reference:* Inglis (21).

There is a lower extension of the Inglis tests, Forms X and Y, for Grades 6–10, by C. Thomas Downing.

Michigan Vocabulary Profile Test, by Edward B. Greene. New York: Harcourt, Brace & World, Inc., 1937–1949. $5.00 per 35 booklets; $2.00 per 35 IBM 805 answer sheets; 40 cents per set of scoring keys; specimen set, 40 cents.

One of the few vocabulary tests that is long enough to yield reliable diagnostic scores. Contains 240 multiple-choice items covering eight fields: human relations, commerce, government, physical sciences, biological sciences, mathematics, fine arts, and sports. Forms Am and Bm. No time limit, about 50 minutes required for administration. Norms are available for Grades 9–12 and each year of college. Author reports that correlations between subdivisions of two forms range from .87 to .94, with a median of .91. Vocabulary profiles for various groups have been identified. *Reference:* Greene (18).

Vocabulary Test for High School Students and College Freshmen, by Arthur E. Traxler. Indianapolis: Bobbs-Merrill Company, 1964. Test-answer sheets (IBM 1230), $3.30 per 35; scoring keys, 80 cents per set; manual, 30 cents; specimen set, 50 cents.

Designed to serve as a basis for corrective work in vocabulary and reading, as well as for evaluative purposes. Two forms, A and B, with 50 items in each. Working time, 15 minutes. Spearman-Brown reliabilities reported by author are .90–.92 for public school groups, .87–.90 for independent school groups. Correlations with Diagnostic Reading Test

comprehension scores for independent school pupils, .64 for Grade 9, .68 for Grade 11. *References:* Traxler (47, 50).

Lincoln Diagnostic Spelling Test, by A. L. Lincoln. New York: Educational Records Bureau, 1941–1944. 8 cents per copy; specimen set, 50 cents. (Also published by Bobbs-Merrill Company, Indianapolis.)

Contains 100 words arranged in cycles to cover ten aspects of spelling ability. Four forms for use at junior and senior high school levels. Words chosen from Lester's *A Spelling Review* and Simmons and Bixler's *The New Standard High School Spelling Scale.* No time limit; administration time about 30 minutes. Fall and spring norms for independent school pupils for all four forms; also estimated public school norms. Spearman-Brown split-half reliability of total score, .93. Median reliability of part scores, .66. Diagnosis is based largely on words representing common spelling rules. Parallel forms reliability of total score: Grade 10, .93; Grade 12, .85. Spearman-Brown odd-even reliability: Grade 10, .93; Grade 12, .93. At tenth-grade level, reliabilities of parts range from .47 to .80, with median of .69. *Reference:* Townsend (36).

Lincoln Intermediate Spelling Test, by A. L. Lincoln. New York: Educational Records Bureau, 1947–1949. 8 cents per copy; specimen set, 50 cents. (Also published by Bobbs-Merrill Company, Indianapolis.)

Arrangement of 100 words in ten categories of ten words each. Similar to Lincoln Diagnostic Spelling Test but on lower level. Four forms; Grades 4–8. Norms for independent school pupils for both fall and spring; also estimated public school norms. Kuder-Richardson reliabilities of total score, .91 to .95. *Reference:* Townsend (38).

Lincoln Primary Spelling Test, by A. L. Lincoln. New York: Educational Records Bureau, 1960. 8 cents per copy; specimen set, 50 cents.

This level of the Lincoln spelling tests, designed for use with pupils in Grades 2–5, contains 144 words arranged in overlapping cycles of 72 words each. It yields scores in six aspects of spelling. Fall and spring independent school norms for Grades 2 and 3 are available, along with estimated public school norms for the range from the spring of Grade 2 to the fall of Grade 5. Four forms, W, X, Y, and Z. *Reference:* Traxler (45).

FOREIGN LANGUAGES

MLA-Cooperative Foreign Language Tests, prepared by 60 language teachers under the general direction of Nelson Brooks, as a cooperative project of the Modern Language Association of America, the Educational Testing Service, and the United States Office of Education, Department of Health, Education, and Welfare. Princeton, N.J.: Cooperative Test Division, Educational Testing Service, 1963. (Copyright by the Modern Language Association of America.) Test booklets containing complete tests in reading and writing, response choices for listening, and printed stimulus materials and pictures for speaking, $5.00 per 10. Booklets for writing test responses, $4.00 per 20. Tapes for listening or speaking, $7.00 each. Scoring keys for booklets, 25 cents per set; IBM 805 answer sheets, $100 per 20; IBM 1230 answer sheets, $25.00 per 500; Digitek answer sheets, $25.00 per 500; directions for administering and scoring (single booklet for all MLA tests), $1.00; norms booklet, $1.00; handbook, $1.00; specimen set for one language containing one form of each level and sample accessories, $2.00.

Tests listening, speaking, reading, and writing competencies in five languages: French, German, Italian, Russian, and Spanish. Prepared under provisions of the National Defense Education Act of 1958, Title VI, Language Development Program. Two levels: Level L intended for secondary school students completing one or two years of study, and college students completing two semesters of study; Level M intended for secondary students completing three or four years of study, and college students completing four semesters of study. Two forms, A and B. Designed especially to meet needs of schools following audio-lingual approach, but reading and writing tests are also suited for a more traditional approach. Tapes required for administering speaking and listening tests. In writing test, student demonstrates his ability by writing both structured and free responses. Reading and listening tests scored objectively; speaking and writing tests scored semi-objectively. Working time: listening, 25 minutes; speaking, 10 minutes; reading, 35 minutes; writing, 35 minutes. Percentile norms by year of study, high school and college, with traditional, audio-lingual, and general group differentiations at high school level. Technical manual not available when this annotation was being prepared, but general quality of the series seems excellent.

Cooperative French Listening Comprehension Test, by Nelson Brooks. Princeton, N.J.: Cooperative Test Division, Educational Testing Service, 1955. Tape recording, $7.00; answer booklets, $3.00 per 25; scoring keys free with answer booklets; examiner's manual containing scripts for both forms and percentile rank tables, $1.00; specimen set without tape, $2.00.

A 30-minute test, administered by tape-recorded selections. Norms based on use of recording, but teachers may read script from manual. Appropriate for students in second year of high school French, or at higher levels of study through fifth semester of college study. One level, two forms (A and B). Norms for public secondary schools, independent secondary schools, and colleges. *Reference:* Buros (8:398–401), Traxler (46) and Vecchione (53).

Cooperative Latin Test, elementary and advanced, by George A. Land. Princeton, N.J.: Cooperative Test Division, Educational Testing Service, 1940–1941. $4.00

per 25 tests; $1.00 per 25 IBM 805 answer sheets; specimen set, $2.00.

Measures reading, vocabulary, and grammar; a total score is also provided. Several forms of this test were constructed, but only Forms Q and R are in print. There are two levels, an elementary level for pupils with three semesters of Latin or less, and an advanced level for those with more than that amount. Working time, 40 minutes. Public school, independent school, and college percentile norms are available. The Scaled Scores on the two forms and two levels are directly comparable. The corrected odd-even reliability of the total score on Form O, an earlier form which was closely similar to Forms Q and R, was .96 for the elementary test and .94 for the advanced test. Reliabilities estimated from the standard error of measurement at the 50-point of the Scaled Scores: elementary test: reading, .75; vocabulary, .94; grammar, .88; total score, .94; advanced test: reading, .51; vocabulary, .74; grammar, .88; total score, .88. Spearman-Brown split-half reliability for total score on Advanced Form Q, based on independent school population, .94.

MATHEMATICS

Cooperative Mathematics Tests, by the staff of the Cooperative Test Division, E.T.S. Princeton, N.J.: Cooperative Test Division, Educational Testing Service, 1962–1963. Prices for the separate tests: booklets, $4.00 per 20; IBM 805 answer sheets, $1.00 per 20; IBM 1230 or Digitek answer sheets, $25.00 per 500; handbook providing directions for administering and scoring as well as technical and interpretive information, $1.00; specimen set with one form of each test from each area and samples of accessories, $2.00.

The tests in this series, published in separate booklets with a single handbook, are as follows:
Arithmetic, Forms A, B, and C, 50 items, 40 minutes, for Grades 7–9. Single total score with percentile norms for each of the three grades. Stresses understanding and application of mathematical principles.
Structure of the Number System, Forms A and B, 40 items, 40 minutes, for modern mathematics classes in Grades 7 and 8. Single total score with percentile norms for each of the two grades. Covers some of the fundamental concepts of modern mathematics, such as the commutative, associative, and distributive laws, number systems, and factors, divisors, and multiples.
Algebra I, Forms A and B, 40 items, 40 minutes, for elementary algebra classes in Grades 8 and 9. Single total score with eighth and ninth grade norms.
Algebra II, Forms A and B, 40 items, 40 minutes, for intermediate algebra classes. Single total score with percentile norms for composite high school group.
Geometry, Forms A and B, two parts, 40 items in each part, 40 minutes for each part, for high school geometry classes. Percentile norms for Part I and for total test, but not for Part II. Composite high school norm group. Part I may

be given alone to survey important results of a typical high school geometry course; total test provides more thorough coverage, including applications of geometry in three-dimensional space (48).

Trigonometry, Forms A and B, 40 items, 40 minutes, for one-semester high school or college courses in trigonometry or for integrated courses in elementary college mathematics. Single total score with percentile norms for both high school and college composite groups.

Algebra III, Forms A and B, 40 items, 40 minutes, for advanced or "college" algebra courses. Single total score, with both high school and college percentile norms.

Analytic Geometry, Forms A and B, 35 items, 40 minutes, for one-semester high school or college courses or for integrated courses in elementary college mathematics. Single total score with both high school and college percentile norms.

Calculus, Forms A and B, two 30-item parts, 40 minutes for each part, covering work in analytical geometry and calculus through the differential and integral calculus of algebraic and transcendental functions. Appropriate for high school and college students who have completed the equivalent of at least a full year of work in the combined areas of analytical geometry and calculus. Single total score with both high school and college percentile norms.

E.R.B. Modern Mathematics Test, by William S. Litterick, Frederic Bonan, Edwin C. Douglas, Foye Perry, Reinhoud H. van der Linde, and Frederick Watson. New York: Educational Records Bureau, 1965. $4.00 per 25 booklets; $1.25 per 25 answer sheets; specimen set, 50 cents.

Constructed by the Educational Records Bureau Committee on Mathematics Tests to fit the mathematics curricula of the seventh and eighth grades in schools with a college preparatory emphasis. Form L available, Form M in preparation. Two parts, with a total of 80 items requiring 80 minutes of working time. Contains both modern and traditional types of material.

Snader General Mathematics Test, by Daniel W. Snader. New York: Harcourt, Brace & World, Inc., 1950. $5.00 per 35 tests; $1.80 per 35 IBM 805 answer sheets; specimen set, 40 cents.

Based on the objectives of a general mathematics course in which materials from the fields of algebra and informal geometry are stressed. In Evaluation and Adjustment Series. Sixty-five multiple-choice items. Forms Am and Bm. Working time, 40 minutes. End-of-year public school percentile norms. Corrected split-half reliabilities of .80 and .84 are reported in the manual. Standard error of measurement is given as 4.8 standard score points. Forms are reported to be closely equivalent in difficulty.

Davis Test of Functional Competence in Mathematics, by David J. Davis. New York: Harcourt, Brace & World, Inc., 1950. $5.00 per 35 booklets; $1.80 per 35 IBM 805 answer sheets; specimen set, 40 cents.

One of the tests in the Evaluation and Adjustment Series. Designed to measure essentials of functional competence in mathematics outlined by Commission on Post-War Plans of the National Council of Teachers of Mathematics. Eighty multiple-choice questions. Forms Am and Bm. Working time, 80 minutes. Grades 9–13. Yields standard scores for which there are middle and end-of-year percentile norms for each grade from 9 through 12. Eight corrected split-half reliability coefficients, each computed on pupils in single grade, range from .81 to .91 according to directions manual. Standard error of measurement about five standard score points.

A Brief Survey of Arithmetic Skills for Grades 5 to 12, Revised, by Arthur E. Traxler. New York: Educational Records Bureau, 1953. Eight cents per test; specimen set, 50 cents. (Also published by Bobbs-Merrill Company, Indianapolis.)

Designed to provide quick and inexpensive, yet dependable, measurement of fundamental arithmetic skills. Forms A and B. Each form contains two parts: Part 1, 40 computation problems; Part 2, ten reasoning problems. Working time, 20 minutes. Median of three corrected split-half reliability coefficients computed at single grade levels, .87; median of four alternate form reliabilities, .75. Data from 127 pupils in Grades 10 and 11 who took both Forms A and B indicate that Form B is slightly easier than Form A, but that difference at median is less than one raw score point. Correlation of total score with Stanford arithmetic, .70. Twenty correlations of total scores with marks in arithmetic or secondary school mathematics range from .25 to .82, with median of .60. All these data based on results for independent school pupils (42).

E.R.B. Modern Elementary Algebra Test, by William S. Litterick, Frederic Bonan, Edwin C. Douglas, Foye Perry, Reinhoud H. van der Linde, and Frederick Watson. New York: Educational Records Bureau, 1965. $4.00 per 25 booklets; $1.25 per 25 answer sheets; specimen set, 50 cents.

Prepared by the Committee on Mathematics Tests of the Educational Records Bureau for elementary algebra courses geared to the "modern" curriculum. Form L available, Form M in preparation. Two parts, with a total of 70 items requiring 80 minutes of working time. Contains both modern and traditional types of material.

Lankton First-Year Algebra Test, by Robert Lankton. New York: Harcourt, Brace & World, Inc., 1965. $4.00 per 35 booklets; $1.80 per 35 IBM 805 answer sheets; specimen set, 40 cents.

This test consists of 55 items intended to measure objectives and content of the first course in algebra. In Evaluation and Adjustment Series. Contains questions on vocabulary and symbols of algebra, fundamental operations, formulas, equations, and solution of problems. Working time, 40 minutes. Results reported in standard scores and public school percentile norms for end of year. Forms Am and Bm. Data indicate that results of these two forms are closely comparable throughout the scale. Corrected split-half reliability coefficients of .84 and .87 and an alternate form reliability of .81 reported in manual.

Seattle Algebra Test, by Harold B. Jeffery, Earl E. Kirschner, John R. Rushing, David Scott, Philip Stucky, and Otie P. VanOrsdall. New York: Harcourt, Brace & World, Inc., 1951. $3.40 per 35 tests; $1.80 per 35 IBM 805 answer sheets; specimen set, 40 cents.

Most standard tests are planned for use at the end of a full year of study or more, but here is a test designed for the end of the first half-year of algebra. In Evaluation and Adjustment Series. Planned to measure knowledge of facts and application of acquired skills and methods. Forty-seven items. Working time, 40 minutes. Forms Am and Bm. Public school percentile norms for end of first half-year. Median of three corrected split-half reliability coefficients reported in manual as .89. Alternate form reliability reported as .87.

Blyth Second-Year Algebra Test, by M. Isobel Blyth. New York: Harcourt, Brace & World, Inc., 1953. $4.00 per 35 test booklets; $1.80 per 35 IBM 805 answer sheets; specimen set, 40 cents.

Planned for use at the end of a second-year course in algebra. In Evaluation and Adjustment Series. Contains 55 items intended to cover the objectives of a typical course. Responses may be entered in test booklets or on separate answer sheets for machine scoring. Working time, 45 minutes. Forms Am and Bm. Public school percentile norms are available. According to the manual, the reliability coefficients range from .82 to .92 with a median of .88.

Seattle Plane Geometry Test, by Harold B. Jeffery, S. L. Merriam, Clifton T. Smith, Roy D. Kellogg, and Richard E. Bennett. New York: Harcourt, Brace & World, Inc., 1951. $4.00 per 35 booklets; $1.80 per 35 IBM 805 answer sheets; specimen set, 40 cents.

Designed to measure knowledge and understanding of plane geometry acquired during first half-year of study. In Evaluation and Adjustment Series. Working time, 45 minutes. Forms Am and Bm. Percentile norms for public school pupils at the end of first half year of study. Average of four corrected split-half reliability coefficients reported in manual as .80. Alternate form reliability, .78. Raw scores on the two forms are closely comparable according to the manual.

Shaycroft Plane Geometry Test, by Marion F. Shaycroft. New York: Harcourt, Brace & World, Inc., 1951. $4.40 per 35 booklets; $1.80 per 35 IBM 805 answer sheets; specimen set, 40 cents.

Planned to measure achievement at the end of a one-year course in plane geometry. In Evaluation and Adjustment Series. Consists of 60 items divided into two parts. Part A is concerned with basic concepts and facts, and Part B with

application and reasoning. Working time, 40 minutes. Forms Am and Bm. Manual reports average of three corrected split-half reliability coefficients as .82. Alternate-form reliability, .80. Reliability of combination of two forms, .89 with standard error of measurement of 3.6 standard score points. Scores on the two forms are directly comparable according to the manual. Public school end-of-year percentile norms are available.

SCIENCE

Cooperative Science Tests, by the staff of the Cooperative Test Division, E.T.S. Princeton, N.J.: Cooperative Test Division, Educational Testing Service, 1964–1965. Prices for the separate tests: booklets, $4.00 per 20; IBM 805 answer sheets, $1.00 per 20; IBM 1230 or Digitek answer sheets, $25.00 per 500; handbook providing directions for administering and scoring as well as technical and interpretive information, $1.00; specimen set with one form of each test from each area and samples of accessories, including handbook, $2.00.

A new series of tests covering the major areas of the junior-senior high school science curriculum. The separate tests are as follows:

General Science, Forms A and B, 60 items, 40 minutes, for Grades 7–9. Single total score with percentile norms for each of Grades 7, 8, and 9. A brief survey of elementary concepts in biology, chemistry, physics, with some items in astronomy, geology, and meteorology. Appropriate for introductory science courses in the specified grade range.

Advanced General Science, Forms A and B, 60 items in Part I and 60 items in Part II, 40 minutes for each part, for Grades 8 and 9. Provides more intensive and comprehensive treatment than that of the General Science test. Part I has items in biology, astronomy, geology, and meteorology; Part II has physics and chemistry content. Suitable for eighth-grade students of average or higher ability and for ninth-grade students in general science courses. Total score percentile norms for each of the two grades.

Biology, Forms A and B, 60 items in each of two parts, 40 minutes each part, for typical high school courses in this subject. Part I deals with human biology and the general structure, characteristics, and processes of living things; Part II is devoted to plant and animal forms. Percentile norms for the part and total scores for composite high school groups.

Chemistry, Forms A and B, 60 items in Part I, 55 items in Part II, 40 minutes for each part, for typical high school courses in this subject. Part I surveys basic principles and concepts; Part II tests ability to apply knowledge in practical laboratory situations, and measures understanding of scientific methods and principles. Percentile norms for the part and total scores for composite high school groups.

Physics, Forms A and B, 60 items in Part I: General Concepts and Principles, and 55 items in Part II: Laboratory. Coverage parallels that of the chemistry test with respect to types of abilities measured. Percentile norms for part and total scores for composite high school groups.

Read General Science Test, Revised Edition, by John G. Read. New York: Harcourt, Brace & World, Inc., 1965. $5.00 per 35 Form E or F test booklets; scoring key, 35 cents each; IBM 805 answer sheets, $1.80 per 35; IBM 805 scoring stencil, 20 cents each; specimen set, 40 cents.

A test in the Evaluation and Adjustment Series. Like other tests in this series, separate answer sheets must be used. Intended as a measure of basic facts and principles of the physical and biological sciences and their applications in a general science course. Seventy-five objective test items. Forms E and F. To be used at end of high school general science course. Working time, 40 minutes. Public school percentile norms are available. Manual reports corrected split-half reliability of .85 and higher.

BSCS High School Biology Test, by Biology Sciences Curriculum Study Test Committee. New York: The Psychological Corporation, 1965. Package of 32 reusable test booklets and 32 IBM 805 answer sheets, $4.80; extra IBM 805 answer sheets, $1.40 per 50; directions for administration and scoring key included with package of test booklets.

Covers the entire year's work in the Blue, Green, or Yellow versions of the high school biology materials prepared by the Biological Sciences Curriculum Study. The items cover both specific knowledge and general concepts. One form, 45 minutes. Norms given in terms of average scores for tenth grade students.

Cooperative Biology Test, Educational Records Bureau edition, by Thomas F. Morrison, Virginia F. Babcock, John K. Bodel, Jr., Donald H. Miller, Charles Tanzer, and Robert F. Woodworth. New York: Educational Records Bureau, 1941–1966. $4.00 per 25 booklets; $1.00 per 25 IBM 805 answer sheets; specimen set, 50 cents.

Devised by the Committee on Biology Tests of the Educational Records Bureau. Based on the objectives and curricula of college preparatory schools. Revised 1964–1966. Forms ERB-RZ, ERB-SZ, and ERB-TZ, each requiring 40 minutes of working time. A 40-minute reading comprehension supplement is under development. No converted scores or public school norms. Independent school norms are available. Spearman-Brown reliability of Form ERB-SZ, based on scores of 270 independent school biology students, .91. Correlations of scores on this form with class marks of pupils in four independent school biology classes range from .72 to .82, with median of .75. *Reference:* Traxler (49).

Nelson Biology Test, by Clarence H. Nelson. New York: Harcourt, Brace & World, Inc., 1965. $5.00 per 35 Form E or F test booklets; $1.80 per 35 IBM 805 answer sheets; specimen set, 40 cents each.

Measures knowledge and understanding of facts, principles, and concepts in the usual biology course, and ability to apply them. Two comparable forms, E and F, each containing 75 objective questions. In Evaluation and Adjustment Series. Separate answer sheets must be used. For use near end of high school biology course. Working time, 40 minutes. Standard scores and end-of-year public school percentile norms are available. Manual reports corrected split-half reliability coefficients of .87 and .88; alternate form reliability of .77. Apparently a well-designed test.

Anderson Chemistry Test, by Kenneth E. Anderson. New York: Harcourt, Brace & World, Inc., 1950. $5.00 per 35 test booklets; scoring key, 35 cents each; IBM 805 answer sheets, $1.80 per 35; IBM 805 scoring stencil, 20 cents each; specimen set, 40 cents.

Based on objectives of high school chemistry course. Comparable forms, Am and Bm, each requiring 40 minutes of working time and consisting of 80 multiple-choice items. Intended for use near end of high school chemistry course. In Evaluation and Adjustment Series. Separate answer sheets must be used. There are standard scores and public school end-of-year percentile norms. Manual reports corrected split-half reliability coefficients of .90 and .93; alternate-form reliability of .87. Seems, in general, to be one of the better chemistry tests, although some inaccuracies noted by one reviewer. See Buros (8:816).

Cooperative Chemistry Test, Educational Records Bureau edition, by Charles L. Bickel, Otis E. Alley, W. Gordon Brown, Curtiss S. Hitchcock, Wendell H. Taylor, and George C. Whiteley. New York: Educational Records Bureau, 1941–1966. $4.00 per 25 booklets; $1.00 per 25 IBM 805 answer sheets; specimen set, 50 cents.

Devised by Committee on Chemistry Tests of Educational Records Bureau. Based on objectives and curricula of college preparatory schools. Revised 1964–1966. Forms ERB-RZ, ERB-SZ, ERB-TZ each requiring 80 minutes of working time. Part I covers concepts and Part II consists of problems involving computations. No public school norms, but independent school norms are available. Spearman-Brown reliability based on scores of 206 chemistry students in independent schools, .92 for Form ERB-SZ. Correlations of scores on this form with school marks in chemistry in four independent schools range from .58 to .73, with median of .68. *Reference:* Traxler (49).

Cooperative Physics Test, Educational Records Bureau edition, by Lester D. Beers, William S. Burton, Forrest W. Cobb, Curtiss S. Hitchcock, Roberta G. Poland, and Richard G. Sagebeer. New York: Educational Records Bureau, 1941–1966. $4.00 per 25 booklets; $1.00 per 25 IBM 805 answer sheets; specimen set, 50 cents.

Prepared by the Committee on Physics Tests of Educational Records Bureau to fit the objectives and curricula of college preparatory schools. Revised 1964–1966. Forms ERB-RZ, ERB-SZ, and ERB-TZ, each requiring 80 minutes of working time. Part I covers concepts and reading comprehension and Part II consists of computational problems. No public school norms, but independent school norms are available. Spearman-Brown reliability based on scores of 236 physics students in independent schools, .85 for Form ERB-SZ. Correlations of Form ERB-SZ scores with school marks in four independent school physics classes range from .34 to .79, with median of .74. *Reference*: Traxler (49).

Dunning Physics Test, by Gordon M. Dunning. New York: Harcourt, Brace & World, Inc., 1950. $5.00 per 35 booklets; $1.80 per 35 IBM 805 answer sheets; specimen set, 40 cents.

A test in the Evaluation and Adjustment Series constructed to measure achievement of objectives of high school physics course. Forms Am and Bm, each including 75 objective items. Working time, 45 minutes. Results expressed in terms of standard scores for which end-of-year public school percentile norms are available. Corrected split-half reliabilities of .90 and .86 are reported in manual. Standard error of measurement, 3.8 standard score points.

SOCIAL STUDIES

Cooperative Social Studies Tests, by the staff of the Cooperative Test Division, E.T.S. Princeton, N.J.: Cooperative Test Division, Educational Testing Service, 1965. Prices for the separate tests: booklets, $4.00 per 20; IBM 805 answer sheets, $1.00 per 20; IBM 1230 or Digitek answer sheets, $25.00 per 500; handbook providing directions for administering and scoring as well as technical and interpretive information, $1.00; specimen set with one form of each test from each area and samples of accessories, including handbook, $2.00.

This new series of tests covers the major areas of the junior-senior high school social studies curriculum. Each test is published in two forms, A and B. The handbook contains classification tables showing the major content areas represented by the items, and indicating the type of cognitive skills required to answer each item. The skills are classified as remembering, understanding, or analyzing. The results are reported in terms of converted scores and percentiles. Working time for each test is 40 minutes. Of the 14 Kuder-Richardson reliabilities reported in the handbook for the series, 11 are .90 or higher and the other 3 are in the range of .87 to .89. The tests and their coverages are as follows:

American History, Junior High School: covers the economic, social, and cultural development of the United States from the period of exploration to the present; deals with government and politics, relations between the United States and other nations and peoples. Approximately 60 percent of the items pertain to the period from exploration to the end of the Civil War.

Civics, Junior High School: the principal areas covered are the Constitution and the federal government; state and local governments; citizenship and political participation; government services, controls, and finances; national defense and international relations.

American History, Senior High School: coverage similar to that of the junior high school level, but greater emphasis (about 60 percent) given to the period from 1865 to the present.

Problems of Democracy, High School: topics included are public opinion, politics, national defense, international relations, constitutional rights, urbanization, labor management relations, and the role of government in the economy.

American Government, High School: places major emphasis on the United States Constitution and federal government, but also deals with state and local governments; covers citizenship and political participation, governmental functions and controls, national defense and international relations.

Modern European History, High School: covers cultural, political, economic, and diplomatic developments in European history from 1450 to the present, with about one third of the content relating to the period before the French Revolution and about one fourth concerning the twentieth century.

World History, High School: approximately 75 percent of the content deals with Western civilization from ancient days to the present; other 25 percent is concerned with historical developments in Eastern Europe, Africa, and Asia; about one half of the items cover the period since 1800.

Crary American History Test, by Ryland W. Crary. New York: Harcourt, Brace & World, Inc., 1965. $4.00 per 35 Form E or F test booklets; IBM 805 answer sheets, $1.80 per 35; specimen set, 40 cents each.

Designed to measure knowledge of historical facts, understanding and interpretation of historical information, and reasoning. One of the tests in Evaluation and Adjustment Series. Separate answer sheets must be used. Working time, 40 minutes. Two comparable forms, Am and Bm, each containing 90 objective items. Results expressed in terms of standard scores for which end-of-year public school percentile norms are available. Independent school norms also available. Corrected split-half reliability coefficients of .87 and .91 are reported in the manual. Corrected split-half reliabilities of .92 and .89 were obtained by Educational Records Bureau for Forms Am and Bm, respectively, based on scores of independent school pupils. Correlations of test scores with school marks in 20 independent school classes in American history range from .36 to .86, with a median of .60 (39).

Cummings World History Test, by Howard H. Cummings. New York: Harcourt, Brace & World, Inc., 1951. $5.00 per 35 test booklets; $1.80 per 35 IBM 805 answer sheets; specimen set, 40 cents.

Designed to measure factual knowledge of world history and understanding of great movements and social trends in development of civilization. Two comparable forms, Am and Bm, each comprising 80 test items and calling for 40 minutes of working time. In Evaluation and Adjustment Series. Raw scores are translated into standard scores for which end-of-year public school percentile norms are available. There are also independent school percentile norms based on April testing program of Educational Records Bureau. Corrected split-half reliabilities of .91 and .94 are reported in the manual. Corrected split-half reliability coefficient of .89 found for independent school group where the range may be somewhat more restricted than is the case with a sample drawn from public schools. Correlations of test scores with grades in world history in ten independent schools range from .36 to .81, with a median of .65 (43). The test seems comparatively valid and reliable for a test of content designed for a single class period.

ANNOTATED LIST OF SILENT READING TESTS

American School Reading Tests: Senior High Schools and College Freshmen, by Willis E. Pratt and Stanley W. Lore. Indianapolis: Bobbs-Merrill Company, 1955. Booklets, $3.85 per 35; specimen set, 50 cents.

Forms A and B, for Grades 10 through 13. Working time, 55 minutes. Yields scores for vocabulary, reading rate, and reading comprehension. Reliability (parallel forms method) reported as .953 for vocabulary, .855 for rate, and .978 for comprehension. Public school percentile norms based on rather small number of cases in Grades 10, 11, 12, and 13 are available.

Cooperative Reading Comprehension Test, by the staff of the Cooperative Test Division, E.T.S. Princeton, N.J.: Educational Testing Service, 1960. Test booklets, $4.00 per 20; IBM 805 or Scribe answer sheets, $1.00 per 20; IBM 1230 or Digitek answer sheets, $25.00 per 500; directions for administering and scoring, 25 cents; manual for interpreting scores, $1.00; student report profile, $1.00 per 20; technical report, $1.00 each; specimen set (including Cooperative English Expression Test), $2.00.

This test, while a part of the Cooperative English Test, is also printed as a separate booklet. Two levels: Level 1 (Forms 1A, 1B, and 1C) for Grade 12, college freshmen and sophomores; and Level 2 (Forms 2A, 2B, and 2C) for Grades 9–12. Form 1C is restricted to college and university use. Each level contains two parts, vocabulary and paragraph reading. Provides scores for vocabulary, speed of comprehension, level of comprehension, and a total score. The level score is obtained by means of a repeating-scale technique, which largely eliminates the influence of speed of reading on the results. Working time, 40 minutes. Public school and independent school percentile norms are available. Independent school norms are based on use of Level 1 in Grades 10–12, Level 2 in Grades 7–9.

Davis Reading Test, by Frederick B. Davis and Charlotte C. Davis. New York: The Psychological Corporation, 1956–1962. $3.50 per 25 test booklets; answer sheets, $2.00 per 50; set of two stencils and manual, 50 cents; specimen set, one form, 75 cents; specimen set, including all forms, $1.50.

Measures reading comprehension skills in the junior high school to college freshman range. Series 1 for grades 11–13, Series 2 for Grades 8–11. Four forms (A, B, C, and D) at each level, with 80 items in each. Level of Comprehension score is based on first 40 items, Speed of Comprehension score derived from total test. Reading passages used as basis for items vary in length from 5 to 30 lines. Working time, 40 minutes. Percentile norms for each grade in range covered. Test-retest reliabilities of both the Level and Speed scores over periods of one to four weeks, as reported in the manual, range from .70 to .89 for Series 1, and from .71 to .93 for Series 2. Correlations with STEP reading and Cooperative Reading Comprehension scores are near .80.

Diagnostic Reading Tests, by Committee on Diagnostic Reading Tests, Inc. (Frances O. Triggs, chairman, Robert M. Bear, Ralph Bedell, John V. McQuitty, George D. Spache, Agatha Townsend, Arthur E. Traxler, and Frederick L. Westover). Mountain Home, North Carolina: The Committee, 1947–1952. Survey Section and four Diagnostic Sections. Specimen set, $4.50. Separate answer sheets may be used except with Section IV, Part I. Survey Section: test booklets, 25 cents each; directions for administering, 25 cents; hand-scoring answer sheets, 4 cents each; IBM 805 or 1230 answer sheets, 7 cents each; scoring stencil or fan key, 25 cents each. Diagnostic Section I: Vocabulary (revised), booklets, 15 cents each; directions, 25 cents; hand-scoring answer sheets, 4 cents each; IBM 805 or 1230 answer sheets, 7 cents each; scoring stencil or fan key, 25 cents. Section II: Comprehension, Auditory and Silent (revised), booklets, 25 cents each; directions, 25 cents; hand-scoring answer sheets, 4 cents each; IBM 805 or 1230 answer sheets, 7 cents each; scoring stencil or fan key, 25 cents. Section III: Rates of Reading, booklets, 15 cents each; directions, 25 cents; hand-scoring answer sheets, 4 cents each; IBM 805 or 1230 answer sheets, 7 cents each; scoring stencil or fan key, 25 cents. Section IV: Word Attack, Part 1, Oral, booklets, 20 cents each; directions, 25 cents; Part 2, Silent, booklets, 15 cents each; directions, 25 cents; hand-scoring answer sheets, 4 cents each; IBM 805 or 1230 answer sheets, 7 cents each; scoring stencil or fan key, 25 cents. Norms for all tests, 50 cents.

Survey Section designed as screening test for all pupils; eight forms, A through H; working time, 40 minutes. Section I: Vocabulary, five scores: English, mathematics, science, social studies, total; Forms A and B; testing time, 40 minutes. Section II: Comprehension, Forms A and B, two parts (Part 1, Silent; Part 2, Auditory); untimed (40–60 minutes). Section III: Rates of Reading, Forms A and B, three parts: Part

1, General, four scores: normal rate of reading, comprehension at normal rate, maximum rate of reading, comprehension at maximum rate; working time, about 30 minutes; Part 2, Social Studies, two scores, rate of reading and comprehension check; working time, about 20 minutes; Part 3, Science, two scores, rate of reading and comprehension; working time, about 20 minutes. Section IV: Word Attack, two parts, Part 1, Oral, individual administration, Forms A and B, working time, about 30 minutes; Part two, Silent, working time, about 30 minutes.

An extensive series of tests constructed by an independent, nonprofit committee whose work was subsidized in the early stages by the Blue Hill Foundation. Tests consist of Survey Section and various Diagnostic Sections designed to be used in studying pupils whose gross weaknesses have been revealed by Survey Section. Public school norms have been prepared for all sections of these tests, although the norms for some of the Diagnostic Sections are not very adequate. Independent school norms for all forms of the Survey Section are available from the Educational Records Bureau. A considerable amount of data on the reliability and validity has been reported by the committee. These data are too varied and detailed for adequate summarization here. In general, reliability coefficients (usually parallel form or Kuder-Richardson) are in the range of approximately .80 to .94. Intercorrelations of parts are substantial, but seem low enough to warrant reporting of separate scores except in the case of different kinds of rate measures used. *References:* the Committee (*10*) and Triggs (*51*).

Diagnostic Reading Tests: Survey Section, Lower Level, by Committee on Diagnostic Reading Tests, Inc. Mountain Home, N.C.: The Committee, 1952–1956. Three parts published in two booklets for Grades 4–8. Booklet I, Part 1, Word Recognition and Comprehension. Booklet II: Part 2, Vocabulary and Part 3, Rate of Reading. Also section IV, Word Attack, Part I, Oral, revised (including test paragraphs, Grades 1–8), an individually administered test, and Part 2, Silent. Test booklets of each type, 20 cents each, except Section IV, Part 2, priced at 15 cents each; directions for each booklet, 25 cents; hand-scoring answer sheets for each booklet, 4 cents each; IBM 805 or 1230 answer sheets, 7 cents each; scoring stencil or fan key for each booklet, 25 cents each, specimen set, including booklets and directions, $1.75.

These tests are designed as a lower level of the Survey Section of the Diagnostic Reading Tests for Grades 7–13. Forms A, B, C, and D. Working time: Booklets 1 and 2, untimed (about 30 minutes for each). Public school and independent school norms are available. Kuder-Richardson and Spearman-Brown odd-even reliabilities of parts fall within the range .82 to .91; reliabilities of total score on Booklet 1, as reported in manual, are from .90 to .93.

Diagnostic Reading Tests, Survey Section: Kindergarten through Fourth Grades, by Committee on Diagnostic Reading Tests, Inc. (Frances O. Triggs, chairman;

Robert M. Bear, George D. Spache, Agatha Townsend (ed.), and Arthur E. Traxler). Mountain Home, North Carolina: The Committee, 1957. Four separate booklets —Reading Readiness (Form B only), Booklet I for kindergarten and Grade 1, Booklet II for Grade 2, Booklet III for Grades 3 and 4—20 cents each; directions for administering, 25 cents each; answer sheets (to be used with Booklet II or III only), hand-scoring, 4 cents each; IBM 805 or 1230, 7 cents each; fan keys or scoring stencils, 25 cents each; specimen set (includes booklet and directions for all parts), $2.50.

Designed to measure reading readiness and reading skills in the early years of the reading program. Two forms, A and B, except for the Readiness booklet, which has been published in Form B only. The scores yielded are: Reading Readiness Booklet, five scores, including relationships, eye-hand coordination, visual discrimination, auditory discrimination, vocabulary; Booklet 1, for Grade 1, 13 scores, including visual discrimination, auditory discrimination (three subscores plus total), vocabulary (three subscores plus total), story reading (two subscores plus total), and a total score; Booklets II and III, for Grades 2, 3, and 4, three scores, including word recognition, comprehension, and a total score. Untimed. Data on reliability and validity not available.

Durrell-Sullivan Reading Capacity and Achievement Tests, by Donald D. Durrell and Helen B. Sullivan. New York: Harcourt, Brace & World, Inc., 1937–1944. Primary Test (both Capacity and Achievement), $6.00 per 35; Reading Capacity Test, Intermediate $3.50 per 35; Reading Achievement Test, Intermediate, $4.50 per 35; manual, 30 cents; specimen set, 60 cents each test.

Designed to provide evidence concerning whether reading achievement of an individual pupil is up to his reading capacity. Intermediate test for Grades 3–6 and Primary test for Grades 2–4. There are two sections, Reading Capacity and Reading Achievement. Primary Test and Intermediate Reading Capacity Test available in one form each; Intermediate Reading Achievement Test available in Forms A and B. Each section contains a word-meaning part and a paragraph-meaning part. The Reading Achievement Test includes a spelling test and a written recall test which may be used at the option of the teacher. Administration time required is 55–65 minutes for the Primary tests, 30–40 minutes for the Intermediate Capacity, and 45–55 minutes for the Intermediate Achievement. Age and grade norms are available. Reliabilities according to publisher are: Reading Capacity score, .89 to .94; Reading Achievement score, .94 to .96; no reliability data are available for subtests. *Reference:* Buros (8:759–760).

Gates Primary Reading Tests, by Arthur I. Gates. Grade 1 and first half of Grade 2. New York: Bureau of Publications, Teachers College, Columbia University, 1926–1958. $1.50 per 35 tests of each type; specimen set

50 cents. A revision of the Gates Primary Silent Reading Tests which were first published in 1926.

Three separate booklets: Type PWR, word recognition; Type PSR, sentence meaning; Type PPR, paragraph reading. Working time, 15 minutes for each of first two types and 20 minutes for Type PPR. Each type exists in Forms 1, 2, and 3. Public school grade norms based on scores of about 250,000 pupils in schools throughout the country are available. The Educational Records Bureau has fall independent school norms for each of the three forms. No published data on reliability and validity.

Gates Advanced Primary Reading Tests, by Arthur I. Gates. New York: Bureau of Publications, Teachers College, Columbia University, 1926–1958. Two types, word recognition and paragraph reading. Printed in separate booklets, $1.50 per 35 tests; 50 cents per specimen set.

These tests are intended for second half of Grade 2 and Grade 3. They fit between the Gates Primary Reading Tests and the Gates Basic Reading Tests. Working time, 15 minutes for Type AWR, word recognition; 25 minutes for Type APR, paragraph reading. Data on reliability and validity are lacking, but, as is true of the Primary Reading Tests, experience indicates that these tests are reasonably valid. Public school grade and age norms are available, and the Educational Records Bureau has independent school norms on all forms, 1, 2, and 3.

Gates Basic Reading Test, by Arthur I. Gates. New York: Bureau of Publications, Teachers College, Columbia University, 1926–1958. $1.50 per 35 booklets for each form of each type; specimen set, 50 cents.

Designed for second half of Grade 3 through Grade 8. These tests are the second revision of the Gates Silent Reading Tests, first published in 1926 and revised in 1943. Three forms, each consisting of five booklets designed to measure the following types of reading ability: Type GS, reading to appreciate the general significance of a paragraph; Type ND, reading to note details; Type UD, reading to understand precise directions; Type LC, level of comprehension; Type RV, reading vocabulary. Time required is 8 to 10 minutes each for Types GS, ND, and UD, and 20 minutes each for Types LC and RV. All responses are recorded in the test booklets. Reliability coefficients reported by the author, based on alternate-form method, are between .80 and .90.

Iowa Silent Reading Tests, new ed., Elementary test, by H. A. Greene and V. H. Kelley. New York: Harcourt, Brace & World, Inc., 1933–1956. $4.50 per 35 tests; $2.45 per 35 answer sheets; machine keys, 60 cents; specimen set, 40 cents.

A revision of the older form published in 1933. Eight subtests include rate, comprehension, directed reading, word meaning, paragraph comprehension, sentence meaning, location of information, (which consists of alphabetizing), and the use of the index. Forms Am, Bm, Cm, and Dm, yielding comparable results. Working time, 49 minutes. Raw scores are converted to standard scores, thus providing a basis for a profile in graphic form. Hand scoring for all forms; machine scoring for Forms Cm and Bm. The authors' reliabilities for the subtests, found by means of the Spearman-Brown formula, range from .61 for sentence meaning to .94 for alphabetizing. The reliability of the median standard score is reported as .93. Reliability coefficients obtained in a study at the Educational Records Bureau are in rather close agreement with the publisher's reliability (37). The Educational Records Bureau has independent school norms for Form Cm.

Iowa Silent Reading Tests, new ed., Advanced test, by H. A. Greene, A. N. Jorgensen, and V. H. Kelley. New York: Harcourt, Brace, & World, Inc., 1927–1943. $6.00 per 35 tests; $2.45 per 35 answer sheets; machine keys, 60 cents; specimen set, 40 cents.

These tests, which consist of Forms Am, Bm, Cm, and Dm, are similar to the elementary tests just described. There are nine subtests: rate, comprehension, directed reading, poetry comprehension, word meaning, sentence meaning, paragraph comprehension, location of information, (including use of index), and selection of key words. Raw scores may be changed into standard scores and arranged in the form of a graphic profile. Data at the Educational Records Bureau on independent school pupils indicate that standard scores on the elementary and advanced forms do not seem to be directly comparable. The score on the test as a whole is the median score, or middle one of the nine part scores when they are arranged in order of size. Working time, 45 minutes. According to authors' manual, Spearman-Brown reliabilities of parts range from .68 for poetry comprehension to .87 for word meaning. Reliability of median standard score, .92. Adapted for machine scoring. Independent school norms for all four forms may be obtained from the Educational Records Bureau.

Nelson-Denny Reading Test, by M. J. Nelson and E. C. Denny. Boston: Houghton Mifflin Company, 1929–1960. Test booklets, $4.95 per 35; self-marking answer sheets, $2.55 per 35; IBM 805 answer sheets, $3.30 per 100; IBM 805 right keys, 50 cents per set; examiner's manual, 42 cents each; class record sheets, 99 cents per 35; specimen set, 75 cents.

This test provides scores for vocabulary, comprehension, and reading rate. The vocabulary test consists of 100 words, and the paragraph test contains nine selections with four questions on each. Working time, 30 minutes. Two forms, A and B. Responses are recorded on an answer sheet, and scoring is facilitated through the use of the Clapp-Young self-marking carbon paper device. Norms based on scores of more than 21,000 high school and college students provided in percentile and grade-equivalent terms for each of Grades 9–16. Special adult norms provided for use with superior students and adults. Useful as a means of surveying reading ability in high schools and colleges.

Traxler Reading Tests, by Arthur E. Traxler. *Silent Reading Test,* Grade 7–10; *High School Reading Test,* Grades 10–12. Indianapolis: Bobbs-Merrill Company, 1934–1942. $4.20 per 35 copies of either test, or 15 cents per copy in smaller quantities; teacher's handbook, 30 cents each; specimen set, 50 cents.

The Silent Reading Test contains three parts: reading rate and story comprehension, word meaning, and paragraph comprehension. Working time, 46 minutes. Forms 1, 2, 3, and 4, the last two of which are adapted for machine scoring. The High School Reading Test contains two parts: reading rate and story comprehension, and main ideas in paragraphs. Suited to machine scoring. Working time, 45 minutes. Forms A and B. Public school percentiles for part scores and total scores are available for both tests. Independent school percentile norms, for Grades 6, 7, and 8 have been prepared for the lower test at the Educational Records Bureau. Reliability of Silent Reading Test, based on correlations of two forms of the test administered to pupils at a single grade level: average reliability of part scores, .80; total score, .92. Average reliability of part scores in High School Reading Test, .81; estimated reliability of total score, .93. Correlation with Cooperative Reading Comprehension Test, with time interval of several months, .71; with Diagnostic Reading Tests: Survey Section, .70 (41).

ANNOTATED LIST OF ORAL READING TESTS

Gilmore Oral Reading Test, by John V. Gilmore. New York: Harcourt, Brace & World, Inc., 1952. $2.50 per 35 record blanks; set of reading paragraphs, $1.80 each; manual of directions, 50 cents; specimen set, 60 cents.

An individual oral reading test designed for Grades 1–8. Forms A and B. Yields three scores: accuracy, comprehension, and rate. Summary check list of difficulties and errors. Grade equivalents for accuracy and comprehension scores. Requires 15 to 20 minutes for administration. A promising appearing oral test on which little research has thus far been done. *Reference:* Buros (8:767–768).

Gray Oral Reading Tests, by William S. Gray. Indianapolis: Bobbs-Merrill Company, 1965. $3.30 per 35 booklets; $1.60 per set of reading passages, one form; manual, 50 cents; specimen set, including examiner booklet and manual for one form, 50 cents.

A successor to one of the oldest reading tests, the Gray Standardized Oral Reading Paragraphs Test. Very useful for individual measurement of oral reading ability of elementary school pupils. Thirteen paragraphs arranged in order of increasing difficulty. Examiner keeps time and records types of errors. Four forms, A, B, C, and D. Separate and combined norms and grade equivalents for boys and girls.

Reading Diagnostic Record for High School and College Students, by Ruth Strang. New York: Bureau of Publications, Teachers College, Columbia University, 1938; revised, 1952. 35 cents per set (manual, record blank, and oral reading passages); 30 cents per set in quantities of ten or more.

A guide for teachers who are making a comprehensive study of reading difficulties of individual students. Contains oral reading test consisting of four passages. Manual of directions and 24-page record blank.

Diagnostic Reading Tests, Section IV, Part 1, Oral, by Committee on Diagnostic Reading Tests, Inc. Mountain Home, N. C.: The Committee. Test booklet, 20 cents; directions for administering, 25 cents.

This test was included in the listing of the Diagnostic Reading Tests, but it may be obtained separately from the rest of the battery, if desired.

ANNOTATED LIST OF READINESS TESTS

Harrison-Stroud Reading Readiness Profiles, by M. Lucile Harrison and James B. Stroud. Boston: Houghton Mifflin Company, 1949–1956. Booklets, $4.20 per 35; letter card, 9 cents each; letter card mask, 9 cents; specimen set, 66 cents.

These tests are based on the assumption that readiness to learn to read includes five abilities, as measured by the following five subtests: Using Symbols; Making Visual Discriminations; Using the Context; Making Auditory Discriminations; Using Context and Auditory Clues. A total score is obtained in addition to scores on these subtests. The sixth subtest is optional. This is an individually administered test that enables the teacher to determine how well a pupil knows the names of capital and lower case letters. One form. For use in kindergarten and beginning of Grade 1. Difficulty level seems somewhat better suited to the kindergarten than to pupils entering the first grade. Working time, 76 minutes. Public school percentile norms are available; independent school percentile norms have been prepared by the Educational Records Bureau. Little information on the reliability and validity of these tests has been published. *Reference:* Buros (8:775–776).

Lee-Clark Reading Readiness Test, 1962 Revision, by J. Murray Lee and Willis W. Clark. Monterey: California Test Bureau, 1931–1962. Booklets, $4.20 per 35; manual of directions, 25 cents each; tape-recorded directions for administration, $5.95; specimen set without tape, 50 cents; specimen set with tape, $6.45.

May be administered either orally by the examiner, or by means of tape-recorded directions. Test 1 (Matching) and Test 2 (Cross Out) are designed to measure visual discrimination and recognition of differences and similarities in letter symbols. Test 3 (Total Vocabulary and Following Instructions) measures concept formation. Test 4 (Identification of Letters and Words) tests the child's ability to recognize and differentiate word symbols. Testing time is about 20 minutes. Norms are provided for the end of kindergarten and the beginning of Grade 1. Spearman-Brown reliabilities reported to be in the range of .83 to .94 for the subtests, .92 for the total score.

Metropolitan Readiness Tests, by Gertrude H. Hildreth and Nellie L. Griffiths. New York: Harcourt, Brace & World, Inc., 1933–1950. $4.90 per 35 booklets; specimen set, 40 cents.

Consist of several subtests designed to measure readiness for reading and a number readiness test. Yields a reading readiness score, a number readiness score, and a total score. Working time, about 60 minutes. Forms R and S. There are public school percentile norms for the kindergarten and beginning of Grade 1, and the Educational Records Bureau has independent school norms. Reported alternate-form reliabilities for public school pupils beginning Grade 1 are as follows: reading readiness score, .83; number readiness score, .84; total score, .89. In a study based on 143 independent school pupils entering Grade 1, a Kuder-Richardson reliability coefficient of .85 was obtained for the number readiness test, and a reliability of .90 was found for the total score. These reliabilities for public school and independent school pupils are in close agreement, and they are fairly high for tests administered at the beginning of Grade 1. There is some evidence that the Metropolitan Readiness Tests have considerable value for predicting achievement in the primary grades. Correlations of scores of 38 independent school pupils on the Metropolitan Readiness Tests and the Metropolitan Achievement Tests, Primary I Battery, with a time interval of about five months were as follows: reading readiness score vs. reading achievement, .79; number readiness score vs. number achievement, .64; total readiness score vs. total achievement, .79. For small groups of independent school pupils, significant correlations were also found between Metropolitan Readiness scores obtained at beginning of Grade 1 and achievement on Metropolitan Achievement Tests, Primary II Battery, administered near the end of Grade 2, and achievement on the Metropolitan Primary III Battery given in the latter part of Grade 3 (40).

New York Test of Arithmetical Meanings, by J. Wayne Wrightstone, Joseph Justman, Morris Pincus, and Ruth

M. Lowe. New York: Harcourt, Brace & World, Inc., 1956. $4.00 per 35 Level 1 booklets; $3.30 per 35 Level 2 booklets; 60 cents per specimen set.

This test may serve as both a numbers readiness test and a test of arithmetical understandings acquired in Grades 1 and 2. One form, two levels. Level 1 is designed to sample concepts acquired before and during the first grade; Level 2 covers arithmetical concepts and processes taught in Grades 1 and 2. Working time, about 60 minutes, arranged in two 30-minute sittings. There are public school percentile norms for each level.

REFERENCES

1. *ACT General Information Bulletin,* Iowa City, Iowa: The American College Testing Program, 1965. Pp. 32.
2. Baron, Denis and Bernard, Harold W. *Evaluation Techniques for Classroom Teachers.* New York: McGraw-Hill Book Company, Inc., 1958. Pd. xi + 297.
3. Bauernfeind, Robert H. *Building A School Testing Program.* Boston: Houghton Mifflin Company, 1963. Pp. xvii + 343.
4. Bloom, B. S. "The 1955 Normative Study of the Tests of General Educational Development," *School Review,* LXIV (March 1956), 110–124.
5. Bradfield, James M. and Moredock, H. Stewart. *Measurement and Evaluation in Education.* New York: The Macmillan Company, 1957. Pp. xiv + 509.
6. Brown, Frederick G. and Wolins, Leroy. "An Empirical Evaluation of the American College Testing Program," *Personnel and Guidance Journal,* XLIII (January 1965), 451–456.
7. Buros, Oscar K. (ed.). *The Fourth Mental Measurements Yearbook.* Highland Park, N.J.: The Gryphon Press, 1953. Pp. xvii + 1164.
8. Buros, Oscar K. (ed.). *The Fifth Mental Measurements Yearbook.* Highland Park, N.J.: The Gryphon Press, 1959. Pp. xxvii + 1292.
9. Buros, Oscar K. (ed.). *Tests in Print.* Highland Park, N.J.: The Gryphon Press, 1961. Pp. xxix + 479.
10. Committee on Diagnostic Reading Tests, Inc. *Diagnostic Reading Tests: A History of Their Construction and Validation.* New York: The Committee, 1952. Pp. 56.
11. Committee on the Evaluation of the Tyler Fact-Finding Study of the American Council on Education. *Conclusions and Recommendations on a Study of the General Educational Development Testing Program.* Washington: American Council on Education, 1956. Pp. xii + 72.
12. Cronbach, Lee J. *Essentials of Psychological Testing,* 2nd ed. New York: Harper & Row, Publishers, 1960. Pp. xxii + 650.
13. Davis, Frederick B. "Fundamental Factors of Comprehension in Reading," *Psychometrika,* IX (September 1944), 185–197.

14. Ebel, Robert L. *Measuring Educational Achievement.* East Lansing, Mich.: Michigan State University, 1965. Pp. 496.

15. Educational Records Bureau. "The Interpretation and Use of Scaled Scores," *1937 Achievement Testing Program of the Educational Records Bureau,* pp. 13–36. Educational Records Bulletin 20. New York: Educational Records Bureau, June 1937. Pp. xii + 134.

16. Flanagan, John C. *The Cooperative Achievement Tests: A Bulletin Reporting the Basic Principles and Procedures Used in the Development of Their System of Scaled Scores.* Princeton, N.J.: Educational Testing Service, December 1939. Pp. v +41.

17. Foster, James M., and Danskin, David G. "The American College Test (ACT) Tested Three Ways," *Personnel and Guidance Journal,* XLIII (May 1965), 904–909.

18. Greene, Edward B. "The Michigan Vocabulary Profile Test After Ten Years," *Educational and Psychological Measurement,* XI (Summer 1951), 208–211.

19. Greene, Harry A., Jorgensen, Albert N., and Gerberich, J. Raymond. *Measurement and Evaluation in the Secondary School,* 2nd ed. New York: Longmans, Green & Co., Inc., 1954. Pp. xxii + 690.

20. Harrison, M. Lucile, and Stroud, James B. *The Harrison-Stroud Reading Readiness Profiles Teacher's Manual.* Boston: Houghton Mifflin Company, 1956. Pp. 24.

21. Inglis, Alexander. "A Vocabulary Test for High School and College Students," *English Leaflet,* XXIII (October 1923), 1–13.

22. Luntz, Lester. "Some Reliability and Validity Data on the Dimond-Pflieger Problems of Democracy Test, Form Am," *1955 Achievement Testing Program in Independent Schools and Supplementary Studies,* pp. 69–72. Educational Records Bulletin 66. New York: Educational Records Bureau, July 1955. Pp. xiv + 80.

23. National Society for the Study of Education. *The Impact and Improvement of School Testing Programs. The Sixty-second Yearbook of the National Society for the Study of Education.* Chicago: The University of Chicago Press, 1963. Pp. xii + 304.

24. North, Robert D. "An Evaluation of the STEP Listening Test for the Independent School Testing Program," *1958 Achievement Testing Program in Independent Schools and Supplementary Studies,* pp. 61–68. Educational Records Bulletin 72. New York: Educational Records Bureau, July 1958. Pp. xii + 79.

25. North, Robert D. "Trial Use of the 1959 Edition of the Metropolitan Achievement Tests in Some ERB Member Schools," *1959 Achievement Testing Program in Independent Schools and Supplementary Studies,* pp. 61–74. Educational Records Bulletin 74. New York: Educational Records Bureau, July 1959. Pp. xii + 104.

26. North, Robert D. "An Appraisal of Independent School Results on the Primary Levels of the Metropolitan Achievement Tests, 1959 Edition," *1960 Achievement Testing Program in Independent Schools and Supplementary Studies,* pp. 55–66. Educational Records Bulletin 77. New York: Educational Records Bureau, July 1960. Pp. xii + 82.

27. North, Robert D. "Results of the ERB Mathematics Tests in the 1962 Spring Program," *1962 Achievement Testing Program in Independent Schools and Supplementary Studies,* pp. 57–60. Educational Records Bulletin 82. New York: Educational Records Bureau, July 1962. Pp. xii + 75.

28. North, Robert D. "The 1964 Edition of the Stanford Achievement Test: Description and Initial Appraisal of Independent School Program Results," *1964 Achievement Testing Program in Independent Schools and Supplementary Studies,* pp. 57–66. Educational Records Bulletin 86. New York: Educational Records Bureau, July 1964. Pp. xii +70.

29. Remmers, H. H., Gage, N. L., and Rummel, J. Francis. *A Practical Introduction to Measurement and Evaluation.* New York: Harper and Row, Publishers, 1960. Pp. xiii + 370.

30. Schwartz, Alfred, and Tiedeman, Stuart C. (with the assistance of Donald G. Wallace). *Evaluating Student Progress in the Secondary School.* New York: Longmans, Green & Co., Inc., 1957. Pp. xi + 434.

31. Smith, Eugene R., Tyler, Ralph W., and the Evaluation Staff. *Appraising and Recording Student Progress,* Chapter X. (Report of the Eight-Year Study of the Progressive Education Association.) New York: McGraw-Hill Book Company, Inc., 1942. Pp. xxiv + 550.

32. Stake, Robert E., and Hastings, J. Thomas. "The Stanford Achievement Battery, 1964," *Personnel and Guidance Journal,* XLIII (October 1964), 178–184.

33. Stalnaker, John M. "Essay Examinations Reliably Read," *School and Society,* XLVI (1937), 671–672.

34. Stalnaker, John M. "The Essay Type of Examination," *Educational Measurement* (ed. by E. F. Lindquist),. pp. 495–530. Washington: American Council on Education, 1951. Pp. xx + 820.

35. Thomas, R. Murray. *Judging Student Progress,* 2nd ed. New York: Longmans, Green & Co., Inc. 1960. Pp. x + 518.

36. Townsend, Agatha. "A Study of the Lincoln Diagnostic Spelling Test," *1943 Achievement Testing Program in Independent Schools and Supplementary Studies,* pp. 49–53. Educational Records Bulletin 38. New York: Educational Records Bureau, June 1943. Pp. xiv + 54.

37. Townsend, Agatha. "A Study of the Revised New Edition of the Iowa Silent Reading Tests," *1944 Fall Testing Program in Independent Schools and Supplementary Studies,* pp. 31–39. Educational Records Bulletin 42. New York: Educational Records Bureau, January 1945. Pp. x + 50.

38. Townsend, Agatha. "A Report on the Use of the Lincoln Intermediate Spelling Test," *1947 Fall Testing Program in Independent Schools and Supplementary Studies,* pp. 40–48. Educational Records Bulletin 49. New York: Educational Records Bureau, February 1948. Pp. xii + 70.

39. Townsend, Agatha. "A Review of the Crary American

History Test," *1953 Achievement Testing Program in Independent Schools and Supplementary Studies.* pp. 67–71. Educational Records Bulletin 61. New York: Educational Records Bureau, July 1953, Pp. xii + 86.

40. Traxler, Arthur E. "Reliability and Predictive Value of the Metropolitan Readiness Tests," *1946 Fall Testing Program in Independent Schools and Supplementary Studies,* pp. 49–58. Educational Records Bulletin 47. New York: Educational Records Bureau, February 1947. Pp. x + 58.

41. Traxler, Arthur E. "Correlations between Scores on Various Reading Tests Administered Several Months Apart," *1949 Achievement Testing Program in Independent Schools and Supplementary Studies,* pp. 78–82. Educational Records Bulletin 52. New York: Educational Records Bureau, July 1949. Pp. xiv + 88.

42. Traxler, Arthur E. "Reliability and Validity of A Brief Survey of Arithmetic Skills, Revised Edition," *1953 Fall Testing Program in Independent Schools and Supplementary Studies,* pp. 76–84. Educational Records Bulletin 62. New York: Educational Records Bureau, February 1954. Pp. xii + 84.

43. Traxler, Arthur E., and Townsend, Agatha. "Some Data on the Results of the Cummings World History Test among Independent School Pupils," *1952 Achievement Testing Program in Independent Schools and Supplementary Studies,* pp. 77–78. Educational Records Bulletin 59. New York: Educational Records Bureau, July 1952. Pp. xiv + 86.

44. Traxler, Arthur E. "Some Data on the Results of the Sequential Tests of Educational Progress (STEP), Level 3, Form A, for Small Groups of Pupils in Two Independent Schools for Girls," *1958 Achievement Testing Program in Independent Schools and Supplementary Studies,* pp. 69–73. Educational Records Bulletin 72. New York: Educational Records Bureau, July 1958. Pp. xii + 79.

45. Traxler, Arthur E. "Some Data on the Difficulty, Reliability, and Validity of a New Spelling Test for the Primary Grades," *1960 Achievement Testing Program in Independent Schools and Supplementary Studies,* pp. 67–73. Educational Records Bulletin 77. New York: Educational Records Bureau, July 1960. Pp. xii + 82.

46. Traxler, Arthur E. "Some Further Information on the Cooperative French Listening Comprehension Test Among Independent School Pupils," *1962 Achievement Testing Program in Independent Schools and Supplementary Studies,* pp. 61–62. Educational Records Bulletin 82. New York: Educational Records Bureau, July 1962. Pp. xii + 75.

47. Traxler, Arthur E. "Development of a Vocabulary Test for High School Pupils and College Freshmen," *1962 Fall Testing Program in Independent Schools and Supplementary Studies,* pp. 67–73. Educational Records Bulletin 83. New York: Educational Records Bureau, February 1963. Pp. xii + 84.

48. Traxler, Arthur E. "Difficulty, Reliability, and Validity of the Cooperative Mathematics Tests: Geometry, Form A, Among Independent School Pupils," *1963 Achievement Testing Program in Independent Schools and Supplementary Studies,* pp. 63–66. Educational Records Bulletin 84. New York: Educational Records Bureau, July 1963. Pp. xii + 83.

49. Traxler, Arthur E. "The 1964 Edition of the Cooperative Biology, Chemistry, and Physics Tests: Difficulty, Reliability, and Correlation With School Marks," *1964 Achievement Testing Program in Independent Schools and Supplementary Studies,* pp. 67–70. Educational Records Bulletin 86. New York: Educational Records Bureau, July 1964. Pp. xii + 70.

50. Traxler, Arthur E. "Some Aspects of the Vocabulary of Independent Secondary School Pupils," *1964 Fall Testing Program in Independent Schools and Supplementary Studies,* pp. 44–49. Educational Records Bulletin 87. New York: Educational Records Bureau, February 1965. Pp. xii + 59.

51. Triggs, Frances Oralind. "The Diagnosis of Reading Deficiencies as an Aid to Remedial Work," *Educational and Psychological Measurement,* VII (Autumn 1947), 638–646.

52. Tyler, Ralph W. *The Fact-Finding Study of the Testing Program of the United States Armed Forces Institute.* Washington: American Council on Education, 1955. Pp. vi + 304 + 35. (Mimeographed.)

53. Vecchione, Nicholas, "A Further Study of the Cooperative French Listening Comprehension Test," *1960 Achievement Testing Program in Independent Schools and Supplementary Studies,* pp. 74–82. Educational Records Bulletin 77. New York: Educational Records Bureau, July 1960. Pp. xii + 82.

Note: The Gates reading tests listed and annotated on pages 91 and 92 are being replaced by the new Gates-MacGinitie reading tests and will not be available after June 30, 1966. Information concerning the new tests may be obtained from the Teachers College Press, Teachers College, Columbia University, New York, N.Y.

CHAPTER VII

Appraisal of Personal Qualities and Interests: Tests and Inventories

ACCURATE, OBJECTIVE INFORMATION IN REGARD to aptitude and achievement, such as may be obtained from the tests listed in Chapters V and VI, is very important in a guidance program, but it fills in only part of the picture for each individual pupil. Most teachers and guidance officers are aware that personal qualities and interests are fully as important in a pupil's academic and out-of-school adjustment as are those more easily measured factors of intelligence and achievement. There is an increasing demand for valid and reliable records of personality development to assist the school in its guidance program.

There are three broad approaches to the evaluation of personal qualities. One of these is by means of tests, usually of the paper-and-pencil sort. A second is by means of more informal procedures involving anecdotal records, ratings, descriptions of behavior, and sociometric devices. A third approach is through the use of projective techniques of a laboratory or clinical nature.

Under ideal conditions, anecdotal records, rating devices, and behavior descriptions undoubtedly have more to offer to a guidance program than do personality tests which, for the most part, are still in an experimental stage in that their validity has not been clearly established. The more informal devices are, however, much more time-consuming than tests. Therefore, it is probable that for some time to come many schools which have established guidance programs will not be able to employ informal evaluative procedures on a school-wide basis— at least until a long and thorough program of teacher education in guidance philosophy has taken place. In the meantime, personality questionnaires and interest inventories furnish almost the only available means of systematically collecting helpful, although admittedly inadequate and imperfect, information in this important area.

In the hands of well-trained clinical psychologists and psychiatrists, projective techniques, as, for example, the Rorschach and the Thematic Apperception Test, are probably the most revealing of all devices for use in studying personality. It is to be noted, however, that it is the expertness of the personnel using these devices, not the devices as such, which lends special validity to their employment in the study of personality. The great majority of schools do not yet employ such specialists, and large numbers do not have access to such services in their own community, in their own county, or even in their own geographical area. Without expertness in their administration, interpretation, and application, the more esoteric projective techniques are likely to be ineffective, or dangerous, or both.

EXTENT OF ATTEMPTS TO MEASURE PERSONALITY

Notwithstanding the nebulousness of this field, there have been numerous attempts to devise instruments for the appraisal of personality. In 1932 Maller (*81*) published a bibliography of some 300 character and personality measures. Hildreth's *A Bibliography of Mental Tests and Rating Scales* (*58*), published in 1933 and revised in 1939, contained 402 titles dealing with the broad field of character and personality, and a supplement (*59*) issued in 1945 added 169 titles. Buros' *Fourth Mental Measurements* Yearbook (*18*) added 62 measures in the field of character and personality, attitudes and

97

opinions, interests, and social adjustment published since 1945. The *Fifth Mental Measurements Yearbook* (*19*) lists a total of 145 instruments of these types. It is probable that the number of unpublished questionnaires and devices for rating personality is even greater.

There are so many inferior instruments purporting to measure personality that busy teachers and counselors cannot find sufficient time to inspect all of them to find the few that hold some promise of serving a practical purpose. The main objective of this chapter is to provide a simple, nontechnical discussion of personality measurement, and a carefully selected list of instruments for counselors who may contemplate using personality measures but who do not have time to survey the whole field in order to find those best suited to their needs. But it is recommended that not even the questionnaires and tests chosen for listing in this chapter be used until these instruments have been carefully studied and until the school has made sure that it is staffed for effective interpretation and use of the personality scores, the meaning of which may seem very obscure to most teachers.

DEFINITION OF PERSONALITY

One obstacle to the measurement of personality is that there is no general agreement on a definition of personality or on the number and nature of the traits of which it is composed. In fact, there is difference of opinion in regard to the existence of generalized personality traits. Some authorities insist that the immediate situation largely determines behavior, and, consequently, personality, which in an individual may change markedly as conditions vary. It is observed, for example, that a boy may be repressed and submissive in the classroom but very expressive and dominant on the playground; or that a pupil may be honest where money is concerned but dishonest when taking a test. Conclusions of this kind were reached nearly 40 years ago in the Character Education Inquiry (*49, 50, 51*), which remains the most extensive study of personality ever conducted.

If it is true that personality is determined by the immediate situation, its adequate measurement becomes an almost impossible task, for innumerable tests will be required in order to obtain an adequate sampling. Even if the tests were available, it would seem that measurement in this broad field would be of doubtful value because the personality of a given individual, from this point of view, would be too unstable ever to be described accurately.

The immediate environmental situation does, of course, color the personality of every individual appreciably. No one feels the same or behaves the same in the office, on the golf course, at a New Year's Eve celebration, and in Sunday morning devotion services. Nevertheless, nearly all individuals display enough consistency in behavior, even under widely varying situations, so that those who know one well know what to expect of him. In other words, within limits, personality qualities seem consistent and relatively permanent in all normal individuals. If an occasional person is so erratic that his specific behavior is utterly unpredictable, that very erratic quality is in itself a dependable basis of prediction, and one that may ultimately cause the individual to be institutionalized unless therapeutic measures are used.

If we accept the more common assumption that personality is a more or less definite set of attributes, made up largely of a number of generalized traits, the fact that there is difficulty in defining it and lack of agreement concerning its components should not be an insuperable obstacle to measurement. A similar situation exists with respect to intelligence, yet tests in that field have been in general use for years and have shown their worth in a guidance program.

For purposes of this discussion, personality will be defined as the totality of an individual's behavior in social situations. Behavior includes not only overt acts but inward feeling tone produced by the situation as interpreted by the individual through introspection. It is necessary to include the inward reaction, since the great majority of personality tests proceed by attempting to obtain from the subject statements about how he feels in various situations. The introspective nature of the usual paper-and-pencil test of personality is the feature which, more than anything else, distinguishes this kind of instrument from intelligence and achievement tests.

Tests of intelligence and tests of achievement in certain fields, as, for example, reading and English, provide much evidence about personality, since intelligence and such abilities as reading and English affect an individual's behavior in a social situation. Mental ability has long been recognized as one of the components of personality. A test of intelligence should, without doubt, be a part of a comprehensive inquiry into the personality of a given individual. But functioning in relationship with intelligence and with the more specialized skills or abilities, there is a whole complex of attributes which have thus far not been analyzed with precision but which undoubtedly play a basic role in adjustment.

Although the words "personality" and "character" have somewhat different connotations, the term "personality tests" is sometimes used as practically synonymous with "character tests"; tests of attitude and interest fall outside the scope of the term. As used in the present discussion, the term "personality" is more inclusive, and certain inventories of interests and social attitudes will be included in this chapter.

Most personality tests are designed to yield a quantitative evaluation of personality traits in the form of scores or divisions on a scale. These scores, considered singly in their numerical form, have little meaning. They are useful only if they make possible a better *description* of personality. It is a valid, reliable, and meaningful *description* of personality that counselors need in guidance. Before introducing a new test for measuring personality, a school would do well to try it out experimentally with a few pupils to see whether or not it contributes to the description of the personality of the individual pupil.

SURVEY OF PROCEDURES FOR APPRAISING PERSONALITY

Instruments for the measurement of personality may be divided into two general classes, global and atomistic. In the first class of instruments of appraisal, personality as a whole is studied qualitatively and intensively by means of projective techniques, while in the latter class an attempt is made to analyze personality into its component parts. The majority of the available personality tests have emphasized the atomistic approach; but there are several noteworthy tests of the global type, and the number of these instruments is increasing.

These two classes of instruments are frequently called projective and nonprojective devices. A projective device is one which stimulates the individual to project his own personality into the test situation, and allows him freedom to do so. There is a helpful distinction here, although, strictly speaking, the term nonprojective is likely to be something of a misnomer, since there is hardly a test of any sort which does not, on occasion, have projective overtones, or which cannot be used as a projective device by a skillful psychologist. The terms "nonstructured" and "structured" are perhaps more nearly descriptive of the basic technique used in the global and atomistic devices, respectively.

FREE ASSOCIATION METHOD

The basic method used in assessing personality as a whole, as exemplified in projective devices or nonstructured instruments, is free association. An old and well-known test which utilizes free association based on a list of stimulus words is the Kent-Rosanoff Free Association Test. This test was published in 1910 in a monograph by Kent and Rosanoff (65) on free association among the mentally ill. The test has been used quite often by research workers in the field of personality, but it has seldom been employed in a school guidance program, probably because it is difficult to interpret a score on a free association test of this type. It has been found useful, however, as a counseling instrument in special cases.

Since the mid-1930s the Rorschach Ink Blot Test (98) has attracted more attention and has been the subject of more research and greater controversy than any other projective test. The research bibliography related to this test is no doubt more extensive than that for any other personality test regardless of type. As early as 1935, Hertz (56) compiled a bibliography of 152 titles dealing with the Rorschach, and numerous articles on the test have been published each year since that date. Buros' *Mental Measurements Yearbooks* (16:88–90; 17:124–132; 18: 202–213; 19:254–273) provide a bibliography of 2297 titles concerning this intriguing instrument. The uniqueness of the test is, no doubt, partly responsible for the widespread interest in it. The stimuli, as the name indicates, are a series of ink blots which are presented visually to the subject with a request that he state what each blot suggests to him. The ink blots were chosen with great care some 45 years ago by Hermann Rorschach, a Swiss psychiatrist and psychoanalyst, who had studied the technique for several years. When the Rorschach technique was introduced in the United States in the early 1920s, little attention was at first paid to it, and most of that was casually given. But gradually some of the leading psychologists began to see possibilities in this instrument and to devote a great deal of time to it. Beck (8, 9, 10), Klopfer (67, 68), Hertz (56, 57), and Rapaport (93) are among the leading authorities in the United States on the interpretation and use of the Rorschach.

Some psychologists believe that the Rorschach is the most valuable test of personality now available for clinical use. However, it is seldom used by school personnel workers, for a long period of training and experience is needed by one who attempts to interpret the responses. The procedure of administration is deceptively simple, but this test definitely should not be used in a counseling situation unless someone who can qualify as a Rorschach specialist is available to study and interpret the responses of the subjects.

There is a somewhat similar newer projective device, the Howard Ink Blot Test by James W. Howard (61). This instrument is claimed to have greater diagnostic sensitivity than the Rorschach, but the supporting evidence for this claim is sparse. Another instrument of this general type is the Holtzman Inkblot Technique, developed by Wayne H. Holtzman and published by The

Psychological Corporation. It has two forms, A and B, consisting of 45 blots in each, and provides percentile norms for 22 response variables in the age range of 5 to adult.

The second most important projective test now used in the United States is, in all probability, the Thematic Apperception Test (84), which was first published by Morgan and Murray in 1935. An extensive report of research on the test carried on in the Harvard University Psychological Clinic, *Explorations in Personality* (87), was published by Murray three years later, and from then on there was extensive interest in the test. This test, popularly known as the TAT, consists of a set of 20 picture cards presenting a variety of social situations which the subject is asked to tell a story about or to explain. Buros' *Mental Measurements Yearbooks* present a bibliography of 610 items pertaining to this test. The use of the TAT is somewhat less involved and difficult than the Rorschach, but it is definitely a clinical instrument and not one for ordinary school use. A detailed and helpful manual for the test was published by Tomkins (113). A modification of the TAT designed for use with Negro subjects has been prepared by Thompson (109).

Among the other free-association or projective tests which have become available in the United States are the Rosenzweig Picture-Frustration Study (100), which exists in a form for children and a revised form for adults; the Horn-Hellersberg Test (55), which is based on drawings from the Horn Art Aptitude Inventory and is designed for ages three and over; the Szondi Test (31), an involved clinical instrument devised by the Rumanian psychologist, Lipot Szondi, and introduced to this country by Susan K. Deri; the Goodenough Draw-A-Man Test, originally published by Florence L. Goodenough in 1926 and revised and extended by Dale B. Harris in 1963, yielding both an IQ and an evaluation of some personal characteristics (47); the Draw-A-Person Quality Scales by Wagner and Schubert (121); the Make A Picture Story (MAPS), equipped with a miniature theater, background settings, and 67 cutout figures; and the Rotter Incomplete Sentences Blank. The last two instruments are published by The Psychological Corporation.

DISGUISED AND PARTIALLY DISGUISED PERSONALITY TESTS

Most personality questionnaires are not tests in the usual sense of the term. They do not try out the individual to determine what he is able to do in a given situation. They are standardized questionnaires which ask the subject how he reacts or feels in various situations. The responses of the individual are useful if he does not know

the most desirable answer, or if he is entirely sincere and honest in his responses. The validity of the test depends largely upon the truthfulness of the responses. It has been shown that it is possible to influence the scores on such a test significantly by instructing the persons taking it to mark the test in such a way that they will get a desirable score.

Since the validity of personality inventories whose purpose is not disguised depends so largely upon the veracity of the responses, the value of such instruments for certain types of testing is greatly curtailed. The usefulness of this type of test for employment purposes, for example, or for testing candidates for entrance to college, is limited. There is a need for personality tests whose purpose is not immediately evident to the subject. Thus far, relatively few such tests have been devised.

The largest group of tests which were thoroughly disguised were those developed in connection with the Character Education Inquiry (49, 50, 51) some 40 years ago, but because they reproduced life situations, many of those employed in that inquiry were too elaborate for school use. Maller utilized a technique similar to that employed in the Character Education Inquiry in devising a group test of honesty in school work known as the Self-Marking Test. He reported reliability coefficients above .90 for this test (81).

An interesting example of a well-disguised personality test which was planned for school use was the Downey Will-Temperament Test. This test, which is now of historical interest only, was devised by June E. Downey (32) as a result of her interest in graphology as a means of expressing personality. The test was dependent entirely upon the subject's responses in situations involving handwriting, and the purpose of nearly all the subtests was well hidden from the subject. Unfortunately, however, numerous studies of the reliability and validity of the Downey test yielded discouraging results. Very few of the coefficients of reliability or validity were high enough to satisfy the criteria for a test that is to be used in individual diagnosis. In the hands of persons thoroughly acquainted with its limitations, the test was occasionally a useful laboratory tool—as, for example, in the Newman-Freeman-Holzinger study of identical twins (88)—but the test was not found to be practicable for general school use.

ADJUSTMENT QUESTIONNAIRES AND PSYCHONEUROTIC INVENTORIES

Although there are obvious limitations to the questionnaire method, the standardized questionnaire, or self-inventory, has become the most common instrument for the measurement of personality. There are so many tests of this type that only a small proportion of them can be included in the present discussion.

The Woodworth Personal Data Sheet is the oldest and one of the best known of the controlled-answer questionnaires. Woodworth based a series of questions calling for "yes" or "no" answers on symptoms that had been mentioned in studies of psychoneurotics. The questionnaire was adapted by Woodworth and Mathews for use with children. Many of the questions in Woodworth's sheet appear in modified form in more recent questionnaires.

In 1928, G. W. and F. H. Allport published the Allport Ascendance-Submission Scale, or the A-S Reaction study (5). This scale, which contains 35 multiple-choice questions for women and 33 for men, has been used in a variety of studies. A revision of the A-S Reaction Study for business use was prepared by R. O. Beckman (11).

One of the older and better known controlled-answer questionnaires for adolescents and adults is the Bernreuter Personality Inventory (13, 14). The research bibliography on this inventory is extensive, although attention to this instrument has declined in recent years. The inventory consists of 125 questions selected from Laird's C2 Test of Introversion-Extroversion, the Allports' A-S Reaction Study, Thurstone's Neurotic Inventory, and an earlier test for self-sufficiency by Bernreuter. The unique contribution made by Bernreuter is that, whereas the tests on which it was based furnished only a single measure of adjustment, Bernreuter scored his test with four different scales, thus making available measures of neurotic tendency, self-sufficiency, introversion-extroversion, and ascendance-submission. In 1934 Flanagan (38), using Hotelling's factor-analysis method, added two more scales for scoring the Bernreuter inventory. Flanagan called his scales self-confidence and sociability. The reliability of the Bernreuter scales compares favorably with that of many intelligence and achievement tests, but their validity, like the validity of nearly all personality tests, remains in doubt. The use of the Bernreuter seems to have decreased considerably since about 1945.

The Bell Adjustment Inventory (12), a test which is in form similar to the Bernreuter, was published in 1934. By means of a much simpler scoring procedure than that used by Bernreuter, Bell secured measures which he called home adjustment, health adjustment, social adjustment, and emotional adjustment. The test is designed for use in high school and college. The few studies of it that have been made suggest that it is one of the better inventories in this field. The adult form of this inventory, published in 1938, has a fifth scale, occupational adjustment.

Bell has also published The School Inventory, which purports to make possible a quick, yet reliable, quantita-tive statement of the school adjustment of senior high school pupils.

Among the available inventories of personal qualities, one which has been rather widely used is the Washburne Social Adjustment Inventory (122). It yields scores for truthfulness, sympathy, alienation, purpose, impulse judgment, control, happiness, and wishes.

The majority of the personality inventories are designed for use among senior high school and college students and adults. Several inventories have been devised, however, for use in the elementary school and junior high school. One of these is the Hildreth Personality and Interest Inventory, by Gertrude Hildreth. Initially published in 1935, with revisions up to 1959, this inventory has proved to be useful with children in the Grade 4–9 range. The IPAT Children's Personality Inventory, by Porter and Cattell, published by the Institute for Personality and Ability Testing in 1959, yields scores on 16 scales for children in the 8–12 age range. The title on the cover page of this test is *What You Do and What You Think*.

There is one battery which is designed to cover all levels from kindergarten to adult. This is the California Test of Personality, prepared by Thorpe, Clark, and Tiegs (112). The tests in this series, which were published from 1939 to 1953, provide a profile of scores on component tests grouped under personal adjustment and social adjustment. These authors have also issued the Mental Health Analysis, 1959 Revision, which is a series of four overlapping batteries covering Grade 4 to the adult level. In this set of tests, the number of questions within each category was increased, and the questions were spread throughout the inventory so that a pattern of desirable responses was less readily perceived by the pupil. The categories were classified under two general headings, liabilities and assets.

A number of the self-inventories of personal qualities, particularly those devised by Cattell and by Guilford and their associates, represent the application of factor analysis to the study of personality. Among the instruments produced by Cattell and his co-workers at the University of Illinois, in addition to the one mentioned above, are the 16-Personality Factor Questionnaire, the IPAT High School Personality Questionnaire, and the IPAT Humor Test of Personality.

Guilford and his associates have prepared the Guilford-Martin Personnel Inventory, the Guilford-Martin Inventory of Factors GAMIN, the Guilford-Martin Inventory of Factors STDCR, and the Guilford-Zimmerman Temperament Survey (42). An attempt is made in the last test to bring together, in one inventory, the factors previously found in the other four inventories. The qualities included in the Guilford-Zimmerman survey are (G)

General Activity, (R) Restraint, (A) Ascendence, (S) Sociability, (E) Emotional Stability, (O) Objectivity, (F) Friendliness, (T) Thoughtfulness, (P) Personal Relations, and (M) Masculinity.

Another technique that has been used to improve the validity of self-inventories is the casting of the items into a forced-choice format, which requires the individual to choose from a set of responses that are approximately equal in social acceptability—ego enhancement, self-effacement, or some other value loading. This technique is designed to prevent the individual from choosing responses with the principal aim of presenting himself in a favorable light. One inventory that utilizes this forced-choice type of item is the Edwards Personal Preference Schedule. It yields scores for 15 needs or motives—such as achievement, deference, order, exhibition, and autonomy—with norms for college students and adults. Other forced-choice questionnaires suitable for use with high school students, college students, and adults are the Gordon Personal Profile and the Gordon Personal Inventory. The Profile has scales for ascendency, responsibility, emotional stability, and sociability. The Inventory is scored for cautiousness, original thinking, personal relations, and vigor.

Among other noteworthy inventories of personal qualities published since 1949 are the Billett-Starr Youth Problems Inventory (1958); KD Proneness Scale and Checklist (1950–1953); Minnesota Counseling Inventory (1953–1957); Minnesota Multiphasic Personality Inventory, revised edition (1951); Mooney Problem Checklist, 1950 revision; Syracuse Scales of Social Relations (1958); Tennessee Self Concept Scale (1965); Thurstone Temperament Schedule (1950); and the Wood Behavior Preference Record (1953). Of these comparatively recent inventories, probably the largest amount of interest has centered on the Minnesota Multiphasic Personality Inventory. Buros' *Third, Fourth,* and *Fifth Mental Measurements Yearbooks* list 779 titles dealing with the *MMPI* (17:103–104; 18:126–130; 19:158–168). The research literature on this inventory is now more extensive than that concerned with any other nonprojective personality test.

ATTITUDE QUESTIONNAIRES AND SCALES

Chave (25) defined attitude as a complex of feelings, desires, fears, convictions, prejudices, or other tendencies that have given a set, or readiness to act, to a person because of varied experiences. In recent years, there have been many attempts to study attitudes, but most of these have not been very successful.

The most extensive and sustained work in attitude measurement was carried on some 35 years ago by Thurstone and his associates at the University of Chicago. This work resulted in an extensive set of scales for the measurement of social attitudes (110, 111). These scales are no longer available, but Thurstone's contributions to the measurement of attitudes deserve some attention. In the first place, Thurstone restricted the field which each instrument was designed to measure. In contrast to some test specialists who take the position that attitude is a broad and general aspect of personality, Thurstone said that attitude is affect for or against a psychological object. In accordance with this definition, his social attitude scales dealt with attitude toward individual social institutions, such as the church, the Constitution, communism, and war. This approach lent definiteness to the measurement of attitudes, but at the same time it required a large number of scales to provide comprehensive measurement in this field.

Thurstone's second contribution to the measurement of attitudes was the technique he developed for the construction of attitude scales. This technique was more elaborate than that used in most of the other investigations of attitudes. The first step in the procedure was the collection of statements about a given social institution from many different sources. The second step was the sorting, by a large number of judges, of the statements into several categories with respect to degree of favorableness toward the institution. The third step was the selection of about 20 statements, ranging from extreme favorableness to extreme unfavorableness toward the institution and the assignment of scale values to these statements. This was done by a statistical procedure based on the sorting by the judges. In scoring, the scale value of each statement with which the subject agreed was noted and a score was assigned which corresponded to the median scale value. Available data indicate that most of the Thurstone scales were fairly reliable. However, apparently because of small demand for measurement devices whose purpose is so highly specific, the publication of these scales was discontinued.

Remmers (94, 95) edited a series of Attitude Scales, the purpose of which is somewhat similar to that of the Thurstone scales. Remmers' method of constructing his scales resembles Thurstone's method in that it utilizes the principle that equally-often-observed differences are equal. The main difference in method is that whereas each of Thurstone's scales was designed to measure attitude toward one definite social institution, an attempt is made in Remmers' scales to measure attitude toward a large group or class of objects, such as attitude toward any school subject or attitude toward any vocation. The scales constructed by Remmers and his students may be used throughout the junior and senior high school and college. Although McNemar (80) and other authorities have criticized generalized attitude scales, these scales continue to serve a useful function in guidance programs when used in conjunction with other data.

INTEREST INVENTORIES

Interests, like attitudes, are difficult to measure with precision, but several useful instruments in this area have been devised. The Allport-Vernon Study of Values (116), which was published in 1931 and revised in 1951, is among the better-known scales for measuring dominant interests. This scale is aimed at the measurement of six basic types of interests: theoretical, economic, aesthetic, social, political, and religious. This classification is based on a scheme of ideal types proposed by Eduard Spranger, a German psychologist. This test is designed for high school and college students.

Because of their importance in guidance, vocational interests have no doubt been studied more intensively than any other type of interest. The Strong Vocational Interest Blanks (104) were for years the most widely used interest questionnaires, and they continue to be among the most extensively employed. The Strong blanks require the subject to indicate if he likes or dislikes various occupations, amusements, school subjects, types of people, and so forth. The men's blank is scored for 51 occupations, five occupational groups, and four other areas—masculinity-femininity, maturity of interest, specialization level, and occupational level. There is also a studiousness scale which was added by Young and Estabrooks (129). The women's blank may be scored with 29 occupational scales and a scale for masculinity-femininity.

The Strong blanks were standardized on the basis of the actual interests of persons in the occupations for which the scales were developed. They were designed primarily for use with college students and adults, and they seldom should be used below the junior year in high school. The reliabilities of the scales average about .85.

The greatest obstacle to the wider use of the Strong blank is the difficulty of its scoring. Since the blank must be scored separately with a scale for each occupation, hours are required to score by hand a single blank. Both the men's and the women's blanks, however, may be scored by special data processing equipment, and the men's blank is also set up for scoring on the IBM 805 Test-Scoring Machine, although this is also a long and tedious process. Scoring by special machines is the only practicable method for use with the Strong blank.

At present the fastest and most economical way of scoring the Strong tests is by means of mechanical equipment located at National Computer Service or Testscor, both in Minneapolis.

Much simpler scoring procedures are used in connection with a vocational interest inventory designed for high school and college use by Glen U. Cleeton (26). This instrument has not been the subject of nearly so much research as the Strong blank.

One of the most promising testing procedures applied in the field of interests is the paired-comparison technique, first exemplified in a doctor's dissertation by Weedon (123). The basis of this technique consists in preparing "preference" items in which each interest to be investigated is paired with every other interest, all stated in terms of behavior. Individuals are then asked to indicate which one of each pair they prefer to do, and the responses are treated statistically. An adaptation of this technique, in which the test items are presented in triads, is found in the Kuder Preference Record—Vocational (70), which was first published in 1934 and which has gone through a number of revisions. The most recent edition provides scores in ten broad areas which are reported in the form of a profile. There is also a verification scale for identifying unreliable scores.

The Kuder Preference Record—Personal, originally published in 1948, is a companion instrument which yields five preference scores and a verification score. The Kuder Preference Records are among the most carefully constructed instruments for the appraisal of interests. At present, the Preference Record—Vocational is probably the most widely used of all the interest measures.

Other interest measures are the Occupational Interest Inventory, by Lee and Thorpe, and the Vocational Interest Analyses, prepared by Roeber and Prideaux. The former inventory purports to measure interests in six fields: personal-social, natural, mechanical, business, the arts, and the sciences. This inventory was criticized by Dulsky in Buros' *Third Mental Measurements Yearbook* (17:667–668) on the basis that the six fields were too large and complex and contained too many diverse occupational activities. Roeber and Prideaux's Vocational Interest Analysis represents an attempt to meet this kind of criticism through providing scores for categories within the broader areas covered by the Occupational Interest Inventory. Research data are not available for an adequate appraisal of the Vocational Interest Analyses or the parent instrument, the Occupational Interest Inventory.

Nearly all available interest measures are intended for use in high schools and colleges and with adults. How-

REPORT FORM—STRONG VOCATIONAL INTEREST BLANK—FOR MEN

#		OCCUPATION	STD. SCORE
1	I	ARTIST	11
2		PSYCHOLOGIST	29
3		ARCHITECT	20
4		PHYSICIAN	27
5		PSYCHIATRIST	31
6		OSTEOPATH	20
7		DENTIST	24
8		VETERINARIAN	12
9	II	MATHEMATICIAN	19
10		PHYSICIST	20
11		CHEMIST	37
12		ENGINEER	40
13	III	PRODUCTION MANAGER	47
14	IV	FARMER	40
15		CARPENTER	25
16		FOREST SERVICE MAN	29
17		AVIATOR	31
18		PRINTER	38
19		MATH. SCI. TEACHER	45
20		INDUSTRIAL ARTS TEACHER	31
21		VOC. AGRICULT. TEACHER	29
22		POLICEMAN	30
23		ARMY OFFICER	43
24	V	Y.M.C.A. PHYSICAL DIRECTOR	25
25		PERSONNEL MANAGER	46
26		PUBLIC ADMINISTRATOR	48
27		VOCATIONAL COUNSELOR	37
28		PHYSICAL THERAPIST	37
29		SOCIAL WORKER	31
30		SOCIAL SCIENCE TEACHER	27
31		BUS. EDUC. TEACHER	45
32		SCHOOL SUPT	27
33		MINISTER	26
34	VI	MUSICIAN	26
35		MUSIC TEACHER	28
36	VII	C.P.A. OWNER	29
37	VIII	SENIOR C.P.A.	53
38		ACCOUNTANT	53
39		OFFICE WORKER	51
40		CREDIT MANAGER	53
41		PURCHASING AGENT	37
42		BANKER	26
43		PHARMACIST	28
44		MORTICIAN	22
45	IX	SALES MANAGER	29
46		REAL ESTATE SALESMAN	24
47		LIFE INSURANCE SALESMAN	18
48	X	ADVERTISING MAN	24
49		LAWYER	20
50		AUTHOR-JOURNALIST	19
51	XI	PRES. MFG. CONCERN	33
52		GROUP I	31
53		GROUP II	48
54		GROUP V	42
55		GROUP VIII	45
56		GROUP IX	28
57		SPECIALIZATION LEVEL	52
58		INTEREST MATURITY	63
59		OCCUPATIONAL LEVEL	56
60		MASCULINITY-FEMININITY	51

Scored by NATIONAL COMPUTER SYSTEMS—1015 South 6th, Minneapolis, Minn. (SEE OTHER SIDE FOR EXPLANATION) FORM SVI–RM

104 **FIGURE 4 (Front).**

Report on Vocational Interest Blank for Men *(Continued)*

Your occupational interests are recorded under the heading "Std. Score" and opposite the appropriate occupations. The score is plotted as shown below:

		STD. SCORE	C			C+	B−	B	B+		A	
	OCCUPATION		0	10	20	30		40		50	60	70
1	ARTIST	44										
2	PSYCHOLOGIST	23										
3	ARCHITECT	55										
4	PHYSICIAN	22										

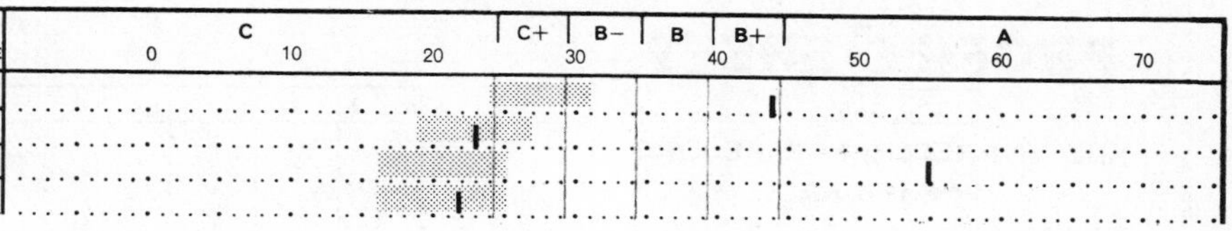

The higher a score to the right of the shaded area the greater the certainty that one has the interests characteristic of that occupation. The lower the score to the left of the shaded area the greater the certainty that one does not have the interests of the occupation. Scores falling within the shaded area are indeterminate: they help sometimes to show, along with other scores, the general trend of one's interests in an occupational group. But generally they can be ignored. Consequently, in the above diagram, the standard scores of 23 for psychologist and 22 for physician are disregarded, and we conclude that the individual has an A rating in the interest of an architect and a B rating in the interest of an artist.

Standard scores of 45 and above are rated A, meaning one has the interests characteristic of men successfully engaged in the occupation. Ratings of B+, B, and B− also indicate possession of the interests characterizing men in those occupations, but at the same time they represent less and less assurance that the classification is correct. The higher the score the greater the certainty the man will continue in the occupation.

About 15 percent of men known to be successful rate B+; about 9 percent rate B; and about 4 percent, B−; and about 2 percent C. Occasionally a successful man rates below B−. On the other hand, many successful men rate B−, B, and B+, and a few rate A in occupations other than the one in which they are engaged.

Occupations included in the same group all correlate highly with one another.

Men's interests change very little from 25 to 55 years of age. They change somewhat from 20 to 25 years and much more so from 15 to 20 years. Consequently, the younger the man, particularly below 20 years of age, the less certainly can his interests be identified in terms of some occupation. Such changes in interests as take place are more likely to result in higher ratings than the reverse. This is particularly true with respect to ratings in Group V.

The ratings from this test should not be viewed as conclusive; they are not guaranteed as correct. Instead they should be viewed as merely suggestive and to be considered in the light of all other information bearing upon one's vocational choice. Occupations rated A and B+ should be carefully considered before definitely deciding against them; occupations rated C, and B− should be carefully considered before definitely deciding to enter them. Remember only a few from among all the hundreds of occupations are reported on here.

This is a test of your interests. Your abilities must also be considered. Interests point the way you want to go, abilities determine how well you can progress, provided also that you are willing to learn and to work.

Scores on the four special scales are for the use of trained counselors and should be explained personally by them. The OL scale indicates whether one's interests are similar to common workmen (a low score) or to business and professional men (a high score). The MF scale indicates whether one's interests are similar to the interests of women or men. The average man scores 50 on both these scales. The IM scale expresses maturity of interests. One's age must be taken into consideration in interpreting this score. It applies only to men between the ages of 15 and 20 years. The Specialization Level scale pertains to college men as to whether or not they would enjoy advanced study and narrow specialization in their work. See "The Use of Vocational Interest Scales in Planning a Medical Career," by Edward K. Strong, Jr., and Anthony C. Tucker, *Psychological Monographs*, No. 341, 1952, Vol. 66, #9.

Edward K. Strong, Jr.
Stanford, California

FIGURE 4 (Back).

NAME *Stevenson, Charles L.*   AGE *17* SEX *M* GROUP *Grade 12*   DATE OF TEST *4-12-65*

Print Last   First   Initial   M or F

Second Revision, January 1950

PROFILE SHEET

for the

KUDER PREFERENCE RECORD VOCATIONAL

Forms CH, CM

BOYS and GIRLS

DIRECTIONS FOR PROFILING

1. Copy the V-Score from the back page of your answer pad to the box at the right.

   If your V-Score is 37 or less, there is some reason for doubting the value of your answers, and your other scores may not be very accurate. *If your V-Score is 45 or more,* you may not have understood the directions, since 44 is the highest possible score. *If your score is not between 38 and 44,* inclusive, you should see your adviser. He will probably recommend that you read the directions again, and then that you fill out the blank a second time, being careful to follow the directions exactly and to give sincere replies.

   If your V-Score is between 38 and 44, inclusive, go ahead with the following directions.

2. Copy the scores 0 through 9 in the spaces at the top of the profile chart. Under "OUTDOOR" find the number which is the same as the score at the top. Use the numbers under M if you are a boy and the numbers under F if you are a girl. Draw a line through this number from one side to the other of the entire column under OUTDOOR. Do the same thing for the scores at the top of each of the other columns. If a score is larger than any number in the column, draw a line across the top of the column; if it is smaller, draw a line across the bottom.

3. With your pencil blacken the entire space between the lines you have drawn and the bottom of the chart. If your score is not shown, draw a line *between* the scores above and below your own. The result is your profile for the *Kuder Preference Record — Vocational.*

   An interpretation of the scores will be found on the other side.

Published by Science Research Associates, Inc.
259 East Erie Street, Chicago 11, Illinois
Copyright 1950, by G. Frederic Kuder.
Copyright under International Copyright Union.
All rights reserved under Fourth International American Convention (1910).
Printed in the U. S. A. Copyright 1948 in Canada.

FIGURE 5 (Front).

Reproduced with permission of Science Research Associates.

SRA Catalog Number 7-293

Your INTEREST PROFILE

Your profile on the *Kuder Preference Record—Vocational* shows your interest in the ten important areas listed across the top of the chart. The profile will also help you learn how you compare with other people.

The lines you drew on the chart show whether your interest is high, average, or low. If your score is above the top dotted line in any column, it is a high score and shows that you like activities in that area. If your score is between the two dotted lines, your interest is about average. If your score is below the bottom dotted line, it is a low score and shows that you dislike activities of that type.

Like most people, you are probably high in some areas, low in some, and average in others. Look at your highest score first. This score shows the type of activities you probably like best. If you have more than one score above the top dotted line, you have a combination of high interests.

Look at your low scores, too. They should be considered in any plans you make because they indicate the kinds of activities you probably do not enjoy. Remember that high interests are not better or worse than low, nor are some interests better than others. It is your own *pattern* of interests that counts.

Here is what your scores on the *Preference Record* mean:

OUTDOOR interest means that you prefer work that keeps you outside most of the time and usually deals with animals and growing things. Forest rangers, naturalists, and farmers are among those high in outdoor interests.

MECHANICAL interest means you like to work with machines and tools. Jobs in this area include automobile repairmen, watchmakers, drill press operators, and engineers.

COMPUTATIONAL interest means you like to work with numbers. A high score in this area suggests that you might like such jobs as bookkeeper, accountant, or bank teller.

SCIENTIFIC interest means that you like to discover new facts and solve problems. Doctors, chemists, nurses, engineers, radio repairmen, aviators, and dietitians usually have high scientific interests.

PERSUASIVE interest means that you like to meet and deal with people and to promote projects or things to sell. Most actors, politicians, radio announcers, au-

thors, salesmen, and store clerks have high persuasive interests.

ARTISTIC interest means you like to do creative work with your hands. It is usually work that has "eye appeal" involving attractive design, color, and materials. Painters, sculptors, architects, dress designers, hairdressers, and interior decorators all do "artistic" work.

LITERARY interest shows that you like to read and write. Literary jobs include novelist, historian, teacher, actor, news reporter, editor, drama critic, librarian, and book reviewer.

MUSICAL interest shows you like going to concerts, playing instruments, singing, or reading about music and musicians.

SOCIAL SERVICE interest indicates a preference for helping people. Nurses, Boy or Girl Scout leaders, vocational counselors, tutors, ministers, personnel workers, social workers, and hospital attendants spend much of their time helping other people.

CLERICAL interest means you like office work that requires precision and accuracy. Jobs such as bookkeeper, accountant, file clerk, salesclerk, secretary, statistician, and traffic manager fall in this area.

The occupations listed for each area on this profile are only examples. Your counselor can help you think of many others that are suggested by your pattern of interests. He can also tell you about many books and pamphlets that will help you learn more about these occupations. You may find that many school courses and leisure-time activities fit into your high interest areas.

Another form of the *Preference Record*, the *Personal*, will help you find out more about the types of things you like to do. It will help you discover, for example, how much you like meeting new people, whether you prefer situations you are familiar with, if you would rather work with ideas or things, how much you prefer pleasant social situations, and if you like to direct others. Your scores in these areas, too, will help you plan your career.

What you can do well depends, of course, on many things in addition to interest. Your abilities are particularly important. Many abilities can be measured by tests. Here, again, your counselor is the person to see.

Try to get as much information as you can about your interests, abilities, and the jobs you want to consider. The more you know about yourself, the more opportunity you have to make wise plans for your future.

345/2-9876

FIGURE 5 (Back).

ever, one new interest inventory, What I Like to Do, by Thorpe, Myers, and Bonsall, is designed for children in Grades 4 through 7. This is among the tests annotated later in the chapter.

Examples of profile forms showing interest inventory results are presented in Figures 4 and 5. The Strong Vocational Interest Blank profile in Figure 4 gives the interest ratings for a high school senior, John J. Cramer. The names of the occupations appear near the left-hand margin of the sheet. Standard scores are shown in the column to the right of the names of the occupations. The standard score scale is also printed across the top of the sheet, and letter ratings (A, B+, B, B−, C+ and C) are applied to different ranges of standard scores. The standard scores of the individual are represented by the short vertical lines opposite the various occupations and below the appropriate numbers printed at the top of the sheet.

The shaded areas for each occupation indicate a range within which scores cannot be interpreted very dependably. Marks falling to the right or left of the shaded areas are likely to be more nearly indicative of the true interests of the individual than marks within this range.

In general, ratings of A indicate close agreement between the interests of the individual taking the test and those of men successfully engaged in the occupation concerned; ratings of B+ show considerable agreement in interests; ratings of B suggest that there may be some correspondence between the interests of the individual and those of persons engaged in the occupations for which these ratings are obtained but that the agreement is not very close; ratings of B−, C+, and C indicate little or no agreement in interests.

The interests of John J. Cramer tend to be similar to those of men in administrative occupations in business. John has an A rating in this group of occupations as a whole (Group VIII, shown on the sixth line from the foot of the sheet), and on the senior CPA, accountants, office worker, and credit manager scales within this group. There also seems to be considerable correspondence between the interests of this boy and those of production managers, mathematics and science teachers, personnel managers, public administrators, and business education teachers, since he has A ratings on the scales for these occupations, too. In addition, there appears to be substantial similarity between John's interests and those of engineers, farmers, and army officers, for he obtained B+ ratings in these three areas. It seems probable that the agreement between John's interests and those of persons engaged in the other occupations for which his blank was scored is moderate, slight, or completely lacking. The ratings on the four scales at the

foot of the sheet signify that John is apparently interested in a rather high level of specialization in his vocational work, is very mature in his interests, has a high level of vocational aspiration, and tends to like work that is of a masculine nature. On the basis of the results of this inventory, one would be inclined to suggest that, in his choice of an occupation, this boy might give serious thought to some type of work calling for managerial interests, such as accounting in a large public accounting firm, or as a public administrator, personnel manager, or sales manager. Engineering and teaching might be other reasonable vocational choices for him. Although these results should, of course, be checked against other information, it seems fairly clear that his interests lie in the general field of business, the engineering or physical sciences, or social service and welfare, rather than in the trades, music, or art.

A profile of the percentiles of a high school senior, Charles L. Stevenson, on the ten scales of the Kuder Preference Record—Vocational is shown in Figure 5. Since the boy's V-Score of 40 is within the 38–44 range, he evidently followed the directions carefully and entered his responses conscientiously. His profile signifies that he has high interest ratings in the scientific, literary, and computational areas. This is a pattern of interests that is similar to that of certified public accountants. Charles ranks low in artistic and clerical interests, and falls within the average range (25th to 75th percentiles) in the other five vocational areas covered by this inventory.

It would be unwise, of course, for an individual to base his vocational choice on the results of a single interest inventory. In counseling practice, results of interest inventories such as the Kuder and the Strong would be considered as only one part of a much larger picture, made up of information concerning background, experience, education, intelligence, achievement, special aptitudes, and health and physical characteristics.

VALIDITY AND RELIABILITY

Although there have been many studies of personality tests, the validity of the various tests in this field has not been established. Summaries of research in this field by Ellis (34) and Ellis and Conrad (35) indicated that the validity of personality measures was generally low in civilian use, but somewhat higher in military practice.

It is very difficult to determine the validity of personality tests because there is no satisfactory criterion with which to correlate the test scores. The ratings of judges are a common criterion in studies of validity, but judges' ratings are not highly reliable, even when the characteristic to be rated is well understood by them. When the trait is intangible and difficult to get clearly in mind, still less confidence can be placed on the ratings. The fact that scores on personality tests usually do not correlate highly with judges' ratings is by no means conclusive evidence that the tests fail to measure the traits which they are intended to measure.

The reliability coefficients for most personality tests and inventories are between .70 and .90. Personality tests thus tend to be as reliable as some of the widely used intelligence and achievement tests. Few, if any, however, have consistently shown reliability as high as the most reliable tests of mental ability or achievement. The most dependable intelligence tests and achievement tests have reliability coefficients as high as .95 to .98. Few reliability coefficients that high have thus far been reported for personality tests.

USES OF RESULTS OF PERSONALITY TESTS

Most personality and interest measures are reliable enough for group studies, and they may be used for research if they can be shown to be reasonably valid.

The majority of these instruments, however, are not reliable enough to be very satisfactory for use in individual diagnosis. Individual scores on personality tests can contribute materially, nevertheless, to the guidance program of the school. Two important uses of these tests are (1) to stimulate the pupils to evaluate critically their own personality characteristics, and (2) to serve as a point of departure in conferences between counselors and individual pupils. Personality tests are also helpful in locating pupils who are poorly adjusted and unhappy, and who need guidance in making emotional and personal adjustment. Tests are sometimes more successful in discovering such cases than are observational or interview procedures, since many maladjusted pupils are so repressed that they give little outward evidence of poor adjustment. If scores on personality tests indicate that there are such cases in the school, a wise counselor will not accept the results unreservedly but will verify them by means of careful observation and well-planned personal interviews with the pupils.

For the purpose of records of growth, anecdotal records, behavior descriptions, and sociometric devices seem preferable to existing personality tests. Some of the rating scales in which the categories are carefully defined and explained in very concrete terms, likewise, provide more valuable records than do most of the personality tests. These types of appraisal will be discussed in the next chapter.

SELECTED AND ANNOTATED LIST OF PERSONALITY AND INTEREST TESTS

The personality tests and inventories (including measures of interests and of study habits) in this section have been selected from a possible list of more than 400. It is believed that they are among the more useful instruments of their respective types, although there is no intention of recommending them to the exclusion of all other personality tests.

Various ways of classifying tests and inventories for measuring character and personality have been suggested by different authors. The following ninefold classification is used in the present discussion: I, records of uncontrolled observations; II, rating devices; III, behavior descriptions; IV, structured self-inventories; V, tests utilizing life situations; VI, paper-and-pencil tests of broad traits or attitudes; VII, scales for specific traits or attitudes; VIII, free association or projective tests; IX, laboratory techniques.

The first three classes include devices to be discussed in the next chapter. The last one is omitted because such instruments can be used in few schools because of the elaborateness of the equipment required. Classes IV, VI, VII, and VIII are represented in this list. The Roman numeral in parentheses following each title indicates the classification of the test or inventory.

Allport, Gordon W., and Allport, Floyd H. *The A-S Reaction Study*.[1] Boston: Houghton Mifflin Company, 1928–1939. Separate forms for men and women. $3.40 per 35 tests; specimen set, 60 cents (IV).

A self-inventory, the purpose of which is to discover the extent to which a person is disposed to dominate or be

[1] It will be observed that the aptitude tests and achievement tests in the two preceding chapters were listed with the name of the test first, followed by the name of the author, while in this list of tests the author's name precedes that of the test. There is a logical reason for this apparent lack of consistency. Many of the aptitude tests and achievement tests are identified with a certain series or battery, *e.g.*, the Cooperative Academic Ability Test, the Stanford Arithmetic Test, and so forth. Most of the personality and interest tests, on the other hand, are customarily identified by the name of the author—although the author's name is not a part of the title of some of them—for instance, the Bell Adjustment Inventory and the Strong Vocational Interest Blank. For this reason, it was thought that the tests annotated in the book could be found more readily if the aptitude and achievement tests were listed according to the name of the test and if the personality and interest tests were listed alphabetically by names of the authors.

dominated by his fellows. A variety of situations is verbally presented and the subject selects for each situation that one of several possible responses which most nearly characterizes his customary behavior. No time limit; 20 minutes usually sufficient. Standardized on college classes but could probably be used in high school. Norms for men and for women are given in the manual. Reliability, .74 to .78. Validity, as indicated by correlation with ratings, .29 to .79. According to authors, the overall validity index would be about .45. This cannot be regarded as a test of a variety of personality qualities, but it is one of the better measures of dominance. *Reference:* Buros (17:51–52).

Allport, Gordon W., Vernon, Philip, E., and Lindzey, Gardner. *Study of Values,* revised. Boston: Houghton Mifflin Company, 1931–1951. $4.00 per 35 tests; specimen set, 60 cents (VI).

A scale for measuring the dominant interests of personality according to Spranger's classification of six ideal types: theoretical, economic, aesthetic, social, political, and religious. The 1951 revision is basically similar to the earlier form, but some of the items have been revised and modernized and the test has a more attractive appearance. Contains two parts arranged in a single booklet. In all, there are 45 items, which call for a total of 120 responses, 20 for each value. The blank is self-administering and may be filled out within a period of 20 minutes. The score sheet provides for showing graphically the scores of an individual on the six values. Norms in terms of means and standard deviations for college students in general, for males and females, and for several adult groups. The population in some of the norm groups is rather small. Data reported by the authors indicate that split-half reliabilities of scales in revised form range from .73 to .90, with a mean reliability coefficient of .82, using a z transformation, whereas the mean reliability for the old form was .70. The repeat reliabilities, with an interval of one month, tend to be somewhat higher. The correlations among the value types tend to be low, which is, of course, desirable. A considerable number of studies of validity have been made by various researchers, but most of these pertain to the unrevised form. The authors are very conservative in their claims for this instrument, but it is one of the better paper-and-pencil measures of personal qualities. *Reference:* Buros (18:156–158).

Baker, Harry J. *Detroit Adjustment Inventories.* Indianapolis: Bobbs-Merrill Company, 1942–1954. 35 booklets with accessories, each level, $4.50; single copy, 15 cents; specimen set, 50 cents; remedial suggestions, set containing one copy of each, $1.50; single copy, any topic, 10 cents (IV).

Also known as "Telling What I Do." A series of four inventories of adjustment problems. A set of remedial leaflets is designed to be given to pupil or parent to assist in correcting the bad or weak habits revealed by the inventory. Delta Form for ages 5–8; Gamma Form for Grades 3–6; Alpha Forms for junior and senior high schools; Self-Analysis

Inventory for adults. Nontimed, requiring 20–50 minutes. Designed to tap four kinds of reactions: habits, social, emotional, and ethical. No reliability data. The small amount of validity information, indicating degree to which inventories distinguish between behavior and nonbehavior cases, is given in manuals. *Reference:* Buros (19:113).

Bell, Hugh M. *The Adjustment Inventory, Revised.* Palo Alto, Calif.: Consulting Psychologists Press, 1962. $3.25 per 25 booklets; $3.75 per 50 IBM 805 answer sheets; scoring keys, $2.00 per set (IV).

Yields 6 scores: Home Adjustment, Health Adjustment, Submissiveness, Emotionality, Hostility, and Masculinity-Femininity. Consists of series of questions to which pupil responds by encircling *yes, no,* or *?.* One form intended for use in Grades 9–14. No time limit; can be completed in about 35 minutes. Norms for high school boys and girls and college men and women are given separately in the manual. Research on earlier edition: Turney and Fee (*119*) reported a study of the use of the Bell Adjustment Inventory in high school guidance. They found reliability coefficients of .74 to .85 for the descriptive classifications and .82 for the total score. Correlations of scores on the inventory with average ratings of 15 judges were low, ranging from .18 to .42. Traxler (*114*) obtained somewhat similar reliability and validity data in a study based on scores of high school pupils. Pedersen (*89*) studied validity of inventory on basis of scores and ratings of freshmen girls in University of Rochester; found evidence of validity of home adjustment, health adjustment, and social adjustment, but not of emotional adjustment. Resnick (*96*) found that the home adjustment score and total adjustment score discriminated between pairs of high, middle, and low achieving high school pupils at the .01 level. Odd-even coefficients of reliability predicted with the Spearman-Brown formula range from .80 to .89. Bibliography of 119 items given in Buros' *Fourth Mental Measurements Yearbook* (18:67–69). *Reference:* Cantoni (*21*).

Bell, Hugh M. *The School Inventory.* Palo Alto, Calif.: Consulting Psychologists Press, 1936–1937. $3.00 per 25; manual and scoring stencil $1.25 (IV).

An inventory for use in investigating pupils' attitudes toward their school. Designed for senior high school pupils who have attended the school in which the test is given for at least three months. Contains 76 questions which are to be answered by encircling *yes, no,* or *?.* Pupils who make high scores tend to be poorly adjusted to the school. The test is practically self-administering. No time limit; most students can complete it within 15 minutes. Scoring time, about one minute. There are norms for high school students which yield descriptions ranging from "excellent" to "very unsatisfactory." The author reports a reliability coefficient of .94, based on the scores of 242 high school freshmen, sophomores, juniors, and seniors. Traxler (*114*) found a reliability of .92 for this inventory; he also obtained a correlation of .54 between scores on the inventory and the pooled opinions of judges. Not a diagnostic instrument; but useful in counseling interviews.

Berdie, Ralph F. and Layton, Wilbur L. *The Minnesota Counseling Inventory*. New York: The Psychological Corporation, 1953–1957. Test booklets, $3.50 per 25; IBM 805 answer sheets with profile sheets, $3.75 per 50; extra profile sheets, $1.90 per 50; manual and hand-scoring keys, 75 cents; manual and machine-scoring keys, $1.00; specimen set, 90 cents (IV).

Designed to be used in connection with the counseling of high school students. Based on items in the Minnesota Multiphasic Personality Inventory and the Minnesota Personality Scale. Yields seven scores: family relationships, social relationships, emotional stability, conformity, adjustment to reality, mood, and leadership. The first three scores relate to areas where students may be making particularly good or poor adjustments, and the other four scores are intended to reflect some of the modes of behavior which students characteristically adopt in meeting life situations. Two additional validating scores provide a check on the thoroughness and frankness with which the questions have been answered. No time limit; most students finish in about 50 minutes. Norms provide for converting raw scores into standard scores separately for the two sexes, for Grades 9–10 and for Grades 11–12. Profile sheet similar to that of MMPI. Spearman-Brown and test-retest reliabilities reported in manual are satisfactory, in general. *Reference:* Buros (19:157–158).

Bernreuter, Robert G. *The Personality Inventory*. Palo Alto, Calif.: Consulting Psychologists Press, 1931–1938. $3.25 per 25 booklets; $2.20 per 50 IBM answer sheets; $2.50 per set of hand-scoring stencils; manual and norms, 25 cents; specimen set, 50 cents (IV).

Measures neurotic tendency, self-sufficiency, introversion-extroversion, dominance-submission, confidence, and sociability. The last two scales were added by Flanagan. Consists of series of questions to which pupil responds by encircling *yes, no,* or *?.* No time limit; requires about 30 minutes. Scoring is complicated; if many blanks are to be scored, it is economical to have the work done by machine scoring at a test service bureau, such as National Computer Service or Testscor in Minneapolis. One form for high school and college students. Percentile norms for high school and college students and for men and women accompany each scale. Bernreuter (*13*) attempted to validate his four scales by correlation with criterion made up from scores on Thurstone's Neurotic Inventory, the Allports' A-S Reaction Study, and Laird's C2 Introversion-Extroversion Test, and secured coefficients which varied from .84 to approximately 1.00. Research literature concerned with this test is so extensive that it is impossible to summarize even the main findings in this annotation. Buros' *Mental Measurements Yearbooks* include bibliography of 299 items published through 1958 (16:80–81; 18:135–139; 19:175–176). Series of articles by Lorge (*74, 75, 76*), together with Flanagan's (*39*) reply

to Lorge's second article, constitute one of best appraisals of the Bernreuter. Research indicates that most of the value of this instrument can be obtained from scoring with Flanagan's two scales, self-confidence and sociability. New studies of this instrument have decreased in number in recent years, and use may have declined as well, partly because some users have found validity rather low in actual practice. However, schools planning to use a personality inventory in their guidance programs can well consider this one, for some 20 years of research and experience have revealed its uses and limitations much more thoroughly than is true of most instruments in this field. *Reference* for information about theory on which inventory was constructed: Bernreuter (*14*).

Billett, Roy O. and Starr, Irving, S. *Billett-Starr Youth Problems Inventory*, New York: Harcourt, Brace & World, Inc., 1958. $5.50 per 35, Junior or Senior level; specimen set, 40 cents each (IV).

A problem checklist for junior and senior high school students. Covers 11 areas: physical health, fitness and safety; getting along with others; boy-girl relationships; home and family life; personal finance; interests and activities; school life; personal potentialities; planning for the future; mental-emotional health and fitness; morality and religion. Junior level is for Grades 7–9, Senior level for Grades 10–12. No time limit, but group administration usually requires 60–75 minutes. Student's score is number of problems checked. Norms given in terms of (1) number of problems per student, by sex and area, for each level of the inventory, and (2) percentage frequency, by sex, of each problem in both levels.

Brainard, P. P. and Brainard, R. T. *Brainard Occupational Preference Inventory*. New York: The Psychological Corporation, 1945–1956. Reusable test booklets, $3.25 per 25; single copy, 20 cents; IBM 805 answer sheets, $2.00 per 50; manual, 25 cents; machine-scoring key, 25 cents; specimen set, 50 cents (IV).

Covers six broad occupational fields for each sex: commercial, mechanical, professional, aesthetic, and scientific—for both boys and girls; agricultural additional for boys only; personal service additional for girls only. Only low level of reading skill required. Percentile norms for Grades 8–12. No time limit, but usually takes about 30 minutes. Normative data based on scores of 9695 pupils in 14 school systems. *Reference:* Buros (19:879–880).

Cattell, Raymond B., Beloff, Halla, and Coan, Richard W. *The High School Personality Questionnaire*. Champaign, Ill.: Institute for Personality and Ability Testing, 1953–1958. $4.00 per 25 booklets; $1.90 per 50 answer sheets; handbook, $2.20; hand-scoring key, 60 cents; specimen set, $3.10 (IV).

Formerly called The Junior Personality Quiz. Test bears title of H.S.P.Q. Yields 14 scores on reportedly independent factors, among which is general intelligence. Designed for use in clinics and in educational and vocational guidance. Age range, 12–17 years. Two forms, A and B. Time for administration, 30–60 minutes. Separate norms for boys and girls, based on more than a thousand cases. *Reference:* Buros (19:142–143).

Cattell, Raymond B., and Stice, Glen F. *The 16 Personality Factor Questionnaire.* Champaign, Ill.: Institute for Personality and Ability Testing, 1949–1957. $6.00 per 25 booklets; $2.25 per 50 answer sheets; $1.80 per 50 profile sheets; $2.70 per 50 combination answer-profile sheets; scoring key, $1.00; handbook, $2.90; specimen set, $4.00. Also a special short form (Form C): test booklets, industrial edition, 40 cents each; Form C handbook supplement, $1.00; scoring key for Form C, $1.00; speci-ment set, $1.00 (IV).

Based on factor analysis of a wide variety of items, many of which are similar to those appearing in other self-inventories of personality. Forms A and B each contain 187 items designed to measure a total of 16 factors. Raw scores are converted to standard scores on a ten-point scale and are expressed in the form of a profile. Form C is a more recent short form consisting of 105 items. Designed for senior high school, college, and adult subjects. Working time, approximately 50 minutes for Forms A and B and 30 minutes for Form C. Norms for college students, general adult population, and 28 occupational groups. In a guidance situation, this test should probably be used only by counselors with clinical training. Corrected split-half reliabilities of the 16 factors, based on sample of 200 drawn from the general population, range from .50 to .88, with a median of .705. These reliabilities are probably as high as could be expected for subscores based on small numbers of items, but they tend to be too low for use of this instrument in individual diagnosis. At the present stage of development of this questionnaire, it is perhaps more suitable for experimental use than for regular use in counseling. *References:* Cattell (22), Buros (19:196–199).

Cleeton, Glen U. *Vocational Interest Inventory,* rev. ed. Bloomington, Ill.: McKnight & McKnight Publishing Company, 1937–1943. $2.50 per 25 test booklets, with manual; IBM 805 answer sheets for machine scoring, 4.5 cents each; machine scoring stencils, 40 cents per set; extra manual, 50 cents; specimen set, 50 cents (IV).

Two forms, one for vocational interests of men and one for vocational interests of women. Designed for use in Grades 9–12 and in college. Can also be used with adults. Each blank contains nine occupational groups and a tenth section on social adjustment. Construction and validation not carried on with the thoroughness of the work on such inventories as the Strong and Kuder. Scoring is very easy in comparison with that of the Strong and most other vocational interest tests. Reliability coefficients reported by the author are relatively high, .82 to .91. Congdon (27) found the inventory valuable in counseling freshmen and seniors in the Colorado State College of Education. *Reference:* Cleeton (26).

Edwards, Allen L. *Edwards Personal Preference Schedule.* New York: The Psychological Corporation, 1953–1959. Booklets, $3.50 per 25; IBM 805 answer sheets, $2.50 per 50; manual and hand-scoring template, 60 cents; manual and hand-scoring keys for IBM answer sheets, $1.50; manual and machine-scoring keys for IBM answer sheets, $1.65; specimen set, 75 cents (IV).

Constructed to measure 15 needs or motives of college students and adults. An attempt is made in the inventory to choose items which minimize tendency to select face-saving or socially desirable responses. One form consisting of 225 paired-comparison statements. Subject is required to choose the statement in each pair which is most characteristic or descriptive of himself. The 15 personality scores yielded by the inventory are (1) achievement, (2) deference, (3) order, (4) exhibition, (5) autonomy, (6) affiliation, (7) intraception, (8) succorance, (9) dominance, (10) abasement, (11) nurturance, (12) change, (13) endurance, (14) heterosexuality, (15) aggression. Raw scores ranging from 0 to 28 on each variable are translated into T-scores and percentiles separately for men and for women. Also yields a consistency score. Working time is about 45 minutes. Corrected split-half reliabilities given in the manual range from .60 to .87, with a median of .78. Likewise, test-retest reliabilities range from .74 to .88, with a median of .79. Reported intercorrelations among the variables are, in general, quite low. Correlations with the Guilford-Zimmerman Personality Inventory and the Taylor Manifest Anxiety Scale are given in the manual. A comparatively promising appearing inventory. Gives evidence of considerable sophistication in test construction. Yields scores, the definitions of which are so stated that they should not be difficult for counselors and students to understand. *Reference:* Buros (19:113–120).

Fitts, William H. *Tennessee (Department of Mental Health) Self Concept Scale.* Nashville, Tenn: Counselor Recordings and Tests, 1964–1965. Booklets, 26 cents each; combination packet of answer sheet, score sheet, and profile sheet, 16 cents each; specimen set, 90 cents each (IV).

A questionnaire consisting of 100 self-description items. Two forms: Counseling Form and Clinical Research Form. No time limit, but usually completed in 10–20 minutes. Vocabulary suitable for individuals 12 years of age or older, reading at sixth-grade level or better. Yields 29 scores, including a Self Criticism score based on ten items taken from the L-scale of the MMPI. Percentile norms based on "broad sample" of 626 individuals in age range of 12–68. Author reports reliabilities for college students over two-week period range from .60 to .92. Validity data given in terms of content validity, differentiation between criteria groups, discrimination within patient groups, and correlations with other personality measures.

Gordon, Leonard V. *Gordon Personal Profile and Personal Inventory*. New York: Harcourt, Brace & World, Inc., 1955–1963. $3.15 per 35 booklets, either Profile or Inventory; IBM answer sheet edition of either, $2.90 per 35; machine scoring keys for either, 80 cents per set; specimen set (combined), 60 cents each (IV).

Forced-choice inventories measuring eight aspects of personality when used in combination. *Profile* yields scores in ascendancy, responsibility, emotional stability, and sociability; *Inventory* yields scores in cautiousness, original thinking, personal relations, and vigor. Percentile norms, by sex, for high school, college, and adults. Short and simple in design, easily and quickly administered. No time limits, but usually take about 15 minutes each. One form. Manual reports considerable evidence of validity, in terms of correlation with independent criteria and internal consistency of component items. These simple, carefully constructed inventories, yielding scores that are not highly technical, will probably appeal to many school and college counselors, as compared with other recently published inventories that are oriented toward clinical and therapeutic uses. *Reference:* Buros (19:124–130).

Gough, Harrison G. *California Psychological Inventory*. Palo Alto, Calif.: Consulting Psychologists Press, 1956–1957. Reusable booklets, $6.25 per 25; answer sheets including profiles, $3.75 per 50; scoring stencils, $4.50 per set; specimen set, $1.00; "Counselors' Kit," $9.75 (IV).

Derived from the Minnesota Multiphasic Personality Inventory, but designed to be used with normal individuals. Contains 480 true-false items. Yields scores on the following 18 scales: dominance, capacity for status, sociability, social presence, self-acceptance, sense of well-being, responsibility, socialization, self-control, tolerance, good impression, communality, achievement via conformance, achievement via independence, intellectual efficiency, psychological-mindedness, flexibility, femininity. For ages 13 and over. Norms based on more than 13,000 cases in 30 states. Manual also gives means and standard deviations for 30 educational, professional, and other types of groups. No time limit, but usually takes 45 minutes to an hour. Manual gives validity data in terms of differences between extreme groups. Reliabilities not given in manual, but Thorndike in his review of the test in Buros' *Fifth Mental Measurements Yearbook* (19:99) states that "application of Kuder-Richardson formula 21 to some of the data reported in the manual suggests that split-half reliabilities would be likely to be in the .70's." While not a simple instrument, it is useful for counseling and research purposes. *Reference:* Leton (72).

Guilford, J. P., and Zimmerman, Wayne S. *The Guilford-Zimmerman Temperament Survey*. Beverly Hills, Calif.: Sheridan Supply Company, 1949–1955. $3.75 per 25 booklets; 75 cents per 25 IBM answer sheets; $2.00 per set of machine-scoring stencils, $2.00 per set of hand-

scoring stencils; manual, 25 cents; profile charts, 50 cents per 25; specimen set, 60 cents (IV).

This inventory is derived from several earlier inventories prepared by Guilford and his associates, including the Nebraska Personality Inventory, the Guilford-Martin Inventory of Factors GAMIN, the Guilford-Martin Inventory I (O Ag Co), and the Inventory of Factors STDCR. Three hundred items, 30 for each of ten traits: (G) general activity, (R) restraint, (A) ascendance, (S) sociability, (E) emotional stability, (O) objectivity, (F) friendliness, (T) thoughtfulness, (P) personal relations, and (M) masculinity. Based on factor analysis studies of personality. One form intended for Grades 9–16 and adults. Nontimed; probable working time, about 50 minutes. Comparatively easy to administer and score, and the obtained scores have psychological meaning. The reliability of the scores is in the neighborhood of .80, and the intercorrelations are low, as reported by the authors. May well be considered for use by counselors in schools and colleges. *References:* Eisele and Cattell (33), Gilbert (42).

Hathaway, Starke R., and McKinley, J. Charnley. *Minnesota Multiphasic Personality Inventory*, revised edition. New York: The Psychological Corporation, 1942–1951. Individual form (the "card set"), $25.50 per set of testing materials including 50 recording sheets; $3.75 per 50 recording sheets. Group form (the "booklet form"), $5.50 per 25 booklets; $1.50 per manual; $4.00 per 50 IBM 805 answer sheets and profile forms; $4.65 per set of machine-scoring stencils with manual; $4.50 per set of hand-scoring stencils with manual (IV).

This inventory takes its origin from studies of personality deviates in mental hospitals. Was first devised as an individual test administered through the use of cards, and was later published in a booklet for group use. Both individual and group forms are available. Separate answer sheets must be used with group form. Consists of 550 statements to which subject responds by indicating "true," "false," or "doubtful (?)," as applied to himself. One form, nontimed; administration time about 40 to 90 minutes. Yields scores for ten personality trends or structures based on scales derived from performance of patients in different psychiatric groupings (hypochondriasis, depression, hysteria, psychopathic deviate, masculinity-femininity, paranoia, psychasthenia, schizophrenia, hypomania, and social introversion) and four scores pertaining to validity of responses: a "lie" scale, a scale derived from number of items placed in the "?" category, an "F" scale on which a high score suggests that the individual may not have understood what he read, and a "K" scale designed to indicate "defensiveness-frankness" in test taking. The K-score is used as a suppressor variable to sharpen the discrimination of the test.

A shortened version consisting of the first 366 items may be used if it is necessary to save time in administration, but the K-scale and the social introversion scale do not apply to this version.

At present, the Minnesota Multiphasic is probably held in higher regard by psychologists in general than any other structured inventory of personality. In recent years, this instrument has no doubt been the subject of more research interest and effort for the assessment of personality than any other instrument except the Rorschach and the TAT. Buros' *Third, Fourth,* and *Fifth Mental Measurements Yearbooks* list a total of 779 titles pertaining to the Multiphasic through the year 1958 (*17*:103–104, *18*:126–130, *19*:158–166). An "Atlas" by Hathaway and Meehl is an authoritative clinical guide for the inventory (*54*). It contains 968 short case histories accompanied by test profiles which were independent of the case summaries. Test-retest reliability coefficients, as given in the manual, range from .46 to .93, with a median of .76. These do not compare favorably with reliabilities reported for some of the other personality measures. In general, the MMPI is primarily an instrument for clinical use by professional psychologists and psychiatrists. It may be used by counselors who majored in psychology, but it is not an instrument for use by teacher-counselors whose preparation is based largely on in-service training. *References:* Hathaway and McKinley (*52, 53*); McKinley and Hathaway (*78, 79*); Hathaway and Meehl (*54*); Meehl and Hathaway (*83*).

Holtzman, W. H. *Holtzman Inkblot Technique.* New York: The Psychological Corporation, 1958–1961. Set A or Set B: 45 inkblots, monograph, scoring guide, and 25 record forms, $32.00; Set A-B: 90 inkblots, monograph, scoring guide and 25 of each record form, $52.00; inkblots alone, A or B, set of 45, $22.00; record forms with summary sheets, A or B, package of 25, $2.75; Monograph, "Inkblot Perception and Personality," $8.00; scoring guide for both forms, $3.00 (VIII).

A projective type of instrument with objective scoring features. The 90 stimulus blots include some that are asymmetric, some in a color other than black, some with visual textures. Parallel forms, A and B, of 45 blots each. One response allowed for each blot. Scoring guide claimed to make scoring results highly reproducible from one scorer to another. Percentile norms for 22 response variables based on eight groups, normal and pathological, ranging from normal five-year-olds to adults, and including clinical populations such as schizophrenics and mental defectives.

Kent, Grace H., and Rosanoff, A. J. *Kent-Rosanoff Free Association Tests.* Chicago: C. H. Stoelting Company, 1910. $4.50 per set, including 50 test blanks and manual (VIII).

Consists of 100 stimulus words. Examiner pronounces each word aloud to the subject, who responds with the first word that he associates with the stimulus word. Authors have reported frequency of response to each word for 1000 individuals. Number of atypical responses is taken as a measure of psychopathic tendencies. Manual for the test is contained in Rosanoff's *Manual of Psychiatry.* Data on reliability not available. *Reference:* Kent and Rosanoff (*65*).

Kuder, G. Frederic. *Kuder Preference Record—Vocational.* Chicago: Science Research Associates, Inc., 1934–1956. Form CH: hand-scoring, record booklets, $12.50 per 20; answer pads, $3.00 per 20; review set, $1.00. Form CM: machine-scoring, record booklets, $12.50 per 20; IBM 805 answer sheets, $5.00 per 100; scoring keys, $7.50 per set; review set, $1.00. Interpretive materials for either form: profile leaflet, boys and girls, 80 cents per 20; profile leaflet, men and women, 80 cents per 20; administrator's manual, 50 cents (IV).

This preference record is one of the two most carefully and scientifically constructed interest inventories, and is probably the most widely used instrument in the field of interests at the present time. Since its publication in 1934, it has gone through two revisions. The first revision resulted in an instrument for the measurement of interests in nine broad areas: mechanical, computational, scientific, persuasive, artistic, literary, musical, social service, and clerical. Form BB for hand scoring and Form BM for machine scoring. In the most recent edition, a scale for outdoor activities was added to the other nine, and a verification score was included in order to help in identifying individuals who fail to follow directions or give careless responses. Form CH for hand scoring and Form CM for machine scoring.

The Kuder Preference Record contains 168 items, each listing three activities. Subject indicates which activity he likes most and which he likes least. Inventory yields a profile of preference scores in the nine or ten areas for which it is scored. Designed for high school and college students and adults. Administered without time limits; approximate time, 40 minutes. All tests administered with separate answer pads for hand scoring or separate answer sheets for machine scoring or hand scoring. Numerous reliability data summarized in manual, derived from repeating the inventory or from Kuder-Richardson formula, fall within the range .80 to .98, indicating comparatively high reliability. Most reported intercorrelations among the scales are fairly low. Correlations of the Kuder record with the Strong blank and various other measures have been reported by Triggs and others (*117, 118, 126*). Manuals report mean profiles for men and for women in variety of occupations. These data useful in counseling. Studies reporting Kuder profiles for different occupations also reported elsewhere in the literature, as, for example, one for public accountants (*63*). Buros' *Mental Measurements Yearbooks* contain bibliography of 419 items through 1958 (*16*:447; *17*:659–660; *18*:734–737; *19*:887–890).

Kuder, G. Frederic. *Kuder Preference Record—Personal.* Chicago: Science Research Associates, Inc., 1948–1953. Form AH (hand-scoring edition): $12.50 per 20 record booklets; $3.00 per 20 answer pads. Form AM (machine-scoring edition): $12.50 per 20 record booklets; $5.00 per 100 answer sheets; $4.00 per set of scoring keys. Profile sheets, 80 cents per 20 (specify whether for boys and girls or for men and women); review set, either form, $1.00 (IV).

Designed to measure preferences for five general kinds of personal and social activities: (1) working with ideas, (2) being active in groups, (3) avoiding conflicts, (4) directing others, and (5) being in familiar and stable situations. Yields scores in these areas which may be graphed in the form of a profile. Also has a V-score or verification score. Type of item and format similar to that of Preference Record—Vocational. Intended for high school and college students and adults. No time limit; administration time about 40 to 45 minutes. Reliabilities (Kuder-Richardson) reported in manual range from .76 to .89. These are a little lower than reliabilities of the Preference Record—Vocational. Most of the reported intercorrelations of the scores on the five scales are rather low. Norms based on 3650 high school boys, 3924 high school girls, 1000 men, and 532 women. Data in manual indicate that certain scales distinguish between satisfied and dissatisfied workers in certain occupations. As yet, few articles reporting research with this instrument have been published.

Kvaraceus, William C. *KD Proneness Scale and Check List.* (Also called *Delinquency Proneness Scale.*) Los Angeles: Western Psychological Services, 1950–1956. $6.50 per 25 scales; $3.50 per 25 checklists; manual and supplement, $2.50; scoring keys, $1.50; kit, $12.00 (II and IV).

Unlike most of the newer personality inventories which are designed to yield several scores purporting to have diagnostic value, this instrument provides simply a total score which is intended to aid in the identification of boys and girls who are susceptible to the development of delinquent patterns of behavior. Consists of two separate pieces of paper, the Proneness Scale and the Proneness Check List. The 74 items in the Proneness Scale are derived from areas in which significant differences between delinquents and nondelinquents have been indicated by the research literature. Among these are family relationships, home conditions, truancy record, school retardation, immaturity, club membership, family mobility, and the like. The check list consists of 58 items distributed among personal factors, environmental factors—home and family, and school factors, which the counselor, social worker, or other person checks as "yes," "no," or "?" with regard to the individual being rated. The scale is designed for Grades 7 through 12; the check list may be used at any age level. Working time for scale, about 25 minutes. Reliabilities of .75 and .81 reported in manual for two small groups. Data reported in the manual which indicate that the Proneness Scale distinguishes between delinquent, nondelinquent, and "high morale" groups with all differences significant at the 1 percent level. Data suggest that the instrument is about equally suitable for use with boys and girls. The check list appears to have face validity, although statistical information on validity seems not to be available. The scale and check list are potentially useful screening devices. They should be helpful to teachers and counselors in identifying adolescents who may need to be referred to a psychologist or psychiatrist. *Reference:* Buros (19:150–151).

Lee, Edwin A. and Thorpe, Louis P. *Occupational Interest Inventory.* Monterey: California Test Bureau, 1943–1956. Test booklets, $5.25 per 35; manual of directions, 50 cents; IBM 1230 answer sheets, 5 cents each; IBM hand-scoring stencils, $2.00 per set; specimen set, 75 cents (IV).

This inventory purports to measure basic occupational interests. It includes six fields of interests: personal-social, natural, mechanical, business, the arts, and the sciences; three types of interests, verbal, manipulative, and computational; and level of interests. One form at each of two levels: Intermediate for junior high school and average adult, and Advanced for senior high school, college, and adult. No time limit; approximate administration time, 30 to 40 minutes. Responses may be entered either in booklet or on separate answer sheets. Based on vocational classifications and job analyses in *Dictionary of Occupational Titles.* Arranged for easy use. Construction of inventory apparently carried on by means of armchair or reasoned approach rather than through more laborious and careful research and statistical analysis. Nevertheless, several of the scores are substantially correlated with certain Kuder scales according to two studies (62, 73). Percentile norms for males, for females, and for composite population. Test-retest reliabilities of the ten scales for 180 ninth-grade pupils with an interval of four weeks between administrations range from .82 to .95 according to data in manual of directions. Little objective evidence of validity thus far reported by authors. *Reference:* Buros (19:892–896).

Mooney, Ross L., and Gordon, Leonard V. *Mooney Problem Check Lists,* 1950 revision. New York: The Psychological Corporation, 1941–1950. Regular edition, $1.90 per 25 copies; specimen set, 50 cents (specify form desired); separate answer sheet edition, reusable booklets, $2.40 per 25; answer sheets, $2.00 per 50 (IV).

A revision of earlier editions of the Mooney Problem Check Lists which were published by the Bureau of Educational Research of Ohio State University. Planned to help individuals identify their personal problems. Intended primarily as an interview aid and counseling device rather than a test. Usual statistical criteria of reliability and validity do not apply. A form for each of four levels: J for junior high school pupils, H for high school pupils, C for college students, and A for adults. Form J consists of 210 items, 30 in each of seven areas: health, physical development; school; home and family; money, work and the future; boy and girl relations; relations with people in general; and self-centered concerns. Forms H and C each contain 330 items, 30 in each of 11 areas. Form A has 288 items distributed among nine areas. Administration is simple. Individual goes through blank and underlines problems troubling him. No time limit; usual time about 30 minutes. A valuable counseling device when used in connection with interviews. Evidence of sensitivity of college form of check list reflecting problem changes as indicated by an independent measure was reported by Gordon (44).

Murray, Henry A. *Thematic Apperception Test*. Cambridge, Mass.: Harvard University Press, 1943. Package of pictures with manual, $6.30; Thompson Modification for use with Negroes, $6.30 (VIII).

This is a free-association or projective technique designed mainly for use in clinical situations. The test materials consist of 31 picture cards devised and arranged so that they provide two series of ten cards each for boys, girls, men, and women. Suitable for ages 7 and over. One form. The TAT is administered individually. The subject is asked to tell a story about each picture. Presumably he identifies himself with the characters in the story and thus reveals his inner emotions, motivations, complexes, and personality conflicts. Administration and interpretation tend to be a rather slow and tedious process, but the instrument has been sufficiently intriguing and promising to motivate a large amount of discussion and research on the part of psychologists. Buros' *Third, Fourth, and Fifth Mental Measurements Yearbooks* list a total of 610 titles through 1958 (17:202–294; 18:263–267; 19:301–306). Reliability data seem not to be available. Aron (1) and Shorr (102) have proposed scoring systems more objective than the original ones.

A modification of the TAT for Negroes was provided by Thompson (109). Manuals for the administration and interpretation of the TAT were prepared by Stein (103), Tomkins (113), and others. A standardized form, prepared by Leopold Bellak for recording and analyzing the stories obtained by means of the TAT, is published by The Psychological Corporation (Bellak TAT Blank, $1.25 per ten; analysis sheet, $1.75 per 100; manual, 35 cents.) *Reference* for information concerning basis of construction: Murray (87).

Remmers, H. H. *Purdue Master Attitude Scales*. Lafayette, Ind.: Division of Educational Reference, Purdue University, 1934–1960. Three cents per scale; 15 cents per specimen set of any one scale (VII).

A series of nine separate, brief scales for measuring attitude toward the following: any homemaking project, any institution, any national or racial group, any practice, any school subject, any teacher, any vocation, any play, any proposed social action, any selection of poetry, any disciplinary procedure; also a high school attitude scale, a scale for measuring attitude toward teaching, and a scale for measuring individual and group "morale." The technique of construction resembles that employed by Thurstone, but the scales are designed to serve broader purposes than the Thurstone scales. Grades 7–16. Forms A and B. Administration time, about five minutes per scale. The average reliabilities of scale for measuring attitude toward high school, one form, .74; two forms combined, .85. Forty-six references through 1951 are listed in Buros' *Mental Measurements Yearbooks* (16:57; 18:89–90).

Roeber, Edward C., and Prideaux, Gerald G. in collaboration with Edwin A. Lee and Louis P. Thorpe. *Vocational Interest Analyses*. Monterey: California Test Bureau, 1951. 10 cents per copy for each of the six analyses or 54 cents for a complete set; IBM 805 answer sheets, 6 cents each (two answer sheets required for any one examinee on all six analyses); scoring stencils, machine scoring, 60 cents; hand scoring, 60 cents; specimen set, 75 cents (IV).

Based on the *Occupational Interest Inventory* by Lee and Thorpe. Designed to increase the usefulness of the older inventory through providing vocational interest analyses in six fields: personal-social, natural, mechanical, business, the arts, and the sciences. Consists of six separate booklets, one for each area. Each booklet contains 120 paired-comparison items. One form, Grade 9–adult. The Vocational Interest Analyses can be administered within one class period of 45 minutes. Procedure is first to give Occupational Interest Inventory to locate field or fields of major interest, and then to administer the appropriate Vocational Interest Analyses, which, in turn, provide a breakdown within the field. For instance, the sciences analysis includes scores for laboratory work, mineral-petroleum products, applied chemistry, chemical research, biological research, and scientific engineering. This procedure seems sound, although there is at least reasonable doubt as to whether the instruments themselves adequately do the job for which they are designed. Analyses are coded with the *Dictionary of Occupational Titles*, but statistical data on their validity are lacking. Test-retest reliabilities reported in manual range from .82 to .94 for a group of 100 twelfth-grade students. These seem satisfactorily high so far as reliability is concerned, but the question of validity remains unanswered, much as it does for most other interest and personality measures.

Rorschach, Hermann. *Rorschach*. New York: The Psychological Corporation; also distributed by C. H. Stoelting Company, Chicago. Many variants of the Rorschach are available from various publishers. The following materials may be purchased from The Psychological Corporation: *Rorschach Psychodiagnostic Plates*; set of ten ink blots, $13.00; individual record blanks (Klopfer and Davidson), package of 35, $3.80; location charts (facsimiles of the ten figures in black and white), $3.60 per 100; Rorschach Slides (Harrower Group Method), the ten inkblots reproduced on Kodaslides, $12.50 per set; Group Rorschach Blank (Harrower), for use with the Rorschach slides with check list for use with Munroe "Inspection Technique" printed on back cover, $4.70 per 25; Rorschach Multiple Choice Blank (Harrower), for use with either cards or slides, $3.00 per 25; specimen set of Harrower blanks, 50 cents. Also, *Rorschach Method of Personality Diagnosis*, by Bruno Klopfer and Helen H. Davidson (an individual record blank developed by

The Rorschach Institute), is available from Harcourt, Brace & World, Inc., New York, at $3.30 per 35 (VIII).

A series of ten ink blots selected by Rorschach from a much larger number of ink blots for their value in diagnosing emotional disorders and first published in 1921. The test is administered individually. The subject is directed to look at each blot and state what it seems to be or what it suggests to him. Free range of responses permitted. Standards have been developed for evaluating responses. Results are reputed to provide information about emotional stability, originality of thinking, adaptability, and other traits, all of which are studied in terms of the whole personality. In a period of 45 years, this device has been developed from an interesting novelty into a veritable institution which is probably the most erudite instrument of appraisal employed by the modern psychologist. Literature relating to this technique is more extensive than that for any other measurement device. Buros' *Mental Measurements Yearbooks* list a total of 2297 titles through 1958 (16:88–90; 17:124–132; 18:202–213; 19:254–273). Despite the numerous studies, statistical data on reliability and validity are inconclusive, although numerous psychologists regard the Rorschach as the most sensitive and useful instrument for the assessment of personality. The Behn-Rorschach Test, a parallel set of ink blots, was prepared by Hans Zulliger and issued by Grune and Stratton, Inc., in 1942. The Psychodiagnostic ink blots, a parallel set of ink blots on slides, was prepared by M. R. Harrower and M. E. Steiner and is distributed by The Psychological Corporation. Original scoring was highly subjective, and much effort has been directed toward objectifying and standardizing the scoring. It is claimed for the Rorschach that it will show the general intellectual level of the subject, while at the same time exploring his emotional traits, but separate measurement of intelligence is advisable. There are numerous books and monographs on the Rorschach technique, among which are those by Klopfer and Kelley (67); B. Klopfer, Ainsworth, W. G. Klopfer, and Holt (68); Beck (8, 9, 10); Munroe (86); Ames and others (6, 7); Halpern (46); and Harrower and Steiner (48). Rorschach's original book, *Psychodiagnostics*, was translated into English and published in 1949 (99).

Strong, Edward K., Jr. *Vocational Interest Blanks*, revised. Palo Alto, Calif.: Consulting Psychologists Press, 1927–1959. Booklets: reusable, $6.00 per 25; expendable (for handscoring), $4.00 per 25; single scoring scales, $1.25 each; IBM 805 answer sheets, $2.50 per 50; NCS answer sheets, $3.25 per 50; profiles, $1.25 per 25. Prices for Form W (women) are same as prices for Form M for men. Prices for Hankes' answer sheets available from Testscor, Minneapolis, Minnesota (IV).

For many years the leading vocational interest inventories, a position they now share with the Kuder records. The purpose of the Strong blanks is not to test interest *in* vocations but to discover the extent to which a person's interests agree with those of persons in various occupational groups. De-

signed mainly for adults and college students, and probably should not be used below the junior or senior year of high school. Separate blanks for men and women. The men's blank is scored for 51 occupations, and the women's blank for 29. The blank is scored separately for each occupation. The men's blank is also scored for five occupational groups. In addition, four special scales—occupational level, masculinity-femininity, specialization level, and interest-maturity—are available for use with the men's blank. A masculinity-femininity scale is also available for the women's blank. Scoring is laborious if done by hand. If separate answer sheets are used, the men's blank may be scored on the IBM 805 Test-Scoring Machine, although this procedure is so long and tedious that it is seldom used. The women's blank has not been adapted for the IBM test-scoring machine. Rapid scoring service on the Strong blanks is available from Testscor and from National Computer Systems, both in Minneapolis.

Results of the Strong blanks are reported on men's or women's profile sheets and interpreted in terms of letter ratings: A, B+, B, B−, C+, and C. Special profile form for public accountants issued by American Institute of Certified Public Accountants. Research on Strong blanks too extensive to be summarized. Some 490 titles concerned with these blanks have been published (16:458–459; 17:670–672, 673–674; 18:748–749; 19:896–900). Average reliability of scales, .80 to .85. *References*: Strong (104, 105, 106, 107, 108).

Thorpe, Louis P., Clark, Willis W., and Tiegs, Ernest. W. *California Test of Personality*. Monterey: California Test Bureau, 1939–1953. $3.50 per 35 of any series; IBM 805 answer sheets for any level except primary, 5 cents each; machine-scoring stencils, 60 cents per set; hand-scoring keys, 50 cents per set; specimen set of any one level, 50 cents (IV).

An extensive battery consisting of five levels: primary series, kindergarten and Grades 1–3; elementary series, Grades 4–8; intermediate series, Grades 7–10; secondary series, Grades 9–14; and adult series. Planned to measure personal adjustment and social adjustment at all levels. Within each main part there are several subtests, the results of which may be graphed in the form of a profile. The test authors report the Kuder-Richardson reliabilities of the five series range from .83 to .93 for personal adjustment, from .80 to .94 for social adjustment, and from .88 to .96 for total score. Reliabilities of the subtests within the two main divisions are presumed to be rather low because of the small number of items in each subtest. *Reference*: Tiegs, Clark, and Thorpe (112).

Thorpe, Louis P., and Clark, Willis W. with Ernest W. Tiegs, consultant. *Mental Health Analysis*, 1959 Revision. Monterey: California Test Bureau, 1959. Test booklets, $3.15 per 35; IBM 805 answer sheets, 5 cents each; scoring stencils, for machine scoring, $1.00 per set; for hand scoring, $1.00; specimen set, any one level, 50 cents (IV).

Constructed for use in assessing the liabilities and assets of an individual or group in the field of mental health. Four levels: elementary, Grades 4–8; intermediate, Grades 7–10; secondary, Grades 9–12 and college; and adults. One form; administration time, about 45 to 50 minutes. Contains 200 questions to which individual responds with "yes" or "no." There is no intermediate or doubtful choice. One hundred items are related to liabilities, with 20 items devoted to each of the following areas: behavioral immaturity, emotional instability, feelings of inadequacy, physical defects, and nervous manifestations. One hundred items have to do with assets, with 20 items in each of the following areas: close personal relationships, interpersonal skills, social participation, satisfying work and recreation, and adequate outlook and goals. There are percentile norms for each of the areas and for the two main divisions of the inventory. Percentiles may be shown in graphic form. Kuder-Richardson reliabilities reported in manual range as follows: liabilities, .92 to .93; assets, .89 to .93; total score, .93 to .96. Reliabilities of subtests are not given, but in view of small number of items these are probably somewhat low. This instrument apparently constructed on a common-sense basis without much in the way of research. Scores on the various liability and asset categories may provide useful counseling information, although statistical evidence on this point is lacking.

Thorpe, Louis P., Myers, Charles E., and Bonsall, Marcella Ryser. *What I Like to Do.* Chicago: Science Research Associates, Inc., 1956. Booklets, $4.00 per 20; IBM 805 answer sheets, $5.00 per 100; machine-scoring stencils, set of 3, $1.50; profile folders, $1.20 per 20; specimen set, $2.00 (IV).

A new interest inventory for Grades 4–7. Planned to measure the child's interests in eight areas: art, music, social studies, active play, quiet play, manual arts, home arts, and science. Administration time is about one hour. National norms by grade and sex.

Thurstone, L. L. *Thurstone Temperament Schedule.* Chicago: Science Research Associates, Inc., 1949–1953. Hand-scoring test booklets with answer pads, $12.00 per 20; extra answer pads, $2.60 per 20; machine-scoring booklets, $12.00 per 20; answer sheets, $5.00 per 100; scoring stencils, $2.50 per set; specimen set, $1.00 (IV).

Designed to describe the important and stable personality traits of normal, well-adjusted individuals. Contains 140 questions to which the subject responds by marking *yes, ?,* or *no.* Yields scores in seven areas of personality: active, vigorous, impulsive, dominant, stable, sociable, and reflective. These areas were derived from factor analysis. Suitable for senior high school pupils, college students, and adults. No time limit; administration time about 15 minutes. May be given with or without supervision. Percentile norms for high school boys and girls and for men and women are available. Percentiles may be shown graphically on a profile form. Emphasis on normal characteristics will appeal to counselors in their daily work. Easily scored and interpreted. Spearman-Brown split-half reliabilities reported in manual range from .45 to .86, with a median of .65. Test-retest reliabilities range from .61 to .82, with a median of .78. These reliabilities are rather low, although probably not lower than would be expected in view of the number of questions in each area. Most of the intercorrelations between the area scores are quite low. A study by Ryans (101) indicates that this schedule may be of some use in discriminating between successful and unsuccessful teachers. A few other validity studies have been reported. *Reference:* Thurstone (110).

Washburne, J. N. *Washburne Social Adjustment Inventory* (Thaspic edition). New York: Harcourt, Brace & World, Inc., 1940. $4.50 per 35; manual for interpreting, 50 cents; machine-scored answer sheets, $2.00 per 35; set of 12 machine keys, $2.40; specimen set, 40 cents (IV).

A group test of social adjustment, consisting of 123 items, some of which call for more than one response. Most of the questions are to be answered by writing *yes* or *no* on a line preceding each question. The scoring key indicates the questions that attempt to get at the same trait or complex, thus providing for a grouping of the questions according to "elements." The aspects of personality for which scores are obtained by means of this inventory are truthfulness, sympathy, alienation, purpose, impulse-judgment, control, happiness, and wishes. One form suitable for all ages above Grade 8. Calls for 30–50 minutes of working time. Reliability coefficients reported in manual are as follows: truthfulness, .73; alienation, .81; happiness, .85; wish, .88; total adjustment score, .92. Reliabilities are not available for the other elements. It is reported that the correlation with intelligence and chronological age is negligible and that the correlations between test elements are also slight. In a study in which the scores of college women on the individual form of the Minnesota Multiphasic Personality Inventory were compared with scores on the Washburne Social Adjustment Inventory, Lough and Green (77) concluded that "the Washburne group test might well serve for a preliminary study of college women students and would aid in identifying those who had personality difficulties." *Reference* concerning origin of the inventory: Washburne (122).

Wood, Hugh B. *Behavior Preference Record.* Monterey: California Test Bureau, 1953. Booklets, $2.80 per 35; IBM 805 answer sheets, 5 cents each; scoring stencils, $3.00 per set; manuals, 25 cents each; specimen set, 50 cents (VI).

Designed to measure knowledge of and preference for different kinds of social behavior in situations the individual is likely to meet in school, home, and community. This inventory is at three levels: elementary, Grades 4–6; intermediate, Grades 7–9; advanced, Grades 9–12. Forms A and B at each level. Each form presents a series of 15 or 20 problems or situations. For each situation, the pupil answers a multiple-choice question indicating what he would do, and then selects from a list of choices the reason for his action. The procedure will appeal to teacher-counselors, although it is rather awkward from the standpoint of a test technician. Yields scores in the following five areas: cooperation, friendliness, integrity, leadership, and responsibility. Also yields a score for critical thinking. Results may be shown in profile form. No time limit; administration time, 30 to 45 minutes. According to manual of directions, reliability coefficients obtained from correlating Form A with Form B range from .65 to .91. Forty-two correlations of test scores with teacher estimates of their pupils on the five characteristics range from .21 to .78, with a median of .57. The median is fairly high for correlation of test scores with this kind of validity criterion. Adequate appraisal must await further research.

Woodworth, R. S., and Mathews, E. *Personal Data Sheet*. Chicago: C. H. Stoelting Company, 1924. $3.75 per 50 copies; specimen set, $1.00 (IV).

One of the oldest personality measures. A revision for high school use based on the original test of emotional stability devised by Woodworth. A questionnaire for obtaining a measurement of the general emotionality and nervous and mental stability of preadolescent and adolescent children. One form. Ages 9–18 years. Norms based on unselected group of 1034 cases. Flemming and Flemming (40) compared scores made by children on the test with ratings of emotional balance made for the children by teachers two years earlier, and found no relation between the tests of emotional stability and the teachers' estimates of emotional balance. The time interval between the ratings and the test is a limitation of the study. Wrightstone (128) found the Woodworth-Mathews sheet fairly valid for diagnosing certain personality disorders of children.

STUDY HABITS AND ATTITUDES

Study habits and attitudes are not precisely qualities of personality, but to a considerable extent they reflect personality characteristics. Inventories of study habits probably more properly have a place in a chapter on personality inventories than in any of the other chapters.

Scales for obtaining scores in the field of study habits, which might be employed in connection with personality or interest inventories that are already widely used, have intriguing possibilities. As mentioned in an earlier section of this chapter, Young and Estabrooks (129) prepared some years ago a "studiousness scale" for the Strong Vocational Interest Blank for Men. Williamson (124, 125) found low correlation between scores on the studiousness scale and the marks of university freshmen.

The following three inventories are among the better-known instruments for the appraisal of study habits, attitudes, and procedures.

Brown, William F., and Holtzman, Wayne H. *Survey of Study Habits and Attitudes*. New York: The Psychological Corporation, 1953. $2.00 per 25 booklets; $1.85 per 50 machine-scorable answer sheets; scoring keys, 50 cents; specimen set, 60 cents (IV).

Consists of 75 statements concerning work and study habits and attitudes to which the individual responds by marking *r*, rarely; *s*, sometimes; *f*, frequently; *g*, generally; or *a*, almost always. One form. Separate answer sheets must be used. Working time about 15 to 25 minutes. Standardized on freshmen in ten colleges but may also be used in counseling eleventh- and twelfth-grade pupils. A special counseling key is available. Separate percentile norms for men and women. Test-retest reliability coefficients of .95 for men and .93 for women with a two-week interval are reported in the manual. For an 11-week interval, the reliabilities are .88 and .84 for men and women, respectively. Correlations of inventory scores of men with one-semester grade-point averages range from .27 to .66 with an average of .42; for women, they range from .26 to .65 with an average of .45. Correlations of the inventory scores with scores on the American Council Psychological Examination are reported to be low. Multiple correlations of study habits inventory and ACE with one-semester grades reported as .63 for women and .73 for men. *Reference*: Holtzman and Brown (60).

Traxler, Arthur E. *Survey of Study Habits*. New York: Educational Records Bureau, 1944. Eight cents per copy; specimen set, 50 cents (IV).

Planned as a checklist of study habits and procedures of pupils in Grades 8–14. Contains 85 suggestions regarding study, such as "do your work regularly from day to day," "look over the work to see that you understand what you are doing," "stick to a task even though it is difficult or disagreeable," "compare viewpoints of different authorities," and so forth. The 85 items, which are grouped according to 17 general headings, were derived in part from mimeographed materials employed in the University of Chicago and from Whipple's *How to Study Effectively*. Subject answers the question "Do you?" about each item and checks in the appropriate spaces under "seldom or never," "sometimes," or "usually or always." Intended mainly as an instrument for counseling on the basis of individual items, but simple scoring procedure may be used. Independent school norms based on this procedure are available for each grade level from Grade 7 through Grade 12. One form. Spearman-Brown split-half reliability, or internal consistency, as follows: 119 independent school pupils in Grade 10, .912; 137 independent school pupils in Grade 12, .908. Correlations with achievement test scores, with school marks, and with teachers' estimates of study habits, tend to be positive but low. Suggested as an instrument for use in counseling interviews rather than as a test. A guide in helping pupils improve study habits and skills is available for use in connection with the checklist (*115*).

Wrenn, C. Gilbert. *Study Habits Inventory*, 1941 revision. Palo Alto, Calif.: Consulting Psychologists Press, 1941. $2.50 per 25 copies; manual and hand-scoring stencil, 25 cents (IV).

The oldest and no doubt the best-known inventory of study habits. Contains 28 items, grouped under A, reading and note taking techniques; B, habits of concentration; C, distribution of time and social relations in study; and D, general habits and attitudes of work. Subject responds to each item by checking in one of three columns headed "rarely or never," "sometimes," and "often or always." Responses are assigned weights according to Wrenn's research data. A total score may be obtained, but it is recommended that more attention be given to the scores on the individual items. One form. Suitable for use with senior high school pupils and college students. There is a manual by Wrenn and Larsen for use in connection with this inventory (*127*). Reported correlations of inventory scores with grade point averages range from .24 to .58.

REFERENCES

1. Aron, Betty. *A Manual for Analysis of the Thematic Apperception Test: A Method and Technique for Personality Research.* Foreword by R. Nevitt Sanford. Berkeley, Calif.: Willis E. Berg, 1949. Pp. xiv + 164. (Lithotyped.)
2. Allen, Robert M. *Introduction to the Rorschach Technique: Manual of Administration and Scoring.* New York: International Universities Press, Inc., 1953. Pp. 126.
3. Allen, Robert M. *Elements of Rorschach Interpretation.* New York: International Universities Press, Inc., 1954. Pp. 242.
4. Allen, Robert M. *Personality Assessment Procedures.* New York: Harper & Row, Publishers, 1958. Pp. xi + 541.
5. Allport, Gordon W. "A Test of Ascendance-Submission," *Journal of Abnormal and Social Psychology,* XXVI (October–December 1931), 231–248.
6. Ames, Louise Bates, and others. *Child Rorschach Responses: Development Trends from Two to Ten Years.* New York: Paul B. Hoeber, Inc., 1952. Pp. 310.
7. Ames, Louise Bates, and others. *Rorschach Responses in Old Age.* New York: The Psychological Corporation, 1954. Pp. 245.
8. Beck, Samuel J. *Rorschach's Test: I, Basic Processes.* Foreword by Willard L. Valentine. New York: Grune & Stratton, Inc., 1944. Pp. xiv + 224.
9. Beck, Samuel J. *Rorschach's Test: II, A Variety of Personality Pictures.* New York: Grune & Stratton, Inc., 1945. Pp. xii + 402.
10. Beck, Samuel J. *Rorschach's Test: III, Advances in Interpretation.* New York: Grune & Stratton, Inc., 1945. Pp. 301.
11. Beckman, R. O. "Ascendance-Submission Test—Revised," *Personnel Journal,* XI (April 1933), 387–392.
12. Bell, Hugh M. *The Theory and Practice of Student Counseling, with Special Reference to the Adjustment Inventory.* Stanford University, Calif.: Stanford University Press, 1935. Pp. 138.
13. Bernreuter, Robert G. "Validity of the Personality Inventory," *Personnel Journal,* XI (April 1933), 383–386.
14. Bernreuter, Robert G. "The Theory and Construction of the Personality Inventory," *Journal of Social Psychology,* IV (November 1933), 387–405.
15. Buros, Oscar K. (ed.). *The Nineteen Thirty-eight Mental Measurements Yearbook.* New Brunswick, N.J.: Rutgers University Press, 1938. Pp. xxii + 416.
16. Buros, Oscar K. (ed.). *The Nineteen Forty Mental Measurements Yearbook.* Highland Park, N.J.: The Mental Measurements Yearbook, 1941. Pp. xxii + 674.
17. Buros, Oscar K. (ed.). *The Third Mental Measurements Yearbook.* New Brunswick, N.J.: Rutgers University Press, 1949. Pp. xvi + 1048.
18. Buros, Oscar K. (ed.). *The Fourth Mental Measurements Yearbook.* Highland Park, N.J.: The Gryphon Press, 1953. Pp. xvii + 1164.
19. Buros, Oscar K. (ed.). *The Fifth Mental Measurements Yearbook.* Highland Park, N.J.: The Gryphon Press, 1959. Pp. xxvii + 1292.
20. Buros, Oscar K. (ed.). *Tests in Print.* Highland Park, N.J.: The Gryphon Press, 1961. Pp. xxix + 479.
21. Cantoni, Louis J. "A Study in Emotional Adjustment: the Correlation of Student and Adult Forms of the Bell Adjustment Inventory over a Period of Thirteen Years," *Educational and Psychological Measurement,* XV (Summer 1955), 137–143.
22. Cattell, Raymond B. "The Description of Personality: Principles and Findings in a Factor Analysis," *American Journal of Psychology,* LVIII (January 1945), 69–90.
23. Cattell, Raymond B., and Luborsky, L. B. "Personality Factors in Response to Humor," *Journal of Abnormal and Social Psychology,* XLII (October 1947), 402–421.
24. Cattell, Raymond B. "Primary Personality Factors in the Realm of Objective Tests," *Journal of Personality,* XVI (June 1948), 459–487.
25. Chave, E. J. *Personality Development in Children.* Chicago: The University of Chicago Press, 1937. Pp. xiv + 354.
26. Cleeton, Glen U. "An Analysis of Women's Vocational Interests," *Report of the Twelfth Annual Meeting,* American College Personnel Association, 1935.
27. Congdon, Nora A. "A Study of Cleeton's Vocational Interest Inventory," *Occupations,* XVIII (February 1940), 347–352.

28. Cronbach, Lee J. *Essentials of Psychological Testing*, 2nd ed. New York: Harper & Row, Publishers, 1960. Pp. xxii+650.
29. Darley, John G., and McNamara, Walter J. "Factor Analysis in the Establishment of New Personality Tests," *Journal of Educational Psychology*, XXXI (May 1940), 321–334.
30. Darley, John G., and Hagenah, Theda. *Vocational Interest Measurement: Theory and Practice*. Minneapolis: The University of Minnesota Press, 1955. Pp. 279.
31. Deri, Susan K. *Introduction to the Szondi Test: Theory and Practice*. New York: Grune & Stratton, Inc., 1949. Pp. xiv+354.
32. Downey, June E. *The Will-Temperament and Its Testing*. Yonkers, N.Y.: World Book Company, 1923. Pp. vi+340.
33. Eisele, Martha C., and Cattell, William C. "The Guilford-Zimmerman Temperament Survey: I, with Rural High School Students," *University of Kansas Bulletin of Education*, VI (November 1951), 12–15.
34. Ellis, Albert. "The Validity of Personality Questionnaires," *Psychological Bulletin*, XLIII (September 1946), 385–440.
35. Ellis, Albert, and Conrad, Herbert S. "The Validity of Personality Inventories in Military Practice," *Psychological Bulletin*, XLV (September 1948), 385–426.
36. Eysenck, H. J. *The Structure of Human Personality*. New York: John Wiley & Sons, Inc., 1953. Pp. xix+348.
37. Ferguson, Leonard W. *Personality Measurement*. New York: McGraw-Hill Book Company, Inc., 1952. Pp. xv+457.
38. Flanagan, John C. *Factor Analysis in the Study of Personality*. Stanford University, Calif.: Stanford University Press, 1935. Pp. x+104.
39. Flanagan, John C. "Technical Aspects of Multi-Trait Tests," *Journal of Educational Psychology*, XXVI (November 1935), 641–651.
40. Flemming, E. G., and Flemming, C. W. "The Validity of the Mathews Revision of the Woodworth Personal Data Questionnaire," *Journal of Abnormal and Social Psychology*, XXIII (January–February 1939), 500–506.
41. Forer, Bertram R. "The Stability of Kuder Scores in a Disabled Population," *Educational and Psychological Measurement*, XV (Summer 1955), 166–169.
42. Gilbert, Claudia, "The Guilford-Zimmerman Temperament Survey and Certain Related Personality Tests," *Journal of Applied Psychology*, XXXIV (December 1950), 394–396.
43. Goldman, Leo. *Using Tests in Counseling*. New York: Appleton-Century-Crofts, Inc., 1961. Pp. xviii+434.
44. Gordon, Leonard V. "The Reflection of Problem Changes by the Mooney Problem Check List," *Educational and Psychological Measurement*, IX (Winter 1949), 749–752.
45. Guilford, J. P. and Guilford, Ruth B. "Personality Factors S, E, and M, and Their Measurement," *Journal of Psychology*, II (1936), 109–127.

46. Halpern, Florence. *A Clinical Approach to Children's Rorschachs*. New York: The Psychological Corporation, 1953. Pp. 288.
47. Harris, Dale B. *Children's Drawings As Measures of Intellectual Maturity—A Revision and Extension of the Goodenough Draw-A-Man Test*. New York: Harcourt, Brace & World, Inc., 1963. Pp. 367, $8.95.
48. Harrower, M. R., and Steiner, M. E. *Large-Scale Rorschach Technique*, 2nd ed. Springfield, Ill.: Charles C. Thomas, Publisher, 1951. Pp. 354.
49. Hartshorne, Hugh, and May, Mark. *Studies in Deceit*. New York: The Macmillan Company, 1928. Pp. xxii+306.
50. Hartshorne, Hugh, May, Mark, and Maller, J. B. *Studies in Service and Self-Control*. New York: The Macmillan Company, 1929. Pp. xxvi+560.
51. Hartshorne, Hugh, May, Mark, and Shuttleworth, F. K. *Studies in the Organization of Character*. New York: The Macmillan Company, 1930. Pp. xxvi+504.
52. Hathaway, S. R., and McKinley, J. C. "A Multiphasic Personality Schedule (Minn.): I, Construction of the Schedule," *Journal of Psychology*, X (October 1940), 249–254.
53. Hathaway, S. R., and McKinley, J. C. "A Multiphasic Personality Schedule (Minn.): III, The Measurement of Symptomatic Depression," *Journal of Psychology*, XIV (July 1942), 63–84.
54. Hathaway, S. R., and Meehl, Paul E. *An Atlas for the Clinical Use of the MMPI*. Minn.: The University of Minnesota Press, 1951. Pp. xliv+800.
55. Hellersberg, Elizabeth F. "The Horn-Hellersberg Test, An Adjustment to Reality," *American Journal of Orthopsychiatry*, XV (October 1945), 690–710.
56. Hertz, Marguerite R. "The Rorschach Ink Blot Test: Historical Summary," *Psychological Bulletin*, XXXII (1935), 33–36.
57. Hertz, Marguerite R. *Frequency Tables to be Used in Scoring Responses to the Rorschach Ink Blot Test: Revised Edition with Code Charts for Locating Responses, Lists of Normal Details, Lists of F+ and F− Responses, Lists of Popular Responses, Indications of Original Responses*. Cleveland, Ohio: Western Reserve University Book Store, 1946. Pp. iv+160. (Lithotyped.)
58. Hildreth, Gertrude. *A Bibliography of Mental Tests and Rating Scales*. New York: The Psychological Corporation, 1933 (rev. 1939). Pp. 295.
59. Hildreth, Gertrude. *A Bibliography of Mental Tests and Rating Scales, 1945 Supplement*. New York: The Psychological Corporation, 1946. Pp. ix+86.
60. Holtzman, Wayne H., and Brown, William F. "Study Habits and Attitudes in the Prediction of Academic Success," *American Psychologist*, VIII (August 1953), 369 (abstract).
61. Howard, James W. *Howard Ink Blot Test Manual*. Brandon, Vt.: Monograph Supplement 10 from July 1953 Issue of *Journal of Clinical Psychology*.
62. Jacobs, Robert. "A Brief Study of the Relationship between Scores on the Lee-Thorpe Occupational Interest

Inventory and Scores on the Kuder Preference Record," *1951 Achievement Testing Program in Independent Schools and Supplementary Studies*, pp. 79–85. Educational Records Bulletin 57. New York: Educational Records Bureau, July 1951. Pp. xiv+86.

63. Jacobs, Robert, and Traxler, Arthur E. "Use of the Kuder in Counseling with Regard to Accounting as a Career," *Journal of Counseling Psychology*, I (1954), 153–158.

64. Jacobs, Robert, and Traxler, Arthur E. "What Manner of Man Is the Average Public Accountant?" *Journal of Accountancy* (April 1954), 465–469.

65. Kent, Grace H., and Rosanoff, A. J. *A Study of Association in Insanity*. Baltimore: Lord Baltimore Press, 1910. Pp. 142.

66. King, Paul T., and Ross, Donald R. "Test Transparency as Related to Test Response," *Personnel and Guidance Journal*, XLIII (March 1965), 669–673.

67. Klopfer, Bruno. *The Rorschach Technique: A Manual for a Projective Method of Personality Diagnosis*, with clinical contributions by Douglas McGlashen Kelley. With 1946 supplement by Bruno Klopfer and Helen H. Davidson. Tarrytown-on-Hudson, N.Y.: World Book Company, 1946. Pp. xv+476.

68. Klopfer, Bruno, Ainsworth, Mary D., Klopfer, Walter G., and Holt, Robert R. *Developments in the Rorschach Technique. Vol. I: Technique and Theory*. Tarrytown-on-Hudson, N.Y.: World Book Company, 1954. Pp. 726.

69. Krugman, Morris. "Projective Techniques in the Assessment of Personality in Schools," *Educational and Psychological Measurement*, XIV (Summer 1954), 272–276.

70. Kuder, G. Frederic. "The Stability of Preference Items," *Journal of Social Psychology*, XI (1939), 41–50.

71. Kuder, G. Frederic. "Expected Developments in Interest and Personality Inventories," *Educational and Psychological Measurement*, XIV (Summer 1954), 265–271.

72. Leton, Donald A. "Personality Ratings of High School Students," *Journal of Educational Research*, LVI (November 1962), 160–163.

73. Lindgren, Henry C. "A Study of Certain Aspects of the Lee-Thorpe Occupational Interest Inventory," *Journal of Educational Psychology*, XXXVIII (October 1947), 353–362.

74. Lorge, Irving. "Personality Traits by Fiat I. The Analysis of Total Trait Scores and Keys by the Bernreuter Personality Inventory," *Journal of Educational Psychology*, XXVI (April 1935), 273–278.

75. Lorge, Irving. "Personality Traits by Fiat II. The Consistency of the Bernreuter Personality Inventory by the Bernreuter and by the Flanagan Keys," *Journal of Educational Psychology*, XXVI (September 1935), 427–434.

76. Lorge, Irving. "Personality Traits by Fiat II. A Correction," *Journal of Educational Psychology*, XXVI (December 1935), 652–654.

77. Lough, Orpha M., and Green, Mary E. "Comparison of the Minnesota Multiphasic Personality Inventory and the Washburne S-A Inventory as Measures of Personality of College Women," *Journal of Social Psychology*, XXXII (August 1950), 23–30.

78. McKinley, J. C., and Hathaway, S. R. "A Multiphasic Personality Schedule (Minn.): II, A Differential Study of Hypochondriasis," *Journal of Psychology*, X (October 1940), 255–268.

79. McKinley, J. C., and Hathaway, S. R. "A Multiphasic Personality Schedule (Minn.): IV, Psychasthenia," *Journal of Applied Psychology*, XXVI (October 1942), 614–624.

80. McNemar, Quinn. "Opinion-Attitude Methodology," *Psychological Bulletin*, XLIII (July 1946), 289–374.

81. Maller, J. B. *Character and Personality Tests*. New York: Bureau of Publications, Teachers College, Columbia University, 1932. Pp. 53.

82. Malloy, John. "The Prediction of College Achievement with the Life Experience Inventory," *Educational and Psychological Measurement*, XV (Summer 1955), 170–180.

83. Meehl, Paul E., and Hathaway, Starke R. "The K Factor as a Suppressor Variable in the Minnesota Multiphasic Personality Inventory," *Journal of Applied Psychology*, XXX (October 1946), 524–564.

84. Morgan, C. D., and Murray, H. A. "A Method for Investigating Phantasies: The Thematic Apperception Test," *Archives of Neurology and Psychiatry*, XIV (1935), 289–306.

85. Mosier, Mary F., and Kuder, G. Frederic. "Personal Preference Differences among Occupational Groups," *Journal of Applied Psychology*, XXXIII (January 1949), 231–239.

86. Munroe, Ruth L. "Prediction of the Adjustment and Academic Performance of College Students by a Modification of the Rorschach Method," *Applied Psychology Monograph* 7 (1945), 104.

87. Murray, H. A., and the workers at Harvard Psychological Clinic. *Explorations in Personality*. Fairlawn, N.J.: Oxford University Press, 1938. Pp. xiv+762.

88. Newman, Horatio H., Freeman, Frank N., and Holzinger, Karl J. *Twins: A Study of Heredity and Environment*. Chicago: The University of Chicago Press, 1937. Pp. xvi+370.

89. Pedersen, Ruth A. "Validity of the Bell Adjustment Inventory When Applied to College Women," *Journal of Psychology*, IX (January 1940), 227–236.

90. Pintner, Rudolf, and Forlano, George. "Four Retests of a Personality Inventory," *Journal of Educational Psychology*, XXIX (February 1938), 93–100.

91. Pintner, Rudolf, and Forlano, George. "Validation of Personality Tests by Outstanding Characteristics of Pupils," *Journal of Educational Psychology*, XXX (January 1939), 25–32.

92. *Pupil Appraisal Practices in Secondary Schools*. Report of Fifth National Conference Sponsored by Office of Education and Commission on Life Adjustment Education for Youth. Circular 363. Compiled by Howard H.

Cummings, Walter H. Gaumnitz, J. Dan Hull, John R. Ludington, and Ellsworth Tompkins. Washington: U.S. Office of Education, 1952.

93. Rapaport, David. *Diagnostic Psychological Testing.* Chicago: The Year Book Publishers, 1946. Pp. 516.

94. Remmers, H. H. "Measuring Attitudes toward Vocations," *Studies in Attitudes: A Contribution to Social-Psychological Research Methods,* pp. 77–83. Bulletin of Purdue University, Vol. XXXV, No. 4. Studies in Higher Education No. 26. Lafayette, Ind.: Division of Educational Reference, Purdue University, December 1934. Pp. 112.

95. Remmers, H. H., and Silance, E. B. "Generalized Attitude Scales," *Journal of Psychology,* V (August 1934), 298–312.

96. Resnick, Joseph. "A Study of Some Relationships between High School Grades and Certain Aspects of Adjustment," *Journal of Educational Research,* XLIV (January 1951), 321–340.

97. Rogers, Carl R. *Measuring Personality Adjustment in Children 9 to 13 Years of Age.* New York: Bureau of Publications, Teachers College, Columbia University, 1931. Pp. 98.

98. Rorschach, Hermann. *Psychodiagnostik: Methodik und Ergebnisse eines Wahrnehmungsdiagnostischen Experiments.* Berne, Switzerland: E. Birchner, 1921. Pp. 174.

99. Rorschach, Hermann, *Psychodiagnostics.* New York: Grune & Stratton, Inc., 1949. Pp. 263.

100. Rosenzweig, Sol, and Sarason, Seymour. "An Experimental Study of the Triadic Hypothesis Reaction to Frustration, Ego-Defense, and Hypnotizability: I. Correlational Approach," *Character and Personality,* XI (September 1942), 1–19.

101. Ryans, David G. *Characteristics of Teachers.* Washington, D.C.: American Council on Education, 1960. Pp. 416.

102. Shorr, Joseph E. "A Proposed System for Scoring the TAT," *Journal of Clinical Psychology,* IV (April 1948), 189–194.

103. Stein, Morris I. *The Thematic Apperception Test: An Introductory Manual for Its Clinical Use with Adult Males.* Reading, Mass.: Addison-Wesley Publishing Company, Inc., 1948. Pp. viii + 95. (Lithotyped.)

104. Strong, Edward K., Jr. *Vocational Interests of Men and Women.* Stanford, Calif.: Stanford University Press, 1943. Pp. xxx + 746.

105. Strong, Edward K., Jr. "The Role of Interests in Guidance," *Occupations,* XXVII (May 1949), 517–522.

106. Strong, Edward K., Jr. "Permanence of Interest Scores over 22 Years," *Journal of Applied Psychology,* XXXV (April 1951), 89–91.

107. Strong, Edward K., Jr. "Interest Scores while in College of Occupations Engaged in 20 Years Later," *Educational and Psychological Measurement,* XI (Autumn 1951), 335–348.

108. Strong, Edward K., Jr. *Vocational Interests Eighteen Years after College.* Minneapolis: The University of Minnesota Press, 1955. Pp. 207.

109. Thompson, Charles E. "The Thompson Modification of the Thematic Apperception Test," *Rorschach Research Exchange and Journal of Projective Techniques,* XIII (December 1949), 469–478.

110. Thurstone, L. L. "The Dimensions of Temperament," *Psychometrika,* XVI (March 1951), 11–20.

111. Thurstone, L. L., and Chave, E. J. *The Measurement of Attitude.* Chicago: The University of Chicago Press, 1929. Pp. xii + 96.

112. Tiegs, Ernest W., Clark, Willis W., and Thorpe, Louis P. "The California Test of Personality," *Journal of Educational Research,* XXXV (October 1941), 102–108.

113. Tomkins, Silvan S. *The Thematic Apperception Test: The Theory and Technique of Interpretation.* New York: Grune & Stratton, Inc., 1947. Pp. xii + 298.

114. Traxler, Arthur E. "The Reliability of the Bell Inventories and Their Correlation with Teacher Judgment," *Journal of Applied Psychology,* XXV (December 1941), 672–678.

115. Traxler, Arthur E. *The Improvement of Study Habits and Skills.* Educational Records Bulletin 41, revised. New York: Educational Records Bureau, 1954. Pp. 40.

116. Traxler, Arthur E. and Vecchione, Nicholas. "Scores of Seniors in Six Secondary Schools on the Allport-Vernon-Lindzey Study of Values," *1959 Achievement Testing Program in Independent Schools and Supplementary Studies,* pp. 75–89. Educational Records Bulletin 74. New York: Educational Records Bureau, July 1959. Pp. xii + 104.

117. Triggs, Frances O. "A Study of the Relation of Kuder Preference Record Scores to Various Other Measures," *Educational and Psychological Measurement,* III (Winter 1943), 341–354.

118. Triggs, Frances O. "A Further Comparison of Interest Measurement by the Kuder Preference Record and the Strong Vocational Interest Blank for Men," *Journal of Educational Research,* XXXVII (March 1944), 538–544.

119. Turney, Austin H., and Fee, Mary. "An Attempt to Use the Bell Adjustment Inventory for High School Guidance," *School Review,* XLIV (March 1936), 193–198.

120. Vernon, P. E., and Allport, Gordon W. "A Test for Personal Values," *Journal of Abnormal and Social Psychology,* XXVI (October–December 1931), 231–248.

121. Wagner, Mazie Earle, and Schubert, Herman, J. P. *D.A.P. Quality Scale for Late Adolescents and Young Adults.* Kenmore, N.Y.: Delaware Letter Shop, 1955. Pp. 23 + 29 unnumbered pages.

122. Washburne, J. N. "A Test of Social Adjustment," *Journal of Applied Psychology,* XIX (April 1935), 123–144.

123. Weedon, Vivian F. "Technique for Determining Interest," *Educational Research Bulletin,* XIII (November–December 1934), 191–197, 231–234.

124. Williamson, E. G. "An Analysis of the Young-Esta-

brooks Studiousness Scale," *Journal of Applied Psychology*, XXI (June 1937), 260–264.

125. Williamson, E. G. "A Further Analysis of the Young-Estabrooks Studiousness Scale," *Journal of Applied Psychology*, XXII (February 1938), 105.

126. Wittenborn, J. R., Triggs, Frances O., and Feder, Daniel D. "A Comparison of Interest Measurement by the Kuder Preference Record and the Strong Vocational Interest Blanks for Men and Women," *Educational and Psychological Measurement*, III (Autumn 1943), 239–257.

127. Wrenn, C. Gilbert, and Larsen, Robert P. *Studying Effectively*. Stanford, Calif.: Stanford University Press, 1941. Pp. 36.

128. Wrightstone, J. Wayne. "Validity of the Woodworth-Mathews Personal Data Sheet for Diagnosing Certain Personality Disorders," *Journal of Educational Psychology*, XXV (January 1934), 39–44.

129. Young, C. W., and Estabrooks, G. H. "Report of the Young-Estabrooks Studiousness Scale for Use with the Strong Vocational Interest Blank for Men," *Journal of Educational Psychology*, XXVIII (March 1937), 176–187.

CHAPTER VIII

Appraisal of Personal Qualities: Rating Scales, Behavior Descriptions, Anecdotal Records, and Sociometric Devices[1]

THE INSTRUMENTS FOR THE APPRAISAL OF personal qualities discussed in Chapter VII were based on the reaction of the individual to a series of questions or situations. Nearly all of them were entirely objective, and most could be scored by machine and the scores handled by data processing equipment. Thus, they were suitable for use with the rapidly growing population in our schools.

A deterrent to the use of the nontest, nonobjective or semiobjective, instruments discussed in the present chapter is the amount of time these instruments require, and this is especially noticeable at present when our schools are bulging with students.

Nevertheless, for those schools that are well staffed in relation to the number of pupils, the collection and systematic recording of nontest information to supplement test data is well worth the effort.

RATING SCALES

Closely related to the self-inventories, which formed an important part of the preceding chapter, are the behavior rating scales, in which the rating of the

pupil is done by counselors, teachers, parents, or others, rather than by the pupil himself.

A limitation to the use of rating scales is that unless the rater is well acquainted with the individual being rated, or has perfected a technique for getting reliable information from persons who do know the subject intimately, the ratings will probably be low in validity. On the other hand, persons are less likely to be biased in their judgments concerning others than in their estimates of themselves, and it has been demonstrated that the reliability and validity of ratings can be increased by combining those secured from several judges concerning the same individual.

There are several well-known and long-used rating scales, such as the Vineland Social Maturity Scale and the Haggerty-Olson-Wickman Behavior Rating Schedules. On the whole, however, the use of instruments designed for the rating of individuals by others, as contrasted with self-rating scales, such as those discussed in Chapter VII, has declined in recent years. Very few new rating scales have been published, while a number of worthwhile scales that were formerly available, such as the Freeman-Kawin Teacher's Rating Scales for Pupil Adjustment, the Hayes Scale for Evaluating the

---

[1] Some of the best work on anecdotal records, behavior descriptions, rating scales, and sociometric devices was done between 1930 and 1955. Hence, many of the references in this chapter are by no means recent, although it will be observed that some work in this field has been done lately.

School Behavior of Children Ten to Fifteen, and the B E C Personality Rating Schedule, by Rulon, Nash, Woodward, and others, have been allowed to go out of print.

One advantage of rating scales over questionnaires is that they may be used with children who are too young to read questionnaires or to evaluate their own reactions. Years ago, Marston (37) published an instrument entitled Introversion-Extroversion in Young Children which could be used in rating traits of children between 2 and 6 years of age. The Merrill-Palmer School published 19 Personality Rating schedules for young children (48). Recently, Cassel issued a more up-to-date Child Behavior Rating Scale (see annotated list).

Schedule B of the Haggerty-Olson-Wickman blank is a graphic rating scale. In this type of scale the pupil is rated with respect to a certain characteristic by placing a check mark at an appropriate place on a continuous line. The rater indicates where he thinks the individual falls between the two extremes of behavior of that particular type. Descriptive statements are sometimes printed below portions of the scale to help define the thinking of the rater. Psychologists tend to prefer the graphic rating scale to other types.

One difficulty with the usual procedure of using rating scales is that the ratings are frequently subject to "halo effect"; that is, the rating assigned to the pupil on one trait often influences the rating which is assigned to him on the next trait. Halo effect can be reduced by having the rater judge all the individuals in the group on a single trait, then rate all the individuals on the next trait, and so forth. Some rating scales provide for the use of the latter procedure. A plan of this kind was recommended for filling out the Behavior Description Form described later in this chapter.

Persons undertaking appraisal of the general development, including the personal qualities, of young children would be well advised to become familiar with the developmental examination tests prepared by Ilg and Ames and explained in detail in their book (28).

ANECDOTAL RECORDS[2]

About 35 years ago, some schools began to use a device for the appraisal of personality known as the anecdotal record. Because it is time consuming, this type of record is not widely used at present. But it is worthy of consideration in any school where the guidance program has the full cooperation of the faculty.

The anecdotal record, as the name implies, involves setting down an anecdote concerning some aspect of pupil behavior which seems significant to the observer. There is no standardized technique for the making and utilizing of anecdotal records, but there are many points of similarity in the plans described by different writers.

Records of this kind were first given wide publicity in a report entitled "Personnel Methods," a supplement to the *Educational Record* published in 1928 by the American Council on Education, but these records were called descriptions of personality.

The term "anecdotal record" apparently originated at the Rochester Athenaeum and Mechanics Institute[3] (45), which was a leading institution in the introduction of such records. In the early 1930's, Wood (63), Tyler (56), and others began to direct the attention of schools to anecdotal records.

Among the various definitions of the anecdotal record, over the years, the following are especially significant:

The anecdotal record is a specialized form of incidental observation. It is a description of the child's conduct and personality in terms of frequent, brief, concrete observations of the pupil made and recorded by the teacher. [Strang (53).]

An anecdotal record is a report of a significant episode in the life of a student. [Raths (46).]

Anecdotes are descriptive accounts of episodes or occurrences in the daily life of the student. [Brown and Martin (12).]

Here used, the anecdotal record is a simple statement of an incident deemed by the observer to be significant with respect to a given pupil. [Zahn (67).]

. . . descriptions of actual behavior taking place in situations noted by the instructor, in contrast with rating scales which provide records only of the summary interpretation of the behavior observed. [Tyler (56).]

As used there [the Rochester Athenaeum and Mechanics Institute], the anecdote is a record of some significant item of conduct; a record of an episode in the life of the student; a word picture of the student in action; the teacher's best effort at taking a word snapshot at the moment of the incident; any narrative of events in which the student takes such part as to reveal something which may be significant about his personality. [Randall (45).]

CHARACTERISTICS OF A GOOD ANECDOTE

The natural tendency of an untrained observer when reporting an incident is to mix fact and opinion,

[2] Anecdotal records and behavior descriptions are discussed in this chapter rather than in the chapters on personnel records because their main purpose is the securing of evaluative data instead of the organizing and relating of different types of evaluations. They are comparable to test papers in that they constitute primary sources of data and not secondary sources as do most other kinds of personnel records.

[3] Now the Rochester Institute of Technology.

but this is not desirable. Objectivity is the essence of a good anecdote.

One who is just beginning to experiment with anecdotes may be helped if he draws an analogy between the writing of anecdotes and good news reporting. A newspaper contains both news items and editorial opinion, but as a rule these are carefully separated. The function of the anecdotal writer, like the function of the news writer, is to report the facts accurately, objectively, and dispassionately.

The following is an anecdote from an untrained observer:

In study hall today, George showed his great desire to get attention, particularly from girls, by whispering and clowning for the benefit of everyone about him whenever he thought the teacher's attention was elsewhere. He seems to be a born trouble-maker who will be a bad influence in this school. I think the principal and his counselor should call him in and take strong action before it is too late.

The phrases "showed his great desire to get attention," "born trouble-maker," and "bad influence in this school" are matters of opinion that have no place in a report of the incident itself. An objective report of what took place would read approximately as follows:

Incident. In study hall today, George whispered frequently and created a disturbance by various antics which attracted the attention of the pupils sitting near him.

This is a brief, clear statement of what took place. Some authorities on this method would limit the anecdotal record to a report of the incident, but most of them agree that it is sometimes desirable to add an interpretation, if it is clearly separated from the incident. The interpretation can well be placed in a separate paragraph or column carefully so labeled:

Interpretation. George seems to be a boy who wants much attention from other pupils, particularly girls. He manages to get some of the attention he craves, but his classmates seem more annoyed and disgusted than amused.

Occasionally a recommendation is also helpful, provided it is separated from both incident and interpretation. It can be placed in a separate short paragraph, as follows:

Recommendation. It would be advisable for George's counselor to find an opportunity to talk with him about his relations with the other students and the school generally, and to make suggestions which may help to improve the boy's adjustment before he becomes a serious problem.

An important advantage in separating the interpretation and the recommendation from the report of what was observed is that persons interested in obtaining an impartial appraisal of the pupil by summarizing many different anecdotes can deal with the incidents and entirely ignore the subjective parts of the record. This procedure will keep the points of view of different teachers from influencing the conclusions.

It may be felt that the mere report of an incident without interpretation is of such slight importance that it can be of little value in helping a counselor to understand a pupil. This opinion is no doubt justified if a single anecdote is considered alone, but ordinarily anecdotes are not used in that way. The anecdotal method is essentially cumulative in nature. While a single incident may not be at all typical of the behavior of the pupil concerned, the assembling and studying of many anecdotes, together with the other information the school has recorded about a pupil, present a pattern of individual personality that is most helpful in a counseling program.

SITUATIONS IN WHICH THE ANECDOTAL METHOD IS APPLICABLE

Should anecdotes be prepared for problem cases only, or should this method be applied to all pupils? Olson (42) developed the problem-behavior journal, which is designed especially for personal and social behavior problems; this plan was used to advantage in the University Elementary School, University of Michigan. The Canadian psychologists, Blatz and Bott (5) likewise made extensive use of the problem-record log by having teachers make journal entries of misdemeanors by weeks. One possible advantage in confining the method to behavior problems is that the number of anecdotes to be prepared will be relatively small, and, consequently, the plan can be introduced into a school without greatly adding to the work of the staff.

However, the majority of those who have worked with the anecdotal method are in favor of using it with all pupils, and Olson and others who have employed the problem-behavior log agree that the method is applicable on a wider basis. It has been pointed out that the use of the anecdotal method with all pupils serves to help direct the attention of teachers toward inconspicuous pupils who otherwise might never be really known by their teachers. Moreover, it is felt that if anecdotes are to present a truly developmental picture for each individual, they should not be confined to problem matters but should contain positive and constructive features, through reporting admirable behavior and outstanding achievement, as well as the other side. The present tendency, therefore, is to regard the anecdotal method as applicable to all pupils and all situations, except on rare occasions when counselors or teachers share confidences with pupils which should not be written down.

Some schools now follow the plan of designating positive anecdotes, or those which are in harmony with character objectives, with a certain type of symbol, and negative anecdotes, or those which are not in harmony with these objectives, with a different type. Thus, one may obtain a rough quantitative measure of a pupil's growth by counting the number of positive and of negative symbols for different time intervals.

STEPS IN AN ANECDOTAL RECORD PLAN

Procedures for the introduction, preparation, and use of anecdotal records have not been standardized, and it would not be desirable to standardize them, but it appears that certain steps are needed when records of this kind are introduced into a school, regardless of modifications to meet the local situation.

ENLISTING COOPERATION

At the outset, the entire faculty of the school should be given an understanding of what is involved in the anecdotal record plan. Willingness to cooperate in trying out the method should be stimulated. Counselors, as a rule, tend to favor the plan, for they can see possibilities of immediate and direct help from it in connection with their work, whereas some of the teachers may at first be unable to see the value of these records, and may feel that they are just an addition to the load they are already carrying. It is the teachers, however, whose attitudes and cooperation are most essential to the success of the plan, for they have a better opportunity to observe pupil behavior than do the other members of the staff. The success of the plan depends largely upon them, for they will write the great majority of the anecdotes.

The introduction of anecdotal records should begin with the development within the faculty of the ideal of individualized education. The anecdotal method rests on an interest in individual boys and girls, a grasp of the concept of individual differences, a conviction that the development of each pupil is more important than the teaching of subject matter, and a knowledge that teaching effectiveness increases in proportion to one's acquaintance with the individuals composing the class. Until the faculty members have reached a point in their thinking where they believe that the study of pupils is at least as important as the teaching of their subject, they are not ready to participate whole-heartedly in the preparation of anecdotal records. Schools whose staff members have already reached that point should find these records an easy and logical next step.

DECIDING HOW MUCH SHOULD BE EXPECTED OF OBSERVERS

When a faculty has decided to try out the anecdotal method, the next step is to arrive at an understanding of what shall be expected of those who are to write the anecdotes. This step involves two dangers. The first is that too much will be attempted and that the staff will become discouraged because so much time is required. The second is that after it has been agreed that anecdotal records are a promising approach to the investigation of pupil personality, the whole matter will be left to the individual whim of each teacher. The probable net result will be that the plan will resolve itself into an expression of good intentions with little or no tangible result. It seems desirable to decide on some reasonable minimum number of anecdotes which each teacher will write each week. It is not easy to say just what constitutes a "reasonable minimum number." Probably the best plan in deciding what can reasonably be expected of observers in a given school is to set aside an experimental week in which each teacher will prepare as many anecdotes as possible, after which a meeting can be held to study the ancedotes and to find out how many of them various teachers have written. This procedure will be advantageous both for showing the number of anecdotes that teachers should be able to write without being overburdened, and for obtaining criticism on the anecdotes which have been prepared.

Another plan is to choose certain aspects of behavior, such as cooperation or punctuality, and to ask all the teachers to observe the pupils and write anecdotes concerned with these particular kinds of behavior. A plan of this kind for limiting the scope of the project has the advantage of focusing the attention of the teachers on a few traits. This helps to keep them from becoming overwhelmed and discouraged in the very beginning by the size of the undertaking.

It may be feared that the writing of anecdotes will become routinized and perfunctory if teachers are asked to submit a certain minimum number. Some people will insist that teachers should be requested to write anecdotes only when they observe behavior that they feel is worth recording. The danger here is that some teachers will not be led to observe the pupils carefully and that they may record only striking behavior that may not be at all typical of the pupil. Behavior is a continuing process, and it is probable that during any class hour every pupil in the group exhibits behavior that brings out his personal qualities in a significant way, if only the observer were alert to see the behavior and grasp its implications. Highly passive behavior may be more significant than active behavior.

PREPARING FORMS

The anecdotal record does not require elaborate forms. In fact, two or three simple ones are usually sufficient. There must be, first of all, forms for the original record to be made by the teacher or other observer. Each faculty member should be supplied with these.

The form for the original record may be placed on a small card, a half-sheet, or an ordinary letter-size sheet.

ANECDOTAL RECORD

Pupil--Class----------------

Date	Place	Incident	Comment

Observer---------------------

FORM 5.

When a card or a half-sheet is used, it is assumed that there will be only one anecdote on each form, while the full-size sheet may serve for the writing of several anecdotes about the same pupil.

A form which should prove adequate in most classroom situations is shown in Form 5. The same four columns can be ruled on the back, if desired. If this is done, five or six anecdotes can frequently be entered on one sheet. The date and the place should be given in connection with each anecdote. The behavior observed should be stated clearly, concisely, and objectively under *incident*. Both interpretation and recommendation can be entered in separate paragraphs under *comment*. It should be understood that there is no necessity for writing anything under *comment* unless the observer feels that a comment will help the counselor understand the incident. The name of the observer should be signed at the bottom of each anecdotal record page.

If a letter-size record sheet of this kind is adopted for classroom use, it may be desirable to supplement it with some small cards, particularly if the members of the staff are encouraged to write anecdotes concerning behavior outside class.

Cards similar to the one illustrated in Form 6 are easily carried and are convenient for making quick notes when there is an occasion to do so.

A third form that some schools may use is one for organizing and summarizing periodically the anecdotes from the various staff members. Other schools may avoid the use of a secondary-entry form of this type through a system of filing the original records. A form for summarizing anecdotes periodically is suggested in Form 7.

The anecdotes should be arranged in chronological order in the periodic summary. The name of the staff member reporting the anecdote should be entered under *observer*. Under *anecdote*, a brief statement of each incident, ordinarily without interpretation or recommendation, will be transferred from the original record.

At the end of each year, the periodic summary sheets may be used in preparing an annual summary for the cumulative record. The annual summary may take any one of several different forms, depending on the nature of the cumulative record employed in the local school. These will be discussed later.

OBTAINING THE ORIGINAL RECORDS

It is seldom convenient for a teacher to write an anecdote at the moment the incident takes place. Many incidents that should be recorded occur during class discussion or immediately before or after class, when a multitude of different things is claiming the attention of the teacher. If the teacher stopped to record significant behavior as it took place, the continuity of the work of the class would be interrupted, and in the minds of the pupils undesirable importance would be attached to the preparation of anecdotes. At most, the teacher can find time merely to jot down the name of the pupil, with perhaps a phrase to call the incident to mind later.

In order to be successful in preparing anecdotes, teachers must learn to observe the behavior of individuals accurately, to remember what took place, and to make a record of each incident later when they are free to give their entire attention to the writing of the anecdotes. For instance, each teacher may set aside a certain period toward the end of each day—perhaps 15 to 30 minutes —for the preparation of anecdotes concerning all the significant behavior incidents they have observed earlier in the day.

One who is engaged in the making of anecdotal records should check occasionally to see how the anecdotes are distributed among the various pupils. It may be found that there are many anecdotes for some pupils and very few or none at all for others. If this proves to be true, attention should consciously be directed toward those quiet members of the group whose behavior is so inconspicuous that their individuality has previously failed to

of the anecdotes they prepare, they can easily make carbon copies when writing the originals, or dittoes of their entire record.

In schools that have well-established counseling systems, the anecdotes for each pupil will naturally be sent to the office of his counselor, where they will be utilized in conferences (although usually not shown to the pupil) and filed in individual folders. In other schools, home-room teachers may be the logical persons to receive the anecdotes. In small schools where the principal is the chief guidance officer, the anecdotes will probably be filed in his office. Anecdotal records should be filed in the office of that functionary who will make the most use of them in guidance.

```
┌─────────────────────────────────────────────────────────────┐
│  Pupil_____Date_____   │
│                                                               │
│  Class_____Place_____   │
│                                                               │
│                          ANECDOTE                             │
│                                                               │
│                                                               │
│                                                               │
│                                                               │
│                                                               │
│                                                               │
│                                                               │
│                                           Observer_____  │
└─────────────────────────────────────────────────────────────┘
```

FORM 6.

impress itself upon the observer. It would be inadvisable to attempt to prepare the same number of anecdotes for all pupils, but it seems fair to assume that in the course of a semester a teacher should be able to write several anecdotes for every pupil in his classes.

CENTRAL FILING

Anecdotes concerning any individual take on added meaning when those written by different observers over a period of time are brought together and compared. It is highly desirable, therefore, that a system be worked out in each school whereby the anecdotal records for each pupil are collected in one place at regular intervals, so that they may be studied in relation to one another. If certain teachers wish to retain in their own files a record

The frequency with which the anecdotes are collected should be determined by the local situation. In some schools they are brought together at the end of each week, whereas in other schools they are collected at longer intervals.

SUMMARIZATION

Even though it is time-consuming, a carefully developed procedure for summarizing anecdotes is highly desirable. When the school reaches the point where the teachers have been trained in the writing of anecdotes and have accepted the preparation of them as one of their responsibilities, it is in the organization and summarization of the anecdotal material that the system is most likely to break down. If all teachers conscientiously

PERIODIC ANECDOTAL RECORD SUMMARY

Pupil_____Grade_____

From_____To_____

Date	Place	Observer	Anecdote

FORM 7.

turn in several anecdotes each day, the wealth of the material obtained may overwhelm the counselors or others responsible for summarizing it, since a great many anecdotes will be collected for nearly every pupil in the school within the course of a year. At the Rochester Athenaeum and Mechanics Institute, for example, the average number of anecdotes reported for 520 students during the first semester of a school year was 46 (45). At this rate, 92 anecdotes for each student would be obtained in one school year. It is no small task to go through so much material for even one student, to discover trends in personality development, and to reduce all that material to a brief, usable statement for the cumulative record.

If there is sufficient staff time available for the making of periodic summaries, perhaps once a month, on blanks similar to the one shown in Form 7, the task of summarizing at the end of the year should be greatly simplified. If the periodic summary consists merely of a chronological arrangement of "boiled-down" statements of the behavior incidents collected from the various staff members concerning each pupil, it can probably be entrusted to intelligent clerical workers. The annual summary, however, which involves interpretation and a statement of trends and growth to be entered on the cumulative record, is no clerical task. It calls for the best knowledge and thinking that are available for this work. Ordinarily, the annual summary should be prepared by the counselor, or better still, by a committee consisting of the counselor, the pupil's teachers, and the psychologist.

If it is the custom in the school to obtain a checking of certain personality traits of each pupil on a rating scale, or if a behavior-description form is employed, the annual summary of the anecdotal material may readily be made to conform to the rating scale or the behavior description. This point will be discussed at greater length in another section of this chapter.

LIMITATIONS AND CAUTIONS IN THE PREPARATION OF ANECDOTES

Several limitations and dangers are inherent in anecdotal records, although these can be minimized by observing certain cautions. A number of these have already been suggested, but a more formal listing of them may be helpful.

1. It is apparent, of course, that an anecdotal record can be valuable only if the original observation is accurate and correctly recorded; otherwise, it may be worse than useless. Court records provide ample evidence that reports of observation are often faulty. Frequently, persons do not see what they think they see nor hear what they think they hear. In the school situation, there is especial danger that some observations will be faulty, for in conducting a class a teacher may be able to give only partial attention to a behavior incident and still keep the discussion moving. Great care must, therefore, be observed. The first rule in the writing of an anecdote is to make sure that the report of behavior is correct. It is far better to omit an anecdote entirely than to turn it in if there is a possibility that it may be incorrect in any detail.

2. Many persons find it extremely difficult to write with complete objectivity, but practice will do a great deal to overcome the tendency to intersperse the report of behavior with statements of opinion. A report of an incident should be as cold and impartial as an X-ray photograph. If the teacher must "let himself go" in describing the incident, he can do so under *comments,* where his remarks will not be prejudicial.

3. A pernicious, but fortunately rare, use of anecdotal records is their employment for the defense of the person making the report. The central purpose of every anecdotal record is to help the entire school staff to obtain better understanding of a given student. Such a record should never be written to explain or justify action on the part of the teacher. Needless to say, if a behavior incident has created an emotional reaction in a teacher, he should not attempt to prepare an anecdote about it.

4. It is evident that there is danger in lifting a behavior incident out of the social setting in which it occurred and in reporting it in isolation. This is true especially when, under the stimulus of group sentiment and action, a pupil may behave in a way that is not typical of him. Observers should remember that a brief description of the background against which an action took place is often essential in the reporting.

5. At best, only a small proportion of the total number of significant behavior incidents for any pupil will find its way into anecdotal records. One who is summarizing and interpreting anecdotal records should guard against a tendency to accept a small number of anecdotes as valid evidence of the total picture. The danger at this point will be minimized as more and more anecdotal material is accumulated.

6. Some persons fear that anecdotes, through preserving a record of unfortunate behavior incidents on the part of certain pupils, may prejudice their success long afterward, when the behavior is no longer typical of them. There is ground for this fear if the school carelessly allows the anecdotes to fall into the hands of irresponsible persons. The original records should be regarded as confidential material for which the counselor, or other person entrusted with the care of them, is personally and professionally responsible. On the other hand, the annual summary of the anecdotes, since it does not report specific incidents but is a general statement of development, is no more confidential than the rest of the cumulative record.

7. It cannot be emphasized too strongly that the adoption of a system of anecdotal records is no small commitment and that it will add inevitably to the load of the entire school, particularly the counselors and the clerical staff. A definite and workable plan for handling the additional clerical work and for summarizing the anecdotes should be developed before the writing of anecdotes is undertaken.

8. It is obvious that the indications in the anecdotal records should be studied and an attempt made to improve

the adjustment of the pupils when the anecdotes show that better adjustment is needed. In this connection, however, a caution should be observed. As Zahn (67) pointed out, adjustment is ordinarily a long-term process. There is some danger that anecdotal records will throw the need for the better adjustment of certain pupils into such high relief that too marked an effort will be made to short-cut the adjustment process. Counselors should remember that personality adaptations frequently involve the formation of new sets of habits, and that time is required for this.

9. Undesirable behavior, because of its nuisance aspect, is likely to make a stronger impression on teachers than desirable behavior. There is some danger, therefore, that the total effect of anecdotal records will be negative rather than positive. The staff members of a school should train themselves to observe and record evidences of growth even more diligently than they note retarded personality development.

10. Occasionally teachers will observe incidents that are not at all typical of the behavior of the pupil concerned. Sometimes these may be of such a character that they should be recorded, but ordinarily it is desirable to "select those illustrations of conduct which are consistent with the personality of the student as you have observed and understood it" (45).

VALUES AND USES OF ANECDOTAL RECORDS

Various uses and values of anecdotal records have been mentioned in preceding sections of this chapter. According to the writers of published articles on the subject, the following are especially noteworthy.[4]

1. Anecdotal records provide a variety of descriptions concerning the unconstrained behavior of pupils in diverse situations. Thus they contribute to an understanding of the core or basic personality pattern of each individual and of the changes in pattern.

2. They substitute specific and exact descriptions of personality for vague generalizations.

3. They direct the attention of teachers away from subject matter and class groups and toward individual pupils.

4. They stimulate teachers to use records and to contribute to them.

5. They relieve individual teachers of the responsibility of making trait ratings, and provide a basis for composite ratings. Moreover, they provide a continuous record, whereas trait ratings are usually made only at certain points in a pupil's school experience.

[4] For additional information concerning values and uses of anecdotal records, see especially Brown and Martin (12), Charters (14), Demming (16), Randall (45), Raths (46), Rothney (50), Wood (63), and Zahn (67).

6. They encourage teacher interest in, and understanding of, the larger school problems that are indicated by an accumulation of anecdotes.

7. They provide the information which the counselor needs to organize conferences with individual pupils. An appropriate starting point for each conference can be found in the data, and the discussion can be kept close to the pupil's needs.

8. They provide data for pupils to use in self-appraisal. Whereas in some cases the anecdotes should not be shown to the pupils, each pupil can profitably study the indications in many of the anecdotes about him in order to decide what he needs to do to improve.

9. Personal relationships between the pupil and the counselor are improved by these records, for they show the pupil that the counselor is acquainted with his problems.

10. Anecdotal records aid in the formulation of individual help programs and encourage active pupil participation in remedial work.

11. They show needs for the formation of better work and study habits and also provide encouraging evidence of growth in these respects.

12. Curriculum construction, modification, and emphasis may be improved through reference to the whole volume of anecdotal record material collected by a school. The anecdotes indicate where there should be general presentation of material in character development to satisfy the needs of the whole school community.

13. An appropriate summary of anecdotes is valuable for forwarding with a pupil when he is promoted to another school.

14. Anecdotal records may be used by new members of the staff in acquainting themselves with the student body.

15. The qualitative statements contained in these records supplement and assist in the interpretation of quantitative data.

16. Collections of anecdotal records may provide the necessary validating evidence for various evaluative instruments. For instance, when the results of the Minnesota Multiphasic Inventory indicate that certain pupils are high in social inversion and others are low, the anecdotal record material for these pupils may be analyzed to find out whether or not the Inventory scores agree with the observations of behavior.

17. Anecdotal records aid in clinical service. When pupils are referred to clinical workers for special study of their problems, there is a great advantage in having these records available for these highly trained workers to interpret. In this connection, Charters (14) made the following significant observation concerning the anecdotal records of the Rochester Athenaeum and Mechanics Institute: "How penetrating the accumulated emphasis of these anecdotes is was put to a test recently when a psychiatrist came to the faculty for information about a student who had been brought to him as a mild case for observation. As he and the supervisor exchanged impressions, it appeared that the psychiatrist had un-

covered no characteristics that were not already recorded among the anecdotes."

SAMPLE ANECDOTES

The following anecdotes, consisting of reports from four different teachers about the same pupil, show clearly a need for counseling to bring about better adjustment (32:197).

Teacher 1. Objective Description: John was late and was told to go to the dean's office for an entrance pass to class. He did not return all period. Another pupil who was late was sent to the same office for a pass, and when he returned was questioned as to the whereabouts of John. The second pupil reported he had not seen him at the dean's office.

Comment: On first writing this anecdote the observer thought that John resented being sent to the dean's office and to show this had cut class. However, the next day it was learned that he had gone to the nurse complaining of illness. To the observer, it represents a shifting of responsibility.

Teacher 2. Objective Description: John became angry when the assignment was longer than he thought it should have been. He said, "I'm not goin' to do that work."

I told him to do what he thought best about it. The next day the assignment was done.

Comment: I believe that John is subject to sudden outbursts of temper. During these times it is useless to talk to him because he seems to expect an argument. I have observed this several times and, after almost every such experience, he does the thing he knows is right, even though he has opposed it.

Teacher 3. Objective Description: Donald, when talking with me, stood beside John's desk. Upon taking his seat, John said, "Donald has the top of my pen." This Donald denied. John insisted, telling him to look in his pocket. There it was found.

Donald immediately handed it to John, saying to me, "He put it there himself. He's always trying to get others in bad."

Comment: I knew John put the top of his pen in Donald's pocket. I have observed that he is very anxious to have attention from boys in the Leaders' Club. He is a member, but does not seem to be entirely taken into the group. Hence his attempts at attention.

Teacher 4. Objective Description: I asked John to sit up front near my desk because he kept annoying his neighbors, even after two warnings.

Comment: John seldom seems to have any work to do, and delights in annoying his neighbors.

The next series of anecdotes, written by an English teacher about a backward pupil, provides encouraging evidence of improvement (32:198–199).

English Teacher. Objective Description: Tom informed me before class that he had finished his library book, *The Story of David Livingstone,* which I helped him select last Friday.

Comment: Tom has the lowest score of any freshman on the Iowa test. He usually labors through a book, if he finishes it at all.

This book he liked very much, and I was proud of this achievement—a book read in one weekend.

English Teacher. Objective Description: Tom answered "Unprepared" when the chairman of the Book Club announced him on the program. I asked to see him after school.

Comment: I knew Tom had a book which he had told me he liked. I asked him whether he had read it all. He said he had, but that he couldn't pronounce the names, and he couldn't make a story out of it for the class. I asked why he had not come for help before our meeting. He said he did not think about doing that.

After more questioning, I came to the conclusion that he would have to get even simpler material. He asked me to find another book for him. There are very few books in the library within his capacity, and they are usually out of circulation.

English Teacher. Objective Description: I sent for Tom before school to give him the library book he requested me to choose for him. He promised to "look it over" and to let me know in class whether he wished to keep it.

By afternoon he informed me he had read 103 pages! "This is interesting," he volunteered.

Comment: That he had finished 103 pages amazed me. Of course, I praised him, and told him of a sequel to the same book.

I have never known the Silver Chief books to fail in their appeal to freshman boys who are very low in their reading ability. We need more books of this caliber.

English Teacher. Objective Description: Before class Tom stopped at my desk to tell me that the librarian had promised to let him know when the sequel to Silver Chief was available.

"Have you finished this one already?" I asked.

He grinned. "Yes, I have."

Comment: This is the same book, that started another boy on his reading "career."

I wish we had more books with such a universal appeal for nonreaders.

English Teacher. Objective Description: Tom was responsible for an oral assignment today. When called upon, Tom shook his head and said he was unprepared.

I asked him to come after school for a talk with me.

English Teacher. Objective Description: Tom is one of my poorest readers, so I wondered at first whether the assignment had been too difficult, but Tom said he knew his assignment without any notes even. Sitting beside my desk, he told his story. I asked him to tell it again, and suggested several improvements. He did it better. I asked him to do it a third time, so that he was thoroughly familiar with it. Then I asked him to go to the rear of the room, and tell his story to me.

"I don't want to do that," he said.

Comment: This is the real difficulty.

English Teacher. Objective Description: Tom was prepared today with his oral report, which he gave without apparent nervousness. It was short, but a real achievement, nevertheless.

Note how the following series of anecdotes present a picture of personality development.[5]

Date	Observer	Anecdotal Record
Sept.	Supervisor	Dorothy's stunt in the Retailing Party was highly original. Her attitude was abrupt and superior. The other girls avoided her.
Nov.	Teacher 9	She monopolized the entire group discussion today.
Dec.	Teacher 8	She told me in conference that the other students do not like her. I tried to explain that it would be desirable to be a little less aggressive and to avoid giving the appearance of feeling superior. She said little in reply and I do not know whether or not I got the idea across.
Jan.	Teacher 7	Dorothy came to me for advice on overcoming characteristics which make students dislike her. She took a difficult assignment in color and design which involved doing a costume analysis and prescription for a classmate who seemed antagonistic to her. She is doing a good job with it.
March	Teacher 7	She gave the other students opportunity to discuss and to work out their share of group assignments.
April	Teacher 7	Several students have told me that they feel she is not so much self-centered as ambitious. They said that she was gaining the cooperation and confidence of nearly all her classmates.
May	Teacher 8	In the sorority, Dorothy has become the person (next to the president) to whom people turn for suggestions, assistance, and leadership. This is true of those who first resented her.

A summary statement for this student's cumulative record might read as follows:

At the beginning of the year, Dorothy's manner was so aggressive, self-centered, and superior that she was very unpopular with the other students. She became aware of her shortcomings and tried, with the help of some of her teach-

[5] Adapted from Wood (63).

ers, to change her behavior. She was so successful that she won the cooperation and confidence of her fellow students, and at the end of the year she was regarded as a leader by her group.

RELATION OF ANECDOTAL RECORDS TO PERSONALITY RATINGS AND BEHAVIOR DESCRIPTIONS

Anecdotal records, when properly prepared, provide rather highly objective information, which need not replace rating or behavior description plans already established in a school, but which may be used as a valuable supplement to established procedures. If a school is using a personality rating scale, the teachers and counselors should be encouraged to keep in mind the traits which are emphasized in the scale and to try to prepare anecdotes which will throw light on these traits.

Some schools, particularly certain progressive ones, have used, for the appraisal of the personality of their pupils, the Behavior-Description plan devised in the early 1940s by the Reports and Records Committee of the Eight-Year Study of the Progressive Education Association (52). This plan was designed to secure and record in permanent form judgments of behavior with respect to the traits which the committee decided, after extensive study, were important. It consists of a "behavior-description" filing and transfer card in the form of a folder, a sheet to be used by the teacher in making a report on the pupils, and a "trait-study" manual containing complete directions. The traits included are responsibility-dependability, creativeness and imagination, influence, inquiring mind, open-mindedness, power and habit of analysis, social concern, emotional responsiveness, serious purpose, social adaptability, work habits, physical energy, assurance, self-reliance, and emotional control. A series of descriptive statements is given in connection with each trait and the teacher indicates the one which describes the pupil best. The trait-rating sheets are sent by the teachers to the records office, where the judgments concerning each pupil are transferred to the individual record folders by clerical service. Space is provided on the pupil's folder for recording the judgments of all his teachers from Grade 7 through Grade 12.

Since the Progressive Education Association was discontinued in 1955, the Behavior Description forms have not been purchasable for some years, but any school is free to use part or all of this plan, which was the result of the thought and cooperative effort of specialists in the field of evaluation and recording procedures. In order

NORTON, ROBERT SAMUEL
LAST NAME / FIRST / MIDDLE

BEHAVIOR DESCRIPTION
(EXPERIMENTAL FORM)

Thomas Jefferson High School
SCHOOL

THIS REPORT DESCRIBES THE CHARACTERISTIC BEHAVIOR OF THE STUDENT IN A NUMBER OF IMPORTANT AREAS. IT SHOULD NOT BE INTERPRETED AS A RATING. INSTEAD ONE SHOULD READ THE DESCRIPTIONS AND ATTEMPT TO GET FROM THEM AN UNDERSTANDING OF THE PERSON DESCRIBED, AND OF HIS FITNESS FOR PARTICULAR OPPORTUNITIES AND UNDERTAKINGS.

DIRECTIONS:

(1) IN GENERAL THE INITIALS OF SUBJECT OR ACTIVITY FIELDS ARE USED IN THE RECORDING IN ORDER TO IDENTIFY THE RELATIONS BETWEEN THE OBSERVERS AND THE STUDENT. A COMPLETE KEY IS GIVEN AT THE TOP OF THE FOLDED-OVER SHEET.

(2) THE SPACES FROM LEFT TO RIGHT, BEING CHRONOLOGICAL, SHOW THE CHANGES OR CONTINUITY IN BEHAVIOR DURING THE PERIOD COVERED BY THE RECORD.

(3) WHILE AGREEMENTS IN DESCRIPTION MAY SHOW A STUDENT'S MOST COMMON BEHAVIOR, THEY MAY NOT BE MORE IMPORTANT THAN AN ISOLATED JUDGMENT WHICH OFTEN HAS GREAT SIGNIFICANCE BECAUSE OF A BETTER BASIS FOR JUDGMENT, OR BECAUSE IT INDICATES A RESPONSE TO SOME PARTICULAR CONDITION.

FIELD OR PERSONALITY

RESPONSIBILITY—DEPENDABILITY

	GRADE 7	GRADE 8	GRADE 9	GRADE 10	GRADE 11	GRADE 12
RESPONSIBLE AND RESOURCEFUL: CARRIES THROUGH WHATEVER IS UNDERTAKEN, AND ALSO SHOWS INITIATIVE AND VERSATILITY IN ACCOMPLISHING AND ENLARGING UPON UNDERTAKINGS.			P	P	P	D
CONSCIENTIOUS: COMPLETES WITHOUT EXTERNAL COMPULSION WHATEVER IS ASSIGNED BUT IS UNLIKELY TO ENLARGE THE SCOPE OF ASSIGNMENTS.	E	E-P	E-AD	SS	E-AD	E-NS-AD
GENERALLY DEPENDABLE: USUALLY CARRIES THROUGH UNDERTAKINGS, SELF-ASSUMED OR ASSIGNED BY OTHERS, REQUIRING ONLY OCCASIONAL REMINDER OR COMPULSION.	NS-SS	NS-SS	E-AD	E-AD	M-F-SS	M-SS
SELECTIVELY DEPENDABLE: SHOWS HIGH PERSISTANCE IN UNDERTAKINGS IN WHICH THERE IS PARTICULAR INTEREST, BUT IS LESS LIKELY TO CARRY THROUGH OTHER ASSIGNMENTS.	AD	AD-MU	M-F-NS	M-F		
UNRELIABLE: CAN BE RELIED UPON TO COMPLETE UNDERTAKINGS ONLY WHEN THEY ARE OF MODERATE DURATION OR DIFFICULTY AND THEN ONLY WITH MUCH PRODDING AND SUPERVISION.	A	M				
IRRESPONSIBLE: CANNOT BE RELIED UPON TO COMPLETE ANY UNDERTAKING EVEN WHEN CONSTANTLY PRODDED AND GUIDED.	M					

CREATIVENESS AND IMAGINATION

	GRADE 7	GRADE 8	GRADE 9	GRADE 10	GRADE 11	GRADE 12
GENERAL: APPROACHES WHATEVER HE DOES WITH ACTIVE IMAGINATION AND ORIGINALITY, SO THAT HE CONTRIBUTES SOMETHING THAT IS HIS OWN.					P	NS
SPECIFIC: MAKES DISTINCTLY ORIGINAL AND SIGNIFICANT CONTRIBUTIONS IN ONE OR MORE FIELDS.	NS	NS-P	P-AD-NS	E-P-AD	E-SS-AD	E-SS-AD
PROMISING: SHOWS A DEGREE OF CREATIVENESS THAT INDICATES THE LIKELIHOOD OF VALUABLE ORIGINAL CONTRIBUTION IN SOME FIELD, ALTHOUGH THE CONTRIBUTIONS ALREADY MADE HAVE NOT PROVED TO BE PARTICULARLY SIGNIFICANT.	E-A-AD	E-SS-AD	E	SS-F	F	D
LIMITED: SHOWS THE DESIRE TO CONTRIBUTE HIS OWN THINKING AND EXPRESSION TO SITUATIONS, BUT HIS DEGREE OF IMAGINATION AND ORIGINALITY IS NOT IN GENERAL HIGH ENOUGH TO HAVE MUCH INFLUENCE ON HIS ACCOMPLISHMENTS.	SS	MU	M-F	M	M	M
IMITATIVE: MAKES LITTLE OR NO CREATIVE CONTRIBUTIONS, YET SHOWS SUFFICIENT IMAGINATION TO SEE THE IMPLICATIONS IN THE CREATION OF OTHERS AND TO MAKE USE OF THEIR IDEAS OR ACCOMPLISHMENTS.		M				
UNIMAGINATIVE: HAS GIVEN PRACTICALLY NO EVIDENCE OF ORIGINALITY OR CREATIVENESS IN IMAGINATION OR ACTION.	M					

FORM 8A (Front).

INFLUENCE

Category	1	2	3	4	5	6
CONTROLLING: His influence habitually shapes the opinions, activities, or ideals of his associates.					P	SS
CONTRIBUTING INFLUENCE: His influence, while not controlling, strongly affects the opinions, activities, or ideals of his associates.	E-NS-SS-AD	P-NS	P-E-SS		E-SS-AD	E-NS-AD-D
VARYING: His influence varies, having force when particular ability, skill, experience or circumstance gives it opportunity or value.	M-A	E-SS-AD	M-NS-F-AD		M-AD	M-F
CO-OPERATING: Has no very definite influence on his associates, but contributes to group thinking and action because of some discrimination in regard to ideas and leaders.		M-Mu	F			
PASSIVE: Has no definite influence on his associates, being carried along by the nearest or strongest influence.						

INQUIRING MIND

Category	1	2	3	4	5	6
GENERAL: Responds with consistent, active and deep interest to any intellectual stimulus and uses to good advantage various sources of information.				P	P	AD-SS
SPECIFIC: Responds with consistent, active and deep interest only to stimuli arising in specific fields or problems. Uses effectively the sources available for such purposes.	AD-SS	AD-P-SS	E-AD-P	E-AD	E-AD-SS	E-NS-D
LIMITED: Somewhat sensitive to stimuli arising from limited fields, but engages in exploration and investigation only when a general plan of attacking the problem is indicated to him.	E-NS	E-NS-MU	NS-F	M-SS-F	M-F	M
DIRECTED: Responds to stimuli in a limited field of interests but is impelled to act only when both the plan and the details of procedure are definitely outlined for him.	A		M	M		
UNRESPONSIVE: Rarely seems to be sensitive to any intellectual stimulus and shows little or no ability to use the tools and methodology of exploration and investigation.	M	M				

OPENMINDEDNESS

Category	1	2	3	4	5	6
DISCRIMINATING: Welcomes new ideas but habitually suspends judgment until all the available evidence is obtained.	AD-SS			AD-F	SS-P-F	AD-SS-D
TOLERANT: Does not readily appreciate or respond to opposing viewpoints and new ideas, although he is tolerant of them and consciously tries to suspend judgment regarding them.	E-AD-P	M-AD-NS-P	M-E-SS-P		M-E-AD	M-E-NS
PASSIVE: Tolerance of the new or different is passive, arising from lack of interest or conviction. Welcomes, or is indifferent to change, because of lack of understanding or appreciation of the new or of that which it replaces.	M-E-NS-A	M-NS-SS-MU	E-F			
RIGID: Preconceived ideas and prejudices so govern his thinking that he usually ends a discussion or an investigation without change of opinion.						
INTOLERANT: Is actively intolerant, resents any interference with his habitual beliefs, ideas and procedures.						

FORM 8A (Front), Continued.

THE POWER AND HABIT OF ANALYSIS; THE HABIT OF REACHING CONCLUSIONS ON THE BASIS OF VALID EVIDENCE

HIGHLY ANALYTICAL: HABITUALLY MAKES AN ANALYTICAL APPROACH TO HIS PROBLEMS, ASSEMBLING THE FACTS, SHOWING A CLEAR PERCEPTION OF THEIR RELATIONSHIPS AND IMPLICATIONS, AND THINKING THROUGH THE SITUATION TO WELL FOUNDED CONCLUSIONS.					
INCOMPLETE: MAKES AN INTELLIGENTLY ANALYTICAL APPROACH TO HIS PROBLEMS BUT IS MORE LIMITED IN ABILITY TO ASSEMBLE THE FACTS COMPLETELY, AND TO SEE THEIR RELATIONSHIPS OR THEIR IMPLICATIONS.	NS	NS-P	P	AD-SS-P	NS
IRREGULAR: ON OCCASION SHOWS UNUSUAL ANALYTICAL POWER BUT DOES NOT DO SO HABITUALLY.	SS	E-SS	AD	M-E-F	E-RD-D
UNDEVELOPED: SHOWS SIGNS OF ANALYTICAL POWER, BUT BECAUSE OF FEARS, THE DOMINATION OF OTHERS, OR SOME OTHER INHIBITING AGENCY HAS NOT YET DEVELOPED IT TO ANY HIGH DEGREE.	AD-A	AD-MU	M-E-F	E-AD-SS	M-SS
LIMITED: IS ABLE TO PURSUE REASONING PROCESSES IF AIDED BY SOME GUIDANCE AND DIRECTION.	E	M	M-F		
PASSIVE: HIS APPROACH TO A PROBLEM IS NOT AN ANALYTICAL ONE, THOUGH HE MAY BE ABLE TO APPRECIATE A TRAIN OF REASONING OR TO FOLLOW ONE LAID OUT BY SOME ONE ELSE.	M				
UNREASONING: SEEMS UNABLE TO ANALYZE EVEN A FAIRLY SIMPLE SITUATION, TENDING RATHER TO RELY ON MEMORY AS A SUBSTITUTE FOR LOGIC. ACCEPTS STATEMENTS AND RESULTS WITHOUT ATTEMPTING TO REASON ABOUT THEM.					

SOCIAL CONCERN

GENERALLY CONCERNED: SHOWS AN ALTRUISTIC AND GENERAL SOCIAL CONCERN AND INTERPRETS THIS IN ACTION TO THE EXTENT OF HIS ABILITIES AND OPPORTUNITIES.					
SELECTIVELY CONCERNED: SHOWS CONCERN BY ATTITUDE AND ACTION ABOUT CERTAIN SOCIAL CONDITIONS BUT SEEMS UNABLE TO APPRECIATE THE IMPORTANCE OF OTHER SUCH PROBLEMS.	SS-AD	NS	AD	E-P	E-NS-AD
PERSONAL: IS NOT STRONGLY CONCERNED ABOUT THE WELFARE OF OTHERS AND RESPONDS TO SOCIAL PROBLEMS ONLY WHEN HE RECOGNIZES SOME INTIMATE PERSONAL RELATIONSHIP TO THE PROBLEM OR GROUP IN QUESTION.	E-NS-M	SS-P-AD-NS	E-P	E-M-SS-AD	M-SS-AD
INACTIVE: SEEMS AWARE OF SOCIAL PROBLEMS, AND MAY PROFESS CONCERN ABOUT THEM, BUT DOES NOTHING.	A	E-M	M-F-NS	F	F
UNCONCERNED: DOES NOT SHOW ANY GENUINE CONCERN FOR THE COMMON GOOD.		MU			

EMOTIONAL RESPONSIVENESS AND CONTROL

TO IDEAS: IS EMOTIONALLY STIRRED BY BECOMING AWARE OF CHALLENGING IDEAS.		NS-SS	NS	SS-AD	NS-SS
TO DIFFICULTY: RESPONDS EMOTIONALLY TO A SITUATION OR PROBLEM CHALLENGING TO HIM BECAUSE OF THE POSSIBILITY OF OVERCOMING DIFFICULTIES.	E-AD	P	P-AD	P-E	AD
TO IDEALS: RESPONDS EMOTIONALLY TO WHAT IS CHARACTERIZED PRIMARILY BY ITS PERSONAL OR SOCIAL IDEALISM.			AD		AD
TO BEAUTY: RESPONDS EMOTIONALLY TO BEAUTY AS FOUND IN NATURE AND THE ARTS.					
TO ORDER: RESPONDS EMOTIONALLY TO PERFECTION OF FUNCTIONING AS IT IS SEEN IN ORGANIZATION, MECHANICAL OPERATION OR LOGICAL COMPLETENESS.	NS	NS	AD	AD	D

NOTE: ANY ENTRY IN RED INK IS A SECOND JUDGMENT MADE LATER IN THE YEAR.

FORM 8A (Front), Continued.

KEY TO OBSERVERS MAKING THE DESCRIPTIONS

THE FOLLOWING ABBREVIATIONS HAVE BEEN USED: IN THE SPACES BELOW ENTER THE TEACHERS' INITIALS.

A—ARTS AD—ADVISOR D—DRAMATICS E—ENGLISH F—FRENCH P—PHYSICAL TRAINING H.R.—HOME ROOM TEACHER

G—GERMAN L—LATIN M—MATHEMATICS MU—MUSIC N.S—NATURAL SCIENCE S.S.—SOCIAL SCIENCES

1959-1960	1960-1961	1961-1962	1962-1963	1963-1964	1964-1965
E = ES	E = GH	E = HAA	E = HAA	E = GC	E = RT
M = LJ	M = LJ	M = GH	M = GH	M = WS	NS = ERB
NS = JCM	NS = JCM	NS = ODS	SS = HCH	SS = HCH	SS = CH
SS = JD	SS = JD	P = CW	P = GB	F = GB	P = REK
A = RN	MU = HV	A = GW	A = LWI	P = LWI	AD = SV
AD = RW	A = GW	AD = RW	AD = LCS	AD = LCS	= LCS
	AD = RW				

Descriptions

	TYPE	GRADE 7	GRADE 8	GRADE 9	GRADE 10	GRADE 11	GRADE 12
SERIOUS PURPOSE							
PURPOSEFUL: HAS DEFINITE PURPOSE AND PLANS AND CARRIES THROUGH TO THE BEST OF HIS ABILITY UNDERTAKINGS CONSISTENT WITH THIS PURPOSE.	1					SS	SS
LIMITED: MAKES PLANS AND SHOWS DETERMINATION IN ATTACKING SHORT-TIME PROJECTS THAT INTEREST HIM, BUT HAS NOT YET THOUGHT OUT GOALS FOR HIMSELF	2	E	SS	E	E-SS-P	E-P-AD	E-D-NS
POTENTIAL: TAKES THINGS AS THEY COME, MEETING SITUATIONS SOMEWHAT ON THE SPUR OF THE MOMENT, YET MAY BE CAPABLE OF SERIOUS PURPOSE IF ONCE AROUSED.	3	SS-NS-AD	E-NS-AD	AD-P	AD-F	F-M	M-AD
UNRELIABLE: MAKES PLANS THAT ARE FAIRLY DEFINITE, BUT CANNOT BE COUNTED ON FOR THE DETERMINATION TO CARRY THEM THROUGH.	4	M-A	M-MU-P	M-NS-F	M	M	
VAGUE: IS LIKELY TO DRIFT WITHOUT THE DECISION AND PERSISTENCE THAT WILL ENABLE HIM TO CARRY OUT HIS VAGUELY CONCEIVED PLANS.	5						
SOCIAL ADJUSTABILITY							
SECURE: APPEARS TO FEEL SECURE IN HIS SOCIAL RELATIONSHIPS AND IS ACCEPTED BY THE GROUPS OF WHICH HE IS A PART.	1		SS	E-P	E-SS-P	E-SS-P	E-SS-D-AD
UNCERTAIN: APPEARS TO HAVE SOME ANXIETY ABOUT HIS SOCIAL RELATIONSHIPS ALTHOUGH HE IS ACCEPTED BY THE GROUPS OF WHICH HE IS A PART	2	E-SS-AD	E-NS-P-AD	NS-AD	M-F-AD	M-AD	M-NS
NEUTRAL: SHOWS THE DESIRE TO HAVE AN ESTABLISHED PLACE IN THE GROUP, BUT IS, IN GENERAL, TREATED WITH INDIFFERENCE.	3	M-NS-A	M-MU	M-F		F	
WITHDRAWN: WITHDRAWS FROM OTHERS TO AN EXTENT THAT PREVENTS HIS BEING A FULLY ACCEPTED MEMBER OF HIS GROUPS.	4						
NOT ACCEPTED: HAS CHARACTERISTICS OF PERSON OR BEHAVIOR THAT PREVENT HIS BEING AN ACCEPTED MEMBER OF HIS GROUP.	5						
WORK HABITS							
HIGHLY EFFECTIVE: A PUPIL HAVING HIGHLY EFFECTIVE WORK HABITS WOULD BE LIKELY TO REACH THE MAXIMUM ACCOMPLISHMENT FOR ONE OF HIS ABILITY.	1				SS	P	SS
ADEQUATE: A PUPIL HAVING ADEQUATE WORK HABITS WOULD ACCOMPLISH ALL THAT WOULD COMMONLY BE EXPECTED OF ONE OF HIS ABILITY.	2	E	E-SS-P	E-P-AD	E-P-AD	E-SS-AD	E-D-AD
PROMISING: WHILE HIS HABITS ARE NOT YET ADEQUATE THEY SHOW PROMISE OF BECOMING SO.	3	SS-AD	NS-MU-AD	M-NS-F	F	M-F	M-NS
LIMITED: HAS WORK HABITS THAT ARE ADEQUATE ONLY FOR SIMPLE SITUATIONS, OR ARE LIMITED BY THE LACK OF DEVELOPMENT OF SOME ELEMENTS THAT MAKE FOR EFFICIENCY.	4	NS	M	M	M		
INEFFECTIVE: HAS NOT DEVELOPED HIS WORK HABITS TO THE POINT WHERE HE CAN WORK EFFICIENTLY.	5	M-A					

FORM 8B (Back).

A MARKEDLY HIGH (H) OR LOW (L) DEGREE OF THE FOLLOWING BEHAVIOR CHARACTERISTICS IS SHOWN BY RECORDINGS IN THE APPROPRIATE SPACES. NO IMPLICATION IS ASSUMED AS TO DESIRABILITY OR UNDESIRABILITY FOR THE PARTICULAR INDIVIDUAL. ANY QUALIFICATIONS OR FURTHER COMMENT SHOULD APPEAR UNDER "GENERAL COMMENT."

		GRADE 7	GRADE 8	GRADE 9	GRADE 10	GRADE 11	GRADE 12
PHYSICAL ENERGY	BEHAVIOR IN RELATION TO VIGOR AND ENDURANCE.	H	P	P-NS	P	P-AD	NS-AD
		L					
ASSURANCE	ABILITY TO MEET SITUATIONS AND PEOPLE EASILY.	H			AD-SS	AD'	AD-SS
		L					
SELF RELIANCE	THE HABIT OF DEPENDING ON ONE'S SELF RATHER THAN ON OTHERS.	H			P	E	E-NS
		L					
EMOTIONAL CONTROL	ABILITY TO RETAIN POISE AND SELF CONTROL.	H	SS	E-NS	E-SS-AD	E-SS-P	E-D-SS-AD
		L					
		H					
		L					

USE H (HIGH), U (USUAL FOR AGE), OR L (LOW) TO INDICATE THE SUCCESS THIS STUDENT HAS HAD IN DEALING WITH

{ ABSTRACT IDEAS AND SYMBOLS
  PEOPLE
  PLANNING AND MANAGEMENT
  THINGS AND MANIPULATION }

ABSTRACT IDEAS AND SYMBOLS	L	U	U	L
PEOPLE	L	U	H	U
PLANNING AND MANAGEMENT	H	H	U	U
THINGS AND MANIPULATION	H	U	U	H

GENERAL COMMENT: THE FOLLOWING SPACE IS TO BE USED FOR SPECIFIC INSTANCES OF BEHAVIOR AND FOR ADDITIONAL INFORMATION THAT AMPLIFIES AND SYNTHESIZES THE DESCRIPTION OF THE STUDENT.

Robert has an unusually pleasing personality and is very well adjusted socially. He is strong and vigorous and has splendid self-control. He is inclined to be practical rather than idealistic. He has shown little evidence of esthetic appreciation or interest in the arts. When he is interested in any project he works with definite purpose and great tenacity, but he is rather indifferent and careless if the subject is outside his interests. Although he has some limitations in habits of work and seriousness of purpose, he possesses considerable self-reliance and force of character, and is well liked by his teachers and classmates.

FORM 8B (Back), Continued.

to make the Behavior Description form readily available, the front and back of this folder, filled out with a sample record, are shown in Forms 8A and 8B.

A slightly abbreviated adaptation of the Behavior Description folder was incorporated into the revised American Council on Education Cumulative Record Cards, which cover all levels from the kindergarten through college (36).

As Wood (63) pointed out, there is no conflict between anecdotal records and behavior descriptions; on the contrary, these plans are supplementary. Anecdotes provide the basic material for behavior descriptions, and there is little doubt that the validity and efficiency of the behavior-description plan is enhanced when there is a wealth of anecdotal material available for reference.

Another scale which is essentially a device for obtaining behavior descriptions under standardized conditions is the Vineland Social Maturity Scale, by Doll (19, 20). A unique feature of this blank is that it yields an age scale and an SQ, or social quotient, roughly analogous to the IQ. The scale may be applied to subjects from birth to 30 years of age.

THE CRITICAL INCIDENT TECHNIQUE OF STUDYING BEHAVIOR AND PERSONALITY

One limitation to the success of anecdotal records is that in many instances teachers attempt to record too many behavior incidents, many of which are trivial and lacking in value for the understanding of personality. Hence the program may get bogged down in a morass of unimportant and confusing detail.

In order to make the description of behavior more selective, more significant, and more readily manageable, John Flanagan has for a good many years advocated the use of a "critical incident" technique in which the recording is confined to those times which the observer believes to be particularly revealing (22). Flanagan has experimented with this technique in military and civilian situations.

Out of the framework of the critical incident technique, Flanagan made available in 1956 a thorough *Personal and Social Development Program* for schools, with emphasis on the elementary school level. The basic materials in this program were a *Performance Record,* a *Teacher's Guide,* and an *Administrator's Manual.* This program is currently undergoing some revision and is out of print.

A similar form devised by Flanagan is *The Perform-*

ance Record, the different forms of which are designed for industrial use and which, like the school record, is based on the critical incident method. The majority of the categories in which critical incidents are to be recorded could be adapted for school use.[6]

AUTOBIOGRAPHIES, BIOGRAPHICAL INVENTORIES, AND SOCIOMETRIC DEVICES

In addition to rating scales, anecdotal records, and behavior descriptions, a number of other informal techniques are being used by schools in collecting information about the personal qualities of individuals.

AUTOBIOGRAPHIES AND BIOGRAPHICAL INVENTORIES

The autobiography is a technique which is readily usable by classroom teachers. It may serve the dual purpose of furnishing a basis for theme writing in English classes and of providing personal information for use by the counselor. Moreover, if the autobiography is analyzed by the school psychologist, it may provide leads to pupils who are in need of special help with problems of adjustment or who have basic feelings of insecurity. Probably because of its informal, unstructured, and nonscientific character, there has been little research on the autobiography. Shaffer (51) found that the autobiography was used by only one fourth of the counselors in a large city school system and that only one half of them had ever seen an autobiography. He also found from ratings obtained from 68 of these counselors that the autobiography was placed next to last in a list of ten counseling techniques. The rank order was as follows: (1) interview, (2) achievement tests, (3) intelligence tests, (4) anecdotal records, (5) oral teacher reports, (6) grades, (7) written teacher reports, (8) personality tests, (9) autobiographies, and (10) questionnaires. He found, nevertheless, in a study of 500 autobiographies, that the technique was useful in gaining understanding of high school pupils. A high percentage of the students wrote autobiographies. Most statements in the autobiographies were honest and accurate. Rapport was not necessary for group administration. The autobiographies identified unadjusted students and added to the understanding of visiting teachers.

A structured or semistructured instrument which

[6] Published by Science Research Associates, Inc., Chicago, Ill., 1955. Review set, $3.00.

serves a purpose somewhat similar to the autobiography is the biographical inventory, or personal history record. Numerous items pertaining to the history, activities, and experiences of the individual are listed in the biographical inventory. The pupil is required to check those items which apply to him or to indicate whether he frequently, sometimes, or rarely engages in the activities listed.

Some experimental work has been done with the biographical inventory in connection with psychological services related to military service, to industry, and to a lesser extent in school situations. Malloy (35) constructed a Life Experience Inventory and studied its value for the prediction of first-semester college marks. The inventory sampled the areas of school experience, self-appraisal, family relationships, and choice and type of friends. It was found that the inventory significantly increased the prediction of college marks over and above that which was obtained from the L-score on the American Council on Education Psychological Examination and the University of Nebraska English Placement Test.

Similarly, in some exploratory work at the Educational Records Bureau, a Personal History Record, devised by Lester Luntz, was filled out by pupils in several secondary schools. With English marks as a criterion, a set of weights for the different items was worked out on the basis of the responses of the boys in one high school. In a validation study on boys in another high school, it was found that the correlation of the Personal History Record scores with English marks was approximately .45, as compared with a correlation of .55 between total scores on the American Council Psychological Examination and English marks. The multiple correlation of the two measures with marks in English was .65 (39). This study and the preceding one suggest that the biographical inventory technique may add a noncognitive measure which will be a useful supplement to a scholastic aptitude test in the prediction of student success, but at present there is not enough research evidence to warrant a definite statement on this point. A clear statement favorable to the use of the life history as a primary tool of personality assessment was made by Dailey (15).

SOCIOMETRIC DEVICES

Since the appearance in 1934 of Moreno's book, *Who Shall Survive*, which was revised in 1953 (38), there has developed a set of techniques, known as sociometry, for assessing the degree of acceptance of an individual by his peers. The research bibliography in this area is now fairly extensive, and new studies are constantly being added. Among those who have been quite active in investigating the values of sociometric techniques are J. Wayne Wrightstone (66) and G. G. Thompson (55).

The application of Moreno's original technique to the school situation involves asking each pupil to indicate the other pupils in his class or group whom he regards as close friends and likes to have in the group and those toward whom he does not feel friendly and would prefer not to have in his group. Questions such as the following are sometimes used: In the seating arrangement we are working out for the class, what two pupils would you like to sit next to you? What two pupils would you not like to sit next to you? Which classmate would you want to help you with your school work? What pupils of the same sex would you invite to accompany you on a hike? Which boys or girls of your class would you like to play with during recess? What pupil of the opposite sex would you invite to a party? The purpose is to measure the extent of acceptance or rejection among the individuals in the group. Some teachers use only the positive items which indicate degree of acceptance, since they feel that it is undesirable to direct the attention of pupils toward individuals who are not socially accepted, even though the responses are always obtained in written form and no information concerning pupils generally accepted or generally rejected is given to the class.

When the summaries of the responses of all pupils to the questions used are available, a graphic representation of acceptance and rejection among the individuals of the group may be prepared in the form of a "sociogram." A published form and directions for collecting and recording sociometric information have been made available in the Bonney-Fessenden Sociograph (7), which is included in the annotated list of instruments later in the chapter.

A second and somewhat different approach to the obtaining of sociometric data is through what has been called the "guess who technique." Various kinds of presumably desirable or undesirable behavior are briefly described, and each pupil is asked to name a pupil in his group who represents a particular kind of behavior. A variation of this technique is to ask the pupils to nominate other pupils in their group for roles in class plays.

It has been generally assumed by those using sociometric procedures that the individuals who are rated the highest in acceptance by their peers are the best adjusted, although there is not clear-cut research evidence on this point. In a study of the relationship between the sociometric rating and the recorded actual behavior of second-grade children, Bonney (7) found that pupils with high peer status were more involved in verbal behavior, tended to possess positive traits, and showed greater personality balance. Brieland (11) found, in an investigation of a variation of the "guess who technique" for use in studying the adjustment of children, that there was more agreement between pupils and teachers on undesirable behavior than on desirable behavior.

In a study reported by Wrightstone (64), the results of two sociometric techniques and the California Test of Personality were correlated against ratings of personal qualities by teachers and supervisors. One of the sociometric techniques involved nomination of classmates as friends; the second involved nomination of classmates as naturally suited for roles in class plays. In the analysis of the sociometric devices, it was found that rejection, or the tendency not to nominate classmates as friends, correlated rather highly with teacher observation, .72. However, the correlations between the California Test of Personality and teachers' ratings were approximately as high, .66 and .74. Fox and Segel (24) analyzed the results of several research studies bearing on the question of adjustment and concluded that the Moreno choice type of social rating had little or no relation to social adjustment.

Instead of the Moreno type of approach, or the partial-rank-order sociometric approach, as it is sometimes called, it is possible to use a paired-comparison procedure in which each pupil is paired with each of the other pupils and the subject is asked to indicate the one in each pair he likes the better. Thus far, there has been little use of the paired-comparison technique, but perhaps more attention should be given to it, since in one study, by Witryol and Thompson (61), it was found that social acceptability scores obtained through the use of the paired-comparison technique were more stable than those obtained by means of the partial-rank-order procedure (median stability coefficient of .96 as compared with .75).

It has been pointed out by some workers in the field of sociometry that the use of a rating scale for obtaining social acceptability scores would be simpler administratively and would lend itself more readily to quantitative expression of the scores for purposes of interpretation and research than the results of more elaborate techniques. Thompson and Powell (55) developed a rating scale and compared it with the partial-rank-order approach. They found advantages in the rating scale and concluded that it was the better research technique. In three studies at the junior high school level, Forlano and Wrightstone (23) found that the Revised Ohio Social Acceptance Scale, Advanced Series, a peer-rating instrument suitable for group administration, showed "some promise and practicality in assessing the quality of social acceptability in a class." This scale requires each pupil to rate each classmate on a five-point scale as follows: (1) very best friends, (2) good friends, (3) not friends but okay, (4) you don't know them, (5) you know them but not friends and not okay to you.

In another study, Justman and Wrightstone (33) compared methods of measuring pupil status in the classroom. One of these was a modified form of the Ohio Social Acceptance Scale. A second was a variant of the "guess who test" which involved the casting of classmates as characters to play given roles in class plays. The third was a modification of Moreno's original approach in which each pupil was asked to select the three pupils liked best and the three liked least. The intercorrelations among these three methods were found to be relatively high, .535 to .958. It was concluded that the modified Moreno approach and the Ohio Social Acceptance Scale could be used interchangeably whereas somewhat different aspects of status were measured by the casting-characters approach.

As was emphasized by Ohlsen (40) teachers need specific suggestions in preparing sociometric measures and using the results. He illustrated the use of the sociogram. Dunlap (21) described a method simpler than the sociogram for recording sociometric data which was devised after six years of experimentation. This is essentially a cumulative record with spaces for recording sociometric data in code once a month for ten months. The data for 40 pupils can be kept on a chart 20 inches square. While it was not regarded as a replacement of the sociogram, Dunlap pointed out that this kind of cumulative record was a useful adjunct to it because of its effectiveness in picturing the individual through time and in helping to spot the individuals who were isolates from the group over a long period. It would seem that this kind of cumulative record ought to lend greater validity to sociometric data, just as a cumulative record of test scores may be regarded with greater confidence than a score resulting from one administration of a single test.

ANNOTATED LIST OF RATING SCALES, BEHAVIOR DESCRIPTIONS, ANECDOTAL RECORDS, AND SOCIOMETRIC DEVICES

Behavior Description form. Reports and Records Committee of Progressive Education Association, 1938. Formerly published by Progressive Education Association which is now out of existence. The form is now in the public domain (III).[7]

---

[7] The Roman numerals used in this section carry forward the classification of instruments for gathering data about personal qualities that was begun in Chapter VII. II refers to rating devices and III to behavior descriptions.

A plan, resulting from intensive work over an extended period of time by the Reports and Records Committee, designed to secure and record in permanent form judgments of teachers concerning traits believed to be important. Consists of a "behavior description" filing and transfer card in the form of a folder, a sheet to be used by the teacher in making a report on his pupils, and a "trait study" manual containing complete directions. The traits included are: responsibility-dependability, creativeness and imagination, influence, inquiring mind, openmindedness, power and habit of analysis, social concern, emotional responsiveness, serious purpose, social adaptability, work habits, physical energy, assurance, self-reliance, and emotional control. A series of descriptive statements is given in connection with each trait and the teacher indicates the one which describes the pupil best. Space is provided on the pupil's card for recording judgments of all his teachers from Grade 7 through Grade 12. *Reference:* Manual for Behavior Description, Reports and Records Committee of the Commission on the Relation of School and College of Progressive Education Association (Eugene R. Smith, chairman). Form may be reprinted or adapted for local use without permission.

Bonney, Merl E., and Fessenden, Seth A. *Bonney-Fessenden Sociograph.* Monterey: California Test Bureau, 1955. Complete set of materials, including directions for administering, recording, and interpreting Sociograph for a class of 40 (one manila folder, one manual, and five sheets of eight perforated answer slips), 60 cents; additional folders (the Sociograph), 25 cents each; additional answer slips, 15 cents each; additional manuals, 25 cents; specimen set, 60 cents (II).

An instrument planned to simplify and organize the collection and interpretation of sociometric data. It consists of a specially printed folder containing an ingenious graph arrangement for the teacher's use in recording data and a detailed manual of instructions. Answer sheets are also available for use in collecting responses from the pupils, although the use of these is not required. Pupils indicate names of their classmates whom they would like to have work on a committee with them, and also indicate, if they wish, those they would prefer not to have on a committee. Spaces and directions are provided for summary and interpretation of data. It is implied in manual that reliability or stability of the group status of individual pupils derived from sociometric data is .90 for a time interval of one week or less, .76 for an interval of two to nine weeks, and .65 for an interval of three months to a year (7).

Cain, Leo F., Levine, Samuel, and Elzey, Freeman F. *Cain-Levine Social Competency Scales.* Palo Alto, Calif.: Consulting Psychologists Press, 1963. Booklets $3.85 per 25, $13.00 per 100, $25.00 per 500; manual, $1.35; specimen set, $1.50 (II).

A scale for rating the behavior and estimating the social competence of mentally retarded children who are trainable.

Consists of 44 items yielding four scores: self-help, initiative, social skills, and communication. Percentile norms for mentally retarded children ages 5–13. Manual may be used by either teachers or clinicians.

Cassel, Russell M. *Child Behavior Rating Scale.* Los Angeles, Western Psychological Services, 1964. 25 scales and manual, $6.00 (II).

Designed for rapid rating of the behavior and personal qualities of preschool, kindergarten, and primary grade children.

Doll, Edgar A., and staff. *The Vineland Social Maturity Scale, Revised.* Minneapolis: American Guidance Services, Inc., 1947. Record blanks, $1.90 per 25; manual, $1.25; specimen set, $1.30 (III).

A social maturity scale standardized for normal subjects from birth to 30 years. A behavior description form rather than a rating scale. One form. Time required for rating an individual, 20–30 minutes. Judgments are recorded by the examiner after interviewing in detail either someone well acquainted with the subject or the subject himself. The manual warns that at least as much care should be used in mastering the technique as is given to acquiring the technique of the Stanford-Binet Scale. The present Vineland scale consists of 117 items arranged in order of difficulty and grouped in six categories: self-help, self-direction, occupation, communication, locomotion, socialization. Examples: Year 0–1, balances head, grasps objects within reach; Year 7–8, tells time to quarter hour, disavows literal Santa Claus; Year 25, systematizes own work, shares community responsibility. Yields a raw score, an age score, and an SQ, which is the subject's age score divided by his life age. A plus score is given for habitual behavior, a minus for absence of behavior, and a ± for occasional behavior. The scale has been used as a developmental measure for normal subjects and also for various types of socially handicapped subjects. *References:* Doll (*19, 20*), and Watson (*59*).

Fels Parent Behavior Rating Scales. Yellow Springs, Ohio: The Fels Research Institute, 1937–1949. $1.00 per set of 30 scales; manual, $1.50; specimen set, $1.00 (II).

A device for use in assessing parent behavior toward the child, as well as various aspects of the home environment. Thirty linear or graphic rating scales, each of which is supplemented by descriptions of points along the scales, are available. The instrument requires two home visits and interviews of about two hours each. Sheets with space to rate ten children on each one facilitate comparisons from child to child. Manual reports reliability data indicating that two sets of ratings by a rater without much experience correlated from .53 to .85. The two sets of ratings showed correlations above .70 on about half the scales. After some years of experience, the same rater made two sets of ratings with an interval of 6 months between them, and the ratings correlated from .62 to .90, with a median of about .80. Ratings of two different raters correlated .26 to .88 on the 30 scales, with 22 of the 30 correlations exceeding .65. Norms for the raw scores are not available. In the hands of an experienced, skillful interviewer, these scales should provide a useful supplement to other counseling devices and procedures (2).

Flanagan, John C. *Personal and Social Development Program.* Chicago: Science Research Associates, Inc., 1956. Classroom Booklet of *Performance Record* incident sheets; *Teacher's Guide; Manual for School Administrators and Supervisors* (III). (Temporarily out of print.)

A carefully worked out and thoroughly explained program of personal development of pupils for use by classroom teachers. Consists of (1) a *Performance Record* on which behaviors which "need improvement" and behaviors "to be encouraged" are listed under eight major areas; (2) a detailed *Teacher's Guide* which explains the materials, principles, and procedures of the program; and (3) a *Manual for School Administrators and Supervisors* setting forth the philosophy of the program and containing ideas for introducing the program, making it meaningful to parents, and integrating it into the curriculum. Intended mainly for the elementary school level.

Haggerty, M. E., Olson, W. C., and Wickman, E. K. *Haggerty-Olson-Wickman Behavior Rating Schedules.* New York: Harcourt, Brace & World, Inc., 1930. $3.00 per 35; specimen set, 40 cents (II).

Designed for the study of behavior problems and problem tendencies in children. Two schedules, A and B. A is for behavior problems—the rater checks each item to indicate the relative frequency of occurrence of the behavior in the child being rated. Schedule B is a graphic rating scale for intellectual, physical, social, and emotional traits. One form only for kindergarten-Grade 12. No time limit, as it is a rating device. Reliability of Schedule B has been reported in various studies. Correlation coefficients vary from .56 to .92 in nursery, elementary, and high school populations. Correlation between Schedule A and Schedule B, .62. A more reliable measure can be obtained by averaging the ratings of several judges. *Reference:* Olson (41).

Wittenborn, J. Richard. *Wittenborn Psychiatric Rating Scales.* New York: The Psychological Corporation, 1955. $2.75 per 25; specimen set, 50 cents (II).

Provides for ratings on 52 symptoms which are combined to yield nine cluster scores. Psychiatric terminology used in defining scores. Not for use by teacher-counselors but may be used by school psychologists, physicians, or professionally trained counselors in cases where severe emotional or mental disorder is suspected. Norms based on 1000 cases admitted to a mental hospital. To be used in rating adolescents or adults. One form which can be filled out by an experienced rater in about 15 minutes.

REFERENCES

1. Abbott, Winona, Reid, Grace L., and Smith, Leo F. "The Anecdotal Behavior Journal," *American Journal of Nursing,* XLIII (October 1943), 928–933.
2. Baldwin, Alfred L., Kalhorn, Joan, and Breese, Fay Huffman. *The Appraisal of Parent Behavior.* Psychological Monographs 63, No. 4, 1949. Pp. vii + 85.
3. Barr, A. S. "On the Use of Anecdotal Records," *Journal of Educational Research,* XXXIV (January 1941), 358–360.
4. Bicker, H. "Using Anecdotal Records to Know the Child," *Fostering Mental Health in Our Schools,* pp. 184–202. Association for Supervision and Curriculum Development, 1950 Yearbook. Washington, D.C.: National Education Association, 1950. Pp. x + 320.
5. Blatz, William E., and Bott, E. A. "Studies in Mental Hygiene of Children. I, Behavior of Public School Children: A Description of Method," *Pedagogical Seminary and Journal of Genetic Psychology,* XXXIV (December 1927), 552–582.
6. Bonney, Merl E. "Social Behavior Differences between Second Grade Children of High and Low Sociometric Status," *Journal of Educational Research,* XLVIII (March 1955), 481–495.
7. Bonney, Merl E., and Fessenden, Seth A. *Bonney-Fessenden Sociograph Manual.* Monterey: California Test Bureau, 1955. Pp. 20.
8. Bonney, Merl E., and Powell, J. "Differences in Social Behavior between Sociometrically High and Sociometrically Low Children," *Journal of Educational Research,* XLVI (March 1953), 481–495.
9. Bonney, Warren C., and McGehearty, Loyce. "Non-Test Pupil Data," *Vocational Guidance Quarterly,* XI (Autumn 1962), 68–72.
10. Bowes, Fern H. "The Anecdotal Behavior Record in Measuring Progress in Character," *Elementary School Journal,* XXXIX (February 1939), 431–435.
11. Brieland, Donald. "Variation of the 'Guess Who' Technique for the Study of the Adjustment of Children," *Journal of Educational Research,* XLV (January 1952), 385–390.
12. Brown, Marion, and Martin, Vibella. "Anecdotal Records of Pupil Behavior," *California Journal of Secondary Education,* XIII (April 1938), 205–208.
13. Budd, G. F. "Anecdotal Record as a Technique for Gathering Data on Professional Laboratory Exercises in Student Teaching," *Evaluation of Student Techniques,* 81–91. Association for Student Teaching, 1949 Yearbook.
14. Charters, W. W. "A Character Development Study," *Personnel Journal,* XII (August 1933), 119–123.
15. Dailey, Charles A. "The Life History Approach to Assessment," *Personnel and Guidance Journal,* XXXVI (March 1958), 456–460.
16. Demming, John A. "Basic Principles for Making Anecdotal Recordings," *Readings in Guidance* (edited by

Crow and Crow), pp. 281–285. New York: David McKay Company, Inc., 1962. Pp. 626.

17. Diederich, Paul B. "Design for a Comprehensive Evaluation Program," *School Review*, LVIII (April 1950), 225–232.

18. Dinkmeyer, Don. "Reconsideration of the Autobiography," *Vocational Guidance Quarterly*, VI (Autumn 1957), 9–11.

19. Doll, E. A. "The Vineland Social Maturity Scale," *Training School Bulletin*, XXXII (March, April, May, June 1935), 1–7, 25–32, 48–55, 68–74.

20. Doll, E. A. "Preliminary Standardization of The Vineland Social Maturity Scale," *American Journal of Orthopsychiatry*, VI (1936), 283–293.

21. Dunlap, Carolyn C. "Recording of Sociometric Data Made Concise and Continuous," *School Review*, LX (April 1952), 225–229.

22. Flanagan, John C. "The Critical Incident Technique in the Study of Individuals," *Modern Educational Problems* (ed. by Arthur E. Traxler), pp. 61–70. Report of the Seventeenth Educational Conference Sponsored by the Educational Records Bureau and the American Council on Education. Washington: American Council on Education, 1955. Pp. viii + 148.

23. Forlano, George, and Wrightstone, J. Wayne. "Measuring the Quality of Social Acceptability within a Class," *Educational and Psychological Measurement*, XV (Summer 1955), 127–136.

24. Fox, W. H., and Segel, David. "Validity of the Choice of Friends Method of Measuring Social Adjustment," *Journal of Educational Research*, XLVII (January 1954), 389–394.

25. French, Joseph L. "Interests of the Gifted," *Vocational Guidance Quarterly*, VII (Autumn 1958), 14–16.

26. Guinouard, Donald E., and Rychlak, Joseph F. "Personality Correlates of Sociometric Popularity in Elementary School Children," *Personnel and Guidance Journal*, XL (January 1962), 438–442.

27. Hamalainen, Arthur E. *An Appraisal of Anecdotal Records.* Teachers College Contributions to Education, No. 891. New York: Bureau of Publications, Teachers College, Columbia University, 1943. Pp. 87.

28. Ilg, Frances L., and Ames, Louise Bates. *School Readiness: Behavior Tests Used In the Gesell Institute.* New York: Harper & Row, Publishers, 1964. Pp. xi + 396.

29. Jarvie, L. L. "The Anecdotal Record as a Means of Understanding Students," *Institute for Administrative Officers of Higher Education Proceedings* (1940), 127–142.

30. Jarvie, L. L., and Ellingson, Mark. *Handbook on the Anecdotal Behavior Journal.* Chicago: The University of Chicago Press, 1940. Pp. xii + 72.

31. Johnson, O. E. "Cumulative Anecdotal Records," *School Executive*, LXI (February 1942), 28–30.

32. Jones, Galen, and Galbraith, Adria. "An Experiment with Anecdotal Records," *Guidance in Public Secondary Schools*, Educational Records Bulletin 28. New York: Educational Records Bureau, 1939. Pp. xxvi + 330.

33. Justman, Joseph, and Wrightstone, J. Wayne. "Comparison of Three Methods of Measuring Pupil Status in the Classroom," *Educational and Psychological Measurement*, XI (Autumn 1951), 362–367.

34. McCormick, C. F. "Anecdotal Record in the Appraisal of Personality," *School and Society*, LIII (January 25, 1941), 126–127.

35. Malloy, John. "The Prediction of College Achievement with the Life Experience Inventory," *Educational and Psychological Measurement*, XV (Summer 1955), 170–180.

36. *Manual for the American Council on Education Cumulative Record Folders for Schools and Colleges.* Prepared by Committee on the Revision of Cumulative Record Cards (Eugene R. Smith, chairman). Washington: American Council on Education, 1947. Pp. iv + 28.

37. Marston, L. R. *The Emotions in Young Children.* University of Iowa Studies in Child Welfare, Vol. III, 1925. Pp. 99.

38. Moreno, Jacob L. *Who Shall Survive?—A New Approach to the Problem of Human Inter-Relations*, rev. ed. Beacon, N.Y.: Beacon House, Inc., 1953. Pp. 763.

39. North, Robert D. "The Experimental Use of a Biographical Inventory in Four Public High Schools," *1955 Fall Testing Program in Independent Schools and Supplementary Studies*, pp. 77–83. Educational Records Bulletin 67. New York: Educational Records Bureau, February 1956. Pp. xii + 84.

40. Ohlsen, Merle M. "Helping Teachers Interpret Sociometric-Test Data," *Journal of Teacher Education*, II (June 1951), 99–104.

41. Olson, Willard C. "Utilization of the Haggerty-Olson-Wickman Behavior Rating Schedules," *Childhood Education*, IX (April 1933), 350–359.

42. Olson, Willard C. "The Diagnosis and Treatment of Behavior Disorders of Children," *Educational Diagnosis*, pp. 363–396. Thirty-fourth Yearbook of the National Society for the Study of Education, Chapter XVIII. Chicago, Ill.: The University of Chicago Press, 1935. Pp. x + 564.

43. Powers, N. E. "An Application of the Marston Introversion Extroversion Rating Scale," *Journal of Educational Psychology*, XIX (March 1928), 168–174.

44. Putnam, J. F. "Toward Improved Information about Pupils," *School Life*, XLIV (January 1963).

45. Randall, J. A. "The Anecdotal Behavior Journal," *Progressive Education*, XIII (January 1936), 21–26.

46. Raths, Louis. *Anecdotal Records.* Bulletin No. 1 (September 1935). Progressive Education Association, Evaluation in the Eight-Year Study, Ohio State University, Columbus, Ohio.

47. Report of Subcommittee on Personality Measurement (D. A. Robertson, chmn.). "Personnel Methods," *Educational Record*, Supplement No. 8 (July 1928), 53–68.

48. Roberts, Katherine E., and Ball, Rachel S. "A Study of Personality in Young Children by Means of a Series

of Rating Scales," *Pedagogical Seminary and Journal of Genetic Psychology*, LII (March 1938), 78–149.

49. Roby, Dale L. "Learning about Pupils: Non-test Tools and Their Uses," *Teachers College Journal*, XXX (December 1959), 65–66.

50. Rothney, John W. M. *Evaluating and Reporting Pupil Progress*, pp. 17–22. Washington, D.C.: National Educational Association, 1955.

51. Shaffer, E. Evan Jr., "The Autobiography in Secondary School Counseling," *Personnel and Guidance Journal*, XXXII (March 1954), 395–398.

52. Smith, Eugene R., Tyler, Ralph W., and the Evaluation Staff. *Appraising and Recording Student Progress*, Chapter X. (Report of the Eight-Year Study of the Progressive Education Association.) New York: McGraw-Hill Book Company, Inc., 1942. Pp. xxiv+550.

53. Strang, Ruth. *Counseling Technics in College and Secondary School*, rev. ed. New York: Harper & Row, Publishers, 1949. Pp. xii+302.

54. Stuart, Sylvia. "Reading the Anecdotal Behavior Record," *The Problems and Techniques Involved in Reading Social Relationships*, pp. 169–173. Fourteenth Yearbook. Claremont, Calif.: Claremont College Curriculum Laboratory, 1949. Pp. viii+192.

55. Thompson, George G., and Powell, Marvin, "Investigation of the Rating Scale Approach to the Measurement of Social Status," *Educational and Psychological Measurement*, XI (Autumn 1951), 440–455.

56. Tyler, Ralph W. "Techniques for Evaluating Behavior," *Educational Research Bulletin*, XIII (January 17, 1934), 1–11.

57. Van Alstyne, Dorothy. "A Record for Describing Attitudes and Behavior in the High School," *Journal of Educational Research*, XXXVII (December 1941), 276–286.

58. Van Alstyne, Dorothy, Hattwick, L. W., and Totten, Helen. "New Scale for Rating School Behavior and Attitudes," *Elementary School Journal*, XXXV (October 1936), 115–121.

59. Watson, Robert I. *The Clinical Method in Psychology*, Chapter II. New York: Harper & Row, Publishers, 1951. Pp. xii+780.

60. Whittenburg, Clarice. "Plea for the Anecdotal Record," *School Executive*, LXIV (June 1945), 44–46.

61. Witryol, Sam L., and Thompson, George G. "Experimental Comparison of the Stability of Social Acceptability Scores Obtained with the Partial-Rank-Order and the Paired-Comparison Scales," *Journal of Educational Psychology*, XLIV (January 1953), 20–30.

62. Wodder, Niels C., and Hall, William E. "An Analysis of Peer Ratings," *Personnel and Guidance Journal*, XL (March 1962), 606–609.

63. Wood, Ben D. "The Major Strategy of Guidance," *Educational Record*, XV (October 1934), 419–444.

64. Wrightstone, J. Wayne. "Assessing Pupil Adjustment by Self-Descriptive and Sociometric Techniques," *Growing Points in Educational Research*, pp. 330–335. Official Report, American Educational Research Association, Washington, D.C.: American Educational Research Association, 1949.

65. Wrightstone, J. Wayne, Justman, Joseph, and Robbins, Irving. *Evaluation in Modern Education*. New York: American Book Company, 1956. Pp. xii+482.

66. Wrightstone, J. Wayne, and others. "Application of Sociometric Techniques to School Personnel," *Journal of Experimental Education*, XX (March 1952), 301–304.

67. Zahn, D. Willard. "Anecdotal Records in Relation to Character Development," *Education for Dynamic Citizenship*, pp. 294–300. Twenty-fourth Annual Schoolmen's Week Proceedings. Philadelphia: University of Pennsylvania, School of Education, January 25, 1937.

CHAPTER IX

Planning and Administering a Testing Program for Guidance Purposes

THE NEWER CONCEPT OF A PROGRAM OF INDI-vidualized instruction and guidance as contrasted with the older practice of mass education is concentrating the attention of administrators, teachers, and counselors at all levels of the school on the need for a great variety of information about each individual pupil (4). In their efforts to obtain records of ability and achievement that have a high degree of objectivity and reliability, an increasing number of schools are carrying on programs of measurement. Consequently, many questions are being asked concerning how a test program should be planned and what kinds of tests should be used.

Tests for a school guidance program may be divided into two broad categories: those to be used systematically and those for special uses. The tests to be used systematically should be given at regular intervals in a program which is carefully planned in every detail and in which every normal pupil in the school participates fully. The tests for special uses should supplement the regular program and should be administered to individuals and groups as needs arise.

A systematic testing program ordinarily includes tests of four general types: (1) group intelligence tests or tests of academic aptitude; (2) tests of reading ability; (3) tests of achievement in the subjects commonly included in the academic curriculum or, if the school is one in which subject-matter lines have been broken down, tests in the broad fields of the curriculum; and (4) interest inventories. There are so many tests of each type and so many new tests are produced each year that most schools, unless they happen to employ specialists in testing, find it a baffling problem to choose from among the available instruments. The following are among the most important guiding principles of test selection.

1. *First, secure a detailed statement of the school's objectives from the faculty of the school itself.* Then choose (or construct) tests that measure the progress of the pupils toward these objectives—or at least toward some of them, for it is improbable that any test or combination of tests will measure the progress of pupils toward all the purposes that a school believes to be important. Try to obtain evidence concerning the degree to which the tests under consideration predict or measure the attainment of the objectives listed by the school. This is an important aspect of test validity.

2. Become familiar with the *Standards for Educational and Psychological Tests and Manuals* (1). This important reference is a revision and combination of *Technical Recommendations for Psychological Tests and Diagnostic Techniques,* published in 1954 by the American Psychological Association, and *Technical Recommendations for Achievement Tests,* published in 1955 by the American Educational Research Association. At this writing, the new revision is being prepared by an APA committee and a joint committee of the American Educational Research Association and the National Council on Measurement in Education and is in draft form. Also refer to reviews of tests in Buros' *Mental Measurements Yearbooks* (5, 7). Use these as general guides in the selection of tests.

3. *Choose tests that have been shown to be highly reliable.* A reliable test is one that measures consistently; that is, if the test is repeated or given in alternate forms, the

results obtained are in close agreement. Try to find studies in which the reliabilities of the tests have been reported from several sources. Remember that split-half reliability coefficients are likely to be spuriously high if they involve a speed factor. This is also true of Kuder-Richardson reliabilities. Give preference to reliability coefficients which result from the administration of different forms of a test and which are based on cases taken from a single grade level rather than from a range of grades.

4. Other things being equal, *select tests for which several comparable forms are available*. This point is important in a regular testing program to minimize practice effects. The opportunities for systematic testing are even more favorable if a new form of the test is issued each year.

5. Other things being equal, *select tests for which adequate, up-to-date norms are available*. It is helpful to be able to compare the achievement of a given pupil with norms of regional or national scope as well as with the local population. Private schools and public schools in residential districts of suburban communities usually find the independent school norms prepared by the Educational Records Bureau of more value than norms for unselected public schools.

6. When a number of different achievement tests are being given to the same group of pupils, *it is helpful to select tests that are scaled on a common criterion group*. Obviously, if the raw scores are translated into derived scores that have the same normative meaning for all tests, comparisons of achievement in different subject fields will be greatly facilitated.

7. Other things being equal, *choose tests that can be scored objectively, rapidly, and inexpensively*. Objectivity of scoring is ordinarily a practical necessity from the standpoint both of reliability of scoring and of economy. Rapidity of scoring is highly desirable to allow results to be used in guidance and instruction before interest has waned. Inexpensive scoring is usually essential since most budgets for testing are limited. In this connection schools should investigate the possibilities inherent in the various kinds of machine scoring now available: IBM Model 1230, Digitek, Lindquist's test scoring service at the University of Iowa (MRC), ETS's SCRIBE, The Psychological Corporation's Psyche and so forth.

A school which can afford to administer on a systematic basis only one test annually to all pupils will do well to select a group test of academic aptitude, for a test of this kind naturally tends to have more uses in guidance in general than tests whose functions are specialized. The present tendency among test specialists is to recommend tests that yield separate verbal and numerical scores or tests that provide comparable scores in several different mental functions in preference to tests that provide only a single total score, mental age, or IQ.

Next to an intelligence test, the test that probably has the most general usefulness is a silent reading test. Reading ability plays so large a part in academic success, particularly in the verbal subjects and in vocational adapt-

ability, that in every guidance program the reading achievement of all pupils should be checked regularly. Moreover, many personality aberrations have their root in the failure of the child to learn to read and thus to make one of the most important of all adaptations to his social environment. Another important reason for measuring reading is that no conclusion concerning intelligence that is based on the usual group test of mental ability is really valid unless the reading ability of the pupil is known.

8. For areas and objectives where no published tests will meet the needs, *construct, or better still, cooperate with classroom teachers in the preparation of, tests or examinations suited to the purposes and curriculum of the local school*. These may be essay examinations, semiobjective tests, or objective tests. Locally prepared instruments of this kind will be more useful if local norms are developed for them. For a good, brief treatment of procedures in planning and preparing local tests and examinations, Englehart's *Improving Classroom Testing* (12) is recommended.

STEPS IN PLANNING AND CONDUCTING A TESTING PROGRAM

The values of measurement depend to a great extent on the care with which the testing program is planned and carried out. The responsibility for the testing program should be centered on a member of the school staff who will give patient attention to the planning of the entire program each year, who will faithfully administer every detail, and who will make it his business to see that the test records of every pupil are complete except where extenuating circumstances make it impossible for the pupil to take the tests. The following rules for administering a testing program have been found useful in actual practice:

1. Select the tests carefully, preferably in cooperation with a faculty committee. If there is a state testing program in your state, consider carefully the tests recommended in connection with that program, for they are usually selected by experts in measurement and guidance. Take into account the tests recommended by an independent organization such as the Educational Records Bureau in connection with its fall and spring testing programs. The tests for those programs are chosen by a committee of administrators and teachers from member schools of the Bureau, working in cooperation with test specialists on the Bureau's staff.

2. Order the tests well in advance of the date on which they are to be used. Allow plenty of time to get all the material ready before the first day of the testing sessions.

Remember that if separate answer sheets are to be used and if the pupils taking a given test are to be tested in several groups at different times, the number of booklets ordered may be only as many as are needed to supply the largest group, since each booklet may be used several times. However, a few additional booklets probably should be ordered in case some of them become so badly mutilated through use that they must be discarded.

3. Plan *in detail* for the administration of the tests. Choose examiners and proctors with great care. If possible, use examiners who have had previous experience in giving standardized tests. If inexperienced examiners must be used, they should be rehearsed beforehand. Remember that some very intelligent people are temperamentally unsuited to the exacting routine of administering a test. You may use such persons as proctors where tests are being given to larger groups, but they should not be placed in charge of the administration of a test. It is ordinarily desirable to have teachers in the lower elementary grades administer the tests to their own classes in order to maintain a feeling of confidence and security in the test situation on the part of these young children.

4. Ditto or otherwise duplicate an examination schedule and see that every person concerned receives a copy of it. The schedule should give the time and place of each test, indicate just where each class which is to take the test is to go, where the pupils who are not taking the test should be during that hour, what material the pupils will need when taking the test, and the name of the faculty member in charge at each examination.

5. Avoid overemphasis on the tests. Urge the teachers to have the pupils take them "in stride."

6. Give pupils who have never taken objective tests an opportunity to examine old tests of this kind. Better still, have them take a short practice test of the objective type. However, for many groups, this step will not be needed, since objective tests are now so common that nearly all pupils except beginners in school are acquainted with them.

7. Do not distribute the tests to the examiners before the day of the examination. Have packages containing the requisite numbers of test booklets (and answer sheets if the tests are to be given with answer sheets) made up and ready for the examiners when the date for the tests arrives.

8. Provide each examiner with a manual and a sample copy of the test several days before the examination, and urge him to study the manual and to practice by taking the test himself. Most errors in the administration of tests are caused by the failure of the examiner to prepare sufficiently beforehand. Make sure that each teacher serving as an examiner is forewarned against giving the pupils any specific information about the content of the tests.

9. Provide each examiner and proctor with a written set of instructions outlining his duties during the examination.

10. When administering tests to large groups:

a. Make arrangements so that there will be no interruptions or distractions during the testing period. Persons should not enter or leave the room unless absolutely necessary.

b. Seat the pupils in alternate chairs, if possible.

c. See that each proctor understands what is expected of him.

d. Make announcements slowly and clearly in a voice that is loud enough to be heard throughout the room. Assume a businesslike and efficient attitude that will command attention, but do not be unnecessarily severe. Remember that some pupils become nervous when faced with an examination.

e. Have proctors supply all pupils with test material and pencils. Announce that the pupils are not to write on the booklets nor to open them until so instructed.

f. Have the blanks on the front of the booklets or answer sheets filled out, and in the case of certain kinds of answer sheets follow the directions for coding them. Be sure to announce the date, how names are to be written, and other items that may need clarification. Spend sufficient time on this step to see that the information is given correctly by the pupils. Ages and birth dates are especially important on tests of academic aptitude.

g. Hold faithfully to the exact wording of the printed directions unless there is an excellent reason for introducing a minor variation in them. The preparation of directions for a test is one aspect of test construction and standardization. The wording of the directions has been carefully thought out by the test author. Don't improvise or introduce short cuts. If you do, you may change the test results significantly.

h. Time the examination with extreme care, using a watch which has a second hand and which has been checked for accuracy. It is advisable to have one of the proctors check your timing to be sure that no error occurs. In some tests accurate timing is the most important single feature of the entire procedure of administering them.

i. Move about the room occasionally to see that all pupils are working on the right part of the examination, but do not stand gazing over a pupil's shoulder until he becomes self-conscious, and do not constantly move nervously from pupil to pupil.

j. Stop the examination immediately when the time is up and collect the booklets.

k. If the tests are administered with separate answer sheets for scoring with the older model of the IBM Test-Scoring Machine (Model 805), make sure that all pupils have made their response marks heavy, black, and glossy, and have erased stray marks before the answer sheets are turned in. One procedure is to allow a few moments for the darkening of the responses and the erasing of stray dots and other marks after the pupils have handed in their booklets but before the answer sheets are collected. If this procedure is followed, the pupils should be very carefully supervised to make sure that none of them mark at random items which they did not reach during the time limit for the administration of the test.

11. As soon as a certain test has been given, have all examiners turn in their booklets promptly. Alphabetize and check the test papers against the class lists.

12. If tests are given with separate answer sheets and if the same booklets are used with successive groups, be sure to have them carefully inspected after each use. Erase all notes, figuring, or other writing; or if there is extensive writing in the booklets discard them. If this step is omitted, the tests of those pupils who receive booklets in which other pupils have written may be invalidated.

13. Except in cases of protracted illness, *see that all absentees make up the examination.* You will find this part of the testing program a great nuisance and you will feel that it is not worth the bother, but it is unavoidable. Complete data are essential if the results are to be used successfully in either teaching or guidance. Moreover, if the pupils once discover that absentees do not have to make up the tests, a few escapists will conveniently be ill every time an examination period arrives.

14. See that the tests are scored promptly. Report the results to the faculty in a form that they can use and provide them with an explanation of the meaning of the results.

15. Have the scores of each pupil entered on an individual cumulative record card and make this card available to both counselors and classroom teachers. The card should also be made available to the parents, if the data are carefully explained in conference.

16. If the school has access to electronic computers, use this equipment to summarize test score evidence concerning individual pupils with respect to particular guidance questions. Although some guidance theorists question whether testing is a legitimate guidance activity, surveys indicate that in the schools themselves "the testing program is the dominating and expanding aspect of guidance." Interpretation of test scores in relation to other data is often difficult, and it may be possible to achieve the goal of sounder interpretation by use of the computer and continuous, longitudinal studies (9).

The following materials furnish two illustrations of step 4 in the foregoing list of suggestions. The first is a set of "General Directions Concerning Fall Testing Program" which was distributed some years ago in mimeographed form to the students in The Hill School, Pottstown, Pa., in connection with the fall program in that school. It illustrates the planning of a special schedule for the testing program for an entire school, without regard to the regular class schedule. The second is a schedule of the spring testing program prepared for the

teachers at Tower Hill School, Wilmington, Del. (see adjoining page). It illustrates directions for a testing program which is to be administered to the regular class groups.

GENERAL DIRECTIONS CONCERNING FALL TESTING PROGRAM[1]

(Do not lose these sheets!)

1. There will be a General School Meeting on **Thursday** evening at 7:45 P.M. in Memorial Hall. All boys, *including day students,* must attend.
2. The tests start on Thursday evening and continue through Saturday noon. There will be no classes on Friday and Saturday.
3. Read carefully Page 2 in order to determine which tests you are to take.
4. Consult Page 3 for the schedule of these tests.
5. Consult the Common Room Bulletin Boards to find out the room in which you will take a given examination. *YOU WILL NOT HAVE ALL YOUR TESTS IN THE SAME ROOM.* Therefore, be sure to consult the Bulletin Board before each test and PLEASE DO NOT WAIT UNTIL THE LAST MINUTE TO DO THIS.
6. Be in your seat in the examination room at least five minutes ahead of the scheduled examination time. EXAMINATIONS WILL START ON TIME! The tests are spaced close together and it is important that everyone be on time.
7. Be sure to have with you at each test a SUPPLY of well-sharpened pencils. Ink must not be used.
8. No one may leave the room until the end of each test. WAIT FOR DISMISSAL. You will need all the time allotted.
9. On each test you must indicate the name of the course you are taking in that subject, giving the exact full name. For example:

6F. Honor English	2F. English
6F. Special English	5F. Mathematics
4F. French A	5F. Geometry
et cetera	

Be sure you know the name of your instructor and how to spell his name.

10. THE MOST IMPORTANT THING IN TAKING THE TESTS IS TO FOLLOW ALL DIRECTIONS VERY CAREFULLY. *Wise* guessing may improve

[1] Prepared by the late Ralph C. Johnson, former assistant headmaster, The Hill School, Pottstown, Pennsylvania.

SPRING TESTING PROGRAM, GRADES 8-12

DATES / PERIOD	April 4 Monday	April 5 Tuesday	April 6 Wednesday	April 7 Thursday	April 8 Friday	April 11 Monday	April 12 Tuesday	April 13 Wednesday	April 14 Thursday	April 15 Friday
I	Eng. 9A / Eng. 8C	↑ ↑	↑ ↑	Lit. 9A / Math. 8A* Math. 8C			Mod. Eur. Hist. A / Contemp. Civilization	French 3A, French 2A, Latin 2A, German 2, French 4	Math. 9B, Math. 11A	
II	Eng. 8A, Eng. 9D, Eng. 10A	↑ ↑ ↑	↑ ↑ ↑	Math. 8A-C* → / Lit. 9D, Lit. 10A		Chemistry → Chemistry	Mod. Eur. Hist. B, Hist. 8B → Hist. 8B	French 1A, Latin 2B, German 1	Math. 12	
III			(Assembly)	Math. 8B → Math. 8B		Biology A	Hist. 8C / Hist. 8C	(Assembly)	Physics → Physics	
IV	Eng. 9C, Eng. 10B	↑ ↑	↑ ↑	Lit. 9C, Lit. 10B			Hist. 8A → Hist. 8A	French 3B, French 2B, Latin 1A	Math. 10A, Math. 9A, Math. 9C	
V	Eng. 12B, Eng. 11A, Eng. 9B, Eng. 8B	↑ ↑ ↑ ↑	↑ ↑ ↑ ↑	Lit. 12B, Lit. 11A, Lit. 9B			Hist. 8A, American Hist. A	Latin 3	↑	
VI	(LUNCH PERIOD)			↑		↑	(LUNCH PERIOD)	(LUNCH PERIOD)	↑	
VII	Eng. 12A, Eng. 11B	↑ ↑	↑ ↑	Lit. 12A, Lit. 11B		General Science → General Science	Biology B, Anc. Hist., Am.Hist.B	French 1B, French 1C, Latin 1B	Math. 11B, Math. 10B	
VIII						General Science				

April 8 Friday (all periods): GOOD FRIDAY — SCHOOL CLOSED

April 15 Friday (all periods): COMPLETE ANY ABSENTEE "MAKE-UP" TESTS; WHEREVER POSSIBLE

*8A and 8C *Math.* groups *combined* for 80" test.

→ Indicates next section of test continued next day in same period.

↓ Indicates 80" test continuing into following period, same day*

All tests are 40" *except* English = 120"; Grade 8 Tests = 80"; Chemistry, Physics, General Science = 80".

Made available through the courtesy of Miss Mary Tayloe Souther, who supervises the testing program at the Tower Hill School, Wilmington, Delaware.

your score. *Wild* guessing may lower it. Don't be a gambler!

The scores you receive on these tests will be recorded on your cumulative record card. Make yourself look as brilliant as possible!

WHICH EXAMINATION DO YOU TAKE? This sheet tells you. Read it carefully.

SOCIAL SCIENCE
Everybody in school *except 2nd Form.*

AMERICAN COUNCIL PSYCHOLOGICAL EXAMI-NATION[2]
Everybody in school *except 2nd Form.*

KUHLMANN-ANDERSON TEST
2nd Form only.

IOWA SILENT READING TEST
Everybody in school *except 2nd Form.*

TRAXLER SILENT READING TEST
2nd Form only.

FRENCH (*advanced*)
Those taking 4F. French A., 5F., 6F., and Special French.

FRENCH (*elementary*)
Those taking 4F. French.

GERMAN
Those taking 4F., 5F., 6F., and Special German.

SPANISH
Those taking 4F. and 5F. Spanish.

MATHEMATICS
Gen. Achievement Math. . . . . 5F. Geom., 5F. and 6F. Math. Mathematics, 7, 8, 9 . . . . . 2F., 3F., 4F., Algebra & 4F. Math.

ENGLISH
Everybody in school.

LINCOLN SPELLING TEST
Everybody in school.

SCHEDULE OF TESTS

Note: The starting time indicates the time that the examiner will start the examination. YOU MUST BE IN YOUR SEAT FIVE MINUTES BEFORE START-ING TIME.

BE SURE TO CONSULT:
1. Page 2—"Which Examinations do you take?"
2. The Common Room Seating Lists.

· · · · · · · · · · · ·

THURSDAY, October 14.
7:45 P.M. General School Meeting in Memorial Hall.
8:15 P.M. Social Science Test.

FRIDAY, October 15.
9.00 A.M. American Council Psychological Examina-tion. Kuhlmann-Anderson Test.
10:45 A.M. All tests in Mathematics.
2:00 P.M. French, German, and Spanish Tests.
7:45 P.M. Iowa Silent Reading Test.
Traxler Silent Reading Test.
9:00 P.M. Lincoln Spelling Test.

[2] The ACE Psychological Examination is now out of print.

SATURDAY, October 16.
9:00 A.M. All English Tests.

AFTER YOU HAVE READ THIS SEE IF THERE ARE ANY CONFLICTS; IF SO, REPORT THEM TO MRS. MERWIN, PERSONNEL OFFICE, *BEFORE NOON ON THURSDAY.*

TEST INFORMATION FOR STUDENTS[3]

Suggestions concerning the taking of objective tests, which may be mimeographed on a single page and given to each pupil, are contained in the following para-graphs:

The purpose of this sheet is to inform you about the general nature of some tests you will take within the next few days. The purpose in giving them is to inform your teachers and counselors about your ability and your needs so that they can provide the best possible learning and guid-ance conditions for you.

Each test contains a large number of questions calling for very brief answers. For most of the questions, several answers are suggested and you will be asked to select the one which you think is right. You should not become discouraged if you find some questions which you are unable to answer, for you are not expected to answer all the questions. Some of the tests are used in several grades and, of course, the pupils in the lower grades are not expected to answer so many questions as those in the higher ones. It is difficult for even the most advanced student to obtain a perfect score.

It is advisable to answer some questions about which you are not entirely sure. If you think you know the answer, you should put it down, even though you are not certain, but you should not guess wildly on questions concerning which you are totally uninformed. In some tests in which a certain proportion of the wrong answers is subtracted from the correct answers, blind guessing may result in a reduction in your score.

There is no passing mark for these tests. Results will be expressed in percentiles which will show how you stand in comparison with other students in the same grade or class who take the same test in many different schools.

Since time is an important element, be sure to have at least two well-sharpened pencils and an eraser. Do not use ink.

Some tests are to be given with special answer sheets so that they may be scored by means of an electrical machine. The examiner will give you special instructions for the marking of these answer sheets. Follow these directions care-fully.

Points to Keep in Mind When Taking the Test
1. Listen *carefully* to all instructions given by the examiner and follow them exactly.

[3] Adapted from a sheet prepared by Ralph D. Britton, formerly of The Loomis School, Windsor, Connecticut.

2. You are not expected to answer *all* the questions but *answer as many as you can.*

3. Work as *rapidly* as you can, spending very little time puzzling over difficult questions. Return to the hard questions if you have time after you have gone through the test.

4. Guess only if you can do so *intelligently.* Don't waste time guessing, if you know nothing about the question.

5. Go to the examination room with *two pencils* and an eraser. If a special pencil is given to you use it *only.*

6. Do not waste your spare time during the days on which the examinations are scheduled, but spend the time as constructively as you would during any school day.

NEED FOR PLAN OF USING TEST RESULTS

It cannot be emphasized too often that the administration of tests is merely a means to an end. The purpose of testing is to obtain data that can be used in improving the instruction, classification, guidance, and adjustment of individual boys and girls. Too often persons in charge of testing programs feel that they have discharged their responsibility when reports of the results have been filed, and any use that is made of the results is left to the initiative of individual staff members.

Every school should have a carefully planned program for using the results of all tests given to the pupils. The first step in this program is to provide each counselor and teacher with a copy of the test results which are of special concern to that particular staff member. The second step is to record the results cumulatively on some meaningful and comparable basis, such as standard scores, grade equivalents, or percentiles. The test scores should be merely one of several important parts of a comprehensive record form which covers several years and contains a digest of all pertinent information about each pupil. Along with the cumulative-record system there should be a vigorous and continuous program of educating the school staff in the interpretation and the use of the records. Test technicians, statisticians, psychologists, psychiatrists, and clinicians can well cooperate in training the school staff. The most important aspect of the training, however, is the daily experience that each staff member should have in using the data in solving the problems of his own pupils, until he habitually turns to objective records as one of the most useful tools in individualizing instruction and fulfilling his guidance function.

REFERENCES

1. American Psychological Association; American Educational Research Association; and National Council on Measurement in Education, Joint Committee (John W. French, chairman). *Standards for Educational and Psychological Tests and Manuals.* (In preparation for probable publication in 1966.)

2. Anderson, Scarvia; Katz, Martin; and Shimberg, Benjamin. *Meeting the Test.* New York: Four Winds Press, 1965. Pp. vi + 184.

3. Bauernfiend, Robert H. *Building a School Testing Program.* Boston: Houghton Mifflin Company, 1963. Pp. xvii + 343.

4. Brown, B. Frank. "An Ungraded High School in Action —A New Educational Development," *Keeping Abreast of the Revolution in Education* (A. E. Traxler, ed.), pp. 120–126. Report of Twenty-eighth Educational Conference sponsored by the Educational Records Bureau. Washington, D.C.: American Council on Education, 1964. Pp. viii + 195.

5. Buros, Oscar K. (ed.). *The Fifth Mental Measurements Yearbook.* Highland Park, N.J.: The Gryphon Press, 1959. Pp. xxvii + 1292.

6. Buros, Oscar K. (ed.). *Tests in Print.* Highland Park, N.J.: The Gryphon Press, 1961. Pp. xxx + 480.

7. Buros, Oscar K. (ed.). *The Sixth Mental Measurements Yearbook.* Highland Park, N.J.: The Gryphon Press, 1965. Pp. xxxvi + 1714.

8. Colver, Robert M. "A Testing Program," *High School Journal,* LXV (November 1961), 64–71.

9. Cooley, William W. "A Computer-Measurement System for Guidance," *Harvard Educational Review,* XXIV (Fall 1964), 559–572.

10. Dallmann, Martha. "Tests and How to Give Them," *Grade Teacher,* LXXIV (January 1962). Pp. 40, 94–95.

11. Davis, Frederick B. "Testing and the Use of Test Results: Test Administration," *Review of Educational Research,* XXXII (February 1962), 7–8.

12. Engelhart, Max D. *Improving Classroom Testing,* What Research Says to the Teacher. AERA-DCT Research Pamphlet Series (Frank W. Hubbard, chairman and editor). Washington, D.C.: National Education Association, 1964. Pp. 33.

13. Findley, Warren G. (ed.). *The Impact and Improvement of School Testing Programs.* The Sixty-seventh Yearbook of the National Society for the Study of Education, Part 2. Chicago, Ill.: The University of Chicago Press, 1964. Pp. xii + 304.

14. Lindquist, E. F. (ed.). *Educational Measurement.* Chapter X. Washington, D.C.: American Council on Education, 1951. Pp. xx + 820.

15. Morris, J. R. "To Test or Not to Test," *Journal of National Association of Secondary-School Principals,* LXV (November 1961), 112–117.

16. Peters, Herman J. "Some Key Sources of Error in Test

Administration," *Clearing House*, XXXIV (November 1959), 161–164.

17. Remmers, H. H., and Gage, N. L. *Educational Measurement and Evaluation*, rev. ed., Chapter XX. New York: Harper & Row, Publishers, 1955. Pp. xiv+650.

18. Sobel, Stuart. "Problems Presented by Large-Scale Testing," *High Points*, XLIV (November 1962), 32–37.

19. *Testing Guide for Teachers*. Prepared by Technical Subcommittee of Independent Schools Advisory Committee with the assistance of the Educational Records Bureau Staff. New York: Educational Records Bureau, 1961. Pp. viii+43.

20. Torrance, E. P. "Testing and Creative Talent," *Educational Leader*, XX (October 1962), 25–29.

21. Traxler, Arthur E. "Administration of the Testing Program," *1963 Achievement Testing Program in Independent Schools and Supplementary Studies*, pp. 75–83. Educational Records Bulletin No. 84. New York: Educational Records Bureau, July 1963. Pp. x+83.

22. Wellman, F. E. "Administration of the Testing Program," *School Life*, XLIV (September 1959), 21–25.

23. West, Doral N. "Reducing Chance in Test Selection," *Personnel and Guidance Journal*, XXXVI (February 1958), 420–421.

CHAPTER X

Scoring, Organizing, and Reporting Test Results

SCORING PROCEDURES

As suggested in the preceding chapter, if a testing program is to be of any great value in the guidance work of a school, it is necessary that the tests be scored accurately and quickly and that the results be reported to the teachers in a form that they can and will use. Unless the whole program is carefully planned, there is danger that the scoring of the tests will be allowed to drag over such a long period of time that the teachers will have lost all interest in them. A still more serious danger is that of inaccuracy of scoring. Objective scoring with an answer key seems such an easy, mechanical procedure that novices in testing are likely to be entirely unaware of the difficulties involved. The work may be placed unknowingly in incompetent hands, for some otherwise intelligent and capable persons seem constitutionally not fitted for a mechanical task such as scoring papers. Sample checking of scoring frequently reveals a surprisingly high percentage of errors, some of which are serious enough to affect the standing of the pupil significantly.

In general, there are four ways of getting the scoring done after the tests have been administered: local hand scoring, local machine scoring, machine scoring at a service center equipped with electronic test processing equipment, and hand or machine scoring and reporting by a service agency.

LOCAL HAND SCORING

If the tests are to be scored manually at the local school, one of the first and most important questions concerns the personnel to be used in the scoring. Probably the most common, but certainly the least satisfactory procedure, is to have the teachers or counselors do the scoring. A teacher may be a good instructor but a very poor scorer.[1] Teachers as a group are probably no more efficient scorers than office clerks; in fact, they are probably less efficient than well-trained office workers. Since the salaries of teachers and counselors are higher (or should be higher) than those of clerks, it obviously is poor economy to use them for scoring.

A more important reason for not assigning the scoring of objective tests to teachers is that this routine drudgery takes valuable time and energy that should be used in planning instruction and guidance. In answer to this statement, it is sometimes insisted by administrators that the scoring of tests is valuable experience for teachers because, they believe, this work acquaints the teachers with the strengths and weaknesses of their pupils. This argument would have validity if a scorer of objective tests were obliged to read each question and evaluate each answer, but that is not the way efficient scoring is done. One compares a key with the answers of the pupils and checks the right and the wrong responses mechanically. It is true that the teacher could take the time to study each pupil's paper while correcting it, but this would not be scoring; it would be diagnosis. Diagnosis by the teacher is necessary, but it should not be confused with the scoring of the papers. It is reasonable to believe that both the diagnosis and the scoring will

---

[1] Arthur E. Traxler. "A Note on the Accuracy of Teachers' Scoring of Semi-Objective Tests," *Journal of Educational Research*, XXXVII (November 1943), 212–213.

suffer if the teacher's attention is thus divided between two unrelated activities.

Although the use of teachers or counselors in scoring is not advised, it is realized that in some schools the instructional and counseling staff will continue to do this kind of work because no other services are available for it. When this is necessary, it is desirable to observe the following rules:

1. Make sure that each teacher understands just how the scoring is to be done.
2. Rescore the first few papers scored by each teacher and make suggestions for the elimination of errors as needed.
3. Thereafter, check the scoring of every fifth or sixth paper and the addition of part scores on all papers.
4. Completely rescore the test booklets when any systematic errors are found, or whenever there is any reason to doubt the accuracy of the scores.

For objective hand scoring that is to be done locally, it is preferable to hire clerks who are specially selected for this purpose. They should be placed under a supervisor, who will carefully check their scoring and insist upon a high standard of accuracy and reasonable speed. The checking of counting and addition is more important than the checking of the scoring of individual items, since it is in counting and adding that large errors are usually made.

LOCAL MACHINE SCORING

The most revolutionary development in the scoring of objective tests has been the application of machine methods to the scoring process. Although there had previously been a number of exploratory attempts to score tests mechanically, the first successful machine scoring method was initiated in the mid-1930s through the production of the electric Test-Scoring Machine (Model 805) of the International Business Machines Corporation. This remarkable timesaving machine has had great influence on test construction, test scoring, and test use for some 30 years. During World War II, it was virtually indispensable in the selection of personnel for a great variety of military assignments. The tests of many millions of high school and college students have been processed on this machine. While this pioneering venture in machine scoring is gradually being replaced by still more efficient methods, this kind of IBM machine scoring will no doubt continue to be used in a good many places for some years to come.

Notwithstanding the wide use of the IBM 805 Test-Scoring Machine for some 30 years, many teachers and even some counselors have never seen one of these scoring machines in operation and have little idea how it works. It seems appropriate, therefore, to discuss this machine at some length, partly as a matter of historical record and partly for the information of teacher-counselors who may be expected to do a better job of test administration if they are acquainted with the requirements of this kind of mechanical equipment.

The idea of a mechanical device for scoring tests goes back 35 years or more. One of the first persons to suggest the feasibility of a machine of this kind was Dr. Ben D. Wood of Columbia University, who saw the need in connection with the great volume of test scoring required by the Pennsylvania study carried on by the Carnegie Foundation for the Advancement of Teaching. President Thomas J. Watson of the International Business Machines Corporation became interested in the idea and various procedures were tried out, but for a time no satisfactory plan was evolved. Finally, Reynold B. Johnson, a young science instructor, who later became director of the Westcoast laboratories of the International Business Machines Corporation, set up a model that became the basis of the first IBM scoring machine.

The IBM 805 scoring machine makes use of the elementary fact that a soft lead pencil will conduct an electric current. Instead of indicating his answers in the test booklet in the usual manner, the pupil records them on an answer sheet of a type with which most students and teachers are now familiar. Each side of the standard answer sheet provides for answers to 150 questions, with a maximum of five choices to each question. Instead of writing the number of his choice for each item in a designated place, as in the ordinary objective test, the pupil indicates it by penciling a heavy mark between the printed lines in the position which represents the number of his choice.

The scoring machine is so constructed that it contains 750 sensing units corresponding to the 750 possible choices on the answer sheet. Each sensing unit is connected in series with a high-resistance coil which allows an infinitesimal but definite amount of electricity to flow through the unit when the connection is made by means of a pencil mark. After the test has been given, the machine is set by means of a master scoring key which divides the current into two circuits—one for the right responses and one for the wrong responses. The answer sheets are then dropped one by one through a slot in the machine and the score is read from an ammeter conveniently placed in front of the operator.

The great advantage of the scoring machine, of course, lies in the fact that it works with the speed of electricity and that it will score up to 150 five-choice items at once, or an even larger number of items having fewer choices. It has been found that on the IBM 805 an experienced operator can score as many as 500 tests an hour with no error of more than one point.

The scoring machine has been equipped with an item analysis unit which makes it possible to secure a graphic record of the number of right responses given by a class or other group to each item in the test. The advantages of this unit for research purposes and for diagnosis and reteaching are obvious.

The scoring machine can be set so that formulas for correcting for guessing, such as R-W in true-false tests, and R-W/4 in five-response tests, are applied automatically and the corrected score is shown on the meter.

A limitation to machine scoring, as far as the classroom use of the tests is concerned, is that although the machine shows the score of the pupil it does not mark each individual item. Therefore, if one wishes to note just what questions a given pupil has answered correctly, it is necessary to resort to supplementary procedures such as the use of a punched-out key that can be superimposed on the pupil's paper, or the overprinting of the key on the answer sheets.[2]

Another limitation of machine scoring is that all items must be phrased in strictly objective form, such as multiple-choice items and matching items. Some persons may try to force all tests into purely objective form even when their content may not be adapted for the objective type of item, although the distributors of the machine, as well as psychologists and test constructors, have taken the precaution of warning users that not all kinds of testing material are at present suitable for machine scoring. However, some interesting experimental work has been done in adapting tests that are not entirely objective, such as completion tests, to objective scoring.[3]

In the beginning, test authors and test publishers varied considerably in their willingness to make the changes necessary in order to set their tests up for machine scoring. If the items had to be changed to make them purely objective it would be necessary to prepare new norms. The proper standardization of a test is a tedious and expensive procedure. So some test authors who already had extensive series of tests in print naturally hesitated to revise their tests for machine scoring. Moreover, if the score is based partly upon speed, it is necessary to go to the additional trouble of equating the results of hand-scored booklets and machine-scored answer sheets, for the use of answer sheets causes those taking tests to work at slower speeds than they would if they marked their answers in booklets.

Many of the older tests were, however, soon adapted for machine scoring, and the majority of the high school and college tests published within the last 20 years are so arranged that the responses may be entered on a separate answer sheet or card for machine scoring. Provision is also made in most of these tests for entering the answers in the test booklet if that procedure is preferred. However, separate answer sheets must be used with many of the newer tests, although hand scoring of the answer sheets with a punched-out key is possible if a scoring machine is not available.

A study by Dunlap[4] indicated that separate answer sheets may successfully be used with objective tests, without loss of accuracy, as low as Grade 4 of elementary school, but many teachers seem doubtful about the advisability of employing them below the junior high school level. It seems to be widely agreed that answer sheets should not be used in the administration of tests to pupils in Grades 1 and 2.

Cost is an important aspect of machine scoring. For a good many years, the International Business Machines Corporation has rented the 805 scoring machine at a charge of approximately $600 a year, which includes servicing the machine.[5] This amount is much less than that for the IBM 1230, which is discussed later, but it is still a large item of expense for a small school. However, such schools can still avail themselves of the advantages of machine scoring, either by means of a cooperative rental arrangement, or through taking advantage of the scoring services offered by various agencies.

The main items of cost, in addition to the rental for the machine, are the test booklets, the answer sheets, the services of an operator for the machine, and the special pencils to be used by the pupils in marking the answer sheets. Answer sheets, of course, would not always be required if the scoring were to be done by hand, but the cost of the answer sheets can usually be saved on the test booklets, for the pupils make no marks on the booklets themselves and ordinarily each booklet can be used several times, provided the booklets are carefully inspected after each administration of the test.

The machine is not difficult to operate and does not require the services of one who is highly trained technically. The wage of an operator will ordinarily approximate that of a superior clerical worker.

In order for this machine to work without error, it is

[2] Arthur E. Traxler. "A Procedure for Overprinting Answer Sheets for Hand Scoring Which Might be Adapted to Local Scoring," *Educational and Psychological Measurement*, VIII (Spring 1948), 65–67.

[3] Clarence F. Willey, "Classroom Scoring of Tests," *Keeping Abreast of the Revolution in Education*, pp. 82–88. Report of Twenty-eighth Educational Conference sponsored by the Educational Records Bureau. Washington, D.C.: American Council on Education, 1964. Pp. viii + 195.

[4] Jack W. Dunlap. "Problems Arising from the Use of a Separate Answer Sheet," *Journal of Psychology*, X (July 1940), 3–48.

[5] A court ruling requires the offering for sale of all IBM tabulating machines. Scoring machines now in operation may be purchased at a rate depending on the age of the machine. Owners of scoring machines may obtain services at a monthly rate, also depending on how old the machine is. Detailed information may be obtained from IBM, Armonk, N.Y.

necessary that the pupils record their responses on the answer sheets with soft lead pencils that are high in graphite content. Since it is almost impossible to maintain uniformity in this respect if the pupils are allowed to supply their own pencils, schools have usually been equipped with a supply of pencils containing soft leads that have been made especially for use with tests that are to be machine scored. These may be regarded as a part of the standard equipment of all schools using machine scoring of this type.

The most difficult problem in machine scoring with IBM 805 equipment occurs in the administration of the tests. If correct scores are to be obtained with this machine, it is necessary that the responses of the individuals be made with heavy, black, glossy marks, and that dots or other stray marks be eliminated. Examiners need to use great care to see that answer sheets turned in are suitable for scoring by machine. Otherwise, it is necessary for clerical workers to spend many hours in darkening responses and erasing stray dots and marks before the answer sheets are run through the machine. In the usual machine-scoring department, a great deal more time is spent in scanning answer sheets and cleaning up stray marks than in the actual scoring of the papers. Procedures for improving this situation have been suggested in other publications.[6]

The relation of machine scoring to the testing program of a school can best be illustrated by the following statement concerning the testing program of a fairly large public high school.

PLAINFIELD PUBLIC SCHOOLS' TESTING PROGRAM

One of the pioneering test-scoring machine installations is in the Plainfield Public Schools, Plainfield, New Jersey. The following tests are administered in the annual program of testing in the high school:

In October:

1. A general test of academic aptitude for all pupils enrolled in the school. In one school year the tests used were the Otis Quick-Scoring Gamma Test in Grades 9 and 10 and the School and College Ability Test (SCAT) in Grade 11.
2. The Diagnostic Reading Tests and the Cooperative Reading Comprehension Tests.

In June:

Cooperative Achievement Tests in the five academic areas for which these tests are prepared. The program

for one year included over 11,080 standardized tests administered, scored, reported, and recorded.

All tests used in the annual program were machine scored. The Plainfield administration has noted that by making test results almost instantly available, the machine has increased the efficiency of the testing program and has decreased the probability of a loss of interest on the part of teachers as compared to that during the time required for hand scoring.

MORE RECENT DEVELOPMENTS IN MACHINE SCORING AND THE NEEDS OF THE LARGE CONSUMER

If test publishers, and users as well, felt that their lives were made more complicated by the IBM 805 scoring machine, in recent years confusion has been compounded by the introduction of at least five new and improved kinds of scoring machines with as many different kinds of new answer sheets.

THE NEW IBM TEST-SCORING MACHINE, MODEL 1230

Recognizing that its pioneer test-scoring machine, the 805, would soon be passé, the International Business Machines Corporation began, about 1956, to experiment with improved scoring equipment that would take advantage of new developments in machine methods and, at the same time, would be within the price range of the large individual consumers and the smaller test service agencies. After several years of experimentation, the IBM test-scoring machine, Model 1230, was released in 1964. The Model 1230 is an optical, or document reader, scoring machine; that is, the answer sheets are fed through the machine below a row of photocells which automatically counts the correct responses and the wrong ones, as determined by a "master" answer sheet, makes the necessary computations, and prints the score or scores on the answer sheet or punches them on cards. Part scores and total scores can be obtained in one operation.

The IBM 1230 answer sheet is similar in size to the one for the older model, 805, but it differs considerably from the older one in appearance. The response positions are horizontal rather than vertical, and there may be space for the testee to record certain identifying information in code. There is space for 200 five-choice questions on one side of a standard answer sheet. A filled-out answer sheet is illustrated in Figure 6.

---

[6] Arthur E. Traxler. "The IBM Test-Scoring Machine: An Evaluation," *Proceedings of the 1953 Invitational Conference on Testing Problems,* pp. 139–146. Princeton, N.J. Educational Testing Service, 1954. Pp. xii + 180.

Please print:

NAME *Johnson,* *Kenneth* *C.* SEX *m* AGE *12* *10*
LAST FIRST MIDDLE M OR F YRS. MOS.

DATE *March 10, 1965* GRADE *7* TEACHER *Miss Hill* BIRTH DATE *May* *19,* *1952*
MONTH DAY YR.

SCHOOL *Lakeview* CITY *Hartsdale* STATE *N.Y.* FORM OF TEST (Circle One) Ⓐ B C

PART 1

IBM 1230 Answer Sheet

USE A NO. 2 PENCIL

MAKE YOUR MARKS
HEAVY AND BLACK

ERASE COMPLETELY
ANY ANSWERS YOU
WANT TO CHANGE

PART 3

PART 2

THE ANSWER SPACES
FOR PARTS 4 AND 5
ARE ON THE OTHER SIDE

Distributed only by Educational Records Bureau, New York, N.Y.   PRINTED IN U.S.A.   IBM H90518

160   **FIGURE 6.**

Unlike the older model, 805, the IBM 1230 scoring machine does not require the use of special pencils by the testees. Regular No. 2 lead pencils are recommended. Light marks are no problem unless they are very light indeed; neither do stray marks or dots ordinarily cause any difficulty. Papers that have two response positions darkened almost equally where only one is required will be rejected by the machine and shunted to a separate pile to be dealt with manually. One difficulty is that an erasure may be read by the machine as a second mark and the paper rejected. There are "thresholds" above and below which the machine will reject, and the scoring-machine operator must determine by experimentation the optimum setting of each threshold. Pupils must use care to have their responses cover the center of each response position, otherwise the machine will not score accurately.

Answer sheets are fed automatically through the machine at the rate of about 1250 an hour, more than twice as fast as a top-notch operator could put answer sheets through the IBM 805. In order to take full advantage of the improved machine, however, its use should be coordinated with punch-card, computer, and data-processing equipment for purposes of reporting the test scores.

The new IBM test-scoring machine is a definite improvement over the Model 805; but probably no kind of "threshold" machine can do the job as fast or as well as elaborate test processing equipment such as that available at the State University of Iowa, which will be discussed later in this chapter.

THE DIGITEK SCORING MACHINE

Another new optical, or document reader, scoring machine is the Digitek,[7] which, like the IBM 1230, was made available in 1964. This machine uses either IBM 805-type answer sheets or Digitek answer sheets. The answer sheets are automatically fed through the machine at a basic speed which is said to be 2500 an hour. Like the IBM 1230, it will do formula scoring and will print part and total scores on the answer sheet. Digitek data-processsing and computer output may be purchased or rented along with the basic scoring machine.

IOWA ELECTRONIC TEST-PROCESSING EQUIPMENT

The most revolutionary contribution to machine scoring in recent years is the electronic test-processing equipment developed under the direction of E. F. Lind-

quist of the State University of Iowa.[8] This equipment consists of a high-speed automatic test-scoring machine in conjunction with magnetic tape storage, a digital electronic computer, and a fast output printer. An 8½-by-11-inch answer sheet, of such compact design that the answers to as many as 960 multiple-choice items may be placed on the two sides of the sheet, is used with the machine. Responses are indicated by heavy black dots in small boxes. An ordinary lead pencil may be used in making the dots. Scanning the answer sheets for double marks or stray dots is not necessary, since the machine automatically takes care of this. The answer sheets are fed through the machine automatically at the basic rate of 6000 an hour. As the answer sheets go through the machine, the marks are sensed photoelectrically from both sides of the sheet simultaneously. The answers are compared with the key of correct answers, and the scores are recorded in digital electronic counters. Thus, scores on as many as 14 different tests involving up to 960 items may be obtained from a single pass of the answer sheet through the machine.

After the scoring process, an electronic computer converts raw scores on as many as 14 tests into derived scores in accordance with a conversion table for each test. These derived scores may be converted scores, percentile ranks, T-scores, age or grade equivalents, or practically any other kind of derived score. If desired, the machine will convert raw scores into two or more derived scores simultaneously.

The scoring machine also "reads" from the answer sheets the examinee's name and other information, which may be in either alphabetical or numerical form. From this information reports of the names of the pupils and all their scores can be printed. The maximum length of a line is 93 characters, of which any 18 may be either alphabetical or numerical. If the number of scores to be reported for each answer sheet is comparatively small, both lists and individual reports can be prepared simultaneously. The machine will also print the necessary headings on the list.

If desired, the machine will provide scores on odd- and even-numbered items separately for each of as many as seven tests so that reliability coefficients may be computed. This is only one of the many research potentialities of the machine which might be listed but which are not of primary concern here.

The services of the Iowa Electronic Test Processing Equipment are made available through a nonprofit corporation, the Measurement Research Center (MRC).

---

[7] Manufactured and distributed by Digitek Corporation, Fairless Hills, Pa.

[8] E. F. Lindquist. "The Iowa Electronic Test Processing Equipmen," *Proceedings of the 1953 Invitational Conference on Testing Problems*, pp. 160–168. Princeton, N.J.: Educational Testing Service, 1954, Pp. xii + 180.

The equipment was placed in use in March 1955, and after several months of experience the general service was offered beginning in January 1956.

MRC offers both standard and special services. The standard "package" service is designed for widely-used multiple-choice test batteries. This standard service is obtained either through the publishers of the tests or through large-scale testing programs which have made arrangements with test publishers.

The standard service includes (1) designing and printing special machine-scorable answer sheets; (2) receiving marked answer sheets from the users; and (3) processing these answer sheets, including (a) scoring of answer sheets, (b) conversion of raw scores to derived scores, (c) computation of weighted combinations of converted scores, (d) printing of list reports of scores in triplicate, and (e) punching of IBM cards, one for each answer sheet, containing the names and scores of the examinees.

The special services for which arrangements may be made include computation of the means and variances of score distributions, intercorrelations among the tests, and odd-even reliability coefficients.

The potential speed of the service is remarkable. It is possible to score up to 100,000 answer sheets with the Iowa equipment within a 24-hour period. However, the speed of service for any particular school depends to a considerable extent upon the scheduling of the work in advance to avoid conflicts with services requested by other users. It is not practicable, of course, to set up this complicated mechanical equipment for a small number of answer sheets, so it may be necessary to hold the answer sheets from a particular school until they can be combined with those from other institutions using the same set of tests, and the whole group of answer sheets is then processed as one job. Reports of results are usually issued within three weeks after the answer sheets are received at the test processing center.[9]

"SCRIBE" SCORING MACHINE OF THE EDUCATIONAL TESTING SERVICE

In the latter 1950s an electronic data processing team at the Educational Testing Service designed an electronic scoring and data transcription device which was then produced by the Norden Division of the United Aircraft Corporation. In 1960 it was installed at ETS in Princeton and given the name "SCRIBE I." It consisted essentially of a paper-handling assembly, a processor, and a

[9] Price quotations on scoring with the Iowa Test Processing Equipment may be obtained from Measurement Research Center, P.O. Box 69, Iowa City, Iowa.

card punch. As test papers are fed through the machine, its electronic scanning system "reads" identifying information, compares the student's responses with the correct responses for the test, punches the information into an IBM card, and stores the information in its magnetic "memory." An improvement of the original machine, known as "Scribe II," has both a card punch and a magnetic tape output and thus can transcribe information either to IBM cards or to tape.

SCRIBE is said to be capable of scoring up to six different tests on a single answer sheet, and to do this at a rate of nearly 100 sheets a minute. An internal checking system makes it possible to score answer sheets with a very high degree of accuracy.

In order to convert the raw scores yielded by SCRIBE to a standard score scale, and to do this with speed and flexibility, and to print out the data, an electronic computer is teamed up with SCRIBE.

This integrated system makes possible very rapid test processing, saves much storage space (since records are stored on magnetic tape rather than on cards), and stores not only the results of current tests but also cumulative-score reports covering a period of years.

SOME ADVANTAGES AND DISADVANTAGES OF AUTOMATIC DATA PROCESSING

Lindquist's MRC test-processing equipment and ETS's SCRIBE could conceivably score all the millions of tests administered annually in the United States, provided the students' responses were entered on suitable answer sheets. Both machines could perform the necessary operations with astonishing speed and accuracy, and perform numerous computations helpful in the interpretation of the results, as well. The use of SCRIBE, it should be noted, is confined largely to ETS's own tests and programs.

Both these huge electronic set-ups are extremely well suited to large testing programs involving thousands or hundreds of thousands of test papers. Small jobs may not fare as well as might be expected because of the problem of scheduling. The actual processing time for, let us say, 200 test papers might not be more than a minute or two, but the working of such a small job into the processing schedule could be a matter of several days.

So, for small and medium-size public schools and for virtually all independent schools, there continues to be a need for the kind of service that can be rendered by means of the IBM 1230 scoring machine, or the Digitek, or even on occasion the older IBM 805 machine. And for some kinds of tests and for tests taken by kindergarten or primary grade children, hand scoring continues to have at least a small place in the work of a service organization and a large place in the local scoring that is still carried on by hundreds of schools.

HAND AND MACHINE SCORING BY A SERVICE AGENCY

Many schools are taking advantage of scoring services made available in state testing programs which now exist in about half the states,[10] or the services provided by various agencies which are national in scope. This plan insures accuracy of scoring and statistical work and relieves the local school of a great deal of routine work. Even when the actual test processing is to be done on electronic equipment, such as that located at the State University of Iowa, schools will often find it advantageous to participate in their own state testing program or in a national testing program carried on by schools of their own type, and leave the detailed arrangements with MRC to the central agency.

Both hand- and machine-scoring services are provided by various state bureaus, and at least one organization of national scope, the Educational Records Bureau. A report of the scoring procedures used by the Educational Records Bureau may perhaps be suggestive to schools that are obliged to do their own scoring locally.

The Educational Records Bureau is a research and service agency which has a membership of more than 950 institutions, most of which are independent or private elementary and secondary schools. It is a self-supporting organization. Its income is derived mainly from its services in connection with scoring and reporting the results of tests for the schools belonging to the Bureau. It constructs only a few tests, but through a committee composed of representatives from its member schools, it selects from the available tests of various publishers those which seem best adapted to the needs of the whole group of schools taking part in the testing. A limited portion of the Bureau's scoring services is available to nonmembers, although it is expected that institutions using the services regularly will become members of the organization.

Two testing programs are conducted annually by the

[10] A survey of the services of statewide testing programs was reported in Arthur E. Traxler, "The Status of Statewide Testing Programs," 1954 Achievement Testing Programs in Independent Schools and Supplementary Studies, pp. 86–92. Educational Records Bulletin No. 63. New York: Educational Records Bureau, July 1954. Pp. xii + 96.

Bureau's member schools. The fall program consists of academic aptitude and reading tests, along with some achievement tests for placement and diagnosis. In the spring, a comprehensive achievement testing program is conducted in all academic subjects at the elementary and secondary school levels. Every member school is free to participate as little or as fully as desired in the testing programs. The schools obtain the tests and complete directions for giving them from the Bureau. The tests are administered by the schools themselves, usually within a specified period, although they are free to utilize the services of the Bureau at other times if they so desire. Some of the schools score their tests locally, but the majority return them for central scoring by the Bureau's staff at a per-test-per-pupil cost. Norms for independent schools are prepared from the results of the tests scored at the Bureau.

Most of the schools participating in the testing programs are independent schools whose enrollments, in comparison with those of public schools, are rather small. The teachers are able to do a considerable amount of diagnostic work with the test results, provided the scored test booklets are returned. Hand scoring, therefore, is still used quite extensively in connection with the independent-school tests.

During a testing program, the tests from as many as 300 schools may be returned to the Bureau almost simultaneously. The careful organization of all details of the scoring and reporting, therefore, is absolutely essential. During the testing season the scoring and processing are set up in departments according to the nature of the work required, and about half of the Bureau's regular staff of 30 persons serve as supervisors of these departments. Most of the actual scoring work is done by part-time employees who have been carefully tested and selected for this work.

Rather extensive experimentation has been done with various screening tests in the selection of scorers. Formerly an intelligence test was administered to applicants for scoring work, but this was discontinued since it does not appear that the results of the usual verbal or quantitative test of mental ability are very highly correlated with success in objective scoring. Some years ago, each applicant for a scoring position was given a scorer's test in which the scoring situation was approximated as nearly as possible. It was found, however, that the accuracy and speed scores on this type of test had rather low correlations with actual success in scoring. At present, the Minnesota Clerical Test is administered to all scoring applicants, and the results of this brief test, along with a personal interview, are providing reasonably good prediction of success in the actual scoring situation.

A scorer is assigned to a certain department and usually works on one particular kind of operation. The work done in scoring tests is always identified by the initials of the scorers so that responsibility can be allocated definitely.

The papers hand-scored by new employees are always completely rescored. After a worker has satisfactorily

When the tests are received from the schools they go to the classification department where they are inspected for discrepancies and carefully separated into the proper groups as determined by number of years of study and other factors. The amount of time that will be needed for scoring is estimated, and the report to the school is scheduled for a certain date.

TABLE 1.   Scores and Percentiles of a Ninth-Grade Class on the Cooperative English Test

School: *Century Day*   City: *New York*   State: *N.Y.*

Grade: *9*   Date of Report: *April 29, 1963*   Date Adm.: *April 8, 1963*

Names of Pupils	Chron. Age	A Mech. of Expression		B₁ Effect. of Expression		C₁ Reading Comprehension					Total English	
		Sc. Sc.	%ile	Sc. Sc.	%ile	Vocab.	Speed	Level	Total	%ile	Sc. Sc.	%ile
1. Barton, Barbara A.	15–5	47	39	49	55	43	54	57	51	43	49	46
2. Blum, John W.	15–3	48	42	53	70	49	46	49	48	29	50	50
3. Denton, Robert D.	14–6	47	39	58	85	57	54	59	57	70	54	67
4. Dickinson, Samuel J.	13–7	64	94	72	98	68	72	73	74	97	72	98
5. Duncan, George W.	14–1	52	56	61	90	59	55	62	59	76	58	79
6. Elkins, George H.	14–11	60	85	60	89	61	59	62	61	82	61	87
7. Feder, Fred	15–8	36	10	40	16	48	34	36	39	6	37	10
8. Frost, Virgil C.	15–1	54	64	64	93	52	46	40	46	21	55	70
9. Haynes, Julie A.	15–4	49	45	46	42	54	52	62	56	66	50	50
10. Hunt, Barbara A.	15–5	56	71	56	79	51	53	54	53	52	55	70
11. Kolnick, Mary	14–11	58	79	64	93	54	53	57	55	61	60	85
12. Livingstone, Martin H.	14–11	50	48	62	91	47	51	51	50	38	54	67
13. McKean, Sarah A.	14–8	49	45	47	47	51	46	54	50	38	48	42
14. McNaughton, Jean	13–11	52	56	59	87	51	51	62	55	61	56	73
15. Prescott, Elsie	15–4	47	39	39	14	49	53	46	49	33	44	28
16. Royer, Laurence	14–3	59	82	60	89	52	58	61	57	70	59	82
17. Simpson, Martha F.	15–7	56	71	62	91	64	54	72	64	89	62	89
18. Smith, Marie A.	15–0	50	48	50	59	50	63	60	58	73	53	63
19. Swanson, John S.	14–8	57	75	62	91	55	68	66	64	89	62	89
20. Thompson, Carol E.	15–2	50	48	51	63	52	48	51	50	38	50	50
21. Wickowsky, Jon	14–10	60	85	63	92	64	60	67	65	91	64	93
Class Median		52.5	56	59.5	87	53.0	53.8	59.0	55.5	61	55.3	70
E.R.B. Median		50.4	50	52.1	50	53.2	53.5	54.4	54.1	50	52.3	50

demonstrated his accuracy, the rescoring is reduced to the checking of one paper in five, except in the case of certain very important tests. However, such operations as the counting of number of right answers, and the addition of part scores in tests containing several sections, are invariably done twice.

As fast as the scoring of a certain type of test is completed, the test booklets are turned over to members of the staff whose responsibility it is to make distributions of the scores and to compute medians, quartiles, and any other statistical data that are needed. The booklets then go to the typists who type alphabetical class lists showing the scores of the various pupils. These lists are made in triplicate. When all distributions and lists have been made and the work has been checked, the various parts of the report are assembled and inspected by the chief scoring supervisor.

The assembled report, together with the school's statistical folders for preceding testing programs, is sent to the desk of another member of the staff, who is trained in psychological measurement and guidance techniques. He dictates an extensive letter in which the results are explained and interpreted in considerable detail for the school to which the report is going. This report is preliminary in nature, unless norms for independent schools based on an earlier testing program are available for the tests included in the report. At the end of the program, independent-school percentiles are computed on the basis of the scores from all participating schools, and a second report showing the percentile ratings of each individual pupil is sent to each school.

Almost the same general plan is followed in connection with the machine scoring that is done at the Bureau, except that each machine operator replaces many scorers.

Data processing equipment is also being used to an increasing extent for conversions, distributions, statistical computations, and the preparation of class lists.

The scoring and reporting procedures of the Educational Records Bureau have been described in considerable detail because during the nearly 40 years that the Bureau has been rendering this type of service to its member schools, these procedures have proved sound, and it is believed that some of them could be followed in local scoring. Such a plan might readily be adopted with modifications in a uniform testing program involving all the schools in a city school system. Careful systematizing and supervision of the scoring work, together with a thorough plan for checking every important operation, insure the accuracy and speed which are the prime essentials of every testing program.[11]

REPORTING PROCEDURES

If a testing program is to be of any real value to a school, it is imperative that the results be placed in the hands of the teachers and counselors as soon as possible.

[11] Among other machine scoring installations and services not described elsewhere in this chapter are those of the California Test Bureau (IBM); Harcourt, Brace & World, Inc. (service by IBM and MRC); Houghton Mifflin Company (IBM); National Computer Systems, Minneapolis (equipment for scoring Strong Vocational Interest Blanks and other tests and for data processing); The Psychological Corporation (Psyche, Modified IBM 805, Digitek); Testscor, Minneapolis (Strong blanks and other tests).

Too often a school will end its testing program with the scoring of the tests, apparently under the mistaken impression that the mere taking of the tests will bring about improvement.

The emphasis in reporting results of tests to the faculty should be on the scores of individuals rather than on group comparisons, although the achievement of groups may well receive some attention. An adequate summary report of the results of tests consists of at least two types of record: (1) distributions of scores by classes, together with medians and quartiles, or means and standard deviations, and (2) alphabetical class lists showing the part scores, total scores, and percentile ratings of individual pupils.

LISTS AND DISTRIBUTIONS OF SCORES

In preparing class lists, it is desirable to show the scores made on the parts of the test, as well as the total score, if such part scores are of sufficient practical importance and reliability to be used as a basis for studying the pupils' performances and for planning teaching procedures. Percentile ranks, standard scores, or other derived measures, as well as raw scores, should be shown on the lists. A sample class list is shown in Table 1.[12]

The preparation of distributions of scores is a straightforward, routine task that any accurate clerk can readily learn to do once he has been shown the elementary procedures involved. The purpose of a distribution is to indicate the number of pupils making scores at each level from highest to lowest, and thus to facilitate the study of both individuals and groups. In most tests, the range of scores is so great that it is not feasible to show every score in the distribution. The scores are therefore grouped thus:

Scores	Number of Pupils
85–89	2
80–84	5
75–79	4
70–74	6
65–69	3

etc.

Sometimes only the bottom score in each interval is written and it is understood that the scores below the

[12] All names in the table are fictitious, but the scores are the actual test results obtained by one class.

next higher one appearing in the table are to be recorded in the same interval. In this case, the illustration just given would appear as follows:

Scores	Number of Pupils
85	2
80	5
75	4
70	6
65	3

etc.

Ordinarily it is advisable to use an interval size of 2, 5, or 10, if the whole range of the scores justifies the use of one of such interval sizes, for the speed of making the distribution will be greater and the chance of mechanical error will be less than if some other size is employed, simply because we are accustomed to grouping numbers in that way. Occasionally, however, intervals of 3, 4, 7, or some other number will be preferable because of the range. As a rule, distributions containing from 10 to 20 intervals are the most practicable. If fewer than 10 intervals are used, the grouping is likely to be too coarse; if more than 20 are employed, the central tendency of the group may be obscured, although this is not always the case.

In making a distribution, of course, one must first tally the scores in the proper intervals and then count the tally marks in order to find the number of scores at each interval. Let us assume, for instance, that the following numbers represent the scores of a class of 31 pupils on an arithmetic test containing 20 problems: 13, 10, 8, 15, 11, 12, 9, 11, 14, 9, 7, 18, 10, 13, 11, 6, 12, 17, 15, 2, 8, 15, 12, 17, 11, 13, 7, 4, 16, 12, and 10. A distribution of the scores in intervals with an interval size of one is shown in the next column. For a group of about 30 pupils, this simple procedure requires only two or three minutes.

If distributions are prepared for the part scores as well as for the total scores yielded by a test, it is helpful to report all of them on the same sheet, particularly if the raw scores have been translated into derived scores that are comparable from one part to another. Distributions of the Scaled Scores made by a class of 21 ninth-grade pupils in an independent school on the Cooperative English Test, Form RX, are shown in Table 2. The class is the same one that furnished the scores for the list given in Table 1.

The Scaled Scores, in intervals of 2, are shown along the left-hand margin. The dotted lines across the distribution columns indicate the independent school medians for Grades 7–12, and the broken lines show the public school medians. The median scores of the class in question are shown graphically by the short horizontal lines,

Score	Tally	F (Frequency)
18	/	1
17	//	2
16	/	1
15	///	3
14	/	1
13	///	3
12	////	4
11	////	4
10	///	3
9	//	2
8	//	2
7	//	2
6	/	1
5		0
4	/	1
3		0
2	/	1

N = 31

and the interquartile range (the range from the 25th to the 75th percentile) of each distribution is marked off by the vertical line. The medians, quartiles, and ranges of the distributions are also stated numerically near the bottom of the page.

It is apparent that the median total English score of this ninth-grade class, 55.3, is a little above the independent school median for Grade 10. The range of total scores

TABLE 2.

Cooperative English Tests, Form RX

SCHOOL Century Day   GRADE 9   DATE April 29, 1963

Scaled Score	A: Mechanics of Expression	B: Effectiveness of Expression	C: Reading Comprehension	Total A + B + C
80				
78				
76				
74				
72		1	1	
70				1
68				
66				
64	1	2	3	1
62	2	4	1	2
60	2	3	2	2
58	3	2	3	2
56	1	1	2	1
54	2		1	4
52	3	1	4	
50	3	2	2	3
48	3	1	1	
46		2		2
44				1
42				
40		1		
38		1	1	1
36	1			
34				1
32				
30				
Total	21	21	21	21
Q3	57.8	62.9	59.8	60.8
MD	52.5	59.5	55.5	55.3
Q1	48.8	50.3	50.6	50.8
Range	36–64	39–72	39–74	37–72

.... Independent School Median, Form RX

– – – – – End-of-year Public School Median

is wide; the lowest score is considerably below the independent school median for Grade 7 and is close to the public school norm for Grade 8; the highest score, on the other hand, is about 12 Scaled Score units above the independent school median for the twelfth grade.

A study of the distributions of part scores shows that the class, as a group, tends to be a little higher in effectiveness of expression than in mechanics of expression and reading comprehension. The median mechanics score is a little lower than the median for reading comprehension. The mechanics median falls between the independent school medians for Grades 9 and 10, while the reading comprehension median is approximately at the independent school median for Grade 10.

The distributions in Table 2 could be analyzed in much more detail, but perhaps enough has been said to show that considerable helpful information about the achievement of a class may be derived from a careful study of a well-planned set of distributions.

STATISTICAL PROCEDURES INVOLVED IN SUMMARIZING AND REPORTING THE RESULTS OF TESTS

The statistical procedures needed in summarizing and reporting test results are very simple. Anyone with a knowledge of sixth-grade arithmetic should be able to master them without difficulty. The only skills necessary are those required for the finding of medians, quartiles, and percentiles. An understanding of how to find means and standard deviations from distributions is also helpful, but not absolutely essential. The whole thing should be kept very elementary if it is to be understood by all the teachers, for in certain fields there are many teachers who are allergic to anything mathematical, but who can perform important guidance functions if they are provided with data in terms which they find meaningful.

The median may be defined as the mid-point in a distribution. If the test scores of a class are arranged in order of magnitude and if there is an odd number of pupils in the class, the median is the middle score. In a class of 33 pupils, for example, the median is the seventeenth score from either end of the distribution. If there is an even number of pupils in the class, the median is the point halfway between the two scores nearest the middle. The finding of the median by counting is thus a very simple process.

When the scores are arranged in a distribution, however, a slightly different procedure must be used, particularly if the interval size is greater than one. Let us consider the distribution of scores on the usage part of one of the earlier forms of the Cooperative English Test, as shown in Table 3. Here the interval size is 2. The steps in finding the median for this distribution are as follows:

1. Divide the number of pupils by 2: $\frac{35}{2} = 17.5$.

2. Start at the bottom of the distribution and add all the numbers of pupils in the different intervals until you reach the interval in which the median falls: $1 + 2 + 3 + 3 + 6 = 15$. The median must fall in the next interval, for if the three cases in that interval were added,

TABLE 3. Distribution of Scores on Usage Part of Cooperative English Test

Scaled Score	Frequency
80	
78	
76	
74	1
72	1
70	3
68	1
66	2
64	1
62	1
60	4
58	3
56	3
54	6
52	3
50	3
48	2
46	1
44	
42	
40	
38	
36	
34	
32	
30	

N = 35

the total would be 18, whereas half of 35 is only 17.5. (Or one may start at the top and use a similar procedure.)

3. The interval in which the median falls includes scores 56 and 57. It is probable that two of the cases in this interval have one of these scores and one has the other, but one cannot tell from the distribution exactly what the scores are. The fairest assumption, therefore, is that the cases are distributed equally throughout the interval. Following this assumption we can compute the median by a simple numerical process. We know that after adding the cases up to the lower limit of the interval we were 2.5 cases short of 17.5. There are three cases in the interval and, as already indicated, the interval size is 2. To find the median, we merely multiply 2.5

by 2, divide the product by 3, and add it to the lower limit of the interval, thus:

$$2 \times 2.5 = 5$$

$$\frac{5}{3} = 1.7 \text{ (rounded to one decimal place)}$$

$$56.0 + 1.7 = 57.7 = \text{median}$$

Here we have assumed that the lower limit of the interval is 56.0 and that the interval runs from 56.0 to 57.9+. From a statistical standpoint, a better assumption is that the limits of the interval are 55.5 to 57.4+, but the reason for preferring this assumption requires a rather involved explanation which will not be taken up here. For most practical purposes, it is satisfactory to use as the lower limit of the interval the lowest whole number falling within the interval.

The whole procedure of finding the median is represented by the following formula:

$$Md = L.L. + \left(\frac{\frac{N}{2} - F\ up}{fmi} \right) h$$

Where Md = median

$L.L.$ = lower limit of interval in which median falls

N = number of cases

$F\ up$ = frequency number up to the interval containing the median

fmi = frequency of the interval containing the median

h = size of class interval

The finding of Q_1 and Q_3, or the 25th and 75th percentiles, involves essentially the same steps as the computation of the median. The formulas are as follows:

$$Q_1 = L.L. + \left(\frac{\frac{N}{4} - F\ up}{fqi} \right) h$$

$$Q_3 = L.L. + \left(\frac{\frac{3N}{4} - F\ up}{fqi} \right) h$$

Let us refer again to the distribution of scores on the usage part of the Cooperative English Test.

$$Q_1 = 52.0 + \left(\frac{8.75 - 6}{3} \right) 2$$

$$= 52.0 + \left(\frac{2.75 \times 2}{3} \right)$$

$$= 52.0 + 1.8 = 53.8$$

$$Q_3 = 64.0 + \left(\frac{26.25 - 26}{1} \right) 2$$

$$= 64.0 + 0.5 = 64.5$$

It is somewhat easier to begin at the top of the distribution and work downward when computing Q_3. If this is done, the equation becomes:

$$Q_3 = U.L. - \left(\frac{\frac{N}{4} - F\ down}{fqi} \right) h$$

$$= 66.0 - \left(\frac{8.75 - 8}{1} \right) 2$$

$$= 66.0 - 1.5 = 64.5$$

The two other measures of central tendency, in addition to the median, are the *mean* and the *mode*. The mode is the most frequent measure in a distribution. It is found by inspection. Where scores are grouped in intervals larger than one, the mode cannot be determined from the distribution, but the *modal interval* can be seen at a glance. For example, in the distribution of scores on the usage part of the Cooperative English Test, the modal interval is 54-55. If two intervals in different parts of the distribution have a greater frequency than any of the others, the distribution is said to be bimodal. The mode is not a very important measure of central tendency, but it is of some value for making a quick inventory.

The mean is simply the arithmetic average. Although it can be found from a distribution, most teachers interested in computing the mean score for a class will find it more convenient to do the work in the familiar way of adding the scores and dividing by the number of pupils, particularly if a calculating machine is available.

The last elementary statistical concept usually essential in reporting test results is the percentile rank, or percentile rating. Notwithstanding the criticism that is sometimes directed toward the statistical properties of percentiles, their simplicity has without doubt caused them to be more extensively used than any other procedure for interpreting test results.

All teachers and counselors, however far removed their own field may be from that of mathematics, can quickly grasp the idea that a pupil's percentile rating on a certain test shows the percent of the pupils in a group that he equals or excels in score—or, even more simply but slightly less accurately stated, the percent of pupils that are below him in score. It is, for example, very easy to explain to a teacher or counselor that Robert Denton's percentile for total English score, as given in Table 1, means that this boy's score on the Cooperative English

Test, as a whole, is up to or above the scores of 67 percent of the independent school ninth-grade pupils who took the test. If the teacher understands further that the percentile ratings range from one to 100, and that 50 is the median or average, it should be clear to her that Robert's score is somewhat above the median for his grade.

The teacher should readily grasp the further ideas that Robert's achievement in mechanics of expression is above that of about two fifths of the independent school ninth-grade group, that his achievement in effectiveness of expression is much higher, surpassing that of more than four fifths of the norm group, and that his total comprehension score exceeds that of a little more than two thirds of the pupils at the ninth-grade level.

Various procedures are used in computing local percentile ranks from a distribution of test scores. A graphic method is favored by some persons, but perhaps the simplest procedure is one which involves the following four steps:

1. Arrange the scores in a distribution that shows every score (interval size of one).
2. Find the cumulative frequency.
3. Find the reciprocal of the number of pupils in the group (divide one by the number of pupils).
4. Multiply each number in the cumulative frequency by the reciprocal.

By means of this procedure, the percentile ranks of the tops of the class intervals are found. It is usually not regarded as worthwhile to compute percentiles based on groups containing less than 100 cases, but the general procedure may be illustrated with a smaller group. For this purpose, we will use the arithmetic scores of the class of 31 pupils mentioned earlier in the chapter. The distribution of these scores is shown in Table 4.

To find the cumulative frequency, simply add up from the bottom of the distribution and write the total frequency up to, and including, each interval.

$$\text{Reciprocal of } 31 = 1/31 = .03226$$

The cumulative frequency at each interval multiplied by .03226 gives the percentile rank of the score in that interval. For example, the cumulative frequency up to and including a score of 16 is 28.

$$28 \times .03226 = .90$$

Therefore the percentile rank of a score of 16 is 90.

When percentiles are found by this procedure, a percentile rating corresponding to a score shows the percent of the scores in a distribution that are *equaled or exceeded* by that particular score.

The percentiles for all the scores on a test can be computed on a calculating machine or by an electronic computer in a very short time. It is advisable to type or duplicate percentile tables for the scores on each test and to use these tables in entering the percentiles on the class lists that are to be sent to the teachers. All this applies, of course, to the computation of local percentiles and may not be necessary in the case of well-standardized tests for which national norms are available. Most test publishers and service agencies now supply complete percentile norms for defined groups on a variety of tests.

TABLE 4. Percentiles Based on Distribution of Arithmetic Scores of One Class

Score	Frequency	Cumulative Frequency	Percentile
18	1	31	100
17	2	30	97
16	1	28	90
15	3	27	87
14	1	24	77
13	3	23	74
12	4	20	65
11	4	16	52
10	3	12	39
9	2	9	29
8	2	7	23
7	2	5	16
6	1	3	10
5	0	2	6
4	1	2	6
3	0	1	3
2	1	1	3
	31		

An up-to-date treatment of norms as well as many other aspects of educational measurement and interpretation is provided in a book by Davis.[13]

[13] Frederick B. Davis, *Educational Measurements and Their Interpretation.* Belmont, Calif.: Wadsworth Publishing Company, 1964.

CHAPTER XI

Use of Results of Objective Tests in Improving the Instructional and Counseling Program of the School

ADMINISTRATIVE AND SUPERVISORY USES OF TESTS

THE RESULTS OF TESTS MAY BE USED IN MANY different ways. Some of the common uses are mainly administrative and supervisory, rather than for purposes of diagnosis, instruction, or counseling. A detailed discussion of the administrative and supervisory uses of tests is outside the scope of this book, but it will perhaps be desirable to enumerate and comment briefly upon some of them. Two types of uses which are closely related to the administration of the school will be discussed in Chapters XIII and XIV. These are the uses of tests in permanent and cumulative school records of pupil progress and in reports to parents.

Another administrative use of tests is in the classification, grouping, and placement of pupils. Tests are employed widely in the classification and placement of new pupils at levels conforming to their ability, and this kind of use will no doubt increase as the tendency to advance pupils on the basis of time served is gradually abandoned. Tests form one of the main bases for the grouping or sectioning of classes studying the same subject in a given school.

A fourth administrative use of tests is in the modification of programs of study of individual pupils. Tests may sometimes show the inadvisability of trying to have individual pupils proceed beyond a certain level in a field

of study. For example, a pupil with a percentile rating of 2 in mathematical aptitude can scarcely be expected to profit from the study of higher mathematics. In similar fashion, tests may show that a pupil has unusual ability in a certain field, and may lead to the modification of his program to permit him to take advantage of that ability.

A fifth use of test results which has both administrative and supervisory relationships is the evaluation of methods and materials of instruction. A school may, for instance, wish to experiment with conventional and with freer methods in the teaching of social studies and to evaluate the results. Or, it may desire to compare the achievement obtained with different textbooks, or with a certain textbook as contrasted with extensive reading materials not confined to any one book. The cautious use of tests in these ways is legitimate, provided all possible influences on the test results are carefully considered and weighed.

Tests may, in the sixth place, serve administrative and supervisory functions by forming an objective basis for suggestions concerning the instruction of individual pupils. For instance, a high school principal, through an analysis of the results of a reading test, may note that certain individuals are very low in general reading achievement, and he may suggest to the English department that the teachers consider what can be done to improve their reading skill. Or the test scores may indicate to the principal that certain pupils should have an opportunity to do additional study of an individual nature, by means of teaching machines and programmed instruction, to improve reading skills.

In addition to these commonly accepted uses of tests, some schools have occasionally employed the results of tests in ways that are of questionable value. For example, administrators and supervisors have sometimes used test results to rate the proficiency of their teachers. Unless all other factors which help to determine test scores are carefully controlled, such a use may result in marked injustice to individual teachers. Among the factors which influence test results are the chronological age of the pupils; their brightness and the number of years of schooling they have had; their individual rate of growth; the school, departmental, and course objectives; the content of the courses; the methods of instruction employed in the school; the effort put forth by the pupils both in their school work and in the taking of the tests; the amount of experience that the pupils have had in taking tests; and the psychological and physical conditions under which the tests were administered. Any one of these factors may have a more potent influence upon the results of the tests of a given class than the teaching ability of the instructor. For instance, in the instruction of an algebra class that has a median intelligence quotient of 90, it is doubtful if even an extremely able teacher could bring its median algebra test score up to the national average. Since it is practically impossible to control all the other factors in the usual school situation, the use of test results for rating teachers is seldom advisable. In fact, it is not too much to say that this practice is the most pernicious use that is ever made of testing in our schools, and that it has done more than anything else to retard the legitimate uses of tests in the study of individuals.

Another common administrative use of test results is the comparison of median scores in the local school with norms that have been established by giving the tests in a large number of other schools. This is a defensible use, if the findings are interpreted with caution and understanding. It should be remembered that the failure of school averages to reach national averages may not indicate inferior instruction. It may be the result of somewhat lower scholastic aptitude in the local school than in the schools from which the norms were derived; it may indicate that the school has made new and valuable innovations in its curriculum that are not measured by the tests; or it may be due to any of several other factors. The school, therefore, should strive to determine, in the light of local conditions, the meaning of the deviation from norms, rather than to assume that high or low average scores are indicative of superior or inferior work on the part of either teachers or pupils (29).

INSTRUCTIONAL USES OF TESTS

MAIN USES OF TEST RESULTS BY THE TEACHER

In the meeting of individual and group needs and abilities, teachers may use test results in the following valuable ways: (1) discovering the scholastic aptitudes of the pupils, and adapting instruction to their individual levels of aptitude; (2) knowing in detail the cumulative achievement record and the achievement status of each pupil, and guiding him in the development of all the types of achievement in the school curriculum which are in line with his abilities; (3) discovering the exceptionally bright or high-achieving pupils and making special provision for them; and (4) diagnosing individual pupil weaknesses and abilities in the different subjects and giving individual help or remedial treatment based on the diagnosis.

It should be noted that there is a distinction between the use of test results as aids to instruction and the use of the tests themselves as goals of instruction. The uses just listed are those in which the findings resulting from tests become aids to instruction, by enabling the teacher to analyze pupil achievement and to discover those aspects in which each pupil is superior and those points in which he needs special help. Such uses are unquestionably sound, for they lend definiteness and purposefulness to teaching. If, however, the content of the tests used in surveying or diagnosing achievement becomes in itself a teaching goal, the practice may be a hindrance to the development of a program of instruction based on a fundamental philosophy, and it will unquestionably tend to invalidate future measurements with the same or similar tests. The danger that tests will, in fact, become goals of instruction has often been cited in the past as a reason for not adopting achievement tests, and it is still an important deterrent to their wider use.

PRINCIPLES GOVERNING THE USE OF OBJECTIVE TESTS IN DIAGNOSIS AND INSTRUCTION

When utilizing test results in diagnosing pupil difficulties, and in planning special help to meet the needs indicated by the tests and other evidence, teachers and counselors would do well to keep the following points in mind:

1. *Test results are valuable in the degree to which constructive use is made of them in securing improved educational and vocational adjustment and distribution.* They are useful only if someone does some thinking about them, and interprets the standing of individuals and groups with reference both to national or local norms and to the past performance and future plans of these

same individuals and groups. If the school is going to realize the potential values of its testing program, it is practically imperative that someone who understands not only the fundamental philosophy or purposes of the school but also the basic philosophy of measurement and guidance, and who is acquainted with the elementary statistical techniques utilized in educational measurement, and who understands the legitimate uses and limitations of individual tests, be assigned the major responsibility for the testing and guidance program and remedial work.

2. *As far as possible, tests should be employed which measure the achievement of the pupils with respect to the purposes of the individual school using the tests.* Since a considerable number of the objectives of most schools are implied rather than expressly stated, the testing program should rarely be restricted to the consciously emphasized local objectives of a school, but it is very important to know the status of the pupils and their rate of growth in relation to purposes which the school does have in mind and for which it is striving. No test, or combination of tests, will measure every attainment a school desires for its pupils, but through wise use of standardized and locally made tests, most of its more important objectives can be evaluated.

3. *No test is infallible.* The best test ever made is not perfectly reliable—that is, if the test were repeated under identical conditions, it is highly improbable that every pupil would make exactly the same score he made before or would maintain precisely the same position in the group of pupils tested. Human nature is, moreover, variable, and an occasional pupil's test score may fail by a wide margin to reveal his true ability or achievement because of obscure psychological factors over which the examiner may have no control and of which he may be unaware. It is, therefore, highly important that a school, in making any major decision about the achievement of a pupil, utilize the results of more than one test of a particular kind, as well as all other available information. In selecting pupils for special remedial work in reading, for example, it is wise to use at least two, and preferably three or more, reading tests. An even better procedure is to test the various basic skills at yearly intervals and to keep a record of the results in comparable units. In this way, not only status at any given time but extent and rate of growth over a period of several years can be determined. This enables the school to discover readily and to analyze marked changes in the progress of any given pupil.

4. *Achievement in a particular subject usually bears a close functional relationship to general intelligence.* Dependable diagnostic work in any subject almost always calls for the use of a good test of mental ability along with the achievement test. Other things being equal,

an individual test, such as the Stanford-Binet scale or one of the Wechsler scales, is to be preferred. If a school does not have the facilities for individual testing, however, such group tests as the Otis Quick-Scoring Mental Ability Tests, the Kuhlmann-Anderson Tests, and the Cooperative Academic Ability Test, which correlate rather highly with individual measures, may be used, preferably at intervals of one year or one semester.

5. *Intelligence tests involving language are not highly valid measuring instruments for pupils who have language difficulties.* For instance, if retarded readers are given a group test of mental ability calling for a considerable amount of reading, the results are ambiguous because it is uncertain whether low scores indicate low intelligence or undeveloped reading ability. It is evident, therefore, that conclusions about the mental ability of such pupils should be held in abeyance until the results have been checked by an individual mental test or a nonlanguage intelligence test.

6. *Scores on all intelligence and achievement tests are influenced, to some extent, by practice.* In other words, the second time a pupil takes a test he will probably do a little better than he did the first time, merely because he will have had experience with the test and will be familiar with its general form. This will be true even though the content may be varied through the use of a different form of the test. Because of the effect of practice, a pupil to whom the tests are new is under a certain handicap in comparison with pupils to whom the tests are familiar, and a single low score by such a pupil should be regarded as inconclusive evidence that he is really inferior in that ability or skill to the extent indicated by his score.

7. *The real cause of a disability may be far removed from the disability as revealed by a test.* A language handicap, for example, may be the result of lack of emotional balance rather than of low learning capacity. Hasty conclusions concerning the reasons for low scores should be avoided, and the assembling and careful analysis of a variety of information about each pupil should be a regular practice. In some instances the advice of medical or psychiatric experts may be imperative for accurate and adequate diagnosis, but the collection of many facts about study habits and personality traits, and the consideration of these facts in relation to scholastic performance, can be done effectively by the school staff itself.

GENERAL PROCEDURES IN DIAGNOSTIC AND INSTRUCTIONAL USES OF TESTS

Although methods of diagnosis and instruction naturally vary considerably from subject to subject, there are certain elements in the general procedure which are common to all basic tool subjects. Regardless of what he is teaching, the teacher who expects to diagnose the difficulties of his pupils and to provide suitable instruction to meet these difficulties will need to go through most of the steps suggested in the following paragraphs:

1. It is sometimes possible for an instructor to make an educational diagnosis with some degree of success without using any measuring instruments whatsoever, just as it is possible for a physician occasionally to diagnose correctly the ills of a patient without utilizing any of the instruments peculiar to his profession. Diagnostic work is unquestionably much more accurate, however, when its basis includes objective data. The first step, therefore, in diagnosis is *to give a suitable test to all the pupils.*

This first step is often accomplished in the regular testing program of the school. If, for example, a school participates extensively in the testing programs of the Educational Records Bureau, it will, in all probability, administer at regular intervals at least one test in each of the basic tool subjects.

Achievement tests are often divided into two general types, *survey* and *diagnostic.* The main difference between these two types lies in the method of scoring. A survey test ordinarily results only in a total score, or, at most, scores in a few of the larger, grosser features of a pupil's achievement in a subject; a diagnostic test not only yields a total score, but also shows achievement with respect to specific elements of the subject. These two types may be illustrated by reference to reading tests. The Metropolitan Reading Test may be regarded as a survey test, since it provides only a score for word knowledge and a score for reading comprehension, in addition to a total score; the Iowa Silent Reading Test, on the other hand, has apparent diagnostic features, for it yields scores in rate, comprehension, directed reading, poetry comprehension, word meaning (social science, natural science, mathematics, and English), sentence meaning, paragraph comprehension, and location of information, including use of the index and selection of key words.

Both survey tests and diagnostic tests have important functions in measurement. Survey tests are often used as the initial step to identify the pupils who need diagnosis; they can, in fact, be used in diagnosis, if the teacher will take the trouble to tabulate and classify the kinds of errors made by individual pupils. Diagnostic tests are highly useful in locating specific weaknesses, especially when followed by interviews with pupils about the parts which gave them difficulty. Some schools use the procedure of giving a survey test in a subject, and following it with a diagnostic test for the pupils who make low scores on the survey test. Other schools prefer to use diagnostic tests with all their pupils in the subjects in which such tests are readily available. Diagnostic tests usually take more time than survey tests. In a regular testing program conducted on an annual or semiannual basis, it is ordinarily desirable to use some tests of each type, as the exclusive use of diagnostic tests would involve more time than most schools would wish to give to testing.

2. After the test data have been assembled in convenient form, the next step is *to study the data carefully* in relation to all available information from other sources. This often entails not only an inspection of the test scores but a careful perusal of the test papers as well. This step should be carried on by the teacher. Detailed diagnosis is excellent preparation for corrective and remedial teaching, for in this way the teacher acquires a familiarity with the difficulties of his pupils that probably he could get in no other manner.

Study of the data will probably reveal at least five groups of pupils: (a) a few pupils whose achievement is very high (percentile of 90 or better for their grade level) on all parts of the test and who may possibly be excused, after their cases have been carefully scrutinized, from some of the routine aspects of the class work in order that they may use their time to better advantage in the development of special abilities and interests; (b) pupils whose achievement is as high as can be expected in view of their scholastic aptitude and their cumulative record of achievement in the subject measured by the test, and who apparently need no other teaching than that which is provided in the regular developmental program of the school; (c) pupils whose achievement in the various aspects of the subject or skill is so uneven that they apparently need special help in certain phases but not in others; (d) pupils who are somewhat low in all parts of the test, but whose difficulties can probably be corrected by group teaching; and (e) pupils who are so seriously handicapped that their cases demand individual attention. The proportions of pupils falling into the different groups will of course vary with the school and with the subject. Some schools follow the practice of giving remedial training in reading and other tool subjects to the lowest fourth of their pupils, regardless of how they stand with respect to national norms.

The teacher, in discovering the pupils who need remedial help, should avoid by all means the naïve assumption that a given grade norm for a test is necessarily an acceptable standard of achievement for all pupils in the grade. A moment's consideration will show that, in fact, the norm may not be a suitable achievement standard for any of the pupils. It is, at best, an average score of a widely distributed school population of that grade level.

If the pupils used in establishing the norm happen to be, in general, rather low in achievement, their average score will probably represent an achievement level that is by no means acceptable for schools in general. On the other hand, selection of superior pupils or differences in emphasis on various aspects of the curriculum may lead to the establishment of norms that are practically unattainable for pupils in certain schools.

Whether or not the grade norm for a test is a suitable standard for average pupils in the group, it is certainly not a desirable standard for exceptionally able pupils or pupils with limited aptitude. Superior pupils may justifiably be regarded as remedial cases if they fall as low as the norm in achievement, whereas some pupils of low ability probably should not be expected to reach the norm or group median, but rather to reach a level of achievement that is consistent with their measured scholastic aptitude. Each pupil must be considered individually in the light of all the evidence at hand. In some subjects, the interests and life ambitions of the pupils must be taken into consideration when making decisions about remedial work. In selecting pupils for remedial work in the *tool* subjects, however, interests and professional or vocational aptitudes of individuals are not so important, for a certain minimum level of skill is required of every pupil in order that he may be able to function successfully in adult life.

In deciding on some of the doubtful cases, the teacher will find it very helpful, if time permits, to retest the pupils individually while she observes their methods of work, and perhaps to have them do certain sections of the test aloud. This method has been found particularly useful in diagnosing arithmetic difficulties (4). The teacher will also find it advantageous to check her diagnosis with the opinions of other teachers of the pupil and with teachers who have had the pupil in preceding years, if these can be secured. When cumulative records of the type recommended by the American Council on Education are kept, it will be much easier and more convenient to study the previous history of the pupil.

3. The third step in the diagnostic and instructional uses of tests is *to set up procedures for the teaching that is needed.* The procedures will, of course, vary greatly with the subject, but some features are similar in all subjects. The first two groups listed in the preceding step do not require special teaching. The pupils in the third group—those low in one or two aspects, but up to acceptable achievement for their grade level in the others—may be taught individually or in small groups of pupils with like deficiencies, or they may be brought into the fourth group at appropriate points. The corrective teaching of the pupils in the fourth group can be mainly group instruction, but the individual needs of the pupils should

not be neglected. It has usually been found that the most effective plan is to organize the group as a regular class which is an integral part of the curriculum, but if this is not feasible the group may be met at study periods or other convenient times. The instruction of the pupils in the fifth group will necessarily be organized for individual teaching or work in very small groups.

4. Before the instruction is begun, *the school should make sure that there is an adequate recent record of the achievement status of the pupils,* so that their progress during the teaching may be measured accurately. Ordinarily the test, or tests, used as a basis of diagnosis will provide this record. If a considerable time elapses between the original measurement and the beginning of the remedial work (if, for example, a test in English usage administered in the spring forms the background for setting up a remedial program in English the following autumn) it is desirable that the pupils who were selected for the remedial teaching should be retested shortly before the beginning of the remedial program. Comparable forms of the test will be needed, of course, if this procedure is followed.

5. The next step is to launch the program of instruction according to a plan that is carefully thought out, yet flexible enough to be modified, if necessary, as the work progresses. A general rule in all remedial and corrective work is that *the teaching should be directed toward the specific difficulties experienced by the pupils.* This means that the diagnosis should be made as definite and detailed as possible. It also means that the teacher must keep the details of the diagnosis in mind in his instruction. Since the needs of the pupils will vary, the work must be highly individualized. Teachers with limited experience in remedial teaching will find some of the better workbook material, or materials designed for programmed instruction, a distinct aid in individualizing instruction.

Care should be taken to avoid goals that are really beyond the ability of the student. Continued driving, after the pupil has reached the limit of his ability, will accomplish little or nothing and may be harmful. Special help should not be allowed to become disguised coercion.

In connection with the remedial teaching, the instructor should remember that environmental factors, both in and out of school, may contribute to the learning difficulties of the various pupils, and he should be alert to opportunities to discover and help relieve maladjustments of this kind. In other words, diagnosis is not something that is finished before instruction begins, but is a continuing process.

The teacher should keep in mind, too, that the root of the difficulty of an individual pupil may be in a faulty mental attitude toward the school or toward the particular subject in which the remedial instruction is being given. Reading cases, for example, are sometimes of this sort; that is, no real disability may be involved. The pupil is simply interested in other activities to the exclusion of reading, and has, therefore, not developed facility in it. The remedy obviously lies in bringing about a changed attitude on the part of the learner.

Pupils of high mental ability who encounter learning difficulties and become remedial cases need a different type of instruction than pupils of low mental ability. Considerable repetition is needed in giving remedial instruction to dull pupils, whereas bright pupils may find repetition so deadening to their interest that they may make little or no improvement. Remedial instruction with pupils who are above average in intelligence is most effective if they are encouraged to make a self-diagnosis of their difficulties and to initiate their own attack, under guidance, upon the solution of their learning problems. At all levels of ability, progress is more rapid if pupils have an opportunity to measure their status at regular intervals and to keep an individual cumulative record of growth.

6. It is desirable to test the pupils a few weeks after the beginning of the teaching with a comparable form of the test used before the teaching was undertaken, in order to find out if the methods in use are producing results. If there are enough forms of the test, retesting at intervals is very helpful. It aids the teacher in planning his remedial program, and enables him to release pupils who no longer need the training. Evidence of progress also encourages the pupils and spurs them on to greater effort. Even if a different test is used and national norms are not available, the relative positions of students can be determined and their response to training noted. *A form of the test originally used should be given, by all means, at the conclusion of the period of teaching, to measure gains.* It is only by careful measurement of progress made under different methods of teaching that the various remedial methods can be properly evaluated. A test should also be administered several months later to measure the permanence of improvement and to find the pupils who still need special help.

7. When the results of the test given at the conclusion of the group instruction have been analyzed, the pupils who are up to the goals originally set should be released from further remedial training, but should probably be kept under observation for a time. Those who have made progress in relation to what may be expected, but are still somewhat low, will require further group instruction, perhaps at less frequent intervals and in certain special aspects. *The pupils who have failed to gain should be scheduled for intensive individual instruction.* Such in-

struction, in order to be successful, may require case study, diagnosis, and supervision of treatment by a psychologist.

The foregoing discussion of diagnostic and instructional uses of tests assumes conventional school organization and classroom instruction of groups. With the rise of teaching machines and programmed learning, and the innovation of the ungraded school, the regular use of measurement in analyzing the progress and planning the study programs of all pupils becomes not merely desirable but essential if positive values are to result from the newer and more flexible methods.

THE USE OF THE RESULTS OF TESTS IN PROVIDING FOR PUPILS OF HIGH ABILITY

If test scores indicate that the bright pupils have already mastered much of the work planned for a given grade, this fact should frequently lead to an enriched program for them. Another way of taking care of the needs of these pupils is to excuse them from aspects of the work in which they test very high, in order that they may do advanced work in keeping with their interests and special abilities. A ninth-grade pupil who reaches the 95th percentile for twelfth-grade pupils on the expression part of the Cooperative English Test may be excused, for example, from formal participation in those activities of the English class designed to train pupils in grammar and correct usage, and may be permitted to give his time, under guidance, to more advanced work in English, or to some other phase of his school program in which he has special interest and in which he has the capacity for independent study. Special promotions or other procedures for accelerating the rate of progress through school and college are also ways of taking care of pupils whose test records are exceptionally high, as, for example, the College Board's Advanced Placement Program. Procedures for acceleration were brought to the foreground during World War II because of the educational demands related to the war effort; and they are, of course, implicit in the current attention to the individualization of instruction which is developing in many places.

USE OF TEST RESULTS IN COUNSELING

The uses of test results in counseling are conditioned by the guidance functions which are carried on in each school. Although these vary considerably from one school to another, there are a number of activities which seem to be common to most guidance programs.

One function of guidance is to *identify weaknesses of individual pupils* and provide for long-time study and treatment. This function is related to those of diagnosis and instruction discussed in the preceding section but, considered as an aspect of guidance, it implies the follow-up of a pupil over a longer period than is usually possible in connection with the work of a single class.

Tests may be used effectively for this purpose. For example, one can follow the case of a pupil who has a deficiency in mathematics and note year after year the changes in score and percentile rank that have resulted from different kinds of treatment. The prediction of the later success of the individual depends not alone on what his achievement is today, but also on what it was last year and the year before, and the year before that. The prognosis for a pupil whose standing was low at secondary school entrance but who has managed to come up to average by the end of secondary school may be better than that for the pupil who has maintained an average record throughout the secondary school grades.

A second function of guidance is to *discover special abilities* that should be developed. If there is sufficient variety in the tests used, one frequently finds that a pupil handicapped in the academic subjects has marked ability in some other area. Tests of clerical and mechanical ability, for instance, are valuable supplements to tests in the academic subjects. The discovery and development of exceptional ability is of great importance for the benefit of society generally as well as for that of the individual pupil.

A third function of guidance officers is to *confer with pupils* from time to time *about achievement*. Such conferences are much more meaningful if the counselor is able to present objective evidence to the pupils. There is no better way to encourage a hard-working pupil than to show him how much he has increased his test scores. Also, there is no more convincing evidence with which to arouse pupils who are not working up to capacity than to show them the decline in their percentile ratings or to compare their achievement test percentiles with their percentiles for academic aptitude. In the latter type of comparison, however, the counselor should be aware that, because of the imperfect correlation between aptitude and achievement, a pupil with exceptionally high academic aptitude percentiles cannot be expected consistently to maintain quite as high percentiles in all aspects of achievement.

A fourth and closely related function of guidance counselors is to *confer with certain pupils about problems of adjustment*. For this purpose, the results of inventories of personality, attitude, and interests may sometimes be used to advantage. The scores on such inventories may not be reliable enough to be given much weight in the total record of the pupil, but the responses to specific items can be very valuable in interviews. An individual's aptitude and achievement scores are also useful in interviews of this kind, and they should be scrutinized closely in cases of personal problems that may grow out of an inability to do the required work of certain classes.

A fifth function of personnel officers in a guidance program is to *confer with parents about the ability, achievement, growth, and school adjustment of their children*. Tests have potential values that few schools, even those with extensive guidance programs, have fully realized. Parents are naturally keenly interested in the test scores of their children and are usually glad to have an opportunity to study objective, impartial evidence concerning ability, achievement, and special aptitudes. One technique that is sometimes employed is to give a general explanation of the meaning of test records to groups of parents and to invite them to visit the office of the staff member in charge of testing for a more detailed explanation based on the records of their own child. A helpful report on this use of test results and other types of recorded material was made by Hilkert (*10*) some time ago, and recently a *Parents' Guide to Understanding Tests* was published by the Educational Records Bureau (*19*).

A sixth function of counselors is to *guide pupils into or away from certain courses* and thus to reduce failure through careful planning based on available evidence. A function similar to this one was mentioned earlier in this chapter in connection with administration, but this is as much a counseling function as an administrative one. Tests can be used extensively in this kind of guidance. Assume that a test yields just two scores, verbal and mathematical, and that a certain pupil has a high percentile rating in the former and a low percentile rating in the latter. These data provide some evidence for guiding the pupil into linguistic subjects and away from mathematical ones, or for the need to help him improve his mathematical ability in some cases. Whereas the scores on one test alone cannot be used with perfect assurance as a basis for action, the evidence piled up from several tests over a period of two or three years may be so strong that the guidance to be given a pupil in the choice of a field of specialization will be indicated beyond reasonable doubt.

A seventh guidance function is to *help pupils and parents make plans for the pupils' careers after graduation*. This includes counseling concerning whether or not the pupil should attend college, assistance in deciding what colleges to apply to, and help in choosing a vocation with, of course, the *decision* always resting with the student himself. Pupils whose public school percentile ratings on academic aptitude and achievement tests are consistently above 75 usually can do successful work in the better colleges, whereas those whose percentile ratings generally fall below the median should be steered away from the more selective colleges toward community colleges, or perhaps advised to go directly into an occupation without attempting to enter college. Pupils considering the most highly selective colleges usually should have percentiles above 90 on public school norms.

Ambitious but dull pupils are sometimes much upset emotionally if, at the end of their secondary school course, they are suddenly confronted with the knowledge that they cannot expect to succeed in college, or that they must be content with attendance at some minor college rather than an outstanding college which they had hoped to attend. However, if achievement test scores are available for each pupil throughout the secondary school, and if these are shown regularly to parents and pupils with an explanation of their meaning, a low-ranking pupil will gradually become aware of and come to accept the fact that his abilities are of a different type from those of academically successful students. Thus, on the basis of this impartial evidence, the student has an opportunity to make adjustment to a nonacademic career by easy stages.

The results of vocational interest inventories as well as the scores on academic aptitude and achievement tests are useful in helping pupils to choose a career. The results of interest inventories should be very carefully interpreted, however, and it should be made clear to the pupil and his parents that these instruments do not measure *ability* for different vocations nor show whether or not the individual can be *successful* in a particular vocation. They do indicate whether an individual is likely to be interested in, and satisfied with, a particular occupation or occupational field.

An eighth function of counselors is to *confer with teachers about individual pupils.* One of the most important aspects of guidance is adjustment, and it is obvious that adjustment between pupils and teachers will be better if each teacher understands the abilities and limitations of the various pupils in his classes. The test scores are valuable both for conferences between counselors and individual teachers, and for staff clinics in which groups of teachers study the problems of different pupils and decide on treatment for their difficulties. One of the essential elements of every testing program is a continuous program of educating teachers in the use of test results. Regardless of how a school's testing program is organized or how many counselors it has, its classroom teachers will

do much of the actual guidance work, broadly conceived, and the value of tests is almost directly proportional to the interest of the teachers in them and their understanding of the results.

Another function of both counselors and teachers is to *make case studies of certain pupils.* The case study is one of the most useful techniques in a guidance program. Not only is it valuable in personnel work with the pupils, but it is an effective way of educating teachers in guidance procedures. The backbone of any case study is evaluation. Tests are needed at the beginning of a study to help determine the nature and degree of the problem which initiated the study, during treatment to measure progress and to redirect training, and at the end to determine the gains made and to indicate what still remains to be done. This function is discussed in detail in Chapter XV.

A tenth guidance function, particularly in college preparatory schools, is to *aid in decisions concerning when pupils are ready to take admission examinations,* such as those of the College Entrance Examination Board, or the American College Testing Program. Although the correlation between scores on objective tests used in the regular program of the school and the results of examinations of the type prepared by the College Board and the ACTP is by no means perfect, there is substantial agreement between them. Even when the College Board tests were mainly of the essay type, a study reported by the Educational Records Bureau years ago indicated that the average correlation between these two types of tests was .67 as compared with a correlation of .63 between school marks and College Board examinations (27). A more recent study of the predictive value of cumulative test records has shown still closer relationship (23). The use of cumulative test records to help decide when students are ready for admission examinations is a practical application of tests to guidance and is one that some schools are finding worthwhile.

The last function of guidance officers which will be mentioned here is to *make reports to colleges and prospective employers.* As already indicated, test results are valuable in reports of both kinds. Test records, together with an appropriate explanation, have been accepted as an integral part of the reports which are sent with the pupil when he is graduated. This is evidenced by the fact that nearly every up-to-date report or transfer form now has space for test results expressed in meaningful, nontechnical terms, such as percentiles. It is true that these records are not always understood by the institutions or the employers to which they are sent, but it is also true that they are much more generally understood than they were in earlier years.

LIMITATIONS TO THE USE OF TESTS IN INSTRUCTIONAL AND GUIDANCE PROGRAMS

Although testing is being used in numerous ways, there are several limitations which restrict the extent and precision of the use of test results. Some tests do not agree very well with the objectives in the organization of modern courses; that is, they do not provide valid measurement of the curriculum with which they are used. As noted earlier, no test is perfectly reliable, and there is always a certain amount of sampling error in even the best test administered under ideal conditions. Users of tests sometimes allow themselves to be misled by the labels or names attached to the tests. For example, if one test is called an academic aptitude test and another is called an achievement test, there is a tendency for users to feel that the tests measure very different things, even when their content is such that there is obviously a great deal of similarity between them. Unless counselors and teachers are aware of these pitfalls, their interpretations of test results are likely to be erroneous.

Probably the most serious limitation to the use of tests in instruction and guidance, as well as in some of the most rapidly developing occupations—and this is particularly true of some of the most promising of the newer tests—is that in many cases no one, not even the test expert, knows just what the relationship of the test data is to future success in various fields. Some tests yield scores, for instance, for such mental traits as verbal, number, space, memory, and reasoning factors. The scores on such tests have a potential value that is very great, but their present usefulness is limited by the fact that we need more information about what the scores mean in terms of the future accomplishment of the individual. The fact that the scores on so many tests cannot be adequately explained in terms of outcomes has caused some people to become considerably discouraged over the possibility of effective use of tests in guidance. This tendency to be skeptical of the guidance values of some of the newer tests grows out of the knowledge that test results expressed in quantitative terms are really useful for guidance purposes only when they can be expressed in meaningful everyday terms, and thus enable one to make a valid qualitative appraisal of the individual and to predict his success in qualitative terms.

The use of objective tests has been criticized in a considerable number of recent articles and several books. Barclay (2) reviewed a number of these contributions to the literature on testing, and provided a thoughtful and helpful appraisal. He found some of the criticisms justified, but also noted instances of bias and faulty logic on the part of the critics of testing.

HOW TO IMPROVE THE USEFULNESS OF TESTS

The lack of complete understanding of the scores obtained from tests should not lead to loss of faith in these devices, for at the present stage of measurement work, when new tests are appearing frequently, and when criteria of success are fluctuating, a paucity of consequential data is to be expected. Although some of the objective tests of aptitude and achievement have been in use for a generation or more, most of the better tests have been prepared within the last 20 years, and several of the more promising tests have been made available within the last ten years. Research is the only means by which the prognostic nature of a test can be adequately investigated; but research techniques are often slow and expensive, and not enough time has elapsed since the publication of the majority of the good tests for research to discover their relationships to fundamental long-time objectives, especially when the objectives themselves may not be stable. It is encouraging to discover that test specialists are showing an increasing awareness of the need for information on the relationship between test data and guidance outcomes, and are beginning to take steps to join forces in attacking the problem.

This fact is evidenced by the cooperation of leading test publishers in plans for a national program for assessing the progress of education which was proposed by a national committee chaired by Ralph W. Tyler (31) and given financial support by the Carnegie Foundation for the Advancement of Teaching.

REFERENCES

1. American Psychological Association, American Educational Research Association, and National Council on Measurement in Education, Joint Committee (John W. French, chairman). *Standards for Educational and Psychological Tests and Manuals.* (In preparation for probable publication in 1965.)
2. Barclay, James R. "The Attack on Testing and Counseling: An Examination and Reappraisal," *Personnel and Guidance Journal,* XLIII (September 1964), 6–15.
3. Berdie, Ralph F. "Testing Programs and Counseling in the Schools," *The Impact and Improvement of School*

Testing Programs, pp. 126–162. The Sixty-second Yearbook of the National Society for the Study of Education, Part II. (Warren G. Findley, ed.). Chicago: The University of Chicago Press, 1963. Pp. xii + 304.

4. Buswell, G. T., and John, Lenore. *Diagnostic Studies in Arithmetic.* Chicago: The University of Chicago Press, 1926. Pp. xiv + 212.

5. Dressel, Paul L. "The Role of External Testing Programs in Education," *Educational Record,* XLV (Spring 1964), 161–166.

6. Durost, Walter N., and Prescott, George A. *Essentials of Measurement for Teachers,* Chapters 7–9. New York: Harcourt, Brace & World, Inc., 1962. Pp. viii + 167.

7. Ebel, Robert L. "Problems of Communication between Test Specialists and Test Users," *Educational and Psychological Measurement,* XIV (Summer 1954), 277–282.

8. Engelhart, Max D. "Testing and Use of Test Results," *Review of Educational Research,* XXVI (February 1956), 5–13.

9. Gustad, John W. "Helping Students Understand Test Information," *Proceedings of the 1955 Invitational Conference on Testing Problems,* pp. 51–59. Princeton, N.J.: Educational Testing Service, 1956. Pp. 152.

10. Hilkert, Robert N. "Parents and Cumulative Records," *Educational Record,* Supplement 13 (January 1940), 172–183.

11. Klausmeier, Herbert J. "Identifying Children through Measurement," *Education,* LXXX (November 1959), 167–181.

12. Lennon, Roger T. *A Glossary of 100 Measurement Terms.* Test Service Notebook No. 13. New York: Harcourt, Brace & World, Inc. Pp. 6.

13. Lindball, C. M. *Testing and Evaluation.* New York: Harcourt, Brace & World, Inc., 1961. Pp. 260.

14. Lundy, C. P., and Shertzer, Bruce. "Making Test Data Useful," *Personnel and Guidance Journal,* XLII (September 1963), 62–63.

15. Lyman, Howard B. *Test Scores and What They Mean.* Englewood Cliffs, N.J.: Prentice-Hall, Inc., 1963. Pp. xv + 223.

16. McCauley, John H. "Reporting Results of the Standardized Testing Program to Parents," *Personnel and Guidance Journal,* XLI (September 1962), 56–57.

17. McLaughlin, Kenneth F. *Interpretation of Test Results.* Washington, D.C.: Superintendent of Documents, 1964. Pp. 63.

18. North, Robert D. "The Use of Multi-Factor Aptitude Tests in Counseling," *Proceedings of the 1955 Invitational Conference on Testing Problems,* pp. 11–15.

Princeton, N.J.: Educational Testing Service, 1956. Pp. 152.

19. *Parents' Guide to Understanding Tests.* New York: Educational Records Bureau, 1964. Pp. viii + 43.

20. Remmers, H. H., and Rummel, J. Francis. *A Practical Introduction to Evaluation.* New York: Harper & Row, Publishers, 1960. Pp. 370.

21. Rosenbeck, Viola. "The Use of Reading Test Results in Counseling," *Personnel and Guidance Journal,* XLII (November 1963), 269–294.

22. Rothney, John W. M.; Danielson, Paul J.; and Hymann, Robert A. *Measurement for Guidance.* New York: Harper & Row, Publishers, 1959. Pp. 378.

23. Spaulding, Geraldine. *The Application of Secondary-School Cumulative Record Data to the Prediction of College Success.* New York: Educational Records Bureau, 1960. Pp. 42. (Mimeographed; unpublished.)

24. Stanley, Julian C., and Ross, C. C. *Measurement in Today's Schools,* 4th ed. Englewood Cliffs, N.J.: Prentice-Hall, Inc., 1964. Pp. 512.

25. *Testing Guide for Teachers.* New York: Educational Records Bureau, 1961. Pp. 43.

26. Thorndike, Robert L., and Hagen, Elizabeth. *Measurement and Evaluation in Psychology and Education,* 2nd ed. New York: John Wiley & Sons, Inc., 1960. Pp. 602.

27. Traxler, Arthur E. "Comparable Tests and School Marks," *1963 Fall Testing Program in Independent Schools and Supplementary Studies,* Educational Records Bulletin No. 19, pp. 83–109. New York: Educational Records Bureau, January 1937. Pp. 112.

28. Traxler, Arthur E., and North, Robert D. "The Selection and Use of Tests in a School Testing Program," *The Impact and Improvement of School Testing Programs,* pp. 211–231. The Sixty-second Yearbook of the National Society for the Study of Education, Part II (Warren G. Findley, ed.). Chicago: The University of Chicago Press, 1963. Pp. xi + 304.

29. Traxler, Arthur E. "Educational Measurement: An Aid to School Administration," *School Review,* LXVIII (Summer 1960), 196–209.

30. Tyler, Leona E. *Tests and Measurements.* Englewood Cliffs, N.J.: Prentice-Hall, Inc., 1963. Pp. 116.

31. Tyler, Ralph W. "Assessing the Progress of Education," *Phi Delta Kappan,* XLVII (September 1965), 13–16.

32. Wellck, Arthur A. "Statewide Tests and Academic Success at the University of New Mexico," *Personnel and Guidance Journal,* XLII (December 1963), 403–405.

33. Wrightstone, J. Wayne. *What Tests Can Tell Us About Children.* Better Living Booklet. Chicago: Science Research Associates, Inc., 1954. Pp. 48.

CHAPTER XII

Basic Principles and Main Types of Pupil Personnel Records

SOME BASIC PRINCIPLES

THE TERM "PERSONNEL RECORDS," AS USED here, includes all the records of the school that are employed in recording information about individual pupils. It does not include financial and business records, or records and reports that deal with groups rather than with individuals.

According to this definition, certain individual school records, such as the school census and attendance data, which are kept partly for purposes of making group summaries, may logically be regarded as personnel records. Records of this sort, however, will not be included in this discussion. The emphasis will be upon records that are maintained for the purpose of facilitating the guidance of each individual pupil.

We are still in a period of transition from haphazard record systems that "just grew" in different schools to systems carefully planned in the light of a study of the conditions and needs of each school. A century and a half ago few schools kept any records at all. Largely through the efforts of Horace Mann, the Daily Register was introduced into the schools of Massachusetts in the 1830s; its use gradually spread throughout the country. This one record book, which consists largely of a record of attendance and promotion, continues, even to the present day, to be practically the sole recording device in some rural schools. As the complexity of urban schools has increased, additional office records and records for transfer of pupil information from department to department, from school to school, and from school system to school

system, perforce have been devised. Many of these record forms have grown up without definite plan or coordination and without relationship to records used in other places. So great is the diversity in personnel record systems that the efforts of regional associations and other organizations to bring some order out of the chaos have, until recently, met with indifferent success.

Some persons, after examining the poorly planned and unwieldy record systems in vogue in many schools, have been inclined to take a very pessimistic view of the possibility of getting the general rank and file of schools to build efficient and significant personnel records. But anyone who tends to despair over the situation may find considerable solace in a comparison of the present personnel records of any school with the kind that were possible, for instance, 200 years ago. For example, in his *History of Education*, Cubberley[1] reported in detail a record that was kept by a Prussian schoolmaster about 1750. This schoolmaster, one Hauberle by name,

... with characteristic Teutonic attention to details, has left on record that, in the course of his 51 years and 7 months as a teacher he had, by a moderate computation, given 911,527 blows with a cane, 124,010 blows with a rod, 20,989 blows and raps with a ruler, 136,715 blows with the hand, 10,235 blows over the mouth, 7,905 boxes on the ear, 1,115,800 raps on the head, and 22,763 *notabenes* with the Bible, Cathechism, singing book, and grammar. He had 777 times made boys kneel on peas, 613 times on a triangular piece of wood, had made 3,001 wear the jackass, and 1,707 hold the rod up, not to mention various more unusual punish-

[1] Ellwood P. Cubberley. *The History of Education*, pp. 455–456. Boston: Houghton Mifflin Company, 1920. Pp. xxiv + 849.

ments he had contrived on the spur of the occasion. Of the blows with the cane, 800,000 were for Latin words; of the rod, 76,000 were for texts from the Bible or verses from the singing book. He also had about 3,000 expressions to scold with, two thirds of which were native to the German tongue and the remainder his invention.

In contrast to this recital of items which two centuries ago were regarded as important in the guidance of pupils, even the most archaic of personnel records now in use seem fairly valuable. The great need at present is to improve the scope, reliability, and organization of the information collected and recorded about pupils, and to train teachers in the intelligent use of this information. The recognition of a number of basic principles should give important impetus to the realization of this goal.

1. *A comprehensive and detailed system of cumulative personnel records is indispensable for the proper functioning of the modern school.* From earliest colonial times down to the beginning of the twentieth century, our schools were mainly rural and village schools. Furthermore, the great majority of the pupils were enrolled in eight-grade elementary schools. This situation had a definite effect on pupil-teacher relationships and on the opportunity for intelligent instruction and guidance, for it was inevitable that the teacher and his pupils should be intimately acquainted. Pupils were often under the same teacher for several years, not merely in one subject, but in all aspects of the life of the school. The contacts of pupils and teacher extended beyond the school, for the teacher knew each pupil in out-of-school relationships. He was in all probability a friend of the pupils' parents. He visited, and sometimes boarded for long periods of time, in each home. The teacher needed no written case history for his pupils. He carried in his mind the history of every one of them. This is not to say that *written* objective records would not have aided the teacher in his work with the pupils. They would have been useful, but they were not indispensable. So he got along either with no permanent records or with the daily register, which was mainly a record of attendance and promotions.

There were secondary schools consisting first of the Latin grammar schools, later of the academies, and finally of the public high schools, but they were small and tended to be selective. The curricula were limited in scope, and the pupils were for the most part those who were getting ready for colleges and professional schools. There was little need, therefore, for either educational or vocational guidance.

With the rapid development of junior and senior high schools during the present century, and with the tendency toward departmentalization even in the elementary school, this homely, intimate picture of the school has changed. Departmentalization contributes to the effi-

ciency of instruction, even in a small school, but as soon as a school has departments, it has teachers seeing only segments of the development of boys and girls. The teacher knows the pupil as a student of English, or a student of mathematics, or as a football player, but he rarely knows the whole individual.

When to this situation there is added another twentieth century influence—namely, the influx of huge numbers of pupils of all economic and ability levels into the schools—there comes into existence a great metropolitan high school, with perhaps 200 teachers and from 5,000 to 10,000 pupils. Each teacher may meet some 200 pupils, in groups of perhaps 40 an hour a day, for one semester, and then receive an entirely new crowd. The only way of establishing an adequate basis for teacher participation in guidance, or for counselors to have the information they need, is to pool the various isolated bits of information that are gleaned by the different persons who have contact with each pupil and to bring them together into one composite picture.

But, one may inquire, when these many items are brought together and put down cumulatively on a record card, is the result actually a picture of the pupil? When dealing with personality, is not the whole greater than the sum of its parts? The answer is, yes, that is true, but the saving feature of the whole plan is the power of synthesis that is inherent in the human mind. When one takes a long-time cumulative record which has been filled out in detail, and studies it with the understanding that comes from experience with such records, one does not get just an impression of a series of details—one gets an impression of unity. *One relates a dozen different items and has something new,* an understanding of personality that is not down on the card but is a result of his ability to assimilate a group of facts and to abstract a generalization. Some persons who insist that guidance must be based on an understanding of the whole personality of the individual are critical of the use of tests and cumulative records because they do not see this fundamental point.

2. *The most important purpose of personnel records is to improve the instruction and guidance of each individual pupil.* Personnel records serve various purposes: they contribute to the administration of the school, they form a basis for reports to higher institutions, and they provide data for research. But, in setting up a system of personnel records, these purposes are secondary. Each item should be evaluated in the light of its contribution to pupil adjustment and development, and a decision concerning whether or not to include a particular item in the record should be based, first of all, on its value to the individual pupil. The items not related to this central purpose, that are necessarily added to the personnel-record system, should be clearly differentiated from those of

major importance, so that they will not be allowed to consume the time and confuse the thinking of persons who are studying the records for the sole purpose of helping the pupil develop normally.

3. *Records are needed that will be continuous over the whole school history from the kindergarten to the junior college, and that will follow the child from school to school.* The bringing together of all available important information about a pupil at any given time, and the recording of the facts in one place so that they may be studied is a great help in understanding the child, but the value of the record is increased manyfold if it is cumulative from year to year. It is self-evident that teachers in a higher grade need the benefit of the experience of teachers who have had the pupil in a lower grade. If a complete record of the child's history in a lower school can accompany him when he advances to a higher level, his new school can place him and deal with him to far greater advantage. Status at any given time is important, but for purposes of guiding a pupil, a knowledge of the amount of growth is even more important.

4. *The personnel records for all pupils should be readily accessible to the entire faculty of the school.* The value of personnel records is almost directly proportional to their use by the classroom teacher. They should be open to inspection by the teachers at all times; in fact, if possible, the teachers should be free to go directly to the records without having to utilize the services of a clerk to obtain access to the material. If there are matters of record about certain pupils that are too confidential to be read by everyone, they should be filed in a separate place. *The freedom of use of the main records should not be impaired by the need for recording occasional confidential bits of information.* All school personnel should observe ethical standards and should be informed about legal responsibilities pertaining to the confidentiality of records.[2] Needless to say, the pupils themselves should not have access to each other's record cards, but each pupil should have an opportunity to study his own cumulative record in consultation with his faculty adviser.

5. *The records system should be simple enough and well enough organized so that the essential facts about any given pupil will be brought together on one central record card or set of cards in such a way that they may be grasped through a few moments of study by busy teachers and counselors who are not highly trained in interpreting records.* Regardless of the extent and complexity of the procedures used in collecting the original data about each pupil, a plan should be evolved for "boiling down" the essential data and recording it in simple,

concise, readable form. The record which the teacher or the counselor uses should be so greatly simplified that the high spots in the whole life of the child can be taken in almost at a glance. Naturally, more extensive and detailed information back of the entries on the cumulative record should be available, but either it should be filed in a different place or it should be arranged in such a manner that it does not interfere with the reading of the main record.

6. *An attempt should be made to keep the records high in reliability and comparability by basing them as far as possible on objective data.* Opinions about pupils are notoriously unreliable, and they should have a minor place in the records. Main dependence should be placed on behavior descriptions, physical and mental measurements, and achievement test scores. School marks are useful if their meaning is carefully defined and if the marks are supplemented and interpreted by written comments. Probably the most important single type of data is scores obtained annually or semiannually on a series of comparable tests.

7. *The records should be uniform in type throughout all the schools of the local system.* Complete uniformity in personnel records may not be either possible or desirable for different schools because of differences in objectives, but the permanent records that are kept in the various schools of one city system should certainly be coordinated. This is particularly important if the elementary school cumulative record goes with the pupil to the junior high school, and the records for both elementary school and junior high school go along with the pupil to the senior high school.

The need for uniformity pertains, of course, to the permanent cumulative record and not necessarily to the "feeders" for the cumulative record, which may conceivably differ from school to school.

8. *The records system should provide for a minimum of repetition of items.* One of the most important reasons why schools hesitate to adopt a really comprehensive and significant system of cumulative records is the amount of clerical work involved in their upkeep. The clerical work can be minimized by planning the system so that needless duplication of items is avoided. A certain amount of duplication is of course inevitable in large schools, since it is not possible to have a single set of cumulative records placed where they are easily accessible to everyone. Where repetition is necessary, and the amount of clerical work excessive, use should be made wherever possible of mechanical or electronic devices.[3]

[2] Thomas Magoon. "Confidentiality of Student Records," *NEA Journal,* LI (December 1962), 29–30.

[3] John E. Dobbin, "Cooperative Plan for Guidance and Admissions, Georgia," *Bulletin of the National Association of Secondary-School Principals,* XLV (April 1961), 194–195.

9. *The building of a personnel records system for a given school does not begin with a consideration of the records themselves; it begins with a study of the nature and purposes of the school and of the pupil.* The whole program of the school impinges upon the record system. A good system of records reflects the purposes of the school and what the school is doing. A new record system may perhaps go beyond the immediate program of the school, and make provision for the recording of types of information that the school is not at the moment ready to provide, but it should by all means be consistent with the purposes of the school. Therefore, the first step in the revision of personnel records is to obtain a statement of the school's objectives. These objectives should not be vague and ethereal, but should be stated in terms of pupil behavior. They should be stated by each department in the school, and they should be specific and detailed rather than general. Once the school has agreed on what it is trying to do, it can proceed to build or to adopt a system of personnel records that will provide for the recording of information about the growth of pupils toward the goals it has set up.[4]

10. *If a school adopts one comprehensive cumulative form as its basic personnel record, it should not only plan this form with meticulous attention to detail, but it should also carefully plan the forms which are to be used in collecting data which will contribute to the main record.* A cumulative record form cannot be regarded as a card for original entry. Obviously, it will seldom, if ever, circulate throughout the faculty so that the various members of the staff may make entries on it. The teachers, counselors, and others will record the information on transient forms of various sorts and they will record it, as a rule, in more detail than it appears on the cumulative record. It is the job of a specially trained staff member to select and summarize the original data and enter it on the permanent card. Obviously, the final entries cannot be more valid, reliable, and meaningful than the original ones. Therefore, the forms for original entry and the directions for filling them out should be set up very carefully.

11. *A detailed manual of directions should accompany the personnel records for the guidance of persons filling out or using the forms.* Some items on the record form, such as the name and address of the pupil, are of course self-explanatory, but others, for example, the personality trait record or the marking system used in the school, require explanation. It is, therefore, desirable to prepare a manual in which the various items will be taken up in

[4] Robert L. Ebel, "The Relation of Testing Programs to Educational Goals," *The Impact and Improvement of School Testing Programs*, pp. 28–44. Sixty-second Yearbook of the National Society for the Study of Education, Part II (Warren G. Findley, ed.). Chicago: The University of Chicago Press, 1963.

order, and directions for recording given and interpretation of the entries explained. An explanation is particularly important if a graphical record of test results is maintained, for the meaning of a graph may not be easily apparent to everyone.

12. *There is a natural and logical relationship between the information on reports made to the parents and the information recorded for purposes of permanent record; this relationship should be taken into account in planning both types of forms.* The reports to the parents are less extensive and usually less detailed than the personnel records maintained by the school, and there are, of course, certain kinds of information that the school may not wish to give to the parents. For example, because of the danger of misinterpretation, it is seldom advisable to report IQs on mental tests to parents. Nevertheless, the reports to the parents and the cumulative records may well have many items in common, and efficiency will be promoted if they are planned in relation to one another.

13. *There is also a natural and close relationship between cumulative records and transcripts of school records which are sent to colleges.* For entrance to some colleges, copies of cumulative records made by the photostatic or other duplicating process may serve in lieu of, or supplementary to, college transcripts. As long ago as 1950, more than half of 1351 secondary schools that replied to a questionnaire on college admission practices indicated that requests from colleges for secondary school cumulative record cards were increasing. For reports to colleges that continue to insist upon the use of their own transcript form, the data on the pupil's cumulative record card may serve as the basis for the filling out of the transcript.

14. *A system of personnel records must not be static; it must be revised frequently, as a school's theory of education matures and its practices change.* The reasons why so many schools are now dissatisfied with their records, and are trying to do something about them are that during the last few years we have been going through a period of rapid change in educational philosophy and practice, and that records systems have been allowed to lag behind other developments. Many schools, for example, are making extensive use of annual programs of comparable tests, but in many cases the cumulative records of the school do not provide adequately for the recording of the test results because they were developed in a period when tests were of minor importance to the school. Similarly, a large number of schools are giving more and more attention to the integration of personality, to social adjustment, and to the development of the student's concept of self, but few permanent record systems make extensive provision for records concerning the development of pupils in these respects. A school

should re-evaluate its personnel records at frequent intervals, discarding those items which are no longer used and adding others which are needed.

15. *It is imperative that a system of personnel records be associated with a program of teacher education in the use of these records.* The education of the teachers begins with the planning of the records. The building of a new system of personnel records should be an all-faculty job, not alone because of the educational value of the work, but also because no innovations in personnel records can be really successful without the full sympathy and participation of the teachers. Naturally, the details of actually drawing up new records will be the work of a selected committee, but the whole faculty should contribute ideas and should help evaluate and revise the new forms before they are put into operation.[5] After the records system is set up, the teachers must be stimulated and encouraged to use the records in connection with their work with their pupils. One excellent means of promoting the use of records is a series of case studies carried on by the teachers themselves and discussed in a series of carefully planned staff meetings. The nature of a program of this kind will be discussed in some detail in Chapter XV.

MAIN TYPES OF PERSONNEL RECORD SYSTEMS

The number of different personnel record forms in use in the schools of this country is unknown, but for a quarter of a century and more it has unquestionably been very large. Surveys of a limited number of schools have identified hundreds of such forms. For example, some 40 years ago in a study of the office practices of only 15 secondary schools, Gray[6] discovered 688 different forms which were classified under 177 descriptive titles, only 12 of which were common to all 15 schools. In another early study, Heck[7] found 1515 different items in a study of the record forms of 131 cities in the United States. Only 11.3 percent of the 1515 items occurred on more than 10 forms, and 50.2 percent of the items occurred only once. Later, Ayer[8] analyzed

the cumulative records used in 200 elementary schools in the state of Texas and found some 300 different items on this type of personnel record. Only 19 items, however, were common to a majority of the cumulative records, and there were 54 items, each of which occurred on only one of the 200 different forms.

A surprisingly large number of forms is required for the administration of the guidance department of any large city school. Becker,[9] for example, listed 31 forms employed in the guidance department of the Samuel Tilden High School, Brooklyn, New York. Similarly, Clark[10] listed 42 guidance forms utilized in the Roosevelt High School, Seattle, Washington, although some of the forms had broader use than for guidance alone. At the college level, the record system may be especially complex, as was brought out by Fulton's analysis of the extensive personnel record system of Syracuse University.[11]

At present, there seems to be a tendency toward some reduction in the number of different personnel records used, and this tendency will no doubt increase as the use of data processing machines and of microfilm becomes more common and as information retrieval devices are perfected.[12]

Nearly all the personnel records used by schools can be classified into a relatively small number of types. We may classify record forms in four different ways: first, according to function; second, according to filing arrangement; third, according to the nature of the centralizing unit; and fourth, according to permanency.

RECORDS CLASSIFIED ACCORDING TO FUNCTION

The grouping of records according to the function they perform is the most familiar way of classifying them. This type of classification for senior high school records was made effectively by Bristow and Proctor.[13] The groups are as follows: (1) forms dealing with registration and classification of students; (2) attendance records; (3) routine permits and passes; (4) reports to parents; (5) health and physical training records; (6) special and cumulative record cards; and (7) reports to colleges and standardizing agencies. Among the forms included in the first group are registration cards, pupils' program cards,

[5] For a discussion of procedures that were followed in one secondary school, see Lester W. Nelson, "Developing a Cumulative Record Card for Local Use," *Guidance in Public Secondary Schools*, pp. 73–78. Educational Records Bulletin No. 28. New York: Educational Records Bureau, October 1939.

[6] M. R. Gray. "The Office Practices of High-School Principals." Unpublished Master's Thesis, Department of Education, University of Chicago, 1927, 54–55.

[7] Arch O. Heck. *Administration of Pupil Personnel*, p. 190. New York: Ginn and Company, 1929.

[8] Fred C. Ayer. *Practical Child Accounting*, pp. 11–12. Austin, Texas: The Steck Company, 1949. Pp. viii + 238.

[9] Elsa Becker. *Guidance at Work in a Large City High School*. New York: New York City Board of Education, 1935. Pp. xii + 125.

[10] Frank Jones Clark. *Guidance Working Materials for Junior and Senior High Schools*. Seattle: The Author, Roosevelt High School, 1936.

[11] Margaret J. Fulton. "Analysis of a Personnel Record System," *Journal of Higher Education*, XXII (April 1951), 209–211.

[12] "Student History Information and Retrieval System," *Data Processing for Education*, III (October 1964), 11.

[13] A. B. Bristow and William M. Proctor. "Senior High School Records and Reports," *Junior-Senior High School Clearing House*, IV (March 1930), 410–432.

course-of-study cards, class lists, forms showing distribution of marks, forms for application for change of course, and forms used in granting permit to change course.

In the second group, attendance records, are included the teacher's daily attendance report, the high school admission card, and the attendance investigation card. The third group covers various brief forms for routine passes and permits, such as permit to go to the library, permit to make up lessons missed on account of absence, and permit for early dismissal. The fourth group, reports to parents, includes not only the regular periodic report on work covered, accomplishment, and growth, but also various special reports, among which are report regarding absence and tardiness, report regarding deficiency in scholarship, report regarding conduct, and report of suspension.

Health and physical training records, which make up the fifth group, include form for reporting pupils to school physician, form for school nurse to use in reporting health inspection, certificate of disability, record of routine medical examination, and, most important of all, the pupil's permanent health record card.

In the sixth class we have what is, without doubt, the most valuable of all the many personnel records that may be maintained by the school, namely, the cumulative record card. This form will be discussed at length and illustrated in the next chapter.

The seventh and last group includes transcript of credits, certificate of recommendation to college, personnel rating blanks, and other forms for reporting to colleges, standardizing agencies and employers. To an increasing degree cumulative record cards are being used to supplement the usual type of report to colleges. As we will see later, at the present time many influences are working toward a radically different type of report to colleges than has been used in the past.

Personnel records for the elementary school and the junior high school may be classified into the same general categories, with the exception of the final group, but fewer records are ordinarily needed at the elementary school level than at the high school level.

RECORDS CLASSIFIED ACCORDING TO FILING ARRANGEMENT

Another way of looking at records systems is to consider the degree to which they are centralized. At one extreme we may postulate a records system which is completely decentralized—that is, one in which each member of the school staff would keep the records which pertained to his own work and in which no attempt would be made to centralize the information about each child. Obviously, a recording plan of this kind is purely hypo-

thetical, for no school could be administered on such a basis. There is a minimum of information about the character of a pupil's work in school which must inevitably be made available in the principal's and the counselor's offices, even though it may in some cases be nothing more than a record of attendance and of marks assigned to the pupils at stated intervals.

The opposite extreme to the recording plan just mentioned would be one in which the teachers and counselors would keep no records at all but would turn all data over to the central office to be filed or entered on cumulative records. No school would attempt to apply such a plan, for in practice it would be almost as faulty as a completely decentralized plan.

There is at present a commendable tendency toward greater centralization of personnel records, and many schools have carried this tendency to the point where they attempt to bring together all important information about each pupil on a single cumulative record. It should be clearly understood, however, that back of any really meaningful cumulative record system there is much detailed and noncentralized information in the records of the various individual teachers and counselors. It is the possession of these detailed and decentralized records that enables the teachers to prepare valid summary reports for the cumulative records.

Some schools that are convinced of the wisdom of centralized cumulative records do not find it practicable to centralize their records to such a degree that they have only one single cumulative record form. In very large schools, the mere consideration of distance from one part of the plant to the other may make it preferable for certain departments to have their own cumulative records and to report only a very abbreviated summary of their own record to be entered on the cumulative record form in the central office. This is true particularly of health and physical education departments. Consequently, cumulative health records have been developed in a good many schools on a parallel to the more comprehensive cumulative records to be found in the principal's office.

RECORDS CLASSIFIED ACCORDING TO THE NATURE OF THE CENTRALIZING UNIT

In general, any one of three plans may be used to bring together and to organize in a central filing system the data about individual pupils. A school may follow the practice of filing loose sheets in cumulative folders, or it may transfer the data annually to a cumulative card or folder, or it may use a combination of the two. Let us see how each one works and consider its advantages and disadvantages.

The cumulative folder should be of the expanding

type, sufficiently large to hold an accumulation of several years' data for a given pupil. It may be used for filing teachers' reports about the pupil, a sample of his work, his test papers, anecdotal records, and any other information that will help to give a comprehensive picture of the pupil as a growing individual.

One difficulty in the use of the cumulative folder is that the accumulation of information will probably after a time become unwieldy, so that the very volume of the data, together with the fact that the information is on loose sheets, makes organization difficult. This difficulty may be met to some extent by utilizing a folder that has separate compartments for different kinds of data.

While a carefully organized folder is no doubt very helpful for a counselor or for anyone who can spend considerable time studying one individual, it is almost impossible for a principal, classroom teacher, or counselor to make a quick appraisal of a pupil through the use of a folder containing many loose papers. In seems desirable, therefore, to have the most significant information recorded on a cumulative record card that can be handled easily and read quickly. Some schools prefer to depend entirely on the cumulative card or set of cards and so do not maintain any cumulative folders at all. This may be a workable plan if the cumulative record card is large and if it is filled out in full, but many of the "shorthand" notations on the cumulative record may lose much of their meaning for subsequent users of the card when they are completely divorced from the original data from which they were abstracted.

A plan that involves the maintaining of both a system of cumulative record cards and a set of cumulative folders seems to be the ideal arrangement, if a school has a sufficient office staff for the handling of such a system. A plan of this kind has three possible variants, which are as follows: (1) the use of the cumulative record as the folder in which the papers containing more detailed information about the pupil are filed; (2) the filing of the cumulative record cards and other information in the same folder; and (3) the maintenance of separate files of folders and record cards. A number of the well-known cumulative record forms can be used in the manner first described, if the school wishes to employ them as file folders as well as record folders. Among these are the cumulative record folders of the American Council on Education, the National Association of Secondary-School Principals, and the Los Angeles City Schools. The main difficulty in the use of the cumulative card as an individual file holder is that it is not large nor durable enough to hold all the papers, if a serious attempt is made to assemble and retain all the significant information about each pupil. Moreover, the utility of a record card which serves as a file folder will be reduced because the card will tend to become soiled and difficult to read, and if filled with papers, cannot be handled quickly and efficiently, either in entering data or in reading the entries that have already been made.

The idea of providing individual folders for filing cumulative record cards along with other papers seems not to have found its way into practice in many schools, but there is one good illustration of such a plan among the record forms that have been devised by individual schools. The Riverside, California, schools have provided for the filing of an educational record, a social and personal record, and a health record along with special data in an 8½-by-11-inch folder.

There is a mechanical difficulty in filing cumulative record cards and other papers in the same folder. After a pupil has been in school for several years, his folder will probably become well filled and rather unwieldy. His cumulative cards cannot easily be consulted without removing the whole folder from the file; yet to take the whole folder out of the file to get one or two items of information about a pupil is time-consuming. Such a plan runs the hazard of discouraging teachers from going to the cumulative records frequently.

Separate files of cumulative record forms and individual folders placed in the same office seem to be the best arrangement. This plan is illustrated by files that have been kept in the records office of the University of Chicago Laboratory Schools. Each pupil's cumulative record from the kindergarten through high school was kept on four "master" cards, and this cumulative record was paralleled by a large cumulative file holder in which samples of the pupil's work, teachers' reports, correspondence between the school and the parents, and other significant data were filed. A plan of this kind efficiently serves the needs of the teacher who wishes to obtain a quick general picture of the pupil's work, or to secure without loss of time certain specific items from the cumulative record, and the case worker or counselor who is making a detailed study of the pupil.

RECORDS CLASSIFIED ACCORDING TO PERMANENCY

Some forms used in guidance departments are designed merely to serve an immediate purpose, such as the summoning of pupils to appear at the counselor's office at a certain time, or as interoffice communication about pupils. Although it is true that if these slips are later filed in the counselor's office they will help to round out the picture concerning the pupil, they are less significant and can be eliminated more readily from consideration than certain other forms.

A second, and much more important, class of guidance

records includes a variety of forms that are intended to be more or less permanent. Under a system in which a record *folder* is the main vehicle for organizing and preserving in a relatively permanent form the counselor's records about individual pupils, these records will be carefully filed in the folder, will be preserved at least until the pupil is graduated, and will serve as the counselor's principal source of cumulative information about each pupil. If there is a comprehensive system of cumulative record *cards,* on the other hand, many of the data will be transferred to the cumulative cards and the forms for original entry will be much less important as permanent sources of information, although they may well be preserved to supplement the cumulative record cards. Illustrations of the semipermanent record forms falling into this category are blanks for securing information about students, reports from schools previously attended by the pupil, forms for teacher estimates concerning pupils, forms for pupils' self-estimates, reports on causes of failure, records of interviews,[14] forms for summarizing the results of one testing program, and forms which pupils may use in giving statements of their vocational interests.

Ingenious counselors and directors of guidance often introduce local innovations to reduce the number of different records and the amount of paper work involved. For instance, in a recent article the central recording and dictating equipment used in one school system for this purpose is explained.[15] Storing pupil records on microfilm is also receiving increased attention.[16]

A third, and still more important, class of counselor's records consists of forms that are designed to provide a permanent and cumulative picture of pupil development. These cumulative records have so close a relationship to the efficiency of the guidance program that a separate chapter may profitably be devoted to a discussion of them.

[14] Lou Utter. "Keeping a Record of Your Counseling Efforts," *Vocational Guidance Quarterly,* VIII (Autumn 1959), 12–14.

[15] Gordon Ellis. "A New Approach to Student Records," *Personnel and Guidance Journal,* XLI (April 1963), 725–729.

[16] John Carruth. "Saving Space with Microfilm," *Educational Executive Overview,* III (August 1962), 51–52; O. C. Lewis. "How to Store Permanent Pupil Records and Save Space," *School Management,* VII (August 1963), 56–58.

CHAPTER XIII

Cumulative Records in a Guidance Program

WHAT THE CUMULATIVE RECORD IS

IN CONTRAST TO SOME OF THE TERMS USED TO characterize pupil personnel records, such as school register, report card, transcript of credits, and permanent record card, the term *cumulative record* is a twentieth-century addition to educational terminology. Cumulative records are rarely mentioned in the literature prior to 1925, and the term did not come into common usage until after 1930. By 1950, the term was beginning to take on common meaning, but in the 1960s the meaning is again being diffused in many places. From a non-technical standpoint, the words *cumulative record* are properly applied to any record that is formed or becomes larger by successive additions. Thus all permanent record forms that are designed to cover a period of years, even though they are very sketchy, may be called cumulative records. The term is also used in a restricted sense to designate the newer type of record forms in which emphasis is placed on objective measurements and personality data, as contrasted with the older type of permanent record that was confined largely to attendance, school marks, and credits. It has sometimes been used, in a still more restricted sense, to apply to the cumulative record forms of the American Council on Education and to adaptations thereof. In the present discussion, *cumulative record* will be used in a rather broad sense and will apply to all records that make provision for the accumulation of significant and comprehensive information about an individual pupil over a period of years—although the illustrations will be drawn mainly from the American Council forms and their adaptations.

VARIATIONS IN RECORD FORMS

Over the years, surveys of cumulative record forms, such as those by Heck (9), Troxel and Koos (25), and Segel (19), show great variations among schools in the number and kinds of items included. Differences in local conditions, of course, make a certain amount of diversity in record forms desirable, but an extremely wide variability in the records of different schools unquestionably creates difficult problems in the exchange of records and in their efficient use by school officers. Herein lies a reason, among others, that some administrators so readily accept the kind of uniform transcript that results from application of data processing equipment to record keeping.

Segel (19) classified the items found on the records of 177 school systems into 17 categories and tabulated the frequency of occurrence of each type of item. The types of items found most frequently were scholarship (marks), school progress, attendance, entrance and withdrawal, home conditions and family history, intelligence test results, social and character ratings, and health. Regardless of the variability in details, it is advisable for a good cumulative record to be based as largely as possible on objective data, to be organized into annual divisions, and to present an all-round picture of individual development rather than one narrowly confined to academic achievement.

In the past, numerous schools have not kept extensive pupil records because of the amount of clerical work required. Now, however, high-speed computers are making good records possible for many more schools.

THE CORE OF THE GUIDANCE PROGRAM

Objective data about individuals are believed to be essential to effective guidance, but there is a danger that a program in which such data have a leading place will become confused and obscured by a multitude of unrelated trivia. A single datum, no matter how objective and valid, is of little value; it is only when data are brought together and related, both laterally and chronologically, that they become meaningful. The device by means of which different kinds of information are brought together and organized is a comprehensive individual *cumulative record*. This record is an important feature of every guidance program that takes its origin from an objective study of the individual. This record ties the loose ends together.

Although the best possible cumulative record cannot in itself insure successful guidance in a school, no plan of advising and counseling students can rise to the level of a thorough guidance program unless it includes a cumulative record *which is understood and used by counselors and teachers alike*. The cumulative record is at once the main technique for the education of the faculty and the strategic organizational device in the whole guidance program.

The value of the cumulative record is recognized in the schools of other countries, as well as in those of the United States. The 26th International Conference on Public Education, meeting in Geneva, Switzerland, in 1963, adopted as one of its recommendations the following:

"It is essential that a cumulative record card be kept throughout the pupil's school life and should include all aspects of his development, such as scholastic achievements and day-to-day behavior; it should be compiled by sufficiently competent teachers; the record is to be kept confidential and be used only for helping educational and vocational guidance" (23:7).

AMERICAN COUNCIL CUMULATIVE RECORD FORMS

Much of the present interest in the comprehensive type of cumulative record can be traced back to the pioneer work that was done in 1928 by the Committee on Personnel Methods of the American Council on Education, and in particular to the work of Professors Ben D. Wood, of Columbia University, and E. L. Clark, of Northwestern University, in devising the original American Council cumulative record folder. Following the work of that committee, the American Council on Education published four cumulative record forms, including a folder for college students, a folder for secondary school pupils, a card for elementary school pupils, and a card that could be used in either the elementary or the secondary school. Approximately half a million of these record forms were distributed; and in addition, the forms influenced the records of many other organizations and countless local school systems.

In 1940, the Council appointed a committee, with Eugene Randolph Smith as chairman, for the purpose of revising the cumulative record forms to take into account the newer trends and progress that had been made in the recording of personnel data by certain other organizations, such as the Progressive Education Association. The Smith committee prepared revisions which included cumulative record folders for junior and senior high schools, for colleges, for Grades 4, 5, and 6, and for the primary grades. This extensive and comprehensive set of cumulative record forms has been widely used for more than 20 years. A more detailed explanation of the nature of these forms will be given later in this chapter.

THE EDUCATIONAL RECORDS BUREAU ADAPTATION OF THE AMERICAN COUNCIL CUMULATIVE RECORD FORM

One of the best-known adaptations of the original American Council form is the Educational Records Bureau Cumulative Record Card for Independent Schools which was devised by Eleanor Perry Wood and Winston B. Stevens. This type of form is illustrated by the records of three pupils in Form 9A, B, and C.[1]

The front of the card, which is made to fit the ordinary letter-size file, is devoted almost entirely to a record of subjects, marks, and credits, and to an extensive test record. The test results are reported in both tabular and graphic form; in fact, one of the distinguishing features of the original American Council form and its adaptations is the gridiron graph in which the results are shown in terms of percentile ratings arranged according to the sigma scale. The back of the card has space for the recording of a variety of less objective data, including information on discipline, home influences and cooperation, mental and emotional factors, physical and athletic development, extracurricular activities and interests, notable accomplishments and experiences, educational plans, and personality. The whole card is planned for a six-year record, and all the data for any given year are confined to a single column so that the cumulative effect is immediately apparent.

This type of record form is easy to understand and

[1] All names and dates in illustrative forms have been changed, but the data are based on real pupils.

NAME LEWIS, PAUL R. BIRTHDATE 12-29-47

	1958-1959	1959-1960	1960-1961	1961-1962	1962-1963	1963-1964
YEAR	1958-1959	1959-1960	1960-1961	1961-1962	1962-1963	1963-1964
SCHOOL	HAWTHORNE					
GRADE	6 6	7 7	8 8 13 13	14 9 9	15 10 10	16 11 11
MENTAL AGE	45-0	16-6 12				
CHRON AGE	11					

SUBJECTS, GRADES AND CREDITS

SUBJECT	1st Sem	2nd Sem
Eng.	A	A
Arith.	B	A
Sci.	A	A
Soc. Stud.	A	A
Art	S	S

SUBJECT	1st Sem	2nd Sem
Eng.	A	A
Arith.	A	A
Sci.	A	B
Soc. Stud.	A	A
Music	S	S

SUBJECT	1st Sem	2nd Sem
Eng.	A	A
Lit.	B	B
Lat.	A	B
Arith.	A	A
Soc. Stud.	A	B

SUBJECT	1st Sem	2nd Sem
Eng. I	A	A
Fr. I	A	A
Alg. I	B	A
Anc. Hist.	A	A

SUBJECT	1st Sem	2nd Sem
Eng. II	A	B
Fr. II	A	A
Pl. Geom.	A	A
Wld. Hist.	A	A

SUBJECT	1st Sem	2nd Sem
Eng. III	B	A
Fr. III	A	B
Alg. II	B	A
Phys.	A	A

ACADEMIC APTITUDE AND READING

TEST	SCORE M.A.	I.Q.	%ile
Kuhlmann-Anderson	45-0	138	90
	15-0		86
Calif. Ment. Mat.	16-6	140	92
Non-Tot. Ment.Fact.			
Traxler Sil. Read.-4	139		97
S.E.B.Jr. Verb.	647		96
Sch. Apt.-DR Num.	639	147	91
Traxler Sil. Read.-1			95
Amer. Council Psych.-1952		126	96
Amer. Council Psych.-1949		147	98
Amer. Council Psych.-1954		133	93

ACHIEVEMENT TEST SCORES AND PERCENTILES

TEST	Score E.A.	%ile
Stan.Ach-Rev.D-Tot.Av.	15.0	95
Av. Read.	12.0	94
Lang. Us.	12.3	94
Av. Arith.	9.9	91
Lit.	13.5	95
Av. Soc. St.	12.2	96
Elem. Sci.	13.5	97
Spell.	11.0	95

TEST	Score E.A.	%ile
Stan.Ach-Rev.H-Tot.Av.		96
Av. Read.	13.7	96
Lang. Us.	14.4+	96
Av. Arith.	14.2	94
Lit.	14.4+	98
Av. Soc. St.	14.4	99
Elem. Sci.	14.1	99
Spell.	14.4+	99
Lat.Coop.Q.8+1yr.	66	94
Vocab.	54	86
Gram.	57	84

TEST	Score E.A.	%ile
Eng.-Coop Z		98
A.-Mech.of Exp.	52	63
C2-Read.Comp.	76	93
Vocab.	63	88
Speed	69	84
Level	86	99
Fr.Coop P.Q.10-2yrs	64	96
Read.	62	97
Vocab.	66	94
Geom.	60	90
Pl.Geom.-Coop Z	64	70
Anc.Hist.-Coop P	73	92

TEST	Score E.A.	%ile
Eng.-Coop Y		98
A.-Mech.of Exp.	68	97
C2-Read.Comp.	66	88
Vocab.	69	85
Speed	66	83
Level	60	71
Fr.Coop.Q.Gr.10-2yrs	87	89
Read.	83	97
Vocab.	89	100
Geom.	79	99
Int.Alg.-Coop T	70	91
Cum.Wld.Hist.-AM	133	97

TEST	Score E.A.	%ile
Eng.-Coop RX		99
A.-Mech.of Exp.	78	99
C2-Read.Comp.	75	93
Vocab.	72	87
Speed	77	94
Level	88	92
Fr.Coop Q.Gr.-3yrs.	90	90
Read.	83	88
Vocab.	79	94
Int.Alg.-Coop T	70	91
Phys.Coop ERB-SX	58	91

SCHOOL GRADES

O PUBLIC ⊕ LOCAL ● INDEPENDENT SCHOOL
TEST PERCENTILES

CUMULATIVE RECORD FOR INDEPENDENT SCHOOLS **FORM 9A (Front).**

NAME	M.F.	BIRTHDATE—PLACE	GEN'L HEALTH	RELIGION	RACE OR NAT'L'TY	OCCUPATION	ADDRESS
LEWIS, PAUL R.		12-29-47 CHICAGO, ILL.	GOOD	EPISC.	AMERICAN	STUDENT	5925 MARYLAND AVENUE CHICAGO ILL.
FATHER LEWIS, GEORGE D.		6-19-18 BUFFALO, N.Y.	EXCELLENT	"	"	PUBLIC ACCOUNTANT	RES. 5925 MARYLAND AVENUE CHICAGO ILL. BUS. 254 N. LASALLE STREET CHICAGO ILL.
MOTHER LEWIS, JOSEPHINE WARD		8-23-23 SPRINGFIELD, MO.	GOOD	"	"	HOUSEWIFE	RES. 5925 MARYLAND AVENUE CHICAGO ILL. BUS.
STEP-PARENT OR GUARDIAN							RES. BUS.

LANGUAGE SPOKEN IN HOME — BEFORE 10— ENGLISH AFTER 10— ENGLISH

TYPE OF COMMUNITY — BEFORE 10— RESIDENTIAL—CITY HOMES & APTS. AFTER 10— RESIDENTIAL—CITY HOMES & APTS.

IF PARENTS SEPARATED GIVE DATE

	1958-59 / 11	1959-60 / 12	1960-61 / 13	1961-62 / 14	1962-63 / 15	1963-64 / 16
YEAR AND AGE						
ADVISER	DABNEY	DABNEY	WINSLOW	WINSLOW	GOFF	GOFF
ATTENDANCE	A REGULAR T	A ABSENT 5 DAYS WITH COLDS T	A REGULAR ATTENDANCE T	A OUT THREE WEEKS WITH PNEUMONIA T	A REGULAR ATTENDANCE T	A REGULAR T
DISCIPLINE	GOOD	FAIR - INCLINED TO BE NOISY	GOOD	EXCELLENT	GOOD	EXCELLENT
HOME INFLUENCES AND COOPERATION	PARENTS INTERESTED AND COOPERATIVE	VERY GOOD	FINE HOME BACKGROUND	ALWAYS WILLING TO COOPERATE	INTERESTED IN HELPING PAUL PLAN HIS FUTURE	SUPERIOR
MENTAL AND EMOTIONAL	VERY INTELLIGENT AND DEPENDABLE. INCLINED TO BE NERVOUS. GETS SO EXCITED IN CLASS HE STUTTERS AT TIMES	STILL SOMEWHAT EXCITABLE AND HIGH STRUNG BUT IS DEVELOPING GOOD SELF-CONTROL	VERY BRIGHT. AN ALL-ROUND GOOD STUDENT	INTELLIGENT AND EMOTIONALLY STABLE	SPLENDID ABILITY. MATERIAL FOR A GOOD COLLEGE	INTELLIGENT AND WELL-BALANCED
PHYSICAL AND ATHLETIC	HEALTH GENERALLY GOOD. SLIGHTLY OVER-ACTIVE THYROID. WEARS GLASSES	GOOD HEALTH EXCEPT FOR OCCASIONAL COLDS. INTERESTED IN BASEBALL	GOOD. A LITTLE NEARSIGHTED BUT VISION NORMAL WITH GLASSES	HAD A SET-BACK WITH PNEUMONIA IN MIDDLE OF YEAR BUT MADE QUICK RECOVERY	VERY GOOD. RAPID PHYSICAL DEVELOPMENT THIS YEAR. OUT FOR BASKETBALL AND TRACK TEAM	GOOD. IS ACTIVE IN BASKETBALL, TRACK & GOLF. RIFLE CLUB
EXTRA-CURRICULAR ACTIVITIES AND INTERESTS	BUILDS MODEL SHIPS. COLLECTS STAMPS. READS MANY BOOKS. HAS DUCKS AND RABBITS FOR PETS	MAKES MODEL SHIPS AND PLANES. INTERESTED IN MILITARY HISTORY AND HISTORY OF THE AIRPLANE	BUILDING MODELS ILLUSTRATING STAGES IN DEVELOPMENT OF AIRPLANE. READING MILITARY AND NAVAL HISTORY	MODEL PLANES AND SHIPS. EXTENSIVE READING IN HISTORY AND SCIENCE. SUMMER CAMP	BOAT BUILDING. OVERHAULING AND RE-BUILDING AUTOMOBILE ENGINE. SUMMER CAMP	BOAT BUILDING. SAILING. MOUNTAIN CLIMBING. COUNSELOR IN SUMMER CAMP
NOTABLE ACCOMPLISHMENTS AND EXPERIENCES	ONE OF THE LEADERS IN HIS CLASS. VERY POPULAR	LEADS THE CLASS IN GENERAL ABILITY. TOOK TRIP TO MEXICO CITY LAST SUMMER	WINNING PERSONALITY MAKES HIM A LEADER. ORGANIZED CLUB OF BOYS INTERESTED IN MODEL SHIPS & PLANES	VICE-PRESIDENT OF HIS CLASS	CLASS PRESIDENT. ELECTED TO STUDENT COUNCIL	STUDENT COUNCIL. RIFLE CLUB TEAM
EDUCATIONAL PLANS	NO DEFINITE PLANS	PLANS TO TAKE COLLEGE PREPARATORY COURSE	INTERESTED IN NAVAL ACADEMY	THINKS HE PREFERS SMALL TO MEDIUM SIZED COLLEGE FOR MEN	IS CONSIDERING HAMILTON, LEHIGH, AMHERST AND SEVERAL OTHER COLLEGES	WILL APPLY TO AMHERST COLLEGE. PLANS TO MAJOR IN SOCIAL SCIENCE
PERSONALITY RATINGS (+2, +1, 0, -1, -2)	A BOY OF EXCELLENT PROMISE	POPULAR & A NATURAL LEADER	ABILITY TO WORK, COOPERATE, ORGANIZE	SPLENDID PERSONAL QUALITIES	SPLENDID PERSONAL QUALITIES	COOPERATION LEADERSHIP / OUTSTANDING PERSONALITY

REMARKS: AN OUTSTANDING BOY IN EVERY WAY. SHOULD BE A REAL ASSET TO HIS COLLEGE. VOCATIONAL AIM IS NOT YET DEFINITE, BUT WILL DECIDE DURING SENIOR YEAR OF HIGH SCHOOL. IS THINKING OF GRADUATE DEGREE IN POLITICAL SCIENCE AND THEN SOME ASPECT OF DIPLOMATIC SERVICE.

FORM 9A (Back).

NAME Nichols, Frank C.   BIRTHDATE 1-3-46

YEAR	1958-1959	1959-1960	1960-1961	1961-1962	1922-1963	1923-1964
SCHOOL	Spring Valley					
GRADE	7	8	9	10	11	12
MENTAL AGE	14-2	15-0	15	16	17	18
CHRON AGE	13	14	15	16	17	18

SUBJECTS, GRADES AND CREDITS

SUBJECT	1st Sem	2nd Sem	SUBJECT	1st Sem	2nd Sem	SUBJECT	1st Sem	2nd Sem	SUBJECT	1st Sem	2nd Sem	SUBJECT	1st Sem	2nd Sem	SUBJECT	1st Sem	2nd Sem
Eng.	C	C	Eng.	C	C	Eng. I	C	C	Eng. II	C	D	Eng. III	C	D	Eng. IV	C	C
Arith.	C	C	Lat.	F	F	Ger. I	D	D	Ger. II	D	D	Fusion Math.	D	D	Chem.	D	C
Soc. Stud.	C	D	Arith.	C	C	Alg. I	C	D	Geom.	C	B	Phys.	D	D	Amer. Hist.	D	C
			Soc. Stud.	D	C	Ang. Hist.	C	C	Biol.	C	C	Econ.	C	C	Prob. of Dem.	D	C

ACADEMIC APTITUDE AND READING

TEST	SCORE M.A.	I.Q.	%ile	TEST	SCORE M.A.	I.Q.	%ile	TEST	SCORE M.A.	I.Q.	%ile	TEST	SCORE M.A.	I.Q.	%ile	TEST	SCORE M.A.	I.Q.	%ile	TEST	SCORE M.A.	I.Q.	%ile
Kuhlmann-Anderson	14-2	111	30	Kuhlmann-Anderson	15-0	108	24	Amer. Council Psych.-1947	81		30	Amer. Council Psych.-1952	87		41	Amer. Council Psych.-1949	111		53	Amer. Council Psych.-1954	101		38
Traxler Silent Read.-3	90		35	Diag. Read. Rate-230 Survey-C TetComp 44				Adv. Div. Mid-Sc.	.156		27															

ACHIEVEMENT TEST SCORES AND PERCENTILES

TEST	SCORE E.A.	%ile	TEST	SCORE E.A.	%ile	TEST	SCORE E.A.	%ile	TEST	SCORE E.A.	%ile	TEST	SCORE E.A.	%ile	TEST	SCORE E.A.	%ile
Stan. Ach. D-Int.	14-4	37	Stan. Ach. Adv.F-Int.	15-8	34	Eng.-Coop. S		34	Eng.-Coop. Z		24	Eng.-Coop. Y		32	Eng.-Coop. RX		24
Av. Read.	9.6	45	Av. Read.	10.5	47	A.-Mech. of Exp.	4.2	13	A.-Mech. of Exp.	4.5	19	A.-Mech. of Exp.	5.3	32	A.-Mech of Exp.	5.3	24
Lang. Us.	10.0	49	Lang. Us.	10.6	37	C2-Read. Comp.	4.7	25	C2-Read. Comp.	3.4	21	C2-Read. Comp.	6.1	62	C2-Read. Comp.	6.5	63
Av. Arith.	8.1	31	Av. Arith.	9.6	36	Vocab.	4.8	35	Vocab.	4.9	33	Vocab.	5.6	47	Vocab.	5.9	51
Lit.	10.3	50	Lit.	11.3	51	Speed	4.9	29	Speed	6.0	61	Speed	6.2	61	Speed	6.7	67
Av. Soc. St.	7.4	18	Av. Soc. St.	8.8	24	Level	4.5	22	Level	5.3	30	Level	6.4	74	Level	6.7	67
Elem. Sci.	8.5	25	Elem. Sci.	9.2	32	Fr-Coop. Gr3-81 yr.	4.8	7	Fr. Coop. Pch4o-1yrs	4.8	7	Int.Alg.-Coop. Z		59	Trig.-Coop. V		54
Spell.	5.9	10	Spell.			Speed Read-1 yr.			Read.	3.8	5	Phys.-Coop.ERB-RX		25	Chem.-Coop.ERB-SX		40
			Vocab.	34	6	Vocab.	3.9	16	Vocab.	5.5	12	Econ.-Coop. S		33	Chem.-Coop.ERB-SX	115	46
			Gram.	38	9	Elem.Alg-Coop. S	5.8	48	Elem. Alg.-Coop. Y	6.5	73				Early Hist.-Am.		
			Math.789-Coop.RO	.57	51	Eng.Hist.-Coop.O	.56	38	Biol.-Coop.ERB-TX	.71	36						

FORM 9B (Front).

CUMULATIVE RECORD FOR INDEPENDENT SCHOOLS

EDUCATIONAL RECORDS BUREAU   21 AUDUBON AVENUE, NEW YORK 32, N. Y.

Key: O PUBLIC   ⊕ INDEPENDENT SCHOOL (LOCAL)   ⊗ SCHOOL GRADES — TEST PERCENTILES

NAME	M. F.	BIRTHDATE—PLACE	GEN'L HEALTH	RELIGION	RACE OR NAT'L'TY	OCCUPATION	ADDRESS
Nichols, Frank C.		1-3-46 St. Louis, Mo.	Good	Protestant	American	Student	535 River Avenue Clayton Mo.
FATHER Nichols, T.D.		6-15-11 Dayton, Ohio	Good	"	English-Amer.	Sales Manager, Eastern Products Co.	RES. 535 River Avenue Clayton Mo. BUS. 2348 Park Street, St. Louis Mo.
MOTHER Nichols, Janet Bauer		10-7-22 Milwaukee Wis.	Fair	"	German-Amer.	Housewife	RES. 535 River Avenue Clayton Mo. BUS.
STEP-PARENT OR GUARDIAN							RES. BUS.

LANGUAGE SPOKEN IN HOME — BEFORE 10— English AFTER 10— English

TYPE OF COMMUNITY — BEFORE 10— Residential AFTER 10— Residential

IF PARENTS SEPARATED GIVE DATE — 1943-64

YEAR AND AGE	1958-59 13	1959-60 14	1960-61 15	1961-62 16	1962-63 17	1943-64 18
ADVISER	Evans	Evans	Pearce	Pearce	Duell	Duell
ATTENDANCE	A Frequent absences because of illness T	A One week- Tonsilectomy T	A Four days absence during year T	A Regular attendance I	A Regular T	A Regular T
DISCIPLINE	Erratic Lacks interest	Fair	Likeable youngster but not very dependable	Real desire to cooperate, but some disagreement between parents over boy	Still lacks self-discipline	Attitude considerably more mature this year
HOME INFLUENCES AND COOPERATION	Seemingly good home background Parents are widely traveled and intelligent	Good cooperation Mother supervises son carefully	Reasonably good Father away a good deal Mother may be overprotective	(see above)	Fair Some tension in home	Good cooperation Parents hope son will go to college
MENTAL AND EMOTIONAL	Fair intelligence but wastes time day dreaming Not much drive	Has difficulty concentrating on his work	Has fair ability but tends to give up when the work is difficult	Still something of a day dreamer except when interested as he was in math this year	Average ability, but below average effort although he is improving	Still easy going, but is showing better general interest and effort
PHYSICAL AND ATHLETIC	Fair health except for frequent colds Interested in all sports	Health better since tonsils out this fall Improving in athletics	Good health Growing rapidly Active in basketball and baseball	Good health Large, strong boy Spends much time in sports	Very good health On basketball team Out for football	Good health Basketball Football
EXTRA-CURRICULAR ACTIVITIES AND INTERESTS	Scouts Summer camp	Scouts	Summer camp Hunting & fishing Likes to tinker with old motors	Rifle club Spends much time watching television	Rifle club Played on town basketball team during summer	Rifle club All sports Boats
NOTABLE ACCOMPLISHMENTS AND EXPERIENCES	Has traveled widely with parents	Went to Europe with parents during the summer		Worked with boy friend building "hot rod" during summer		Worked in manufacturing plant three months past summer
EDUCATIONAL PLANS	None as yet	None	No definite plans beyond high school graduation	No plans for college Thinks he will go to work after high school	Plans not clarified Would like to go to college if he could make the basketball team	No definite educational plans but talks of preparing for business career like his father's
PERSONALITY RATINGS (+2, +1, 0, -1, -2)	Somewhat disorganized	Average for boys his age	Happy-Go-Lucky youngster	Cooperation; Initiative, Industry; Workmanship	Relaxed and careless	Pleasant but not forceful

REMARKS: General scholastic aptitude and achievement somewhat below average for his group. Has much interest and ability in sports but lacks mental drive. Is popular with his classmates, but is not a leader.

FORM 9B (Back).

NAME _Crawford John S._   BIRTHDATE _2-9-45_

YEAR	1960-1961	1961-1962	1962-1963	1963-1944		
SCHOOL	Underhill				SUBJECT	SUBJECT
GRADE	9	10	11	12		
MENTAL AGE	9	10	11	12		
CHRON AGE	16	17	18	19		

SUBJECTS, GRADES AND CREDITS

ACADEMIC APTITUDE

TEST	SCORE M.A	I.Q.	%ile	TEST	SCORE M.A	I.Q.	%ile	TEST	SCORE M.A	I.Q.	%ile	TEST	SCORE M.A	I.Q.	%ile
Amer. Council Psych-1946 Tot.	82		47	Amer. Council Psych-1952 Tot.	88		30	Amer. Council Psych-1949 Tot.	101		35	Amer. Council Psych-1954 Tot.	103		22
Q-Score	38		62	Q-Score	42		33	Q-Score	45		58	Q-Score	43		59
L-Score	44		35	L-Score	46		19	L-Score	56		24	L-Score	60		31

ACHIEVEMENT TEST SCORES AND PERCENTILES

TEST	SCORE E.A	%ile	TEST	SCORE E.A	%ile	TEST	SCORE E.A	%ile	TEST	SCORE E.A Mid.Sc.	%ile
Burg. Read. Rate-G Tot. Comp.	2.38	41	Eng.-Coop Z	45	24	Iowa Sil.Read-Adv.Tot.	172	31	Iowa Sil.Read-Adv.Com.	179	34
Eng.-Coop S			A-Mech.of Exp.	51	25	Eng.-Coop Y			Eng.-Coop RX		34
A-Mech.of Exp.	4.3	22	C2-Read Comp.	54	31	A-Mech.of Exp.	54	36	A-Mech.of Exp.	55	31
C2-Read Comp.	4.7	25	Lit Comp & App Coop R	59	34	C2-Read Comp.	51	17	C2-Read Comp.	56	29
Lit Comp & App Coop R	4.9	16	Fr.Coop P Gr.10-2yrs	4.9		Lit Comp & App Coop T	47	3	Lit Comp & App Coop T	52	10
Fr. Coop Q Gr.9-1yr	2.9	10	Lat.Coop P Gr.10-3yr	6.2		Fr.Coop R Gr.11-3yrs	64	23	Fr.Coop R Gr.12-4yr	66	6
Lat.Coop Q Gr.9 Adv.	5.1		Int.Alg.-Coop Y		57	Lat.Coop Q Gr.11-3yrs	64	7	Lat.Coop Q Gr.12-4yrs	55	2
Elem.Alg.-Coop Y	6.1	57	Biol.Coop ERB-TX	112	83	Pl.Geom.-Coop Z			Phys.Coop ERB-SX	4.9	82
Gen.Sci.-Coop Y	6.5	79				Chem.Coop ERB-RX	80	77	Crary Amer.Hist.-Am	110	30

GR %ile
99
98
96
93
89
84
77
69
60
50
40
31
23
16
11
7
4
2
1

SCHOOL GRADES ○
TEST PERCENTILES
○ PUBLIC   ⊕ LOCAL   ● INDEPENDENT SCHOOL

CUMULATIVE RECORD FOR INDEPENDENT SCHOOLS   EDUCATIONAL RECORDS BUREAU   21 AUDUBON AVENUE, NEW YORK-32, N. Y.

FORM 9C.

use, except for the fact that the graph of test scores, although the clearest phase of the record to one familiar with graphs of this kind, may seem somewhat puzzling to persons who have had no experience with it. As already indicated, the percentile scale at the left is based on the sigma scale, and the distance between successive percentiles is much smaller near the median than at the extremes. The median, or 50th percentile, is marked by the heavy line going horizontally across the graph. The symbols at the top—Jy, Au, S, O, and so forth—stand for the months of the year. As a convenience, the months are grouped according to school years rather than calendar years.

The percentile data that are shown in the table of scores are also entered in the graph. The small dots on the graph show the placement of the various percentiles, the dots being identified by the abbreviated names of the tests printed near them. For example, when the first pupil, Paul R. Lewis (Form 9A), was in the sixth grade, his Kuhlmann-Anderson mental age, 15–0, corresponded to an independent school percentile rating of 86 on a test taken in October, 1958. The dot has been placed under "O" and opposite the level of 86 in the percentile scale, and has been labeled "M.A." to indicate that it stands for the percentile rating on mental age. The percentile shows that the pupil's mental age was up to or above those of 86 percent of the independent school sixth-grade pupils whose results were used in the norms for the Kuhlmann-Anderson test.

The percentile points for tests that are in the same subject field from year to year are connected by lines so that one can readily follow a particular type of aptitude or achievement throughout the whole period covered by the test. For example, one of the lines in the illustration runs from the Stanford elementary science percentile in Grade 6 to the Stanford elementary science percentile in Grade 7, thence to the science percentile in Grade 8, and so forth. Achievement percentiles are connected by solid lines, academic aptitude percentiles by broken lines, and chronological age percentiles by dotted lines.

The test record of Paul R. Lewis is an exceptionally favorable one. The graph shows at a glance that all his academic aptitude and achievement scores were well above the independent school median throughout the six-year history. In fact, except for Latin reading in Grade 8, elementary algebra and mechanics of expression in Grade 9, and speed and level of reading comprehension in Grade 10, all his scores were at or above the 84th percentile, or at least one standard deviation above the median for the independent school population.

The boy's scholastic record is shown near the top of the card. Notwithstanding the limitations in letter grades unsupported by comments explaining the grades, it is evident that the pupil's school work is in agreement with his very high test record.

The information given on the back of the card, as shown in Form 9A, verifies the impression that Paul Lewis is an outstanding boy. Not only is he a good student, but he is a leader of his classmates, and he is reported to have excellent personal qualities. The boy obviously has the ability and preparation for very successful work in a highly selective college, and one would predict that he will make a fine record in college if he continues to be serious in purpose. It may be observed in passing that a record of this kind furnishes a far better basis for prognosis of college success than is provided simply by a transcript of credits and an admission form filled out by the school when the pupil is near the end of his secondary school course.

The cumulative record of the second boy, Frank C. Nichols (Form 9B), is quite different from the record just examined. Frank is somewhat, although not greatly, older than the average pupil of the same grade level, and he is, in most respects, below the median in academic aptitude and achievement as compared with the independent school group. However, he improved his standing considerably during the last two years of high school, and in his senior year he came up to an average record for his grade level.

The back of this boy's card shows that he comes from a good home, is in good health, and is inclined to be athletic, that he has had advantages of travel and other experiences, but that he is easygoing, lacks initiative, and has as yet no thoroughly defined goal. It seems unlikely that this boy would profit by college attendance, although he might make a reasonably creditable record in a community college or other college whose student body is not highly selected, if he had a definite objective in life. An attempt should be made to determine his vocational interests by means of interviews, the Strong Vocational Interest Blank, the Kuder Preference Record, and other procedures.

As a rule, there is considerable correlation in the results of the different tests, so that the points plotted to represent the scores of a pupil tend to fall in the same general area in the graph. Occasionally, however, the graph of percentiles brings out clearly special aptitudes for certain subjects that might otherwise be undiscovered. For example, consider the test record of John S. Crawford (Form 9C). This boy's scores on most of the tests taken during a four-year period are in the lower half of the scores of the independent school group, but his scores on the science tests—general science, biology, chemistry, and physics—are all in the highest fourth of the independent school distributions for these subjects. Obviously, as far as knowledge is concerned, the prognosis for this boy's success is much better in science than in the other subjects in which he was tested, although he is also somewhat better in mathematics than in the rest of the subjects.

THE AMERICAN COUNCIL FORMS

The American Council cumulative record folders which were prepared by the Smith committee differ from many forms of this kind in that they place less emphasis on subjects, credits, and marks, and more emphasis on behavior descriptions and evaluation of personal qualities. They also allow more space for synthesis and interpretation. An illustrative case, entered on the record card for junior and senior high schools is shown in Form 10.

It will be seen that the card makes provision for a six-year record, which would ordinarily include Grades 7 to 12. There is space near the top of the first page for a summary of the previous school record and for two photographs, the first of which would presumably have been obtained near the time of entrance to the junior high school and the second of which would show the pupil shortly before graduation from high school.[2]

It is intended that the record of academic achievement will consist of much more than grades and credits. Five columns are provided under each year so that each teacher may, if it seems feasible, appraise the pupil with respect to such types of development as work habits, ability to think logically, mastery of technique, oral and written communication, and over all achievement in the course. If it seems desirable to estimate achievement at the end of each semester, one of these categories can be dispensed with, and two of the five columns may be used for appraisal of achievement. The indications of kinds of evaluation are intended as suggestions only, and the committee has purposely left the headings to be filled in by the school so that this portion of the card will be quite flexible and can be made to fit into the local situation.

Considerable space in the center of the card is allowed for the record of test scores in three areas—academic aptitude, reading, and achievement. Results of other tests, such as personality or interest tests, might also be entered in the space provided for the achievement tests.

Below the test record, space is provided for the interpretation of test results and their relation to academic achievement on a two-year basis. An alternate form of the card is printed in which this space has been given over

[2] Photographs in personnel record forms are prohibited by law in some states.

to a percentile graph for schools which desire a graphic, as well as a tabular, record of the test results.

Considerable space near the bottom of the front side of the card is allowed for interests and experiences, educational and occupational plans, health and physical characteristics, and discipline. There is also a small segment for an indication of financial aid. Attendance accounts for only a very limited area, since a detailed attendance report is not important for purposes of the cumulative record. The main purpose of noting attendance in a personnel form is to provide a notation of long periods of absence or of frequent tardiness, since these items of information sometimes help in the interpretation of problems of pupil adjustment.

The top portion of the back of the card gives pertinent information concerning home background and family history. Most of the back of the card is taken up with an extensive description of behavior, to which all staff members who are well acquainted with the pupil should contribute. The description of behavior closely parallels the behavior description form developed during the Eight-Year Study of the Progressive Education Association by a committee of which Dr. Eugene Smith was chairman. Notes and postschool and follow-up information complete the card.

The sample record for Martin Lee Robbins shows how the form may be used to present a comprehensive history of the development of an individual pupil during the junior and senior high school years. This boy entered Grade 7 of the Gillispie Junior High School at the age of 11 years, 9 months, after attendance from the kindergarten to the sixth grade at the Packer Elementary School. His work had been average in the elementary school and no special learning difficulties had been noted. He was thought to be in rather poor health. He progressed at a regular rate through the junior and senior high schools, making passing grades in all subjects. During this period, he had three counselors, one throughout the junior high school, another for Grades 10 and 11, and a third for his senior year.

The record of academic achievement in this school system was based on a three-step scale, H for high, U for usual, and L for low. Ratings were assigned in each subject for work habits, ability to think logically, and oral and written communication; achievement marks, in terms of H, U, and L, were assigned at the end of each semester. This boy was rated U in most respects, although he received a number of H's, particularly in mathematics, and several L's, especially in oral and written communication. His rating for academic achievement tended to be a little better in the senior high school than in the junior high school.

On the whole, the boy had approximately an average

Student Record Card

LAST NAME	FIRST	MIDDLE	NICKNAME	RELIGION	DATE AND PLACE OF BIRTH	SEX	COLOR
ROBBINS	MARTIN	LEE JR.		BAPTIST	12-12-46 PHILADELPHIA PA.	M	W

ADDRESS AND TELEPHONE: 4127 SOUTH 26TH STREET — MAIN 4-9605

PHOTOS (Dated)

PREVIOUS SCHOOL RECORD: Names and Types of Schools Attended, Achievement in Subjects and Activities, School Difficulties Encountered, Summary of Test Results

Attended Packer Elementary School from Kindergarten through 6B. Did very well in arithmetic and social studies. Did average work for his ability in other subjects. No special learning difficulties except in language usage. Health rather delicate.

Name and Type of School Attended	GILLISPIE JR. H.S.	SAME	SAME	ROOSEVELT Sr. H.S.	SAME	SAME
COUNSELOR	MILDRED D. CARSON	SAME	SAME	G. L. OWEN	SAME	HARLAN KENT
AGE (As of Sept. 1)	11-9	12-9	13-9	14-9	15-9	16-9
SCHOOL YEAR AND GRADE	7H 1958-59 7B	8H 1959-60 8B	9B 1960-61 9B	10H 1961-62 10B	10B 1962-63 11B	12B 1963-64 12B

ACADEMIC ACHIEVEMENT

These columns are for analyses of development in fields indicated, and some estimate of achievement. L = Low; U = Usual; H = High.
(Headings might include work habits, ability to think logically, ability to think, achievement communication 1st Sem, 2nd Sem.)

Subject						
English — Written Exp.						
Oral Exp.						
Literature						
Lang. — Latin						
French						
Math. — Gen. Math.						
El. Algebra						
Plane Geom.						
Algebra II						
Science — Gen. Science						
Biology						
Chemistry						
Physics						
Social Studies — Social Studies						
Problems of Democracy						
American History						
Other Subjects — Art						
Mech. Draw.						
Woodwork						
Music						
Physical Education						
Metal Work						

TEST RECORD

	TEST	Mo.	Score	%ile
	KUHLMANN-ANDERSON	13-10 / 13-1	IQ 119 / 117	MA 21 / 40
	CALIF. SHORT FORM MENTAL MAT. TEST	14-1 / MA 110		25 / 38
	AMER. COUNCIL PSYCH.-1947	0	80	39
	AMER. COUNCIL PSYCH.-1952	0	95	42
	AMER. COUNCIL PSYCH.-1948	0	110	48
	AMER. COUNCIL PSYCH.-1954	0	110	55

ACADEMIC APTITUDE (Use M.A. and I.Q. if Preferred)

READING

TEST	Mo.	Score	%ile
TRAXLER SILENT	0	91	44
TRAXLER SILENT	0	94	35
IOWA SIL. ADV. AM	0	167	55
DIAG. READ. RATE	0	225	27
SURVEY-E TO COMP	0	72	46

ACHIEVEMENT AND OTHER TESTS

Reading	228	41	230	34	A. Mech. Exp.	43	18	A. Mech. Exp.	49	28	A. Mech. of Exp.	54 34
Vocabulary	231	35	238	38	C-2 Read Comp.	51	41	C-2 Read Comp.	54	57	C-2 Read Comp.	62 69
Arith. Fund.	291	76	298	67	Lat.Coop.Q.Elem.Tot.Ap.	49	30	Lat.Coop.R.Adv.Tot.Ap	59	46	Fr. Coop.S-Low Tot.Ap.	44 42
Arith. Prob.	259	70	264	64	Reading	50	29	Reading	53	50	Reading	41 39
English	218	9	222	7	Vocabulary	44	27	Vocabulary	59	42	Vocabulary	48 45
Literature	229	37	231	39	Grammar	54	40	Grammar	61	50	Grammar	47 75
Science	244	65	234	53	Elem.Alg.-Coop.Q Ap.	68	74	P. Geom.-Coop R Ap.	71	84	Int.Alg.-Coop S	67 85
Spelling	216	12	231	20	Gen.Sci.-Coop Q Ap.	56	46	Biology-Coop X Ap	58	35	Chemistry-Coop X Ap	67 64

Test (cont.)		
A. Mech. of Exp.	58	43
C-2 Read Comp.	62	52
Fr. Coop.O-Adv.Tot.Ap	63	50
Reading	57	50
Vocabulary	63	44
Grammar	68	66
Amer.Hist.-Coop Z Ap	60	37
Physics-Coop Z Ap	66	56

INTERPRETATION OF TEST RECORD AND ITS RELATION TO ACADEMIC ACHIEVEMENT

(In the interpretation of test scores consider differences in norms used. In transferring records indicate basis of norms)

This boy is fairly high in academic aptitude. His class work and his test scores are on the whole about average. He is retarded in mechanics and effectiveness of oral and written communication. On the other hand, he is a promising mathematics student.

Martin is still approximately average in school work and test scores. Good ability in mathematics is offset by weakness in oral and written communication, but he is improving in the latter area.

This boy has shown more than normal growth in his school work during the last two years and is now somewhat above average scholastically. He has made noteworthy improvement in communication. Mathematics continues to be his best field.

ATTENDANCE (Reasons if irregular)

	Fair
	Attendance irregular because of illness
	Absent one month with scarlet fever
	Fair - some illness
	Good
	Good

SIGNIFICANT ACTIVITIES AND ACCOMPLISHMENTS THAT GIVE EVIDENCE REGARDING INTERESTS AND POWERS

INTERESTS REPORTED BY STUDENT

	Reading
	Boy Scouts
	Fishing
	Reading and elementary experiments in electricity
	Reading and elementary electrical engineering
	Electrical Engineering

EXPERIENCES IN SCHOOL

	Made scenery for school play
	Glee Club, Metal Club
	Glee Club, Metal Club
	Glee Club, Senate
	Glee Club, Basketball

OUT OF SCHOOL AND SUMMER EXPERIENCES

	Camp
	Camp
	Camp
	Worked as messenger
	Worked on farm
	Worked for Electrical Service Company

NOTE TYPE, DURATION, HOURS PER WEEK, EARNINGS AND OTHER SIGNIFICANT FACTS

WORK EXPERIENCES

	None
	Carried paper route each evening
	Eight weeks work in summer as Western Union messenger at $35 a week
	Two months work on farm during summer. Board, room and $50 a month
	Work in wiring division of Electrical Company 12 weeks during summer $2.00 an hour

FINANCIAL AID (Type and Amount)

Educational and Occupational Plans

By whom	
Pupil	Pupil and parents have no plans. Boy is quick at arithmetic and should do well in some type of office work.
Parents	The boy is good in mathematics and uses his hands well.
Counselor	No definite plans
	Plans not matured. Boy likes mechanical problems in which he can use his knowledge of mathematics.
	Likes mathematics and shop work - particularly metals
	Martin thinks he would like to study to become an electrical engineer. His interests and aptitudes would seem to fit him for this field.
	Has applied for Carnegie Tech. Wants to study electrical engineering

HEALTH AND PHYSICAL CHARACTERISTICS (Vigor or lassitude; assets, disabilities or limitations)

	Very small for age. Tires easily. Complains of pains in legs
	Still small and thin. Does not look well. Interviewed mother and asked her to have complete physical exam.
	Growth retardation still evident. Not much endurance. Needs frequent rest. Mother is cooperating in health program for him.
	Health and general physical appearance beginning to show improvement
	Gained 4 inches in height and 20 pounds in weight within last year. Is still below average size but looks much better
	Continued improvement in general health and physique. Looks fit and is taking an interest in sports.

DISCIPLINE (Academic / Personal)

	Nervous and restless and rather shy
	Is becoming noisy. Whistles and shouts
	Noisy. Picks quarrels with other boys. Seems to try to compensate for small size.
	Is trying to overcome noisy habits and is gaining in self-control
	Much better self-control. Normally mischievous
	Shows increased maturity and self-discipline

NOTE SIGNIFICANT ITEMS: Health, decease of either parent, birthplaces, citizenship, changes in type of occupation of parents, language spoken, type of community, study conditions or other factors such as "broken home".

Both parents were born in the United States and have spent most of their lives in Philadelphia. They were separated in 1957, the year before Martin entered Junior High School. The father lives at the Y.M.C.A. He seldom sees the family and apparently has little interest in them. Martin feels this strongly. The mother has had to obtain a court order to get support for herself and the children. The family lost their home through the father's neglect. Their present residence is in one of the poorer and more crowded sections of the city.

Family	ROBBINS	Type of Occupation	Education Degree and Kind	Religion
Father	HARVEY N.	GARAGE MECHANIC	TWO YEARS HIGH SCHOOL	BAPTIST
Mother	LAURA	HOUSEWIFE	HIGH SCHOOL GRADUATE	BAPTIST
Step Parent or Guardian				

Siblings	Sex			Birthdate
RAYMOND	M	REPAIRMAN CON-EDISON	HIGH SCHOOL GRADUATE	1943
FLORENCE	F			1945
HELEN	F			1948
GEORGE	M			1951

DESCRIPTION OF BEHAVIOR (Made by all those who have had sufficient opportunity to observe the pupil)

Key to persons making the descriptions below: Ad-Advisor, Ag-Agriculture, Ar-Arts, D-Dramatics, E-English, F-French, G-German, HR-Home Room teacher, HE-Home Economics, L-Latin, M-Mathematics, Mu-Music, NS-Natural Science, SS-Social Science; Others.

RESPONSIBILITY

Description	Ratings
Responsible and Resourceful: Carries Through Whatever is Undertaken, and Also Shows Initiative and Versatility in Accomplishing and Enlarging Upon Undertakings.	M SH / Mu Ad / M / M
Conscientious: Completes Without External Compulsion Whatever is Assigned But is Unlikely to Enlarge the Scope of Assignments.	SH / SH / Ap / NS Ad
Generally Dependable: Usually Carries Through Undertakings, Self-Assumed or Assigned by Others. Requiring Only Occasional Reminder or Compulsion.	E SS Mu NS L E L / NS / Ap NS Ad E F
Selectively Dependable: Shows High Persistence in Undertakings in Which There is Particular Interest, But is Less Likely to Carry Through Other Assignments.	E Art SS Ad Art PE / L E / PE / E SS PE SS PE
Unreliable: Can Be Relied Upon to Complete Undertakings Only When They Are of Moderate Duration or Difficulty and Then Only With Much Prodding and Supervision.	PE / PE
Irresponsible: Cannot Be Relied Upon to Complete Any Undertakings Even When Constantly Prodded and Guided.	PE

CREATIVENESS

Description	Ratings
General: Approaches Whatever He Does With Active Imagination and Originality, So That He Contributes Something That is His Own.	SH / SH / NS / NS
Specific: Makes Distinctly Original and Significant Contributions in One or More Fields.	
Promising: Shows a Degree of Creativeness That Indicates the Likelihood of Valuable Original Contribution in Some Field, Although the Contributions Already Made Have Not Proved to Be Particularly Significant.	Mu SH M / SH / NS / NS / E
Limited: Shows the Desire to Contribute His Own Thinking and Expression to Situations, But His Degree of Imagination and Originality is Not, in General, High Enough to Have Much Influence on His Accomplishments.	E Art E / E / E
Imitative: Makes Little or No Creative Contributions, Yet Shows Sufficient Imagination to See the Implications in the Creation of Others and to Make Use of Their Ideas or Accomplishments.	Art
Unimaginative: Has Given Practically No Evidence of Originality or Creativeness in Imagination or Action.	

INFLUENCE

Description	Ratings
Controlling: His Influence Habitually Shapes the Opinions, Activities, or Ideals of His Associates.	SH / SH / M / Ap / M / SH M E Ad NS Ad PE
Contributing Influence: His Influence, While Not Controlling, Strongly Affects the Opinions, Activities, or Ideals of His Associates.	M SS E / M / Ad / NS E Ap NS SS PE SS E E
Varying: His Influence Varies, Having Force When Particular Ability, Skill, Experience or Circumstance Gives it Opportunity or Value.	Ad E / Mu E / NS
Co-Operating: Has No Very Definite Influence on His Associates, But Contributes to Group Thinking and Action Because of Some Discrimination in Regard to Ideas and Leaders.	Mu Art SS / Mu PE / L PE / F
Passive: Has No Definite Influence on His Associates, Being Carried Along by the Nearest or Strongest Influence.	PE Art / PE / F

ADJUSTABILITY

Description	Ratings
Secure: Appears to Feel Secure in His Social Relationships and is Accepted by the Groups of Which He is a Part.	Ad NS
Uncertain: Appears to Have Some Anxiety About His Social Relationships Although He is Accepted by the Groups of Which He is a Part.	M Ad NS M NS Ad / SH / SS / E SS PE
Neutral: Shows the Desire to Have an Established Place in the Group, But is, in General, Treated With Indifference.	M Mu M / Ad NS / E L PE F / PE F / SS Mu / PE Ad
Withdrawn: Withdraws From Others to an Extent That Prevents His Being a Fully Accepted Member of His Group.	SH Ad E L

CONCERN for OTHERS

Selectively Concerned: Shows Concern by Attitude and Action About About Certain Problems of Welfare of Persons.

Personal: Is Not Strongly Concerned About the Welfare of Others Unless a Situation Materially Affects Him.

Inactive: Professes Concern About Welfare of Others But Does Nothing.

Unconcerned: Shows Little or No Concern For the Welfare of Others.

SERIOUS PURPOSE

Purposeful: Has Definite Purposes and Plans and Carries Through to the Best of His Ability Undertakings Consistent With This Purpose.

Limited: Makes Plans and Shows Determination in Attacking Short Time Projects That Interest Him But Has Not Yet Thought Out Goals for Himself.

Potential: Takes Things as They Come, Meeting Situations Somewhat on the Spur of the Moment Yet May Be Capable of Serious Purpose if Once Aroused.

Vacillating: Makes Plans That Are Fairly Definite, But Cannot Be Counted on for the Determination to Carry Them Through.

Vague: Is Likely to Drift Without the Decisiveness and Persistence That Will Enable Him to Carry Out His Vaguely Conceived Plans.

GRADE

(Rating codes entered across the grade columns — e.g. Ad, SH, M, E, NS, SS, PE, L, F, Mu, Art)

EMOTIONAL STABILITY

Describe Typical Behavior and Significant Variation in it With Respect to Such Factors as Apathy, Excitability, Over-Sensitiveness, Stability

- Nervous and excitable. Seems to lack stability. Ill at ease with adults.
- His nervous condition is probably due partly to ill health and partly to "broken home" circumstances.
- Average mental ability and school achievement. Very immature physically, pale little chap. He is a wizened, pale little chap. Emotionally & socially health is definitely delicate and needs careful watching.
- Is beginning to grow and is improved in appearance. Shows greater control. Less given to exhibitionism.
- Favorable development in appearance and manner. Is becoming much more mature and is now able to control his emotions well.

Additional Comments About Behavior

- Small and tense. Becomes noisy when excited. Wants attention from other boys his age.
- He is so under-sized that the other boys tease him and make him more noisy and excitable
- School work is average or a little below. He does well in mathematics but his English usage is poor. The boys call him "shrimp" and he tries to compensate by showing off. Talk to mother.
- Outside work such as the job he had during the summer is helping to develop his confidence and self-reliance.
- He is literally outgrowing his childish mannerisms

Tentative Synthesis and Suggestions for Guidance Made During, or at Close of, Each School Year

- Continues to be restless and noisy. Seems to feel insecure.
- Noisy manner is probably partly an attempt to escape from insecure conditions at home.
- The academic situation is fairly satisfactory although not at all outstanding except in mathematics. Personal characteristics and health continue to be problems. Slight improvement is due to good cooperation from mother. Urge teachers to help build up feeling of security.
- The boy's improved personal qualities this year are probably as much a result of natural growth as anything else, although cooperation of mother and teachers in helping relieve tensions at home has also been valuable
- Surprisingly rapid all round development. Interest in electrical engineering. Outlook is good unless economic and family relationships at home become too difficult

---

POST SCHOOL AND FOLLOW-UP INFORMATION

College _____ Dates

Other Schools

Work

Marriage

Civic Activities

NOTES: Notwithstanding an unfavorable prognosis at the beginning of the junior high school period, this boy has shown unusually rapid all-round developments, particularly during the last two and a half years. He should make at least an average record in the study of electrical engineering in college and should be moderately successful if he chooses that field as a life vocation. Difficult financial problem in plan to go to college. Will have to work his way for most part, although older brother has promised to give what financial help he can. Expects to enter Temple University in fall and to hold part time job while attending college.

1941 Revision of American Council on Education Cumulative Record Card for Junior and Senior High Schools, Washington, D. C.

DEMOCRAT PRINTING COMPANY, MADISON, WISCONSIN

FORM 10 (Back).

test record with rather high percentiles predominating in mathematics. His percentiles in language usage and mechanics of expression were low in the earlier years but they increased somewhat near the end of the high school period.

The boy was small and frail when he entered the junior high school. He was of a nervous temperament, and tended to try to compensate for his smallness and weakness in comparison with the other boys by being noisy and by adopting a rather belligerent attitude. His attendance was quite irregular at first, because of illness. During the senior high school period, the boy grew rapidly and his health became much improved. These physical factors in turn affected his personality, and he became much more mature, assured, and generally likable.

No clear-cut educational or vocational interests were reported by the boy while he was in junior high school, but during the last two years of senior high school he developed a definite interest in electrical engineering. He had some valuable summer work experiences during the senior high school period.

Martin's home situation was not favorable. He was one of five children in a family whose economic circumstances were somewhat inferior. His mother and father had been separated shortly before he entered the junior high school, and his father thenceforth saw his family infrequently and took little interest in their support. This situation had a marked effect upon the boy, especially during the first two years of the junior high school.

The description of behavior for this student shows how the judgments of different teachers can be brought together and coordinated to show variations in behavior in different situations during a single school year, and to bring out a pattern of development over a period of years. It is interesting to see that in nearly all the categories for which the behavior description form is applicable, this pupil developed from a low or rather mediocre status in Grade 7 to a fairly high position in Grade 12.

It will be observed that in using the description of behavior, it is not necessary for every teacher of the pupil to provide judgments concerning all aspects of his behavior if there are certain categories concerning which an individual teacher may have little or no information. For example, the mathematics teachers and the social studies teachers did not provide descriptions of the behavior of this pupil under the heading of creativeness since the nature of the subjects taught by these teachers was such that they had little opportunity to observe the pupil in situations calling for creativeness.

As one studies a thorough record of this kind, he acquires a feeling of familiarity with the individual's background, aptitudes, achievements, interests, experiences, and personal qualities, even though he may never have seen the pupil or have known anything concerning him previously. When such a record is supplemented by more informal knowledge and information acquired through acquaintance with the student, it becomes an invaluable basis for sound, well-considered, intelligent counseling.

NATIONAL ASSOCIATION OF SECONDARY-SCHOOL PRINCIPALS CUMULATIVE RECORD AND TRANSCRIPT

A cumulative record form whose organization is somewhat like that of the American Council forms was published by the National Association of Secondary-School Principals and copyrighted in 1958. This is a six-year record designed to cover the following general areas: academic achievement, test record, personality estimate, health, work experience, interests and activities, data explaining extreme variation between test results and actual achievement in class, educational and vocational plans, attendance, home background, follow-up, and guidance notes. An interesting feature of this form is that the various categories of the record are printed down the center in the manner of a railroad timetable. The purpost of this arrangement is to reduce eye movement and make for easier reading.

A transcript form for use in summarizing and reporting a student's secondary school record to college or employer was also copyrighted in 1958 by the NASSP. In 1964, the NASSP published a new Secondary-School Record—Transcript and Student Description Summary. This form was developed jointly by the NASSP-AACRAO[3] Committee on School-College Relations and the Educational Testing Service, and it has been widely accepted by schools and colleges. It is shown as Form 11. (These forms may be obtained from NASSP, but permission to reprint or reproduce locally is not granted.)

CUMULATIVE RECORDS EMPLOYED IN DIFFERENT SCHOOL SYSTEMS

A school which is revising its record forms will find it helpful to examine cards which have been published for general distribution, such as those which have just been considered. Some schools may find that records of this kind are so closely adapted to their needs that they can adopt them in their entirety, but no school should decide to take over a ready-made record form without first considering carefully its own objectives and program.

[3] American Association of Collegiate Registrars and Admission Officers.

Other schools may find it more desirable to adopt portions of published record forms but to incorporate these portions into a new form of their production. This can be done readily, since the American Council forms and the Educational Records Bureau forms are not copyrighted.

Still other schools may wish to adopt an entirely new approach to their record forms instead of copying parts of any available forms. Even these schools, however, can obtain valuable ideas concerning arrangement of data on the card from a study of forms that have been prepared either by national organizations, such as the American Council on Education and the National Association of Secondary-School Principals or by committees in local school systems. In recent years, many schools have printed new record forms that are obviously the results of much thought and work but which are so poorly arranged that much more time is required for a counselor to get the essential information from them than is needed when well-organized forms are used.

It is impossible to present in this book more than a few of the many admirable cumulative records which have been devised by school systems throughout the country. The cumulative records of the following school systems will be shown and briefly discussed: Providence, Rhode Island, Public Schools; Junior and Senior High Schools of Los Angeles, California; secondary schools of Newark, New Jersey, and Minneapolis, Minnesota, Public Schools. Those of the Phoenix, Arizona, high schools will be briefly described.

As already indicated, the cumulative record is so extensive and so important that it is necessary, for purposes of study, to consider it apart from the other records of the school. The consideration of the cumulative record without regard to the other school records, however, may confuse our thinking unless a word of warning is issued. It should be remembered that in the case of every cumulative record, the cumulative form is just one important aspect of a whole complex record system. It does not stand alone but is supported by a whole array of suplementary records.

PROVIDENCE PUBLIC SCHOOLS CUMULATIVE RECORD CARD

One of the oldest, most firmly established, and most influential guidance programs in the United States was developed in the Providence, Rhode Island, Public Schools by Dr. Richard D. Allen, Assistant Superintendent of Schools. This program was maintained under Dr. Allen's direction during his lifetime and was then carried forward under the direction of his successor, Dr. Elmer R. Smith. It is currently maintained by the Assistant Superintendent, Dr. Edmund A. Quinn, and Mr. Bernard J. Buonanno,

Supervisor of Guidance and Placement, and with the active interest of Superintendent James I. Hanley. The Providence Cumulative Record Form for Junior and Senior High Schools was revised recently and the new card was adopted in September, 1963. It is shown as Form 12.

The top of the front side of the card provides for a seven-year record of subjects, marks, and credits. Below that, there is ample space for a record of the results of tests including College Board and scholarship tests, objective tests of various kinds, academic aptitude tests, and tests of other aptitudes and interest inventories.

The back of the form allows for more informal entries pertaining to home environment, adjustment, physical and medical factors, activities and interests, accomplishments, work experience, and plans for the future. The lower portion of that side of the form has space for ratings on a variety of personality qualities, some of which are reminiscent of the behavior description portion of the American Council cumulative record form. Provision is also made for recording information with regard to promotion, graduation, a summary of the scholastic record, and names of colleges to which transcripts are sent.

A wealth of information is thus made available on a form which folds to fit a 5-by-8-inch file drawer.

LOS ANGELES CUMULATIVE RECORD FORMS FOR JUNIOR AND SENIOR HIGH SCHOOLS

The cumulative record for junior and senior high schools in Los Angeles, California (Form 13), consists of a folder printed on all four sides. The inside of the folder consists mainly of a detailed record of subjects, marks and credits arranged by half-year intervals from Grade 7 through Grade 12. Provision is made for recording progress in work habits and cooperation, as well as for marks in subjects studied.

The front portion of the outside of the folder is given over to information concerning family and home background and especially to a record of scores on tests of scholastic capacity and educational achievement and inventories of interests and personal qualities. The extensive allowance of space for test data is admirable, although provision is not made sequentially for the test data, as it is for the record of class work, and the names of the parts of certain tests or inventories are printed on the record form, which make it difficult to change from one test to another as better tests are developed.

The back page of the outside of the folder is desirably left with only slight structure so that a variety of significant information concerning the individual may be noted there.

SECONDARY-SCHOOL RECORD—TRANSCRIPT

STUDENT INFORMATION	SCHOOL INFORMATION

STUDENT INFORMATION

Last Name	*First Name*	*Middle Name*

Home Address

Parent or Guardian

Previous Secondary School Attended (if any)	*Date Left*

Date of Birth	*Sex*	☐ *Withdrew* ☐ *Was or Will Be Graduated*	*Month*	*Year*

SCHOOL INFORMATION

School Name

School Address

School Accredited By	☐ State System ☐ Reg. Accred. Assoc.	*School Phone Number*

NON-PUBLIC ☐ PUBLIC ☐	*Enrollment in Grades* —12	*Percent Graduates Entering College* 4 Yr. Col.	2 Yr. Col. and Other

Passing Mark	*Honors Mark (if any)*	LOWEST NUMERICAL EQUIVALENT			
		A	B	C	D

CLASS RECORD
Include Subjects Failed or Repeated

YEAR	SUBJECTS	IDENTIFY LAB TV SEMINAR SUMMER	IDENTIFY HONORS ACCEL AD. PL. ETC.	MARKS 1ST. SEM.	FINAL OR 2ND. SEM.	CRED OR UNIT	STATE EXAM. SCORES
9 19____ 19____							
10 19____ 19____							
11 19____ 19____							
12 19____ 19____							

EXPLANATION OF HONORS COURSES

RANK IN CLASS   BASED ON_____SEMESTERS

☐ EXACTLY   ☐ APPROX. _____ IN CLASS OF _____

FINAL RANK _____

Check Appropriate Rank Information

☐ ALL SUBJECTS GIVEN CREDIT   ☐ ALL STUDENTS
☐ MAJOR SUBJECTS ONLY   ☐ COLL. PREP. STUDENTS ONLY

Explain Weighting of Marks in Determining Rank

OUTSTANDING ACTIVITIES, HONORS, AWARDS

TEST RECORD

DATE	NAME OF TEST	RAW OR STD. SCORE	PERCENTILE SCORE	NORM GROUP	DATE	NAME OF TEST	RAW OR STD. SCORE	PERCENTILE SCORE	NORM GROUP

Date	*Signature*	*Title*

FORM 11 (Front).

Reprinted with permission.

SECONDARY-SCHOOL RECORD—STUDENT DESCRIPTION SUMMARY

Last Name	*First Name*	*Middle Name*	*School*	*State*

SUMMARY OF DESCRIPTIVE SCALES

(specify number at each level)

SUMMARIZED BELOW ARE THE DESCRIPTIONS MADE BY TEACHERS OF GRADE(S) ☐ 10 ☐ 11 ☐ 12

---

(1) PARTICIPATION IN DISCUSSION (SELF-INITIATED)
———— always involved, often initiates discussion
———— usually participates
———— often participates
———— occasionally participates
———— seldom participates
———— not applicable

(2) INVOLVEMENT IN CLASSROOM ACTIVITIES
———— very high in all activities
———— active, usually shows genuine interest
———— mild, politely attentive
———— languid, attention often wanders
———— distracted, does other things during class
———— vacillates greatly

(3) PURSUIT OF INDEPENDENT STUDY
———— considerable study and major project(s)
———— considerable study or major project(s)
———— some study and minor project(s)
———— some study or minor project(s)
———— no evidence of independent study
———— not applicable

(4) EVENNESS OF PERFORMANCE
———— exceptionally consistent
———— even, varies no more than one mark
———— slightly uneven, often varies one mark
———— uneven, often varies two marks
———— erratic, performance fluctuates greatly

(5) CRITICAL AND QUESTIONING ATTITUDE
———— often challenges
———— sometimes challenges
———— occasionally is skeptical
———— sometimes probes
———— rarely questions
———— not applicable

(6) DEPTH OF UNDERSTANDING
———— excellent insight
———— good understanding
———— some insight
———— little insight
———— poor understanding
———— not applicable

(7) PERSONAL RESPONSIBILITY
———— always accepts fully
———— usually accepts fully
———— partially accepts
———— sometimes refuses
———— often refuses

(8) CONSIDERATION FOR OTHERS
———— always considerate of others' rights and feelings
———— usually considerate
———— courteous, little evidence of consideration
———— sometimes inconsiderate
———— often inconsiderate
———— inadequate opportunity to observe

COMMENTS

HEALTH   DO YOU KNOW OF ANY HEALTH FACTORS (PHYSICAL OR EMOTIONAL) OF WHICH THIS COLLEGE SHOULD BE AWARE IF THIS STUDENT MATRICULATES?
☐ NO   ☐ YES   *(Please Explain on Separate Sheet)*

RECOMMENDATION TO COLLEGE   *If school policy precludes any recommendation, please check here* ☐

Date	*Signature*	*Title*

FORM 11 (Back).

NEWARK CUMULATIVE RECORD FOR SECONDARY SCHOOLS

The cumulative record for the secondary schools of Newark, New Jersey, which was carefully developed over a period of several years, illustrates a kind of form which is more definitely oriented toward guidance than the records of many other school systems. The front and back of the basic form, 12-by-17½-inches, which folds to fit a file 9-by-12-inches, are devoted entirely to guidance information. There is a separate card for the record of academic achievement which may be used as an insert for the folder. The entire cumulative record is shown in Forms 14A and 14B.

The front of the folder covers the following areas: family data, personal data, conferences with parents or agencies concerned with the individual pupil, attendance, health data, social and recreational experiences, work experiences, interests and hobbies, educational and vocational goals, and a behavior description which bears some resemblance to the behavior description developed in the Eight-Year Study of the Progressive Education Association, which was discussed in a preceding chapter.

The back of the folder provides for a detailed test record, and for extensive interpretative and follow-up comments on the test findings by the counselor. If this portion of the record is actually used, it should prove to be one of the most valuable parts.

A well-planned, detailed manual of instruction was prepared by a committee for use with the cumulative record. The introductory statement is worth reproducing in full:

A cumulative record serves as a complete and up-to-date picture of each pupil as he progresses through our schools. It reflects all phases of his development—physical, mental, social, vocational, etc. It furnishes scientific data for guidance purposes to teachers, counselors, and all others interested in his adjustment to life both in school and out of school. Through their expert observation and notations, recorded comments, recommendations, and follow-up, counselors build up a veritable case study in outline form. When confidential material is added by means of inserts, the record brings into clear focus an intimate three-dimensional portrait of the pupil's whole personality in his school, home, and community—his total environment.

However, the real value of any record is measured by the extent to which it is analyzed and utilized. Recommendations noted, but never acted upon, are mere gestures hardly worth the time and effort of recording. Records filed neatly in cabinets are time-wasting irritations unless they represent vital problems which are in the process of solution. Easy accessibility and frequent use will make these records important to the pupil, his teachers, parents, social workers, and others who may be called upon to assist the pupil to achieve a happy life adjustment.

The record is a guidance tool and should contain all pertinent information necessary for effective guidance, and only that. In addition to use in school guidance, records are often requested by army and navy officials, courts, and the Bureau of Missing Persons. Every necessary identification should therefore be accurately and fully recorded.

The dignity and self-respect of each pupil should be maintained at all costs. Nothing detrimental to his success in life should be recorded in permanent form. From time to time, he may be shown his record, including the confidential material placed in the folder as inserts to be destroyed when their usefulness has been outlived.

MINNEAPOLIS PUBLIC SCHOOLS CUMULATIVE RECORD CARDS

For many years, the Minneapolis, Minnesota, Public Schools have been in the forefront of large city school systems in the development of cumulative records and in the provision of detailed manuals for recording and using the records. Their forms, recently revised, may be of special interest, since a portion of them is adapted for data processing and the use of gummed labels. Another interesting characteristic of the Minneapolis cumulative record is that it provides for a continuous, coordinated record from Grade 1 through Grade 12. This feature has long been characteristic of the cumulative records of that school system.

The cumulative record folder is reproduced as Forms 15A, B, C, and D, and an unusually thorough health record is shown as Form 15E.

The elementary school record is shown on Card A, the front of the cumulative record folder. It provides for identifying information, the pupil's school record from kindergarten through Grade 6, teacher comments, and data on home and family background, all arranged in parallel columns.

Card B is designed as the secondary school record, going from Grade 7 through Grade 12. The arrangement of data on this card is similar to that for the elementary school record. The arrangement of the information in annual columns permits visual apprehension of the progress of the pupil from year to year.

Card C is given over entirely to the pupil's test record. Provision is made for the recording of results of individual ability tests and group ability and aptitude tests in the usual manner in the upper left-hand portion of the card. The rest of the card is concerned mainly with scholastic achievement tests for both elementary and secondary schools. This part of the card is divided into several large rectangles which have been carefully measured and arranged to allow for the recording of grades and test data through the use of gummed labels which have been put through data processing equipment.

The drudgery of writing achievement test results on the cards is eliminated by the self-explanatory nature of the labels. There is also a space on Card C for the recording of scores on interest inventories and other measures.

The back of the cumulative record, Card D, provides for information on withdrawals and readmissions, participation in activities, social work and psychological services, educational and vocational plans, counselor comments, and a brief follow-up record.

Form 15E is an excellent form for recording the pupil's health record, including disease history, communicable disease protection, and physician's notes and recommendations.

The Minneapolis cumulative record folder and the accompanying handbook could serve as valuable reference material for any course in guidance.

CUMULATIVE RECORD OF PHOENIX UNION HIGH SCHOOL SYSTEM

An especially elaborate cumulative record has been devised for use in the Phoenix Union High School System, Phoenix, Arizona. It is a more elaborate and extensive record form that can readily be displayed in this book, but a brief description of the record system and of the recording procedure used with it may be helpful. A more detailed report was given by Ellis (4).

The record itself consists of a heavy, expandable folder. The inserts are fastened to each side of cardboard sheets which may be turned like the pages of a book. The insert pages consist of (1) essential information for counseling, (2) family data, (3) a record of subjects, grades, and credits, (4) test data expressed in stanines, and (5) gummed label entries, including such items as interview summaries, health data, disciplinary action, honors awards, withdrawals, follow-up, and other personal data.

Individual cumulative records of this kind, of course, could not be maintained for a high school system enrolling some 25,000 pupils if it were necessary to depend upon clerical work alone. Data processing equipment provides a large part of the information for entering in the cumulative record, particularly the family data, the scholastic record, and the test data. The gummed label entries, including interview summaries, health data, and other kinds of entries, some of which may be anecdotal in nature, are typed by means of a unique remote dictating and central recording system known as the IBM "Executary Remote Systems." The Systems make it possible for each telephone in the school to be used as a dictation instrument, with the record made on tape in the central cumulative records room. A staff member may use any telephone in his school and dictate into the central recorder. The dictation is typed in the central records

room and referred back to the originator for checking. Only that portion which the pupil's counselor considers suitable for public examination finds its way, by means of gummed labels, into the pupil's official cumulative record.

Gordon Ellis reported in 1963 that this record system was in use in four of the ten high schools in the Phoenix Union High School System and that other schools would be added to the list in the near future. The success of the records system will bear watching, since it represents experimentation with procedures not previously reported elsewhere.

COOPERATIVE PLAN FOR GUIDANCE AND ADMISSION

There is unquestionably a trend toward greater use of data processing equipment and gummed labels in maintaining cumulative records, particularly in large school systems, as well as in some statewide systems. The Educational Testing Service has spearheaded a major undertaking directed toward the development and maintenance of cumulative records, all entries of which lend themselves to data processing. The prototype of this movement is ETS's Cooperative Plan for Guidance and Admission.

This plan, as well as the general question of how schools could use electronic data processing techniques in improving their student personnel services, was discussed in a helpful paper by Walton (26). He justified the introduction of information processing techniques into student record keeping and use on the ground that the demands for improvement in education, both in quantity and quality, are growing at a rapid pace. In order to keep up with the demand, very detailed student records may be accumulated in taped "memory" from which computer-generated reports may be prepared at intervals as needed.

A portion of the cumulative record form (or student records folder) developed for CPGA is shown as Forms 16A and B. The main form for the Cooperative Plan for Guidance and Admission consists of (1) an extensive student records folder which is maintained by the school through a combination of entries in ink and data on pressure sensitive labels, (2) a student profile record which is filled out by the school largely through the darkening of appropriate code boxes, and (3) a comprehensive student report which is generated by the electronic data processing equipment from the coded information on the student profile record. The comprehensive student report is printed in five copies, presumably at the end of the junior year and again at the end of the senior year. There are pockets in the student records folder for filing of a copy of the comprehensive student report, as well as the student profile

| | | | M-F | BIRTH DATE | | BIRTH PLACE | | | PROOF OF AGE | VACCINATION |

| LAST NAME | | FIRST NAME | | MIDDLE NAME | | | | | | |

| DATE 1 | RESIDENCE | | DATE 3 | RESIDENCE | | | DATE 5 | RESIDENCE | | |

| 2 | | | 4 | | | | 6 | | | |

DATE OF ENTRY										
FROM SCHOOL										
TO SCHOOL										
HOME ROOM										
YEAR										
DATE OF ENTRY										
TO SCHOOL										
HOME ROOM										

GRADE		GRADE		GRADE		GRADE		GRADE		GRADE		GRADE		
E		E		E		E		E		E		E		
M		M		M		M		M		M		M		
S		S		S		S		S		S		S		
ScG		ScG		Sc		Sc		Sc		Sc		Sc		
F		F		F		F		F		F		F		

GG		GG		GG		GG		GG		GG		GG		
PH		PH		PH		PH		PH		PH		PH		
PT		PT		PT		PT		PT		PT		PT		
SCt		SCt		SCt		SCt		SCt		SCt		SCt		
DAYS ABSENT		DAYS ABSENT		DAYS ABSENT		DAYS ABSENT		DAYS ABSENT		DAYS ABSENT		DAYS ABSENT		
TIMES LATE		TIMES LATE		TIMES LATE		TIMES LATE		TIMES LATE		TIMES LATE		TIMES LATE		
UNITS EARNED		UNITS EARNED		UNITS EARNED		UNITS EARNED		UNITS EARNED		UNITS EARNED		UNITS EARNED		

TEST RECORD FOR SENIOR HIGH USE ONLY (ATTACH COLLEGE BOARD AND SCHOLARSHIP SCORES)

(JR. HIGH)   SUPPLEMENTARY OBJECTIVE TESTS

DATE	GRADE	NAME	ER	EV	ES	E	MP	MF				

(JR. HIGH)   ACADEMIC APTITUDE TESTS   (SR. HIGH)

DATE	GRADE	NAME	NUMERICAL	LETTER	%ILE

(SR. HIGH)

DATE	GRADE	NAME	MARK	%ILE	DATE	GRADE	NAME	MARK	%ILE	DATE	GRADE	NAME	MARK	%ILE

APTITUDE TESTS AND INTEREST INVENTORIES

PICTURE

FORM 12 (Front).

208

FATHER (NAME)   MOTHER (INCLUDE MAIDEN NAME)   STEP-PARENT OR GUARDIAN (NAME)

PARENT'S RESIDENCE IF DIFFERENT

COUNSELOR AND DATE

HOME ENVIRONMENT

SOCIAL MENTAL AND EMOTIONAL ADJUSTMENT

PHYSICAL AND MEDICAL FACTORS

EXTRA-CURRICULAR AND LEISURE-TIME ACTIVITIES AND INTERESTS

NOTABLE ACCOMPLISH-MENTS EXPERIENCES AND AWARDS

WORK EXPERIENCES

EDUCATIONAL AND VOCATIONAL PLANS

(BLUE FOR JR. HIGH)	PERSONALITY RATING			(RED FOR SR. HIGH)	DATE AND CAUSE OF LEAVING
MOTIVATION	PURPOSELESS	VACILLATING	USUALLY PURPOSELESS	EFFECTIVELY MOTIVATED	HIGHLY MOTIVATED	PROMOTION FROM JR. HIGH SCHOOL
INDUSTRY	SELDOM WORKS EVEN UNDER PRESSURE	NEEDS CONSTANT PRESSURE	NEEDS OCCASIONAL PRODDING	PREPARES ASSIGNED WORK REGULARLY	SEEKS ADDITIONAL WORK	GRADUATION FROM SR. HIGH SCHOOL / TRANSFERRED TO
INITIATIVE	MERELY CONFORMS	SELDOM INITIATES	FREQUENTLY INITIATES	CONSISTENTLY SELF-RELIANT	ACTIVELY CREATIVE	
INFLUENCE AND LEADERSHIP	NEGATIVE	COOPERATIVE BUT RETIRING	SOMETIMES IN MINOR AFFAIRS	CONTRIBUTING IN IMPORTANT AFFAIRS	JUDGMENT RESPECTED MAKES THINGS GO	
CONCERN FOR OTHERS	INDIFFERENT	SELF-CENTERED	SOMEWHAT SOCIALLY CONCERNED	GENERALLY CONCERNED	DEEPLY AND ACTIVELY CONCERNED	OTHER CAUSES FOR LEAVING
RESPONSIBILITY	UNRELIABLE	SOMEWHAT DEPENDABLE	USUALLY DEPENDABLE	CONSCIENTIOUS	ASSUMES MUCH RESPONSIBILITY	
INTEGRITY	NOT DEPENDABLE	QUESTIONABLE AT TIMES	GENERALLY HONEST	RELIABLE, DEPENDABLE	CONSISTENTLY TRUSTWORTHY	COLLEGE TRANSCRIPTS SENT TO
EMOTIONAL STABILITY	HYPEREMOTIONAL / APATHETIC	EXCITABLE / UNRESPONSIVE	USUALLY WELL BALANCED	WELL-BALANCED	EXCEPTIONALLY STABLE	
PERSONAL NEATNESS	CARELESS	OCCASIONALLY CARELESS	USUALLY NEAT	BETTER THAN AVERAGE	EXCEPTIONAL	
AT TIME OF LEAVING	DATE	GRADE	DATE	GRADE		

REMARKS

SCHOLASTIC RECORD	
FINAL AVERAGE	
STANDING IN CLASS	
NUMBER IN GRADUATING CLASS	

LAST NAME   FIRST NAME   MIDDLE NAME

FORM 12 (Back).

PUPIL'S NO.

SOCIAL SECURITY NO.

(THIS CUMULATIVE RECORD IS CONFIDENTIAL INFORMATION FOR PROFESSIONAL PERSONNEL USE)

PHOTOGRAPHS

CUMULATIVE RECORD
JUNIOR AND SENIOR HIGH SCHOOLS
LOS ANGELES, CALIFORNIA
LOS ANGELES CITY HIGH SCHOOL DISTRICT
REVISED 1963

LAST NAME | FIRST | MIDDLE

CHECK SEX M F

DATE OF BIRTH MONTH DAY YEAR | PLACE OF BIRTH CITY | STATE | HOW VERIFIED

PRIOR SCHOOL SCHOOL NAME | CITY | STATE

1. IDENTIFICATION DATA

GRADE LEVEL WHEN PHOTOGRAPHS TAKEN

ALL SUBJECTS RECORDED IN THIS SECTION ARE GRADE LEVEL OF COLUMN IN WHICH POSTED, UNLESS OTHERWISE INDICATED.

POLIO IMMUNIZATION: 1 ☐ : 2 ☐ : 3 ☐ : EXEMPT ☐

2. JUNIOR HIGH SCHOOL RECORD

GENERAL SUBJECT FIELD	B-7 SPECIFIC SUBJECT TITLE	SUBJ. GRADE LEVEL	SEM. PER. CREDITS	MARKS IN SUBJECTS	WORK HABITS	COOPERATION	A-7 SPECIFIC SUBJECT TITLE	SUBJ. GRADE LEVEL	SEM. PER. CREDITS	MARKS IN SUBJECTS	WORK HABITS	COOPERATION	B-8 SPECIFIC SUBJECT TITLE	SUBJ. GRADE LEVEL	SEM. PER. CREDITS	MARKS IN SUBJECTS	WORK HABITS	COOPERATION	A-8 SPECIFIC SUBJECT TITLE	SUBJ. GRADE LEVEL	SEM. PER. CREDITS	MARKS IN SUBJECTS	WORK HABITS	COOPERATION	B-9 SPECIFIC SUBJECT TITLE	SUBJ. GRADE LEVEL	SEM. PER. CREDITS	MARKS IN SUBJECTS	WORK HABITS	COOPERATION	A-9 SPECIFIC SUBJECT TITLE	SUBJ. GRADE LEVEL	SEM. PER. CREDITS	MARKS IN SUBJECTS	WORK HABITS	COOPERATION
SCHOOL																																				
DATE OF ENTRANCE																																				
DATE OF LEAVING																																				
LEFT TO																																				
SEMESTER ENDING																																				
ADVISER																																				
ENGLISH																																				
SOCIAL STUDIES	GEOG.						HIST. GEOG.						U.S. HIST. GEOG.	1					U.S. HIST. GEOG.	2					WLD. HIST. GEOG.	1					WLD. HIST. GEOG.	1				
MATHEMATICS																																				
SCIENCE																																				
FOREIGN LANGUAGE																																				
PRACTICAL ARTS																																				
FINE ARTS																																				
PHYSICAL EDUCATION																																				

JUNIOR HIGH SCHOOL COMPLETION: GRADUATION WITH DIPLOMA ☐   SPECIAL TO HIGH SCHOOL ☐   DATE

3. EXPLANATION OF MARKS AND ABBREVIATIONS

A SUPERIOR
B BETTER THAN AVERAGE
C AVERAGE
D BARELY PASSING
FAIL FAILURE
INC INCOMPLETE
NM NO MARK: ATTENDANCE LESS THAN 3 WEEKS
NO CR INCOMPLETE NOT MADE UP
W WITHDRAWAL (SUMMER SCHOOL MARK ONLY)

E EXCELLENT
S SATISFACTORY
U UNSATISFACTORY

AE ACADEMICALLY ENRICHED CLASS FOR ABLE PUPILS
EMR CLASS FOR THE EDUCABLE MENTALLY RETARDED
H HONORS CLASS FOR ACADEMICALLY GIFTED PUPILS
LI LOW INDEX CLASS FOR SLOW LEARNERS
NES CLASS FOR NON-ENGLISH SPEAKING PUPILS
R REMEDIAL CLASS FOR EDUCATIONALLY RETARDED PUPILS OF AVERAGE OR ABOVE AVERAGE ABILITY

4. TRANSMITTAL RECORD

DATE	CUMULATIVE RECORD OR TRANSCRIPT SENT TO:	DATE	LETTER OF RECOMMENDATION SENT TO:

FORM 13(a).

Used with permission of Los Angeles City Schools.

5. SENIOR HIGH SCHOOL RECORD

ALL SUBJECTS RECORDED IN THIS SECTION ARE GRADE LEVEL OF COLUMN IN WHICH POSTED, UNLESS OTHERWISE INDICATED.

	B-10		A-10		B-11		A-11		B-12		A-12	
	CURRENT	CUMULATIVE	CURRENT	CUMULATIVE	CURRENT	CUMULATIVE	CURRENT	CUMULATIVE	CURRENT	CUMULATIVE	CURRENT	CUMULATIVE
SCHOOL												
DATE OF ENTRANCE												
DATE OF LEAVING												
LEFT TO												
SEMESTER ENDING												
ADVISER												
MAJOR SEQUENCE												
ENGLISH	ENG.	B10	ENG.		ENG.							
SOCIAL STUDIES					U.S. HIST. 1		U.S. HIST.		U.S. GOVT.			
SCIENCE												
MATHEMATICS												
FOREIGN LANGUAGE												
BUSINESS EDUCATION												
HOMEMAKING												
INDUSTRIAL ARTS												
FINE ARTS												
WORK EXPERIENCE												
PHYSICAL EDUCATION												
TOTAL SEMESTER PERIODS CREDIT												

6. EXTRA YEAR IN SENIOR HIGH SCHOOL

	CURRENT	CUMULATIVE
SCHOOL		
DATE OF ENTRANCE		
SEMESTER ENDING		

7. GRADUATION DATA

MAJOR SEQUENCE

APPROXIMATE RANK	NO. IN GRADUATING CLASS
GRADE-POINT AVERAGE	EXPLANATION: BASIS: 8 SEMESTER PERIODS A:4 B:3 C:2 D:1 FAIL:0

DATE OF GRADUATION FROM SENIOR HIGH SCHOOL

MONTH   DAY   YEAR

8. CERTIFICATION (FOR USE ON PHOTOSTAT COPY ONLY)

DATE THIS TRANSCRIPT ISSUED:

I CERTIFY THAT THE INFORMATION HEREON IS CORRECT.

(SIGNED)

(PRINCIPAL)

HIGH SCHOOL

FORM 13(b).

LAST NAME   FIRST   MIDDLE

9. INFORMATION CONCERNING HOME

NAME		SEP.	DEAD	DATE
FATHER				
MOTHER (INCLUDE MAIDEN NAME)				
STEPFATHER				
STEPMOTHER				
GUARDIAN				

DATE   OCCUPATION OF PARENT OR GUARDIAN   RELATIONSHIP

YEAR FIRST REPORTED FOR STATE GIFTED PROGRAM:

10. ADDRESSES

	HOME ADDRESS	PHONE
DATE		

	BUSINESS ADDRESS	PHONE
DATE		

11. HOME BACKGROUND

DATE	LANGUAGE BACKGROUND
	SIBLINGS—OLDER
	SIBLINGS—YOUNGER
	OTHER DATA

12. SCHOLASTIC CAPACITY TESTS

INTELLIGENCE AND ACHIEVEMENT TEST RESULTS RECORDED AS A SINGLE DIGIT ARE ON A STANINE SCALE FROM 1 (LOW) TO 9 (HIGH)

DATE	GRADE	TEST (NAME, LEVEL, FORM)	C. A.	VERBAL INDEX	NON-VERBAL INDEX	TOTAL INDEX

DATE	GRADE	TEST (NAME, LEVEL, FORM)	C.A.	GRADE	VERBAL INDEX	NON-VERBAL INDEX	TOTAL INDEX

13. INTEREST INVENTORIES; APTITUDE TESTS; AND PERSONALITY MEASURES

O. I. I. (LEE-THORPE)

	DATE	GRADE	FORM	SCORE	% ILE
L. A. ACTIVITY					
1. AESTHETIC					
2. COMMERCIAL					
3. MECHANICAL					
4. NATURAL					
5. SCIENTIFIC					
6. SOCIAL					

		SCORE	% ILE	SCORE	% ILE
A. PER.-SOC.					
B. NATURAL					
C. MECHANICAL					
D. BUSINESS					
E. ARTS					
F. SCIENCES					
VERBAL					
MANIP.					
COMP.					
TOTAL					

LEVEL

KUDER

	DATE	GRADE	FORM	SCORE	% ILE
0. OUTDOOR					
1. MECHANICAL					
2. COMPUTA.					
3. SCIENTIFIC					
4. PERSUASIVE					
5. ARTISTIC					
6. LITERARY					
7. MUSICAL					
8. SOC. SERV.					
9. CLERICAL					

14. EDUCATIONAL ACHIEVEMENT TESTS

DATE	GRADE	TEST (NAME, LEVEL, FORM)	C.A. TO DATE	INDEX	X.A. GR. PL. TO DATE	READING VOCAB.	READING COMPR.	ARITHMETIC REAS.	ARITHMETIC FUND.	LANG.	SPELL.	OTHER TESTS

15. HEALTH

FORM 13(c).

16. SIGNIFICANT INFORMATION Report information concerning family and home relationships, attendance, maturation characteristics, interests and activities, education and vocational plans. For detailed comments use separate sheet. Date and sign entry on both forms.

SENIOR HIGH

TENTH

ELEVENTH

TWELFTH

JUNIOR HIGH

SEVENTH

EIGHTH

NINTH

18. HONORS AND AWARDS (DATE AND SIGN EACH ENTRY)

17. REFERRALS TO SCHOOL SERVICES OR COMMUNITY AGENCIES
(DATE AND SIGN EACH ENTRY)

19. OTHER NOTES (DATE AND SIGN EACH ENTRY)

FORM 13(d).

34-H-103-30M-2-64 (STK. NO. 8138001)

213

CUMULATIVE RECORD
SECONDARY SCHOOLS. NEWARK. N. J.

FAMILY DATA

| PUPIL'S LAST NAME | FIRST | MIDDLE | SEX M F | DATE -19 |

	OCCUPATION	EDUCATION	LANGUAGE SPOKEN	DATE & PLACE OF BIRTH	PLACE OF BIRTH	ADDRESS	TELEPHONE
FATHER							
MOTHER							
STEP-PARENT							
SIBLINGS { NUMBER OLDER / NUMBER YOUNGER }							
DATE OF RECORDING						SEE INSERT NO. ☐ ☐	

PERSONAL DATA

SIGNIFICANT HOME CONDITIONS: PARENTAL. COMMUNITY. HEALTH. SOCIAL.

PREVIOUS SCHOOL RECORD: SCHOOLS ATTENDED. ACTIVITIES. HONORS. TEST SUMMARY.

SEE INSERT   Elementary School Cumulative Record

CONFERENCES
WITH PARENTS. RELIGIOUS. SOCIAL OR WELFARE AGENCIES; CLINICS; BUREAU OF CHILD GUIDANCE; BUREAU OF ATTENDANCE; OTHERS.

	SIGNATURES. DATE			SIGNATURES. DATE
				SEE INSERT NO. ☐ ☐

JUNIOR HIGH SCHOOL

SCHOOL							
COUNSELOR							
YEAR & GRADE	7B¹⁹	7A¹⁹	8B¹⁹	8A¹⁹	9B¹⁹	9A¹⁹	
AGE (AS OF SEPT. 1)							
DAYS ABSENT							
TIMES TARDY							

SENIOR HIGH SCHOOL

SCHOOL						PATTERN OF STUDIES
COUNSELOR						
YEAR & GRADE	10B¹⁹	10A¹⁹	11B¹⁹	11A¹⁹	12B¹⁹	12A¹⁹	
AGE (AS OF SEPT. 1)							
DAYS ABSENT							H. S. CREDITS
TIMES TARDY							COLLEGE UNITS

HEALTH DATA: GENERAL HEALTH. VISUAL AND HEARING ACUITY. CARDIAC CONDITION. RESULT OF TUBERCULIN TEST. LUNG X-RAY. EXCLUSION FROM GYM.

PHYSICAL	

GENERAL STABILITY. EVIDENCE OF EMOTIONAL INSECURITY. E.G. MOODINESS. AGGRESSIVENESS. SPEECH DIFFICULTIES.

MENTAL		SEE INSERT NO. ☐ ☐

FORM 14A (Front).

Used with permission of the Newark Public Schools.

EXPERIENCES: EVIDENCE OF SIGNIFICANT ACTIVITIES, PLANNED PROGRAM FOR LEISURE TIME

RECOMMENDATIONS

SOCIAL & RECREATIONAL
- In School
- Out of School
- Camp-Travel

WORK
- Chores
- Employment
- Type & Wages

INTERESTS & HOBBIES

BEHAVIOR DESCRIPTION
- Industry / Work Habits
- Social Adjustment
- Initiative
- Cooperativeness
- Leadership
- Dependability
- Emotional Stability
- Attitude Toward Authority
- Sense of Humor

SUMMARY
PERSONALITY INTEGRATION

ED. & VOC. GOALS

TRANSFER TO _____ SCHOOL _____ GRADE _____ DATE

REASON FOR DROPOUT _____ DATE

FOLLOW-UP REPORT

GRAD. RANK | NO. IN CLASS

FORM 14A (Front), Continued.

215

CUMULATIVE RECORD

DEPARTMENT OF GUIDANCE
SECONDARY SCHOOLS
BOARD OF EDUCATION
NEWARK 2, N. J.

FORM 14A (Back).

TEST RECORD

JUNIOR HIGH SCHOOL

TYPE TEST	SCH. GR.	DATE	NAME OF TEST	CA	MA	IQ	% ILE	SCH. GR.	DATE	SUBJ. GR.
INTELLIGENCE TEST										
ACHIEVEMENT TEST				SUBJ. GR	SUBJ. AGE	% ILE				
READING										
ARITHMETIC										
ADDITIONAL TESTS										

SENIOR HIGH SCHOOL

NAME OF TEST	CA	MA	IQ	% ILE
	SCORE	PERCENTILE POSITION		
		SCHOOL	CITY	OTHER

COUNSELOR'S INTERPRETATION AND FOLLOW-UP OF TEST FINDINGS

INTERPRETATION OF TEST RESULTS IN LIGHT OF MENTAL ABILITY, PUPIL PERSONALITY, BACKGROUND AND HEALTH

EVIDENCES OF COMMENDABLE ACHIEVEMENT OR BEHAVIOR

FORM 14A (Back), Continued.

ACADEMIC ACHIEVEMENT

SECONDARY SCHOOLS, NEWARK, N. J.

LAST NAME   FIRST

ADDRESS

PATTERN OF STUDIES

7B 19 | 7A 19 | 8B 19 | 8A 19 | 9B 19 | 9A 19 | 10B 19 | 10A 19 | 11B 19 | 11A 19 | 12B 19 | 12A 19

SCHOOL ATTENDED

YEAR & GRADE

DAYS ABSENT

TIMES TARDY

ENGLISH

LANG.

MATH.

SOCIAL STUDIES

U.S. HISTORY

SCIENCE

MUSIC OR ART

TECHNICAL, BUSINESS, OTHER

PHYSICAL EDUCATION

HEALTH

HIGH SCHOOL CREDITS

GRADUATED FROM

H. S. CREDITS COLLEGE UNITS

TOTAL

ED. & VOC. PLANS

TRANSFERRED TO   SCHOOL   GRADE   DATE

REASON FOR DROPOUT   DATE

GRADUATED FROM   HIGH SCHOOL   RANK   NUMBER IN CLASS   DATE

IMMEDIATE   LONG RANGE

FORM 14B.

218

record and a student achievement and guidance report. The senior-year report serves both as a permanent record and as the student's official transcript for reports to colleges or employers.

The comprehensive student report is shown as Form 17. Of particular interest are the portions of the report having to do with academic summary and academic record. These parts, when filled out by the data processing equipment, save the school personnel countless hours of time.

A possible limitation to the CPGA plan is its comparative inflexibility; it is necessary to code the information that is fed into the computers, and all schools adopting the plan must use precisely the same form (8). Thus, the creativeness of schools in producing cumulative records adapted to their own situation would be somewhat reduced. Nevertheless, the CPGA plan would seem to be a boon to many large schools and school systems that are overwhelmed by the necessity of keeping records on thousands of pupils. That the plan has already been widely accepted by state and city school systems attests to its place as a major contribution to modern education.

A very promising rapid and accurate new development in the production of cumulative records by means of electronic data processing equipment has been described and explained by Dr. E. F. Lindquist of the Measurement Research Center, State University of Iowa.[4]

A SUGGESTED SIMPLIFIED CUMULATIVE RECORD

Most of the cumulative record forms that have been discussed in this chapter make provision for a rather extensive recording procedure annually for each pupil. This is true especially of the records that are adapted for use with pressure-sensitive labels and automatic data processing equipment. However, it is probable that for some years to come many schools, particularly smaller schools and those in states that have not yet adopted a uniform record for statewide use, will not be ready to take advantage of the most advanced procedures for rapid recording of data on cumulative records. Moreover, the very wealth of information provided on such records may cause some schools to hesitate to adopt them, both because of the amount of clerical service that is required even when considerable use is made of data processing equipment, and because they may feel that their staff is not yet ready to use intelligently the multitude of data that would be made available concerning each individual. For the time being, such schools may wish to maintain their cumulative

records on a somewhat less ambitious basis. A record form (Forms 18A and B) is therefore suggested as an intermediate step toward the modern and extensive cumulative record.

This form is similar in many respects to the Educational Records Bureau cumulative record card, but it omits the graph of percentile ratings on the test results and it provides more space for comments and notes. The top portion of the back page is very much like one section of the American Council folder. A section for behavior description is provided, but this is much less extensive than the one on the American Council form.

This form is obviously not original; it consists rather of a rearrangement and "boiling down" of categories which have appeared on other records. Schools are entirely free to make use of any of the ideas presented on the card without obtaining special permission.

BASIC CONCEPTS IN THE CONSTRUCTION OF A CUMULATIVE RECORD SYSTEM

As indicated in the preceding chapter, a committee that sets out to devise a cumulative record plan for a school system should begin with a study of the school itself, in order to determine what the school is doing and what it hopes to accomplish. The first step is to secure a list of objectives. Once this has been accomplished, the committee will naturally wish to find out what has been done in other places that can be utilized in meeting the recording needs of the local school. An examination of samples of records developed in other school systems will, no doubt, reveal items which are suited to the local situation, but the discovery of these items will not be the major outcome of such a study. The most important result of a study of the more carefully prepared records now available is the development of certain basic concepts which will have a very important influence on the kind of records set up by a school.

Some of the more important concepts which pervade the best cumulative records produced thus far are as follows:

1. THE CONCEPT OF THE CHILD AS A DEVELOPING ORGANISM

Even the best of records consists of a series of snapshots taken at various points in a child's development. These must be combined in such a way that one studying the records sees not the snapshots but a motion pic-

[4] E. F. Lindquist. "Maximizing the Use of Guidance Data in Individualizing Education," *Modern Educational Developments: Another Look.* New York: Educational Records Bureau, 1966. (In press.)

MINNEAPOLIS PUBLIC SCHOOLS

ELEMENTARY SCHOOL RECORD

NAME (Last, First, Middle)

Birth Date   Sex   Name of Father   Birthplace

Name of Mother   Birthplace

Grade

Birthplace

Last School Attended — if from another System

Year 19___	Kindergarten	19___	Grade 1	19___	Grade 2	19___	Grade 3	19___	Grade 4	19___	Grade 5	19___	Grade 6

Room   Room   Room   Room   Room   Room   Room   Room

School

Days Pres.   Days Abs.   Times Tardy

Attendance Remarks

Health/Phy.Ed.
Language
Mathematics
Reading
Science
Social Studies

TEACHER COMMENTS

Days Pres.   Days Abs.   Times Tardy

Attendance Remarks

TEACHER COMMENTS

Family Status

Father's Occ.

Mother's Occ.

Number of Children	Position in Family

Teacher's Sig.

Referred to:

12 ABCD CUMULATIVE RECORD FOLDER (50M 7-64) Vocational School Print Shop

FORM 15, CARD A.

SCHOLARSHIP CODE: 1 = Above Average   2 = Average   3 = Below Average

Used with permission of Minneapolis Public Schools.

MINNEAPOLIS PUBLIC SCHOOLS

SECONDARY SCHOOL RECORD

FINAL RECORD

H.S. %ile Rank _____
Date of Grad. _____ Rank _____
No. in Class _____ Gr. Pt. Av. _____

NAME (Last, First, Middle) _____
Birth Date _____

GRADE 11 RECORD

Col. Apt. _____ Eng. %ile _____
No. in Class _____ Rank _____
Gr. Pt. Av. _____ Eng. %ile _____ Rank _____
H.S. %ile Rank _____

GPA
A = 4
B = 3
C = 2
D = 1
F = 0

Year 19__ - __

| Grade 7 | Room _____ |
| School _____ | |

Subject	Mark
English	
Social Studies	
Mathematics	
Science	
Art	
Music	
Industrial Arts	
Home Economics	

Physical Education

Days Pres.	Days Abs.	Times Tardy

Attendance Remarks

TEACHER COMMENTS

Grade 8 19__ Room _____

Subject	Mark
English	
Social Studies	
Mathematics	
Science	
Art	
Music	
Industrial Arts	
Home Economics	

Physical Education

Days Pres.	Days Abs.	Times Tardy

Attendance Remarks

TEACHER COMMENTS

Grade 9 19__ Room _____

Subject	Mark
English	
Social Studies	
Science	

Health/Phy.Ed.

Days Pres.	Days Abs.	Times Tardy

Attendance Remarks

TEACHER COMMENTS

Grade 10 19__ Room _____

Subject	Sem. 1	Sem. 2	Cr.
English 1-2			
History 1-2			

Physical Education

Days Pres.	Days Abs.	Times Tardy

Attendance Remarks

TEACHER COMMENTS

Grade 11 19__ Room _____

Subject	Sem. 1	Sem. 2	Cr.
English 3-4			
History 3-4			

Health/Phy. Ed.

Days Pres.	Days Abs.	Times Tardy

Attendance Remarks

TEACHER COMMENTS

Grade 12 19__ Room _____

Subject	Sem. 1	Sem. 2	Cr.
English 5-6			
Modern Problems			

Days Pres.	Days Abs.	Times Tardy

Attendance Remarks

PERSONALITY TRAITS

			Reliability	1 2 3 4
Cooperation	1 2 3 4			
Initiative	1 2 3 4		Ability to get along with people	1 2 3 4
Judgment	1 2 3 4			
Leadership	1 2 3 4		Work Habits	1 2 3 4

TEACHER COMMENTS

Family Status _____
Father's Occ. _____
Mother's Occ. _____

Number of Children	Position in Family

Teacher's Sig. _____
Referred to: _____

Mark 1 semester courses ①

FORM 15, CARD B.

SCHOLARSHIP CODE: A = Sup.   B = Ab. Av.   C = Av.   D = Bel. Av.   F = Failure
CITIZENSHIP CODE: 1 = Outstanding   2 = Acceptable   3 = Unsatisfactory

PERSONALITY TRAIT CODE:
1 = Sup.   2 = Above Av.   3 = Average   4 = Bel. Av.

MINNEAPOLIS PUBLIC SCHOOLS

NAME (Last, First, Middle)

INDIVIDUAL ABILITY TESTS

Date	Grade	Test	C. A.	M. A.	I. Q.	Nat. %ile

GROUP ABILITY AND APTITUDE TESTS

Date	Grade	Test	R. S.	Norm.	%ile

SCHOLASTIC ACHIEVEMENT TESTS

Elementary

Secondary

INTERESTS AND OTHER MEASURES

FORM 15, CARD C.

222

MINNEAPOLIS PUBLIC SCHOOLS

NAME (Last, First, Middle)   Birth Date

ADDRESSES — WITHDRAWALS — READMISSIONS

Date	Addresses or Reason for Withdrawal	School

ACTIVITY EXPERIENCES

O = Officer   A = Active   P = Participate
Place appropriate mark under appropriate grade level.

Activity	7	8	9	10	11	12	Activity	7	8	9	10	11	12
Student Council							Annual						
							Debate						
Class Officer							Dramatics						
							Honor Roll						
H. R. Officer							National Honor Society						
							School Paper						
							Special Honors						
Athletics													
							Clubs						
Work Experiences													
Part-Time Work Program													

COMMENTS

Social Work

Psychological Services

EDUCATIONAL AND VOCATIONAL PLANS

Date	
9	
10	
11	
12	

FOLLOW-UP RECORD

	Give Date	Transcripts sent to:
Residence		
College or other Schools		
Employment		
Marriage		

FORM 15, CARD D.

223

LAST NAME	FIRST AND MIDDLE NAMES	M	F	DATE OF BIRTH	GRADE	NAME OF SCHOOL OR BUILDING
						1. 2. 3.

PUPIL'S HEALTH RECORD

REQUIRED BY LAW FOR ALL CHILDREN OF SCHOOL AGE. APPROVED BY STATE DEPARTMENT OF EDUCATION AND STATE DEPARTMENT OF HEALTH. THIS CARD SHOULD FOLLOW THE PUPIL, IF HE IS TRANSFERRED.

ADDRESS (in pencil)

FATHER OR GUARDIAN'S NAME AND ADDRESS

PHONE

IN CASE OF EMERGENCY

CALL ___ PHONE

FAMILY PHYSICIAN ___ PHONE

FAMILY DENTIST ___ PHONE

SIGNIFICANT PAST HISTORY

	YEAR		YEAR		YEAR
ALLERGY		FREQ. COLDS		RHEUMATIC FEVER	
CHICKEN POX		GERMAN MEASLES		SURGERY	
CONVULSIONS		MEASLES		TONSILLITIS	
DIABETES		MUMPS		TUBERCULOSIS	
DIPHTHERIA		ORTHOPEDIC		WHOOPING COUGH	
EMOTION. DIST.		POLIOMYELITIS			

COMMENTS:

COMMUNICABLE DISEASE PROTECTION

	ORIGINAL SERIES COMPLETED	BOOSTER DATES									DATE / RESULT							
DIPHTHERIA											MANTOUX	/	/	/	/	/	/	/	/
TETANUS																			
POLIO											CHEST X-RAY	/	/	/	/	/	/	/	/
WHOOPING COUGH																			
OTHER											SMALLPOX VACCIN.	/	/	/	/	/	/	/	/

TO BE COMPLETED BY PHYSICIAN

DATE	NOTE SIGNIFICANT HEALTH APPRAISAL FINDINGS	RECOMMENDATIONS FOR TREATMENT	IF UNABLE TO PARTICIPATE FULLY IN SCHOOL PROGRAM — SPECIFY CHANGES

12E (60M 11-63) Vocational School Print Shop

MINNEAPOLIS PUBLIC SCHOOLS

FORM 15, CARD E (Front).

224

| GRADE | DATE | VISION SCREENING | | | HEARING SCREENING | | | DENTAL |
		R	L	COMMENTS	R	L	COMMENTS	COMMENTS
K								
1								
2								
3								
4								
5								
6								
7								
8								
9								
10								
11								
12								

ANECDOTAL COMMENTS

DATE		SIGNATURE	TITLE

LAST NAME	FIRST AND MIDDLE NAMES	M	F	DATE OF BIRTH	GRADE	NAME OF SCHOOL OR BUILDING
						1. 2. 3.

FORM 15, CARD E (Back).

225

STUDENT INFORMATION

STUDENT NUMBER

LAST NAME	FIRST NAME	MIDDLE NAME		ENTRY/WITHDRAWAL/RE-ENTRY

DATE OF BIRTH	PLACE OF BIRTH (CITY, COUNTY, STATE)	SEX M F	RACE	FROM WHAT SCHOOL

ADDRESS (NUMBER, STREET)	PHONE NO.	DATE FIRST ENTERED

CHANGE IN ADDRESS	PHONE NO.	DATE WITHDRAWN

CHANGE IN ADDRESS	PHONE NO.	REASON

NO. OF OTHER CHILDREN IN FAMILY OLDER: YOUNGER:	FATHER DECEASED? YES ☐ NO ☐	MOTHER DECEASED? YES ☐ NO ☐	PARENTS SEPARATED? YES ☐ NO ☐	

HOBBIES/SPECIAL ABILITIES	DATE RE-ENTERED

GENERAL HEALTH EXCELLENT ☐ VERY GOOD ☐ GOOD ☐ FAIR ☐ POOR ☐	PHYSICAL DISABILITIES	SPECIAL CIRCUMSTANCES

SERIOUS ILLNESSES	CHURCH PREFERENCE

PARENT INFORMATION

PLACE PRESSURE SENSITIVE TEST LABEL HERE	PLACE PRESSURE SENSITIVE TEST LABEL HERE	FATHER'S NAME

STUDENT RESIDES WITH PARENTS ☐ OTHER:	MOTHER'S MAIDEN NAME

NAME IF OTHER THAN PARENT

OCCUPATION OF FATHER	OCCUPATION OF MOTHER

BUSINESS ADDRESS OF FATHER	BUSINESS ADDRESS OF MOTHER

BUSINESS PHONE	COUNTRY OF BIRTH	BUSINESS PHONE	COUNTRY OF BIRTH

EDUCATION	FATHER 6 7 8 9 10 11 12 COLLEGE 1 2 3 4 OTHER
	MOTHER 6 7 8 9 10 11 12 COLLEGE 1 2 3 4 OTHER

TEST DATA

NAME	DATE GIVEN	TEST FORM	TEST SCORE	TYPE OF SCORE	NORMS USED	PERCEN-TILE

PRELIMINARY SCHOLASTIC APTITUDE TEST

PLACE PRESSURE
SENSITIVE TEST
LABEL HERE

PLACE PRESSURE
SENSITIVE TEST
LABEL HERE

FORM 16(a).

Used with permission of Educational Testing Service.

COUNSELING NOTES

EDUCATIONAL AND OCCUPATIONAL PLANNING

	EDUCATIONAL PLANS				VOCATIONAL PLANS	
GRADE 8	TERMINATION	DATE	GRADE 8		OCCUPATION	DATE
9			9			
10			10			
11			11			
12			12			

HONORS AND AWARDS

DATE	NAME	DESCRIPTION

GEORGIA STUDENT RECORDS FOLDER
©1961 EDUCATIONAL TESTING SERVICE

FORM 16(b).

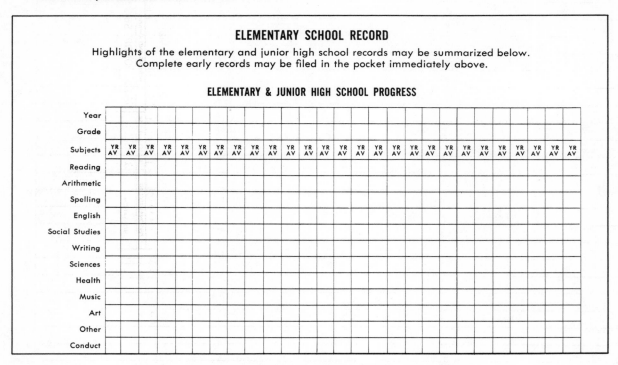

↑ STUDENT ACHIEVEMENT AND GUIDANCE REPORT ↑

At the end of each academic year, the Student Achievement and Guidance Report is summarized into the Student Profile Record in the middle frame of the folder. After posting, the Report is permanently filed in the pocket immediately above. Detailed records of grades and non-academic performance thus may be obtained by reference to this section.

ELEMENTARY SCHOOL RECORD

Highlights of the elementary and junior high school records may be summarized below.
Complete early records may be filed in the pocket immediately above.

ELEMENTARY & JUNIOR HIGH SCHOOL PROGRESS

| | | | | | | | | | | | | | | | | | | | | | | | | | | | | | | |

Year
Grade
Subjects
Reading
Arithmetic
Spelling
English
Social Studies
Writing
Sciences
Health
Music
Art
Other
Conduct

Use "Permanent" type ink to make entries on the folder.

FORM 16(c).

ture—a continuous story of an important segment in the life of an individual.

2. THE CONCEPT OF CONTINUITY IN EDUCATION FROM THE KINDERGARTEN THROUGH COLLEGE

For administrative purposes we divide the educative process into certain artificial units—elementary school, junior high school, senior high school, junior college, and so forth. Between each two units there is a break calling for adjustments on the part of both pupils and teachers. Continuous records, with provision for passing them freely from one school to another, can do much to improve the articulation between successive units, and thus greatly improve both the adjustive and the distributive aspects of guidance.

3. THE CONCEPT OF ORGANIZATION ACCORDING TO TIME SEQUENCE

Some cumulative records present a confused picture; they may contain much useful data, but considerable

time and energy must be expended merely in going over the record and in getting the essential facts arranged in relationship one to the other. One of the most helpful contributions to record keeping that has ever been made is the principle of organization according to time sequence. Busy administrators, teachers, and counselors find records in which the data are clearly classified by school years, and often by months within each year, a welcome contrast to records that are not arranged chronologically. No school, in setting up a new record system, can afford to neglect the need for making the cumulative record inherently a growth record.

4. THE CONCEPT OF COMPARABLE MEASUREMENT

A cumulative record without measurement is like a picture out of focus—there results a blurred and indistinct impression of the individual, but the whole lacks definiteness and assurance. It may be objected that measurement may very easily give a false impression of definiteness,

228   TECHNIQUES OF GUIDANCE

COMPREHENSIVE STUDENT REPORT

STUDENT INFORMATION

NAME: WARNER, NATALIE B

SEX	BIRTH DATE	STATE OF BIRTH
F	8/ 6/48	GA

PARENT OR GUARDIAN: WARNER, WILLIAM

HEALTH | PHYSICAL DISABILITY

CURRICULUM	FR	SO	JR	SR
ACADEMIC	0	0	0	

	FR	SO	JR	SR
DAYS ABSENT	5	2	3	
DAYS TARDY	0	0	1	

SCHOOL INFORMATION

SCHOOL NAME: ROCKY HILL H S
LOCATION: ATLANTA, GA

MEANING OF GRADES						
A	B	C	D	COR. INF.	PASSING	HONORS
95	87	79	70	90	87	70

CLASS PD (MIN)	MEETING WEEKS WEEK	WEEKS/YEAR
55	5	36

CEEB SCHOOL NUMBER	CLASS SIZE	GRAD YEAR	UNITS REQ
110170	430	64	18

SCHOOL ACCREDITED BY: STATE, REGION
OTHER SECONDARY SCHOOLS ATTENDED | DATE LEFT

ACADEMIC SUMMARY

RANK IN CLASS DATA

	POINTS	UNITS	AVERAGE	RANK	GROUP SIZE	%ILE STANDING
COMPLETE CLASS:	72.3+	19	= 3.80	4	IN 430	= 99
ACADEMIC GROUP (ACADEMIC COURSES ONLY):	60.5+	16	= 3.78	4	IN 260	= 99
COMPLETE CLASS WEIGHTED:	77.3+	19	= 4.07	3	IN 430	= 99

COMPOSITE TEST: PRELIMINARY SCHOL APT T

VERBAL TEST SCORE	MATH TEST SCORE	CONVERTED VERBAL COURSE SCORE	CONVERTED MATH/SCIENCE COURSE SCORE	CONVERTED ALL COURSE SCORE	VERBAL COMPOSITE	MATH/SCIENCE COMPOSITE	ALL COURSE COMPOSITE
62	65	71	71	74	64	66	67

ACADEMIC RECORD

AREA	AVERAGE
LANG ART	4.0
FOR LANG	3.5
MATH	3.8
SCIENCE	3.9
SOC STUD	4.0

VERBAL COURSE AVG. 3.7
MATH/SCIENCE COURSE AVG. 3.8

GRADE 9

SUBJECT	1	2	UNIT	GROUP	MISC
ENGLISH 1	A	A	1		
FRENCH 1	A	A	1		
LATIN 1	B	B	1		
ALGEBRA 1	B	A	1		
GEN SCI 1	A	A	1		
PHYS ED 1	A	B	.50		
MIX CHOR1	A	A	.50		

UNITS TOWARD GRADUATION 6
GRADE 9 AVERAGE 3.7

GRADE 10

SUBJECT	1	2	UNIT	GROUP	MISC
ENGLISH 2	A	A	1	HM	
FRENCH 2	A	B	1		
LATIN 2	B	B	1		
PLN GEOM	A		.50		
SLD GEOM	A	A	.50		
BSCS GRN	B	A	1	HM	
PHYS ED 2	A	A	.50		
MIX CHOR2	A	A	.50		

UNITS TOWARD GRADUATION 6
GRADE 10 AVERAGE 3.7

GRADE 11

SUBJECT	1	2	UNIT	GROUP	MISC
ENGLISH 3	A	A	1	HM	
FRENCH 3	A	A	1	HMCL	
FREN CONV	A		.50		
TRIGNMTRY	A	A	1		
CHM BND	A	A	1	HM	
ADV CHEM	A		.50	HMCL	
AM HIST 1	A	A	1		
PHYS ED 3	A	A	.50		
MIX CHOR3	A	A	.50		

UNITS TOWARD GRADUATION 7
GRADE 11 AVERAGE 4.0

OTHER GRADES

GRADE	SUBJECT	1	2	UNIT	GROUP	MISC
12	CBAP ENGL				H	
12	PHYS SSC				HM	
12	AM GOVT 1					
12	WLD HIST1					
12	PHYS ED 4					
12	MIX CHOR4					
12	PERS TYPE					

OTHER GRADE AVERAGE 4.0

TEST RECORD

GRADE	TEST INFORMATION
9	DIFFERENTIAL APTITUDE NRM:GRD 9 SCOR:%ILE
	SCHOL 95 , VERB 95
	NUMER 90 , ABST 85
	SPACE 60 , MECHL 85
	CLERL 45 , L-SPL 85
	L-SEN 80
9	SCH&COLL ABIL TST LVL3 NRM:GRD 9 SCOR:% BND
	VERB 96-99,QUANT 99-00
	TOTAL 99-99
9	SEQNT TST ED PROG LVL3 NRM:GRD 9 SCOR:% BND
	READ 92-00,WRITE 83-94
	LISTN 73-90,SOC S 89-95
	SCIEN 82-95, MATH 86-95
9	CO-OP ACH H S MATH Z NRM: 1 YR ST SCOR:% ILE
	E ALG 95
10	OTIS QCK-SCR M A GAMMA NRM:GRD 10 SCOR:I Q
	SCORE 125
11	PRELIMNARY SCHOL APT T NRM:GRD 11 SCOR:STAND
	VERB 62 MATH 65
11	NATIONL MERIT SCHOL QT NRM:COLLEG SCOR:STAND
	ENGL 23 MATH 25
	SOC S 27 N SCI 15
	WORD 19 TOTAL 22

EXTRA-CURRICULAR

ACTIVITY	FR	SO	JR	SR
SOCIAL CLUB			3	3
DEBATNG CLB			3	2
STD COUN BD				2
JOURNLM CLB			3	3
FUT TEACHRS				2

WORK RECORD

JOB	FR SUM	SO TERM	SO SUM	JR TERM	JR SUM	SR TERM	SR SUM
CLERCL OCC						1	
CLERCL OCC					17		
ACCT&BOOKP						9	
NURSEMAID	9	1	1	1	9	1	
WRITING						1	

PERSONAL RECORD	FR	SO	JR	SR
MOTIVATION	1	1	1	1
INDUSTRY	1	1	1	1
INITIATIVE	1	1	1	1
INFLUENCE-LEAD	1	1	1	1
CONCERN-OTHERS	1	1	1	1
RESPONSIBILITY	1	1	1	1
INTEGRITY	1	1	1	1
EMOTIONAL STABILITY	1	1	1	1

HONORS AND AWARDS
NATL HONOR SOC
LETTER CLUB

SIGNATURE: John Barr Prin. Sept 3 1963
TITLE | DATE

FORM 17 (Front).

Natalie's interest and ability levels are high in many areas, particularly in biography, marine biology, and foreign languages. At present, she is considering careers in journalism and as a teacher of English or foreign languages.

When her father was killed in an auto accident during Natalie's first year of high school, the chances of attending college for the four Warner children seemed dim. Since that time, her mother has obtained a position with the Family Service Group and with her help and scholarship aid, Natalie should be able to meet her expenses.

At present, Northwestern is Natalie's only choice of college. Her high school faculty feels that she should be able to maintain a high level of scholarship there. It is a pleasure to recommend this serious, wholesome, and unspoiled child who has such a serious desire to continue her education.

9/3/63	*Ethel Thomas*	College Counselor
Date	Signature	Title

SPECIAL SYMBOLS

✱ Information insufficient for reporting and computing purposes. Grades and units not included in computations or averages. If an improper composite test entry is coded, summary composites have not been developed.

Information improperly coded or insufficient for reporting purposes. Computations of averages or composites are not affected. If "grade taken" information is not available, grade level average only will be affected.

& Additional information not reported due to space or code limitations. Supplementary information should be added by the high school. For courses coded as "other," grade points and units are not included in area averages or academic group calculations.

Colleges have action to take in completion of this Report **one year** after its receipt. At that time, colleges are to send a transcript of student progress to the Secondary School for completion of its records.

STUDENT INFORMATION

Code #	Days Tardy and Days Absent
0	None
1	One
2	Two
3	3-4
5	5-7
8	8-11
12	12-16
17	17-21
22	22-26
27	27 or more

HEALTH

Code #	Illness Interfered with Studies
0	Not at all
1	To slight degree
2	To moderate degree
3	To appreciable degree
4	To serious detriment of progress.

SCHOOL INFORMATION

Meaning of Grades — The number printed below any grade letter is the lowest grade possible for receipt of that letter grade. **Col. Rec.**—The minimum alphabetic grade for college recommendation. **Grad. Year**—The expected year of graduation. **Units Req.**—The total number of Carnegie Units required for graduation.

ACADEMIC SUMMARY

All Academic Averages are based on assigned values of A=4, B=3, C=2, D=1, and F=0. Rank in Class and Percentile Standing are based on the student's course average (grade points divided by units earned) compared to the course averages of his classmates for each of the separate classifications. Complete class data are based on the total class for all courses taken by the students. Academic group calculations are presented only for those students in the academic curriculum and are based on academic courses only. Complete class-weighted data include all students and all courses. The calculations assign one additional value (A=5, B=4, etc.) for courses tracked as high and high-middle and one less value (A=3, B=2, etc.) for courses tracked as middle-low or low—Composite test notes the testing program employed at a school from which composites have been computed.

Converted Verbal Course Score, Converted Math/Science Course Score, and Converted All Course Score place each of these in-school averages on a scale to which composite test scores can be conveniently transposed. After the appropriate test subscores are transposed to this scale, the converted course scores are adjusted by one half the difference in means between class distributions of the course scores and the test scores. From these components, the following composites are developed:

$$\text{Verbal Composite} = \frac{\text{Transposed Verbal Test Score} + \text{Adj. Verbal Course Score}}{2}$$

$$\text{Math/Science Composite} = \frac{\text{Transposed Math Test Score} + \text{Adj. Math/Science Course Score}}{2}$$

$$\text{All Course Composite} = \frac{2 \text{ Trans. Verbal Test Score} + 2 \text{ Trans. Math Test Score} + 3 \text{ Adjusted All Course Score}}{6}$$

All composites reflect relative measures of student ability and should not be regarded as direct predictions of college freshman grades. Technical details with regard to adjustments, conversions, transpositions, composites and other computations may be found in the publication "Interpretations from Comprehensive Student Reports"— ETS, 1963.

ACADEMIC RECORD

Field Averages are computed from final grades awarded in all courses taken in separate fields of Language Arts, Foreign Language, Mathematics, Science, and Social Studies. The Verbal Course Average is calculated from final grades in all courses in Language Arts, Foreign Language, and Social Studies. The Math/Science Course Average is calculated from final grades in all courses in Mathematics and Science.

GROUPING

A notation will appear in this space only if students in that course were homogeneously grouped.

Code	Tracking Group	Definition
H	High Group	Advanced Placement (CEEB)
HM	High-Middle Group	Content geared to the above average or superior learner
M	Middle Group	Middle Group
ML	Middle-Low Group	Content adjusted to accomodate a low average learner
L	Low Group	Remedial

MISC.

This column takes note of the following information.

Code	Definition
S	Summer Course
LB	Laboratory Course
TV	Television Course
SM	Seminar Course
CL	Course on College Campus

OTHER GRADES

The "Other Grades" area may include course work from the 8th and/or 12th grade. The column entitled **GRADE** will note the specific grade in which the subject was taken.

TEST RECORD

GR-Grade Taken	% ILE-Percentile
NRM-Denotes the test norm group	IQ-Intelligence Quotient
SCOR-The type of score reported	GRD P-Grade Placement
% BND-Percentile Band	RAW S-Raw Score
STAND-Standard Score	STA 9-Stanine

EXTRA-CURRICULAR ACTIVITIES

Student Performance is rated on the following five point scale.

Code #	Activity
1	President, captain, editor, or group leader doing a high quality job.
2	Other elected officers, appointed officer, a letter man effecting his responsibilities.
3	An effectively contributing participant or varsity member.
4	Member of Junior-Varsity or general participant.
5	A disinterested and uncooperative member.
X	Student participated but was not rated.

WORK RECORD

The work record is divided into Summer and Term classifications for each of the four school years.

Code #	Hours Worked/Week
1	1-8
9	9-16
17	17-24
25	25-32
33	33 #

PERSONAL RECORD

Personal characteristics are rated on a scale one through five, one being the highest possible rating, five the lowest. The characteristics are those on the Personality Record of the National Association of Secondary School Principals. Schools are instructed to average three independent ratings for each trait.

FORM 17 (Back).

and that there will be a tendency to read too much into the test scores. This is true if the measurement is made at only one point in the pupil's history and if the interpretation is placed in unskilled hands. But a program of comparable measurements, conducted annually by competent persons, should result in well-placed confidence, in definite evidence of achievement and growth, tempered by an awareness of the limitations that are involved in all objective data relating to living human beings.

The measurement program should be as broad and as thorough as the resources of the school will permit, for the more inclusive the data, the less the chance of drawing incorrect conclusions. It is desirable for the measurement program to include annual records of anthropometric data, health examinations, academic aptitude tests, achievement tests in all subjects studied by the pupil, measures of creativity if such are available, and a limited number of personality and interest inventories.

5. THE CONCEPT OF GRAPHICAL PRESENTATION OF NUMERICAL DATA

In one sense, the idea of presenting test results and other numerical data graphically has been negated by automatic data processing equipment and pressure-sensitive labels for recording test scores. In another sense, however, data processing should save enough time so that it would be easier for schools to prepare graphic records of their test results. Some of the newer data processing equipment can produce graphs as one form of output.

Most people have rather definite opinions about graphs. Some persons are opposed to them either because they do not understand them or feel that many people cannot make them out; others, among whom are some mathematicians, prefer to deal with numbers rather than graphs, because they know that numbers can be manipulated in ways that graphs cannot. On the other hand, there are those who want a picture of everything and feel that they can better make their interpretations if they are able to see data in graphic form.

To meet these individual preferences, it is desirable to present data in the cumulative record both numerically and graphically. Aside from personal preference, there is an excellent psychological basis for using graphs to supplement numerical data wherever possible. The principle is really a dual one. In the first place, the mind can apprehend position more quickly than it can apprehend numerical value, and, in the second place, a group of positions can be taken in at a glance, while a group of numbers cannot be digested with one sweep of the eyes. The numbers must be brought into consciousness and interpreted one after another before a generalization can

be drawn concerning whether a pupil stands high or low in aptitude, achievement, and so forth. Therefore, in interpreting numbers—for example, test scores or grades—one is forced to go from the particular to the general. In interpreting a graph, however, one may work either way; he may, if he wishes, get his generalization before he particularizes, or even, if he is in a great hurry, generalize without particularizing at all. Thus, one will glance at a series of cumulative records of aptitude and achievement, as entered on the Educational Records Bureau cumulative record card, and say, even while glancing at them, "This boy is high in ability and achievement; this one is low; this one has good ability, but his achievement is not up to capacity"; and so forth.

By no other device could such rapid generalizations be achieved. This point is of great importance and should be carefully considered by every records committee. It is safe to say that the average person—even the average teacher—has to learn to like records which are new and strange to him. In the beginning, if he is faced with a mass of detail in records, his natural tendency is to avoid them, for they make his head ache and are otherwise distasteful. But if he can go to the record and get a quick picture of the aptitude and achievement of a problem pupil within a few seconds, he will use the records because they save his time and help him in his work. Certainly, the use of records should not stop with a general impression concerning only certain aspects of a pupil; but, in the beginning, the general picture obtained from the graph is the best single point of contact in the popularization of the records within the faculty. Moreover, the general impression given by the graph will continue to be useful even to those who are very familiar with cumulative records, for each detail is seen in relation to the whole objective record, just as a detail in a picture takes on added meaning when seen against a background.

A main deterrent to graphical representation of test data is the time it takes to make the graphs. But this time is well spent, if understanding is increased. For this reason, graphs continue to be used in the cumulative records which the Educational Records Bureau prepares for some of its members; and the schools say they find this part of the record especially valuable.

6. THE CONCEPT OF BEHAVIOR DESCRIPTION

One of the outstanding contributions to record keeping has been the observation that if one secures a record of a pupil's behavior, not complicated by the opinion of the person who sets it down, one then has a rather objective record. The result is not a record than can readily be treated quantitatively, but nevertheless, in dependability, it compares favorably with a numerical record. Re-

NAME HOME ADDRESS TELEPHONE BIRTH DATE

YEAR

SCHOOL

GRADE

CHRON. AGE

Notes on Elementary School Experience:

| FIELD OF STUDY | FIELD OF STUDY | FIELD OF STUDY | FIELD OF STUDY | FIELD OF STUDY | FIELD OF STUDY |

RECORD OF CLASS WORK

COMMENT

	TEST	Sc. I.Q. %ile°	TEST	Sc. I.Q. %ile	TEST	Sc. I.Q. %ile	TEST	Sc. I.Q. %ile	TEST	Sc. I.Q. %ile
ACADEMIC APTITUDE	TEST	Sc. P.S. Gr. %ile°	TEST	Sc. P.S. Gr. %ile	TEST	Sc. P.S. Gr. %ile	TEST	Sc. P.S. Gr. %ile	TEST	Sc. P.S. Gr. %ile
READING	TEST	Sc. P.S. Gr. %ile°	TEST	Sc. P.S. Gr. %ile	TEST	Sc. P.S. Gr. %ile	TEST	Sc. P.S. Gr. %ile	TEST	Sc. P.S. Gr. %ile

ACHIEVEMENT TESTS & OTHER TESTS

Explanatory notes concerning test scores and percentiles

NOTES

°indicate basic Group (public school, independent school, local, etc.)

PRINCIPAL'S RECOMMENDATION:

This space reserved for notes by College Admissions Officer or Employer:

FORM 18 (Front).

232

NAME   ADDRESS   TELEPHONE

BIRTHDATE   BIRTHPLACE

FAMILY	OCCUPATION	EDUCATION	RELIGION	HEALTH	DECEASED DATE
FATHER					
MOTHER					
STEP PARENT OR GUARDIAN					
SIBLINGS		BIRTHDATE			

Note here everything of significance concerning health of members of family, place of birth, citizenship, language spoken in the home, study conditions, type of community in which the family has lived, or any other matters which simplify significantly the description of the home.

YEAR AND AGE				
COUNSELOR				
ATTENDANCE				
ACADEMIC				
DISCIPLINE PERSONAL				
IN SCHOOL				
INTERESTS OUT OF SCHOOL				
VOCATIONAL EXPERIENCES				
NOTABLE ACCOMPLISHMENTS				
HEALTH AND PHYSICAL VIGOR				
EDUCATIONAL AND VOCATIONAL PLANS				
RESPONSIBILITY DEPENDABILITY				
CREATIVENESS AND IMAGINATION				
INFLUENCE				
SOCIAL ADJUSTMENT				
COUNSELOR'S NOTES				
REMARKS				

BEHAVIOR DESCRIPTION

FORM 18 (Back).

233

gardless of whether one prefers the anecdotal record plan or the Behavior Description form which evolved out of the Eight-Year Study, or some other plan, provision should certainly be made for a description of behavior in any new cumulative record form that is set up. To neglect this aspect of the record is simply to fail to take into account one of the most fruitful recent trends in the philosophy of education. This is the balance wheel in the records system—or, to change the metaphor, it is an appropriate foil for any tendency to overemphasize academic marks and achievement test data.

Finally, there is an emergent concept that may ultimately affect the recording of the results of measurement. This concept, which is not yet widely enough recognized to be listed as one that records committees can utilize, is the idea of a common scale for all test data—a scale that is based on a defined group. Perhaps the best illustrations of the application of this concept are the converted scores used with the tests of the College Entrance Examination Board and the Scaled Score system which was used with the older edition of the Cooperative Achievement Tests. When school people generally come to understand a system of this kind and to realize its advantages, such a plan may largely replace the recording of test results in terms of raw scores and percentiles.

REFERENCES

1. "An Easy Way to Maintain Student Records," *School Management,* V (July 1961), 42–43.
2. Bowman, Howard A. "Techniques for Graphical Representation of Pupil Personnel Data to Indicate Individual Deviates and to Provide a Basis for More Adequate Guidance," *Educational and Psychological Measurement,* XII (Autumn 1952), 490–502.
3. *Cumulative Record Folder: Recording and Use.* Handbook for School Personnel. Minneapolis, Minn.: Minneapolis Public Schools, 1963. Pp. 25. (Mimeographed.)
4. Ellis, Gordon. "A New Approach to Student Records," *Personnel and Guidance Journal,* XLI (April 1963), 724–726.
5. Fibel, Luria R. "Uniform Reference Form," *College and University,* XXXVI (Winter 1961), 210–211.
6. Fulton, Margaret J. "Analysis of a Personnel Record System," *Journal of Higher Education,* XXII (April 1951), 209–211.
7. Gaddis, Edwin A. "Cumulative Record System that Promotes Guidance," *National Elementary Principal,* XXXIV (September 1954), 172–174.
8. Goldman, Leo. "Cooperative Plan for Guidance and Admission," *Personnel and Guidance Journal,* XLII (September 1963), 64–68.
9. Heck, Arch O. *Administration of Pupil Personnel.* New York: Ginn and Company, 1929. Pp. xx + 480.
10. Johnson, Andrew. "An Addition for the Cumulative Record," *Junior College Journal,* XXXII (November 1961), 167–173.
11. Jones, Galen, and Galbraith, Adria. "Genesis of a Guidance Program," *School Executive,* LXII (May 1943), 32–34.
12. Kaczhowski, Henry R. "The Current Status of Cumulative Records," *Vocational Guidance Quarterly,* VII (Summer 1959), 211–213.
13. *Manual for the Secondary-School Record.* Washington, D.C.: National Association of Secondary-School Principals, 1964. Pp. 23.
14. Morrison, Wilma. *The School Record: Its Use and Abuse in College Admissions.* New York: College Entrance Examination Board, 1961. Pp. 15.
15. Ohles, J. F., and others. "Cumulative Record: A Case Study of a Committee in Operation," *Clearing House,* XXXVI (May 1962), 531–535.
16. O'Neill, J. H. "Cumulative Record as a Guidance Service," *Catholic School Journal,* LIV (December 1954), 317–319.
17. "Personnel Methods," *The Educational Record Supplement.* Washington: American Council on Education, 1928.
18. Proff, Fred C. "The Use of Appraisal Data by Guidance and Personnel Workers," *Review of Educational Research,* XXX (April 1960), 141–147.
19. Segel, David. *Nature and Use of the Cumulative Record.* U.S. Office of Education Bulletin 1938, No. 3. Washington, D.C.: Government Printing Office, 1938. Pp. 48.
20. Smith, Eugene R. "Modernizing Records for Guidance and Transfer." *Educational Record,* Supplement 13 (January 1940), 17–33.
21. Spaulding, Geraldine. *The Application of Secondary-School Cumulative Record Data to the Prediction of College Success.* A Report of Research Conducted under a Grant from the College Entrance Examination Board. New York: Educational Records Bureau, 1960. Pp. 42. (Mimeographed.)
22. Steve, R. T. "Cumulative Record," *NEA Journal,* LI (May 1962), 48.
23. *The Recommendations of the 26th International Conference on Public Education Sponsored by UNESCO and the International Bureau of Education,* Geneva, July 1963. Washington, D.C.: Office of Education, Division of International Studies and Services, October 1963. Pp. 17.
24. Traxler, Arthur E. "How to Use Cumulative Records," *Educational Digest,* XIII (October 1947), 9–11.
25. Troxel, Oliver L., and Koos, Leonard V. "An Analysis of High School Record Forms," *Proceedings of the Tenth Annual Meeting of the National Association of Secondary-School Principals,* pp. 33–57. Bulletin of the National Association of Secondary-School Principals, No.

11. Cicero, Ill.: Department of Secondary-School Principals of the National Education Association, 1926.

26. Walton, Wesley W. "Data Processing as an Administrative Tool for Cumulative Records," *Innovation and Experiment in Modern Education,* pp. 65–79. Report of Twenty-ninth Educational Conference sponsored by the Educational Records Bureau. Washington, D.C.: American Council on Education, 1965. Pp. viii + 159.

27. Wood, Ben D. "The Need for Comparable Measurements in Individualized Education," *Educational Record,* Supplement No. 12 (January 1939), 14–31.

28. Warnken, Robert G., and Siess, Thomas F. "The Use of the Cumulative Record in the Prediction of Behavior," *Personnel and Guidance Journal,* XLIV (November 1965), 231–237.

CHAPTER XIV

Reports to the Homes

IT IS WIDELY RECOGNIZED THAT CORDIALITY AND mutual understanding between the school and the homes of the pupils are important in a guidance program. The relations of the school with the home may take many forms, but the one type of contact that can be counted upon to reach every home served by the school is the periodic report of pupil progress. Reports to the home are therefore a major technique in the functioning of a program of individual guidance, just as they are in school administration and public relations. In summarizing a study of recording and reporting of pupil progress at the secondary school level, Vredevoe and Lindecamp (42) said, "The study revealed that no part of the program of communication with parents is of greater importance or influence than that which attempts to report achievement, growth, or progress of the individual pupil in the school."

Report cards are one of the oldest of the forms used by the school, probably antedating all record forms except the school register. The original purpose of report cards was to inform parents how their children were getting along in school, and this has been their main function at all times. The best reporting technique is that which gives the parent the most complete and reliable information about the school history of his child, within the limits of the time that both teachers and parents can be expected to spend on this matter. The information sent to the home obviously should be based on those kinds of achievement and growth which the school is trying to develop in its students.

Report cards are only one of several devices for informing parents concerning the school achievement and growth of their children. In place of report cards, some schools employ letters written by teachers, letters written by pupils, personal interviews, or visits to the home.

Some type of report form, however, continues to have a place in the reporting systems of the great majority of schools. In general, reporting procedures continue to be a good deal more conservative and traditional than one would infer from reading some of the articles in current literature purporting to set forth newer practices.

MARKING SYSTEMS

Although a detailed treatment of the theory and practice of marking falls outside the scope of this book, it is impossible to discuss report cards without giving some attention to it. The plan used by the school to grade its pupils is always of great concern to pupils and parents, and the literature relating to marking systems has grown voluminous. The most common marking plans are the percentage system, the symbolic or categorical system, the dichotomous system, and some type of mark, such as the accomplishment quotient, to indicate the relationship of the pupil's achievement to his ability.

The percentage system is the oldest and, in most ways, the least satisfactory plan of marking. Numerous objections against it have been advanced. One of the most important is that its three reference points—0, 100, and the passing mark—are not stable and cannot be rigidly defined. Another valid criticism of this time-honored plan is that it provides for much finer distinctions than human judgment has the capacity to make. Nevertheless, a considerable number of schools cling fondly to this procedure, even though it is not in harmony with modern techniques of appraisal.

The symbolic or categorical system is one in which letters, such as A, B, C, D, and F, or numbers, as I, II,

III, IV, and V, are used to characterize the achievement of the pupils. It is usually a five-point system, although sometimes it includes three, seven, or even nine groups. One argument in favor of it when contrasted with the percentage plan is that persons are able to form fairly valid judgments concerning individuals by classifying them into about five groups, whereas an attempt to classify them into 101 groups is futile.

The symbolic system may be clarified and rendered definite by relating it to the normal curve. One common plan for a five-point system is to assign a mark of C to all pupils falling between plus and minus 0.5 sigma; B to those between plus 0.5 sigma and plus 1.5 sigma; D to those between minus 0.5 sigma and minus 1.5 sigma; A to those above plus 1.5 sigma; and F to those below minus 1.5 sigma. In a normal distribution, this results in approximately the following percentages of the different marks: A, 7 percent; B, 24 percent; C, 38 percent; D, 24 percent; and F, 7 percent. The marks in this system may be further clarified by paragraph statements supporting them.

The staff members of a considerable number of schools, believing that comparisons among pupils are invidious, have minimized these comparisons as much as possible by adopting a system in which a dichotomy is created. The only grades they routinely assign are *pass* or *fail, satisfactory* or *unsatisfactory, mastery* or *failure to master*. It is stated in favor of this plan that since all pupils who do satisfactory work receive the stamp of official approval, harmful competition is greatly minimized. Nevertheless, it must be admitted that a good many schools that have tried this plan have not found it wholly satisfactory, but have gradually and half-unconsciously abandoned it and returned to a symbolic system. The first step away from the dichotomous system is usually the addition of a middle group because of the feeling that *pass* and *fail* do not take care of the situation. A little later, perhaps an honors group is added, and soon the school finds itself using a five-point system, even though its grouping may not be called A, B, C, D, and F. In fact, the attempt to classify the school achievement of all pupils as satisfactory or unsatisfactory is at variance with what we know about the distribution of individuals or any characteristic. They are not readily divided into two clear-cut groups, for they vary all the way from extremely favorable to very unfavorable, and most of them cluster near the average.

Some 30 or 35 years ago, the accomplishment quotient, or AQ, popularized by Franzen, had a flurry of popularity which has largely abated but is of historical interest. This plan was designed so that AQ equalled educational age divided by mental age, or EQ divided by IQ. It is an interesting commentary upon the thinking that is sometimes done about marking, that some persons who were vigorously opposed to placing pupils along a scale and comparing them with one another subscribed to the accomplishment quotient, which is simply a ratio between the placement of a pupil on two scales in which he is compared with other pupils. Presumably, the reason that they were willing to accept in one instance what they rejected in the other was that they felt that the accomplishment quotient gave every child the same chance to stand high—the dullard as well as the bright pupil. As a matter of fact, it did not. The pupils with high IQs were placed under a handicap by this plan, so that their accomplishment quotients tended to be lower than those of their less fortunate classmates. One of the bases of this phenomenon is opportunistic. Teachers often tend to prod the slow pupils, and to let the bright ones shift for themselves, notwithstanding the growing national attention to the gifted. Consequently, the dullards often do better in comparison with their IQ because of more attention, and not from any inward drive. The other basis is statistical. Stated briefly, everyone tends, because of chance errors that are inherent in every measuring instrument, to regress toward the mean of the group on a series of tests. A pupil who makes a very low score on an intelligence test will probably do a little better on subsequent tests of achievement—at least there is a greater chance that he will do better than that he will do worse. Similarly, a pupil whose intelligence score is very high has less chance of making higher average scores on several additional tests than he has of making lower scores.

In some schools, the general idea of the AQ is employed even though the Accomplishment Quotient, as such, is not used. These schools attempt to take ability into consideration in the assignment of grades. It should not be thought that this procedure eliminates comparison among pupils, for one cannot obtain either a quantitative or a qualitative expression of the ability of the individual pupil except in relation to that of other pupils. An IQ of 115, for example, is derived from norms resulting from the testing of a large and presumably unselected group of children of the same age as the pupil in question. Nevertheless, when intelligently employed, the marking of pupils on the basis of their ability may be a fruitful plan, if the limitations already noted in the discussion of the AQ are kept in mind. For example, according to Keller (*18*), Sewanhaka High School, Floral Park, New York, for nearly 18 years successfully used marks that showed a pupil's achievement in relation to his ability. Teachers had test data in their class roll books concerning their pupils' IQ, reading grade level, and so forth, and they gave careful consideration to these data in assigning marks. Apparently there were no serious objections from parents, colleges, or employers to this marking procedure, and there is reason to believe that it may have had a salutary effect upon the holding power of the school. In 1952, the percentage of dropouts in this high school was only 13 as compared with 50 percent for the state as a whole.

A number of years ago, some people became convinced that all marking systems were inherently bad, and went on record as being opposed to the assignment of any marks whatsoever to the pupils in their schools. Three main arguments were advanced against the use of marks. The first had its origin in research; the second resulted from logical inference, supported by experience; and the third arose from considerations of mental health.

Beginning with the work of Starch and Elliott about 1912, many studies have been concerned with the reliability of school marks. The evidence of those studies is so well known that it does not need to be presented here. Suffice it to say that Starch and Elliott (38), Wood (45), Ruch (37), and others years ago showed convincingly that the reliabilities of the ordinary school marks based on the traditional essay-type examinations are too low to satisfy the criteria for individual guidance. Even for examinations three hours in length, the reliability coefficients usually fall within the range .60 to .80. It is true that the reliability of marks can be improved by basing them on the results of objective tests, or by using procedures to objectify the judgments of the instructors, but all too few schools have made a serious attempt to place the grading of their pupils on a more objective basis.

The second objection to marking arises out of the observation that marks are general statements of achievement, whereas specific statements are needed in guidance. It may be stated syllogistically as follows: general statements about pupils are of limited value in a guidance program; marks are very general summary statements involving a multitude of unanalyzed variables; therefore, marks have limited guidance value. The validity of the criticism is at once apparent to anyone who conducts a case study of a pupil whose marks are unsatisfactory. One is immediately confronted with the problem of collecting a variety of specific facts about the pupil's achievement which will give the marks meaning, reveal the sources of the difficulty, and provide leads for intelligent remedial treatment.

The third argument against marking is the one most frequently advanced by certain modern schools and is also the one which is most vigorously debated. This objection to marking is that assignment of marks causes pupils to compare themselves with each other, and leads to an unwholesome state of competition in which the less able pupils are predestined to lose, and consequently develop feelings of frustration, inferiority, and inward rebellion. It may be pointed out, in reply to this argument,

that ability to obtain high marks is just one of many ways in which pupils vary and that the elimination of marking will not thereby create a Utopian institution in which all pupils work together on a basis of complete equality. It may also be insisted that children who experience complete frustration because of low marks and who are unable to find a compensatory source of satisfaction are already mentally and emotionally sick, and are in need of special therapeutic treatment and guidance. Regardless of opinion on this point, the first two arguments against marking are sufficient to give any school pause if it is committed to a practice of indiscriminate marking based on nothing more tangible than teacher opinion and general appraisal on a subjective basis. Marks reach their greatest value when they are supported by objective data and when they provide information concerning the *specific* strengths and weaknesses of students.

TRENDS IN FORMS FOR REPORTS TO PARENTS

A number of useful studies of report forms have been made since about 1930. The following outline of the trends in reports is based in part on studies reported by Hill (17), Messenger and Watts (24), Pugsley (28), Hansen (14), Brantley (4), Metteer (25), Strang (40), De Pencier (9, 10), Roelfs (33, 34), Duckworth (12), Vredevoe and Lindecamp (42), and Lewis and McCrea (20).

Before note is taken of general trends in reporting procedures, it should be observed that, on the whole, there are some differences between the characteristics of reports in elementary and in secondary schools. Elementary schools have been comparatively free to experiment with new or novel procedures, and many have taken considerable advantage of this freedom. Secondary schools, in part because they must keep records and issue reports which will eventually satisfy not only parents but colleges and employers as well, have been slower to depart from traditional kinds of reports.

The difference between the trends in elementary and secondary school reports is brought out by findings in surveys by De Pencier (9) and Roelfs (33, 34). In a study of trends in reports of pupil progress in the elementary grades over a 12-year period, De Pencier found that the conference or personal interview was emphasized in literature more than any other method. On the other hand, Roelfs, in an analysis of reports employed in 154 junior high schools, found that a printed form of some type was used in every one of these schools.

Home letters are a common way of reporting by

elementary school teachers, even in school systems that lay no claim to "progressive" methods, but the use of this way of reporting is still rather rare in secondary schools.

A newer reporting procedure is not necessarily better than an older one, and it may prove to be actually less satisfactory when it is time-tested. In the long run, it will turn out to be an improvement only if it gives parents a better overall understanding of the school progress of their children than was provided by the older procedure. It is not possible to say, on the basis of objective criteria, that the reporting to homes done by elementary schools is any better than that carried on by secondary schools. It can only be said that elementary school reporting procedures are, in general, less conventional and less formal than the reporting procedures of secondary schools. Some of the specific differences between elementary and secondary school reports will become more apparent in connection with the following statements of general trends.

1. *There is some dissatisfaction with systems of marking that encourage comparison of pupils with one another.* In the first edition of this book, it was stated that there was *growing* dissatisfaction. The more recent surveys do not indicate that this dissatisfaction continues to grow. In fact, there is some indication that there is now a reversal in trend, and that there is developing some dissatisfaction, particularly on the part of parents whose children are college bound, with systems of marking that give no indication of how a child compares with his peers. As one parent is reported to have said in connection with one of the noncomparative systems of marking, "After six years all I know about Paul's school work is that he is always trying."

Moreover, the dissatisfaction with conventional marking plans probably has never been so widespread as one might think from a perusal of articles on the subject. Those who are not satisfied with the traditional marking plan seem to be more articulate and more vociferous than those who are. At any rate, studies fail to show that comparative marking was ever abandoned in more than about 10 percent of the reports sent to homes.

An important criticism of conventional reporting plans is not so much that comparisons are made, but rather that the nature of the comparisons is not clarified for parents. Le Baron (19) stressed the point that the basis of comparison must be made clear, and has referred to Olson's "organismic age" as a scale on which individual comparisons may be based. As Olson explained in his book, *Child Development* (27), organismic age is a technique for showing progress of the individual pupil in relation to the average pattern of progress of all children of the same age. Organismic age is based on development in mental age, reading age, height age, weight age, dental age, grip age, and carpal age. Olson urged that a pupil's

school achievement is a function of his total growth and not solely a matter of curriculum or method. It seems obvious that the employment of such a scheme of reference would facilitate the use of the growth and progress type of report which is now increasing in favor in some places.

2. *For years, there has been a trend in report cards away from percentage marking toward a scale with fewer points.* This was shown clearly some 30 years ago when the findings of Hill (17) in 1935 were compared with those of Chapman and Ashbaugh (6) obtained in 1925. The study by Chapman and Ashbaugh showed that in 1925, 29 percent of the elementary school cards, 23 percent of the junior high school cards, and 37 percent of the high school cards used only percentages in marking. In Hill's study, it was found that only 8 percent of the elementary cards, 12 percent of the junior high school cards, and 15 percent of the high school cards employed percentage marking only. Both investigators showed that symbol-percent scales[1] were utilized in 34 percent of the cards. Chapman and Ashbaugh reported only 31 percent using symbolic scales in 1925, whereas Hill found 54 percent using such scales in 1935.

That the trend away from percentage marks has been continued in more recent years is shown by Roelfs' (33) study at the junior high school level in 1954, in which it was found that only two out of 154 junior high schools cooperating in the survey used percentage marks.

Marking and reporting systems with a very small number of steps, such as S and U, or S-U and H (for honors), are frequently recommended, but both Hill's 1935 study, and Roelf's 1954 survey indicated that in actual practice the five-point scale, such as A, B, C, D, and F, was far more common than other types. Eighty-one percent of Roelf's 154 junior high schools used five-point marking scales; 12 percent employed more divisions; while only 3 percent used fewer divisions, such as S-U. It is to be noted that Roelf's study did not include elementary schools. The proportion of elementary schools marking on the S-U basis is undoubtedly somewhat larger. For example, in a survey reported by Strang (40) which included both elementary and secondary schools, in Nassau County, New York, conducted in 1952, 41 of 126 schools stated that they used S-U marks on report cards, while 56 employed the A, B, C, D type of marking, and 29 used numerical marks. A further analysis of these data as reported by Strang is reproduced in Table 5.[2]

3. *There is at least a slight trend toward the reporting of pupil progress in relation to ability.* As stated by

---

[1] For example, A, B, C, D, F, defined by percentages, as A = 95–100, and so forth.
[2] Reprinted with permission of Dr. Strang and *The School Executive.*

Rogers, Rupright, and Gerich (35), "The secondary school is moving toward a means of reporting that considers pupil progress in the light of individual abilities." Attention was called earlier in this chapter to the successful use of this method of reporting over a long period in one high school, Sewanhaka High School, Floral Park, New York (18).

TABLE 5. Methods of Reporting Pupil Progress in Nassau County, New York

Reporting Methods	Type of Report Card Marks			
	Numerical	Letter (A, B, C, D)	Letter (S-U)	Total Schools
Cards only	5	17	6	28
Cards and letters	3	0	4	7
Cards and conferences	6	12	13	31
Cards, letters, and conferences	15	27	18	60
Total	29	56	41	126

4. *There is a widespread tendency for report cards to include an evaluation of traits other than subject matter achievement alone.* Most cards give some space to rating character traits and conduct habits, although in many cards the trait ratings are very general and perhaps not very meaningful. Roelfs (34) found that behavior was reported in nine out of ten junior high schools. The average number of traits or habits mentioned on the cards studied by Hill (17) was 5.6. According to White (44), there is a trend toward ratings in terms of requisite behavior in connection with each course, rather than an overall grade, and this observation is confirmed by some of the other studies.

5. Messenger and Watts (24) observed in their summary in 1935 that *there was a clear tendency to use descriptive rather than quantitative reports.* This tendency has been continued and apparently strengthened since that time. It is a tendency which may not be wholly commendable. A combination of descriptive and quantitative reporting may be the better plan. Certainly, the ultimate purpose of all reporting is clear and accurate description, but quantitative reports may lend greater precision to descriptions, if properly interpreted and used.

6. As was noted earlier, *in some secondary schools and many elementary schools, formal reports have been replaced by notes or letters to parents.* These may be written by the principal, by the teachers, or by the pupils themselves. A still larger number of schools follow the practice of supplementing the more formal report of marks with notes and letters. Moreover, studies show

that the great majority of report cards carry some kind of form letter to the parents. Although these messages are sometimes brief, and even curt, they usually contain helpful information and suggestions. A list of items discussed in report letters, together with the percentage of cards in which the items appeared, was given by Hill as shown in this column (17:118).[3]

The informal letter to parents, supplemented by conferences as needed, is the preferred means of reporting given by a good many present-day writers on reports to the homes. It has even been said that "the best report

Items Discussed in Letter	Percent of 443
Request for harmony and cooperation	41
Invitation to confer with teachers	35
Invitation to visit the school	32
Request to sign and return the card	31
The importance of regular attendance	20
Explanation of marks	19
Explanation of frequency of issuance	18
The purpose of the report card	14
Meaning of parent's signature—it does not necessarily signify approval	13
Request that parents study card carefully	9
Explanation of absence and tardy excuses	9
Character and citizenship as school aims	8
Importance of home study	5
Purposes and aims of the school	4
Bases of promotion	4
Explanation of the failing mark	2
Parent-Teacher Association meeetings	2
Miscellaneous (20 different items)	14

form is a blank sheet of paper in the hands of a well-qualified teacher." This is a kind of catch phrase which sounds well and has wide appeal, but in most school situations it has one basic difficulty. It simply is not true. Most teachers will do a better job of reporting if they may make use of a report form which provides at least some general guideposts to remind them of the essentials which should be included in their reports. Moreover, when the informal letter is used as the sole means of reporting, some difficulties are encountered with regard to keeping permanent records of what has been reported. Carbon copies of the letters may be maintained in a file, but these become bulky and are not easily reviewed in order to find out what specific items have been reported and what progress has been made by the individual pupil. The information given in informal letters tends to become rather widely diffused. As noted by Le Baron (19), there is a danger that informal notes will tell parents "less and less about more and more."

Certainly, notes and letters to parents have an im-

[3] Reprinted with Dr. Hill's permission.

portant supplementary function to play in reporting, and some teachers may be able to use them successfully as the sole means of reporting, but it remains to be demonstrated that their use on a school-wide basis over a long period is superior to, or even equal to, the use of intelligently prepared report forms which take account of major educational objectives.

7. *Noteworthy attempts are made in some of the more recent report cards to analyze and diagnose a pupil's achievement in terms of the objectives of the school.* Such attempts were not very common in the past. For example, Pugsley (28) found in an analysis of report cards used in certain schools in New York State in the 1930s that reporting was still highly traditional, and that main emphasis remained on common knowledge and skills. Of 63 report cards examined, only six had some sort of statement of the aims and purposes of education, and in only four was there a clear relationship between the stated aims and the group of items in which accounting was made.

Analysis of reporting procedures in the 1950s and 1960s indicates a good deal more attention to reporting on the basis of objectives. In his analysis of new procedures in marking and reporting, White (44) called attention to the newer philosophy, which is first to state objectives and then to evaluate the attainment of pupils in terms of these objectives. Roelfs (34) noted, in his survey of junior high school report forms, that a considerable number of junior high schools were attempting to improve subject matter evaluation by the analysis of each subject into skills or habits, and appraisal on the basis of these detailed items. Bolmeier (3) in setting forth ten principles pertinent to marking and reporting pupil progress, stressed the point that evaluation should bear a close relationship to objectives which are considered important to the course, and he presented an appraisal report in actual use which included six of the most significant factors or objectives applicable to most secondary school subjects.

One important educational objective, healthful living, seems to be neglected in most report forms. Duckworth (12), for example, found that health data were included on only five of 24 forms which he analyzed.

8. *Reports are being sent at less frequent intervals, and in some schools only when there is specific occasion for communication with the home.* This tendency was noted by Messenger and Watts (24) and by Hill (17) in the 1930s, and apparently it has received increased emphasis in the meantime. Hill in his analysis of report cards found that about half of them were sent out six times a year; one fourth were sent monthly; while 15 percent were sent only four times a year. Roelfs (34), in his analysis of junior high school report forms, found

that 49 percent were sent every six weeks, a figure which agrees with that of Hill, but 45 percent were sent four times a year as compared with only 15 percent in Hill's survey. However, one third of the junior high schools sent special reports to the homes as needed. De Pencier (9), in her study of trends in reporting pupil progress in the elementary grades from 1938 to 1949, likewise found a trend toward less frequent issuance. An important point in favor of less frequent reports is that teachers can do a more thorough job of reporting if they are not required to make the reports too frequently.

9. According to White (44), *there is also a trend toward shorter reports forms.* However, there is so much variation in the size of report cards that it is difficult to generalize. Duckworth (12) observed that the cards he examined varied in size all the way from 39 to 247 square inches.

10. *Parents are sometimes asked to cooperate in designing report cards and also to take part in plans of reciprocal reporting and in parent-teacher conferences.* De Pencier (10) described a workshop in Springfield, Delaware County, Pennsylvania in the cooperative planning of report cards. The workshop was made up of representatives of parents, teachers, the administration, and the Board of Education. The group developed two report forms, one for Grade 1 and one for Grades 2–6. Two general areas were covered, "personal and social growth" and "scholastic growth." The card for Grades 2–6 included a total of 53 items grouped under certain heads. Reporting was done three times a year, supplemented by conferences between parents and teachers twice a year. The conferences with parents were scheduled in October and March on school time. A manual of instructions for parents was also prepared.

Flickinger (13) called attention to a two-way report form which was described in the June 14, 1949 issue of *Better Schools,* the weekly news bulletin of the Cincinnati school system. The form, a 4-by-6-inch sheet, carried a note which invited the cooperation of parents in providing information concerning their children which would be helpful to the school. One side of the form was used for the school's report, and the reverse side was used for the replies of the parents.

Some schools have experimented with abandoning report cards altogether, in favor of regularly scheduled conferences with parents. For example, Buswell (5) quoted from the *New Jersey Educational Review* for December, 1948, which reviewed practices in some northern New Jersey schools in which report cards had been eliminated: "Instead of sending report cards, twenty teachers in three townships of Warren County send for parents for fifteen-minute conferences four times a year. An evening or a school afternoon is given up to appointments. . . . For parents the conferences frequently add up to a much needed adult-education course."

Other schools have tried substituting a parent-teacher conference for report cards in one or more of the reporting periods. Bringing the child into this conference is also being tried out. A plan of this kind, for instance, has been reported as definitely successful by sixth grade teachers in one of the Portland, Oregon, schools (20).

Parent-teacher conferences as a means of reporting must be carefully planned if maximum values are to be obtained from them. D'Evelyn (11) provided a manual on individual parent-teacher conferences for teachers of young children.

Not only should the conferences be planned with care, but so far as possible the information given to the parents, concerning the progress of their children, should be based on objective evidence of ability and achievement. As stated by Le Baron (19), "If we will use the best available knowledge of child study and child development to arrive at accurate and meaningful evaluations of individual potential and achievement, there is no doubt that parents will welcome personal conferences as the best way to develop a practical program of guidance for their children."

11. *In some schools, pupils cooperate in devising report cards and in evaluating their own achievement.* In the revision of her earlier publication, *Reporting to Parents,* Strang (39) emphasized reporting as a cooperative responsibility and pointed out the possibility of having pupils participate in their own evaluation. McCleary (21) described the development and use of a pupil self-analysis inventory for Grades 7 and 8 which was based mainly on pupil suggestions during class discussion. The items in the inventory were stated in terms of specific behavior. The pupil was also asked what, in his own opinion, was the greatest problem which kept him from improving. The pupils check themselves on this inventory and the teacher evaluates each pupil on another copy of the form. Then parent-teacher conferences are held, after which teacher reports are sent home. It was found that the pupil could discuss the report with his parents in terms specific enough to enable them to evaluate his development. This reporting procedure was worked out in The Laboratory Schools of the University of Illinois.

12. *There is a recognizable trend toward better administration of procedures of reporting to parents.* In calling attention to this trend, White (44) mentioned that one way in which it is being manifested is through the sending of reports for different children at different times rather than sending all reports at one time. This procedure allows teachers more time to give thorough consideration to the evaluation of each pupil, and also attempts to minimize interpupil comparisons.

Valid and thorough reports to parents call for a great deal of the time of teachers. This is especially true where written reports are supplemented by parent-teacher conferences. Administrators are recognizing that the development of understanding of the progress of their children on the part of parents is an important aspect of instruction, and they are showing increasing willingness to allow sufficient time in the regular school day for conferences between teachers and parents, conferences in which the pupils also frequently share.

Modern school administrators also attempt to provide the means whereby teachers may obtain reliable and valid objective information relative to the aptitudes and achievement of their pupils. As Brantley (4) has said, "The implication is that the school officials know the capacity, interests, and the ability of the individual so well that they can report on whether or not he is making the most of his opportunities. Such an assumption means that wide use must be made of standard tests, personality ratings, and interest questionnaires."[4]

13. *Finally, since about 1962, there has developed in some of the larger school systems a trend toward the preparation of reports to homes through the use of electronic data processing equipment.* For instance, Cuttitta (7) of the New York City Public Schools discussed the use of data processing machines in report card production, as well as in test scoring, scheduling, and accumulating attendance data.

CRITERIA FOR REPORT FORMS

In an article on the character of a reporting system, Tibbetts (41) gave a good summary of 13 criteria for report cards. The criteria are as follows:

1. A report which requires a minimum amount of clerical work.
2. A report to which the community is educated.
3. A report which promotes understanding both within the home and the school.
4. A report which will inform parents of progress in all phases, physical and social as well as mental.
5. A report which states in simple terms the philosophy of the school; in other words, the ultimate goals of education.
6. A report which includes adjustment to life as well as to school subjects.
7. A report which sets up a standard of value of work for its own sake rather than for marks or other emoluments.
8. A report which is suitable to the age level for which it is made.

[4] Quoted with Mr. Brantley's permission.

9. A report which is understandable to the child himself.
10. A school record which includes both objective and subjective material.
11. A type of record which, in case of transfer, facilitates early and proper adjustment of the child in his new situation.
12. A record and report which shall take into consideration the child as an individual as well as the child as a member of a social group.
13. A type of record and report which will indicate scholastic achievement, individual adjustment, and social growth.

SUGGESTIONS FOR IMPROVING REPORTS TO THE HOMES

Reavis (29) quoted comments by Lyle M. Spencer in an issue of the *Junior Guidance Newsletter*. Spencer said that schools had tried many schemes of reporting and that out of these experiments had come five suggestions.

1. Set up a cooperative parent-teacher committee to improve your present report form.
2. Encourage teachers to develop ways of making their marks more reliable and uniform. For example, use standardized achievement tests.
3. Provide space on the report card for both teacher and parent comments.
4. Don't confine reports to report cards. Send informal letters to parents between report cards and also use personal conferences to supplement cards.
5. See that report cards, as well as supplementary reports, "accentuate the positive." Include positive suggestions that parents can follow to help their child, and also tell them what the school plans to do.

BASIC PRINCIPLES OF REPORTING

In a well-written article on principles pertaining to marking and reporting pupil progress, Bolmeier (3) discussed ten principles which are as follows:

1. The marking and reporting system should be in harmony with the philosophy of education held by the school for which the reporting system is to be used.
2. The marking and reporting system should be designed and utilized primarily for the purpose of benefiting the pupil rather than the teacher.
3. The marking and reporting system should be developed democratically with the cooperative participation of the persons concerned.
4. The marking and reporting system should be sufficiently

analytical to be meaningful and informative to pupils, parents, and counselors.
5. The number and nature of the factors to be marked should bear a relationship to objectives which are considered germane to the course.
6. Each factor on the appraisal report should be marked with symbols which are immediately meaningful to all persons who have occasion to review the report.
7. The frequency of preparing reports and submitting them to the homes should be determined on the basis of relative values.
8. The manner in which the appraisal reports are submitted to the parents should be determined by the relative importance of economy and the assurance that they reach their intended destination.
9. The appraisal reports may be used to compute whatever final marks are required, but not to revive the antiquated principle of competition.
10. The marking and reporting system should be evaluated continuously and modified, when deemed desirable, in accordance with the same democratic principles by which it was originally designed.

TYPES OF REPORT FORMS WITH ILLUSTRATIONS

The following illustrative report forms have been selected to represent certain types from a wide variety of forms collected by the Educational Records Bureau. So many forms for reports to homes containing helpful suggestions were available that the problem of selection was a difficult one, and in the case of some of the types represented, the report forms used by several other school systems would have served equally as well as the ones chosen for illustrative purposes.

OLD-TYPE REPORT CARD

Before the newer plans for reporting are taken up, it may be well to present one or two illustrations in order to call to mind the formal type of report that was used traditionally in our schools. The most reactionary report which came to light in this survey was a brief *punishment report* from a house of reformation. It is reproduced (Form 19) with fictitious names and with the address of the institution deleted.

It is perhaps stretching a point to include this type of report in the present book, for it is highly improbable that even the most unenlightened school would employ such a report at the present time. It is offered as a reminder of a philosophy and practice of dealing with young people that was widely accepted two or three generations ago, and that still persists in certain types of institutions.

It constitutes an interesting contrast to most of the illustrative report forms which follow.

Form 20 will serve to indicate the main features of the traditional report card that is still used in some schools, although unquestionably in a decreasing number. It is apparent that this is a monthly report card to inform the parents about the attendance of their child and his achievement in the different school subjects. Achieve-

Clara Mason No. 5794

PUNISHMENT REPORT

House of Reformation

Date 3/17/41

Reported by .... F. C. Horner

For .... Coming to Bldg without permission

25 lashes
Back 1 grade

W. J. Brown, Supt.
H. of R.

FORM 19.

ment is indicated by means of a symbol-percent scale. The only reference to personality or behavior appearing on the card is the one word "Conduct."

It should be stated that this report form, or even the one shown in Form 19, is not per se a bad form if it reflects the educational philosophy of the school in which it is used. Notwithstanding the inadequate and undesirable features of these forms, an attack should not be made upon the cards themselves but rather upon the educational philosophy back of them. As Bolmeier (1) appropriately pointed out, the first step in the modernization of report forms is the re-examination and redefinition of the objectives of the school.

FORMAL REPORT CARDS SUPPLEMENTED BY PERSONALITY REPORT

Some schools that still retain the formal report card on school achievement have taken a step ahead by supplementing this card with a second report on character or

Pupil_____

MEANING OF MARKS E—Excellent .. 90-100 S—Satisfactory 75- 90 P—Poor . . . .65- 75 F—Failure . Below 65	1st Period 4 Weeks	2nd Period 4 Weeks	3rd Period 4 Weeks	4th Period 6 Weeks	Semester
Days Present					
Days Absent					
Times Tardy					
Conduct					
Arithmetic					
Art					
Auditorium					
Civics					
History					
Home Economics or Manual Training					
Language					
Library					
Literature					
Music					
Physical Training					
Physiology-Hygiene					
Science (N.S.& Geog.)					
Reading					
Spelling					
Writing					
Sunday School Credit					

FORM 20.

personality. The card shown in Form 21, for example, was devised for optional use as a supplement to the card shown in Form 20.

In this card, 12 character traits have been listed and briefly defined, and provision has been made for marking the pupil as excellent, satisfactory, improving, or unsatisfactory in each trait. Although certain aspects of this form could be improved, it furnishes some worthwhile information, and it helps to keep the attention of the

CHARACTER DEVELOPMENT

MEANING OF MARKS: E—Excellent. S—Satisfactory. I—Improving. U—Unsatisfactory.

PERIOD	1st	2nd	3rd	4th	Semester
1. HEALTH Physical appearance and health habits.					
2. SPORTSMANSHIP Attitude of fair play; give and take; loyal cooperation and obedience.					
3. WORK Willingness and diligence in performing tasks; an efficient workman; appreciates dignity of manual labor.					
4. BEAUTY Interest in and love of the beautiful.					
5. THRIFT Care of one's own property, that of the school or others; wise use of time and money; habit of saving; school savings account.					
6. COURTESY Consideration of others; good manners.					
7. NATURE Interest in and love of nature; care of animal and plant life.					
8. LEISURE Worthy use of; worthwhile hobbies and interest; wholesome out-of-school activities.					
9. SERVICE Readiness to assist others; obliging and willing service.					
10. WONDER The imaginative faculty; wholesome curiosity.					
11. COOPERATION Good team worker.					
12. SELF-RELIANCE Independence; self-confidence; accepts responsibility; initiative; doesn't hesitate to try.					

FORM 21.

pupils, parents, and teachers from being focused exclusively upon subjects, marks, and credits.

MARKS IN EACH SUBJECT SUPPORTED BY COMMENT

In some schools, it is felt that marks are not inherently bad, but that when they stand alone they do not tell enough. Some of these schools have adopted the practice of supporting the mark with a descriptive and interpretative statement written by the teacher. One plan for doing this is to have the mark and supporting comment for each subject written on a separate card. This plan simplifies the administration of the reporting, but it is probably more helpful to the parent in getting a complete picture of the pupil's achievement if all the marks and comments are brought together on a single report form. A simple report form of the latter type, which has been used in an independent school, is reproduced as Form 22.

A somewhat similar general idea of reporting is found in the Elementary Pupil-Home Report of the Garfield Heights City Schools, Garfield Heights, Cleveland, Ohio,

Mathematics Arithmetic		
Algebra		
English Composition		
Grammar		
Literature		
Speech		
Spelling		
French		
Geography		
History		
Latin		
Science		
Writing		

Art		
Crafts		
Music		
Physical Education		
Deportment		
Effort		
Study Habits		
Social Attitudes		

Comments:

Number of school days_____

Absences_____

Latenesses_____

_____
Room Teacher

_____
Director

FORM 22.

which is illustrated in Form 23. In this form, however, the different subjects or areas in which marks are assigned are briefly defined, and two marks are given, one for achievement and one for effort. Another feature of this report form is that it provides extensive space for parent comments.

ANALYTIC REPORT BUTTRESSED BY TEACHER-PARENT CONFERENCES

A reporting plan based on a combination of a detailed report form and conferences between teacher and parents is used in the elementary grades of the Webster Groves, Missouri, Public Schools. The report form consists of a small folder in which an attempt is made "to give diagnostic insight into the progress of each child in *subject areas* and in *social attitudes and personal skills.*" The outside and inside portions of the pupil progress report for Grades 5 and 6 are shown as Forms 24A and B. The reports are supported by two teacher-parent conferences annually.

LETTERS SUBSTITUTED FOR REPORT CARDS

The report form which, of course, gives teachers greater freedom than any other is the home letter. Among the schools that led a movement in this direction some years ago was the school system of Newton, Massachusetts, which abandoned report cards in the early 1930s (30). Since report letters to parents are, of course, extremely variable, no attempt will be made here to illustrate this type of reporting.

NO SET FORM FOR ALL TEACHERS OR DEPARTMENTS —SEPARATE MULTILITHED OR PRINTED FORMS REPRESENTING TEACHER OR DEPARTMENTAL OBJECTIVES

Another plan for introducing flexibility into the reporting, which does not involve abandonment of report cards, is to have each teacher or each department construct forms for progress reports for the particular subjects or department involved. This kind of report form may readily be changed—as often as the objectives of the courses change.

GROWTH REPORT IN TERMS OF OBJECTIVES FOR EACH GRADE

As already indicated, many schools now base their reports on objectives. In most of these schools, the tendency is to have the objectives formulated by a committee

of teachers, and after careful consideration, incorporated into a printed form. The objectives should be those of the entire program of the school, not simply hastily conceived objectives set up for purposes of reporting.

Among the report forms that illustrate a rather detailed listing of objectives, or desired outcomes of education, are those that have been used in the Cincinnati Public Schools; the Fresno, California, City Schools; the Oklahoma City Public Schools; the Omaha, Nebraska, Public Schools; and the Pasadena, California, Public Schools. The reports used in the Pasadena Elementary Schools will be taken as examples in this discussion. There are separate reports for the kindergarten, for Grades 1 and 2, and for Grades 3 through 6. Since these are similar in general features, the forms for Grades 3–6 only will be reproduced and discussed here.

The reporting plan used in Pasadena represents an interesting coordination of the conference report and the progress report. There are four reporting periods. Parent-teacher conferences are held for the first and third reports; the forms illustrated in Forms 25 and 26 are employed as guides for the conferences and are filled out in duplicate as a record for the parent and the teacher of what took place and what was agreed upon in the conference.

The progress report illustrated in Form 27 is sent to parents at the end of the second and fourth reporting periods. It will be seen that the progress report furnishes a rather detailed listing of objectives for the different school subjects and also within the area of social responsibilities, work and study habits, and safety. A conference report is also used at the end of the year.

This somewhat elaborate system of reporting was developed by a committee of teachers, principals, and central office staff members who worked in cooperation with a lay advisory committee. A splendid manual of instruction was prepared as a guide for school personnel in the use of the forms and the total reporting plan (31). This reporting procedure represents a compromise between the informal parent-teacher conference and the more conventional way of reporting to parents. It is designed to bring out the best features of both approaches to the reporting problem.

DUAL SYSTEMS OF REPORTING—RATING IN TERMS OF OBJECTIVES AND ASSIGNMENT OF MARKS IN THE DIFFERENT COURSES

Two of the most important objections to school marks are (1) that they too often represent hasty and unreliable judgments by teachers concerning their pupils, and (2) that usually no one has any very clear idea of what a given mark means. The various items that should be

Parent - Please examine this report; make whatever comments you care to make, in the proper space, below; sign your name, indicating that you have seen the report; and return it to your child's teacher, immediately. You may keep this report at the end of the school year.

Parent Comment - First Report Period:

_____ Parent Signature

Parent Comment - Second Report Period

_____ Parent Signature

Parent Comment - Third Report Period:

_____ Parent Signature

FORM 23 (Back).

ELEMENTARY PUPIL·HOME REPORT

Garfield Heights City Schools

Pupil _____

School Year _____

Grade _____

Teacher _____

Attendance Record:	Report No.			
	1	2	3	Yr.
Days Present				
Days Absent				
Times Tardy				

This student has been assigned to grade ____ for next school Year.

Used with permission of the Garfield Heights City Schools.

FORM 23 (Front).

ACHIEVEMENT RATING:
A.- Outstanding
B.- Above Average
C.- Average
D.- Below Average
E.- Below promotion level

EFFORT RATING
G - Good
F - Fair
P - Poor

SUBJECTS

READING: Phonics, vocabulary, speed, comprehension, oral reading, outside reading, workbook, Weekly News.

LANGUAGE: Mastery of assigned work. Correct oral and written usage. Oral and written self-expression.

SPELLING: Mastery of assigned words. Application in other written work.

WRITING: Mastery of letter formation spacing and neatness.

SOCIAL STUDIES: Mastery of content as demonstrated in class discussions and in written work.

SCIENCE AND HEALTH: Mastery of content as demonstrated in class discussions, in practice of health habits, and in contributions to class activities.

MATHEMATICS: Mastery of mathematical principles and number processes. Accuracy. Application of principles and skills.

PHYSICAL EDUCATION: Class participation. Mastery of physical fitness and other skills. Sportsmanship.

MUSIC: Appreciation of music and application through singing, rhythms, special study and creative activities.

ART: Expression of creative ideas, and growth in use of materials.

WORK HABITS: Attention to instructions and explanations. Care in following directions. Neatness and order. Promptness in beginning and ending tasks. Ability to work independently.

SOCIAL BEHAVIOR: Courtesy, cooperation, respect for rights and property of others.

Report columns (each with EFFORT TO ACHIEVE: G, F, P; ACHIEVEMENT RATING: A, B, C, D, E; Teacher Comment):

FIRST REPORT	SECOND REPORT	THIRD REPORT	FOURTH REPORT / YEAR'S AVERAGE

FORM 23 (Inside).

SCHOOL DISTRICT OF WEBSTER GROVES

Webster Groves, Missouri

PUPIL PROGRESS REPORT

Grades 5 and 6

A NOTE TO PARENTS -

Education of children is a cooperative enterprise in which the parents and school personnel work together for progress in academic and behavioral practices of children.

Teacher-parent conferences seem to offer a maximum opportunity for mutual understanding of a child's growth and needs. This report is not a substitute for conferences but is a supplement for the information of parents and the record of the school. It attempts to give diagnostic insight into the progress of each child in subject areas and in social attitudes and personal skills.

We are interested in the way your child makes use of the opportunities which the school offers him and invite your continued cooperation.

GEORGE W. BROWN, Superintendent.

Pupil's Name -

School: Year: 19 ___ - 19 ___

Teacher -

Principal -

Used with permission of the Webster Groves Public Schools.

FIRST SEMESTER

TEACHER'S COMMENTS

PARENT'S COMMENTS AND SIGNATURE

SECOND SEMESTER

TEACHER'S COMMENTS

ATTENDANCE REPORT

SEMESTERS	I	II
Days present		
Days absent		
Times Tardy		

ASSIGNED TO:

GRADE:

ROOM:

FORM 24(a).

250

ACADEMIC PROGRESS

LEGEND:

Letter mark assigned to subject:
- E - is above average of child's class
- G - is average
- S - is average but not at ability level
- P - is below average of class

	SEMESTER I					SEMESTER II				
MARKS	Excellent	Superior	Satisfactory	Shows Improvement	Needs to Improve	Excellent	Superior	Satisfactory	Shows Improvement	Needs to Improve
READING										
Understanding of what is read										
Speed										
Scope and variety										
Interest in vocabulary building										
LANGUAGE										
Speaking clearly and concisely										
Growth in using correct English										
Organization of written work										
Proofreading										
Creative expression										
SPELLING										
Mastery of spelling lesson										
Retention and use of words										
Application in written work										
WRITING										
Formation of letters										
Spacing of letters and words										
ARITHMETIC										
Accuracy in computation										
Reasoning ability										
SOCIAL STUDIES										
Understanding of concepts										
Retention of information										
Participation										
Resourcefulness										
Interpretation of maps and globes										
PHYSICAL EDUCATION										
Physical Skills										
Application of rules										
Cooperation										
Sportsmanship										

ACADEMIC PROGRESS

	SEMESTER I					SEMESTER II				
MARKS	Excellent	Superior	Satisfactory	Shows Improvement	Needs to Improve	Excellent	Superior	Satisfactory	Shows Improvement	Needs to Improve
SCIENCE										
Understanding of vocabulary										
Ability to form conclusions										
Research										
HEALTH										
Knowledge of Health facts										
Health habits										
ART										
Skills										
Creativity										
MUSIC										
Interest										
Participation										
Intelligent listening to music										

GROWTH IN HABITS AND TRAITS

	SEMESTER I					SEMESTER II				
MARKS	Excellent	Superior	Satisfactory	Shows Improvement	Needs to Improve	Excellent	Superior	Satisfactory	Shows Improvement	Needs to Improve
WORK AND STUDY HABITS										
Attention to plans and directions										
Use of time										
Neatness and accuracy										
Cares for materials and supplies										
Self evaluation										
PERSONAL AND SOCIAL TRAITS										
Cooperation										
Courtesy and consideration										
Care for school property										
Responsibility										
Self-discipline										
Citizenship										

FORM 24(b).

251

PASADENA CITY SCHOOLS

PASADENA, CALIFORNIA

School_____

Date_____

DEAR PARENTS:

Conferences are being scheduled between parents and teachers for the purpose of reporting pupil progress.

The conference is to provide an opportunity for personal and direct two-way communication between home and school concerning the progress of your child.

A more profitable discussion will result if thought has been given to some of the following: your child's health, his interests, his attitude toward school and any observations you have made concerning him.

Because of the large number of conferences that must be scheduled by each teacher, it is necessary to limit each conference to not more than thirty minutes. It will help if you are on time for your appointment.

Will it be convenient for you to come to school for a conference on_____

_____at_____o'clock?

Please indicate on the attached slip.

Sincerely,

_____

— —

It will not be convenient for me to come at the suggested time for a conference. I will contact you to make arrangements for another conference date.

_____
Signature of Parent

— —

I will come to school for my conference with you on_____

at_____o'clock.

_____
Signature of Parent

175-420 WSN 10578 6-61

FORM 25.   Used with permission of the Pasadena City Schools.

252

PASADENA CITY SCHOOLS
PASADENA, CALIFORNIA

CONFERENCE REPORT

NAME_____SCHOOL_____DATE_____

The purpose of the conference is to provide an opportunity for personal and direct two-way communication between the home and the school. The school program is planned to promote growth in fundamental skills and knowledges, work habits, citizenship, and social adjustment. The conference emphasizes the child's progress as an individual, his growth in terms of the teacher's understanding of his ability and his progress in terms of established grade norms.

SIGNIFICANT BEHAVIOR AND ATTITUDES:
(Possible areas to be considered are health, citizenship, work habits, family and peer relationships, special interests and aptitudes, goals set for child by parent, child's attitude toward school.)

_____

_____

_____

_____

_____

YOUR CHILD:
Is doing his best work in_____

_____

_____

Needs to improve in_____

_____

_____

TEST RESULTS:
Standardized tests in skill subjects give insight into only a part of the total school program. It is important to remember that test scores are not absolutes—various factors may condition results of a test given at any one time. However, it is believed that these results are valuable if considered with other factors relating to the child's school progress. On recent tests your child placed as follows:

_____   _____

_____   _____

_____   _____

SUGGESTED WAYS TO HELP THE CHILD:_____

_____

_____

_____

_____   _____
Signature of Teacher   Signature of Parent

175-423 WSN 10581-Rev. 4-64

FORM 26.

Used with permission of the Pasadena City Schools.

PASADENA CITY SCHOOLS

PASADENA, CALIFORNIA

PROGRESS REPORT

GRADES 3, 4, 5, 6

YEAR 19_____ - 19_____

Dear Parents:

It is the policy of the Pasadena City Board of Education to provide a superior school system, with emphasis on a quality program of instruction for children of all abilities. This includes a strong program in the basic skills and citizenship education as well as in the creative arts, health, and physical education.

The school wishes to help your child develop to the best of his or her ability. Continuous attention must be given to the development of good work habits and the importance of helping each child develop his or her fullest capabilities both as a student and a person.

Your child's progress is given in terms of the average range of achievement expected at each grade level. In addition, the report indicates areas where improvement may be needed.

The first report is in the form of a parent-teacher conference so that there may be a mutual exchange of information between the teacher and the parent.

Please feel free to discuss your child's progress with the teacher or principal at any time. Sympathetic understanding and close cooperation between the home and the school are essential if the child is to develop to the fullest capacity. By working together, the home and the school can help each boy and girl to make the best progress.

ROBERT E. JENKINS
Superintendent of Schools

Pupil's Name _____

School _____

Grade _____

175-429 WSN 10587 Rev. 4-64
FORM 27 (Front).   Used with permission of the Pasadena City Schools.

taken into consideration in the assigning of the marks have not been clearly identified and set down so that teachers, pupils, and parents will all know just what the basis of the marks is. If the elements that make up the marks are clearly stated, the marks themselves may be useful as summary indices of achievement; and it must be admitted that they are, regardless of their merit, still necessary evils in transcripts sent to many higher institutions. It would probably be desirable for critics of marks to turn their attention not to the marks themselves but to improvement in the methods used by schools in arriving at them, and to the need for eliminating the extreme emphasis that is sometimes placed on marks as goals.

If marks are made the lesser phase of a dual system of reporting, their so-called evils will be greatly minimized. The use of a dual reporting plan may be illustrated by reference to a procedure that was employed in the University of Chicago High School (later replaced by letter-grade reports to parents prepared on IBM equipment and supplemented by an annual teacher-student conference).

The first step in this plan was the formulation of a complete list of objectives for each course through a series of departmental meetings. In addition to the specific objectives for each course, the school as a whole accepted the following objectives for habits of work.

Teacher's Comments

Parent's Comments

SECOND REPORT

Teacher's Signature..................

Principal's Signature..................

Parent's Comments

Parent's Signature..................

THIRD REPORT

Teacher's Comments

Teacher's Signature..................

Principal's Signature..................

Parent's Signature..................

FOURTH REPORT

Teacher's Comments

Teacher's Signature..................

Placement for next year—Grade..................

Principal's Signature..................

RECORD OF ATTENDANCE	First and Second Report	Third Report	Fourth Report	Total for Year
Days present..........				
Days absent..........				
Times tardy..........				

The symbols used report your child's progress, growth and achievement in relation to standards for the grade.

A Excellent
B Good
C Average
D Below Average
F Fails to Meet Minimum Requirements

(+ or — used after a grade or after one of the sub-heads indicates strength or weakness.)

SKILLS AND KNOWLEDGE

	Second Report	Third Report	Fourth Report

READING
Reads with understanding
Shows interest in reading
Reads a variety of materials
Works out new words
Reads fluently
Enjoys good literature

MATHEMATICS
Understands number concepts
Computes accurately
Applies reasoning to thought problems

WRITTEN ENGLISH
Expresses ideas clearly
Shows originality
Uses correct English

ORAL ENGLISH
Speaks clearly and distinctly
Uses correct English
Expresses ideas easily
Listens

	Second Report	Third Report	Fourth Report

SPELLING
Learns assigned spelling words
Uses correct spelling in written work

SOCIAL STUDIES (History—Geography—Civics)
Acquires knowledge of historical facts
Acquires knowledge of geography
Acquires knowledge of civics
Acquires and organizes reference material
Plans for class activities
Participates in group discussion and activities
Possesses manual skills

HANDWRITING
Writes legibly
Produces neat written work

ART
Works to develop a variety of skills
Expresses ideas creatively

MUSIC
Takes part in group singing
Works to develop basic music skills
Responds to rhythm

SCIENCE
Works to develop observation skills
Shows growth in knowledge of science

HEALTH EDUCATION

PHYSICAL EDUCATION
Participates in group games
Uses equipment properly
Exhibits good sportsmanship
Demonstrates skill in physical activities

FORM 27 (Inside).

SPANISH (comments)..

       Second Report..

....

       Third Report..

....

       Fourth Report..

....

SCHOOL CITIZENSHIP

SOCIAL RESPONSIBILITIES

	Second Report	Third Report	Fourth Report
Is cooperative			
Is courteous			
Accepts suggestions for improvement			
Exercises self-control			
Shows self-confidence			
Accepts responsibility			
Exercises leadership			
Gets along well with others			
Understands and observes safety rules			
Respects property rights			
Respects rights of others			
Is punctual			

WORK AND STUDY HABITS

Makes good use of time			
Follows directions			
Works independently			
Listens attentively			
Does neat work			
Uses materials wisely			
Is thorough in his work			
Completes assignments			

1. Persistence in overcoming difficulties.
2. Tendency to work independently.
3. Promptness in completing work.
4. Application during study.
5. Attention to class activities.
6. Participation in class activities.
7. Effectiveness in following directions.

In the English Department, separate objectives were set up for each course. In each of the other departments, a common list of objectives was accepted for all the courses within the department, although it was recognized that the emphasis on those objectives would vary from one course to another. Report sheets for the different lists of objectives were mimeographed, and on each sheet provision was made for rating the pupil on each objective in one of five categories—excellent, good, fair, poor, and very poor.

The method was to send a detailed report in terms of the purposes of each course to the parents at the end of each semester. No marks were reported at this time. A week or two after the detailed reports were made, the marks were sent out. The marks were on a five-step scale —A, B, C, D, and F. Since the parents had already had an opportunity to study a detailed analysis of the strengths and weaknesses of the pupil before the marks were received, they were accepted merely as a supplementary and incidental item of information. In fact, it was found that the pupils could usually predict their own marks accurately merely from a study of the analysis of their achievement in terms of the purposes of the course. Three

THE UNIVERSITY OF CHICAGO

The University High School

SEMESTER REPORT, ENGLISH------------------------------------

Student--Date------------------
       Last Name   First Name

NOTE.—This report rates the pupil on his attainment of the purposes of the course and on his habits of work. The ratings are made with reference to standards for the class. Omission of a rating on any item means insufficient evidence.

Purposes	Very Poor	Poor	Fair	Good	Excel-lent
Language					
1. Adequacy of content in papers and talks					
2. Organization of papers and talks					
3. Paragraph structure					
4. Sentence structure					
5. Vocabulary, diction					
6. Punctuation					
7. Manuscript form and appearance					
8. General accuracy of manuscripts					
9. Spelling					
10. Handwriting					
11. Understanding of grammar					
12. Effectiveness of oral expression					
Reading and Literature					
13. Effectiveness in reading					
14. Range of reading					
15. Acquaintance with literature					
Habits of Work					
16. Persistence in overcoming difficulties					
17. Tendency to work independently					
18. Promptness in completing work					
19. Application during study					
20. Attention to class activities					
21. Participation in class activities					
22. Effectiveness in following directions					

Comments (if any):

Pupil's Grade-----------   ----------------------------
                                 Instructor
Used with permission of The University of Chicago High School.

FORM 28(a).

THE UNIVERSITY OF CHICAGO

The University High School

SEMESTER REPORT, SCIENCE_____

Student_____Date_____
     Last Name   First Name

NOTE.—This report rates the student on his attainment of the purposes of the course and on his habits of work. The ratings are made with reference to standards for the class. Omission of a rating on any item means insufficient evidence.

Purposes	Very Poor	Poor	Fair	Good	Excellent
1. Command of significant information and relationships					
2. Ability to apply principles in new situations					
3. Ability to plan an experiment and to draw conclusions from experiments					
4. Interest in science					
5. Scientific attitude: Openmindedness; habit of not jumping at conclusions; etc.					
6. Effectiveness in logical thinking					
7. Effectiveness in oral expression					
8. Effectiveness in written expression					
Habits of Work					
9. Persistence in overcoming difficulties					
10. Tendency to work independently					
11. Tendency to work effectively with others					
12. Promptness in completing work					
13. Neatness of papers handed in					
14. Application during study					
15. Attention to class activities					
16. Participation in class activities					
17. Effectiveness in following directions					

Comments:

Pupil's Grade_____   _____
                                        Instructor

FORM 28(b).

THE UNIVERSITY OF CHICAGO

The University High School

SEMESTER REPORT, SOCIAL STUDIES III................

Student_____Date_____

Last Name   First Name

NOTE.—This report rates the pupil on his attainment of the purposes of the course and on his habits of work. The ratings are made with reference to standards for the class. Omission of a rating on any item means insufficient evidence.

Purposes	Very Poor	Poor	Fair	Good	Excel-lent
1. Acquisition of basic information					
2. Mastery of basic reading skills					
a. ability to recognize main ideas					
b. ability to recognize data pertinent to a given question					
c. understanding of basic social studies concepts					
3. Ability to express ideas orally					
a. presentation					
b. organization					
c. adequacy of content					
4. Ability to express ideas in written form					
a. organization					
b. adequacy of content					
5. Ability to make generalizations and inferences based upon facts					
6. Ability to apply previously acquired information and principles in new situations					
7. Interest in current affairs					
8. Courtesy and cooperation in group situations					
Habits of Work					
9. Persistence in overcoming difficulties					
10. Tendency to work independently					
11. Promptness in completing work					
12. Application during study					
13. Attention to class activities					
14. Participation in class activities					
15. Effectiveness in following directions					

Comments:

Pupil's Grade_____

_____

Instructor

FORM 28(c).

260

sample report forms, not currently in use, developed under this plan are reproduced as Forms 28A to 28C.

Detailed reports in terms of the objectives of each course are not only valuable in informing parents about the achievement and progress of their children, but they are of great assistance in the individualization of instruction and in guidance, and they have a logical relationship to the cumulative record system of the school. They can be used effectively in individual conferences with both parents and pupils.

A PROGRESS REPORT

Forms prepared by a subcommittee of the Reports and Records Committee of the Progressive Education Association for reporting progress represent one of the most interesting and forward-looking approaches to techniques of reporting to parents, even though these forms first appeared some 20 years ago. The Progress Report, which is printed in two forms, A and B, is shown reduced in size as Forms 29A and 29B.

The Progress Report makes provision for each teacher to appraise the pupil in five areas: success in achieving the specific purposes of the course, progress in learning to think, effectiveness in communicating ideas, active concern for the welfare of the group, and general habits of work. It also allows for indication of serious deficiency in certain special work habits. The principal difference between the two forms is that Form A is arranged with columns for the subject fields and provides for a five-point description under each heading and in relation to each area of progress, while Form B has columns for the five descriptive categories and calls for the writing of the names of the subject fields in the proper boxes. Form A is the more conventional, but Form B provides the more graphic picture for the reader and may force more exactness in thinking when the report is made out. Both forms were used experimentally with success by the schools participating in the Eight-Year Study of the Progressive Education Association.[5]

THE USE OF CUMULATIVE RECORDS IN REPORTING

In schools which maintain individual records for their pupils and which are fortunate enough to be able to get the parents to come to the school for individual interviews at regular intervals, it would seem that no report form other than the cumulative record card should be needed. Three essential aspects of an adequate system of

reporting are: ability, present status, and growth. The cumulative record based in part upon objective measurement seems to be more successful in presenting these three indispensable kinds of information than any other report form that has yet been devised.

THE NEED FOR EXPERIMENTATION WITH VARIOUS PLANS OF REPORTING

Any school which abandons the traditional form of report and begins to search earnestly for better procedures will find itself embarked upon an interesting adventure that calls for a great deal of time and energy on the part of a faculty committee, an adventure that will probably need to be carried on for at least two or three years, and perhaps much longer. It is seldom feasible for a school to adopt the report forms devised for some other school system, although valuable ideas can be secured from studying report forms developed in other places, and especially from reviewing the experience of other schools in constructing and using new types of forms.

One of the most striking examples of what may be involved in a search for better reporting techniques is furnished by an experiment described by William L. Wrinkle, formerly director of the College High School, Colorado State College of Education, in his book, *Improving Marking and Reporting Practices* (47). Wrinkle's book provides what is probably the most authoritative and challenging discussion of marking and reporting procedures thus far made available. It is based on a school-wide study of the improvement of reporting practices carried on continuously during a ten-year period. During that time the experiment ran practically the whole gamut of forms of reporting that have ever been undertaken by a school or dreamed up by a professor of education for the edification of his students. The College High School tried in succession: (1) detailed reports in terms of objectives; (2) summary statements by the counselors at the close of each quarter in the form of notes and letters written to parents; (3) scale-type evaluations; (4) conferences with parents; (5) checklists based upon questions that always or nearly always arose in the conferences between parents and teachers; (6) a simplified evaluative report which would be easily interpreted by the student and his parents and which would focus their attention on the major objectives of the school; and (7) report forms based on objectives stated as the desired kinds of behavior the school was trying to develop in its students.

[5] Now that the Progressive Education Association is no longer in existence, there is no agency for the distribution of these forms. They are in the public domain and schools are free to use them.

RECOMMENDATIONS FOR NEXT YEAR
(Used only on the next to the last report)

At the present stage of the work the pupil seems, in the subjects listed:

Likely to profit by continuance of the subject_____

_____

Able to complete the course but with question of the value of continuing it for another year_____

_____

Likely to be unsuccessful in completing the course_____

_____

(For upper classes only) to show promise for continuing the work successfully at an advanced institution_____

_____

GENERAL COMMENT

This comment is intended to give opportunity for presenting information that will make the picture of the pupil's progress more complete. When there are significant interests, abilities, limitations, or contributions made by the pupils, they will be mentioned.

_____
Adviser's Signature

_____
Parent's Signature if the Report Is Returned

Name of School_____

Progress Report of_____
Pupil's Name

_____
Grade   Date

This report has been prepared for the purpose of presenting information about the development of the pupil. It is an analysis of strengths and weaknesses made by all the pupil's teachers and is intended to prove helpful for present and future guidance of the pupil concerned. The symbols used are abbreviations of the following descriptions of development.

O. The pupil has reached an outstanding stage of development in the field and characteristic indicated; that is, a stage distinctly above that usual for pupils of the same age and similar opportunities.

H. A stage of development somewhat higher than usual, perhaps with promise of eventually reaching a superior level.

U. Approximately the usual stage of development for age and opportunity.

L. Sufficiently below the usual stage to need particular help from home and school or greater effort on the part of the pupil.

S. The pupil is seriously below an acceptable standard.

Advisers and subject teachers are glad to explain or supplement this report by conference with parents. Please arrange appointments by telephone.

Attendance Report through_____

Days Absent_____

Days Tardy_____

EXPLANATIONS OF SYMBOLS: (See complete description on front cover.)
O, is outstanding; H, is above usual; U, is at usual stage; L, is below the usual stage; S, seriously below usual stage.
SPECIFIC WORK HABITS ARE CHECKED ONLY WHEN THEY ARE SERIOUSLY BELOW AN ACCEPTABLE STANDARD.

	English	Social Studies	Mathematics	Science				
Success in achieving the specific purposes of the course								
Progress in learning how to think								
Effectiveness in communicating ideas — Oral								
Effectiveness in communicating ideas — Written								
Active concern for the welfare of the group								
General habits of work								

Any entry opposite one of the following indicates that the pupil is seriously below an accepted standard in this respect:

Accuracy in following directions	_____
Efficient use of time and energy	_____
Neatness and orderliness	_____
Self-reliance	_____
Persistence in completing work	_____
Thoughtful participation in discussion	_____
Conscientiousness of effort	_____

REPORTS AND RECORDS COMMITTEE OF THE PROGRESSIVE EDUCATION ASSOCIATION. PRINTED IN U.S.A. R.F.B. 1024

Used with permission of Dr. Eugene R. Smith, Chairman of the Committee.

FORM 29(a).

RECOMMENDATIONS FOR NEXT YEAR
(Used only on the next to the last report)

At the present stage of the work the pupil seems, in the subjects listed:

Likely to profit by continuance of the subject............

Able to complete the course but with question of the value of continuing it for another year...........................

Likely to be unsuccessful in completing the course..........

(For upper classes only) to show promise for continuing the work successfully at an advanced institution.............

GENERAL COMMENT

This comment is intended to give opportunity for presenting information that will make the picture of the pupil's progress more complete. When there are significant interests, abilities, limitations, or contributions made by the pupils, they will be mentioned.

Adviser's Signature

Parent's Signature if the Report Is Returned

Name of School.............................

Progress Report of...........................
Pupil's Name

Grade   Date

This report has been prepared for the purpose of presenting information about the development of the pupil. It is an analysis of strengths and weaknesses made by all the pupil's teachers and is intended to prove helpful for present and future guidance of the pupil concerned. The headings of the columns are abbreviations of the following descriptions of development.

Is Outstanding: The pupil has reached an outstanding stage of development in the characteristic and field indicated: that is, a stage distinctly above that usual for pupils of the same age and similar opportunities.

Is above Usual: The pupil has reached a stage of development somewhat higher than usual, perhaps with promise of eventually reaching a superior level.

Is at Usual Stage: The pupil is at approximately the usual stage of development for age and opportunity.

Is below Usual: The pupil is sufficiently below the usual stage in this field to need particular help from the home and school or greater effort on the part of the pupil.

Is Seriously Below: The pupil is seriously below an acceptable standard in the field indicated.

Advisers and subject teachers are glad to explain or supplement this report by conference with parents. Please arrange appointments by telephone.

Attendance Report through.........................

Days Absent..........

Days Tardy..........

THE SUBJECT FIELD OR OTHER RELATIONSHIP OF THE TEACHER AND THE PUPIL IS FOUND UNDER THE DESCRIPTION AND OPPOSITE THE CHARACTERISTIC DESCRIBED.

	Is Outstanding	Is Above Usual	Is at Usual Stage	Is Below Usual	Is Seriously Below
Success in achieving the specific purposes of the course					
Progress in learning how to think					
Effectiveness in communicating ideas — Oral					
Effectiveness in communicating ideas — Written					
Active concern for the welfare of the group					
General habits of work					

Any entry opposite one of the following indicates that the pupil is seriously below an accepted standard in this respect:

Accuracy in following directions	
Efficient use of time and energy	
Neatness and orderliness	
Self-reliance	
Persistence in completing work	
Thoughtful participation in discussion	
Conscientiousness of effort	

REPORTS AND RECORDS COMMITTEE OF THE PROGRESSIVE EDUCATION ASSOCIATION. PRINTED IN U.S.A. R.F.B. 1024

FORM 29(b).

STUDENT EVALUATION REPORT

The Secondary School of Colorado State College of Education at Greeley

.... 193....

| Student | Curriculum area | Activity | Date |

Fifty desired outcomes of the total school program have been selected for the purpose of evaluation, record and report. The first ten listed below are general outcomes with which all teachers and all areas of the program are concerned. Evaluations of these general outcomes should be indicated by each teacher reporting. From the remaining items each teacher will report on those relating to the area in which he is working.

Five letters are used to indicate evaluations:

H HONORS: He would be noticeably outstanding in a large group of students of similar age and school level.
S SATISFACTORY: He has demonstrated the ability which should be expected of a student of similar age and school level.
N NEEDS TO MAKE IMPROVEMENT: He has not demonstrated the ability which should be expected of a student of his age and school level.
U UNSATISFACTORY: He is very noticeably weak in the demonstration of the ability being evaluated.
O NO EVALUATION: An evaluation cannot be made at this time because (1) the teacher is not sufficiently acquainted with the activities of the student to permit an evaluation, (2) the activity does not permit a demonstration of the ability, or (3) the student has not shown any observed evidence of the ability.

These evaluations are not competitive; they merely indicate how well the student has done certain things which he should do. Specific interpretations of these outcomes are presented in the bulletin "The Interpretation of the Desired Outcomes and Procedures in the Evaluation of the Student."

General Outcomes

—Self-direction
—Social adjustment
—Participation
—Breadth of interests
—Personal attractiveness
—Oral expression
—Written expression
—Basic reading skills
—Location of learning material
—Care of material and equipment

General Arts

—Tool skills and techniques
—Planning, drawing and designing
—Selection of materials
—Application of mathematical skills
—Creative ability

Commercial Education

—Accuracy	Each ability is checked with specific reference to the course in which the student is enroled—typewriting, shorthand, etc.
—Legibility	
—Neatness	
—Speed	

—Application of mathematical skills
—Ability to apply the skill acquired

Physical Activities

—Health practices
—Coordination and skill in physical activities
—Aggressiveness
—Knowledge of rules and techniques
—Adaptation of techniques

General Language Arts

—Clearness and distinctness of speech
—Poise and self-confidence
—Voice quality
—Choice of reading materials
—Understanding of dramatization
—Understanding of contemporary affairs
—Creative ability

The Foreign Languages

—Comprehension in silent reading
—Rate in silent reading
—Comprehension of the spoken language
—Ability in oral usage
—Interest in language
—Understanding of the contributions of foreign peoples to present civilization

Journalism

—Skills in journalistic writing
—Skills in journalistic reading

Science and Social Studies

—Selection and use of learning techniques and procedures
—Application of the scientific method
—Interpretation and construction of graphic and statistical materials
—Application of mathematical skills
—Understanding of contemporary affairs
—Understanding of related background
—Creative ability

Mathematics

—Accuracy in the use of numbers
—Facility in the use of numbers
—Understanding of mathematical terms and concepts
—Application of the scientific method
—Interpretation and construction of graphic and statistical materials

Music

—Basic skills and understandings
—Interest in development of musical abilities

Additional comments (continue on reverse side)

Teacher..   Supervising Teacher...

Used with permission of William L. Winkle.

FORM 30.

Some of the objectives identified were general to all courses, some were semigeneral, some were common to two or more courses and activities, and some were objectives of particular courses or activities. The student evaluation report used in the sixth stage of the experiment and an example of the report in terms of objectives developed and used at the end of the experiment are shown in

Forms 30 and 31, respectively. The latter form is for reporting to parents on progress in exploratory mathematics. The first seven objectives listed are general ones which would appear on report forms for other courses, but most of the other objectives are specific to this particular course.

The two forms shown are worth careful study, for

EVALUATION OF STUDENT ACHIEVEMENT AND PROGRESS IN MATHEMATICS COLLEGE HIGH SCHOOL OF COLORADO STATE COLLEGE OF EDUCATION AT GREELEY

STUDENT _____ COURSE OF ACTIVITY _____ DATE OF REPORT

EXPLORATORY MATHEMATICS

EVALUATIONS ARE MADE IN TERMS OF WHAT MIGHT BE EXPECTED NORMALLY OF A STUDENT OF SIMILAR AGE AND GRADE PLACEMENT. O – OUTSTANDING, S – SATISFACTORY, N – NEEDS TO MAKE IMPROVEMENT. U – UNSATISFACTORY. IE – INSUFFICIENT EVIDENCE.

Evaluation by
Student Teacher

OBJECTIVES

1. He directs his individual activities effectively, begins work promptly, makes good use of his time, requires a minimum of supervision, does more than the minimum that will be accepted, meets his responsibilities promptly, works effectively when left on his own responsibility, and is regular in attendance except for good cause.

2. He intelligently follows plans and directions, listens to and reads directions carefully, and follows and completes plans and directions which have been set up.

3. He gets along well with others, is considerate of the rights and wishes of others, is courteous and tolerant, controls his temper, conforms to reasonable social standards, and adjusts to varied social situations.

4. He takes an active part in group living, participates in group planning, volunteers his services, and does his share in group activities.

5. He speaks correctly and effectively, has a pleasant voice, speaks clearly, adjusts his voice to the size of the group, has adequate vocabulary to express himself interestingly, and speaks with ease and confidence.

6. He is careful of his personal appearance, keeps clean physically, takes good care of his nails, hair, and teeth, selects becoming clothes, keeps clothes neat and clean, has good posture, and avoids distracting habits.

7. He takes good care of personal and school materials and equipment, shows respect for property, doesn't waste materials or subject equipment to unnecessary wear, returns loaned materials when due, and immediately reports breakage and loss.

8. He reads mathematical materials with ease and understanding.

9. He uses the problem solving method, recognizes problems, states them clearly, selects appropriate sources of information, collects and records information, and arrives at accurate conclusions or solutions.

10. He uses correctly the basic skills in mathematics, uses accurately the fundamental combinations in adding, subtracting, multiplying, and dividing whole numbers; uses common and decimal fractions accurately; and selects the correct process in solving problems.

11. He computes with reasonable speed.

12. He checks the accuracy of his work by the use of approximation and common sense judgment.

13. He checks his written work neatly, legibly, and in good form.

14. He uses easily and accurately, the ruler, compass, and protractor.

15. He accurately constructs and identifies the basic plane geometric figures.

16. He applies the basic skills in mathematics in his use of letters and symbols.

17. He solves algebraic exercises and problems on the basis of understanding rather than the mere application of mechanical skill.

18. He shows sufficient aptitude to justify encouraging him to enroll in the full year course in plane geometry.

19. He shows sufficient aptitude to justify encouraging him to enroll in the full year course in algebra.

STUDENT _____ TEACHER _____
(Teacher's comments, particularly on N, PN, and U Evaluations, are written on the opposite side.)

Used with permission of the Colorado State College of Education at Greeley.

FORM 31.

they represent the end product of years of study and experimentation. But, as Dr. Wrinkle appropriately warned in the introductory chapter of his book, "You should not expect to turn to the last chapter of this book and find the perfect report form. It won't be there. I have never seen one and I am sure you haven't. I doubt if there is one. For what might be good in one school might not be good in another. Each school has to work out its own forms and practices on the basis of its own objectives, its own philosophy, and its own staff."

It is interesting to note that after years of experimentation with a variety of reporting procedures, the College High School arrived at a relatively simple form for reporting in terms of desired outcomes of the school program. This seems to be in line with the experience of other schools. If any generalization can be made as a result of the survey of report forms presented in this chapter, it is that *careful thinking and experimentation on the part of the school faculty seem naturally to lead to reports to parents in terms of the larger general educational objectives, supplemented by the major learning objectives in the various departments of the school.*

A brochure by Rothney (36) is a valuable selective summary and interpretation of research on evaluating and reporting pupil progress. This brochure was prepared at the request of the American Educational Research Association and was written especially for the classroom teacher. Among the topics discussed are: the purposes of evaluation, evaluation in terms of objectives of education, assessment of school achievement, assessing personal-social development, what, how, and when we should evaluate, who should evaluate, and procedures of reporting pupil progress.

The most encouraging aspect of present-day reporting is not that perfect report forms have been developed or that the best ways of making reports have been discovered, but that hundreds of schools are experimenting with a variety of new plans, and that some of these schools are publishing their experiences so that other schools may benefit by them. As Rothney said in the final paragraph of his brochure: "Research has provided many alternatives to uncritical passive acceptance of programs of evaluating and reporting that accomplish less than they might because they are static. Those alternatives are for classroom teachers and research workers to appraise continuously our evaluation programs and to persist in their attempts to determine the effectiveness of methods for reporting pupil progress" (36:31).

REPORTING WITH AUTOMATIC DATA PROCESSING

As mentioned earlier in this chapter, increased use of electronic data-processing equipment will expand

REPORT CARD
OAK RIDGE HIGH SCHOOL
OAK RIDGE, TENNESSEE
THOMAS H. DUNIGAN, PRINCIPAL

FORM 32.

and speed up reports to the home. It is possible to get a large amount of information into the relatively brief space of a report form prepared in this way, provided the information is coded. This newer type of report form is illustrated by the report card recently devised for the Oak Ridge High School, Oak Ridge, Tennessee, as furnished by Miss Sarah R. Ketron, director of guidance. The card is shown as Form 32. Miss Ketron comments, "Our teachers like this new form; it summarizes the items on the former cards. We hope the course purposes, listed on the former cards, are conveyed in conferences and orientation sessions."

Home reports prepared through the use of IBM punched cards or other mechanical means save untold hours of teacher time. It is hoped that schools adopting these procedures, as they unquestionably will in increasing numbers, will see to it that machine preparation of home reports does not stifle initiative and experimentation, and reduce communication between school and home to a deadly mechanical uniformity in which counseling might have little or no part. "The machine cannot and, indeed, should not become a substitute for professional decision-making; a decision having been made, however, automatic processing promises the removal of part of the 'paper curtain' blocking professional creativity" (7).

REFERENCES

1. Bolmeier, E. C. "Analytical Appraisal Report of Pupil Progress," *School Review*, LI (May 1943), 292–299.
2. Bolmeier, E. C. "What's In a Mark?" *School Executive*, LXII (May 1943), 25.
3. Bolmeier, E. C. "Principles Pertaining to Marking and Reporting Pupil Progress," *School Review*, LIX (January 1951), 15–24.
4. Brantley, G. D. "An Analysis of Current Practices in the Use of the Report Card," *Bulletin of the National Association of Secondary-School Principals*, XXVI (January 1942), 67–76.
5. Buswell, G. T. "Report Cards," *Elementary School Journal*, XLIX (February 1949), 316–317.
6. Chapman, H. B., and Ashbaugh, E. J. "Report Cards in American Cities," *Educational Research Bulletin*, IV (October 7, 1925), 291–293.
7. Cuttitta, Frederick. "Automatic Data Processing for the Schools," *High Points*, XLVI (November 1964), 28–31.
8. Dawson, M. A. "Report Cards without Marks," *Journal of Education*, CXVIII (December 2, 1935), 532–534.
9. De Pencier, Ida B. "Trends in Reporting Pupil Progress in the Elementary Grades, 1938–1949," *Elementary School Journal*, LI (May 1951), 519–523.
10. De Pencier, Ida B. "Cooperative Planning and Report Cards," *Elementary School Journal*, LIII (January 1953), 254–257.
11. D'Evelyn, Katherine E. *Individual Parent-Teacher Conferences*, rev. ed. New York: Bureau of Publications, Teachers College, Columbia University, 1963. Pp. 97.
12. Duckworth, B. R. "A Superintendent's Study of Report Forms," *Educational Research Bulletin*, XXVI (May 1947), 128–131.
13. Flickinger, Alice. "Two-Way Report Card," *Elementary School Journal*, XLIX (March 1949), 375–376.
14. Hansen, Rowena. *Report Cards for Kindergarten and Elementary Grades*. Leaflet 41. Washington: Office of Education, 1931.
15. Harris, Fred E. "Three Persistent Educational Problems: Grading, Promotion, and Reporting to Parents," *Bulletin of the Bureau of School Service*, XXVI (September 1953), 1–92. Lexington, Ky.: College of Education, University of Kentucky.
16. Herrick, Theral T. "Working With Parents to Improve Guidance," *Readings in Guidance* (ed. by Crowe and Crowe), pp. 346–350. New York: David McKay Company, Inc., 1962. Pp. 626.
17. Hill, George E. "The Report Card in Present Practice," *Educational Method*, XV (December 1935), 115–131.
18. Keller, Irwin. "A More Comprehensive and Significant Marking System," *Bulletin of the National Association of Secondary-School Principals*, XXXVI (January 1952), Pp. 70–78.
19. Le Baron, Walter A. "What Shall We Tell the Parents?" *Elementary School Journal*, LI (February 1951), 322–326.
20. Lewis, Robert, and McCrea, David. "Three Around the Conference Table," *Elementary School Journal*, LXI (November 1960), 72–75.
21. McCleary, Lloyd E. "A New Technique in Reporting Pupil Progress," *School Review*, LXIII (March 1955), 160–163.
22. McCowen, Emeline, and Bryan, Roy C. "Reporting to Parents on Pupil Progress," *Elementary School Journal*, LVI (September 1955), 32–34.
23. McQuagge, Carl L. "This High School Uses Two Grades Per Course," *Nation's Schools*, LII (August 1953), 48–49.
24. Messenger, Helen R., and Watts, Winifred. "Summaries of Selected Articles on Report Cards," *Educational Administration and Supervision*, XXI (October 1935), 539–550.
25. Metteer, W. M. "How California Elementary Schools Report to Parents," *California Journal of Elementary Education*, X (February 1942), 135–151.
26. Morris, L. "Evaluating and Reporting Pupil Progress," *Elementary School Journal*, LIII (November 1952), 144–149.
27. Olson, Willard C. *Child Development*, 2nd ed. Boston: D. C. Heath and Company, 1959. Pp. 508.
28. Pugsley, C. A. "Do Schools Report to Parents in Terms of School Objectives?" *Educational Method*, XV (October 1935), 15–20.

29. Reavis, W. C. "Report Cards," *School Review*, LX (April 1952), 199–200.
30. "Report Cards Abandoned by Newton Public Schools," *Journal of Education*, CXVI (November 6, 1933), 452.
31. *Reporting Pupil Progress*. Manual of Instruction for the Use of School Personnel in Pasadena Elementary Schools. Pasadena, Calif.: Pasadena City Schools, Division of Instructional Service, September 1954. Pp. 27.
32. Robinson, J. B. "Reporting Pupil Progress in the Elementary Schools," *Baltimore Bulletin of Education*, XXVI (June 1949), 1–10.
33. Roelfs, R. M. "Reporting Pupil Progress in the Junior High School," *Bulletin of the National Association of Secondary-School Principals*, XXXVIII (February 1954), 71–79.
34. Roelfs, R. M. "Trends in Junior High School Progress Reporting," *Journal of Educational Research*, XLIX (December 1955), 241–249.
35. Rogers, Virgil M., Rupright, Esther, and Gerich, Jerry. "Improved Methods of Reporting Pupil Progress," *School Executive*, LV (October 1950), 19–22.
36. Rothney, John W. M. *Evaluating and Reporting Pupil Progress*. Washington, D.C.: National Education Association, March 1955. Pp. 33.
37. Ruch, G. M. *The Objective or New-Type Examination*, Chapter III, "Objections to the Traditional Examination," pp. 70–111. Chicago: Scott, Foresman and Company, 1929. Pp. 478.
38. Starch, Daniel, and Elliott, E. C. "The Reliability of Grading High School Work in English," *School Review*, XX (September 1912), 442–457; "The Reliability of Grading High School Work in History," *School Review*, XXI (December 1913), 676–681; "The Reliability of Grading High School Work in Mathematics," *School Review*, XXI (April 1913), 254–259.
39. Strang, Ruth. *Reporting to Parents*, rev. ed. New York: Bureau of Publications, Teachers College, Columbia University, 1948. Pp. 108.
40. Strang, Ruth M. "Reporting Pupil Progress," *The School Executive*, LXXII (August 1953), 47–50.
41. Tibbetts, V. H. "Determining the Character of a Record System," *Progressive Education*, XIII (May 1936), 355.
42. Vredevoe, Lawrence E., and Lindecamp, Charles D. "How Shall We Make the Recording and Reporting of Pupil Progress More Meaningful?" *Bulletin of the National Association of Secondary-School Principals*, XXXVII (April 1953), 179–185.
43. Warnock, Emma. "Reaction of Parents and Children toward a Parent-Teacher-Pupil Conference Plan of Reporting," *Teachers College Journal*, XXVI (November 1954), 25–26.
44. White, M. Judson. "New Procedures in Marking and Reporting," *High School Journal*, XXXVI (April 1953), 202–207.
45. Wood, Ben D. *Measurement in Higher Education*. New York: Harcourt, Brace & World, Inc., 1923. Pp. 337.
46. Wrinkle, William L. "Six Years of an Experiment in Marking and Reporting in the Secondary School of the Colorado State College of Education," *Guidance in Public Secondary Schools*, pp. 86–114. Educational Records Bulletin 28. New York: Educational Records Bureau, October 1939. Pp. x+330.
47. Wrinkle, William L. *Improving Marking and Reporting Practices in Elementary Schools*. New York: Holt, Rinehart and Winston, Inc., 1947. Pp. 120.

CHAPTER XV

Case-Study Procedures in Guidance

ORIGIN OF CASE STUDIES

THE CASE-STUDY TECHNIQUE, WHICH HAS AS-sumed an important place in educational procedures, is of ancient origin. It is reported that the oldest known case study is a record of child placement presumably made about 4000 B.C.[1] From that time down to the present, case-study procedures have occasionally been employed, but it was not until the latter part of the nineteenth century that case studies were placed on a well-organized basis in connection with certain professions.

One of the most important developments of the case-study method was in the field of law. Case studies were initiated in the Harvard Law School about 1870 as a device for training students to think about fundamental principles. In the nineteenth century the medical profession began to develop a literature of medicine based on the accurate observation and recording of cases. The case study has now become a fundamental aspect in the training of medical students. Case-study procedures were soon adopted by sociologists because of their obvious value in social investigation. Psychologists were slower to take over the case-study method because, until fairly recently, they were seldom interested in the whole personality. The case study is now a basic method in both psychology and psychiatry.

Schools did not begin to adopt case-study practices until they had been tried out extensively by several of the other professions. As long as teachers were interested mainly in teaching subject matter to groups of pupils, they had no real need for case studies. The modern tendency, how-ever, to redirect education to take account of individual differences, and the emphasis on mental hygiene and guidance have brought into sharp focus the need for understanding each pupil. Consequently, a large number of schools have turned to the case-study method as an indispensable aid in making adequate provision for their pupils, particularly for pupils who deviate from the average in any important respect.

WHAT THE CASE-STUDY METHOD IS

The term "case study" has been employed in two types of investigation. A study in which real or assumed situations are presented for discussion as a means of arriving at basic principles in a given field or of examining an individual's or a group's understanding of principles has been called a case study. Law case studies are of this type, and some cases along this line have been prepared in the field of educational guidance. For example, a widely-used case-study instrument, known as *The Case of Mickey Murphy*, prepared by Warren R. Baller,[2] is designed to give teachers in training an opportunity to interpret a series of situations concerning an adolescent boy and thus to reveal their understanding of growth and development.

A detailed study of an individual, conducted for the purpose of bringing about better adjustment of the person who is the subject of the investigation, is also known as a case study. It is mainly in the latter sense that the term will be employed in this book.

In a case study of this kind, all available data about

[1] Ruth Strang. *Counseling Technics in College and Secondary School*, rev. ed. New York: Harper & Row, Publishers, 1949.

[2] Warren R. Baller. *The Case of Mickey Murphy: A Case Study Instrument for Evaluating Teachers' Understanding of Child Growth and Development, Form T, Enlarged Edition.* Lincoln, Neb.: University of Nebraska, 1955; Robert L. Baker and Richard E. Schutz. "A Criterion Factor Analysis of the Case of Mickey Murphy," *Personnel and Guidance Journal*, XL (November 1961), 282–285.

an individual are surveyed, and the significant items are assembled, organized, and studied in order that the nature and the causes of difficulties may be discovered, and that treatment designed to remove the difficulties may be planned and carried out. Thinking will perhaps be clarified if a distinction is made between case studies and case histories. A case history presents the story of an individual in as complete and as objective form as possible. It does not interpret the data, and it does not, in itself, bring to a focus the information on the present problems faced by the individual. If the school maintains a complete cumulative-record system, it has many of the elements of a continuous and up-to-date case history for every pupil in the school.

Since the first task in making a case study is to get the facts about the individual, the initial stages of the case study are almost identical with the case history. Thus, if the school has a cumulative-record system, a great part of the arduous work of gathering data for case studies is accomplished as a matter of routine; and by means of information-retrieval methods the data may be made available almost instantaneously. The case study, however, goes far beyond the case history. A case history is to a considerable extent a clerical task, but keen intelligence and insight are called for in making a case study. The facts available in the case history are marshaled and interpreted, and a diagnosis is made which will serve as a starting point for treatment.

A question may be raised whether the treatment of the case is a part of or a procedure that follows the case study. The case studies and case-study outlines appearing in educational and psychological literature exhibit no uniformity in this respect. Some case studies end with the diagnosis; others report extended treatment and the success that attended the treatment. Notwithstanding the fact that treatment is not included in some case studies, it should be clearly understood that every case study implies treatment; otherwise there would be no point in making the study. After the facts have been analyzed and a tentative diagnosis formulated, treatment should follow and, if possible, should become a part of the case-study record. Whether the treatment is recorded as a part of the case study will depend, to a large extent, on how the case is handled. If the person who initiates the case study also applies the treatment, a record of the treatment will ordinarily be added to the case study. If the case is referred to another person for treatment (for example, if a case of personality adjustment is referred to a psychiatrist), it may not be practicable to report the treatment in the case study. In cases treated by a specialist in psychiatric problems, facts are sometimes discovered which are of such a confidential nature that they should not be set down in writing. In cases of learning-difficulty treated in the school, the case study

will be much more valuable if it is concluded with a report of the nature of the treatment and of the progress of the pupil during treatment.

ASSEMBLING AND ORGANIZING DATA IN A CASE STUDY

In a case study of a pupil, usually the first step is to collect from the school records all important information pertaining to the pupil. The question of whether a given item is important will depend on the nature of the case. If the purpose of the study is to discover the causes of, and to prescribe treatment for, an observed difficulty (for example, inability to deal with situations involving numbers), only those items in the records which may contribute to an understanding of the difficulty are of immediate importance. Even in a specialized case of this kind, however, it is desirable to get a complete picture of the pupil, since a particular difficulty can best be interpreted against the background of his whole personality.

If the study is undertaken, not for the purpose of alleviating special difficulty, but for the purpose of arriving at a thorough understanding of the pupil, so that he may be assisted to better adjustment wherever need may manifest itself, every item of information may be important, and the whole record of the pupil should be carefully scrutinized. In schools maintaining cumulative records, including data on the social history, aptitudes, achievement, and personality, the first step of the investigation will be concerned mainly with the pupil's cumulative record card.

Although the school records should supply much helpful information, even the best of records will not provide complete data. As a rule, the data are entered at regular intervals, and there will usually be a period of several weeks between the time of the last entry on the record and the time of making the case study. The case investigator will, therefore, find it necessary to interview those who have contact with the pupil, including classroom teachers, homeroom teacher, physical education instructor, librarian or study-hall supervisor, adviser, and, possibly, parents. Notes should be made after each of these interviews, or, better still, each of the teachers and other school officers who are in contact with the pupil should be asked to write out a brief statement concerning the child's attainments, growth, and personality.

A third step is to interview the pupil himself and perhaps to give him additional tests. The school records may sometimes provide all the test data necessary, but, if the case is one of learning difficulty in a certain subject, it is improbable that the survey test scores in the school records will furnish an adequate basis for diagnosis. For example, if the case is one of reading disability, a diagnostic silent reading test and an oral reading check test should be employed as a minimum. If the difficulty seems to be in the field of personality, one of the more promising personality inventories, such as the California Test of Personality or the Heston Personal Adjustment Inventory, may be given—not so much for the purpose of record as for the purpose of securing responses which will form a convenient starting point of interview.

When reasonably complete data about the pupil have been collected, the case should be written up, and a tentative diagnosis and plan of treatment should be formulated. Although a case study could conceivably be conducted without making a written record, the necessity of putting it into writing forces the investigator to clarify his thinking about the individual and provides excellent training in stating, organizing, and interpreting the facts. Even though the plan is to include the progress of treatment as a part of the study, the case should be written up before treatment starts, and, when treatment is applied, this record should be amplified from time to time. When a written record has been made of the case, it will be very helpful to present the case study to the pupil's teachers, and to secure their reactions and further suggestions before proceeding with a plan of handling the case.

OUTLINES FOR CASE STUDIES

There is no set way of making a case study. The outlines will vary with the nature of the case and the preferences of the person conducting the study. If the school maintains a cumulative-record system in which comparable data for a pupil are recorded in organized fashion from year to year, it may be desirable to have the outline of the case study up to the point of diagnosis agree with the outline of the cumulative record. A considerable number of outlines have appeared in the case-study literature, three of which are presented here for illustrative purposes.

Demming's Case-Study Outline[3]

Description of the Case
  A. Name
  B. Address

[3] John A. Demming. "Case-Study Outline," in *Readings in Guidance* (ed. by Lester D. Crow and Alice Crow), pp. 283–285. New York: David McKay Company, Inc., 1962. (Used with permission.)

  C. Appearance
  D. Age
  E. School
  F. Grade
  G. Name of parents or guardians
  H. Period covered by observations
  I. Sources of information
  J. Definition of problems
Home Background and Family History
  A. Family characteristics and history
    1. Inventory of family members
      a. A list of members of the family and others living in the home
    2. Age of each of family members
    3. Physique and health of each of the members of the family
    4. Physical handicaps of family members
    5. Education and abilities
      a. Length of schooling of parents and siblings
      b. Present occupation of parents and occupational history
      c. Special abilities and disabilities
    6. Estimates of the attitudes of parents toward children, toward each other, toward the school, and toward the interviewer
    7. Interests and hobbies of family members
    8. Ideals and goals of family members
    9. Social status, relationships, and activities
    10. Emotional adjustments of family members
  B. Physical, socioeconomic and cultural environment
    1. Description of the community in which the child now lives
    2. Description of previous communities in which the child has lived
    3. Description of the neighborhood and the house where the child now lives
    4. Description of socioeconomic and educational background of neighbors
    5. Description of socioeconomic status of the child's home
Physical Development and Medical History
  A. Early Development
    1. Birth history
    2. Infancy
      a. Early patterns of development
    3. Development in areas of elimination, bowel and bladder
    4. Development of locomotion
    5. Development of language
    6. Other aspects of early development
  B. Health record
  C. Present physical condition
    1. Present resistance to disease
    2. Diet

3. Height and weight
4. Parent's concepts of child's present physical condition
5. General observation of child's physical condition

Intellectual Development
  A. Preschool history
    1. Nursery school and kindergarten
  B. Standardized test results
  C. School grades
  D. Other evidences of intellectual development

Social Development and Present Social Status
  A. Early social development
  B. Social relationships with peers
    1. Status in various peer groups
  C. Social relationships with adults
  D. Acceptance of the social and moral codes
  E. Learning of sex roles
  F. Manners and related social skills
  G. Leadership qualities
  H. Ascendancy
  I. Cooperative behavior

Character and Personality
  A. Self-concept
  B. Ego ideal
  C. Needs
  D. Presses
  E. Major conflicts
  F. Interests
  G. Independence
  H. Responsibility
  I. Curiosity
  J. Persistence
  K. Values
  L. Sentiments

Appraisal, Interpretation, and Recommendations
  A. An appraisal of the child as a whole person
  B. Interpretation of all of case history material to provide inferences as to the nature of the determining forces which have led to his present adjustment patterns
  C. Recommendations
    1. Statements of hypotheses concerning possible remedial steps that might be effective in promoting more wholesome adjustment

A. J. Jones' Adaptation of Henry C. Morrison's Outline of the Case Method[4]

I. Information
  A. Symptoms

4 Arthur J. Jones. *Principles of Guidance*, 4th ed. pp. 229–231. New York: McGraw-Hill Book Co., Inc., 1951; adapted from: Henry C. Morrison, *The Practice of Teaching in the Secondary*

The first step is always to get at the facts that indicate that the child is a problem case; not his history but the symptoms that have been noted. This involves finding his chronological age, the marks received in various subjects, instances of misconduct, latenesses and absences from school, etc.

All statements must be actually verified. They must be taken from school records when possible and only first-hand information accepted. The information thus obtained will often be sufficient to show that the case is not a problem one at all. Care should be taken here to exclude all that does not have to deal with present symptoms. History is valuable only as it throws light upon the causes of symptoms, but when gathering data on symptoms, history should be excluded. When the data are in, they should be written up and summarized.

  B. Examination

With the symptoms noted, more precise information regarding the case is obtained by various tests and examinations. These are, of course, selected with reference to the needs of the particular case. Some of these are given here:
    1. Psycho-physical
      a. Vision—normal
      b. Hearing—normal
      c. Coordination (neuromuscular)—no good tests are available, but careful observation will give helpful data
      d. Speech—normal
    2. Health
      a. Vital index (height-weight ratio)
      b. Nutrition
      c. Teeth
      d. General physical condition
    3. Educational
      Standard tests of various kinds suitable to the grade of the pupil. These are to be used to discover any fundamental weaknesses in his previous training and also to check up on the marks he has received.
    4. Mentality
      General intelligence test. It is best to give several types to avoid accidental results.
  C. Health and Physical History
    Very careful and exact information should be obtained not only of serious illnesses, scarlet fever, measles, etc., but of other illnesses and

School, rev. ed. pp. 646–666. Chicago: University of Chicago Press, 1931. (Used with permission of the McGraw-Hill Book Company, Inc., and The University of Chicago Press.)

operations for adenoids, tonsils, and any accidents that may have affected the health or resistance. If possible, a complete record of growth in height and weight and physiological maturity should be obtained and carefully recorded.

    D. School History
        1. Promotions
        2. Kind of work done
        3. Changed location—home and school
        4. Quality of schools attended
        5. Relation with individual teachers
    E. Family History
        1. Ancestry, parents, brothers and sisters, nationality, mental and criminal history, etc.
        2. Economic status and history
            The previous and present financial and economic situation of the family
        3. Cultural resources of the home
            Education and training of parents; books, music, and cultural atmosphere of the home
        4. Relation with the home—with parents and brothers and sisters
        5. Attitude of parents toward society
        6. Adjustment of parents to American standards
        7. Control exercised by parents of children—kind and amount of control
    F. Social History and Contacts
        The pupil's social background outside the school and the home
        1. Church and Sunday school, Boy Scouts, etc.
        2. Associates
        3. Summer camps
        4. Gang affiliations
        5. Abnormal sex history
        6. Court record

II. Diagnosis

This is the working hypothesis of the cause or explanation of the symptoms or the problem and results from a careful analysis of all the data obtained. It is not necessarily delayed until all the evidence is in, for guesses or hypotheses are actually being made and leads followed up at many stages, but the final diagnosis is not actually made until the evidence is in. Possibly, the better statement would be that every guess or lead is followed until the worker is reasonably sure from the evidence that it is correct.

III. Treatment

Out of the diagnosis grows the definite systematic treatment. It often happens that the treatment shows that the diagnosis was not correct. In this case, we must go back for further investigation. In one sense, the treatment may be considered as a step in the verification of the hypothesis; in another, it is itself a

guess or an hypothesis set up as a possible remedy that itself needs verification by the final step.

IV. Follow-up

It is very necessary to know the results of the treatment in order to check the accuracy of the diagnosis and to modify, if necessary, the treatment. It also aids in later cases that may be similar in nature.

McCallister's Outline for Case Studies in Remedial Reading[5]

1. Introductory statement—a brief statement which gives the reader the setting of the case
2. Preliminary survey of reading ability
    a. Performance on tests
    b. Reports of instructors concerning school work of pupils
3. Analysis of reading deficiencies
    a. Power of comprehension and interpretation
    b. Rate of reading
    c. Power of perception and recognition
4. Analysis of contributing influences which aid in explaining the origin and cause of deficiencies
    a. Mental ability
    b. Vocabulary
    c. Physical history and health status
    d. School history
    e. Personality traits
5. Diagnosis of the case—a descriptive statement of deficiencies with explanation of causes
6. Remedial instruction
    a. Plan of instruction
    b. Types of instruction
7. Progress of instruction—an evaluation of the effectiveness of remedial measures
    a. Practice records
    b. Improvement as shown by eye-movement records
    c. Improvement in performance on standardized tests
    d. Reports of instructors concerning school progress
    e. Evaluation of remedial instruction
8. Significant observations—an interpretation of the more significant facts about the case

Strang[6] has classified and discussed the content of a case history under the following headings:
1. First impression of the person and his problem
2. Family history, including information about the emotional relationships in the home and neighborhood
3. Developmental history

[5] James M. McCallister. *Remedial and Corrective Instruction in Reading*, pp. 108–126. New York: Appleton-Century-Crofts, Inc., 1936. (Used with permission of the author and the publisher.)
[6] Ruth Strang, *op. cit.*, pp. 208–209.

4. School history
5. Data on the child's present mental ability and achievement (from standard tests, informal tests, and observation)
6. Educational and vocational plans
7. Interpretation and synthesis of data, with indications for treatment

This outline is simple and clear, and it includes one feature that is omitted from some of the other outlines, namely, "Educational and vocational plans."

The following outline was set up by a school psychologist as a guide for teacher-advisers in making case summaries, which may be regarded as abbreviated case studies.

> Introductory statement
> Physical condition
> Mental ability
> Achievement in school
> Study habits
> Attitude toward work
> Interests and special abilities
> Personality
> Summary

In connection with the work of a laboratory school, a school psychologist and a psychiatrist cooperated in a series of case studies. The psychologist carried on the initial stages of each study and provided a tentative diagnosis. The psychiatrist then took the case over, basing his treatment on a more adequate diagnosis than the psychologist was prepared to make. The outline used by the psychologist in reporting the cases to the psychiatrist could readily be applied to case studies by a classroom teacher. The outline included the following steps:

> Introductory statement—identification, age, school grade, etc.
> Intelligence
> Scores on achievement tests
> School progress
> Summary of teachers' statements
> Learning defects
> Social history
> Health history
> Personality problems
> Observation of pupil
> Summary
> Tentative diagnosis

All the case-study outlines that have been presented in this section have many elements in common. The specific type of outline to be used is not important. Pre-

sumably each teacher will wish to formulate his own outline. The main thing is to present the major facts in an orderly fashion and to formulate a plan for using them in understanding and helping the pupil.

THE CASE-STUDY METHOD ILLUSTRATED

Among the books published over the years which contain valuable case studies of school pupils were those by Reavis; Smithies; Brewer; Sayles; McCallister; Bennett, Seashore, and Wesman; Rothney; Rothney and Roens; Everett; and Snyder.[7] Two significant case studies based on cumulative records were reported by Mrs. Hawkes in Chapter IV of *Guidance in Public Secondary Schools,* published by the Educational Records Bureau. Fifteen case studies written by classroom teachers were included in Chapter XII of the same book (13).

In his book, *The High School Student: A Book of Cases,* Rothney presented 27 carefully-chosen and well-written case studies grouped under the following headings: the troubled ones, the ones in trouble, the happy ones, the physically handicapped, and the quiet ones. General principles, problems, and methods of case studies were also discussed in Rothney's book (20).

A Reading Difficulty Case

The following case study was taken from an unpublished report of the senior writer when he was a psychologist in a laboratory school. The illustration consists of a case study of reading difficulty in which treatment and progress of treatment, as well as the history of the case, are reported. The procedures utilized in the study are not highly technical, and they could readily be employed by either teachers or counselors.

Introductory Statement. Fred entered the subfreshman class of the high school at the age of 13 years, 1 month. His scores on all reading tests taken at the time of entrance were rather low and appeared to indicate reading deficiency. He was therefore placed in the corrective reading section of subfreshman English, in which special attention was given to reading. He did fairly good work in that class and his test scores at the end of the year indicated that he had made considerable progress in reading.

Fred's mother, however, was of the opinion that the boy had gained very little in reading ability during the year. She feared that he was so handicapped in reading that if special steps were not taken he would never be able to do the ex-

[7] All these books are listed in the references at the end of the chapter.

tensive reading required in the advanced years of high school and in college. The librarian of the high school, likewise, observed evidence of continued retardation in reading. Because of these facts and also because his scores on reading tests were still considerably below the median of his class, special work in reading was undertaken with Fred at the beginning of his freshman year in high school and was continued throughout the year.

General Ability. Fred's scores on intelligence tests during his first year in the high school are shown in Table 6.

TABLE 6. Intelligence Test Results of a Ninth-Grade Boy

Test	IQ	Norm	Median IQ of Class	Quarter Rank in Class[a]
Otis Self-Administering	102	100	107.0	3
Ohio Psychological	105	100	110.4	3
Stanford-Binet Scale	109	100	....	..

[a] 1 is the highest quarter.

The results of all three tests show that Fred has normal intelligence. His IQ was between 100 and 110 on all the tests. On the group tests, he was below the median but above the lowest quartile of his class. On the individual test he showed a mental age of 14 years, 11 months at a chronological age of 13 years, 8 months. The examiner who administered the Binet test to Fred made the following note on his test blank: "Fred is very deliberate in his attack upon problems. He works slowly but is usually correct in his conclusions. His type of response is *reflective*." There is little doubt that Fred has sufficient mental ability to do acceptable, although probably not outstanding, work in the high school.

Social and School History. Fred is of German stock. His grandparents came to America from Austria and Germany. Three generations on the paternal side have been engaged in the medical profession. Fred has a brother and a sister, both of whom are pupils in the same high school. The economic status of the family is good. A large and comfortable home is maintained and there are two servants. The boy is much interested in a variety of outdoor sports and has playmates his own age.

Fred is large and mature-looking for his age. The school physician examined him and found that his health in general was good. Bitten fingernails were the only evidence of nervousness. The vision in his right eye was found to be quite defective and the physician recommended that he have his eyes retested for glasses. Fred wears glasses now when reading.

If Fred has any serious personality problems, they have not appeared in his work in the high school. He seems to be well adjusted to the social group. Several of his teachers have commented upon his good attitude, his cooperation, and his willingness to profit by criticism.

All of Fred's elementary school training was received out-side this school system. His progress through the elementary school was not entirely normal. He repeated one-half year and made up the last half of the sixth grade in the summer. During the first semester that Fred was in the subfreshman class of the high school he had considerable difficulty with the work. At the end of the first semester he had incomplete work in United States history and art appreciation. His written papers were not good because of weakness in spelling, punctuation, and sentence structure, and he required a considerable amount of reteaching. According to the reports of his teachers, Fred did much better work during the second semester of his subfreshman year and he has continued to do acceptable work this year. Fred has not had serious difficulty in school except in reading.

Evidences of Reading Deficiency. Scores made by Fred on reading tests since he entered the high school are compared with the test norms and class medians in Table 7.

The table shows two general facts concerning the pupil's reading ability. First, Fred was retarded in reading in comparison with the grade norm and the median of his class. Of twelve scores, nine were below standard. In five cases where class medians were available, the pupil's scores were decidedly below the medians.

The second conclusion about Fred's reading skill that can be drawn from the test scores is that there was considerable gain during his subfreshman year. The gains shown are as follows:

Test	Time Elapsed	Points Gained
Monroe Silent Reading— Rate	12 months	9
Monroe Silent Reading— Comprehension	12 "	2
Thorndike-McCall	12 "	12
Traxler Silent Reading	12 "	20
Sangren-Woody	9 "	24

In spite of these gains, however, the fact that Fred was still below the norm on three of the four tests made remedial work during his freshman year advisable.

Fred was observed, while reading, by the librarian and the psychologist early in the present year and a number of difficulties were noted. These will be brought out in the diagnosis of the case.

Diagnosis of Reading Difficulties. The greatest difficulty revealed in Fred's test scores was a marked slowness in rate of reading. Retardation in rate appeared in every timed reading test administered to him. His rate score on the Monroe Standardized Silent Reading Test in the beginning of his subfreshmen year was 77 as compared with a norm of 84 and a class median of 109.3. His score on this test near the beginning of his freshman year was slightly above the grade norm, but was below the class average. On the Sangren-Woody Reading Test, Fred made rate scores of 16.3 and 16.4 at the beginning and the end of his subfreshman year. The grade norm is 21. In the various forms of the Traxler Silent Reading Test he read consistently at a rate of about two words a second, whereas the minimum acceptable rate for his grade is three words a second. His inferior rate of reading was probably due partly to his slow rate of associating ideas with words. This hypothesis is supported by the fact that the speed with which he did a test of rate of association was considerably lower than the average.

The retardation in rate of reading undoubtedly tended to lower Fred's comprehension scores in some of the tests, particularly the Monroe test. However, his rather low scores on the Thorndike-McCall Reading Scale, which has generous time limits, indicate that he was somewhat retarded in ability to comprehend the meaning of reading material, even when he had plenty of time to ponder over it.

Fred's reading vocabulary was not quite as extensive as that of the median pupil in his class, but it was practically up to the grade norm. In fact, his score on the vocabulary parts of the Sangren-Woody and the Traxler tests equaled or exceeded the norm.

training in reading given to Fred this year were directly in line with the diagnosis of difficulties. They were as follows:

1. To foster an interest in reading.
2. To build up habits of independent reading.
3. To increase rate of reading as far as native rate of reaction would permit.
4. To develop greater power of understanding reading material.
5. To utilize incidental opportunities to increase the reading vocabulary. Formal training in this respect seemed unnecessary.
6. To overcome the tendency to reverse certain letters.

Treatment of the Case. The remedial treatment of the pupil was planned to achieve the purposes that were outlined. The first and most important needs were to plan a

TABLE 7.   Scores on Standardized Reading Tests

Test	When Administered	Score	Grade Norm	Class Median
Monroe Silent Reading				
Rate	Subfreshman Year	77	84	109.3
Comprehension	" "	28	25.4	33.0
Monroe Silent Reading				
Rate	Freshman Year	86	84	89.0
Comprehension	" "	30	25.4	27.3
Thorndike-McCall	Subfreshman Year	47	56.0	61.7
" "	Freshman Year	59	61.5	....
Inglis Vocabulary	Subfreshman Year	38	45.0	47.3
Traxler Silent Reading				
Form 1	Subfreshman Year	61	80.0	100.0
Form 3	" "	71	80.0	....
Form 4	Freshman Year	81	89.0	....
Sangren-Woody, Form B	Subfreshman Year	61.3	84.0	....
Form A	" "	85.4	91.0	....
Gray Standard Oral Reading	Freshman Year	37.5	48.0	....

It was discovered early in the individual work with Fred that he manifested a tendency toward that type of reading confusion known as "reversals." That is, he sometimes confused letters which looked alike except that their orientation from left to right was opposite one to the other. This tendency was unquestionably present in the case of *b* and *d,* although it was not noted for any other pairs of letters and was not observed in the case of any pairs of words. The case did not appear to be a very serious one, since no reversals except *b* and *d* were noted.

Fred was not greatly interested in reading when he entered the high school and the training in reading given in the English class during his subfreshman year did not succeed in building up an interest of this kind. His mother stated at the beginning of the present year that he read very little at home and that she would be glad if he would read just one book and really enjoy it.

Aims of Remedial Work. The purposes of the remedial

program of reading that would stimulate interest and lead to habits of reading. In this part of the work, the remedial teacher had the full cooperation of the school librarian. At the beginning of the year, the librarian drew up an extensive and varied reading list for Fred, and throughout the year she was very helpful in supplying books and making additional suggestions.

The pupil met with the remedial teacher one period each week during the 11:00 o'clock hour. Usually the meeting was held on Wednesday. At this meeting the independent reading of the pupil during the next week was planned. Usually the manner of planning followed was for the remedial teacher to select two or three widely different books from the reading list supplied by the librarian and to have Fred examine them and choose the one that he preferred to read. It was generally planned that the pupil should finish the book and return it at the next meeting on the following week. Sometimes, when the book was exceptionally long or

Fred's schedule of regular class work was heavier than usual, more than a week was spent on a book. The pupil reported the amount of independent reading done each week. Usually a few minutes were spent in discussing the content of a book. No attempt was made in connection with this type of reading to check rigidly on Fred's comprehension of the material. It was kept in mind that the purpose was to build up interests in recreative reading and it was felt that the aim would be defeated if the reading was made a task to be done. The *Kuder Book List*, a list of 500 titles related to the interest categories of the Kuder Record—Vocational, is a helpful guide for independent reading in this kind of remedial work.

As a rule, most of the time in the remedial period was spent on the McCall-Crabbs Test Lessons, Book IV. The plan of using the book was as follows: Five lessons were covered at each meeting. The regular three-minute limit was used for each lesson. After Fred had finished a lesson, he read his answers to the questions to the examiner, marked the ones that were wrong, and translated his raw score into a "G–Score" by means of a table. He then worked out correct answers for the questions he had answered incorrectly, and read aloud and answered the questions that he had failed to cover during the time limit. This oral work at the end of each lesson (except those lessons finished within the time limit) assured the thorough understanding of each lesson. It also gave opportunity for constant check on reversals of *b* and *d*, since the questions were of the four-response type (responses *a, b, c, d*), the pupil indicating his answer by reading the letter preceding the answer he thought was right.

The plan of using lessons that were timed stimulated the pupil to read at his maximum rate. He took much interest in his G–Scores and, with the aid of the teacher, kept a graph of the G–Scores from week to week.

The McCall-Crabbs Test Lessons were sometimes made the basis of informal vocabulary work. The remedial teacher soon found that Fred could nearly always work out the right answer for every question unless the material contained words unfamiliar to him. Occasionally the material was varied by using one of the volumes of *Real Life Stories* instead of the McCall-Crabbs lessons.

After each of the meetings with Fred, the remedial teacher wrote a brief summary of the work carried on during the period. If this entire record were included in the present report it would be needlessly long. The following excerpts illustrate the type of record made:

Friday, October 28. Fred read five of the McCall-Crabbs Test Lessons. Rate slow; comprehension good. (A continuous record of these lessons is kept on another sheet.) He selected and read a story in *Real Life Stories*. His rate was slow—about half a page per minute. He said that the story was interesting. His attitude was excellent.

Wednesday, December 7. Fred returned *The Prince and the Pauper*, which he had finished. He had also read 275 pages in *Famous Frontiersmen*. He retained it to finish before next Wednesday. Fred is also going to read

short stories for his literature class and will report the titles to me. He read McCall-Crabbs Test Lessons 11 and 12. An improvement in speed was evident. A tendency to confuse *b* and *d*, when these letters stand alone, which had been noted in preceding lessons, was observed again. When it was mentioned to him, he acknowledged the difficulty. I told him not to worry about it and that it would probably disappear with practice in reading. He read aloud the first chapter of Van Loon's *Ancient Man*. He had practically no difficulty with pronunciation and was able to give the thought orally quite well. Fred did the Gates Pronunciation Test without error. I asked him the meaning of several words and found only one that he didn't know. Fred spent the last part of the hour reading ahead in the book, *Famous Frontiersmen*.

Wednesday, April 19. As Fred was absent from school last Wednesday, this was his first meeting with me for two weeks. He returned Hawes' *Mutineer*, which he had finished. He said that he found it rather dull at first, but interesting after he got into it. The reading during the period covered McCall-Crabbs lessons 63–67. The average G–Score was 7.5, the best record he has made thus far. Fred chose the *Story of Ab* to read during the next week.

Progress of Treatment. Fred and the remedial teacher spent a total of 30 class periods (including testing periods) on the work in reading. The pupil was interested in the reading and cooperated with the teacher in every way. Evidence of his interest is found in the amount of independent reading done during the year. The following is a list of books read:

Britt, *The Boys' Own Book of Frontiersmen*
DuPuy, *Uncle Sam, Detective*
Mark Twain, *The Prince and the Pauper*
Johnston, *Famous Frontiersmen*
Green, *Roy Andrews, Dragon Hunter*
Parker, *Book of Electricity*
Spivak, *Georgia Nigger* (selected independently)
Gaston, *Modern Lives*
Driggs, *The Adventures of Arnold Adair, American Ace*
Garland, *Boy Life on the Prairie*
Masefield, *Martin Hyde*
  Hoof and Claw
Hawes, *Mutineer*
Waterloo, *Story of Ab*
  Lance of Kanana
——— *Electricity for the Farm House*

Fred also read one of Thompson-Seton's book of animal life and several short stories, including some by Poe and one by Conan Doyle.

Near the end of the year the plan of having Fred choose his books from the library rather than from a reading list was adopted. His selections tended to be in the field of science. Although Fred's tastes in fiction are not yet very mature, his interests in nonfiction—especially scientific books—are quite mature. Fred's science teacher reports that he is far ahead of most of his classmates in his understanding of that field.

All 94 test lessons contained in the McCall-Crabbs Book IV were read during the year. Occasionally, this work was varied by selections from other material, but Fred showed a preference for reading in the McCall-Crabbs book because he could see his score in reading and could note his progress from week to week.

Results of the Remedial Work. Evidence of Fred's improvement in reading during the remedial period is of four kinds, which are as follows:

1. Gains in G–Score on McCall-Crabbs Test Lessons.
2. Improvement in scores on reading tests.
3. Reports of teachers.
4. Results of observation of the pupil.

McCall-Crabbs G–Score. The authors of the McCall-Crabbs Test Lessons have provided for changing raw scores directly into G–Scores or grade scores. That is, a G–Score of 5.0 on lesson 10 is equal to a G–Score of 5.0 on lesson 15 and every other lesson. Thus, the G–Scores are directly comparable. Some of the lessons do not seem to be very well standardized, but it is probable that if the G–Scores for several lessons are averaged, the errors appearing in standardizing various lessons will tend to cancel each other. At any rate, the scores offer a fairly satisfactory measure of reading ability in terms of grade norms.

Fred's record of G–Scores, with the scores for all the lessons given on any one date averaged, is shown graphically in Figure 7. The pupil's lowest score was 4.3 on October 28, the first time the test lessons were given, and the highest score was 8.0 on May 31, the date on which the test lessons were discontinued. This gain was equivalent to the progress that might normally be expected in 3.7 grades. A part of the improvement was doubtless due to familiarity with the type of lesson used in the McCall-Crabbs books and to better methods of attack on this kind of lesson. These factors do not, however, explain all the improvement. After a number of lessons of this type had been done by the pupil, one can reasonably assume that he had become thoroughly adjusted to the reading situation set up in the lessons and that familiarity with that kind of lesson would thenceforth cause little, if any, gain in score. Nevertheless, he continued to improve to the end of the training period. A genuine gain in reading ability is therefore indicated.

Scores on Reading Tests. Fred's progress in reading ability during the year is indicated by the scores on five reading tests shown in Table 8.

Improvement was made on every test. The larger gains were in comprehension, vocabulary, and oral reading. The gain in rate of reading was insignificant according to the results of the Monroe test and the Traxler test. The small gain on the Sangren-Woody test, in which rate of reading is very important, also suggests that Fred did not improve materially in speed of reading. In spite of the fact that the gain in rate was negligible, the remedial training was worthwhile because of the large growth in comprehension.

Reports of Teachers. The comments made by Fred's teachers in the regular reports at the end of the year do not show deficiencies in reading. They indicate that Fred's work was satisfactory except in his written papers, which showed marked deficiencies in spelling and handwriting. Apparently, Fred is not now markedly deficient in reading ability; if he were, the deficiency would be reflected in his class work.

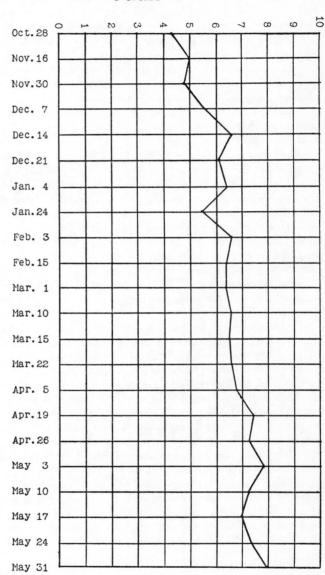

FIGURE 7.

A report made by the librarian on Fred's application in the library may be included in this section. She observed him for 20 minutes on November 22 and again for 20 minutes on May 8 and made a graphic record of her observations. Although the book Fred was reading when the second observation was made was harder to understand than the one he was reading when the first observation was taken, his second record was considerably better than the first one. The observation was not carried on long enough to provide a very reliable sampling of the pupil's study habits, but it may be concluded that the results offer some evidence of improvement in application during the year.

Observations by Remedial Teacher. The written comments made by the remedial teacher after each meeting with the pupil indicate that Fred showed slow, but consistent, growth in reading ability during the period. One of the most encouraging signs of better reading ability was that

TABLE 8. Improvement in Test Scores During Remedial Teaching

Test	Before Remedial Training	After Remedial Training	Gain in Points	Grade Equivalent at End of Period of Teaching
Sangren-Woody Reading	85.4	87.2	1.8	8.3
Thorndike-McCall Reading Scale	59.0	61.0	2.0	8.9
Monroe Silent Reading				
Rate	86.0	89.0	3.0	10.0
Comprehension	30.0	34.0	4.0	12.7
Gray Oral Reading	37.5	46.0	8.5	....
Traxler Silent Reading				
Rate	24.0	24.0	0.0	
Vocabulary	21.0	29.0	8.0	
Comprehension	36.0	42.0	6.0	
Total score	81.0	95.0	14.0	10.0
Average grade equivalent	....	....	....	9.6ᵃ

ᵃ This rough index of the pupil's grade equivalent at the end of the period of training is simply an arithmetical average of the grade equivalents on the four different reading tests. In order to avoid over-weighting the Monroe Silent Reading Test in the composite, the grade equivalents for rate and comprehension on the Monroe test were first averaged, and this average was used along with the grade equivalents derived from the other three tests in computing the average.

the tendency to experience reversals—the confusion of *b* and *d*—that had been noticeable during the fall semester had apparently disappeared by the end of his freshman year. This came about without the use of any of the special corrective devices that are sometimes employed in these cases. It is not known at present, however, whether or not the pupil is permanently cured of the tendency.

Summary and Recommendation. Fred evidently made significant improvement in reading ability during a period of approximately eight months in which he met with the reme-

dial teacher for one class period a week. His largest gains were in power of comprehension. He continued to be a slow reader, but nevertheless he was able to read fast enough to do the work of the ninth grade satisfactorily. He also developed an interest in reading which showed signs of continuing beyond the period of training. Of six objectives set up at the beginning of the teaching, five were reached. The one which was not accomplished dealt with increasing the rate of silent reading.

It appears that Fred is now approximately at the reading standard for the ninth grade, although he is below the median of his class in the high school. He plans to continue doing a large quantity of informal reading during the summer vacation. The remedial teacher should interview him early in the new fall semester in regard to progress and should utilize the opportunity provided by the interview to test his reading ability again. Unless marked loss in skill is found, further remedial instruction will be inadvisable, especially in view of the fact that his written English expression will probably need some special attention. The pupil is mature in his attitude, earnest in purpose, and appears to have reached the point in his development where he can guide himself in his reading.

A Case of Behavior and Learning Difficulty

The next case study was made by a high school teacher who was a student in a graduate class in case studies. It illustrates the kind of case report frequently prepared in the normal course of the regular school activities.[8]

Reason for the Study. Robert has been in disciplinary and academic difficulty in the junior high school which he now attends. Two years ago, after entering Grade 7–1, his teachers felt that he was not prepared adequately for this grade level, and he was therefore placed back in Grade 5. He has come up through the fifth and sixth grades fairly satisfactorily, but he is now repeating 7–1b. Because of his constant demand for attention, he is a disturbing element in the classroom, and he has been sent frequently to the principal's office for disciplinary action. Further, in the light of the results of two tests of scholastic aptitude, it is felt that he has not been achieving at a level compatible with his ability.

Tentative Hypothesis. From information given in the school's records, from talks with his teachers, and from observations of Robert both in the classroom and in personal interviews, the case worker feels that Robert's problem may be basically an emotional one stemming from his home environment.

Personal and Family History. Robert is 13 years, 10 months old. He is a slender, nice-looking boy, with a quick smile, and he has the usual amount of excess energy found in boys of his age. He shows some evidence of neglect in that he is usually in need of a bath and his clothing is ill-

[8] Based on a report written by Basil B. Emerson and used with his permission.

fitting and often ragged. He often has dark circles about his eyes, and interviews have brought out that sometimes he has little sleep because he is allowed to stay up late attending a professional basketball game or a boxing or wrestling match. In spite of his unhygienic appearance, he seems well nourished and in good health.

Robert is the youngest of six children. The father, age 49, drives a truck for the city garbage collection department. The mother, age 43, works in a factory office. Both are reportedly in good health. Neither parent had more than an eighth-grade schooling. His two sisters are married and live at Robert's home with their husbands. The older sister has four children, the eldest of which is a boy of 5 years. Both sisters finished Grade 11–1 in high school. The eldest brother finished Grade 9 and is now in the ground forces of the Air Corps. Another brother quit school while in Grade 10–1. He is now unemployed and is waiting until he is old enough to enlist in the Army. The boy next older than Robert attends a vocational high school. All 13 of these people live in a six-room dwelling which is in a state of dilapidation.

The school records show that Robert transferred to his junior high school from an elementary school in a neighboring community. Very little information came on his transfer card. The only childhood disease listed is chicken pox when he was 7 years old.

The school record of attendance and teachers' marks is as follows:

| | Grades | | | |
	5	6	7 1st half	7 2nd half
Days absent	6	5	0	3/2
Times tardy	3	3	1	4
Behavior	Poor	Poor	Fair	Improved
Reading	70	70	—	—
Writing	75	75	—	—
Spelling	85	50	85	80
Mathematics	60	65	80	78
History and social studies	78	65	80	85
Geography	50	50	—	—
Shop	75	70	—	—
Drawing	—	—	85	—
Music	—	—	85	85
General science	—	—	50[a]	65
English	60	50	78	75

[a] Robert obtained a grade of 95% on the examination, but failure to hand in a notebook resulted in a failing grade.

The following results were obtained from objective tests administered to Robert:

General Intelligence Tests:	IQ
Binet, Grade 4, June	100
Otis Group Test of Mental Ability, Grade 6, Nov.	101
Calif. Test of Mental Maturity, Grade 6, April	100

New York State Reading Progress Tests (%ile for the grade)	Grade 6, Oct.	Grade 7, Oct.	Grade 7, April
Detailed understanding	60%ile	78%ile	
General thought	21%ile	21%ile	
Word meaning	42%ile	32%ile	
Grade level		6.1	6.9

Calif. Test of Personality, Elementary, Form A, Grades 4–9	Gr. 7, Dec.	Gr. 7, May
	%iles	%iles
I. Self-adjustment		
a. Self-reliance	20	70
b. Sense of personal worth	25	35
c. Sense of personal freedom	1	45
d. Feeling of belonging	15	40
e. Withdrawing tendencies (freedom from)	30	60
f. Nervous symptoms (freedom from)	30	95
II. Social adjustment	10	45
a. Social standards	1	60
b. Social skills	15	45
c. Antisocial tendencies (freedom from)	15	20
d. Family relations	5	60
e. School relations	10	15
f. Community relations	20	55
Total adjustment	15	55

Kuder Preference Record (%iles for male adults)	Gr. 7, March
Mechanical	34
Computational	75
Scientific	21
Persuasive	56
Artistic	66
Literary	83
Musical	92
Social Service	29
Clerical	46

MacQuarrie Test of Mechanical Ability, Gr. 7, May 50%ile

The intelligence and reading test results indicate that Robert is of average mental ability, but that he is somewhat low in reading achievement. The results of the other tests are discussed later in this report.

Diagnosis and Plan of Treatment. The difficulty in this case seems to be one of emotional adjustment. The boy appears to feel that he is not recognized as he should be, either at home or at school. Apparently another individual, probably the sister's child, has moved into the limelight in the home situation. To compensate for being pushed aside, Robert has resorted to more overt actions to regain his former position. Some of his teachers do not understand the problem; consequently, Robert is thwarted in his attempts at school. As a result of this frustration, he has become rebellious, especially toward those who do not try to understand him.

The plan of treatment logically follows three avenues: first, an attempt to improve the home relationships; secondly, an attempt to bring about better understanding of Robert by his teachers; and, lastly, an attempt to improve Robert's attitudes toward school and his family.

Treatment and Check of Diagnosis. The last part of the plan was undertaken first. Weekly interviews of from 20 to 45 minutes were held. It was extremely difficult for Robert to "stay put" during the initial talks with him. No coercion was used upon him to reveal anything he did not wish, nor was he forced to stay in the interview. He willingly took the objective tests, but volunteered little information about himself or his family. When at the end of one interview a home visit was mentioned, he protested so vehemently that this part of the plan was postponed in order to preserve the rapport that had been established with him.

It was discovered that Robert was extremely fond of sports and that he joined the school "Y" and "Boys' Club" for this reason. Robert plans to go to high school and later to become a mechanic. In discussing his school subjects and his teachers, Robert said that he liked mathematics and physical education but disliked English and science. Such remarks as "Most teachers have me do things I'm not interested in"; "There's nothing to do at home"; "I don't like to stay in when I'm home"; and "Kids bother me at home" reveal something of his problem and tend to support the original diagnosis.

The individual counseling consisted of explanations of the processes of growth, how attitudes change as we grow, and the necessity for tolerance of other people's opinions and regard for their rights. The advantages of high school were discussed, and the greater variety of sports and athletics was stressed. The last few interviews were more fruitful; he contributed more to the conversation and seemed less anxious to leave.

The second part of the plan was to relieve some of Robert's restraints in school by talking to his teachers. Most of them were concerned about him, and had a good grasp of his problem. His English teacher was very sympathetic, even though Robert showed a dislike for this subject. She said, "Robert is very fidgety in class, but he is not really a disturbing child. I believe he is not supervised enough at home. He may be upset by home environment." His mathematics teacher found no fault with him at all, saying, "His attitude in my class is excellent; he works and does well in mathematics." The science instructor, however, had an unfavorable view of Robert. She felt that his attitude in class was poor and that he could not be trusted. The comment of the physical education instructor was "Robert has lots of energy and enthusiasm for sports. He is usually the leader of his group." Most of those interviewed, including the janitors, felt that Robert was a "likable kid."

Evaluation of Treatment. Since the case work with Robert had not been completed when this report was written, it was not expected that the treatment provided thus far would be very effective. Both the principal and the guidance counselor, however, separately stated that Robert's behavior had improved and that he was doing better work in school. The counselor said, "Robert hasn't been sent to the office for disciplinary action this term, although he has had detention a few times."

It will be observed that there was an improvement in Robert's grades this term and that his reading grade level was raised from 6.1 to 6.9. The most striking change is seen in the test results on the California Test of Personality, Elementary Form A, Grades 4–9. Granted that the results of a paper-and-pencil personality test must be interpreted with caution, these results do indicate considerable improvement in Robert's personality pattern. When interpreted in the light of the observations of this case worker and of Robert's teachers, the results seem fairly valid and are, indeed, encouraging.

The Kuder Preference Record was given more for the purpose of gaining rapport with Robert than for determining any particular interests. The results of the Kuder inventory may be questionable for a boy of this age and ability.

The results of the MacQuarrie Test of Mechanical Ability suggest that while Robert is average for his grade level, he probably has less mechanical ability than would be required for one who is going into this field as an occupation. It would be unwise, however, to draw any definite conclusion from just one paper-and-pencil test of this kind.

In evaluating the treatment, it should be pointed out that the fact that Robert had someone who was taking a personal interest in him may alone have been of more value than the actual procedures used. Good rapport was eventually established, and the data available indicate a fair measure of success.

Follow-up. Obviously, it would be incorrect to say that Robert has made the desired adjustment and that no further special attention is needed. It would also be grossly unfair to the boy to drop his problem now. Three steps in follow-up are planned: (1) to obtain the results of his final work and grades in Grade 7–1b for this term and to discuss these with his teachers; (2) to suggest that the faculty study his problem next school term by the case-conference method and to plan a common program of help for him; and (3) to visit Robert's parents and to attempt to help them understand his need for more attention, affection, supervision, and personal care.

POINTS TO BE OBSERVED IN MAKING A CASE STUDY

PLANNING THE CASE STUDY

The following points are offered as suggestions for those who are contemplating the making of a case study for the first time:

1. Select a case in which you are really interested, both from the standpoint of the nature of the case and the personality of the individual concerned.

2. If possible, choose a pupil from one of your classes who, you feel, needs attention and help and who will probably cooperate well with you.

3. When considering various pupils, give some thought to the shy, quiet, retiring pupils. Pupils of this type are sometimes more suitable subjects for case study than pupils whose difficulties or behavior cause them to be noticed.

4. Plan only as much as you feel that you can accomplish. If you contemplate a thorough case study, including treatment, it will probably be best to confine your study during the first year to one pupil. If you prefer to make brief case summaries, you can perhaps do several, or even summaries for an entire class if it is small.

COLLECTING THE DATA

Some of the main points with respect to collecting the data were set forth earlier in this chapter. An additional point is that in interviewing the pupil and in testing him to get further data about his difficulties, care should be used not to place him on the defensive. He should not be made to feel that he is a culprit or that he is in any way an extreme deviate from his fellow pupils. The meeting ground of the case investigator and the subject should be one of sharing in the solution of the pupil's problems. If the case investigator can enlist the interest of the pupil and can get him to take the initiative from the beginning, the prognosis for the successful solution of the pupil's problems is excellent.

WRITING UP THE CASE

As already indicated, there is no one pattern for writing up the case, but certain general principles should probably be observed.

1. Write objectively, simply, and with directness. Although you should be vitally interested in the case, your report of it should not reflect personal bias. The description of the case should be as objective and the interpretation should be as impersonal as possible. This does not mean that you should avoid interpretation and inference, but it does mean that you should distinguish meticulously between the facts you have discovered and the interpretation or diagnosis based on these facts.

2. In the report of the case, use both general statements and specific illustrations. General statements about intelligence, achievement, and personality are much more convincing if they are supported by some definite data.

3. Eliminate irrelevant items; confine the case report to a few typewritten pages.

APPLYING AND EVALUATING TREATMENT

Persons who are inexperienced in making case studies often find that the study moves along smoothly until they reach the stage of applying treatment, but that this stage presents problems which seem baffling. The observation of a few suggestions may help to clarify these problems.

1. A case investigator should not attempt to apply treatment for difficulties that are entirely outside his experience. If he does make such an attempt, it is probable that he will become involved in an embarrassing situation and that he may do the pupil more harm than good. If the problem is one of learning in his own or a related field, he should be able to handle it. If the problem is one of reading or study difficulty, as many cases are, he should be able to offer the pupil valuable help in reading and studying the content of his own special field and perhaps of other fields. The case investigator can also handle many problems that are volitional, which are caused by lack of interest, or which are of a minor behavior character. If the case involves learning adjustments that are entirely foreign to his experience, or if it includes obscure personality disorders, the investigator should frankly recognize his inability to meet the situation and should conclude his report with a recommendation for referral.

2. During the period of treatment, the case investigator should keep a careful journal record of the progress of treatment. He should not depend upon his memory but should write up each interview with the pupil and each significant observation just as soon as possible. Not all of what is written in the journal will find its way into the case report, but a complete journal record is of inestimable help in making a final report at the end of the period of treatment.

3. If the case is the kind that lends itself to measurement (for example, if it involves achievement in a certain skill or school subject), comparable tests should be administered at the beginning and the end of the treatment. Such tests will take the evaluation of the treatment out of the realm of speculation, and will sometimes reveal significant progress under conditions where no conclusions about growth could be made on the basis of observation alone.

4. After a case has been released from treatment, it should be followed up, and the individual kept under observation for a few months to make sure that a relapse does not take place. This is especially important in cases involving skills such as reading, spelling, and arithmetic. Some pupils who make marked gains on tests during a period of teaching will tend to return to their old habits later unless they are carefully supervised.

DISTRIBUTION OF CASE STUDIES

If each member of a school faculty should undertake one case study, it may be anticipated that the studies will naturally represent a wide sampling of types of cases. Nevertheless, it will probably be advisable for the faculty to spend some time together in planning the studies to make sure that various kinds are represented. Learning cases in different fields of study will probably account for the largest number of studies. It is to be hoped, however, that some persons will have the temerity to undertake studies of behavior problem cases. Most of the case studies will no doubt be concerned with problem pupils, but a few of them should certainly be directed toward understanding and planning adjustments for very superior pupils. Finally, it will be helpful if some members of the staff will study average pupils in order to investigate the value of case reports for the great middle group in the school population.

It is also possible to carry on a case study as a group project, with each of several members of the school staff contributing different kinds of information about the individual. This sort of procedure has been well described by Fisher in the following statement:[9]

The details employed in using this procedure at the school are as follows: A child was selected who had been referred to the psychologist as a behavior problem. Each teacher who was involved was assigned a specific duty for the conference. One teacher reported on the child's home conditions; his classroom teacher reported on his classroom behavior; his school history, from the time of entrance to the present, was described; the school nurse presented his medical history; and the psychologist reported his findings. At the conclusion, the available information was summarized, and the faculty joined in open discussion which culminated in the proposal and the adoption of a plan of action.

It is felt that the method helped everyone who came into contact with the child to see the many-sided picture which is responsible for his present behavior.

VALUE OF CASE STUDIES

Several schools which participated some years ago in the Public School Demonstration Project[10] of the Educational Records Bureau experimented extensively with a plan of having case studies carried on and written

up by classroom teachers. Their experience indicated that the following values resulted:

1. A considerable number of the pupils in the school who were most seriously in need of careful individual attention and guidance were subjects of detailed study. Not every case study brought about improvement, but it is believed that the net result constituted a real gain.

2. Each case investigator acquired a better understanding of cumulative records and a greater insight into the relationship of these records to the immediate needs of the pupils. It seems probable that the teachers profited as much from the case studies as did the pupils.

3. The case studies formed a basis for group discussions between the different teachers of each pupil. Thus, cooperative work between teachers in different departments, and between teachers and counselors, was fostered.

The preparation of case studies by classroom teachers is relatively a new educational procedure in many schools, and there is need for further investigation of what can be done in this field. It is highly desirable for schools that are experimenting with case studies to have them presented in written form, for it is through such reports that other schools may be shown how cumulative histories of aptitude, achievement, and personality factors can be made to contribute to the classroom teacher's understanding of individual pupils and to the individualization of instruction. Thus, an accumulation of written case studies may constitute an important contribution to guidance procedures at all levels of the school.

REFERENCES

1. Baker, Robert L., and Schutz, Richard E. "A Criterion Factor Analysis of The Case of Mickey Murphy," *Personnel and Guidance Journal*, XL (November 1961), 282–285.
2. Barbe, W. "Preparation of Case Study Reports," *Education*, LXXIX (May 1959), 570–574.
3. Bennett, George K., Seashore, Harold G., and Wesman, Alexander G. *Counseling from Profiles: A Casebook for the Differential Aptitude Tests*. New York: The Psychological Corporation, 1951. Pp. 96.
4. Brewer, John M., and others. *Case Studies in Educational and Vocational Guidance*. New York: Ginn and Company, 1926. Pp. xxiv + 244.
5. Callis, Robert, Polmantier, Paul C., and Roeber, Edward C. *A Case Book of Counseling*. New York: Appleton-Century-Crofts, Inc., 1955. Pp. xii + 352.
6. Cassel, R. N. "Clinical Diagnostic Case Study Procedure for a School Psychologist," *Journal of the National*

[9] Bernard Fisher. "A Psychologist's Evaluation of Teachers' Reports and Suggestions for Their Improvement," *Educational Administration and Supervision*, XXXVIII (March 1952), 175–179.
[10] See *Guidance in Public Secondary Schools*, Chapter XII. Educational Records Bulletin 28. New York: Educational Records Bureau, 1939.

Association of Deans of Women and Counselors, XXIV (October 1960), 23–27.

7. Cherveric, Emily. "Cases in Vocational Counseling—A Potential Drop-Out in Mid-Sophomore Year," *Vocational Guidance Quarterly*, X (Summer 1962), 242–243.

8. Demming, John A. "Basic Principles for Making Anecdotal Recordings," *Readings in Guidance* (edited by Crow and Crow), pp. 281–285. New York: David McKay Company, Inc., 1962.

9. Everett, Samuel (ed.). *Programs for the Gifted: A Casebook in Secondary Education*. Fifteenth Yearbook of the John Dewey Society. New York: Harper & Row, Publishers, 1961. Pp. 299.

10. Fisher, Bernard. "A Psychologist's Evaluation of Teachers' Reports and Suggestions for Their Improvement," *Educational Administration and Supervision*, XXXVIII (March 1952), 175–179.

11. Gaw, E. A. "Case Study Techniques Developed in the Office of a University Dean of Women but Suggestive for Other Personnel Workers," *Journal of Higher Education*, XIV (January 1943), 37–40, 58.

12. Gleason, Clyde W. "How Revealing Are Case Histories?" *Vocational Guidance Quarterly*, IV (Winter 1955–1956), 39–40.

13. Hawkes, Anna Rose. "The Cumulative Record and Its Uses," *Guidance in Public Secondary Schools*. Educational Records Bulletin No. 28, Chapter IV. New York: Educational Records Bureau, 1939. Pp. x+530.

14. Jarvie, L. L. "Interpretation of Case Studies," *Occupations*, XVIII (April 1940), 488–494.

15. Jones, Arthur J. *Principles of Guidance and Pupil Personnel Work*, 5th ed. New York: McGraw-Hill Book Company, Inc., 1963. Pp. vi+306.

16. Lawson, Douglas E. "Development of Case-Study Approaches," *Educational Forum*, XVI (March 1952), 311–317.

17. McCallister, James M. *Remedial and Corrective Instruction in Reading*, pp. 108–158. New York: Appleton-Century-Crofts, Inc., 1936. Pp. xviii+300.

18. Morrison, Henry C. *The Practice of Teaching in the Secondary School*, Chapter XXX. Chicago: The University of Chicago Press, 1931. Pp. x+688.

19. Reavis, W. C. *Pupil Adjustment in Junior and Senior High Schools*. Boston: D. C. Heath and Company, 1926. Pp. xviii+348.

20. Rothney, John W. M. *The High School Student: A Book of Cases*. New York: Holt, Rinehart and Winston, Inc., 1953. Pp. xvi+272.

21. Rothney, John W. M., and Roens, Bert A. *Counseling the Individual Student*. New York: Holt, Rinehart and Winston, Inc., 1949. Pp. viii + 364.

22. Sarbin, Theodore R. "The Case Record in Psychological Counseling," *Journal of Applied Psychology*, XXIV (April 1940), 184–197.

23. Sayles, Mary B. *Child Guidance Cases*. New York: The Commonwealth Fund, 1932. Pp. xxiv+584.

24. Smithies, Elsie M. *Case Studies of Normal Adolescent Girls*. New York: Appleton-Century-Crofts, Inc., 1933. Pp. x+284.

25. Snyder, William U. (ed.). *Casebook of Non-Directive Counseling*. Boston: Houghton Mifflin Company, 1947. Pp. x+340.

26. Strang, Ruth. *The Role of the Teacher in Personnel Work*, 4th ed., Chapter XIV. New York: Bureau of Publications, Teachers College, Columbia University, 1953. Pp. 491.

27. Traxler, Arthur E. (ed.). *Guidance in Public Secondary Schools*, Chapter XII. Educational Records Bulletin No. 28. New York: Educational Records Bureau, 1939. Pp. x+330.

28. Wofford, K. V. "Understanding the Reading and Speech Difficulties of Children: A Case Study," *Elementary English Review*, XXI (December 1944), 305–311.

29. Womer, Frank B., and Frick, Willard B. *Personalizing Test Use: A Counselor's Casebook*. Ann Arbor, Mich.: Bureau of School Services, University of Michigan, 1964. Pp. 102.

CHAPTER XVI

The Role of the Teacher in Guidance

WITH THE INCREASED PROFESSIONALIZATION of guidance, the direct participation of teachers in the guidance program has been decreasing in many schools. The schools that are adequately staffed with professionally trained counselors are indeed fortunate, but, even in these schools, the success of the guidance program depends in considerable degree upon the sympathetic understanding and cooperation of the teachers.

The relationship of the teacher to the guidance program may be considered in two ways. First, there is the obvious connection with guidance which teachers have in school systems where all instructors, or certain selected ones, are designated as guidance officers, each being responsible for a group of perhaps 20 or 30 pupils. Second, there is the connection with guidance which each teacher has in her regular classroom and extracurricular activities, regardless of the system of guidance followed in the school. This chapter will be concerned mainly with the second of these relationships—that which exists in the ordinary daily contacts between teacher and pupils.

It is common knowledge that the average public high school teacher carries a heavy load. He or she must teach from 100 to 200 or more pupils distributed through four, five, or even six classes; participate in the extracurricular program of the school; prepare lesson plans; read and correct papers; give special help to slow pupils; handle minor behavior problems; make out reports; and often take an important part in the out-of-school life of the community. If participation in a guidance program seems to be just another routine responsibility added to an already heavy load, enthusiasm for the program will naturally be lacking among the teaching staff. A teacher can be expected to contribute whole-heartedly to such a program only if the relationship of guidance to the job already being done is clearly understood. It is hoped that the following list of questions and answers will help to clarify this relationship.

I. Is It Desirable to Combine the Functions of Guidance and the Functions of Teaching in the Same Person? Should Not Guidance Procedures Be Carried on by Specially Trained Persons Entirely Separate from Teaching?

The answer is that to some degree these functions are always combined in the same persons. All teachers carry on guidance and will continue inevitably to do so. The question is not whether teachers shall engage in guidance, but whether the guidance they provide shall be unplanned and incidental, or planned and purposeful. It is true that the guidance program should be under the direction of one who has specialized in this field, and that a staff of specially trained counselors is needed if the program is to reach its greatest effectiveness, but these specialists can succeed only if they have the full and active cooperation of the teachers. In schools that have only one guidance officer, who is frequently on a part-time basis, most of the actual counseling must be done by the teaching staff, because it is physically impossible for one person to keep in close contact with several hundred pupils. Although the principal and the assistant principals often assume much of the work of counseling, it is probable that the most effective guidance can be done when administration and counseling are divorced. The best guidance relationship is obtained when pupil and counselor meet as nearly as possible on an equal footing, with the relationship completely freed of all implications of authority or coercion. Teachers, because of their closer contacts with the pupils, are frequently in a better position to provide the conditions needed for effective counseling than are other members of the staff.

285

II. If I Try to Do Guidance Work When My Schedule Is Already Full, Will Not This Extra Load Reduce My Teaching Efficiency?

It is true that learning to use test results and cumulative records and studying guidance philosophy and the application of guidance techniques do require a considerable amount of a teacher's time at first, and it may call for some reduction in other types of service in the beginning; but in the end it should greatly increase teaching efficiency, for it will lead the teacher to become better acquainted with the abilities and needs of the different pupils, and will help the teacher see them as individuals rather than merely as members of a group.

The study of the philosophy and methodology of guidance is in a sense an extra, although necessary, load for the teacher. The process of guidance itself is not, however, an extra load, for it is work that the teacher already engages in, and it has for its ultimate goal the same objectives that good teaching has—the maximum adjustment and growth possible for every individual. Under the normal conditions of teaching in an elementary or even a secondary school there can be no sharp dividing line between instruction and guidance. These two processes are inextricably related in every classroom and in every extracurricular activity in which both pupils and teachers engage.

III. What Can I Do About the Guidance of the Pupils in My Classes, Whom I See in Groups for Forty or Fifty Minutes Each Day, Most of Whom I Did Not Even Know by Name Before They Entered the Class, and About Whom I Know Little or Nothing?

This is a live question, presenting a situation which is typical in almost all large public high schools. One might answer the question by asking another—What can you do about *teaching* under such conditions? Even if the teacher were interested only in the formal presentation of subject matter, an adequate job could not be done until he or she had ascertained whether or not the background of the pupils was sufficient to make the class presentations comprehensible. It is obvious that the first thing to be done in meeting the situation for either instructional or guidance purposes is to *study the pupils*. It is here that some of the most important instruments in guidance will be found indispensable. If a comprehensive testing program has been carried on, the test scores will provide information about the present aptitude and achievement of the pupils. If cumulative records have been kept in the school, a variety of information about home background, health, interests, extracurricular activities, and growth in achievement, as well as present status of achievement, will be available in compact and readable form. Lacking standardized test scores and cumulative records, the teacher will find the problem of becoming acquainted with the needs of the pupils much more difficult, and its solution will depend on the teacher's ingenuity in devising her own methods for getting the necessary information.

Much of the guidance that teachers do is necessarily through group procedures rather than through individual conferences. Alert teachers who have studied their pupils will see opportunities to carry on group guidance in connection with their regular teaching. For example, most pupils need guidance in study habits. The nature of study varies so much from subject to subject that probably the most effective guidance in study habits will be carried on in connection with the actual classwork. Time spent on guidance of this type in the classroom is certainly a legitimate function of instruction.

IV. What Can I Do to Help Make the Testing Program of the School Effective?

Teachers can make a very important contribution to the testing program of the school through critically evaluating the achievement tests in the light of the objectives and content of their courses. Such an evaluation calls for more than general impressions. A detailed checking of each item in the test should be made, with notations indicating whether or not the test question samples something the school is trying to do. Such analyses should be most helpful in interpreting the results of the tests. No test can be expected to fit a particular curriculum exactly, but the correspondence should be fairly close.

The teachers can also aid with the testing program by sending information to the principal, which may be passed along to the publishers, about questions which experience indicates are not valid.[1] The actual experience of teachers in the field is one of the best aids in the revision and improvement of tests.

Still another way in which teachers can assist in securing valid results with tests is to see to it that the new pupils in their classes who have not previously had experience in taking standardized tests are made acquainted with the general nature of the objective tests they are to take before the tests are administered. A few minutes spent in making an explanation and displaying sample questions to a group of inexperienced pupils may place them in a much better position to show their real ability when the tests are given. Needless to say, the actual forms of the tests which are to be employed in the testing program should not be used for this purpose.

A fourth contribution that the teacher can make to

[1] For example, this is a common practice in connection with the spring achievement testing program of the Educational Records Bureau.

the guidance program is to explain the results to the pupils in either group or individual discussions. It is also legitimate, after the tests have been given, to use some types of scored test papers as teaching devices; but not much time should be spent in this way and care should be used to avoid allowing the tests to determine the content of the courses.

V. What Use Can I Make of Cumulative Records and How Can I Contribute to the Records?

The teacher can use cumulative records in getting the essential facts about the ability and achievement of the class at the beginning of the term; and thus within a few days after the course has begun (or even before it has begun) information will be available that could not be collected in less than several weeks by the usual procedure of gradually becoming acquainted with the pupils through day-to-day contacts. So, from the beginning, the teacher can plan for group activities with some assurance, and can also take into account the special needs of individual pupils.

The cumulative records will be a constant source of information for the teacher in connection with individual conferences and special help for the various pupils. Each card should provide an up-to-date case history in summary form. A teacher cannot be expected to carry in mind the essential facts about each pupil, but if the school has a cumulative record system the facts should be looked up when they are needed.

An important part of the cumulative record has to do with social adjustment, personality, mental and emotional factors, activities and interests, accomplishments, experiences, and plans. Tests in these fields are still highly experimental, and the main reliance for the filling out of this part of the card must be placed upon the observations of persons who have contacts with the pupil. The classroom teachers of each student will have the best opportunity to contribute to this part of the card. Teachers should form the habit of noting down brief anecdotal records about their pupils and of forwarding them to the proper office for entering in condensed form on the pupil's cumulative record, or dictating them into the central recording system if one is available. Over a period of years, such uncontrolled observations, collected from a large number of teachers and assembled in the same part of the record card, are extremely revealing and provide invaluable data for future guidance.

VI. How Can I Make Maximum Use of Cumulative Test Histories in Diagnosing the Learning Difficulties and Improving the Instruction of My Pupils?

The point which will bear repetition is that conducting testing programs and keeping cumulative records

are only means to an end. As has been stressed in Chapter XIII, these procedures will be valuable in direct proportion to the degree to which the records are used constructively in the improvement of instruction and guidance. After every testing program, the scores and percentile ratings of each pupil should be studied in order to find his points of strength and weakness—and in the case of subjects that are continuous over a period of several years, the pupil's growth since the last test was taken should be noted.

One plan for doing this is to have the guidance officer or psychologist make a survey of the test scores of the entire school in order to find the pupils whose grade scores are low and the subjects in which they are deficient, and to refer these cases to the proper teachers for more careful analysis. Pupils who are very slow should be scheduled for special help.

The use of test results in instruction has three distinct aspects, as follows: (1) the improvement of instruction in the regular curriculum of the school; (2) the planning of corrective and remedial work for retarded pupils; and (3) the provision of special programs for superior pupils. In connection with the first aspect, it has been found that a tabulation of the percentage of correct responses made by a class on each item of a standardized test is very useful in helping a teacher see those points that need greater emphasis in instruction. This procedure is to be recommended if it is kept in mind that the purpose is to discover the areas in which groups of children are strong or weak, and then to decide what should be done about the situation. Care should be used to avoid making the specific test items themselves objectives of instruction. Tests are at best samplings of basic skills, information, and understanding, and they should not be permitted to determine the curriculum of the school. The evaluation of responses to particular items, and even to whole sections of the test, should be in terms of the teacher's objectives for the particular course covered by the test. The fact that the pupils may make low scores on certain parts of the test may not mean that the teacher should give special attention to the matters covered by those parts. It may mean only that the objectives in that particular school are different in some respects from the objectives of the test makers. Nevertheless, the tabulation and study of quantitative data concerning the success of the pupils on the different items in the various tests used is a procedure that some schools are finding very helpful in reappraising and improving their courses. The item-counter unit on the International Test-Scoring Machine, Model 805, is a distinct aid to this kind of use of test results, as far as machine-scored tests are concerned.

At the beginning of the year each teacher can profitably spend several hours studying the test histories of the pupils in her class and noting at least the following points: (1) the general level of the academic aptitude and achievement of each pupil in relation to the basic criterion group and to the members of his own class; (2) the achievement of the pupils in the teacher's special field as compared with their achievement in other fields; (3) the achievement of the pupils in the different parts of the test covering the teacher's special field (if this information is available); and (4) the probable readiness of the class as a whole to proceed with the course without taking preliminary preparatory steps.

In the planning of remedial and corrective work in connection with a testing program, four steps are ordinarily required of a teacher: (1) a survey of the scores on each test to select the pupils who are low; (2) the diagnosis of the difficulties of the pupil with low scores—a step which may call for the administration of additional diagnostic tests; (3) the planning of corrective teaching either in regular classes or in groups meeting at special times; and (4) the assignment of pupils to these special help groups for the duration of their deficiency. An additional step may also be needed: the provision of individual instruction for pupils who are too handicapped to profit by group instruction—although extensive individual instruction is seldom practicable in a remedial program conducted in public schools, because of the heavy regular teaching load that each instructor carries.

Many studies have been made of diagnostic and remedial work in connection with the basic skills of reading, arithmetic, language usage, spelling, and handwriting, and the more effective methods are fairly well established.[2] In most of the high school subjects, however, the use of test results in analyzing difficulties and in planning special help is still a pioneer field. One of the most significant contributions that could be made by teachers in public schools would be to set up and validate some techniques for doing this type of work.

Much emphasis should be placed on the third aspect of the use of test results—the provision of special programs for superior pupils. Although much theorizing has been done by educators in recent years about the desirability of providing for pupils with exceptional ability, the carrying of these ideas into action is still largely neglected by many schools. Consequently, even pupils whose test results at the time of entrance to high school indicate that they are above the average for high school graduates in English usage, acquaintance with literature, under-

standing of the world of science, or other aspects of the work of the secondary school, are too often put through the same routine as their less gifted classmates. If here and there throughout the country, enlightened teachers, with the consent of their high school principals, courageously break with tradition—to the extent of releasing their outstanding pupils from a portion of the regular work of their classes so that they will be free to carry on individual study under guidance—and keep cumulative records of the progress of these pupils, this example will have marked effect in freeing the superior pupils in the schools of the United States from useless and deadening routine.

VII. How Can I Help My Pupils to Become Better Adjusted to Their In-School and Out-of-School Environments?

This question is directed toward the most vital part of the guidance program. The contributions that a teacher can make to adjustment are innumerable. When it is discovered that a pupil is poorly adjusted, the general rule is to assemble the facts, analyze them, form a tentative hypothesis about the nature of the difficulty, plan treatment, apply it, observe the effect, and revise treatment as needed until the difficulty appears to have been removed. The teacher's most obvious relation to adjustment of pupils is in learning situations. If the pupil's failure is in the teacher's special field, the study of the cumulative record should help the teacher to diagnose the failure, to prescribe and administer treatment, and to effect a cure. If the failure to adjust is due to difficulty with a related field (for example, inability to write up science experiments because of English deficiency) the facts can be marshaled and reported to the proper department. Teachers have long cooperated in adjustment matters of this sort.

Another type of adjustment problem to which teachers can and usually do contribute is the type sometimes known as the "problem of inconvenience." Problems of inconvenience include the minor behavior difficulties that temporarily upset the routine of a classroom. Such problems, being overt in nature, usually do not indicate serious maladjustment on the part of the pupils who cause them, but teachers are ordinarily anxious to help work out adjustments because these matters are so annoying to them. The cumulative record—particularly the less objective part of it—may furnish valuable leads concerning the pupil's behavior and possible ways of modifying it.

All teachers know that there are many matters of personal and social adjustment in which they may aid pupils who seek their advice. Teachers have always helped with this kind of adjustment, but they should remem-

---

[2] For further information on this point see *The Use of Test Results in Diagnosis and Instruction in the Tool Subjects*, 2nd ed., Educational Records Bulletin 18, pp. 17–35. New York: Educational Records Bureau, 1949. Pp. vi + 82.

ber that in all such cases, they can do a better job if they will utilize the information that can be obtained from complete and carefully kept records.

Much more serious problems of pupil adjustment are likely to be deeply hidden and may escape observation altogether, unless teachers are alert for them. The shy, introverted, imaginative pupil may be more seriously maladjusted than the worst trouble-maker in the class. Teachers who have not had courses dealing with psychological and psychiatric problems will be much more competent to assist with the more obscure and difficult problems of adjustment if they will become acquainted with the writings of leaders in these fields, or with recent textbooks and studies dealing with various aspects of child and adolescent psychology. Teachers may thus improve their ability to discover individuals needing guidance in mental hygiene; but they should be careful not to arrive at hasty conclusions about the nature of the difficulties, for psychiatric symptoms usually are not overtly related to their cause, but are secondary symptoms developed as a healing process. These symptoms should be recognized and reported, but the teacher will seldom, if ever, be prepared to provide adequate interpretation or treatment for them.

Although the adjustive aspects of guidance do have, in some instances, obscure and technical ramifications that call for the assistance of experts, a considerable part of the work of guidance is neither mysterious nor highly technical. Good teachers have always been guidance officers, as well as instructors, and they always will be. The philosophy and techniques of a guidance program are for the most part simply a means of helping the school staff do better what it would, by virtue of necessity, attempt to do anyway.

VIII. How Can I Help My Students to Become Interested In, to Choose Among, and to Develop Life Careers?

Even though many young people of school age are not yet ready to choose a career, they should gradually accumulate information concerning different fields of endeavor —many of which are new and are developing rapidly— and they should make tentative explorations through reading, lectures, and discussion. As stated by Ashcraft, "The officers, trustees, and members of the National Vocational Guidance Association want to emphasize to our teacher colleagues the important contribution they make in pointing out the relationship of the subject matter they teach to various careers and successful performance in occupations." (33:3).

Today's students face great complexities in developing their abilities toward suitable and satisfying life work.

Teachers and counselors need to combine their efforts to help young people to understand themselves, to see the subject matter of each field in relation to their own strengths and limitations, and to appreciate the need for developing broad abilities and skills to meet the vocational demands of tomorrow—as hundreds of new occupations are developed to meet new needs and hundreds of others are rendered obsolete or relegated to places of minor importance. This is primarily a *learning* situation, and the teacher, more than anyone else, can open doors through which the student may glimpse his own future.

REFERENCES

1. Arbuckle, Dugald S. "The Teacher as a Counselor," *High School Journal*, XL (May 1957), 285–289.
2. Arthur Philip, Brother. "Vocational Guidance by the Classroom Teacher," *Bulletin of the National Catholic Education Association*, LII (August 1955), 376–382.
3. Association for Supervision and Curriculum Development. *Guidance in the Curriculum.* 1955 Yearbook of the Association for Supervision and Curriculum Development. Washington, D.C.: National Education Association, 1955. Pp. xvi+232.
4. Baker, Robert L., and Doyle, Roy P. "Teacher Knowledge of Pupil Data and Marking Practices at the Elementary School Level," *Personnel and Guidance Journal,* XXXVII (May 1959), 644–647.
5. Baron, Denis, and Bernard, Harold W. *Evaluation Techniques for Classroom Teachers.* New York: McGraw-Hill Book Company, Inc., 1958. Pp. 297.
6. Boyd, Gertrude A. "Parents and Teachers Team Up to Give Prevocational Guidance," *Vocational Guidance Quarterly*, VI (Autumn 1957), 12–14.
7. Cohen, Nancy K. "Must Teaching Be a Prerequisite for Guidance?" *Counselor Education and Supervision*, I (Winter 1961), 69–71.
8. Coleman, William. "Assisting Teachers in Using Test Results," *Personnel and Guidance Journal,* XXXVI (September 1957), 38–40.
9. Detjen, Ervin Winfred, and Detjen, Mary Ford. *Elementary School Guidance,* 2nd ed. New York: McGraw-Hill Book Company, Inc., 1963. Pp. 256.
10. Dunsmoor, Clarence C., and Miller, Leonard M. *Principles and Methods of Guidance for Teachers,* rev. ed. Scranton, Pa.: International Textbook Company, 1950. Pp. xii+400.
11. Durr, William K. *The Gifted Student.* Fairlawn, N.J.: Oxford University Press, 1964. Pp. 296.
12. Farwell, Gail F., and Peters, Herman J. "The Guidance Function of the Classroom Teacher," *Guidance Readings for Counselors,* pp. 496–499. Chicago: Rand, McNally & Company, 1960. Pp. x+691.

13. Garrison, R. H. "Teaching as Counseling," *Junior College Journal,* XXXIV (October 1963), 12–15.

14. Gass, G. Z. "Guidance in Russia: Bibliography," *Personnel and Guidance Journal,* XXXVIII (September 1959), 34–39.

15. Hall, E. C. "What the Teacher Should Know about Psychiatry," *Progressive Education,* XXXI (November 1953), 54–56.

16. Hoyt, Kenneth B. "How Well Can Classroom Teachers Know Their Pupils?" *School Review,* LXIII (April 1955), 228–235.

17. Hudson, George R. "Counselors Need Teaching Experience," *Counselor Education and Supervision* (Spring 1961), 24–27.

18. Johnston, Edgar G., Peters, Mildred, and Evraiff, William. *The Role of the Teacher in Guidance.* Englewood Cliffs, N.J.: Prentice-Hall, Inc., 1959. Pp. 276.

19. Kaback, Goldie Ruth. "The Role of the Teacher in a School Guidance Program," *Education,* LXXV (March 1955), 466–470.

20. Krugman, Morris. "Appraisal and Treatment of Personality Problems in a Guidance Program," *Education in a Free World* (ed. by Arthur E. Traxler), pp. 114–121. Report of the Nineteenth Educational Conference Sponsored by the Educational Records Bureau and the American Council on Education. Washington, D.C.: American Council on Education, 1955. Pp. vi+164.

21. Levine, Madeline S. "Guidance: A Positive Factor in Teacher Education," *Personnel and Guidance Journal,* XXXIV (January 1956), 271–275.

22. Matthews, Blanche. "The Classroom Teacher and Guidance," *Bulletin of the National Association of Secondary-School Principals,* XXXIV (May 1950), 124–134.

23. Morris, Glyn A. *Practical Guidance Methods for Principals and Teachers.* New York: Harper & Row, Publishers, 1952. Pp. xiv+266.

24. Rich, Jeanne, and Bardon, Jack I. "The Teacher and the School Psychologist," *Elementary School Journal,* LXIV (March 1964), 318–323.

25. Ross, Vivian. *Handbook for Homeroom Guidance.* New York: The Macmillan Company, 1954. Pp. xiv+134.

26. Santavicca, G. G. "What Homeroom Teachers Should Know," *Occupations,* XXX (February 1952), 351–355.

27. Schiff, Albert. "Teachers and Counselors Can Work Together," *Readings in Guidance* (ed. by Crow and Crow), pp. 180–183. New York: David McKay Company, Inc., 1962. Pp. 626.

28. Shane, Harold G., and McSwain, E. T. *Evaluation and the Elementary Curriculum,* rev. ed. New York: Holt, Rinehart and Winston, Inc., 1958. Pp. 446.

29. Stouffer, George A. W., Jr. "Behavior Problems of Children as Viewed by Teachers and Mental Hygienists," *Mental Health,* XXXVI (April 1952), 271–285.

30. Stouffer, George A. W., Jr., and Owens, Jennie. "Behavior Problems of Children as Identified by Today's Teachers and Compared with Those Reported by E. K. Wickman," *Journal of Educational Research,* XLVIII (January 1955), 321–331.

31. Stowig, R. Wray. "The Teacher's Responsibility for Pupils' Mental Health," *Elementary School Journal,* LXIX (March 1964), 310–317.

32. Strang, Ruth. *The Role of the Teacher in Personnel Work,* 4th ed. New York: Bureau of Publications, Teachers College, Columbia University, 1953. Pp. 491.

33. Tennyson, W. Wesley, Soldahl, Thomas A., and Mueller, Charlotte. *The Teacher's Role in Career Development.* A Minnesota Department of Education Publication revised and reprinted by the National Vocational Guidance Association Division of the American Personnel and Guidance Association. Washington, D.C.: National Vocational Guidance Association, 1960; revised, 1965. Pp. 107.

34. Willey, Roy, and Dunn, Melvin. *The Role of the Teacher in the Guidance Program.* Bloomington, Ill.: McKnight & McKnight Publishing Company, 1964. Pp. 487.

CHAPTER XVII

Follow-up of Students and School Leavers

ASPECTS OF A SCHOOL FOLLOW-UP PROGRAM

THERE ARE FOUR DISTINGUISHABLE ASPECTS OF follow-up work in guidance. In the first place, there is the incidental follow-up of pupils which counselors and teachers carry on as a part of their normal activities in the school. Counselors frequently follow up interviews with individual pupils, to note the effect of the counseling given, or to gather additional information, or to assist the pupil further with his problems of adjustment. Teachers follow up pupils who have had special help with learning problems in order to note progress and forestall recurrence of the difficulties. Individual cumulative record cards are prepared as one phase of the guidance program, and these records may be regarded as a systematic follow-up procedure applied to all pupils—superior, average, and slow. No school could function as a unit without carrying on a considerable number of follow-up activities. Abandonment of these activities would lead to a thoroughly chaotic situation.

A second type of follow-up work is to be found in connection with individual pupils who have served as bases of case studies or who have received intensive remedial help in certain fields. It would be unwise to carry on a detailed case study or to provide remedial teaching for a pupil during a period of a few weeks and then drop the case. Nearly all psychological or psychiatric work in education presupposes that the case of the individual pupil will be followed up over a period of at least a year after the treatment has been discontinued, in order to evaluate the results of the work and to note whether further progress is being made. Unfortunately, in the busy environment of the school, where dozens of pupils constantly need special attention, this important phase of case-study and remedial work is too often neglected.

A third aspect of follow-up work in guidance is to be found where schools have evolved a systematic procedure for following up pupils from one unit of the school to the next higher one. For instance, a sixth-grade teacher may follow up each of her pupils when they advance to the junior high school, or a junior high school counselor may follow up the pupils in his advisory group throughout the three grades of the senior high school. An illustration of the latter type of provision was furnished by the Providence Public Schools, where the seventh-grade counselors made one-year follow-up studies in cooperation with counselors in Grade 10, eighth-grade counselors carried on two-year follow-up studies in conjunction with the counselors in Grade 11, and counselors at the ninth-grade level conducted three-year follow-up studies jointly with the twelfth-grade counselors. The Providence follow-up plan was explained in detail by Allen (2:166–170) and was confirmed as of 1964 in a letter by Mr. Bernard J. Buonanno, supervisor of guidance and placement.

The fourth aspect of follow-up work is the one toward which attention especially needs to be directed, because for the most part this phase of the guidance programs leaves much to be desired. This has to do with the follow-up of graduates and other school leavers. Its importance in the development of a guidance program which actually functions in the lives of the individual young people can hardly be overemphasized. One may well question whether a school has discharged its full guidance responsibility if it gives a pupil careful attention while he is in school, but abruptly terminates its interest in him when he drops out or is graduated. Rather, it would seem that the school should help him get adjusted to his postschool environment and that the guidance activities should be "tapered off" gradually.

The population included in a thoroughgoing follow-up plan should represent all kinds of students that the school has served. As Eckert has said, "Studies based on graduates alone neglect the very persons from whom the faculty stands most to learn—the pupils who dropped out because of serious financial difficulties, inadequate course offerings, or lack of counsel on personal problems" (12: 107).

The last aspect of follow-up work—the one having to do with graduates and school leavers—is the main concern of this chapter. According to Troyer and Pace, the techniques of this kind of follow-up study have been of two main types. Such studies have dealt with the activities, behavior, or practices of the individuals included in the study, or they have sought to find out the opinion of the respondents about the value of their previous educational experiences (56). In a review of 18 follow-up studies, however, Lorenzen (32) found that only six reported any investigation of opinion. Lorenzen stated that much of the research on follow-up studies is poorly reported; anyone who reads carefully the literature in this field will probably agree with this statement. It seems advisable for any school which intends to undertake follow-up work to give careful consideration to the purposes, nature, procedures, and desirable characteristics of a follow-up plan.

PURPOSES AND NATURE OF FOLLOW-UP OF SCHOOL LEAVERS

Young people who leave school, either by graduation or by dropping out, are followed up for one or more of three main purposes. First, there is the altruistic desire to help the individual with problems of vocational, educational, and social adjustment after he goes from the school and while he is getting himself established elsewhere. As a rule, more attention is given to college or vocational adjustment than to the other types, although not infrequently adjustment to a vocation depends in part upon the successful resolution of personal factors in the individual's make-up.

A second purpose of follow-up studies is to gather data for use in evaluating the instructional and guidance programs of the local school. This is an extremely important purpose. For instance, Patterson and Fotiu (40) followed up 155 cases to determine the effectiveness of counseling by the Highland Park, Michigan, Guidance Center, and concluded that advisement was generally "successful in assisting students in selecting educational or vocational

programs which can be pursued by them with satisfactory progress." Likewise, Oppenheimer (38) reported a ten-year follow-up of the class of 1940 of the Woodrow Wilson High School, Washington, D.C. More recently, Brown (9) reported that the Highland Park, Illinois, High School had surveyed its graduates who had gone on to college to find out how well the school had prepared them. This follow-up was used to strengthen the school's curriculum and guidance program for college-bound students. More than 600 students distributed among 178 colleges cooperated in the study. English and study habits were very frequently mentioned as needing special attention. The follow-up program subsequently was expanded to include graduates who went directly into the work force.

The chief criterion of the value of a guidance program is its influence on the postschool lives of the individuals who have received the counseling services. The administration of a school can have no clear idea of the worth of its guidance program, or the mistakes that are being made, or the phases which should be stressed more, or those which should be changed, unless data are available concerning outcomes—that is, concerning what is happening to the product of the school.

A third purpose of follow-up studies of school leavers is to gather information of general interest concerning those who have left. Such studies are intended to help all social agencies, including schools, deal with the problems of youth more intelligently. For instance, Rothney, in concluding a report of a follow-up of members of the 1951 graduating classes of four Wisconsin high schools, suggested "that the figures we have given, and the extent to which school people are aware of them, may assist us in keeping at least one foot on the ground in the planning of education for Wisconsin youth." (44:10). Later, through the cooperation of a group of Wisconsin high schools, Rothney (45) reported a ten-year follow-up of graduates under the title "Counseling Does Help." Rothney has been one of the most consistent contributors to follow-up research on the value of guidance services.

The majority of the comprehensive follow-up studies reported over the years belong in this same category. Among these may be mentioned the study by Eckert and Marshall, *When Youth Leave School* (13), carried on as one part of the Regent's Inquiry in New York State; Eurich and Pace's (15) follow-up study of Minnesota graduates; a study by R. L. Thorndike under the title "Tests and Long-Time Prediction of Vocational Choice" (55); a study on "Job Appropriateness: A One-Year Follow-up of High School Graduates," carried on by Latham (30) under the direction of John C. Flanagan; a 2- to 17-year follow-up study of the clinical features of hysteria in 41 children by Robbins and O'Neal (42);

Hollinshead's *Who Should Go to College* (27); the comprehensive study of school leavers carried on by Dillon for the National Child Labor Committee (11); and, especially, the American Institute for Research's Project TALENT, discussed near the end of this chapter (17).

The great need at present is for the careful planning of continuous follow-up studies to be carried on by local school systems to serve the first and second purposes mentioned. The state education departments of a number of states, including especially Illinois and California, have undertaken to assist schools in planning and conducting follow-up studies. Follow-up work in several states is discussed later in this chapter.

In follow-up studies of graduates and other school leavers, the following types of information have been found useful in counseling programs:

1. Occupational distribution of school leavers.
2. Occupations in which employment is increasing.
3. Occupations in which employment is decreasing.
4. Time elapsed between school leaving and employment.
5. Success of graduates and nongraduates in employment.
6. Extent to which former students are engaged in the vocations they had in mind in school.
7. Degree to which vocational training pursued in school carries over into life.
8. Influence of such factors as age, sex, intelligence, health school achievement, home background, and marital status on occupational adjustment.
9. Earnings of school leavers in various occupations.
10. Occupational conditions which have hindered progress.
11. Extent to which graduates are engaged in further study.
12. Success of graduates in higher institutions.
13. Factors that influence the migration of young people.
14. Ways in which students feel that their school training has been most beneficial.
15. Ways in which the school has failed to meet educational or vocational needs.
16. How data processing and computers are changing occupations and occupational goals.

PROCEDURES IN FOLLOW-UP STUDIES

The two main procedures used in gathering information in follow-up studies are questionnaires and interviews. Both procedures have certain limitations. It is not uncommon to find, in the literature, reports of follow-up studies in which less than half of those to whom questionnaires were sent replied. Eckert suggested that "to detect certain kinds of bias, such as lesser cooperation from persons who failed to make satisfactory adult adjustments, it may be necessary to interview a random sampling of nonrespondents and compare findings with

those already secured from respondents" (12:107). Rothney and Mooren (47) have also discussed sampling problems in follow-up research.

In certain school systems, such as the Providence Public Schools, which have had much experience with follow-up studies, procedures have been developed for insuring a large proportion of returns. In an effort to get complete cooperation, Ledvina (31) discussed procedures involved in the "100 percent follow-up."

Interviews are time-consuming and costly and are seldom practicable in the case of individuals who have left the community, but more detailed and perhaps more accurate information can be obtained in this way than by means of questionnaires. In some of the more recent follow-up plans, there is a tendency to submit a questionnaire to all school leavers and to select from those returning the inquiry forms a representative sampling to be interviewed. In other surveys, the interview has carried the entire burden of collecting data for the study. For instance, Barahal and Brammer (6) used what was termed the "permissive evaluation interview" in getting the opinions of 100 Stanford University freshmen concerning the extent and character of the counseling they had received in high school. The figures they gave on the basis of these interviews did not support any tendency to hold an exalted opinion of the status of high school counseling. Nearly half of the group were not able to provide a rating because they felt they had had no counseling in high school. Of the remainder, 23 freshmen thought that their high school counseling was poor, and 21 indicated that it was fair, while only two rated it excellent, and seven said that it was good. However, it is believed, or at least hoped, that guidance in high schools has become more effective since that study was made.

In both questionnaires and interviews, the replies to questions of opinion about the values of training received in school may, because of what Wrenn (60) has called the "old oaken bucket" reaction, be somewhat too favorable. Everyone tends to remember pleasant experiences and to forget the unpleasant ones. When one has been out of school a few years, his memory of school life tends to be colored by sentiment, and he is liable to exaggerate the values derived from the school program. Nevertheless, helpful leads concerning needed improvement in the school are frequently obtained by presenting questions of opinion in the inquiry form.

The treatment of some of the data obtained in follow-up studies is a simple straightforward task. Data on types of occupation and salaries are of that sort. The analysis of those types of data involving covariance and causal relationship is, however, exceedingly intricate and baffling, and even competent research men sometimes draw questionable conclusions about the relationships of certain factors. It can be shown readily, for example, that number of years of schooling and standing in class are related to vocational success, but one is not justified in inferring a causal relationship without controlling other variables. The correlation may be due to the influence of intelligence upon the factors concerned. This is but one illustration of the need for interpreting with caution the data obtained in follow-up surveys.

A considerable number of helpful publications dealing with procedures in follow-up studies are now available. In a publication of the California Test Bureau, Brewster and Zeran (8) outlined the steps to be taken in conducting a follow-up study. Cuony (10) discussed the follow-up study in the junior high school orientation program.

The Illinois Department of Public Instruction has published a useful bulletin, by Henderson and Goerwitz, entitled *How to Conduct the Follow-up Study* (25). Topics discussed in this bulletin include the following: why the follow-up study is needed, the instruments used in ing a follow-up study. Cuony (11) discussed the follow-up study, how to summarize the findings, and how to interpret the findings and use them to accomplish the purposes of the study. There is an appendix showing instruments used in the follow-up study, and summary sheets which may be used in summarizing the information on each of the 56 real-life problems of high school youth.

Similarly, the Bureau of Occupational Information and Guidance of the California State Department of Education issued a *Guide for Making a Follow-up Study of School Drop-outs and Graduates* (22). This guide was prepared for use in connection with a state-wide study of dropouts and graduates. In addition to an explanation of the procedures of the follow-up, the guide shows the questionnaire used in the study, as well as the form used by schools in notifying the Department of their intention to participate.

Earlier, the Michigan State Board of Education issued a publication, *Follow-up of Secondary School Graduates* (19), which furnished "a comprehensive statement of the purposes, procedures, and outcomes of follow-up studies." This publication was used in the Michigan study of the secondary school curriculum.

Procedures in making and utilizing follow-up studies of school leavers were discussed by Sando (48) and by Fleming (18). A report of an actual follow-up study was included in each discussion.

An informal follow-up procedure that any teacher might use was described by Putman (41), a secondary-school teacher who followed up 150 graduating seniors of the class of 1951 between the first and second years after graduation. No questionnaire was employed; instead, Putman used informal procedures such as casual conversation with the individuals themselves or other interested

parties, and talked with classmates, friends and relatives, and employers. He also made use of news notes in local and state newspapers and college publications. A running file was kept on each graduate. In this way, useful information was obtained about the post-high school activities of 79 percent of the graduating class, a high percentage in view of the number in the Armed Forces at that time.

Although most follow-up studies have been carried on at the secondary school level, there is also a need for colleges to follow up their dropouts and graduates. Goertzen and Strong (20) reported a 12-year follow-up study among small colleges and universities of the Pacific Northwest. Pace (39) outlined the principles underlying follow-up studies of college graduates and discussed certain weaknesses that ought to be avoided. He then described three follow-up studies based on a series of opinion and attitude scales which could be scored so that the results could be treated statistically. He also illustrated the pattern for analyzing the results. Procedures such as Pace presented should be helpful in improving the design and breadth of follow-up studies and in bringing about closer relationships between these studies and the fundamental objectives of education.

THE CONTINUOUS FOLLOW-UP SURVEY

Occasional surveys of school leavers, carried on intermittently, provide a certain amount of useful information for counseling purposes, but they do not satisfactorily meet either the purpose of helping the individual or the purpose of furnishing data on the product of the school. Under the conditions of a haphazard program of this kind, many former students who need help will escape attention, and up-to-date information on the circumstances surrounding school leavers will be lacking.

As Myers (35) pointed out, the ideal follow-up plan is the continuous survey conducted as an integral part of a school's counseling program. Some schools have inaugurated this type of survey. In the senior high schools of the Providence, Rhode Island, Public Schools, a plan of this kind has been in operation for years. The plan, which was described in an article by Allen (2), involves a follow-up survey of each class, one, three, and five years after the class has been graduated. The class counselor is responsible for making the study, although he may call upon the central office for a certain amount of clerical assistance.

Briefly, the mechanics of the plan are as follows: a counselor stays with the same class throughout the three-year senior high school period. In the orientation course

294   TECHNIQUES OF GUIDANCE

at the eleventh- and twelfth-grade levels, he introduces materials to help prepare the class for its own follow-up survey, and he stresses the importance of such surveys to both the individual and the school. The first year after the class is graduated, the counselor drops back to Grade 10 and begins the guidance of another class. At the same time, he makes a one-year follow-up study of his former class. Through the cooperation of class officers, and by means of questionnaires, telephone calls, and interviews, he manages to maintain a proportion of replies that usually reaches 98 to 100 percent.

The next year the counselor makes no follow-up study, unless he has been responsible for an earlier class, but the following year, when his present counseling group is in Grade 12, he makes a three-year survey of the preceding class. The fourth year, the counselor has a new tenth-grade counseling group and he makes his first follow-up survey of the class just graduated. The next year, the earlier class is ready for its five-year follow-up. Henceforth, the counselor has one follow-up study to make each year, but never more than one. Needless to say, the difficulties of securing replies are greater in the three-year and five-year follow-up surveys than they are after an interval of only one-year, but even in the five-year follow-up, the counselors customarily manage to get returns from more than 85 percent of the members of the class.

When all available questionnaires are in, the counselor himself treats them statistically and writes a report of his study, which is then duplicated in the central office for distribution to all advisers, principals, and staff officers. Finally, the studies of all advisers of that particular grade are combined to form a composite city-wide study.

A somewhat similar follow-up plan, involving one-, three-, and five-year follow-up studies, was recommended years ago by the Implementation Commission of the National Association of Secondary-School Principals as the result of its study of occupational adjustment carried on under the direction of Landy (29). The need for follow-up of all school leavers, including dropouts as well as graduates, was emphasized in that study, which was based upon data obtained from 1000 school leavers from six representative school systems. The study also pointed to the need for better placement facilities and for postschool counseling service. Only about 5 percent of the people studied secured their first jobs through the school authorities.

It appears from the literature on guidance that comparatively few schools have thus far undertaken continuous follow-up studies. One such study was reported by Gurr (23), of the East Bakersfield, California, High School. She submitted a simple postal-card questionnaire (shown later in this chapter) to the classes of 1947 through 1949. Replies were received from the same per-

sons at successive stages of their post-high school experience.

The Denver Public Schools issue at regular intervals an excellent series of triennial survey reports which include follow-up studies of graduates both in college and in business and industry (53, 54).

Aumack and Douglass (3) described a follow-up plan developed by the guidance office of the Compton Junior College which was continuous in the sense that 20 successive classes of students leaving the junior college were followed up. The main purpose was to gather information about the services of the junior college. The following conclusion concerning the value of the study appears in the report: "If the time and energy consumed in the making of the study were finally usable only by the guidance office at Compton Junior College, the results would have justified the expenditure, but its applications reach into many other areas. . . . The implications of the study will be carried into even broader areas of the community college concept by introducing pertinent facts into the curriculum meetings with the entire faculty."

FORMS USED IN FOLLOW-UP SURVEYS

Representative forms which have been used in follow-up studies of high school graduates and other school leavers are shown in Forms 33 to 36.

STATE-WIDE AND COUNTY-WIDE FOLLOW-UP STUDIES

In an earlier section of this chapter, reference was made to bulletins and brochures developed by state departments of education in a number of states in order to explain purposes, plans, and procedures of follow-up studies to schools. The plan worked out in one of those states, California, was used in a cooperative study of school dropouts and graduates which resulted in a comprehensive report entitled *Now Hear Youth* (36).

A follow-up study of early school leavers in Kentucky, sponsored by the Kentucky Association of Colleges, Secondary Schools, and Elementary Schools, was reported by Hecker (24). Pupils leaving Kentucky high schools during the period 1948 to 1950 served as the basis of the study. Data were presented on the extent and causes of early school leaving. In order to reduce the number of dropouts, certain guidance procedures were recommended, including detection and diagnosis of maladjust-

JUNIOR PLACEMENT SERVICE
Providence Public Schools
20 Summer Street
Providence, Rhode Island

Placement Office   DExter 1-9400

FOLLOW-UP STUDY
Senior High School Graduate

1. Your name _____ Date _____
   First   Last   Maiden

2. Address _____ Telephone _____

3. Schools or colleges attended after graduation: Day   Evening

| | | Date | | |
Name of School	Course	Entered	Date Left	Reason for Leaving
. . . .	. . .	. . .	. . .	. . . .
. . . .	. . .	. . .	. . .	. . . .
. . . .	. . .	. . .	. . .	. . . .
. . . .	. . .	. . .	. . .	. . . .

4. Positions held since graduation: Starting with present position

| | | Date | | |
Firm Name	Address	Entered	Date Left	Position Held
. . . .	. . . .	. . .	. . .	. . . . . .
. . . .	. . . .	. . .	. . .	. . . . . .
. . . .	. . . .	. . .	. . .	. . . . . .
. . . .	. . . .	. . .	. . .	. . . . . .

5. Armed Services:

| | | Date | Date | |
Branch of Service	Rank Held	Entered	Discharged	Reason
. . . .	. . .	. . .	. . . . .	. . . .
. . . .	. . .	. . .	. . . . .	. . . .
. . . .	. . .	. . .	. . . . .	. . . .

6. Marital Status:
   Single . . . . Married . . . . . Date of Marriage . . . . .

   No. of Children:
   Sons . . . . . . Daughters . . . . . .

FORM 33(a).   Used with permission of Providence Public Schools.

(con't)

7. In what community activities have you participated?
    Such as:

    Civil Defense . . . .

    Red Cross . . . .

    P.T.A. . . . .

    Others . . . .

    . . . .

8. What subjects, training, experiences which you had in school have been most
    useful to you?

    . . . .

    . . . .

9. Are there any subjects or experiences you wish you could have had in school?

    . . . .

    . . . .

10. Are there any remarks you wish to make concerning the present school pro-
    gram as you know it?

    . . . .

    . . . .

11. What hobby or hobbies are you interested in?

    . . . .

    . . . .

12. Would you like to participate in a hobby activity with members of your class?

    Yes . . . .   No . . . .

    What hobby?

    . . . .

13. Other remarks and suggestions: (You may use other side for additional remarks)

    . . . .

    . . . .

FORM 33(b).

Year in college { Freshman / Sophomore / Junior / Senior }

Name..........

College or university..........

Are any of your present courses selected with a vocation in mind?..........

If so, what vocation?..........

When did you decide on this vocation?..........

Did you select any of your high-school courses with this vocation in mind?..........

Was your high-school preparation adequate for the work that you are now taking?.......... If not, how was it weak? (Be specific.)..........

Do you find it necessary to work harder in college than you worked in high school?..........

Comment:..........

Have you received any honors or awards in college?.......... If so, what were they?..........

Have you taken part in any extra-curriculum activities?.......... If so, what ones? (Include athletics.)..........

Have you held office in any organization?.......... If so, what?..........

In the light of your present experience, could you have planned your work in the University High School so that it would have been more profitable to you?..........

In what way?..........

FORM 34.

Year in college { Freshman / Sophomore / Junior / Senior }

Name..........

College or university..........

Is the school year divided into semesters or quarters?..........

	Courses	Hours	Marks	Grade points
Semester or Quarter — First				
Second				
Third				

Total grade points.......... Grade points possible..........

Rank in class: Percentile.......... If not available, in what quarter of the class does this student rank? Upper.......... Upper middle.......... Lower middle.......... Lower..........

Has the student received any honors during the present year?..........

If so, what?..........

Have you any evidence concerning citizenship of the student?..........

If so, check one of the following: Low.......... Average.......... High..........

Comment:..........

FORM 35.

ment in the elementary school, the use of a comprehensive cumulative record system, and the scheduling of carefully planned conferences of the homeroom teacher with the pupil and his parents.

A report of a statewide follow-up study in Virginia was given by Miller (33). The study was carried on during 1948—1949 of those students who were graduated or who dropped out of high school in 1939–1940. A questionnaire was submitted, to which 50 percent of the graduates and 25 percent of the dropouts responded. A significant finding of the study was that more than half of the former students had had little or no help of a guidance nature. A series of recommendations was drawn from the information obtained in this survey.

---

1. Are you employed?_____ Or are you furthering your formal education?_____

2. What is the nature of your work, or in what college are you enrolled?_____

3. What courses taken at E.B. do you feel were particularly valuable?_____

4. What courses do you feel were least valuable?

_____

5. Have you suggestions as to courses of study, counseling, etc.?_____

6. Your name and address, if you please.

From Miriam B. Gurr, "Continuous Follow-up Study," *California Journal of Secondary Education*, May, 1951. Used with permission of the California Association of Secondary School Administrators.

FORM 36.

Follow-up studies may have especially significant and worthwhile outcomes if the cooperative effort in the studies is extended beyond the school personnel and is made community-wide. This observation is pointed up by follow-up studies of graduates and dropouts carried on in Cabarrus County and Duplin County of North Carolina, as reported by Ellis (14). It was stated that "the primary method used in the Cooperative Project was that of involving lay-professional committees in the identification and study of school problems." The major outcomes in Cabarrus County were (1) greater understanding of the dropout problem among lay citizens; (2) a large number of changes in the school program; and (3) desire for lay-professional evaluation of the schools. In Duplin County, the study led to a concrete and far-reaching outcome in that seven high schools were consolidated into three large modern schools.

The factual information which served as the basis of these studies was obtained by means of interviews, many of which were conducted by citizens of the respective communities. It was concluded that "the lay-citizen in-

terview technique opens up promising possibilities for acquainting lay-citizens with a wide variety of school problems."

FOLLOW-UP AS A TECHNIQUE OF COMPREHENSIVE, LONG-TERM RESEARCH

In recent years, some of the leaders in research have turned their attention to long-range follow-up as a means of gathering research data on a statewide or nationwide basis. The follow-up studies by Rothney and his associates in Wisconsin were mentioned earlier in the chapter. The most ambitious, comprehensive, and sustained follow-up program ever undertaken is Project TALENT (16), now being carried on by the American Institutes for Research under the direction of John C. Flanagan and John T. Dailey. Many articles giving an overview of this project have been published. The project is supported by a grant from the Cooperative Research Program of the United States Office of Education, the National Institute of Mental Health, the Office of Naval Research, and the National Science Foundation. In the planning stages, the project staff had the cooperation of advisory panels in educational research, testing, counseling and guidance, and manpower and sociology.

The objectives of Project TALENT were (1) to survey available talent, (2) to identify interests, aptitudes, and background factors of high school pupils, (3) to determine the effects of lack of interest and motivation, (4) to identify factors affecting vocational choice, (5) to indicate predictors of creativity and productivity, (6) to determine the effectiveness of various kinds of educational experience, and (7) to study procedures for realizing individual potential. The project developed its own tests and inventories in line with these objectives.

The two-day battery was administered in the spring of 1960 to 445,000 pupils in Grades 9, 10, 11, and 12 in 1353 schools throughout the country, of which 987 schools were used to form a stratified random sample. These constituted approximately 5 percent of the high schools in the United States. More than 2000 items of information were collected on each student.

A series of follow-up studies was planned for one, five, ten, and twenty years after each class was graduated from high school. By 1964, the project had issued six major reports. The sixth of these reports contained detailed information concerning the characteristics of American high school students in 1960, as well as procedures and results of the first one-year follow-up study carried on in

1961 (17). Approximately 70 percent of the graduates responded to the follow-up questionnaire.

It will be many years before the values of this mammoth follow-up study can be fully assessed. Project TALENT has already provided valuable information about the status of the American high school student at the beginning of the sixties. The follow-up aspects, however, will largely determine the success of the study in reaching its objectives. It is to be noted that a study of such proportions is made possible only by substantial financial support from agencies of the federal government and by the availability of electronic data-processing equipment and high-speed computers.

SALIENT CHARACTERISTICS OF A FOLLOW-UP PLAN

The following are among the characteristics of a desirable plan for following up school leavers:

1. It is planned to serve the needs of both the individual and the school.
2. It begins before the students leave school.
3. It is continuous.
4. It includes all school leavers—those dropping out as well as those being graduated.
5. Each class is followed up for at least five years.
6. Procedures are used to insure returns from 80 percent or more of those to whom the questionnaire is sent.
7. A representative sampling of each group is interviewed in order to obtain more extensive and detailed information than can be included in a questionnaire.
8. Responsibility for making follow-up studies is decentralized so that each class adviser follows up his own classes as they leave school.
9. The adviser's analysis of the data is made available to other school functionaries and is combined with those of other advisers in order to give a complete picture for the school system.
10. Conclusions concerning causal relationships are drawn with caution.
11. The significant items from each individual's return are transferred to his cumulative record card.
12. The follow-up plan is coordinated with a postschool counseling service.
13. So far as possible, the cooperation of lay citizens is obtained in collecting, studying, and using the follow-up data.

The inauguration of a continuous follow-up service may seem to place a considerable additional burden upon a school staff, but it has been found in practice that a program of this kind is more than worth the additional labor and expense. It helps the school administration, the counselors, the placement office, and the young people who furnish the replies. Perhaps more important than any of these, it benefits the boys and girls still in school, since it helps to bring about needed improvements in the entire school program.

REFERENCES

1. *After Teen-Agers Quit School.* Bulletin 150. Bureau of Labor Standards, U.S. Department of Labor. Washington, D.C.: Government Printing Office, 1952. Pp. v + 30.
2. Allen, Richard D. *Organization and Supervision of Guidance in Public Education,* pp. 166–176, 297–308, 331–369. Sweet Springs, Mo.: Inor Publishing Company, 1937. Pp. xxii + 420.
3. Aumack, Gordon D., and Douglass, Lucile A. "Experiences of Compton College Guidance Office in Developing a Twenty-Year Educational Follow-up Survey," *Junior College Journal,* XXII (November 1951), 158–163.
4. Baer, Max F., and Roeber, Edward C. *Occupational Information: The Dynamics of Its Nature and Use.* Chicago: Science Research Associates, Inc., 1958. Pp. 494.
5. Ball, W. N. "What Is an Effective Follow-up Program for High School Leavers?" *Bulletin of the National Association of Secondary-School Principals,* XXIX (April 1955), 335–337.
6. Barahal, George D., and Brammer, L. M. "What Do College Freshmen Think of Their School Counseling," *California Journal of Secondary Education,* XXV (October 1950), 328–331.
7. Berdie, Ralph F., with chapters by Wilber L. Layton and Ben Willerman. *After High School—What?* Minneapolis: The University of Minnesota Press, 1954. Pp. xii + 240.
8. Brewster, Royce E., and Zeran, Franklin R. *Techniques of Follow-up Study of School Leavers.* Monterey: California Test Bureau, 1947. Pp. 4.
9. Brown, Fern G. "High School That Learns from Its Graduates," *NEA Journal,* LI (December 1962), 26.
10. Cuony, Edward. "The Follow-up Study in the Junior High School Orientation Program," *Personnel and Guidance Journal,* XL (May 1962), 812–814.
11. Dillon, Harold J. *Early School Leavers: A Major Educational Problem.* Publication 401. New York: National Child Labor Committee, 1949. Pp. 94.
12. Eckert, Ruth E. "Studies of Former Students as a Measure of School Success," *High School Journal,* XXXIV (April 1951), 106–109.
13. Eckert, Ruth E., and Marshall, Thomas O. *When Youth Leave School.* New York: McGraw-Hill Book Company, Inc., 1938. Pp. 360.
14. Ellis, G. Gordon. "Involvement of Lay Citizens in School

Follow-up Studies," *High School Journal*, XXXVIII (April 1955), 264–271.

15. Eurich, Alvin C., and Pace, C. Robert. *A Follow-up Study of Minnesota Graduates from 1928 to 1936*. Minneapolis: University of Minnesota Committee on Educational Research, 1938. Pp. 41.

16. Flanagan, John C. "Project TALENT: A Progress Report," *Measurement and Research in Today's Schools*, pp. 99–108. Report of Twenty-fifth Educational Conference sponsored by the Educational Records Bureau and the American Council on Education. Washington, D.C.: American Council on Education, 1961.

17. Flanagan, John C., Davis, Frederick B., Dailey, John T., and others. *The American High-School Student*. Technical Report to the U.S. Office of Education, Cooperative Research Project No. 635. Pittsburgh: Project TALENT Office, University of Pittsburgh, 1964.

18. Fleming, R. L. "How to Make and Utilize Follow-up Studies of School Leavers?" *Bulletin of the National Association of Secondary-School Principals*, XXXVI (March 1952), 74–84.

19. *Follow-up of Secondary School Graduates*. Leads to Better Secondary Schools in Michigan, No. 1 Lansing, Mich.: Michigan Study of the Secondary School Curriculum, State Board of Education, 1943. Pp. 70.

20. Goertzen, Stan M., and Strong, Donald J. "Counseling Practices in the Small Colleges and Universities of the Pacific Northwest: A Twelve-Year Follow-up Study," *Personnel and Guidance Journal*, XLI (November 1962), 254–259.

21. Green, Donald A. "A Study of Talented High School Drop-outs," *Vocational Guidance Quarterly*, X (Spring 1962), 171–172.

22. *Guide for Making a Follow-up Study of School Dropouts and Graduates*. Sacramento, Calif.: Bureau of Occupational Information and Guidance, California State Department of Education, 1950. Pp. 23.

23. Gurr, Miriam B. "Continuous Follow-up Study," *California Journal of Secondary Education*, XXVI (May 1951), 302–305.

24. Hecker, Stanley E. *Early School Leavers in Kentucky*. Bulletin of the Bureau of School Service, College of Education, University of Kentucky, Vol. XXV, Lexington, Ky.: University of Kentucky, 1953. Pp. 80.

25. Henderson, Kenneth B., and Goerwitz John E. *How to Conduct the Follow-up Study*. Illinois Secondary School Curriculum Program Bulletin 11. Springfield: Illinois Department of Public Instruction, 1950. Pp. 142.

26. Herrman, Lyndon, and Cottle, William C. "An Inventory to Identify High School Dropouts," *Vocational Guidance Quarterly*, VI (Spring 1958), 122–123.

27. Hollinshead, Byron S. *Who Should Go to College*, with a chapter on "The Role of Motivation in Attendance at Post-High-School Educational Institutions," by Robert J. Havighurst and Robert R. Rodgers. Published for the Commission on Financing Higher Education. New York: Columbia University Press, 1952. Pp. xvi+190.

28. Humphreys, J. Anthony, Traxler, Arthur E., and North,

Robert D. *Guidance Services*, Chapter X. Chicago: Science Research Associates, Inc., 1960. Pp. xv+414.

29. Landy, Edward; Berry, John R.; Hayes, Byron C.; and Long, C. Darl. *The Occupational Follow-up and Adjustment Service Plan*. New York: The Occupational Adjustment Study of the National Association of Secondary-School Principals, 1940. Pp. 96.

30. Latham, A. J. "Job Appropriateness: A One-Year Follow-up of High School Graduates," *Journal of Social Psychology*, XXXIV (August 1951), 55–68.

31. Ledvina, L. M. "100 Per Cent Follow-up," *Personnel and Guidance Journal*, XXXIII (October 1954), 90–93.

32. Lorenzen, Stanley H. "Opinion Reactions in High School Follow-up Studies," *Bulletin of the National Association of Secondary-School Principals*, XXXIII (January 1949), 119–126.

33. Miller, Leonard M. "Graduates and Drop-outs in Virginia," *School Life*, XXXIV (March 1952), 87, 93–95.

34. Munger, Paul F., Brown, D. F., and Needham, John T. "NDEA Institute Participants Two Years Later," *Personnel and Guidance Journal*, XLII (June 1964), 987–990.

35. Myers, George E. "Follow-up: The Stepchild of the Guidance Family," *Occupations*, XXVII (November 1948), 100–103.

36. *Now Hear Youth: Report of the California Cooperative Study of School Drop-Outs and Graduates*. Sacramento, Calif.: State Department of Education, 1953. Pp. 69.

37. O'Neill, J. H. "Follow-up Services in Guidance," *Catholic Schools Journal*, LVII (December 1957), 23–24.

38. Oppenheimer, Celia. "Ten-Year Follow-up of the Class of 1940," Bulletin of the National Association of Secondary-School Principals, XXXVII (March 1953), 77–80.

39. Pace, C. Robert. "Follow-up Studies of College Graduates," *Growing Points in Educational Research*, pp. 285–290. Official Report of 1949 Meeting. Washington, D.C.: American Educational Research Association, 1949.

40. Patterson, R. L., and Fotiu, P. G. "Effectiveness of Guidance Center Counseling," *Journal of Educational Research*, XLVI (January 1953), 359–363.

41. Putman, John A. "Use of Community Resources in a Follow-up Study," *Personnel and Guidance Journal*, XXXII (March 1954), 409–410.

42. Robbins, Eli, and O'Neal, Patricia. "Clinical Features of Hysteria in Children, with a Note on Prognosis; a Two to Seventeen Year Follow-up Study of 41 Patients," *Nervous Child*, X, No. 2 (1953), 246–271.

43. Roeber, Edward C., Smith, Glenn E., and Erickson, Clifford E. *Organization and Administration of Guidance Services*, 2d ed. New York: McGraw-Hill Book Company, Inc., 1955. Pp. x+294.

44. Rothney, John W. M. "What Are Your 1951 High School Graduates Doing Now?" *Wisconsin Journal of Education*, LXXXVI (April 1954), 9–10.

45. Rothney, John W. M. "Counseling Does Help!" *Vocational Guidance Quarterly*, VI (Autumn 1957), 15–18.

46. Rothney, John W. M. "What Are High School Graduates Doing Ten Years After High School?" *Vocational*

Guidance Quarterly, XIII (Winter 1964–1965), 134–136.

47. Rothney, John W. M., and Mooren, Robert L. "Sampling Problems in Follow-up Research," *Occupations*, XXX (May 1952), 573–578.

48. Sando, Rudolph F. "How to Make and Utilize Follow-up Studies of School Leavers," *Bulletin of the National Association of Secondary-School Principals,* XXXVI (March 1952), 66–74.

49. Schultz, Merlin W. "Student Opinions of a High School Guidance Program," *Personnel and Guidance Journal,* XLI (April 1963), 709–715.

50. Snepp, D. W. "These Things Happened to Our 1953 Graduates," *Clearing House,* XXVII (April 1954), 494–497.

51. Strong, Edward K., Jr., "Nineteen-Year Follow-up of Engineer Interests," *Journal of Applied Psychology,* XXXVI (April 1952), 65–74.

52. Terry, I. G. "Ten Year Follow-up Study of Cooperative Part-time Pupils," *Industrial Arts and Vocational Education,* XLII (April 1953), 115–118.

53. *The Denver Public Schools Look at 1962 High School Graduates in College.* Highlights from the 1963 Evaluation Study Directed by the Division of Instructional Services. Denver, Colo.: Denver Public Schools, 1963. Pp. 20.

54. *The Denver Public Schools Look at 1962 High School Graduates in Business and Industry.* Highlights from the 1964 Evaluation Study Directed by the Division of Instructional Services. Denver, Colo.: Denver Public Schools, 1964. Pp. 37.

55. Thorndike, Robert L. "Tests and Long-Time Prediction of Vocational Choice," *Strengthening Education at All Levels* (ed. by Arthur E. Traxler). Report of Eighteenth Educational Conference sponsored by Educational Records Bureau and American Council on Education, pp. 114–132. Washington, D.C.: American Council on Education, 1953. Pp. vi+156.

56. Troyer, Maurice, and Pace, C. Robert. *Evaluation in Teacher Education.* Washington, D.C.: American Council on Education, 1944. Pp. xii+368.

57. Turchin, Samuel. "The Drop-out Returns to Evening High School," *High Points,* LXIV (December 1962), 53–56.

58. Walker, R. M. "Follow-up Really Works," *Occupations,* XXIX (February 1951), 328–330.

59. Wiegman, Robert R., and Jacobson, Paul B. "How Well Did They Know?" *Journal of Higher Education,* XXVI (May 1955), 267–270.

60. Wrenn, C. Gilbert. "A Critique of Methods Used in Follow-up Studies of Students," *Harvard Educational Review* X (May 1940), 357–363.

61. Young, R. J., and Holman, W. "Follow-up: New Variety," *Clearing House,* XXVIII (January 1954), 295–297.

CHAPTER XVIII

Guidance in the Adjustment of Individuals

A GUIDANCE PROGRAM OBVIOUSLY CONSISTS OF more than the techniques discussed in this book. Familiarity with, and skill in using these techniques should greatly increase a counselor's effectiveness, but it should be clear to everyone that the techniques are tools or means to an end, and that intelligence, understanding, sympathy, and insight are required of a counselor in the application of these techniques to the guidance of individual boys and girls.

The science of guidance is applied by counselors and teachers who are not highly trained in psychology more readily to the *distributive* phases of guidance than to the adjustive aspects. One who is well informed concerning the educational and vocational opportunities for young people, so far as it is possible to be informed in this period of accelerated change, and who has command of the procedures for obtaining broad and reasonably accurate information about individuals can help students make appropriate kinds of educational and occupational choices with considerable confidence and with a large measure of success. This aspect of guidance, of course, contributes to the adjustment of the individual, but these adjustive functions are indirect and may not be fully realized by either counselor or student.

Even though a good many persons participating in a school guidance program have had little professional training for counseling, they can be very helpful to individual pupils in connection with the *overt, immediate problems of adjustment.* The more common general areas into which these problems fall are pupil-teacher relationships, relationships with other pupils, relationships between pupils and parents, study difficulties, and minor behavior difficulties. This type of problem is usually specific, and ordinarily it is either recognized by pupil and counselor from the outset, or it emerges and is identified in the course of one or two interviews. Not infrequently, this kind of problem can be solved quickly through the planning of a definite and immediate course of action. Information is often a large component of counseling in these areas. When the counselee has obtained the information he seeks from the counselor, and when he has learned what the alternatives are, he can reach a decision as to what he ought to do.

More important adjustment problems are deep-seated, are woven into the fabric of the individual's personality, are not overtly related to symptoms, and are to be resolved largely through growth and development over a considerable period of time. It is in this area that the average counselor is most likely to fall down on the job because of lack of knowledge and skill in psychotherapy. There is danger that he will either completely overlook or ignore the difficulty and do nothing about it, or will misinterpret the difficulty and try to apply treatment directly to the symptoms. Even when he correctly diagnoses the problem he may get into deep water if he tries to prescribe and direct a program of treatment himself.

There is no easy solution for the lack of preparation of a large proportion of school guidance functionaries to handle difficult and obscure cases of poor adjustment. But consideration of certain fundamentals may sharpen the awareness of counselors to these problems and help them avoid some of the pitfalls.

WHAT IS ADJUSTMENT?

Occasionally in the use of the term adjustment we imply that the most desirable state is one in which the individual is perfectly happy and satisfied with all aspects

303

of his life, and one in which he has reached the level in all his contacts with his environment that he would be glad to see persist through his life. Seldom, if ever, is this kind of adjustment achieved by an individual in all his relationships, and it would not be a desirable kind of adjustment even if it were realized. Complete adjustment in all aspects of life would lead to extreme mental and physical stagnation. Much of the motivational power of living would be lost.

A certain degree of dissatisfaction is wholesome and stimulating. Man's realization that he has not reached his goals is one of the great driving forces both for individuals and for social groups. Much of the work of the world is done by those who are somewhat unadjusted but who have lofty aspirations and strong drives to attain their goal. In fact, some of the most outstanding contributions to our civilization, particularly in the fields of literature and music, have been made by men who were decidedly neurotic. This is not to imply that the bringing about of better adjustment all along the line is not desirable; but it is well to keep in mind that adjustment is always relative, and that occasional evidence of maladjustment is usual and does not set one off from the normal or even the superior group.

In the last analysis, the best-integrated and adjusted individuals seem to be those who have established some reasonable goals, in line with their interests and abilities, and who have settled down to work toward those goals seriously and steadily, but without unusual tension. It is highly desirable for advisers to keep in mind the *integrative and adjustive nature of purposeful behavior* in connection with the therapeutic aspects of their counseling work.

THE DANGER OF LABELS

In every area in which thinking is done, vocabulary is, of course, extremely important, not only as a vehicle of thinking but as a guide to and a determiner of thinking. The truth of this observation is especially apparent when the personality adjustment of an individual is being considered. To the lay mind, the word *psychoneurotic* has a connotation that is damning to the individual concerned; yet it is a generic term which covers everything from mild neuroses to personality aberrations that merge with the psychotic and call for institutional treatment. In reality, the term has little meaning until the nature of the difficulty is defined.

An illustration of the need for especial care in the application of technical terms to individuals is furnished by the cases of some of the veterans returning at the end of World War II and after the Korean War. The Armed Forces designated a considerable number of men unfit for military service because of psychoneuroses. Where a given individual was concerned, this may have been significant with respect to his ability to adjust to civilian life, or it may have had little or no significance. There is a positive correlation between external conditions—between physical, mental, and emotional pressure—and neurotic tendency. Many individuals who cannot withstand, over a long period, rigorous and exacting conditions such as those found in military life, get along very well in a civilian environment. It is probably no exaggeration to state flatly that every individual without exception may become neurotic if he is placed in an environment which subjects him to continuous emotional tension or to a continuous series of problems which he cannot solve.

It is of the utmost importance for counselors to keep in mind one basic tenet of modern psychology. This tenet is that individuals can never be clearly separated into the normal and the abnormal, or into the emotionally adjusted and the neurotic, but rather that *abnormal psychological phenomena are either exaggerations or disguised developments of normal psychological phenomena.* Counselors who keep this important principle constantly in mind will be in much less danger of allowing the jangle fallacy resulting from names and labels to obscure their thinking concerning individual cases.

MECHANISMS OF ESCAPE FROM REALITY

Major problems which seem insoluble to the individual concerned are the chief source of emotional disorders. The characteristic abnormal reaction to a baffling problem is some type of retreat from reality. Avoidance of reality may be attempted in many ways. Some of the milder forms of escape are *repression,* or forgetting the unpleasant experience or problem; *rationalization,* or the advancement of plausible but incorrect reasons to justify a course of action or explain a failure; *phantasy,* or daydreaming in which one achieves imaginary fame or success, performs wonderful feats, or renders outstanding service; and *projection,* or attempts to divert attention from one's own problems by dwelling on those of others or attributing to others his own shortcomings. These means of avoiding facing problems are undesirable, but they are very common among normal individuals. Their mechanism is not highly complex, and school counselors should be able to recognize them and to help individuals who are being counseled understand how they function and how they can be overcome.

A more serious mode of escape from difficult problems or unwelcome situations is the development of temporary *mental or physical ills or incapacities* which force the individual out of the activities he wishes to avoid. For example, a boy who fears he will fail a difficult examination may develop an upset stomach on the morning of the examination day and have to spend the day in bed; or an extremely timid girl who is frightened at the thought of having to make a talk in her English class may come down with a nervous headache. These mechanisms of escape may take place not merely once, but each time a difficult situation is encountered. Occasionally they represent deliberate malingering, in which case they are more reprehensible but not so serious psychologically. Not infrequently, however, the individual is made actually sick by the difficulty he faces. He is not pretending illness, and he is probably not even aware of the relationship between his indisposition and his desire to escape an intolerable situation.

Hysterical-like symptoms such as those just described are likely to be baffling, but they are not insoluble in a counseling situation in which the counselor is able to enlist the active cooperation of the individual in analyzing his symptoms and going to the root of the trouble. In rare instances, however, the mechanism of hysteria may be completely beyond the counselor's experience and beyond any contribution he can make to a treatment of the case, except to report what he observes.

The outward manifestation of hysteria in the technical sense is a disease symptom. The number of diseases that may be simulated by a hysterical person is almost infinite. An inquiry into the mechanism of hysteria would call for an extensive study of the theories of various psychologists, including especially Janet (*17*) and Freud (*9*). The explanation advanced by Freud is interwoven with his concept of sex as the great motivating force in human life. Regardless of what theory is accepted, the modern treatment of hysteria calls for analysis by an expert in psychology or psychiatry and a program of re-education.

It is not probable that school counselors will encounter cases of major hysteria, for the withdrawal reactions of children and adolescents in school are rarely so extreme. An awareness of the symptoms of marked maladjustment may help counselors occasionally, however, to recognize incipient abnormal tendencies and to take steps to bring these cases to the attention of specialists in the early stages when adjustment can readily be brought about.

One of the primary functions of counselors is to help young people learn to meet problems frankly and courageously, and to accept frustration philosophically. All persons have limitations; no one can excel in everything. Failure can be reduced by setting goals that are within the capacity of the individual, but even under the best planning possible, every individual will have his failures and everyone will meet some problems—vocational, social, or personal—which are clearly insoluble as far as he is concerned. When one of these immovable barriers is encountered, an individual may either persistently refuse to accept the reality of the situation until he experiences a disintegration of personality, or he may find compensatory activities and other outlets around which he can achieve such an integration of personality that he may emerge from the experience stronger than before. Everyone will agree that the counselor has extremely important work to perform in this connection, but no one has ever been able to give him a blueprint of how to proceed, although it may be helpful to list the steps in a usual counseling situation where the primary purpose is therapeutic.

STEPS IN COUNSELING FOR ADJUSTMENT

The traditional concept of counseling is the giving of advice. While this limited definition of counseling is no longer accepted by counselors with professional training, it is still widely held by pupils and laymen. According to this concept, a student goes to his counselor with a problem, or the counselor calls him in, and then the counselor talks the situation over with the student, and out of his broader knowledge and more mature experience offers suggestions for the student to consider and presumably to act upon. This will no doubt always be an important phase of counseling, for in the experience of every student there may arise emergencies of urgent and immediate import concerning which the advice of an experienced and understanding friend is greatly needed. The need for early resolution of the difficulty may outweigh the desire to make the counseling relationship a growth experience for the individual.

These instances, however, are exceptional. In the more common counseling situation, the modern emphasis is upon the sharing of experiences and not upon the counselor's accepting responsibility for the solution of problems. The more skillful counselor, who is seeking to help the student to better adjustment, is likely to let the individual do the larger share of the talking while, by means of timely questions, he shrewdly and subtly directs the line of thinking until, in the end, the student himself will seem to have thought the problem through and to have decided upon a course of action almost independently. It is here that counseling loses much of its scientific character and takes on the guise of a highly sensitive art.

This approach to counseling not only is likely to be more successful in the immediate situation, but it has for its more remote objective the development in the individual of a confident, independent, and thoughtful attitude that will lead him to make a determined effort to solve his own problems whenever they arise.

The following list indicates the steps that may take place during successful counseling for adjustment:[1]

1. The student asks his counselor for help and states the situation as he sees it.
2. The counselor and student discuss the situation until the problem is clearly defined.
3. The counselor leads the student to talk about the problem at length. In the beginning, the individual's statements about the problem will in all probability be negative. That is, he will talk about how difficult the problem is or how unendurable the situation, and how thoroughly disgusted he is with the whole business.
4. Instead of criticizing this attitude, the counselor accepts it as normal and logical. He does not show approval, but he avoids creating antagonism by trying to force a different attitude at this point.
5. After the individual has "talked himself out," the counselor, by means of appropriate suggestions, leads him to begin consideration of the positive side of the situation.
6. The counselor accepts the positive suggestions of the individual calmly and thoughtfully, and voices approval when the individual seems to be on the right track.
7. As the subject talks on the positive side, he begins to develop insight and to formulate a plan of action.
8. The counselor allows the individual to do most of the planning, but keeping in mind the accumulated information he has about this student, he tries to steer him into a course of action consistent with his abilities and with the problem at hand.
9. The individual puts his plan into action, thereby acquiring further understanding of the problem.
10. He develops an integrated and successful program of action, loses his need for the counselor, and terminates the guidance relationship as far as it applies to this problem.

This outline of the development of a counseling situation is, of course, very general, and in actual practice certain steps frequently will be merged and will not occur in exactly this sequence. The important point is for the counselor to help the subject take positive and appropriate action which is self-initiated and is therefore likely to persist and to contribute to the personal growth of the individual.

[1] A more detailed outline and discussion was given by Carl R. Rogers in his *Counseling and Psychotherapy*. Boston: Houghton Mifflin Company, 1942.

CHARACTERISTICS AND PROFESSIONAL TRAINING DESIRABLE FOR COUNSELORS

The techniques discussed in the other chapters of this book will, when used intelligently, provide much of the data for a dependable guidance program. Familiarity with these procedures will help the work of every counselor, but the point which will bear repetition is that close attention to them does not alone constitute guidance. It is through the intelligence, understanding, skill, and personality of the counselor himself that life is given to these techniques. The personal qualities of a school's counselors are among the most important determiners of the excellence of its guidance program. Probably not more than one fourth of the teachers in a school have the qualities required for superior work in the guidance of young people. The characteristics needed for successful counseling of individuals include:

1. An intelligent view of the philosophy of individual guidance and the relation of guidance to a broad educational program.
2. A genuine interest in, liking for, and faith in people.
3. Ability and willingness to know and understand individuals before attempting to guide them.
4. A sincere and businesslike attitude, tempered by a sense of humor.
5. An easy and cordial manner in meeting and talking with people.
6. Ability to approach the main problem in a discussion without abruptness but without vacillation.
7. Ability to control the interview and still take a self-effacing position.
8. Skill in asking the right questions at the right time and in keeping silent at the right places during an interview.
9. Awareness of one's own strengths and limitations as a counselor, combined with a willingness to undertake what one is competent to do, and to admit inability to provide treatment for certain individuals or certain kinds of difficulty.
10. Sufficient knowledge of various theories of personality to understand what different kinds of overt behavior may mean in terms of adjustment.

With regard to the last category, many counselors— until recently the majority—have not specialized in psychology. Much of their training in psychology must be acquired through in-service reading and experience. Their reading is certain to bring them into contact with various theories concerning the organization of personality, including those of Jung, Kretschmer, Adler, and Freud. Jung has stressed introversion-extroversion; Kretschmer, constitutional types; Adler, compensation and struggle for power; Freud, sex, broadly defined, and psychoanalysis. Freud's theories are likely to be both highly intriguing and very comfusing for one not professionally trained in psychiatry. Historically, the usual first reaction was to reject and even to ridicule Freud's whole point of view, for his analysis of maladjustment in terms of repressed sex impulses—in particular, his emphasis upon infantile sex drives—seemed at first thought to be far-fetched and even bizarre. Without question, there has been a great deal of misinterpretation and exploitation of Freud's theories by incompetent persons, and there has been and still is much popular misinformation about his contribution to psychology.

Nevertheless, Freudian psychology is so closely interwoven with modern psychiatry that guidance people in schools cannot choose to ignore Freud if they expect to enlist the cooperation of experts in the handling of difficult and obscure cases. The principal contributions to, and applications of, Freudian psychology have in recent years passed from Germany to America. A competent and especially thorough and critical appraisal of Freud's work from the American point of view was given a quarter of a century ago in the writings of the late Karen Horney (15). Freud's own introductory book on psychoanalysis was translated into English by Joan Riviere (9). A simplified, nontechnical statement of an important aspect of Freud's point of view is that mental health calls for two essential ingredients—the ability to love and the ability to work (20).

Those who are specialists in psychology are likely to have their moments of doubt as they contemplate the guidance scene in the United States, and observe, even today, classroom teachers whose training has been in English or mathematics or social studies performing guidance functions and making certain tentative explorations and probings into the personality of the pupils they counsel. They are inclined to wonder sometimes, even though they may not voice their fears, whether more harm than good may not come from such an arrangement. The whole thesis of this book, however, is that counselors who are not professional psychologists are capable of performing the *distributive functions* of guidance and many of the *less involved adjustive functions*, provided they will become acquainted with and use the techniques for knowing individuals and helping the individuals to know themselves. Every guidance program should be so organized that the services of one or more specialists in mental therapy is available for the treatment of the more involved cases. Teacher-counselors can contribute to the treatment of these cases by observing pupils accurately and with some understanding of the problems involved, and by reporting their observations to the specialists. They can increase their effectiveness in this regard by means of carefully selected pro-

fessional reading, through summer-session and extension courses in mental hygiene, and especially by participation in NDEA Counseling and Guidance Training Institutes (26). Graduate courses in guidance and personnel work are offered in more than 300 colleges and universities in the United States (22).

REFERENCES

1. American Personnel and Guidance Association. "Counselor: Professional Preparation and Role: Statement of Policy," *Personnel and Guidance Journal*, XLII (January 1964), 536–541.
2. Angers, William P. "The Psychological Significance of Adlerian Concepts in Counseling," *Vocational Guidance Quarterly*, VIII (Spring 1960), 139–143.
3. Appell, M. L. "Self-Understanding for the Guidance Counselor," *Personnel and Guidance Journal*, XLII (October 1963), 143–148.
4. Baker, John Q., and Wagner, Nathaniel N. "Social Class and Mental Illness," *Teachers College Record*, LXVI (March 1965), 522–536.
5. Baldwin, Alfred L. *Behavior and Development in Childhood*. New York: Holt, Rinehart and Winston, Inc., 1955. Pp. 637.
6. Baller, Warren R., and Charles, Don C. *The Psychology of Human Growth and Development*. New York: Holt, Rinehart and Winston, Inc., 1961. Pp. xiii+432.
7. Bordin, Edward S. *Psychological Counseling*. New York: Appleton-Century-Crofts, Inc., 1955. Pp. x+410.
8. Erickson, Clifford E. *The Counseling Interview*. Englewood Cliffs, N.J.: Prentice-Hall, Inc., 1950. Pp. viii+174.
9. Freud, Sigmund. *A General Introduction to Psychoanalysis*. Authorized English translation of revised edition by Joan Riviere. Garden City, N.Y.: Doubleday & Company, Inc., 1943. Pp. 412.
10. Gorlow, Leon, Hoch, Erasmus L., and Telschow, Earl F. *The Nature of Nondirective Group Psychotherapy*. New York: Bureau of Publications, Teachers College, Columbia University, 1952. Pp. xiv+144.
11. Grant, Claude W. "How Students Perceive the Counselor's Role," *Personnel and Guidance Journal*, XXXII (March 1954), 386–388.
12. Gray, Susan W. *The Psychologist in the Schools*. New York: Holt, Rinehart and Winston, Inc., 1963. Pp. 416.
13. Green, Sidney L., and Rothenberg, Alan B. *A Manual of First Aid for Mental Health in Childhood and Adolescence*. New York: Julian Press, Inc., 1953. Pp. vi+278.
14. Hahn, Milton E., and MacLean, Malcolm S. *Counseling Psychology*, 2nd ed. New York: McGraw-Hill Book Company, Inc., 1955. Pp. xii+312.
15. Horney, Karen. *New Ways in Psychoanalysis*. New York: W. W. Norton & Company, 1939. Pp. 313.

16. Hoyt, Kenneth B., and Loughary, John W. "Acquaintance With and Use of Referral Sources by Iowa Secondary School Counselors," *Personnel and Guidance Journal*, XXXVI (February 1958), 388–391.

17. Janet, Pierre. *Major Symptoms of Hysteria.* New York: The Macmillan Company, 1929. Pp. x + 345.

18. Koeppe, Richard P., and Rothney, John W. M. "Evaluation of First Steps in the Counseling of Superior Students," *Personnel and Guidance Journal*, XLII (September 1963), 35–39.

19. Lehner, George F. J., and Kube, Ella. *The Dynamics of Personal Adjustment,* 2nd ed. Englewood Cliffs, N.J.: Prentice-Hall, Inc., 1963. Pp. 492.

20. Levinson, Harry. "What Is Mental Health?" *Think,* XXXI (March–April 1965), 24–28.

21. Lindgren, Henry Clay. *Psychology of Personal and Social Adjustment.* New York: American Book Company, 1959. Pp. 534.

22. Lovejoy, Clarence G. *Lovejoy's Guidance Digest,* XVII (March 1965), 5.

23. Madison, Peter. *Freud's Concept of Repression and Defense.* Minneapolis: The University of Minnesota Press, 1961. Pp. 205.

24. Murphy, Gardner. "New Vistas in Personality Research," *Personnel and Guidance Journal*, XL (October 1961), 114–122.

25. Nancarrow, James E. "Guidance Means Help," *Bulletin of the National Association of Secondary-School Principals,* XLV (May 1961), 1–5.

26. *National Defense Counseling and Guidance Training Institutes Program: Basic Facts.* Washington, D.C.: Superintendent of Documents, Government Printing Office. Pp. 9.

27. Neumeyer, Martin H. *Juvenile Delinquency in Modern Society,* 2nd ed. New York: D. Van Nostrand Company, Inc., 1955. Pp. x + 336.

28. Ojemann, Ralph H. *Personality Adjustment of Individual Children.* Department of Classroom Teachers and American Educational Research Association. Washington, D.C.: National Education Association, 1954. Pp. 32.

29. Ojemann, Ralph H. "The Significance of a Causal Orientation in Human Development," *Keeping Abreast of the Revolution in Education,* pp. 47–55. Report of Twenty-eighth Educational Conference sponsored by Educational Records Bureau. Washington, D.C.: American Council on Education, 1964. Pp. viii + 195.

30. Ramsey, Glenn V. "The Referral Task in Counseling," *Personnel and Guidance Journal*, XL (January 1962), 443–447.

31. Robinson, Francis P. "Modern Approaches to Counseling 'Diagnosis,'" *Journal of Counseling Psychology,* X (Winter 1963), 325–333.

32. Rogers, Carl R. *Counseling and Psychotherapy.* Boston: Houghton Mifflin Company, 1942. Pp. xiv + 450.

33. Rogers, Carl R., and Dymond, Rosalind F. (eds.). *Psychotherapy and Personality Change.* Chicago: The University of Chicago Press, 1954. Pp. x + 448.

34. Samler, Joseph. "Basic Approaches to Mental Health," *Personnel and Guidance Journal*, XXXVII (September 1958), 26–31.

35. Schneiders, Alexander A. *Personnel Adjustment and Mental Health.* New York: Holt, Rinehart, and Winston, Inc., 1955. Pp. xviii + 588.

36. Sinick, Daniel. "Is There a Social Role for Vocational Counselors?" *Vocational Guidance Quarterly,* XII (Spring 1964), 192–193.

37. Smith, Henry Clay. *Personality Adjustment.* New York: McGraw-Hill Book Company, Inc., 1961. Pp. 617.

38. Symonds, Percival M. "Implications for the Counselor," *Education,* LXXVI (December 1955), 246–248.

39. Tyler, Ralph W. "We Are Learning More and More About Human Behavior. What Are the Implications for Education?" *NEA Journal,* XLIV (October 1955), 426–429.

40. Walquist, G. L. "How Machine Processes Save Counselor Time," *California Journal of Secondary Education,* XXXII (November 1957), 442–445.

41. Warters, Jane. *Techniques of Counseling,* 2nd ed. New York: McGraw-Hill Book Company, Inc., 1964. Pp. 478.

42. Wrenn, C. Gilbert. "The School Counselor's Task," *Education Digest,* XXVIII (November 1962), 16–19.

CHAPTER XIX

Counseling as a Learning Function:
A Meeting Ground of Viewpoints

WHAT APPROACH TO COUNSELING?

THE PUBLICATION OF CARL R. ROGERS' BOOK, *Counseling and Psychotherapy* (41), in 1942, marked the beginning of an extensive debate over the philosophy and techniques of clinical counseling which enlivened psychology and guidance for some years. Strong differences of opinion persisted for more than a decade, but the intensity of the disagreement has greatly diminished during more recent years as proponents of different viewpoints have come to understand each other's position better and have found a great deal of common ground.

The opposing groups in the debate, which sometimes took the shape of a controversy, were commonly designated as the directive and the nondirective. The terms "directive" and "nondirective" were largely misnomers. Even before Rogers' influence, strictly directive counseling was abandoned in many places; it is seldom practiced today, even though it was common practice during the first quarter of this century. Trained counselors of whatever persuasion clearly understand the importance of meeting the counselee on equal terms, and of making the counseling process a sharing of knowledge, experience, and viewpoint.

The counselors first designated as "nondirective" came to regard themselves as not strictly nondirective but as "client-centered" or "counselee-centered" or "student-centered"; this is an attitude which has found great favor throughout the profession.

A FOOTNOTE TO HISTORY

In order to see the whole matter in perspective, it is necessary to go back in time into the nineteenth century to the work of Freud and his disciples. Freud's develop-

ment of psychoanalysis was largely nondirective. The subject was encouraged to express himself, to talk and keep on talking, to bring up from his subconscious the memories and thoughts and feelings long suppressed and to take a good look at them. A major role of the psychoanalyst was to stimulate the subject to express his innermost thoughts; the subject, not the analyst, did most of the talking.

But Freud, as a medical man, was always aware of the need for complete and accurate diagnosis. The catharsis of confession was an important element but was not in itself enough. It was not assumed that the patient could work out his own salvation without outside assistance. A central purpose of getting the subject to talk himself out was to bring to light long-hidden thoughts and emotions that would serve as the basis of diagnosis by the professionally trained analyst.

Freud's influence began to be felt in this country early in the twentieth century. The writings of one of Freud's leading disciples, Otto Rank, were translated and applied by Jessie Taft (39, 40), in a very helpful way. The Philadelphia Child Guidance Clinic, under the direction of Frederick H. Allen, and other centers stressed the dynamics inherent in the therapeutic work which had been emphasized by Freud and Rank (1).

At the turn of the century, another influence which was to impinge mightily upon the guidance movement had its beginning. Impressed by the success of the application of precise, objective methods of research in the physical world, Rice, Thorndike, Judd, Freeman, Courtis, and other young psychologists and educators developed a conviction that similar methods could be applied to the study of the mind of man. It will be recalled that this was the heyday of Newtonian physics. Man inhabited a corner of a neatly conceived, mechanical, deterministic universe. The new Titans of the world of science were only at the beginning of their work. Einstein was just in the process of publishing the three papers that were to shake classical physics from its foundation. Max Planck had only tentatively enunciated his quantum theory and was not himself ready to accept all its implications. The renaissance of physical science was nearly 25 years in the future, and it would be still another quarter of a century before its impact upon thinking in the social science fields would be felt to an appreciable degree.

So the science of psychometrics was born. Measures of aptitudes, achievement, and certain aspects of personal qualities were developed and improved. These were not wholly precise, but they gave good approximations of the qualities they were intended to measure, and they took much of the guesswork out of the appraisal of individuals.

Leaders in the guidance movement began to apply these instruments diagnostically. The clinical use of tests in diagnosis, as a step in counseling, became standard procedure.

Rogers' paramount contribution was that he made the counselee the center, not only as object but also as process. There was a kind of dualism in Freudian psychotherapy—diagnosis by the analyst or counselor and catharsis through expression by the patient. The approach of psychometrically oriented counselors was that of the scientific method—gather the data about the counselee, analyze it, form a hypothesis concerning the problem (diagnose), develop a plan mutually with the counselee for meeting the problem, put the plan into action (test the hypothesis), evaluate the progress of treatment (reappraise the hypothesis) and make needed adjustments in hypothesis and treatment, and carry the plan forward until the problem is solved. An actual counseling case is seldom carried out in such a formal way, but the basis of the scientific method is present in some degree. Rogers, in a sense, by-passed both diagnosis by the psychotherapist and the scientific method of the psychometrician. He expressed faith in the ability of the counselee to carry out the whole process of problem-solving through his own self-expression. This faith was accepted by Rogers' immediate followers, although more recently it has been modified to some extent in actual practice.

Thus a new school of counseling came into being which had wide appeal. It interested professional psychologists because it represented a new orientation in thinking; it appealed to social case workers and religious workers because of its expression of faith in the individual; and, one suspects, it intrigued many young persons entering upon work in the field of guidance because it seemed to them to offer a kind of ritual whereby adjustment counseling and depth therapy could be carried on by persons without a great deal of background in profes-

sional psychology and with practically no understanding of psychometrics or measurement. So the "nondirective" or "client-centered" school of psychotherapy and counseling developed with extreme rapidity.

DIFFERENCES BETWEEN "STRUCTURED" AND CLIENT-CENTERED COUNSELING

What has been called directive counseling might more properly be termed a structured approach to counseling. Guidance workers who take this structured approach prefer to begin by gathering information concerning the individual's abilities, achievements, and interests as a basis for interviewing him. A large part of this information is accumulated routinely in nearly all modern schools simply as a result of holding classes, assigning marks, conducting testing programs, and carrying on other school activities, the essential data from which find their way into the cumulative record. The client-centered view demands that the whole procedure be based on individual counseling and that items of information about the individual either develop as by-products of the process or be introduced as needed.

A guidance worker who is committed to structured counseling customarily retains a considerable degree of control over the interview; participates much as he would in ordinary conversation, except that he keeps in mind that the conversation has a purpose; shares the experiences with the counselee; gives information, including the results of tests; makes suggestions; and takes an active part in planning with the counselee. A client-centered counselor acts more as a catalytic agent. He does less talking, and he spends much of his time listening and encouraging the counselee to express himself.

Virtually all trained counselors now accept the view that a counselee needs a warm, permissive atmosphere for his thinking, unrestricted by overt diagnosis or value judgments on the part of the counselor; that is, all accept the view that the counselee and his needs are the focal point of the counseling, and all desire it to be a growth experience for him—even though it is recognized that sometimes emergency situations arise where temporarily this may not be the main objective.

Counseling, as we have been discussing it, is a very young profession, and its guidelines are by no means determined and agreed upon. There are doubts and differences of opinion as to how much help the counselor should give the counselee.

There is a large and probably growing group of counseling leaders who question whether the counselor should undertake to influence the counselee at all in the decision-making process. It is felt by these persons that counseling can too readily become directive and coercive, and that the main objective, of helping the individual to become a self-sufficient person whose decisions grow out of a realistic concept of himself, may be defeated.

There is, of course, another point of view. This one has been voiced rather timidly by some counselors, particularly the younger ones who are still finding their place in the profession. In general, it has been school administrators and other noncounseling school personnel who have spoken out most vigorously concerning this side of the counseling function. They prefer to see counselors assume responsibility for some activities that are closely related to administration and instruction. It is here that the real issue, so far as an issue exists, is joined.

At the same time, certain guidance leaders have in recent years taken a rather definite view that the counselor does, and inevitably must, influence his counselee. One of the most influential and convincing of these spokesmen is Williamson, who has said, "The history of pedagogy, as well as that of therapy, indicates that some types of direct-assistance from outside the individual's own capacity seem to be needed to achieve inner growth." And, again, "The counselor himself—his style of living —is an important counseling technique. Counselors are in the 'influence business' " (58).

Williamson presents the view that counseling is, and must be, value-oriented, and not open-ended, and that the counselor must make values explicit. In counseling about values, Williamson points out that the student must be helped to understand the options open to him and must be free to make his own choice. In this way, he is in agreement with other counseling authorities that, as Sorenson has pointed out (49), a major goal of personnel workers should continue to be the increasing of the freedom of the individual student to make decisions by introducing him to more rather than fewer alternatives.

However, where a need for therapy is indicated, there is, as Williamson (58) insisted years ago, a question as to whether it is possible for the counselor to avoid direct influence, and a related question as to whether the counselor exerts less influence on behavior when he simply interprets or clarifies than when he predicts, suggests, or advises.

STRENGTHS AND LIMITATIONS OF THE
CLIENT-CENTERED APPROACH

Unquestionably, counseling has seen a great revolution during the last 25 years, and a marked development for the better—a development given great impetus by

Title V of the National Defense Education Act of 1958. It is undoubtedly true that in the past all education, including counseling, has been overdirective. When Rogerian therapy burst upon a startled guidance world in the mid-1940s, attention was centered, first of all, on the most obvious aspect, the techniques. The general reaction tended to be critical toward the neutral role of the counselor. It soon became apparent, however, that this approach should be evaluated on a more professional and more valid basis. Since what was then called "nondirective counseling" was essentially intuitive, it was difficult to evaluate its outcomes objectively. However, favorable evidence for its effectiveness was fairly soon reported in various studies, among which were those of Lipkin (28), Raimy (38), Snyder (48), and Watt (56).

At the same time that the newer approach came into wider and wider acceptance, it was pointed out by some guidance workers that only a comparatively small proportion of the counseling contacts involving students were those where personal, social, or emotional problems were involved. Most of them were educational-vocational —Jones (24), Hahn and Kendall (17). Obviously, when a student goes to his counselor about a minor change in his program or with a request for information about where he could get suggestions for overcoming spelling errors in his written papers, it is hardly appropriate for the counselor to attempt to probe deeply into his emotional life and adjustment or try to have the student work out the answer for himself instead of giving him the simple and direct help he needs. Even in such an uncomplicated counseling situation as this, however, the student, of course, is and should be the center of the process, and the suggestions offered by the counselor should be appropriate for him as an individual.

All this brings us back to the question of how much in the way of direct help or suggestions it is professionally appropriate and ethically right for the counselor to give the student. For example, in the problems of college choice or vocational choice, should the counselor suggest specific colleges or vocations to the individual? In this regard, the actual practice of counselors on the firing line may on occasion be at variance with the position of some of the theorists. In a discussion of whether directiveness or client-centeredness is a desideratum in college counseling, Mink and Sgan (32) said, "Counselors cannot afford to be insensitive to the needs of certain clients for well-structured and positive suggestions." There is always the danger that in the initial stages of the counseling relationship students who feel that they are getting nothing in the way of positive help from the counselor will become discouraged and break contact.

Hitchcock (22) has appropriately called attention to the fact that expanding educational opportunities and the increasing flexibility of the curriculum place an ever greater responsibility on the counselor. One is inclined to wonder whether the very multitude of choices now open to the student does not present such a bewildering situation to some individuals that they desperately need a little assistance in the decision-making process. If they don't get it from the counselor, will they not sometimes be inclined to obtain it from less professional sources? Also, the image of the counselor's role on the part of students needs to be kept in mind. Even college students, as Drasgow (*14*) has pointed out, not infrequently wait for the counselor to approach *them* and offer help.

At the same time, guidance workers must not allow initiative to become disguised coercion. This word of caution is particularly appropriate for guidance in the smaller schools, especially in rural areas, where guidance is likely to be the responsibility of a special teacher rather than a professionally trained counselor. Chase (*10*) pointed out that these teachers need to learn to be less directive, to use a problem-method approach, and to suggest readings which will help the student consider the alternatives among which he must decide, rather than to follow their natural tendency to give direct advice.

In order to be productive, each counseling event must establish a relationship between two individuals directed toward the understanding and eventual resolution of a problem faced by one of them. The prime ingredients are the personality, intelligence, information, and maturity of both parties to the counseling relationship. It may be frustrating and futile to undertake to decide in advance what approach will be taken. In a short, well-stated plea for eclecticism in counseling, Branan (*5*) would have counselors in training thoroughly exposed to the various theories of counseling so that they might choose and apply the best from each theory for the particular client being counseled.

ENTER THE ECLECTIC

Recognizing values in both "directive" and "client-centered" approaches to counseling, many modern personnel workers are taking an eclectic position. They constantly try to keep in mind the advantages and limitations of all schools of counseling and to select, in the case of each counselee, those procedures that seem most appropriate to the immediate situation.

The eclectic point of view was stressed some years ago by Hamrin and Paulson (*18*) in their extensive discussion of counseling. Along a similar line, Cottle (*12*) called attention to some common elements in all systems of counseling. Among these are acceptance of the client as he is; emphasis on growth of the client's capacity to solve his own problems; an atmosphere of frankness and

honesty; breadth and depth of knowledge about people on the part of the successful counselor; ability to handle communication in the interview; changes in the feelings and attitudes of the client, as he progresses in the interviews, from those of confusion, uncertainty, and negation, to those which are organized and positive; and structuring of the limits which are developed to determine how the counseling will proceed.

The majority of the counselors working in present-day schools and colleges are believed to be eclectic in their procedures, regardless of whether theoretically they place themselves in that category.

SIMILARITIES AND DIFFERENCES IN COUNSELING VIEWPOINT AND PRACTICE—A RECAPITULATION

All counseling worthy of the name is client-centered, in that the counseling is based upon the counselee and his needs. Counseling that is not thus oriented is pointless and perhaps worse than useless. Counselees are by common consent the focal point of the process. However, this does not mean that counseling is necessarily "client-centered" in a narrow, technical sense.

But a real difference exists in approaches to and procedures of the counseling relationship. A large and growing group of theorists and professional counselors—the present-day counterpart of the nondirective school—believe that counseling should be largely unstructured, or at any rate that it should derive such structuring as takes place from the emergent interests, desires, needs, and problems as expressed by the counselee in his relationship with the counselor. A convincing word-picture of the kind of "client-centered" counseling that may be carried on by a trained and mature counselor or therapist has been presented by Rogers:

> It would mean that the therapist feels this client to be a person of unconditional self-worth: of value no matter what his condition, his behavior, or his feelings. It would mean that the therapist is genuine, hiding behind no defensive façade, but meeting the client with the feelings he is experiencing. It would mean that the therapist is able to let himself go in understanding this client; that no inner barriers keep him from sensing what it feels like to be the client at each moment of the relationship; and that he can convey something of this empathetic understanding to the client. It means that the therapist has been comfortable in entering this relationship fully, without knowing cognitively where it will lead, satisfied with providing a climate which will permit the client the utmost freedom to become himself.[1]

Clearly, this level of counseling is an ideal growth relationship, which can hardly be reached in actual prac-

[1] Reprinted from Carl R. Rogers' *On Becoming a Person*, pp. 184–185. Boston: Houghton Mifflin Company, 1961. (Used with permission of the author and the publisher.)

tice even by many counselors with extensive professional training. Many guidance workers, administrators, and laymen believe that most counselors will succeed better if they structure the relationship to a somewhat greater extent and if they begin with a basis of objective data concerning their counselees—data of which test scores are an important aspect, but only one aspect. The devotees of unstructured, or nonstructured, counseling tend to see this approach as a weakness, as evidence of insecurity in the counselor, and a desire on his part to achieve a sense of security by exerting dominance over the counselee. Such an imputation of motives would be difficult to justify. Many guidance workers sincerely believe that they can be more effective in helping the counselee if they bring to the relationship some objective information about the individual's abilities, achievements, and interests, and if they are able to draw on this knowledge in the counseling interview.

Majority theory no doubt supports the former viewpoint, but it is believed that majority practice in American schools is more nearly in line with the latter belief. The question is not which group is the more devoted to or understanding of the high calling of counseling, or which one has the greater faith in the individual young person as he searches for understanding of himself and his relationship to the environment. The question is a more practical one. Regardless of what may be ideal in theory or in the advanced practice of some leaders, can we, at the present stage of the development of guidance, expect each one of the thousands of guidance workers in our schools to be a psychotherapist, a psychiatrist without portfolio, or even a knowledgeable psychologist?

Great progress has been made since mid-century, and a still more advanced stage will be reached, but some objective-oriented guidance persons continue to believe that, for the present, most counselors can advantageously structure their counseling interviews at least to some extent through the use of the objective information available to them in the student's cumulative record. They hope that this information will give them at least some indication of the uniqueness of each counselee and enable them to approach the individual helpfully in terms of the kind of person he is. This brings us full circle, back to the eclectic.

COUNSELING AS A LEARNING FUNCTION

The tendency of many counselors in educational institutions to assume an eclectic position in their work is believed to be desirable as far as it goes. But eclecticism, in itself, is hardly enough. The eclectic is an opportunist and a borrower. He has no definite philosophy around which to orient his work. He needs some guideposts of his own.

The concept of counseling as a learning activity may furnish the kind of orientation he needs. This concept may be a mutually agreeable meeting ground for the different schools of counseling. Williamson, representing the scientific approach to counseling, has said "To me, the counselor may be thought of as a special kind of teacher, with primary concern for the individual's personality development, normal and deviate as well" (57).

In his book, *Client-centered Therapy*, Rogers included a chapter on "Student-centered Teaching," in which he stressed the close relationship that is possible between client-centered counseling and learning. In discussing the instructor who takes the client-centered approach, Rogers says, "He has confidence in the fact that, in this atmosphere which he has helped to create, a type of learning takes place which is personally meaningful and which feeds the total self-development of the individual as well as improves his acquaintance with a given field of knowledge" (43).

In the first chapter of their book, *Student Personnel Work as Deeper Teaching*, Lloyd-Jones and Smith called attention to the relationship between guidance and teaching in these words, "This book attempts to set forth the view that student personnel workers should not so much be expert technicians as they should be educators in a somewhat unconventional and new sense. Student personnel workers have many opportunities through their work to contribute to the development of students, to help them learn many lessons and skills of vital importance for their fulfillment as whole persons within a democratic society" (30:12).

The Pepinskys, likewise, stated a theory of counseling as a learning situation in which the modification of the counselee's behavior takes place. They said at one point, "To bridge the gap between present and past and future behavior, or between behavior inside and outside the counseling situation, linking hypothetical constructs are needed. The concept of learning provides one such connection" (34:71). And, further on, they stated that "the counseling situation is conceived as one where distinctly social learning can take place and where a significant function of the counselor is to facilitate that social learning" (34:143).

In an article discussing similarities and differences between psychotherapy and education, Symonds said, "With the passage of years, the function of psychotherapy is conceived to be that of assisting in belated personality development, while education, too, has accepted greater responsibility for the all-round development of the individual instead of for isolated segments of his personality. Methods of the two disciplines, too, have become more and more alike until some writers suggest that they are almost identical" (54:61).

It is evident that a good many leaders in personnel work are now thinking along somewhat similar lines. The time may now be appropriate for rather detailed and explicit discussion of the concept that counseling is a learning experience—or if one prefers to state the matter in reverse, the concept that instruction may well draw upon and utilize the procedures of counseling which are largely client-centered along the lines of the classroom method advocated by Cantor (9).

If one inquires into the history of counseling in the United States, he will note that this kind of service developed later than, and somewhat aside from, the instructional program. In the earlier stages of personnel work, it was thought that counseling should help solve students' personal and vocational problems that interfered with learning, but that the function of counseling was different from that of instruction. Thus, an unfortunate dualism developed, with counseling in a secondary and often definitely subordinate position in relation to instruction.

As personnel work has matured, however, and as the aims and processes of education have, at the same time, been re-examined, it has become increasingly clear that, when the objectives of education are stated and analyzed, the important objectives stress the growth and development of the individual and draw upon principles of guidance as fully as they do upon principles of learning. The ultimate purposes of counselors and teachers are not only similar, they are virtually identical. Not only do the aims of instruction and counseling coincide, but their processes likewise have identical elements. The classroom furnishes an important environment for the appraisal of the individual, for his character development, and for his formulation of life goals. Similarly, the educational possibilities of the personnel program—health, social adjustment, group activities, vocational exploration, and so forth—are almost unlimited.

While emphasis will properly be determined by the primary responsibility of the individual staff member, to an increasing degree the activities of instructors are taking on the functions of both instruction and personnel work without changing appreciably the fundamental long-term educational goals.

Arbuckle (2) called attention to the fact that the teacher is traditionally involved with product and ideas rather than with process and people. The educator must learn to function to a large degree as a counselor rather than as an educator alone.

Counseling is the central process by means of which

guidance of the individual student is carried on. Counseling lends meaning and purpose to guidance. The most important long-term purpose of counseling is to improve the adjustment and self-reliance of the counselee so that he will develop increasing ability to solve his own problems. This is also a major aim of teaching.

It should be emphasized that a great deal of learning necessarily takes place before counseling can be carried to a successful conclusion. Counseling is a learning experience for both the counselor and the counselee. Let us first consider the kinds of learning that are required of the counselor.

THE COUNSELOR'S LEARNING

The counselor must, in the first place, acquire what is often a new set of attitudes toward the counseling function. A new counselor, or one who is preparing for counseling either through graduate courses or through in-service training, usually undergoes this kind of experience. Often his first inclination, particularly if he enters the field of counseling after experience as an instructor, is to assume a somewhat directive and dominating role in his relationship with his counselees. Many writers have referred to the difficulties that counselors who come from teaching have in overcoming an authoritarian approach. This tendency is increased by the fact that many students who turn to the counselor for assistance expect him to assume this kind of role and almost thrust it upon him.

The counselor usually finds, however, that he is able to make a larger contribution to individual development if he plays a secondary role, or if, at any rate, he is willing to meet the counselee on an equal footing. Thus, the counselor gradually relinquishes his earlier concepts concerning his relationship with students, and replaces them as time goes on with concepts and attitudes more appropriate to the counseling situation. In other words, he develops a new concept of himself and a new understanding of the position of the counselee. For, as Yates and Schmidt (63) indicated, many of the pressures, anxieties, and tensions felt by the client may also be experienced to a degree by the counselor in training.

The counselor must, in the second place, learn a variety of techniques for the collection and summarization of information about individuals. He needs to learn the nature and purposes, the uses and limitations, of the main counseling tools and tests, and to acquire much information concerning, and experience with, a number of specific tests of each kind. For instance, it is generally assumed that a counselor of school or college students will be intimately acquainted with such common and widely-used measures as the School and College Ability

Test, the Otis Quick-Scoring Mental Ability Test, the California Test of Mental Maturity, the Kuhlmann-Anderson Tests, the Diagnostic Reading Tests, the Davis Reading Tests, the Cooperative English Test, the Iowa Tests of Basic Skills, the Differential Aptitude Tests, the Strong Vocational Interest Blanks, the Kuder Preference Records—Vocational and Personal, the Minnesota Multiphasic Personality Inventory, and many other instruments for the measurement of mental ability, achievement, aptitudes, interests, and personal qualities.

The counselor needs to learn how to choose tests that are appropriate for a given measurement situation, either group or individual. For instance, assume that a student has sought the advice of his counselor because of uncertainty with regard to vocational goals. If it develops in the interview that testing is needed and mutually agreed upon, the counselor will probably find it desirable to begin with an instrument which measures interests in broad fields and to follow this measure up with tests of aptitude in areas where the greatest concentration of interests appears to be, or to employ portions of an aptitude test battery such as the Flanagan Aptitude Classification Tests.

It is desirable, too, for the counselor to learn about less formal procedures for collecting information: anecdotal records, self-inventories of personal qualities, and even projective techniques, such as the Thematic Apperception Test and the Rorschach—although the use of the last instrument calls for intensive training which many counselors have not had an opportunity to obtain. It is helpful for the counselor to learn thoroughly the technique of writing and summarizing anecdotal records and of training others to prepare records of this kind.

The counselor must learn how to bring all these kinds of information together on cumulative records, and how to interpret each record in terms of the growth of the individual as well as his status.

Some authorities on counseling fear that tests and other kinds of objective or semiobjective information will be used by poorly trained counselors as devices to place them in authority over students. This danger does exist, but the better corrective procedure is not to discard valuable tools but to redouble efforts to train counselors in their proper use.

In the third place, the counselor must learn the technique of the interview. He needs to know how to use the interview for various purposes: to collect information, to give information, to maintain personal contact with counselees and give them an opportunity to raise questions, to uncover problems, and to consult with counselees about educational, vocational, and personal problems. The counselor must learn to adapt interview techniques so that they are suited to his own personality rather than

copied from someone else, however successful the other person may be. He needs to know how to put the counselee at ease gracefully and, at the same time, get down to the business of the interview without loss of time. He needs to learn how to encourage an outgoing attitude and a tendency to take the lead on the part of the counselee and, at the same time, to keep control of the interview so that it does not degenerate into an aimless discussion.

In the case of counselee-initiated interviews, the counselor must learn how to "size up" the motives of the counselee and to sense whether the problem which the counselee first brings up is the main one or whether the problem is only a kind of trial balloon which the counselee sends up while he is deciding and mustering his courage to begin talking about the real problem. The manner and understanding of the counselor may determine whether or not the counselee will bring the real problem out into the open at all.

The following are among the more important suggestions that the counselor may well keep in mind in learning interview techniques:

Form the habit of preparing carefully for each regularly scheduled interview. Go over the counselee's cumulative record with care beforehand. Pay particular attention to evidences of growth. However, do not let the habit of careful preparation interfere with the need to see counselees immediately when they bring pressing problems for discussion.

Begin the interview on a friendly and informal note, but maintain a businesslike atmosphere and get on with the main purpose of the interview without loss of time.

Encourage the counselee to do most of the talking. If the counselee expresses himself fully, the counselor's opportunity to learn about him and his problems is increased, and often the counselee begins to achieve insight through self-expression. At the same time, the counselor should not hesitate to enter into the interview where he can contribute to the counselee's thinking and where entry seems necessary in order to bring the discussion back on the main track.

Take a permissive and understanding attitude but maintain an objective point of view. Help the counselee to understand and to keep clearly in mind that he himself has the main responsibility for the solution of his problem.

Toward the end of the interview, summarize the discussion and help the counselee identify the essentials of his problem and plan a course of action. This planning should be a cooperative procedure between the counselor and the counselee.

End the interview on as constructive a note as circumstances permit. Either schedule a follow-up interview or leave the door open for future counseling interviews at the discretion of the counselee.

In the fourth place, and most important, counseling is a learning experience for the counselor in the sense that he must strive constantly throughout the counseling process to learn everything he can about the individual counselee. It is a long-standing and somewhat shopworn axiom of individualized education that "before you teach a pupil you must first learn him." Similarly, before you counsel a student you must first learn as much as you can about the kind of individual he is. This learning comes about through a study of the individual's background; through reports of other instructors, both oral and written; through additions to and interpretation of items in the individual's cumulative record; through interviews with the student, and, on occasion, with his parents; and at times through staff conferences, where all available information about the individual is pooled and interpreted. Learning about the individual also takes place in successive interviews during the counseling process. Oftentimes, counseling and diagnosis, or learning about the counselee, go forward together.

Except in rare cases where the finding of an immediate answer for a crucial problem outweighs everything else, the growth and self-improvement of the counselee is a more important consideration than questions which are raised by either the counselor or the counselee as the immediate subject of counseling. The counselor must learn patience. He must restrain his natural impulse to show the student at once what the counselor believes to be the right way. Time must be allowed for the counselor to study the counselee, for the counselee to study and understand himself, and for decisions to mature.

THE COUNSELEE'S LEARNING

Now let us examine the learning process of the counselee—that is, the student's learning in a counseling situation.

The process of learning for the counselee is even more extensive than for the counselor, but in some respects, the two are parallel. *At the outset, the counselee, like the counselor, needs to learn a new set of attitudes.* The counselee is likely, in the beginning, to think of the counselor either as a minor disciplinarian who will call him in for a serious talk if he gets into trouble, or as a person to whom he can go with a problem and quickly obtain a ready-made solution. It is necessary for him to learn that, as a rule, the counselor has no disciplinary function, and also that the counselor is not a trouble shooter who will listen to a student's tale of his difficulties and then come up with a quick answer.

At first, the counselee tends to think of the counselor as one who *advises* rather than *counsels*. He may go to the counselor, state a problem which is troubling him, and then in effect say, "Well, there it is. What do I do now? Your business is to advise students, isn't it?" He will learn that a wise and well-trained counselor does not allow himself to make the counselee's problems his own or to become emotionally involved with the counselee, but instead uses his experience and training in helping the counselee think through his problem and work out his own solution. He will discover that the counselor, because of his greater knowledge and experience, is ready and able to make suggestions at appropriate points and even to guide the counselee's thinking at times, but that he never, or almost never, tells the counselee exactly what to do. "The professional counselor does not counsel anybody into anything; he helps people reach their own decisions about what to do" (*14*). At first, the counselee may find this a new and perhaps baffling concept of the counseling relationship; it is only through personal experience that he learns that this is the best way.

A second area of learning for a student who is introduced to a personnel program has to do with certain group procedures. He is likely to come into contact with these procedures soon after he enters the institution. In a strict sense, these group relationships are not counseling at all, for counseling ordinarily takes place where just two individuals—the counselor and a single counselee —are involved. Group guidance, or group learning, however, is closely related to counseling in that the group work will meet certain general problems of many of the students and thus reduce the need for individual counseling.

Among the kinds of group guidance which provide learning situations for counselees are meetings to orient them to the life of the institution, courses providing orientation and exploration in the field of the vocations, and courses of training in study habits and skills—including corrective reading for individuals who are retarded in reading ability.

Many students need special help with the development of efficient study procedures, elementary processes of English expression, arithmetic, and spelling, which ought to have been learned much earlier. It is in reading, however, that the need is particularly acute. Ability to read well is essential to adjustment to all educational levels above the primary grades. Knowledge of and facility in work-type reading skills grow in importance as the student advances through the school, until at the college and adult levels these are among the first essentials for the mastery of an educational program. A student whose reading is markedly retarded will almost inevitably have problems of personal and social adjustment. Similarly, a student who is badly adjusted emotionally may have reading difficulties on that account. A reading specialist cooperating in the counseling program can do much to help solve some of the more difficult adjustment cases.

A third area of learning for the counselee has to do with the meaning of various kinds of devices used to appraise him. He needs to learn what tests of intelligence, achievement, interests, and personal qualities are designed to do, and to understand that the results of these measures are useful in counseling him only if he gives full cooperation and follows all instructions faithfully when they are administered to him. He needs to learn the meaning of such concepts as converted scores and percentiles. Even percentiles, which are perhaps the simplest basis for acquainting counselees with their test results, are often misunderstood because they are confused with percentage grades.

The counselee needs to learn the uses and limitations of tests of specific aptitudes and inventories of interests and personality. Results of measures of interests, for example, are nearly always regarded by counselees as indicative of aptitude unless the difference is carefully explained to them.

Further, the counselee needs to understand how the entries on his cumulative record are interrelated and how they provide a continuing picture of his growth and development. If his test results are recorded cumulatively in graphic form, a careful explanation of the basis of the graph is required. While certain concepts important for the test specialist, such as standard errors of scores and the effect of regression on test results, can hardly be made explicit for the average counselee, still he can with practice acquire a reasonably effective understanding of the interpretation of his own record and an understanding of the need for considering these data in relation to the other information on his cumulative record.

A fourth area of learning, and the most important of these, is the student himself. Through interviews with his counselor the student can clarify his own self-concept, and by means of available measures he can check various aspects of this concept quantitatively. He needs to assess as objectively as possible his general ability, his special aptitudes, his achievement in different areas of study, his interests, and his personal qualities. Senior high school pupils and college students should have access to their own test results (with the possible exception of IQs and data on clinical measures in the field of personality), and they should have ample opportunity to learn through discussion with their counselor the interpretation of the test information about themselves. In this connection,

it should be kept in mind by both the counselor and the counselee that national norms may not be as appropriate a basis for interpretation as norms derived for different educational or occupational groups.

The counselee's learning about himself is a continuous process and is, of course, the key to all intelligent long-term planning.

Finally, counseling is a learning function because, if it is successfully carried on, the counselee learns a new way of thinking about himself and about his problems and plans. He learns to weigh evidence concerning himself and the possibilities open to him impersonally, to reach his own decisions, if not independently at least with full understanding that they are *his* decisions, and to act upon these decisions in a mature manner. If counselors succeed in leading their counselees to adopt this kind of behavior habitually in reaching decisions and to carry such behavior over into later life, this accomplishment alone will make counseling one of the most important of all the learning experiences educational institutions provide for their students.

In conclusion, it is hoped that this discussion will help teacher-counselors appreciate that counseling is basically a learning function, subject in large measure to the same laws of learning which are applicable in the classroom, but with the emphasis not on subject matter but on the growth process of the individual student. This view of counseling will remove much of the vagueness and mystery from counseling activities, and will naturally and inevitably lead to the integration of these activities with the instructional program of the institution.

REFERENCES

1. Allen, Frederick H. *Psychotherapy with Children.* New York: W. W. Norton & Company, 1942. Pp. 331.
2. Arbuckle, Dugald S. "The Learning of Counseling: Process Not Product," *Journal of Counseling Psychology,* X (Summer 1963), 163–168.
3. Berdie, Ralph F.; Layton, Wilbur L.; Swanson, Edward O.; and Hagenah, Theda. *Counseling and the Use of Tests: A Manual for the State-wide Testing Programs of Minnesota.* Minneapolis: The University of Minnesota, 1959. Pp. 178.
4. Bergstein, Harry B., and Grant, Claude W. "How Parents Perceive the Counselor's Role," *Personnel and Guidance Journal,* XXXIX (May 1961), 698–703.
5. Branan, John M. "Eclecticism in Counseling," *Vocational Guidance Quarterly,* XII (Spring 1964), 208–209.
6. Brant, Richard M. "Self: Missing Link for Understand-

ing Behavior," *Mental Hygiene*, XL (January 1957), 24–33.

7. Buckham, Kenneth. "Junior High School Counselor: Herself and Her Work," *Journal of the National Association of Deans of Women and Counselors*, XX (October 1963), 7–14.

8. Callis, Robert. "Counseling," *Review of Educational Research*, XXXIII (April 1963), 179–187.

9. Cantor, Nathaniel. *Dynamics of Learning*. Buffalo, N.Y.: Foster and Stewart Publishing Corp., 1950. Pp. x + 296.

10. Chase, Harold. "Problem Method and Nondirective Guidance," *Agricultural Education Magazine*, XXXVI (January 1964), 132–133.

11. Clark, Francis E. "The Counselee Is a Learner," *Junior College Journal*, XXV (May 1955), 537–541.

12. Cottle, William C. "Some Common Elements in Counseling," *Personnel and Guidance Journal*, XXXII (September 1953), 4–8.

13. Drasgow, James. "College Graduates Ask for More Counseling," *Vocational Guidance Quarterly*, VI (Spring 1958), 124–126.

14. Drasgow, James. "Are You Counseling or Advising," *Vocational Guidance Quarterly*, VII (Spring 1959), 193–195.

15. Evraiff, William. *Helping Counselors Grow Professionally—A Casebook for Counselors*. Englewood Cliffs, N.J.: Prentice-Hall, Inc., 1963. Pp. 376.

16. Goldman, Leo. *Using Tests in Counseling*. New York: Appleton-Century-Crofts, Inc., 1961. Pp. 434.

17. Hahn, Milton E., and Kendall, William E. "Some Comments in Defense of 'Non-Nondirective' Counseling," *Journal of Consulting Psychology*, XI (April 1946), 74–81.

18. Hamrin, Shirley A., and Paulson, Blanche B. *Counseling Adolescents*. Chicago: Science Research Associates, Inc., 1950. Pp. x + 372.

19. Harmon, Donald, and Arnold, Dwight L. "High School Counselors Evaluate Their Formal Preparation," *Personnel and Guidance Journal*, XXXIX (December 1960), 303–306.

20. Harrison, Edna L. "The Elementary School Counselor and the Gifted Underachiever," *Personnel and Guidance Journal*, XLI (April 1963), 716–719.

21. Hill, George E., and Green, Donald A. "The Selection, Preparation, and Professionalization of Guidance and Personnel Workers," *Review of Educational Research*, XXX (April 1960), 115–130.

22. Hitchcock, Arthur A. "The Counselor Looks at the Secondary School Curriculum," *Bulletin of the National Association of Secondary-School Principals*, XLVII (April 1963), 62–68.

23. Hobbs, Nicholas. "The Compleat Counselor," *Personnel and Guidance Journal*, XXXVI (May 1958), 594–602.

24. Jones, Edward S. "Gradations of Directiveness in Counseling," *Educational and Psychological Measurement*, VII (Autumn 1947), 559–563.

25. Kaplan, Bernard A. "The New Counselor and His Professional Problems," *Personnel and Guidance Journal*, XLII (January 1964), 473–478.

26. Keppers, George L. "Selection (If Any) of Graduate Students in Guidance and Counseling," *Vocational Guidance Quarterly*, IX (Winter 1960–1961), 90–94.

27. Kindig, Waldro J. "The Principal Looks at the Counselor's Role in the Curriculum," *Bulletin of the National Association of Secondary-School Principals*, XLVII (April 1963), 68–71.

28. Lipkin, Stanley. "The Client Evaluates Nondirective Psychotherapy," *Journal of Consulting Psychology*, XII (June 1948), 137–146.

29. Livingston, Inez B. "Is the Personnel Worker Liable?" *Personnel and Guidance Journal*, XLIII (January 1965), 471–474.

30. Lloyd-Jones, Esther, and Smith, Margaret R. (eds.). *Student Personnel Work as Deeper Teaching*. New York: Harper & Row, Publishers, 1954. Pp. xii + 362.

31. McGowan, John F., and Schmidt, Lyle D. *Counseling: Readings in Theory and Practice*. New York: Holt, Rinehart and Winston, Inc., 1962. Pp. 637.

32. Mink, Oscar G., and Sgan, Mathew. "Does Counselor Approach Really Matter?" *Vocational Guidance Quarterly*, XI (Spring 1963), 204–206.

33. Olsen, LeRoy C. "Success for New Counselors," *Journal of Counseling Psychology*, X (Winter 1963), 350–355.

34. Pepinsky, Harold B., and Pepinsky, Pauline Nichols. *Counseling: Theory and Practice*. New York: The Ronald Press Company, 1954. Pp. viii + 308.

35. Peters, Herman J., and Mueller, William J. "The Counseling Function," *Review of Educational Research*, XXX (April 1960), 131–140.

36. Pierson, George A., and Grant, Claude W. "The Road Ahead for the School Counselor," *Personnel and Guidance Journal*, XXXVIII (November 1959), 207–210.

37. Pohlman, Edward, and Robinson, Francis P. "Client Reaction to Some Aspects of the Counseling Situation," *Personnel and Guidance Journal*, XXXVIII (March 1960), 546–551.

38. Raimy, Victor C. "Self Reliance in Counseling Interviews," *Journal of Consulting Psychology*, XII (June 1948), 153–163.

39. Rank, Otto. *Truth and Reality: A Life History of the Human Will* (trans. by Jessie Taft). New York: Alfred A. Knopf, Inc., 1936. Pp. x + 194.

40. Rank, Otto. *Will Therapy: An Analysis of the Therapeutic Processes* (trans. by Jessie Taft). New York: Alfred A. Knopf, Inc., 1945. Pp. 208.

41. Rogers, Carl R. *Counseling and Psychotherapy*. Boston: Houghton Mifflin Company, 1942. Pp. xiv + 450.

42. Rogers, Carl R. "The Attitude and Orientation of the Counselor in Client-centered Therapy," *Journal of Consulting Psychology*, XIII (April 1949), 82–94.

43. Rogers, Carl R. *Client-centered Therapy*. Boston: Houghton Mifflin Company, 1959. Pp. 560.

44. Rogers, Carl R. *On Becoming a Person*. Boston: Houghton Mifflin Company, 1961. Pp. 420.

45. Rothney, John W. M. "Counseling Does Help!" *Vocational Guidance Quarterly*, VI (Autumn 1957), 15–18.

46. Routh, Thomas A. "The Importance of 'Body' Language in Counseling," *Vocational Guidance Quarterly*, VI (Spring 1958), 134–137.

47. Sherman, Robert. "The School Counselor: Generalist or Specialist?" *Counselor Education and Supervision*, I (Summer 1962), 203–211.

48. Snyder, William U. "An Investigation of the Nature of Nondirective Psychotherapy," *Journal of General Psychology*, XXXIII (October 1945), 193–223.

49. Sorenson, Garth. "Pterodactyls, Passenger Pigeons, and Personnel Workers," *Personnel and Guidance Journal*, XLIII (January 1965), 430–437.

50. Stefflre, Buford, King, Paul, and Leafgren, Fred. "Characteristics of Counselors Judged Effective by Their Peers," *Journal of Counseling Psychology*, XI (Winter 1964), 335–340.

51. Stewart, C. C. "A Bill of Rights for School Counselors," *Personnel and Guidance Journal*, XXXVII (March 1959), 500–503.

52. Stiller, Alfred. "The High School Guidance Counselor," *Bulletin of the National Association of Secondary-School Principals*, XLV (May 1961), 150–159.

53. Strang, Ruth. "What Does Research Say About Techniques?" *Journal of the National Association of Deans of Women and Counselors*, XVIII (June 1955), 162–166.

54. Symonds, Percival M. "Education and Psychotherapy," *Journal of Educational Psychology*, XL (January 1949), 1–32.

55. Tyler, Leona E. *The Work of the Counselor*, 2nd ed. New York: Appleton-Century-Crofts, Inc., 1961. Pp. xvi + 327.

56. Watt, George D. "An Evaluation of Nondirective Counseling in the Treatment of Delinquents," *Journal of Educational Research*, XLII (January 1949), 343–352.

57. Williamson, E. G. "Counseling and the Minnesota 'Point of View,'" *Educational and Psychological Measurement*, VII (Spring 1947), 141–155.

58. Williamson, E. G. "Directive versus Nondirective Counseling," *California Journal of Secondary Education*, XXV (October 1950), 332–336.

59. Williamson, E. G. "Preventive Aspects of Disciplinary Counseling," *Educational and Psychological Measurement*, XVI (Spring 1956), 68–81.

60. Williamson, E. G. "Value Orientation in Counseling," *Personnel and Guidance Journal*, XXXVII (April 1958), 520–528.

61. Williamson, E. G. "The Meaning of Communication in Counseling," *Personnel and Guidance Journal*, XXXVIII (September 1959), 6–14.

62. Williamson, E. G. "The Counselor as Technique," *Personnel and Guidance Journal*, XLI (October 1962), 108–111.

63. Yates, J. W., and Schmidt, Lyle D. "The Counselor's Self-Concept," *Vocational Guidance Quarterly*, VII (Spring 1959), 151–154.

64. Kruger, Albert H. "Counselor Holding Power: Clinical vs. Client-Centered," *Personnel and Guidance Journal*, XLIII (June 1965), 981–984.

CHAPTER XX

Group Work in Guidance

THE MAIN EMPHASIS IN THIS BOOK IS UPON guidance of the *individual*, as it must be in any serious discussion of guidance services. In the totality of his aptitudes, experience, environment, understandings, emotional needs and drives, and aspirations, each individual is a unique entity which finds no exact counterpart in any other individual. An intelligent personnel program can never lose sight of this uniqueness.

Yet, individuals have much in common. Young people of the same age and grade level, living in the same community, are alike in many ways. They have shared numerous experiences, their lives are to some extent molded by similar environmental influences, and they are concerned with many of the same problems. And subgroups, determined on the basis of sex, interests, vocational goals, or a variety of other factors, consist of individuals who are still more alike than young people in general. Guidance workers need to be aware of these common denominators, which help to determine natural groupings, and to take advantage of them. The dynamics of the group may contribute to individual development over and beyond the guidance worker's own influence.

GROWING ATTENTION TO GROUP GUIDANCE

Although some group guidance activities have been carried on ever since guidance services were begun in schools, attention to group work has increased in recent years. Periodic summaries of the literature carried on during the last 15 or 20 years, such as those in the *Review of Educational Research*, list numerous articles and monographs on group guidance, group counseling,

and group therapy. Koile (47) indicated that group activities were probably the most prevalent guidance services in contemporary schools. Support for this impression is found in the many studies and articles dealing with group guidance in recent years. Colleges may have less interest in group guidance, as suggested in a report of a survey by Headley (36), but even so a considerable number of reports of group work at the college level have been made available. It is obvious that certain aspects of the college environment, such as residence halls, furnish a ready-made locus for a variety of group activities, but it is especially at the secondary school level that many kinds of experiments in group guidance are blossoming in abundance.

WHY GROUP GUIDANCE?

An important reason why there is so much attention to group work in guidance is, of course, that it saves time in dealing with matters that are common to the pupils. In many schools, understaffed guidance services are overburdened with an ever-growing number of counselees, and guidance functionaries see no possibility of handling all problems through individual counseling. Often they are driven, out of sheer necessity, to carry on some of their guidance activities with groups, regardless of their own judgment concerning the relative merits of individual and group work. For instance, Hobbs (37) called attention to the advisability of using group therapeutic methods because of the comparatively small number of trained workers available to aid the many persons needing their services.

A *second reason* is that group work is naturally suited to certain kinds of guidance activity, particularly those which are basically instructional in character—such as the furnishing of information about occupations or helping new students learn about the school. The need for individual instruction is no greater under these conditions than it is in algebra or general science; in both kinds of situations individual attention is frequently called for within the framework of the group.

A third reason, as Woolf and Woolf (85) pointed out, is that a group approach helps an individual to discover that others have needs and problems similar to his. Moreover, as mentioned by Hoppock (38), group guidance focuses collective attention on common problems. In this way it may help an individual more readily find a solution for a problem than he could if he went at it alone, even under the guidance of a friendly, permissive counselor.

A *fourth reason* for group guidance is that it may be used to prepare the way for individual counseling. Rapport may be more readily established with a student, and his understanding quickened, if he is oriented through group procedures before individual counseling is begun. In a controlled study carried on by Richardson and Borow (63), for example, individual counseling following group orientation was compared with individual counseling not preceded by group orientation; the results favored the oriented group on 19 of 25 criteria, and the differences on 6 of these were statistically significant.

All the reasons for group guidance thus far mentioned stress the value of group work as a substitute for or an aid to individual guidance. But there is a *fifth reason* for group work, which in the view of many psychologists justifies group activity in its own right. These workers stress the therapeutic character of discussion, of thinking and searching for values within a group of one's own peers. Here the focus is not upon information but upon attitudes, emotions, motivations, self-concepts, and the whole range of personality qualities. This is peculiarly the habitat and the happy experimental ground of group psychotherapy, sociometry, psychodrama, sociodrama, and group dynamics. No one can be entirely sure what is coming forth of demonstrated value, but the vocabulary of this area is expansive and impressive, and the possibilities are intriguing.

The reason the possibilities are intriguing is that they hold out some promise that group work in guidance, expertly carried on, is not merely a short cut, a makeshift, a substitute for individual counseling, but a new thing, a self-justifying entity, a unique contribution, a complement to individual work. A good deal more research will be needed before one can say just how rosy this particular horizon is.

While there is, for all these reasons and others, a generally favorable attitude toward making the most of group work in guidance, occasional current commentary on the place of group guidance in our schools is somewhat less than enthusiastic. For example, Koile (47), in the article mentioned earlier in this chapter, recognized the worth of group guidance objectives and procedures, but he regretted that we have in our schools a dual program of group work—group guidance and classroom instruction. He urged that the aims and functions of group activities in guidance be incorporated into a more adequate concept and practice of instruction. He indicated that if this were done there would be no need for activities called "group guidance." Wide acceptance of this viewpoint and an attempt to apply it would seem to imply a renewed emphasis on the development of teacher-counselors in the program of teacher-training institutions.

THE STATUS OF GROUP WORK IN GUIDANCE

ASSUMED VALUES

Although group procedures are widely used in guidance programs, the values of these procedures are, for the most part, assumed rather than demonstrated. A statement made by Hoppock in his book some years ago is still applicable today: "Up to the present time, most of what has been done in group guidance has been done because it seemed like a good idea. Only in rare instances has anyone attempted to find out whether or not the anticipated results were in fact achieved" (38).

That the worth of group work in guidance is not established by extensive research does not, however, set group guidance off from individual counseling. Most of what is done in the guidance field arises out of a combination of reasoning and faith, rather than out of certain knowledge that these particular procedures are beneficial to either the individual or the group.

But it may appropriately be pointed out that the opportunities for research on the outcomes of group guidance are probably superior to those for research on the values of individual counseling. Statistical techniques are more readily applied to the group than to the individual. That full advantage is not being taken of these opportunities is brought out by reviews of research on group procedures in guidance published during the past 20 years (1, 24, 48, 49, 75, 80, 88, 89). All call attention to the dearth of research in this area and make suggestions concerning kinds of research that can profitably be conducted.

CONFUSION IN TERMINOLOGY

As is often true of a field experiencing growing pains, there is lack of clarity in the terminology applied to different kinds of group work in guidance. In some places, the group work is called "group counseling," although until recently specialists in the field tended to be critical of this term, since counseling is traditionally a relationship between two individuals—a counselor and a counselee. However, the term "group guidance" received ready acceptance by guidance workers. It is a more inclusive term than "group counseling," and covers preparatory and orientation activities, as well as courses having to do with occupations. Though, in a review of research on group procedures after 1960, Wright (89) found that "group counseling" received by far the greatest attention of the activities of group guidance, and that "the attention given to group counseling was accompanied by greater acceptance of this procedure as a valid concept of counseling per se." As mentioned by Bonney and Foley (7), the increased demand for public school counseling, along with the shortage of personnel, have created a demand for group counseling.

Froehlich (23) proposed the term "multiple counseling" to designate individual counseling carried on in a group, and he sponsored some research along this line, as is noted in another section of this chapter. There do not seem to be many references to "multiple counseling" in recent literature, perhaps because "multiple counseling is often regarded as synonymous with "group counseling," the more familiar term.

Due in part to the entrance of increasing numbers of clinical psychologists into the guidance field, there have recently been many references to "group therapy" in guidance. Just where "group guidance" leaves off and "group therapy" begins is anyone's guess. There is no clear dividing line between the two, although there are differences in comprehensiveness and in emphasis. As Redl (60) pointed out, the use of the term "group therapy" requires recognition of a psychology of group life. There would probably be general agreement with the viewpoint of Lifton that group therapy in an educational setting may be considered to be operating in any group where the *emphasis* is upon providing members of the group with opportunities to explore their own feelings and attitudes, rather than upon the imparting of information (48:156). This emphasis is also present in group counseling, although probably not to the same degree. Group counseling may be regarded as standing between classroom instruction and group therapy and as sharing the purposes and procedures of both.

Along with group therapy, "group dynamics" is another term somewhat foreign to the everyday language of guidance. Not only so, but group dynamics carries within its field other rare terms which are peculiarly its own, such as "syntality" (group personality) and "synergy" (total energy of the group).

Caldwell and Mahler (11), proposed that group guidance, group counseling, and group therapy be distinguished on the basis of meaningful differences in process and in group composition.

As an overall term embracing the entire field under discussion, the phrase "group work in guidance" would seem to be inclusive enough and innocuous enough to satisfy almost everyone.

GENERAL PURPOSES OF GROUP WORK

Wrenn (86) proposed that the counselor should become aware of the value of the various kinds of group learning experiences, and that he should locate between classroom group guidance and group psychotherapy the particular job of the counselor in using planned group experiences to supplement individual counseling.

The purposes of group work in guidance are of four main kinds. One important purpose is the *orientation* of individuals to an unfamiliar environment or to new experiences. For a good many years, both colleges and large secondary schools have made use of a carefully planned program of orientation of new students to the institution; the major part of such a program is handled on a group basis. "Freshman orientation week" has long been a familiar term in high schools and colleges. Largely through group meetings, new students are introduced to the physical plant, courses of study, rules, and customs of the institution. This is a worthwhile guidance purpose in which the administrative and counseling functionaries of the school cooperate. In a report on group approaches to student personnel services in higher education, Kirkbride (46) found orientation activities to be among the most common of the group activities used.

Orientation toward different areas is also carried on through group work in guidance throughout the school year. By this means, students are often introduced to the wide variety of educational opportunities available after high school graduation and to the logical order that may be discerned in what is otherwise an extremely complex and confusing vocational world.

A second and closely related purpose of group work is the provision of *learning experiences* which are, or at any rate which may be, somewhat different from the learning experiences of the curriculum of the school. These may be closely related to the regular classroom, but are often apart from it. Among the purposes in this kind of group work in guidance are the development of more efficient study procedures, understanding of the use of the library, the study of opportunities afforded by different colleges to which the school sends its graduates, and exploration of some of the occupations in which there is a large amount of common interest.

A third purpose of group work is the setting of a *background for individual counseling*. An individual may be more ready to recognize the need for counseling and to seek the counselor's help if he is in a group where problems similar to his are objectively discussed. Or the nature of tests and the meaning of test results may be explained and discussed in guidance groups, so that when a pupil has an interview with his counselor to consider what his own test results mean in terms of educational and vocational plans, a good deal of time may be saved in getting down to the business of the conference. Or pupils may in a group situation check themselves on a self-inventory of personal qualities, after which they may be invited to see their counselor individually about any items in the inventory which they would like to discuss, so far as these items are of personal concern to them. The group may be used in many other ways to set the stage for individual work.

The last purpose of guidance group work to be listed here is *adjustment and therapy*. While this area is often regarded as the particular prerogative of individual counseling, in many cases an approach to it may more readily be made through the group. Acceptance of the fact that one has a problem with which help is needed may grow out of group discussions; and sometimes group activities, particularly in connection with the extracurriculum, may help to resolve personal difficulties. For instance, Rossberg and Jaques (67) concluded that the individual counseling relationship was insufficient to achieve counseling goals aimed at the individual's various relationships to different social groups.

As pointed out by Gorlow, Hoch, and Telschow (30), some authorities emphasize therapy *in a group* through the insight and effort of the group leader, while others emphasize therapy *by the group*. These, of course, are not necessarily unrelated. Although the intention may be to stress one kind of therapy or the other, both may operate in the same group situation with different individuals, or even with the same individual.

AVENUES OF GROUP WORK: LEARNING

The general means of group work in guidance are those which are designed as learning situations, those where student activity is the predominant characteristic, and those centered on adjustment or therapy. These overlap and merge into one another, but certain kinds of group work may be identified and described within each of these areas.

REGULAR ACADEMIC CLASSES

A large amount of guidance takes place, and has always taken place, incidentally in classrooms. Regardless of their philosophy of education, most teachers in elementary and secondary schools are not concerned with subject matter alone but are interested in their pupils as persons. Many of them purposely find opportunities to use the classroom as a means of guidance, even though they may not think of themselves as guidance functionaries.

English literature, for example, affords innumerable opportunities for the discussion of personal adjustment, moral values, and interpersonal relations, all in an objective way, since attention is centered upon characters in fiction and not upon the immediate problems of the persons in the class.

In science, the social implications of atomic energy and other new developments may be brought out in such a way that they tend to promote new concepts of social responsibility on the part of the individuals in the group. Social studies classes provide an almost unlimited field for guidance in intergroup relations and in the development of attitudes toward virtually all social institutions. Even in such an impersonal field as mathematics, there are group guidance possibilities, as, for example, through the provision of information on the kinds of vocational opportunities available to persons with thorough mathematical training.

The classroom is, in fact, an almost ideal ready-made group guidance laboratory. The main obstacle to greater use of the classroom in guidance is shortcomings in teacher personnel. For the most part, teachers need a more extensive background in psychology and greater understanding of the psychology of the group if they are to take advantage of the opportunities to perform guidance activities in such a way that this work will be merged with instruction and make for effective learning.

Group counseling sessions designed to strengthen academic work may be helpful to many students. Spielberger, Weitz, and Denny (72) found that anxious college freshmen who regularly attended group counseling sessions showed more academic improvement than those who were not counseled or who did not attend regularly.

THE HOMEROOM

For years the homeroom type of organization has been common in hundreds of high schools, and in many of these it is the principal avenue of group guidance. This kind of organization of group guidance services presupposes interest in and training for guidance on the part of all teachers in the school. Where this supposition becomes an actuality, the homeroom may be a very effective basis of group work. In the usual school situation, however, there is likely to be rather wide variation in the guidance values individual pupils obtain from their homerooms, depending upon the personality, ability, and training of their homeroom teacher.

In recent years, the homeroom has come in for a good deal of criticism, partly because too often its main purpose seems to be to serve administrative convenience, in the making of announcements, taking attendance, and so forth, rather than to serve guidance purposes. In a critical article, Vontress (79) maintained that homerooms are wasteful of time, and that guidance services through homerooms are unjustifiable. McFarland (51) described the five main causes of lack of effectiveness of the homeroom as lack of time, failure to understand the purposes of the homeroom, indifference of teachers, lack of trained personnel, and inadequate program planning, and he suggested ways of improvement. In a report of a survey of 268 secondary schools, McCorkle and O'Dea (50) furnished information on problems of making the homeroom more effective in guidance.

Although the homeroom may often have limited values, homeroom teachers have an especially favorable opportunity to know their pupils thoroughly. Sachs (69) found that homeroom teachers possessed more information about pupils than did teacher-counselors and had better rapport with them. Similarly, Wagner (80) found that homerooms were making an effective contribution to desirable relationships between pupils and teachers, but that there was much need for better organization of the group guidance content of homerooms. Harris (35) presented a strong statement concerning the value of the homeroom in personality development, and maintained that the homeroom program can be an effective procedure if it is

used mainly for guidance rather than for purposes of administration. He proposed suitable topics for the first and second semesters of a tenth-grade course in homeroom guidance.

There are various publications which are designed to help homeroom teachers do a better job. Among these, a *Handbook for Homeroom Guidance,* prepared by Ross (66) out of her own experience, is full of practical suggestions for developing homeroom spirit, for organizing the homeroom under student officers, for group programs, and for individual counseling within the framework of the homeroom.

COURSES IN OCCUPATIONS AND CAREER CONFERENCES

Courses designed to provide information about a wide variety of occupations and to give pupils opportunities to make exploratory studies of occupations of particular interest to them are among the more obvious means of group guidance at the secondary school level. This kind of course is given various titles, such as "occupations," "life careers," or "self-appraisal course." Rice (62) found, in 1948, that the occupations course was taught in all 48 states, although the percentage of students enrolled was rather small.

The occupations course may be offered on a noncredit basis, but it is preferably a credit course which is given standing equivalent to that of the other courses and which is financed out of the school's instructional budget. It ought to be taught by a member of the faculty who has had work experience and who is willing to keep abreast of current developments in the vocational field.

Basic materials for the occupations course include those by Forrester (22) and Baer and Roeber (4), the *Dictionary of Occupational Titles* (18), films setting forth the essentials of different occupations, and much bulletin and pamphlet material issued at frequent intervals by the United States Office of Education. Forrester's book is an extensive guide to occupational literature for students and counselors. Baer and Roeber recognize in their book that the rapid development of new occupations for which considerable training is needed make it necessary for many young people to be prepared for more than one vocational career.

In connection with many courses in occupations, the practice is followed of having representatives of different occupations in the community speak to the class. However, the value of this procedure is likely to vary a good deal, since not every representative of his field is an effective speaker.

Career conferences or career days constitute a somewhat similar kind of group work in guidance. As mentioned in Chapter III, the career conference is now an annual event in a good many high schools. It is a carefully planned series of meetings intended to give pupils information which will help them plan their educational and vocational future. It may involve all pupils in the secondary school and may make extensive use of outside speakers (39). Sinick and Hoppock (70) have encouraged research on the teaching of occupations and have reported periodically on such research by states.

GROUP VISITS

Visits and trips to local industrial establishments and to other places of interest form another common means of guidance through groups. These may be planned in connection with the course in occupations or other classes or they may be separately organized. Schools occasionally sponsor extensive summer trips for older students; these trips have both educational and guidance values.

CASE CONFERENCES AND GROUP PROJECTS

A fifth frequently used means of group work is the case conference. The purposes of this kind of procedure are partly learning and partly adjustment. The usual procedure is to outline for the group a case involving a problem or a set of problems of a hypothetical young person, and to initiate discussion of the case leading to proposed solutions and considerations of these proposals. In the course of discussion, some individuals may identify themselves with the case or may see applications of certain aspects to difficulties of their own.

Serving a purpose closely similar to that of the case conference is the group project. Wrenn, Hein, and Schwarzrock (87) developed a series of brief projects on such questions as "Why work?" and "How can I plan my future?" This little book seems best suited to a grade range of approximately 7 to 10.

AVENUES OF GROUP WORK: STUDENT ACTIVITY

Often the student activity program of a school is carried on without clear perception of the relation between the student activities and the guidance services of the institution. Some years ago, Williamson (83) called attention to the need for better recognition of the role of directors of activities in well-balanced programs of personnel work.

EXTRACLASS ACTIVITIES

In many schools the activities outside the regular curriculum too often go on in a haphazard manner without any conscious attempt to integrate them into a planned personnel program. This is still true, notwithstanding the fact that for years it has been recognized that there is a need for improved administrative and faculty attitude toward the extracurriculum and for coordinating academic and nonacademic experiences, as evidenced by the writings and reviews of Charters and Harvey (14), Gjerde and Alcorn (26), Johnson (44), Terry and Olson (76), and others. The characteristics of extraclass activities that make them potentially so effective in the total program of guidance are that they are an *active* process, that many aspects, such as clubs, are largely *student* initiated and carried forward, and that opportunities for *freedom of expression,* with a minimum of adult supervision, are present. Club advisers and athletic coaches have especially favorable opportunities to make the work they do with groups serve guidance purposes.

Since extraclass activities are largely voluntary—except for a requirement, perhaps, that everyone take part in at least one activity—there is a constant need for motivating a larger amount of participation. In this connection, Anderson (2) described a successful experiment in which activity periods were staggered through the high school day instead of concentrating them in the late afternoon hours.

RESIDENCE HALLS

Dormitories and residence halls have long been recognized as a natural basis of group work in personnel services at the college level, and in boarding schools at the secondary and elementary school levels. The contributions of the college residence hall, particularly in human relations, were described by Thompson (77), who discussed processes in group living, which, she felt, produced democratic values. In a more recent article, Gonyea and Warman (29) presented various perceptions of the role of the student dormitory counselor.

Under an enlightened institutional administrative system, residence halls are largely student governed and organized, and they afford a variety of opportunities for orientation, for furnishing information, for providing a setting for individual counseling, and for personal growth. Omer (56) prepared a handbook in which she discussed residence halls as laboratories of work at Stephens College, outlined the work of the residence counselor, described techniques for implementing major functions including group guidance techniques, and gave an evaluation of the program.

Fraternities and sororities, of course, present many of the same opportunities as residence halls for group personnel work at the college level. A still more inclusive unit which has similar advantages is the student union, or community center, which is also found in some of the larger secondary schools. Humphreys (41) described some going programs of student unions and discussed the significance of these centers of the life of an educational institution.

SOCIOMETRIC TECHNIQUES

In Chapter IX, sociometric techniques were discussed from the standpoint of their contribution to evaluation; but these procedures are equally important, or perhaps more important, as ways of bringing about better adjustment of individuals within the group. They help the pupils express and make definite their preferences among their classmates, and help certain group patterns to emerge so that the teacher's, or guidance leader's, understanding of the relative social adjustment and security of the pupils in his guidance group is increased (19).

AVENUES OF GROUP WORK: ADJUSTMENT AND PSYCHOTHERAPY

The means of group guidance which are aimed primarily at adjustment and therapy are still evolving, but a number of these have been used enough to warrant an attempt to identify and describe them. Bonney and Foley (7) pointed out that, after the establishment of a counseling group, there is a critical transition stage from an atmosphere which is essentially social to one that is therapeutic. A conflict develops between fear of social disapproval and hope for psychotherapy. It was suggested that the counselor present the view that, although personal problems may not be a suitable subject for a social group, they are suitable for discussion in a counseling group. Needless to say, the discussion should be centered on problems in which all members of the group share, at least to some extent. The integrity of each individual should be carefully protected.

MULTIPLE COUNSELING

As mentioned earlier in the chapter, Froehlich (23) used the term "multiple counseling" to designate situations in which a counselor works simultaneously with several counselees. The work takes place in the framework of the group, yet the individual is constantly kept

in mind. Driver (20) carried on a series of three experiments in which she attempted to evaluate multiple counseling as used with groups of high school pupils and university students. There were eight groups which were organized around a problem or interest which was common to the members of the group. Almost all the persons in her groups felt that multiple counseling was enjoyable and worthwhile. Individual counseling was used to complement the group sessions. The multiple counseling appeared to facilitate rapport and make the individual counseling more efficient. Wright (88) presented a practical and helpful article in which he discussed the nature of multiple counseling, presented reasons for using this procedure, considered when to use it, and dealt briefly with the difficult question of how to practice multiple counseling.

Multiple counseling has possibilities for use with groups of parents, as well as pupils. Mink (52) found some evidence that multiple counseling was more effective with parents than with pupils.

CHECKLISTS AND INVENTORIES

Another means of fostering adjustment is through the use of checklists and inventories. These, administered in a group, can be used to identify problems which may serve as a basis of individual counseling and of group discussion in general terms, without relating these problems specifically to any one individual. One such instrument is the Mooney Problem Check List (53) described in Chapter VII.

PSYCHODRAMA AND SOCIODRAMA

The therapeutic and cathartic values of role playing, and the dramatization of problem situations as represented in the psychodrama and the sociodrama, were urged upon American psychologists and educators by Moreno (54), a Viennese psychologist who came to this country some 25 years ago. The principles of sociodrama as derived from Moreno's experimental work were explained by Jennings (43), who showed how the method could be used in the classroom. She stressed particularly the need for a warming-up period, for respect for the individual pupil's area of reticence, and for a graduated sequence of situations, and advised extensive use of the social-laboratory conditions present in every classroom. Splaver (73) has published a little booklet of 30 ten-minute playlets intended to promote discussion of teen-age problems.

Thus far, the techniques of the psychodrama and the sociodrama seem to have been used more with groups of pupils having serious emotional problems than with "normal" groups. It is possible, however, that these procedures will gradually come to play a larger part in the usual school situation. Some years ago, Slavson (71) indicated that there was growing acceptance of Moreno's position that group therapeutic procedures are not merely expedients or substitutes for individual therapy, but can stand on their own merits as treatments yielding values which may not be attained through individual methods.

But this remains a major question. As Lifton (48) has pointed out, the relationship of group therapy to the normal person still needs to be more clearly delineated; for if it is defined as a specified treatment for psychologically disturbed persons, the number of institutions and individuals interested and engaged in group therapy will almost certainly be very limited.

GROUP PSYCHOTHERAPY

As indicated earlier, group therapy is not a very precise term, for it has been used in different ways by different workers. However, the basic procedure which seems to characterize such efforts is to stimulate free expression on the part of members of the group concerning a common problem, and to develop and nurture a permissive atmosphere which will encourage spontaneous verbalization and discussion freed as far as possible from inhibitions that might result from value judgments on the part of the guidance worker. There seems to be a relation between the extent and pattern of verbal expression and the outcome of this kind of therapy. This relationship was investigated by Peres (58), who found decided differences between the patterns of conversation for those who were benefited and those who were not benefited. He also reported an increase in the value of the group work for the benefited group after the therapy was concluded.

Evidence of the value of permissive group therapy has been obtained in various other studies, such as one by Rashkis and Shaskan (59), who used permissive group psychotherapy with 22 neuropsychiatric battle casualties. The MMPI was applied before and after therapy, and a reduction was found in the scores on the depression, hysteria, paranoia, and psychasthenia scales.

NEED FOR MORE EVALUATION OF GROUP WORK IN GUIDANCE

Although programs of group work in guidance, as well as individual counseling, are rapidly increasing in number, there is still a dearth of convincing research as to the value of these procedures. For the last 20 years, all writers who have taken a close look at the evidence,

as in the periodic summaries in the *Review of Educational Research*, agree on one point: there is much need for further evaluation of the procedures and contributions of group work to guidance services.

Research with human beings, even under the conditions of the classroom where procedures are usually structured to a considerable degree, is always difficult. It is doubly so in a guidance group, where the permissiveness essential to personal development may be antithetical to well-conceived experimental design. Moreover, as Patterson (57) has indicated, the objectives of guidance are not readily made sufficiently specific, nor are the criteria of progress toward the objectives always clearly identified. So, even when serious attempts at research are made, the outcomes are frequently inconclusive.

Hence, we cannot say with confidence at present what the relative merits of different methods of group work in guidance are, or how the advantages of group work in counseling compare with those of individual counseling. And there is only fragmentary research evidence that any type of counseling, or even a combination of group and individual counseling, is measurably better than no counseling at all. Perhaps this state of affairs is inevitable in the still early stages of a young profession.

Notwithstanding the lack of research results in this area, numerous school and college guidance workers have become convinced out of their own experience that group work has an important place in guidance services. But personal experience and faith may not be a sufficient basis on which to build a sound profession. For both group and individual work in guidance—but particularly for the various group approaches—we need much more evidence that our techniques contribute to self-understanding and self-reliance, help individuals solve their own problems, improve their ability to adjust to the rapidly changing environment of the modern world, and enhance their contributions to the welfare of their fellow men.

REFERENCES

1. Adams, Georgia May; Bennett, Margaret E.; Berg, Irwin A.; and Johnson, Claude S. "Guidance Through Groups," *Review of Educational Research*, XVIII (April 1948), 184–193.
2. Anderson, Kenneth E. "A 'Float' Activity Schedule: An Experiment," *School Activities*, XIX (October 1947), 45–46.
3. Attwell, Arthur A., and Odom, Robert R. "Guv'ners: Venture in Group Guidance," *Elementary School Journal*, LXIV (December 1963), 124–130.

4. Baer, Max F., and Roeber, Edward C. *Occupational Information: Its Nature and Use,* 3rd ed. Chicago: Science Research Associates, Inc., 1964. Pp. 494.

5. Bennett, Margaret E. *Guidance and Counseling in Groups, Second Edition.* New York: McGraw-Hill Book Company, Inc., 1963. Pp. xii + 421.

6. Beymer, L. "Communicating Test Results in Groups of Pupils," *Teachers College Journal,* XXXV (November 1963), 45–46.

7. Bonney, Warren C., and Foley, Walter J. "The Transition Stage in Group Counseling in Terms of Congruence Theory," *Journal of Counseling Psychology,* X (Summer 1963), 136–138.

8. Bradford, Leland P. (ed.). *Human Forces in Teaching and Learning.* Selected Reading Series Three. Washington, D.C.: National Education Association, 1961. Pp. 102.

9. Broedel, John, and others. "The Effects of Group Counseling on Gifted Underachieving Adolescents," *Journal of Counseling Psychology,* VII (Fall 1960), 163–170.

10. Burack, Marvin. *Group Guidance Units for Upper Elementary Grades in the Chicago Public Schools.* Chicago: Board of Education, 1959. Pp. 115.

11. Caldwell, Edson, and Mahler, Clarence A. *Group Counseling in Secondary Schools.* Chicago: Science Research Associates Inc., 1961. Pp. 78.

12. Callis, Robert, Polmantier, Paul C., and Roeber, Edward C. *A Casebook of Counseling.* New York: Appleton-Century-Crofts, Inc., 1955. Pp. xii + 352.

13. Caskey, O. L. "Guidance Role of the Teacher," *Clearing House,* XXIX (April 1955), 499.

14. Charters, Werrett W., and Harvey, C. C. "Twelve Questions on the Future of Our Extracurricular Program," *Clearing House,* XIX (September 1944), 3–7.

15. Cohn, Benjamin, and Sniffen, A. Mead. "A School Report on Group Counseling," *Personnel and Guidance Journal,* XLI (October 1962), 133–138.

16. Cohn, Benjamin; Combs, Charles F.; Gibian, Edward J.; and Sniffen, A. Mead. "Group Counseling, an Orientation," *Personnel and Guidance Journal,* XLII (December 1963), 355–358.

17. Davis, Donald A. "Effect of Group Guidance and Individual Counseling on Citizenship Behavior," *Personnel and Guidance Journal,* XXXVIII (October 1959), 142–145.

18. *Dictionary of Occupational Titles.* Washington, D.C.: Superintendent of Documents, 1965.

19. Dineen, Mary Ann, and Garry, Ralph. "Effect of Sociometric Seating on a Classroom Cleavage," *Elementary School Journal* LVI (April 1956), 358–362.

20. Driver, Helen I. "Small-Group Discussion as an Aid to Counseling," *School Review,* LIX (December 1951), 525–530.

21. Ford, Donald H. "Group and Individual Counseling in Modifying Behavior," *Personnel and Guidance Journal,* XL (May 1962), 770–773.

22. Forrester, Gertrude. *Occupational Literature: An Annotated Bibliography, 1964 edition.* New York: The H. W. Wilson Company, 1964. Pp. 675.

23. Froehlich, Clifford P. *Multiple Counseling—A Research Proposal.* Berkeley, Calif.: Department of Education, University of California. Undated. Pp. 7. (Mimeographed.)

24. Froehlich, Clifford P. "Group Guidance Approaches in Educational Institutions," *Review of Educational Research,* XXIV (April 1954), 147–155.

25. Froehlich, Clifford P. "Must Counseling Be Individual," *Educational and Psychological Measurement,* XVIII (Winter 1958), 681–689.

26. Gjerde, Clayton M., and Alcorn, Marvin D. "Selected References on Extra-Class Activities," *School Review,* LXIII (April 1955), 236–241.

27. Glanz, Edward C. *Groups in Guidance: The Dynamics of Groups and the Application of Groups in Guidance.* Englewood Cliffs, N.J.: Allyn and Bacon, Inc., 1962. Pp. 429.

28. Goldman, Leo. "Group Guidance: Content and Process," *Personnel and Guidance Journal,* XL (February 1962), 518–522.

29. Gonyea, George G., and Warman, Roy E. "Differential Perceptions of the Student Dormitory Counselor's Role," *Personnel and Guidance Journal,* XLI (December 1962), 350–355.

30. Gorlow, Leon, Hoch, Erasmus L., and Telschow, Earl F. *The Nature of Nondirective Group Psychotherapy.* New York: Bureau of Publications, Teachers College, Columbia University, 1952. Pp. 143.

31. Greenleaf, Walter J. *Occupations and Careers.* New York: McGraw-Hill Book Company, Inc., 1955. Pp. xiv + 580.

32. Gribbons, Warren D. "Evaluation of an Eighth Grade Group Guidance Program," *Personnel and Guidance Journal,* XXXVIII (May 1960), 740–745.

33. Hahn, Milton E., and MacLean, Malcolm S. *Counseling Psychology.* 2nd ed. New York: McGraw-Hill Book Company, Inc., 1955. Pp. xii + 302.

34. Harris, Brother Philip. "Group Techniques Sell Guidance," *Personnel and Guidance Journal,* XXXIV (November 1955), 161–163.

35. Harris, Brother Philip. "Using Homeroom for Guidance in Personality Development," *Catholic Educational Review,* LVII (February 1959), 97–105.

36. Headley, Robert R. "University Extension Counseling Services," *Adult Education,* I (June 1951), 189–190.

37. Hobbs, Nicholas. "Group Psychotherapy in Preventive Mental Hygiene," *Teachers College Record,* L (December 1948), 195–199.

38. Hoppock, Robert. *Group Guidance: Principles, Techniques, and Evaluation.* New York: McGraw-Hill Book Company, Inc., 1949. Pp. xiv + 394.

39. *How to Plan Career Conferences for Teen Agers.* (Also a Check List of Career Planning Activities.) Washington, D.C.: Chamber of Commerce of the United States.

40. Hoyt, Kenneth B., and Moore, Gilbert D. "Group

Procedures in Guidance and Personnel Work," *Review of Educational Research*, XXX (April 1960), 158–167.

41. Humphreys, Edith. *College Unions—A Handbook on College Community Centers*. Ithaca, N.Y.: Association of College Unions, Cornell University, 1946. Pp. 244.

42. Hutson, P. W. "Foundations of the Curriculum for the Education of Homeroom Teachers," *Personnel and Guidance Journal*, XL (April 1962), 698–702.

43. Jennings, Helen Hall. *Sociometry in Group Relations: A Manual for Teachers* 2nd ed. Washington, D.C.: American Council on Education, 1959. Pp. 105.

44. Johnson, Burges. *Campus versus Classroom*. New York: Ives Washburn, Inc., 1946. Pp. 305.

45. Kemp, C. Grafton. "Behaviors in Group Guidance (Socio Process) and Group Counseling (Psyche Process)," *Journal of Counseling Psychology*, X (Winter 1963), 373–377.

46. Kirkbride, Virginia R. "Group Approaches to Student Personnel Services in Higher Education," *Journal of the National Association of Deans of Women and Counselors*, XXIV (April 1961), 127–131.

47. Koile, Earl A. "Group Guidance—A Fringe Activity," *School Review*, LXIII (December 1955), 483–485.

48. Lifton, Walter M. "Group Therapy in Educational Institutions," *Review of Educational Research*, XXIV (April 1954), 156–165.

49. Lifton, Walter M. *Working with Groups*. New York: John Wiley & Sons, Inc., 1961. Pp. 238.

50. McCorkle, David B., and O'Dea, J. David. "Some Problems of Homeroom Teachers," *Personnel and Guidance Journal*, XXXII (December 1953), 206–208.

51. McFarland, John W. "Developing Effective Homerooms," *School Review*, LXI (October 1953), 400–405.

52. Mink, Oscar G. "Multiple Counseling with Underachieving Junior High School Pupils of Bright-Normal and Higher Ability," *Journal of Educational Research*, LVIII (September 1964), 31–34.

53. Mooney, Ross L., and Gordon, Leonard V. *Mooney Problem Check List: 1950 Revision*. J–for junior high schools; H–for high school students; C–for college students; A–for adults. New York: The Psychological Corporation, 1950.

54. Moreno, Jacob L. *Psychodrama*, Vol. I. New York: Beacon House, Inc., 1946. Pp. 430.

55. Ohlsen, Merle M., and Oelke, Merritt C. "An Evaluation of Discussion Topics in Group Counseling," *Journal of Clinical Psychology*, XVIII (July 1962), 317–322.

56. Omer, Mary Isabel. *A Handbook for Residence Counselors*. Stephens College, Columbia, Mo.: The author, 1949. Pp. 161.

57. Patterson, C. H. "Program Evaluation," *Review of Educational Research*, XXXIII (April 1963), 214–224.

58. Peres, Hadassah. "An Investigation of Nondirective Group Therapy," *Journal of Consulting Psychology*, XI (August 1947), 159–172.

59. Rashkis, Harold A., and Shaskan, Donald A. "The Effects of Group Psychotherapy on Personality Inventory Scores," *American Journal of Orthopsychiatry*, XVI (April 1946), 345–349.

60. Redl, Fritz. "Resistance in Therapy Groups," *Human Relations*, I (August 1948), 307–313.

61. Redman, C. "Group Guidance in the Homeroom Program," *Kentucky School Journal*, XLII (November 1963), 28.

62. Rice, Mabel C. *National Summary of Offerings and Enrollments in High School Subjects, 1948–1949*. Washington, D.C.: Office of Education, May 1951. Pp. 4. (Mimeographed.)

63. Richardson, Harold, and Borow, Henry. "Evaluation of a Technique of Group Orientation for Vocational Counseling," *Educational and Psychological Measurement*, XII (Winter 1952), 587–597.

64. Riegert, Norbert, "Unit on Occupations," *Catholic School Journal*, LX (December 1960), 23–25.

65. Rinn, John L. "Group Guidance: Two Processes," *Personnel and Guidance Journal*, XXXIX (March 1961), 591–594.

66. Ross, Vivian. *Handbook for Homeroom Guidance*. New York: The Macmillan Company, 1954. Pp. 132.

67. Rossberg, Robert, and Jaques, Marceline. "The Role of the Group in Patient Evaluation, Counseling, and Management," *Personnel and Guidance Journal*, XL (October 1961), 135–142.

68. Rusalem, Herbert, and Daren, Hyman. "Vocational Counseling of the Slow Learner," *Journal of the National Association of Deans of Women and Counselors*, XXIII (April 1960), 110–116.

69. Sachs, Georgia May. *Evaluation of Group Guidance Work in Secondary Schools*. Berkeley, Calif.: University of California Press, 1945. Pp. 120.

70. Sinick, Daniel, and Hoppock, Robert. "Research by States on the Teaching of Occupations," *Personnel and Guidance Journal*, XXXIX (November 1960), 218–219.

71. Slavson, Samuel R. *The Practice of Group Therapy*. New York: International Universities Press, Inc., 1947. Pp. 271.

72. Spielberger, Charles D., Weitz, Henry, and Denny, J. Peter. "Group Counseling and the Academic Performance of Anxious College Freshmen," *Journal of Counseling Psychology*, IX (Fall 1962), 195–204.

73. Splaver, Sarah (ed.). *Socio-Guidramas*. Springfield, N.J.: Methods and Materials Press, 1955–1963. Pp. 12.

74. Stockey, Merrel Richard. *A Comparison of the Effectiveness of Group-Counseling, Individual-Counseling, and Employment of Adolescent Boys with Adjustment Problems*. Doctor's Thesis. Ann Arbor, Mich.: University of Michigan Press 1961, pp. 97. *Dissertation Abstracts*, XXII (November 1961), 491.

75. Strang, Ruth, and Wollner, Mary. "Guidance Through Groups," *Review of Educational Research*, XV (April 1945), 164–172.

76. Terry, Paul W., and Olson, Perry T. "Selected References on the Extra-Curriculum," *School Review*, LIX (April 1951), 237–242.

77. Thompson, Florence M. "The Use of Dormitories for Social Education," *Educational and Psychological Measurement,* VII (Spring 1947), 141–155.

78. Volsky, Theodore, and Hewer, Vivian H. "A Program of Group Counseling," *Journal of Counseling Psychology,* VII (Spring 1960), 71–73.

79. Vontress, Clemmont E. "Quackery in the Homeroom," *Clearing House,* XXXVIII (September 1963), 23–25.

80. Wagner, Josephine E. "Factors Conducive to the Effective Functioning of the Homeroom Organization," *Bulletin of the National Association of Secondary-School Principals,* XXX (January 1946), 88–100.

81. Warters, Jane. "Guidance through Groups," *Review of Educational Research,* XXI (April 1951), 140–148.

82. Willey, Roy DeVerl, and Strong, W. Melvin. *Group Procedures in Guidance.* New York: Harper & Row, Publishers, 1957. Pp. 548.

83. Williamson, Edmund G. "Student Activities—An Integral Part of Student Personnel Work," *Educational and Psychological Measurement,* IV (Spring 1944), 3–12.

84. Woal, S. Theodore. "A Project in Group Counseling in a Junior High School," *Personnel and Guidance Journal,* XLII (February 1964), 611–612.

85. Woolf, Maurice D., and Woolf, Jeanne A. *The Student Personnel Program.* New York: McGraw-Hill Book Company, Inc., 1953. Pp. 416.

86. Wrenn, C. Gilbert. *The Counselor in a Changing World.* Washington, D.C.: American Personnel and Guidance Association, 1962. Pp. 195.

87. Wrenn, C. Gilbert, Hein, R. G., and Schwarzrock, S. P. *Planned Group Guidance.* Minneapolis: American Guidance Services, Inc., 1961. Pp. 76.

88. Wright, E. Wayne. "Multiple Counseling: Why? When? How?" *Personnel and Guidance Journal,* XXXVII (April 1959), 551–557.

89. Wright, E. Wayne. "Group Procedures," *Review of Educational Research,* XXXIII (April 1963), 205–213.

90. Wright, E. Wayne. "A Comparison of Individual and Multiple Counseling for Test Interpretation Interviews: with Comment by M. M. Ohlsen," *Journal of Counseling Psychology,* X (Summer 1963), 126–135.

CHAPTER XXI

Reading Resources for Guidance Workers

Contributions to personnel work in schools and colleges are to be found in an extensive body of literature. No guidance worker can be expected to be acquainted with all the books, monographs, and studies that are related to personnel work, but he will be aided materially in meeting the great variety of day-to-day problems of counseling pupils if there is available in the professional library of the school a selected list of reading resources to which he can turn when he does not know the answer to a particular problem.

This chapter represents an attempt to provide such a list. Most of the more than 250 references chosen were published since 1955 and about half since 1960, but some materials from an earlier period were included where they seemed particularly significant and useful. No doubt some references fully as worthwhile as those included escaped attention in the preparation of this reading list. It is believed, however, that the present list would enable a guidance worker to obtain information or expert judgment on almost any question in his field; and for many guidance problems a variety of points of view may be obtained from these reading references.

CHILD PSYCHOLOGY AND MENTAL HYGIENE

It is highly desirable for everyone who performs guidance functions to have some training in individual and group psychology. A well-organized overview of how applied psychologists function is provided in Anastasi's *Fields of Applied Psychology* (4). A part of the book is on counseling psychology.

Regardless of the counselor's professional background in this field, the availability of some of the better reference books in child and adolescent psychology will assist his work; his library should contain such books.

CHILD PSYCHOLOGY

For the beginning worker in this field, Strang's *An Introduction to Child Study* (191), which is in its fourth edition, is a helpful reference. Jersild's *Child Psychology* (106), now in its fifth edition, has also long been a standard reference work. Prescott's *The Child in the Educative Process* (154) is a book by a well-known authority in the field.

A book by Baldwin, *Behavior and Development in Childhood* (9), includes a good, sensible discussion of psychoanalytic theory. Other books in this field are Forest's *Child Development* (55) and Olson's *Child Development* (144). The NSSE Yearbook, *Child Psychology*, edited by Stevenson (186), presents a view of research areas in the psychology of the normal child. In order to have a functional understanding of child behavior, it is necessary to describe the behavior, to locate the action in the general form of the child's life, to clarify the initial appearance of the action, and to determine what maintains the action.

ADOLESCENT PSYCHOLOGY

A useful book with which to start a study of adolescent psychology is Strang's *The Adolescent Views Himself* (190). Among other aspects, this book considers educational and vocational goals, and ways in which the young person achieves success. Jersild's *The Psychology of Adolescence* (107) likewise considers development goals and discusses physical and mental growth, social life, vocations, values, and the influence of heredity and environment, as well as the psychological repercussions of early and late maturity. A well-known book by Crow and Crow, *Adolescent Development and Adjustment,* which is in its second edition (*38*), contains a series of chapters on adolescent experiences, development, behavior motivations, and adjustments. The authors place particular emphasis on the environmental demands in the building of personality. Nixon's *The Art of Growing: A Guide to Psychological Maturity* (*140*) deals with problems of growing up in the American culture. It is concerned with the later adolescent period; that is, with ages approximately 17 to 22.

Studies in Adolescence, edited by Grinder (*77*), contains selections from authorities who present a variety of viewpoints on adolescent behavior. The concentration on research studies makes this a worthwhile reference.

DYNAMICS OF ADJUSTMENT

Books that go somewhat more directly into the psychology of adjustment than the general texts in child or adolescent psychology are also useful in the counselor's library. Among the books in this area are Lindgren's *Psychology of Personal Development* (*122*), and Lehner and Kube's *The Dynamics of Personal Adjustment* (*118*). The general topics covered by Lehner and Kube's book are: why it is important to understand ourselves; origin, nature, and development of emotional and psychological needs; dynamics and principles of adjustment; and goals and processes of improving adjustment. The treatment of frustration, defense mechanisms, neuroses, and psychoses as presented in this book should be particularly helpful to guidance workers in acquiring a background for individual counseling.

MENTAL HYGIENE

The counselor should be acquainted with the relation of mental hygiene to personal guidance, and although he will find this subject discussed in some of the general references on child and adolescent psychology, several books dealing with mental hygiene can profitably be included in his library. General treatments which may serve as textbooks for classes or reference books for counselors are Kaplan and Baron's *Mental Hygiene and Life* (*111*), Lindgren's *Mental Hygiene in Education* (*121*), Schneiders' *Personal Adjustment and Mental Health* (*170*), and Bernard's *Mental Hygiene for Classroom Teachers* (*16*). The book by Kaplan and Baron includes many practical examples from situations drawn from life. Lindgren's book is simple, yet comprehensive, and it

shows close acquaintance with school situations, the classroom, and home. It should prove valuable for administrators as well as teachers and counselors.

EXCEPTIONAL CHILDREN

Most school counselors deal mainly with normal children and young people, but they also need insight into the psychology of exceptional children. A comprehensive treatment of this subject was made available by Cruikshank (*39*). A little book by the internationally known British psychologist, Burt, *The Causes and Treatment of Backwardness* (*24*), provides a nontechnical discussion which teacher-counselors should find helpful. Wallin's book, *Education of Mentally Handicapped Children* (*215*), likewise, places emphasis on understanding and helping mentally handicapped children who do not call for clinical treatment.

Assistance in providing for children at the other end of the intelligence scale may be found in a book, *Bright Children,* by Cutts and Moseley (*41*). In this area, the studies of Elizabeth Monroe Drews are particularly helpful (*46*).

Up-to-date overviews of the education of exceptional children, both the gifted and the handicapped, have been made available by Dunn (*47*) and by Gowan and Demos (*72*). The latter book contains a useful chapter on the identification, diagnosis, and treatment of emotionally disturbed children.

The child who is exceptional, not because he is a mental deviate, but because he commits overt acts against society is likely to precipitate crises which his counselor must help to resolve. Among the books dealing with the child offender or juvenile delinquent are those by Neumeyer (*139*), Robison (*159*), and Tappan (*197*).

CLINICAL COUNSELING AND PSYCHOTHERAPY

In everyday terms, clinical counseling is intensive and frequently long-continued individual counseling, which is intended to help the person gain insight into his own problems, and grow in understanding so that he will be able to work out an adjustment that he finds satisfying and that is socially desirable. Many guidance problems do not call for the intensity and depth of treatment that would place them in the clinical-counseling category. But, when instances requiring clinical counseling do arise, the way the guidance worker handles them is very important. Much has been written about clinical counseling and psychotherapy during the last 15 or 20 years. Some of the more important books are included in this section.

The English translation of Freud's *A General Introduction to Psychoanalysis* (59) is helpful in gaining an understanding of the historical background of nondirective therapy. Rogers, whose book *Counseling and Psychotherapy* (162), published in 1942, was the first comprehensive presentation of his nondirective or client-centered point of view, carried his work forward in his book, *Client-centered Therapy* (163), published in 1959. Rogers, in cooperation with Dymond, reported research work in client-centered counseling at the University of Chicago Counseling Center under the title, *Psychotherapy and Personality Change* (164). Other books on therapeutic counseling are those of Porter (153) and Slavson (178). In his book Slavson illustrated treatment with a number of case studies from a child guidance clinic.

A recent book by Cameron, *Personality Development and Psychopathology: A Dynamic Approach* (27), brings the behavioral sciences to bear on psychodynamics. It helps to round out the counselor's philosophy and his frame of reference.

Counseling and Psychotherapy with the Mentally Retarded, edited by Stacey and DeMartino (183), is a useful reference for counselors of the mentally handicapped.

An eclectic viewpoint in counseling was presented in books by Thorne (204) and Hahn and MacLean (86). Thorne regards therapy as directed toward the replacement of emotional-compulsive behavior with deliberate rational-adaptative behavior growing out of emphasis on intellectual resources. Similarly, Pepinsky and Pepinsky (148) presented counseling as a learning situation for bringing about personality growth and adjustment. Another authoritative book in this field is *Psychological Counseling* by Bordin (18).

Since counselors occasionally find it necessary to refer involved and difficult cases for psychiatric attention, they need a general knowledge of the field and functions of psychiatry. One of the best books on this subject for general use is Hinsie's *Understandable Psychiatry* (98). Hinsie has an unusual gift for writing about a technical field in nontechnical language.

EDUCATIONAL GUIDANCE, COUNSELING, AND PERSONNEL WORK

During the past 15 years, the number of textbooks and general treatises on guidance, counseling, and personnel work has been greatly increased. There are now many comprehensive, well-written books on guidance services at all levels of the school.

Many influential books that have a general bearing on guidance have also been made available in recent years. For example, Conant's *The American High School Today* (33) contained a number of recommendations for guidance in secondary schools, and these recommendations carried a large amount of weight throughout the country. John Gardner's book, *Self-Renewal* (63), is not intended as a guidance book, but it treats masterfully one of the basic concepts for the counselor, and thus contributes to guidance literature on "becoming."

GENERAL TEXTBOOKS

One of the most helpful treatments of guidance is Jones's *Principle of Guidance* (110), now in its fifth edition. This book in its successive editions has been a standard work for 30 years or more. The present edition discusses the meaning and function of guidance, the organization of guidance in schools, essential information, methods of guidance, new areas, and the present status of guidance.

Recent books designed to serve as the basis of an introductory course in guidance or for the purpose of introducing teachers in training to the field of guidance services are Moser and Moser's *Counseling and Guidance: An Exploration* (136), which introduces the student to present-day theories and practices; Patterson's *Counseling and Guidance in Schools* (147), which serves as a first course in guidance presenting the client-centered approach; Ohlsen's *Guidance Services in the Modern School* (143); and Humphreys, Traxler, and North's *Guidance Services* (103), dealing with the meaning, history, and social and psychological foundations of guidance services, their major procedures and techniques, their practical application to pupil problems, and their organization.

Other useful general works on guidance published within the last ten years or less are Arbuckle's *Pupil Personnel Services in American Schools* (7); Blanchard and Flaum's *Guidance, A Longitudinal Approach* (17); Johnson, Stefflre, and Edelfelt's *Pupil Personnel and Guidance Services* (109); Mathewson's *Guidance Policy and Practice* (132); Rosecrance and Hayden's *School Guidance and Personnel Services* (165); Stoops's *Guidance Services* (187); Stoops and Wahlquist's *Principles and Practices in Guidance* (188); and Andrew and Willey's *Administration and Organization of the Guidance Program* (6). The last book approaches guidance administration as a part of educational administration, with emphasis on the dynamics of human relations.

ORGANIZATION AND ADMINISTRATION OF GUIDANCE

Most of the general textbooks in this field devote some attention to the planning, organizing, and administering of a guidance program, but certain books are directed more specifically toward this aspect of the development of guidance programs. A useful book of this kind is Zeran and Riccio's *Organization and Administration of Guidance Services* (230). In addition to organizational practices, the book includes information on the analysis of the individual, counseling services, placement and follow-up, and evaluation of the services. Peters and Shertzer's *Guidance: Program Development and Management* (152) indicates how to initiate, develop, and appraise a school guidance program.

The United States Office of Education's *Organization and Administration of Pupil Personnel Service Programs in Selected School Systems* (145) describes illustrative programs in eight school systems in urban communities.

THEORIES OF COUNSELING

Most contemporary textbooks on guidance give some attention to theories of counseling. Stefflre edited a book, *Theories of Counseling* (185), which presents four major theories designated as the vocational trait and factor theory, the client-centered theory, the behavioral theory, and adaptations of psychoanalytic methods. Contributors include E. G. Williamson, Leonard D. Goodstein, Donald L. Grummon, Paul T. King, and William Ratigan.

In a thoughtful article, Lortie (125) discussed three diverse, contradictory roles of the counselor: administrator, advocate, and therapist. He insisted that these must be resolved in moving counseling toward professionalization.

SCHOOL COUNSELING

Books which cover the range of the counselor's work and create an understanding of the day to day problems of counseling have an important place in the library of a guidance worker. *The Counselor in a Changing World* by Wrenn (226) is a report of the Commission on Guidance in American Schools. It discusses the main elements in the school counselor's task, and considers the social forces that will create change in the future.

Other useful books on counseling are *The School Counselor* by Byrne (25), *Helping Counselors Grow Professionally* by Evraiff (52), *Counseling in the Secondary School* by Glenn E. Smith (180), *The Work of the Counselor* by Tyler (211), and *Techniques of Counseling* by Warters (217). Byrne's book is intended as a

text for a first course in counselor education. Evraiff's book, as the title indicates, is intended to help in promoting the personal and professional growth of counselors. Tyler's book is organized around the tools of the counselor. Warters presents an up-to-date treatment of the techniques of both individual counseling and group work.

Ability to counsel with parents as well as children has an important bearing upon the success of a guidance program. Counseling with parents of young children is discussed in a book by Leonard, Van Deman, and Miles (119).

SECONDARY SCHOOL GUIDANCE SERVICES

A considerable number of the publications in the field of guidance have to do with guidance services at particular levels of the school. Guidance had its earliest development, and for many years its most vigorous and extensive growth, at the secondary school level; so it was natural for much to be written about guidance work in this unit of the school system.

The importance of developing a strong program of guidance in the junior high school is highlighted by the fact that a number of recent books have dealt with guidance services at this level alone. Two such books are *Guidance in the Junior High School* by Cottingham and Hopke (35) and *Junior High School Guidance* by Johnson, Busacker, and Bowman (108). The former book develops the details of an organized guidance program on the basis of information obtained from some 300 junior high schools; the latter covers the services and activities of junior high school guidance broadly conceived.

A practical and helpful book on high school guidance is *Guidance Services in the Secondary School* by Hatch, Dressel, and Costar (94). The Office of the Los Angeles County Superintendent of Schools issued *Guiding Today's Youth* (84), a revision of an earlier publication, which presents secondary school guidance in practical and realistic terms.

PERSONNEL WORK IN HIGHER EDUCATION

Books on personnel work in colleges and universities began to make their appearance in the latter 1930s. In recent years, a considerable number of books aimed entirely or mainly at personnel work in higher education have been published. Perhaps the outstanding one is *Student Personnel Services in Colleges and Universities*, by Williamson (219), long a leader in this field. The book stresses assistance to students in solving their own personal and educational problems. Among others of current value are Mueller's *Student Personnel Work in*

Higher Education (137), and *Essential Student Personnel Practices for Junior Colleges* by McDaniel (126). A book by Hardee, *The Faculty in College Counseling* (90), may be of special interest because it sets forth the functions of the faculty adviser to students, and considers advising by the faculty in relation to the entire program of college counseling.

INTEGRATION OF HIGH SCHOOL AND COLLEGE PERSONNEL PROGRAMS

Some of the references mentioned in the sections on secondary school guidance and personnel work in college call attention to the need for coordination and integration of the personnel programs of high schools and colleges. This need was stressed in Woolf and Woolf's *The Student Personnel Program: Its Development and Integration in the High School and College* (224). Further emphasis on the coordination of guidance services at these two levels of education was given some years ago in *Improving Transition from School to College*, edited by Traxler and Townsend (210). This book reported an extensive survey of college admission practices as viewed by colleges and secondary schools, which was carried on by the Committee on School and College Relations of the Educational Records Bureau. The study was in part replicated by the committee ten years later, and a summary was reported in an Educational Records Bureau brochure, *Admission to American Colleges* (2). Integration of high school and college guidance services was strongly urged in *Secondary School-College Cooperation: An Obligation to Youth*, a publication of the American Association of Collegiate Registrars and Admission Officers (171). A recently formed organization devoted to the objective of furthering high school-college cooperation is the Committee to Form a National Council on School-College Relations (NCSCR).

GUIDANCE IN ELEMENTARY SCHOOLS

In the earlier years of the guidance movement, very little was written about guidance at the elementary school level. It seems to have been more or less assumed that guidance functions could be handled effectively by elementary school classroom teachers without special assistance. Since about 1950, however, there has been a definite trend toward greater attention to guidance services for elementary school children. The Thirty-third Yearbook of the Department of Elementary-School Principals of the National Education Association, under the title *Guidance for Today's Children* (81), included chapters by many different authors having to do with the adjustment problems of elementary school pupils. *Guid-*

ing the Young Child, a book prepared by a committee of the California Schools Supervisors Association and edited by Heffernan (97), dealt with the problems of the social, personal, and learning adjustments of children as they enter school. A practical book, *Guiding Today's Children* (83), is a revision of an earlier bulletin prepared by the Division of Research and Guidance of the Office of the Los Angeles County Superintendent of Schools.

A small book by Detjen and Detjen, *Elementary School Guidance* (43), and a longer one by Willey, *Guidance in Elementary Education* (218) could serve as textbooks in courses on the subject. Peters, Riccio, and Quaranta's *Guidance in the Elementary School* (151) contains a series of articles published from 1950 to 1962 and could well serve as supplementary reading material. A book by Hatch and Costar (93) clarified the role of guidance in the elementary school and dealt in a simple and very practical way with guidance procedures at this level. Cottingham's *Guidance in Elementary Schools* (34) furnished a thorough and well-organized treatment of the philosophy, principles, and actual practices in guidance at the elementary school level.

GUIDANCE IN DIFFERENT KINDS OF INSTITUTIONS AND FOR VARIOUS GROUPS

Recently the American Personnel and Guidance Association has published a short book by Warburton, *Stimulating Guidance in Rural Schools* (216), which reports on the encouraging effect NDEA aid is having on the development of guidance in rural schools. A book on *Counseling in Catholic Life and Education* was published some years ago by Curran (40). Dame and Brinkman's *Guidance in Business Education* (42) is illustrative of the need for guidance services in particular vocational fields.

Reference was made in an earlier section to a book by Kenneth W. Hamilton in which the problems, techniques, and resources of guidance work with handicapped persons are discussed under the title *Counseling the Handicapped in the Rehabilitation Process* (87).

READINGS IN GUIDANCE

Some of the best thinking in the field of guidance services is brought together in such books as *Readings in Guidance: Principles, Practices, Organization, Administration*, edited by Crow and Crow (37); *Guidance Readings for Counselors*, edited by Farwell and Peters (53); and *Counseling: Readings in Theory and Practice*, edited by McGowan and Schmidt (127). Crow and Crow's book contains 95 articles selected from school counseling manuals and guides and from professional journals. Although it is some years old, mention should be made of *The Yearbook of Education, 1955: Guidance and Counseling,* edited by Hall and Lauwerys (*199*). This publication included chapters contributed by a large group of guidance specialists in Europe and America.

The fall, 1962, number of the *Harvard Educational Review* (*79*) was devoted to the topic "Guidance—An Examination," in which various authorities contributed their scholarly and critical views on the subject.

A growing problem for guidance workers is that of keeping abreast of current guidance literature in educational and psychological journals and other periodicals. *Personnel Literature* (*150*), a bi-monthly publication of the United States Civil Service Commission, can be of definite aid in this connection. It lists and briefly annotates books, pamphlets, periodical articles, and other publications received in the library of the Civil Service Commission. Unpublished dissertations and microfilms are also listed. While many of the items listed are more pertinent to industry than to education, school counselors may well make use of this periodical.

GROUP WORK

Within the last ten years, much has been written about group work in guidance. A large proportion of this material is in periodical literature, some of which was listed at the end of Chapter XX, but several books on the subject are now available. A leading book of this kind is Bennett's *Guidance and Counseling in Groups* (*13*), which covers developments in both research and practice. Kemp's *Perspectives on the Group Process—A Foundation for Counseling with Groups* (*113*) is a book of readings which may serve as a basic course for group counselors or teachers.

Guidance in connection with homeroom activities was discussed in a book by Vivian Ross (*166*).

Books and manuals which may serve as guides to the specific group guidance activities may be of considerable help to the guidance worker if they are not used too routinely. A small book by Wrenn, Hein, and Schwarzrock, *Planned Group Guidance* (*228*), which was mentioned in a preceding chapter, contains a series of 38 discussion projects with outlines of procedures. A longer book by Norris, Zeran, and Hatch, *The Information Service in Guidance: Occupational, Educational, Social* (*142*), should also serve a useful purpose.

Books dealing with the psychology of classroom instruction are closely related to the field of group guidance. One of these is *Psychology in Teaching* by Henry P. Smith (*181*).

THE TEACHER AS A GUIDANCE WORKER

The procedures of group guidance and the methods of a modern teacher who makes the pupil the focal point of instruction are scarcely distinguishable one from the other. A considerable number of books written especially to help the teacher participate in guidance services have been published since the middle 1950s. One of the more recent of these is *Teacher's Guide to Group Vocational Guidance* by Shertzer and Knowles (*175*). Earlier books by well-known authors are *The Role of the Teacher in Personnel Work* by Strang (*189*) and *Student Personnel Work as Deeper Teaching,* edited by Lloyd-Jones and Smith (*124*).

BOOKS FOR THE PROSPECTIVE COLLEGE STUDENT

Books about college, written especially for high school pupils, help both the teacher and the counselor provide guidance oriented toward college. Among these books are *How to Prepare for College* by Lass (*117*), *Complete Planning for College* by Sulkin (*193*), and *Your College Education—How to Pay For It* by Splaver (*182*). The last book contains information concerning the various financial aid programs.

VOCATIONAL GUIDANCE

Although educational and vocational guidance cannot and should not be clearly differentiated, certain books are so closely related to the vocational guidance aspect of personnel work that special attention should be drawn to them.

HISTORY AND SCOPE OF VOCATIONAL GUIDANCE

In recent years, clinical counseling and psychotherapy carried on by trained psychologists and counselors and directed toward personal and social development have become increasingly important in guidance theory and practice; but it is well for every guidance worker to keep in mind that the origin of the guidance movement in the United States and much of the impetus of this movement was in the need for better vocational adjustment and placement on the part of thousands of young people, and that *in the minds of many laymen the vocational guidance function is the main justification for the introduction of a guidance program into our schools and for its support through public funds.* An appreciation of the earlier history and scope of vocational guidance may be obtained through such publications as Brewer's *History of Vocational Guidance: Origins and Early Development* (20) and the *Encyclopedia of Vocational Guidance,* edited by Oscar Kaplan (112). A more recent and briefer survey of the history of guidance services, with special reference to vocational guidance, may be found in Chapter VI of *Guidance Services* by Humphreys, Traxler, and North (103).

TEXTBOOKS ON VOCATIONAL GUIDANCE

Forrester's *Methods of Vocational Guidance* (56) has long been a standard text in this field. *Man in a World at Work,* edited by Borow (19), was written in recognition of the fiftieth anniversary of the National Vocational Guidance Association. Its four major parts are concerned with the roots of vocational guidance, the occupational kaleidoscope, research horizons, and the professional practice of vocational guidance. Psychological approaches to vocational guidance were presented in *The Psychology of Occupations* by Anne Roe (160) and in *The Psychology of Careers* by Super (194).

Although it is not intended primarily as a textbook, the Sixty-fourth Yearbook of the National Society for the Study of Education, Part I: *Vocational Education,* edited by Barlow (10), provides a comprehensive treatment of vocational education, and could well serve as a text and as a basis for vocational education in the future.

OCCUPATIONAL INFORMATION

Among the writers who have contributed much published information about occupations are Baer and Roeber, Shartle, Forrester, and Hoppock. Baer and Roeber's *Occupational Information: The Dynamics of Its Nature and Use* (8) discusses occupational structure and functioning. Shartle's book, *Occupational Information: Its Development and Application* (174) was considerably revised in the third edition published in 1959. The revised edition of Forrester's *Occupational Literature: An Annotated Bibliography* (57) gives its major attention to literature published since about 1960. Hoppock's *Occupational Information* (101) is a revision of his well-known *Group Guidance.*

In recent years, there has been a trend toward an organized attempt to introduce occupational information to children in the elementary school. Willa Norris's *Occupational Information in the Elementary School* (141) is a practical and helpful book on the theory and methods of furnishing occupational information from the kindergarten through the sixth grade.

OCCUPATIONAL AND CAREER CHOICE AND DEVELOPMENT

Two small books on career development published by the College Entrance Examination Board are Tiedeman, O'Hara, and Baruch's *Career Development: Choice and Adjustment* (205) and *Career Development: Self-Concept Theory* by Super, Starishevsky, Matlin, and Jordaan (196). *Occupational Choice* is a recent revision of an earlier book by Ginzberg, Ginsburg, Axelrad, and Herma (68). Sifferd prepared a straightforward text, *Selecting An Occupation* (177), which includes methods of studying occupations and finding employment opportunities.

EMPLOYMENT NEEDS AND OPPORTUNITIES

One of the most difficult problems met by the modern guidance worker whose functions include vocational counseling is to keep informed on the present and future needs for workers in different occupations, and on the potential opportunities for their counselees in various lines of work—particularly in new and rapidly growing fields. This is a continuing problem which the counselor must meet through his own efforts, but various publications contain helpful information and suggestions relative to the question. Among these are Willis and others. *Education for a Changing World of Work* (221), the report of the President's panel of consultants on vocational education, and *Why People Work: Changing Incentives in a Troubled World* by Levenstein (120). Venn's *Man, Education, and Work: Postsecondary and Technical Education* (213) vigorously presents the thesis that the national economy and social structure will suffer great damage unless provision is made for more and better education on the semiprofessional, technical, and skilled levels. Personnel workers at the higher educational levels will be interested in a recent book, *Managers for Tomorrow* prepared by the staff of Rohrer, Hibler, and Replogle, a firm of industrial psychologists, and edited by Charles D. Flory (54). This book considers personality factors in the development of executives.

INTERESTS AND THEIR MEASUREMENT

The field of interests is closely related to vocational and educational guidance choice and placement.

It is also one of the broad categories that counselors must explore before they are fully equipped to understand the individual child. Strong carried on the most sustained studies of interests that are related to vocational choice. His book, *Vocational Interests of Men and Women* (192), is still a classic in the field, and it has been supplemented by a number of more recent studies reported in various places in educational literature by the same author. As stated in Chapter VII, the Strong Vocational Interest Blanks for Men and for Women were being revised and updated at the time this book was under revision.

A different approach to the measurement of interests is represented by the Kuder Preference Record. The *Administrator's Manual for the Kuder Preference Record —Vocational* (114) contains valuable information relative to the classification of occupations according to major interests as indicated by this instrument.

TESTING IN A GUIDANCE PROGRAM

In order to study the individual child adequately and to help him understand himself, the counselor must, of course, be familiar with the meaning, interpretation, and use of test results,. Many books on testing are available, and the counselor should certainly have one or more of these at hand.

GENERAL TEXTS

Five excellect general textbooks in this field are Remmers, Gage, and Rummel's *A Practical Introduction to Measurement and Evaluation* (157); *Measurement in Today's Schools*, a thorough revision by Julian C. Stanley (184) of a book originally written by the late C. C. Ross; Gerberich, Greene, and Jorgensen's *Measurement and Evaluation in the Modern School* (66); Thorndike and Hagen's *Measurement and Evaluation in Psychology and Education* (203); and Berdie, Swanson, Hagenah, and Layton's *Testing in Guidance and Counseling* (15). The guidance worker who does not have a background in testing may wish to start with less extensive and formidable reading, such as Leona Tyler's small book, *Tests and Measurements* (212) or Froehlich and Hoyt's *Guidance Testing* (62), or two brochures published by the Educational Records Bureau: *Testing Guide for Teachers* (198) and *Parents' Guide to Understanding Tests* (146).

Gronlund recently made available a book, *Measurement and Evaluation in Teaching* (78), in which prin-

ciples and procedures are emphasized and lengthy descriptions of tests are avoided, and which presents evaluation as an integral part of the teaching-learning process. For counselors concerned with interpreting scores on the Scholastic Aptitude Test there is a monograph, *College Board Score Reports: A Guide for Counselors* (32).

BOOKS ON PSYCHOLOGICAL TESTING

Two books by competent authorities on the testing of mental and personal qualities are *Psychological Testing* by Anastasi (3) and *Essentials of Psychological Testing* by Cronbach (36). Anastasi's book deals with the principles of psychological testing, general classification tests, differential testing of abilities, and the measurement of personality characteristics. Another book in this general area is *Theory and Practice of Psychological Testing* by Freeman (58).

ACHIEVEMENT TESTING

The most authoritative and comprehensive book on measurement in the field of education was *Educational Measurement*, edited by Lindquist (123). This book, which was published in 1951, is still helpful, but is in need of some revision. It contains chapters contributed by 20 specialists in measurement, and was prepared during a period of about five years with the cooperation of numerous other authorities in the testing field. It consists of three parts: (1) the functions of measurement in education, (2) the construction of achievement tests, and (3) measurement theory. It definitely is not an elementary book, but it is one of the most important and valuable books ever published in the measurement field.

A recent book by Travers *An Introduction to Educational Measurement* (208) is also a good reference in this field. It contains four parts: background for educational measurement, measuring the intellectual outcomes of education, measuring personality development, and predicting pupil progress. Other useful books in which the measurement of educational achievement is emphasized are: Greene, Jorgensen, and Gerberich, *Measurement and Evaluation in the Elementary School*, 2d ed. (74) and *Measurement and Evaluation in the Secondary School*, 2d ed. (75), and Torgerson and Adams, *Measurement and Evaluation for the Elementary School Teacher* (206). This last book includes the evaluative process, the study of individuals, the improvement of instruction, administrative and supervisory aspects, and implications for corrective procedures.

VOCATIONAL AND PERSONNEL TESTING

The most comprehensive book concerned with testing for purposes of guidance toward vocations is *Appraising Vocational Fitness by Means of Psychological Tests* by Super and Crites (*195*). This book serves a purpose somewhat similar to that formerly served by Bingham's classic *Aptitudes and Aptitude Testing*, which has been out of print for some years. The breadth of the book may be inferred from the following headings: Intelligence, Proficiency, Clerical Aptitude, Manual Dexterities, Mechanical Aptitude, Spatial Visualization, Aesthetic Judgment and Artistic Ability, Musical Talent, Batteries for Specific Occupations, Interests, and Personality and Temperament. Portions of the general texts mentioned earlier are also applicable to this section.

APPRAISAL BY MEANS OF TESTS AND OTHER DEVICES

A book by Adams, *Measurement and Evaluation in Education, Psychology, and Guidance* (*1*) is concerned with the basic principles and procedures of testing, the study of individuals, the use of tests in improving instruction, and measurement and evaluation in administration, supervision, and guidance. Other books in this area are *Judging Student Progress* by Thomas (*200*) and *Evaluation in Modern Education* by Wrightstone, Justman, and Robbins (*229*).

MENTAL MEASUREMENTS YEARBOOKS

Counselors who have the problem of selecting tests for various purposes should have access to Buros's *Mental Measurements Yearbooks* (*22, 23*). These yearbooks not only provide an extensive and detailed listing of the newer tests and the newer books on measurement, but also contain hundreds of test reviews written by measurement specialists. Although some of the reviews are subjective and reflect the personal bias of the writers, the reviews, as a whole, provide the best appraisal of objective tests available anywhere.

CRITICISM AND EVALUATION OF TESTS AS APPRAISAL DEVICES

Within the last decade a good many books and articles on tests and testing have been written for popular consumption. Some of these have been highly critical of educational and psychological testing, and a few have been biased and misinformed. But, on the whole, their publication has been salutary, for they have led to a re-examination of the strengths and weaknesses of testing by scholars in the field. A carefully prepared book dealing with the social impact of testing is *The Search for Ability*, by David A. Goslin (*71*). Chauncey and Dobbin wrote an objective, dispassionate appraisal of testing techniques and the uses of tests under the title *Testing: Its Place in Education Today* (*30*).

CASE STUDIES

Books dealing wholly or in part with case studies are very valuable references in connection with any guidance program. One of the best of these books is *The High School Student: A Book of Cases* by Rothney (*167*). Detailed case records of 27 boys and girls are reported in this book and are classified into certain groups, such as the troubled ones, the ones in trouble, the quiet ones, and so forth. The book also contains discussion questions and a chapter on "Principles, Problems, and Methods."

The first part of a study by Rothney and Roens, *Guidance of American Youth* (*168*), contains case reports for ten pupils, including not only information about the nature of each case but also progress of counseling, and follow-up several years later. Illustrative of case work in clinical counseling, verbatim reports of five cases each were given by Callis, Polmantier, and Roeber in *A Casebook of Counseling* (*26*).

In a publication of The Psychological Corporation, *Counseling from Profiles: A Casebook for the Differential Aptitude Tests,* Bennett, Seashore, and Wesman (*12*) approached case work from the standpoint of measurement with an extensive test battery, and showed how test profiles along with other information could be used in brief case studies of pupils in the junior and senior high schools.

While some case studies reported in educational and psychological literature are more extensive and elaborate than would be found in the usual school situation, other reports illustrate the kind of study that teachers or counselors should be able to handle. For instance, a chapter in which 15 case studies prepared by classroom teachers were presented was included in the Educational Records Bureau report of the Public School Demonstration Project, *Guidance in Public Secondary Schools* issued some 25 years ago (*209*). Recently, Womer and Frick reported 25 brief case studies illustrating the use of test results for a variety of counseling situations, in their *Personalizing Test Use: A Counselor's Casebook* (*223*).

CUMULATIVE RECORDS

Because some kind of cumulative record is widely used in guidance programs, reports dealing with the nature and use of cumulative records are likely to be of particular interest to personnel workers. Cumulative records of test results are illustrated and discussed in Humphreys, Traxler, and North's *Guidance Services* (*103*) and the Educational Records Bureau's *Testing Guide for Teachers* (*198*). The *Manual for Cumulative Records* published by the American Council on Education (*130*) is not just a manual for the American Council Cumulative Record Forms but it provides a well-planned introduction to the history, uses, and procedures of introducing and maintaining records of the cumulative type. Discussions and illustrations of the uses of cumulative records are likewise found in various journal articles and monographs.

STUDIES RELATED TO GUIDANCE

Notwithstanding recent progress, the comparatively young field of guidance does not yet have a clearly defined body of principles and procedures founded upon research of its own. From the beginning, it has been characterized by a considerable degree of confusion and uncertainty, for it is a meeting ground, and in a sense a battleground, of a host of professional workers whose basic experience and training are in many different areas—medicine, psychiatry, psychology, education, psychometrics, religion, social work, and industry. These specialists from other fields bring their opinions and beliefs and prejudices, as well as their more objectively based knowledge, to bear upon guidance practices.

Guidance literature is replete with statements calling attention to the need for more and more research. Guidance functionaries do not themselves seem greatly inclined to fill the vacuum with studies of their own. Many guidance workers and counselors seem temperamentally unsuited to the task of carrying on serious research. They are inclined to be warm, outgoing personalities who like to deal with people—as they should be if counselees are going to turn to them in large numbers for help. Not infrequently, they are much concerned with the theoretical basis of counseling, and sometimes they develop fine theories for which there is not much objective support. For research is a lonely business—a business which seems particularly suited to introverts. So guidance services go forward and expand out of a background which is perhaps 5 percent research and 95 percent faith.

There are, nevertheless, hundreds of studies which have some relationship to the understanding and guidance of the individual child—studies reported in educational and psychological journals, doctoral dissertations, psychological monographs, and many other places. Counselors cannot be expected to be familiar with all these, but they should have a bowing acquaintance with some of the more significant investigations, and, even more important, they should know where to turn for references dealing with research on their problems. The more important research on "student personnel work" and "student records and reports" up to 1960 is reviewed in the third edition of the *Encyclopedia of Educational Research,* edited by Harris and Liba (*92:1415–1442*). Persons desiring to obtain a rather thorough historical background of research in the field of guidance and personnel work might advisedly begin by reading these two sections of the *Encyclopedia.*

Perhaps the most comprehensive and systematic periodic summary of research on personnel work is to be found in the *Guidance, Counseling, and Personnel Services* issue which appears at intervals of three years in the *Review of Educational Research* published by the American Educational Research Association. An idea of the scope and organization of this issue of the *Review* may be obtained from a listing of the chapter titles which appeared in the April 1963 number (*80*). These were "Foundations," "Elementary and Secondary School Programs," "Higher Education Programs," "Selection, Preparation, and Professionalization of Specialists," "Counseling," "The Appraisal Function," "Vocational Development Process," "Group Procedures," and "Program Evaluation."

STUDIES RELATED TO THE DISTRIBUTIVE FUNCTION OF GUIDANCE

In performing that counseling function having to do with the distribution of individuals to educational and vocational opportunities, counselors must make a special effort to look into the future. They need the results of studies which will help them understand trends in supply and demand for different kinds of workers. Automation is profoundly changing many vocations, eliminating many, and creating a host of new ones. An exceedingly important and valuable little booklet on this subject is *Automation: The Threat and the Promise,* edited by Miller and Swanson (*135*). This publication contains papers by Diebold, Winn, Gross, and Samler. These are not reports of research, but they are based on the results of research, and they are perhaps as authoritative as anything the counselor could read on the subject of automation and the manpower revolution.

More extensive, although somewhat older references, are Wolfle's *America's Resources of Specialized Talent*, a report of the Commission on Human Resources and Advanced Training (*222*), and *A Policy for Skilled Manpower* by the National Manpower Council (*138*). The latter book calls attention to shortages in fields requiring a high degree of talent and training, and urges increased effort to improve the training, guidance, and use of manpower.

In a recent study, Harbison and Myers urged that the development of human resources is a more reliable index of the modernization and growth of nations than any other single measure. Their study was reported in *Education, Manpower, and Economic Growth: Strategies of Human Resource Development* (*89*).

Studies pertaining to relations between secondary and higher education furnish the counselor with a background for better educational guidance. Historically, one of the most influential studies of this kind was the study of the relations of secondary and higher education in Pennsylvania, carried on under the auspices of the Carnegie Foundation for the Advancement of Teaching and reported in *The Student and His Knowledge* by Learned and Wood (out of print).

A number of more recent studies have important implications for guidance from secondary school to college. Among the most comprehensive was a set of four related projects sponsored by The Fund for the Advancement of Education, on which a progress report was made during the 1950s in the publication *Bridging the Gap Between School and College* (*21*). One of these studies was based upon cooperation between three schools and three colleges in developing a coordinated program of general education; a second study had to do with ways of meeting the needs of exceptionally endowed students in secondary schools; a third was concerned with admission to college with advanced standing; and the fourth study was centered around the early admission of students to college. The first of these studies was reported at somewhat greater length in a book published by the Harvard University Press (*65*).

Among reports of other studies having implications for the counseling of college-bound students are *Who Should Go to College* by Hollinshead (*99*), *The Impending Tidal Wave of Students* by Thompson (*201*), *A Survey of the Education of Gifted Children* by Havighurst, Stivers, and DeHaan (*96*), *General Education: Explorations in Evaluation*, the final report of the Cooperative Study of Evaluation in General Education of the American Council on Education, by Dressel and Mayhew (*45*), and *Improving Transition from School to College*, a study of college admission by the Committee on School and College Relations of the Educational Records Bureau

(*210*). The Bureau committee's study of college admission was followed up by a study of the adjustment of college freshmen based on a questionnaire submitted to about 500 freshmen, a report of which was made in *College Freshmen Speak Out* by Townsend (*207*). A later study at the high school level by the same committee was reported in *High School Students Speak Out* by Mallery (*129*).

STUDIES PERTAINING TO ADJUSTMENT

Studies of the character and behavior of children and adolescents obviously help counselors understand individual counselees. Among studies of this kind, Havighurst and Taba reported an investigation of *Adolescent Character and Personality* (*95*) in which they identified personality types among 16-year-old youths.

The rise of psychotherapy and client-centered procedures has naturally led to an interest in research on the values of these procedures. Although enthusiasm in this area seems to have run considerably ahead of research, a growing number of studies is becoming available. Rogers and Dymond led the way with some advanced research in client-centered counseling at the University of Chicago Counseling Center in their book, *Psychotherapy and Personality Change* (*164*).

The level of aspiration of children and adolescents is related both to their distribution to educational and vocational opportunities and to their adjustment. Procedures for changing aspiration in young people are, therefore, an important area of research. Drews (*46*) carried on research, supported by the Educational Media Branch of the United States Office of Education, on "The Effectiveness of Special Training With Audio-Visuals in Changing Aspirations in Intellectually Superior Students." The study was in process of publication at the time this book was being prepared.

STUDIES PERTAINING TO BROAD VALUES OF AND NEEDS FOR GUIDANCE

Rothney and Roens' study, *Guidance of American Youth* (*168*), was a very thorough study of the procedures and outcomes of counseling. Longitudinal and follow-up procedures were used with a large group of pupils who had had continuous counseling during the five years in which they attended Grades 8 through 12.

A number of reports on guidance needs and outcomes has been issued by the University of Minnesota, which has always been a leader in objective evaluation in the guidance area. These studies include *Guidance Procedures in High School* by Wrenn and Dugan (*227*),

After High School—What? by Berdie (*14*), and *A Study of Participation in College Activities* by Williamson, Layton, and Snoke (*220*).

A recent book of readings in studies related to the guidance field is *Psychological Studies of Human Development,* by Kuhlen and Thompson (*116*).

STUDIES OF THE MEASUREMENT OF MENTAL ABILITIES AND OF THE RELATION OF ABILITY TO CAREER CHOICE AND PERFORMANCE

In their book, *10,000 Careers,* Thorndike and Hagen (*202*) reported comparisons of the results of aptitude tests taken by 10,000 men in military service with their performance in postwar careers.

By means of a questionnaire Ginzberg and Herma followed up a group of Columbia University students with high intellectual potential and found that 10 to 15 years after their time at Columbia, social and personal factors had interacted to shape career patterns and levels of achievement. Their study is reported in *Talent and Performance* (*69*).

In recent years, a large number of research workers have reported studies based on the SRA Tests of Primary Mental Abilities by the Thurstones, and studies of other tests yielding profiles of mental abilities, such as the Differential Aptitude Tests, the California Test of Mental Maturity, and the Holzinger-Crowder Uni-Factor Tests. Research on these tests and numerous others is reviewed every three years in the "Educational and Psychological Testing" number of the *Review of Educational Research* (*50*). This is the counselor's best source of information concerning research on tests of mental ability, tests of special aptitude, tests of achievement, and projective and nonprojective measures of personality.

VISUAL AIDS TO GUIDANCE

Since projectors for 16mm sound film are standard equipment in most colleges and secondary schools, instructors of guidance courses, guidance directors, and persons in charge of guidance workshops should be alert to opportunities to use guidance films in promoting understanding of pupil behavior, problems encountered by young people, and procedures of organizing and administering guidance. Films such as *Counseling Adolescents* (*237*), *Getting Along with Parents* (*239*), *Learning to Study* (*243*), *Personality and Emotions* (*249*), *Prepare Through Education* (*251*), *College Perspectives* (*236*), and the other films listed in the last section of the bibli-

ography can be used to advantage in educating counselors and teachers in guidance procedures. Most of them are designed to be shown to students, as well. Information about films that are available without charge may be found in Horkheimer and Diffor's *Educators Guide to Free Films* (*232*). A publication on *U.S. Government Films for Educational Use—1963* was prepared by Reid, Grubbs, and Clugston (*233*).

ANNOTATIONS, REVIEWS, BASIC GUIDANCE KITS

In order to keep posted on the ever-growing literature on guidance and personnel work, counselors should have access to some of the more important annotations, book reviews, and packaged informational materials in the field. Abstracts of articles on guidance and counseling, educational guidance, and educational measurement, as well as on the whole range of the field of psychology, are presented in *Psychological Abstracts* (*155*), published bi-monthly by the American Psychological Association. Reviews of books pertinent to guidance are published each month during the school year in the *Personnel and Guidance Journal* (*149*). Science Research Associates, which began publication of guidance materials about 1940, has considerably expanded its offerings in recent years. Among these materials, the *Basic Guidance Kits I and II* (*11*), consisting of well-designed books and pamphlets, should prove useful to both the beginning guidance worker and the experienced counselor.

REFERENCES*

1. Adams, Georgia Sachs. *Measurement and Evaluation in Education, Psychology and Guidance.* New York: Holt, Rinehart and Winston, Inc., 1964. Pp. 608, $8.95.
2. *Admission to American Colleges.* Sixth Report of Committee on School and College Relations of Educational Records Bureau. New York: Educational Records Bureau, 1964. Pp. 28, 50¢.
3. Anastasi, Anne. *Psychological Testing,* 2nd ed. New York: The Macmillan Company, 1961. Pp. 671, $7.95.
*4. Anastasi, Anne. *Fields of Applied Psychology.* New York: McGraw-Hill Book Company, Inc., 1964. Pp. 621, $8.95.
5. Anderson, Scarvia, Katz, Martin, and Shimberg, Benjamin. *Meeting the Test.* New York: Four

* All starred references are especially recommended.

Winds Press, 1965. Pp. 184, $3.50.

6. Andrew, Dean G., and Willey, Roy DeVerl. *Administration and Organization of the Guidance Program.* New York: Harper & Row, Publishers, 1958. Pp. 330, $5.50.

7. Arbuckle, Dugald S. *Pupil Personnel Services in American Schools.* Englewood Cliffs, N.J.: Allyn and Bacon, Inc., 1962. Pp. 419, $7.25.

8. Baer, Max F., and Roeber, Edward C. *Occupational Information: The Dynamics of Its Nature and Use.* Chicago: Science Research Associates, Inc., 1964. Pp. 495, $7.50.

9. Baldwin, Alfred L. *Behavior and Development in Childhood.* New York: Holt, Rinehart, and Winston, Inc., 1955. Pp. 637, $7.95.

10. Barlow, Melvin L. (ed.). *Vocational Education.* Sixty-fourth Yearbook of the National Society for the Study of Education, Part I. Chicago: The University of Chicago Press, 1965. Pp. 301, $5.00.

11. *Basic Guidance Kits I and II.* Chicago: Science Research Associates, Inc. Approximately 1950–1965. Twenty-four books and monographs. $59.00 both sets; $40, Kit I; $22.50, Kit II.

12. Bennett, George K., Seashore, Harold G., and Wesman, Alexander G. *Counseling from Profiles: A Casebook for the Differential Aptitude Tests.* New York: The Psychological Corporation, 1951. Pp. 96, $1.75.

*13. Bennett, Margaret E. *Guidance and Counseling in Groups,* 2nd ed. New York: McGraw-Hill Book Company, Inc., 1963. Pp. 440, $7.75.

14. Berdie, Ralph F., with chapters by Wilbur E. Layton and Ben Willerman. *After High School—What?* Minneapolis: The University of Minnesota Press, 1954. Pp. 240, $4.25.

15. Berdie, Ralph F., Swanson, Edward O., Hagenah, Theda, and Layton, Wilber F. *Testing in Guidance and Counseling.* New York: McGraw-Hill Book Company, Inc., 1963. Pp. 286, $6.95.

16. Bernard, Harold W. *Mental Hygiene for Classroom Teachers.* New York: McGraw-Hill Book Company, Inc., 1961. Pp. 498, $6.95.

17. Blanchard, Howard L., and Flaum, Laurence S. *Guidance, A Longitudinal Approach,* Minneapolis: Burgess Publishing Company, 1962. Pp. 333, $4.95.

18. Bordin, Edward S. *Psychological Counseling.* New York: Appleton-Century-Crofts, Inc., 1955. Pp. 410. (Out of print.)

19. Borow, Henry (ed.). *Man in a World at Work.* Boston: Houghton Mifflin Company, 1964. Pp. 606, $8.25.

20. Brewer, John M. *History of Vocational Guidance: Origins and Early Development.* New York: Harper & Row, Publishers, 1942. Pp. 344. (Out of print).

21. *Bridging the Gap between High School and College.* Progress Report on Four Related Projects Supported by The Fund for the Advancement of Education. New York: The Fund for the Advancement of Education, 1953. Pp. 128.

*22. Buros, Oscar K. (ed.). *The Fifth Mental Measurements Yearbook.* Highland Park, N.J.: The Gryphon Press, 1959. Pp. 1292, $22.50.

*23. Buros, Oscar K. (ed.). *The Sixth Mental Measurements Yearbook.* Highland Park, N.J.: The Gryphon Press, 1965. Pp. xxxvi + 1714, $32.50.

24. Burt, Sir Cyril. *The Causes and Treatment of Backwardness.* New York: Philosophical Library, Inc., 1953. Pp. 128. (Out of print.)

25. Byrne, Richard H. *The School Counselor.* Boston: Houghton Mifflin Company, 1963. Pp. 296, $6.00.

26. Callis, Robert, Polmantier, Paul C., and Roeber, Edward C. *A Casebook of Counseling.* New York: Appleton-Century-Crofts, Inc., 1955. Pp. 352, $5.00.

27. Cameron, Norman. *Personality Development and Psychopathology: A Dynamic Approach.* Boston: Houghton Mifflin Company, 1963. Pp. 793, $8.75.

28. Carroll, Herbert A. *Mental Hygiene: The Dynamics of Adjustment,* 4th ed. Englewood Cliffs, N.J.: Prentice-Hall, Inc., 1964. Pp. 416, $7.00.

29. Cass, James, and Birnbaum, Max. *Comparative Guide to American Colleges.* New York: Harper & Row, Publishers, 1965. Pp. 576, $8.95 cloth; $3.95 paper.

*30. Chauncey, Henry, and Dobbin, John E. *Testing: Its Place in Education Today.* New York: Harper & Row, Publishers, 1964. Pp. 240, $4.95.

31. Cole, Luella, and Hall, Irma N. *Psychology of Adolescence,* 6th ed. New York: Holt, Rinehart and Winston, Inc., 1964. Pp. 668, $7.50.

32. *College Board Score Reports: A Guide for Counselors.* New York: College Entrance Examination Board, 1963. Pp. 45, 1–5 copies free.

33. Conant, James B. *The American High School Today.* New York: McGraw-Hill Book Company, Inc., 1959. Pp. 140, $1.95, paper.

34. Cottingham, Harold F. *Guidance in Elementary Schools.* Bloomington, Ill.: McKnight & McKnight, Publishing Company, 1956. Pp. 400, $5.50.

*35. Cottingham, Harold F., and Hopke, William. *Guidance in the Junior High School.* Bloomington, Ill.: McKnight & McKnight Publishing Company, 1961. Pp. 390, $6.00.

*36. Cronbach, Lee J. *Essentials of Psychological Testing,* 2nd ed. New York: Harper & Row, Publishers, 1960. Pp. 650, $7.50.

37. Crow, Lester D., and Crow, Alice (eds.). *Readings in Guidance: Principles, Practices, Organization, Administration.* New York: David McKay Company, Inc., 1962. Pp. 626, $3.95.

38. Crow, Lester D., and Crow, Alice. *Adolescent Development and Adjustment,* 2nd ed. New York: McGraw-Hill Book Company, Inc., 1965. Pp. 544, $7.95.

39. Cruikshank, William M. *Psychology of Exceptional Children and Youth,* 2nd ed. Englewood Cliffs, N.J.: Prentice-Hall, Inc., 1963. Pp. 623, $7.95.

40. Curran, Charles A. *Counseling in Catholic Life and*

Education. New York: The Macmillan Company, 1952. Pp. 488, $5.75.

41. Cutts, Norma E., and Moseley, Nicholas. *Bright Children*. New York: G. P. Putnam's Sons, 1953. Pp. 238. (Out of print.)

42. Dame, J. Frank, and Brinkman, Albert R. *Guidance in Business Education*. Cincinnati, Ohio: South-Western Publishing Company, 1954. Pp. 298, $4.00.

*43. Detjen, Ervin W., and Detjen, Mary F. *Elementary School Guidance*, rev. ed. New York: McGraw-Hill Book Company, Inc., 1963. Pp. 256, $5.95.

*44. *Dictionary of Occupational Titles*. Volumes I and II. Washington, D.C.: Superintendent of Documents, 1965. Vol. I, $5.00; Vol. II, $4.25.

45. Dressel, Paul L., and Mayhew, Lewis B. *General Education: Explorations in Evaluation*. The final report of the Cooperative Study of Evaluation in General Education of the American Council on Education. Washington, D.C.: American Council on Education, 1954. Pp. 298, $3.50.

46. Drews, Elizabeth Monroe. *Creative Intellectual Style in Gifted Adolescents; Being and Becoming: A Cosmic Approach to Curriculum Revision*. Research under NDEA, Title VII. East Lansing, Mich.: The author, Michigan State University, 1965.

47. Dunn, Lloyd M. (ed.). *Exceptional Children in the Schools*. New York: Holt, Rinehart, and Winston, Inc., 1963. Pp. 580, $6.00.

48. Dunsmoor, Clarence C., and Miller, Leonard M. *Principles and Methods of Guidance for Teachers*, rev. ed. Scranton, Pa.: International Textbook Company, 1950. Pp. 400, $4.00.

49. Durost, Walter, and Prescott, George A. *Essentials of Measurement for Teachers*. New York: Harcourt, Brace & World, Inc., 1962. Pp. 167, $4.25.

50. "Educational and Psychological Testing," *Review of Educational Research*, Vol. XXXV. Washington, D.C.: American Educational Research Association. (February 1965), Pp. 101.

51. Erickson, Clifford E. *The Counseling Interview*. Englewood Cliffs, N.J.: Prentice-Hall, Inc., 1950. Pp. 174. (Out of print.)

*52. Evraiff, William. *Helping Counselors Grow Professionally*. Englewood Cliffs, N.J.: Prentice-Hall, Inc., 1963. Pp. 384, $6.50.

53. Farwell, Gail F., and Peters Herman J. (eds.). *Guidance Readings for Counselors*. Chicago: Rand McNally & Company, 1960. Pp. 691, $6.75.

54. Flory, Charles D. (ed.). *Managers for Tomorrow*. New York: New American Library of World Literature, Inc., 1965. Pp. 326, $5.95.

55. Forest, Ilse. *Child Development*. New York: McGraw-Hill Book Company, Inc., 1954. Pp. 286, $7.95.

56. Forrester, Gertrude. *Methods of Vocational Guidance*, rev. ed. Boston: D. C. Heath and Company, 1951. Pp. 461, $7.00.

57. Forrester, Gertrude. *Occupational Literature: An An-notated Bibliography, 1964 Edition*. New York: H. W. Wilson Company, 1964. Pp. 675, $8.50.

58. Freeman, Frank S. *Theory and Practice of Psychological Testing*, 3rd ed. New York: Holt, Rinehart and Winston, Inc., 1962. Pp. 720, $7.95.

59. Freud, Sigmund. *A General Introduction to Psychoanalysis*. Authorized English translation of revised edition by Joan Riviere. Garden City, N.Y.: Doubleday & Company, Inc., 1943. Pp. 412. (Out of print.)

60. Froehlich, Clifford P. *Guidance Services in Smaller Schools*. New York: McGraw-Hill Book Company, Inc., 1950. Pp. 352. (Out of print.)

61. Froehlich, Clifford P. *Guidance Services in Schools*, 2nd ed. New York: McGraw-Hill Book Company, Inc. 1958. Pp. 383, $6.95.

62. Froehlich, Clifford P., and Hoyt, Kenneth B. *Guidance Testing*. Chicago: Science Research Associates, Inc., 1959. Pp. 438, $7.50.

63. Gardner, John W. *Self-Renewal*. New York: Harper & Row, Publishers, 1964. Pp. 142, $3.50.

64. Garrison, Karl C., and Force, Dewey G., Jr. *The Psychology of Exceptional Children*, 3rd ed. New York: The Ronald Press Company, 1959. Pp. 586, $6.50.

65. *General Education in School and College*. A Committee Report by Members of Faculties of Andover, Exeter, Lawrenceville, Harvard, Princeton, and Yale (Alan R. Blackmer, chairman). Cambridge, Mass.: Harvard University Press, 1952. Pp. 142.

*66. Gerberich, J. Raymond, Greene, Harry A., and Jorgensen, Albert N. *Measurement and Evaluation in the Modern School*. New York: David McKay Company, Inc., 1962. Pp. 622, $6.95.

67. Gesell, Arnold, Ilg, Frances, and Ames, Louis. *Youth: Years Ten to Sixteen*. New York: Harper & Row, Publishers, 1956. Pp. 542, $5.00.

68. Ginzberg, Eli; Ginsburg, Sol W.; Axelrad, Sidney; and Herma, John L. *Occupational Choice*. New York: Columbia University Press, 1963. Pp. 271, $6.00.

69. Ginzberg, Eli, and Herma, John L. *Talent and Performance*. New York: Columbia University Press, 1964. Pp. 280, $5.00.

*70. Glanz, Edward C. *Foundations and Principles of Guidance*. Englewood Cliffs, N.J.: Allyn and Bacon, Inc., 1964. Pp. 429, $7.50.

*71. Goslin, David A. *The Search for Ability*. New York: Russell Sage Foundation, 1963. Pp. 204, $4.00.

72. Gowan, John Curtis, and Demos, George D. (eds.). *The Guidance of Exceptional Children*. New York: David McKay Company, Inc., 1965. Pp. 450, $3.95.

73. Green, Sidney L., and Rothenberg, Alan B. *A Manual of First Aid for Mental Health in Childhood and Adolescence*. New York: The Julian Press, 1953. Pp. 278. (Out of print.)

74. Greene, Harry A., Jorgensen, Albert N., and Gerberich, J. Raymond. *Measurement and Evaluation in the Elementary School*, 2nd ed. New York: David McKay Company, Inc., 1953. Pp. 617, $5.75.

75. Greene, Harry A., Jorgensen, Albert N., and Gerberich, J. Raymond. *Measurement and Evaluation in the Secondary School,* 2nd ed. New York: David McKay Company, Inc., 1954. Pp. 690, $5.50.

76. Greenleaf, Walter J. *Occupations and Careers.* New York: McGraw-Hill Book Company, Inc., 1955. Pp. 580, $6.96.

77. Grinder, Robert E. (ed.). *Studies in Adolescence.* New York: The Macmillan Company, 1963. Pp. 540, $4.50.

78. Gronlund, Norman E. *Measurement and Evaluation in Teaching.* New York: The Macmillan Company, 1965. Pp. 420, $6.50.

79. "Guidance—An Examination," *Harvard Educational Review,* XXXII (Fall 1962), 373–524.

80. "Guidance, Counseling, and Personnel Services," *Review of Educational Research,* XXXIII (April 1963), 141–226.

81. *Guidance for Today's Children.* Thirty-third Yearbook of Department of Elementary-School Principals. Washington, D.C.: National Education Association, 1954. Pp. 278, $3.50.

82. *Guidance, 1964.* Department of Elementary-School Principals. Washington, D.C.: National Education Association, 1964. Pp. 76, 75¢.

83. *Guiding Today's Children.* Division of Research and Guidance, Office of Los Angeles County Superintendent of Schools. Monterey: California Test Bureau, 1959. Pp. 295, $4.75.

84. *Guiding Today's Youth.* Division of Research and Guidance, Office of Los Angeles County Superintendent of Schools. Monterey: California Test Bureau, 1962. Pp. 411, $5.95.

85. Gulliksen, Harold. *Theory of Mental Tests.* New York: John Wiley & Sons, Inc., 1950. Pp. 486, $8.50.

86. Hahn, Milton E., and MacLean, Malcolm S. *Counseling Psychology,* 2nd ed. New York: McGraw-Hill Book Company, Inc., 1955. Pp. 302, $6.50.

87. Hamilton, Kenneth W. *Counseling the Handicapped in the Rehabilitation Process.* New York: The Ronald Press Company, 1956. Pp. 296. (Out of print.)

88. Hamrin, Shirley A., and Paulson, Blanche B. *Counseling Adolescents.* Chicago: Science Research Associates, Inc., 1950. Pp. 380, $7.00.

89. Harbison, Frederick, and Myers, Charles A. *Education, Manpower, and Economic Growth: Strategies of Human Resource Development.* New York: McGraw-Hill Book Company, Inc., 1964. Pp. 229, $7.50.

90. Hardee, Melvene D. *The Faculty in College Counseling.* New York: McGraw-Hill Book Company, Inc., 1959. Pp. 391, $7.50.

91. Hardee, Melvene D. (ed.). *Personnel Services in Education.* The Fifty-eighth Yearbook of the National *Society for the Study of Education,* Part 2. Chicago: The University of Chicago Press, 1959. Pp. 303, $4.50.

*92. Harris, Chester W., and Liba, Marie R. (eds.). *Encyclopedia of Educational Research,* 3rd ed., pp. 1415–1442. A Project of the American Educational Research Association. New York: The Macmillan Company, 1960. Pp. 1564, $25.00.

93. Hatch, Raymond N., and Costar, James W. *Guidance Services in the Elementary School.* Dubuque, Iowa: William C. Brown Co., 1961. Pp. 202, $3.95.

94. Hatch, Raymond N., Dressel, Paul, and Costar, James. *Guidances Services in the Secondary School.* Dubuque, Iowa: William C. Brown Co., 1963. Pp. 206, $3.95.

95. Havighurst, Robert J., and Taba, Hilda. *Adolescent Character and Personality.* New York: John Wiley & Sons, Inc., 1949. Pp. 316, $5.95.

96. Havighurst, Robert J., Stivers, Eugene, and DeHaan, Robert F. *A Survey of the Education of Gifted Children.* Supplementary Educational Monographs No. 83. Chicago: The University of Chicago Press, November 1955. Pp. 114.

97. Heffernan, Helen, and The California School Supervisors Association. *Guiding the Young Child,* 2nd ed. Boston: D. C. Heath and Company, 1959. Pp. 362, $7.00.

98. Hinsie, Leland E. *Understandable Psychiatry.* New York: The Macmillan Company, 1948. Pp. 359, 95¢, paper.

99. Hollinshead, Byron S. *Who Should Go to College.* Staff Study for the Commission on Financing Higher Education. New York: Columbia University Press, 1952. Pp. 190. (Out of print.)

100. Hollis, Joseph W., and Hollis, Lucille U. *Organizing for Effective Guidance.* Chicago: Science Research Associates, Inc., 1965. Pp. 460, $6.75.

*101. Hoppock, Robert. *Occupational Information,* 2nd ed. New York: McGraw-Hill Book Company, Inc., 1963. Pp. 546, $7.95.

102. Horrocks, John E. *The Psychology of Adolescence: Behavior and Development,* 2nd ed. Boston: Houghton Mifflin Company, 1951. Pp. 614, $7.75.

*103. Humphreys, J. Anthony, Traxler, Arthur E., and North, Robert D. *Guidance Services,* rev. ed. Chicago: Science Research Associates, Inc., 1960. Pp. 414, $7.00.

104. Hurlock, Elizabeth. *Child Growth and Development.* New York: McGraw-Hill Book Company, Inc., 1956. Pp. 384, $6.50.

105. Hutson, Percival W. *The Guidance Function in Education.* New York: Appleton-Century-Crofts, Inc., 1958. Pp. 608, $7.50.

106. Jersild, Arthur T. *Child Psychology,* 5th ed. Englewood Cliffs, N.J.: Prentice-Hall, Inc., 1960. Pp. 506, $7.95.

107. Jersild, Arthur T. *The Psychology of Adolescence,* 2nd ed. New York: The Macmillan Company, 1963. Pp. 468, $6.75.

108. Johnson, Mauritz, Busacker, William, and Bowman, Fred Q., Jr. *Junior High School Guidance.* New York: Harper & Row, Publishers, 1961. Pp. 275, $4.50.

*109. Johnson, Walter F., Stefflre, Buford, and Edelfelt,

Roy A. *Pupil Personnel and Guidance Services.* New York: McGraw-Hill Book Company, Inc., 1961. Pp. 407, $6.95.

*110. Jones, Arthur J. *Principles of Guidance*, 5th ed. New York: McGraw-Hill Book Company, Inc., 1963. Pp. 306, $6.50.

111. Kaplan, Louis, and Baron, Denis. *Mental Hygiene and Life.* New York: Harper & Row, Publishers, 1952. Pp. 422, $4.95.

112. Kaplan, Oscar J. (ed.). *Encyclopedia of Vocational Guidance,* Volumes I and II. New York: Philosophical Library, Inc., 1948. Pp. 1422.

113. Kemp, C. Gratton. *Perspectives on the Group Process —A Foundation for Counseling with Groups.* Boston: Houghton Mifflin Company, 1964. Pp. 388, $5.95.

114. Kuder, G. Frederic. *Administrator's Manual for the Kuder Preference Record—Vocational, Form C.* Chicago: Science Research Associates, Inc., revised 1960. Pp. 24, 50¢

115. Kuhlen, Raymond G. *The Psychology of Adolescent Development.* New York: Harper & Row, Publishers, 1952. Pp. 675, $7.75.

116. Kuhlen, Raymond G., and Thompson, George G. (eds.). *Psychological Studies of Human Development,* 2nd ed. New York: Appleton-Century-Crofts, Inc., 1963. Pp. 638, $3.75.

117. Lass, Abraham H. *How to Prepare for College.* New York: David White Co., 1964. Pp. 466, $5.95.

*118. Lehner, George F. J., and Kube, Ella. *The Dynamics of Personal Adjustment,* 2nd ed. Englewood Cliffs, N.J.: Prentice-Hall, Inc., 1963. Pp. 481, $6.95.

119. Leonard, Edith M., Van Deman, Dorothy D., and Miles, Lillian E. *Counseling with Parents in Early Childhood Education.* New York: The Macmillan Company, 1954. Pp. 330, $5.00.

120. Levenstein, Aaron. *Why People Work: Changing Incentives in a Troubled World.* New York: Crowell-Collier Publishing Co., 1962. Pp. 320, $3.95.

121. Lindgren, Henry Clay. *Mental Hygiene in Education.* New York: Holt, Rinehart and Winston, Inc., 1954. Pp. 574, $6.95.

122. Lindgren, Henry Clay. *Psychology of Personal Development.* New York: American Book Company, 1964. Pp. 491, $6.90.

123. Lindquist, E. F. (ed.). *Educational Measurement.* Washington, D.C.: American Council on Education, 1951. Pp. 820, $6.00.

124. Lloyd-Jones, Esther McD., and Smith, Margaret R. (eds.). *Student Personnel Work as Deeper Teaching.* New York: Harper & Row, Publishers, 1954. Pp. 362. (Out of print.)

125. Lortie, Dan C. "Administrator, Advocate, or Therapist? —Alternatives for Professionalization in School Counseling," *Harvard Educational Review,* XXXV (Winter 1965), 3–17.

126. McDaniel, J. W. *Essential Student Personnel Practices for Junior Colleges.* Washington, D.C.: American Association of Junior Colleges, 1962. Pp. 54, $1.25.

127. McGowan, John F., and Schmidt, Lyle D. (eds.). *Counseling: Readings in Theory and Practice.* New York: Holt, Rinehart and Winston, Inc., 1962. Pp. 637, $7.95.

128. McLaughlin, Kenneth F. *Interpretation of Test Results.* Washington, D.C.: U.S. Government Printing Office, 1964. Pp. 63, 30¢.

*129. Mallery, David. *High School Students Speak Out.* New York: Harper & Row, Publishers, 1962. Pp. 171, $3.75.

130. *Manual for the American Council on Education Cumulative Record Folders for Schools and Colleges.* Washington, D.C.: American Council on Education, 1947. Pp. 28, 30¢.

131. Marzolf, Stanley S. *Psychological Diagnosis and Counseling in the Schools.* New York: Holt, Rinehart and Winston, Inc., 1956. Pp. 415, $5.50.

132. Mathewson, Robert H. *Guidance Policy and Practice,* 3rd ed. New York: Harper & Row, Publishers, 1962. Pp. 397, $6.00.

*133. Miller, Carroll H. *Foundations of Guidance.* New York: Harper & Row, Publishers, 1961. Pp. 464, $6.00.

*134. Miller, Frank W. *Guidance Principles and Services.* Englewood Cliffs, N.J.: Charles E. Merrill, Inc., 1961. Pp. 426, $6.50.

*135. Miller, G. Dean, and Swanson, Edward O. (eds.). *Automation: The Threat and the Promise: The Role of the Counselor in the Manpower Revolution.* Twin City Vocational Guidance Association, Branch of National Vocational Guidance Association. Washington, D.C.: American Personnel and Guidance Association, 1964. Pp. 78.

136. Moser, Leslie E., and Moser, Ruth S. *Counseling and Guidance: An Exploration.* Englewood Cliffs, N.J.: Prentice-Hall, Inc., 1963. Pp. 432, $6.95.

137. Mueller, Kate Herner. *Student Personnel Work in Higher Education.* Boston: Houghton Mifflin Company, 1961. Pp. 570, $6.95.

138. National Manpower Council. *A Policy for Skilled Manpower.* New York: Columbia University Press, 1954. Pp. 300, $4.50.

139. Neumeyer, Martin H. *Juvenile Delinquency in Modern Society,* 3rd ed. Princeton, N.J.: D. Van Nostrand Company, Inc., 1961. Pp. 426, $6.50.

140. Nixon, Robert E., M.D. *The Art of Growing: A Guide to Psychological Maturity.* New York: Random House, Inc., 1962. Pp. 159, $1.95, paper.

141. Norris, Willa. *Occupational Information in the Elementary School.* Chicago: Science Research Associates, Inc., 1963. Pp. 243, $5.95.

142. Norris, Willa, Hatch, Raymond N., and Zeran, Franklin R. *The Information Service in Guidance: Occupational, Educational, Social.* Chicago: Rand, McNally & Company, 1960. Pp. 598, $7.00.

*143. Ohlsen, Merle M. *Guidance Services in the Modern School,* 2nd ed. New York: Harcourt, Brace & World, Inc., 1964. Pp. 515, $6.95.

144. Olson, Willard C. *Child Development.* Boston: D. C. Heath and Company, 1959. Pp. 508, $7.00.

145. *Organization and Administration of Pupil Personnel Service Programs in Selected School Systems.* Washington, D.C.: Superintendent of Documents, 1961. Pp. 73. (Out of print.)

146. *Parents' Guide to Understanding Tests.* New York: Educational Records Bureau, 1963. Pp. 43, $1.00.

147. Patterson, C. H. *Counseling and Guidance in Schools.* New York: Harper & Row, Publishers, 1962. Pp. 382, $5.25.

148. Pepinsky, Harold B., and Pepinsky, Pauline Nichols. *Counseling: Theory and Practice.* New York: The Ronald Press Company, 1954. Pp. 307, $5.50.

149. *Personnel and Guidance Journal.* Washington, D.C.: American Personnel and Guidance Association. (Ten issues annually.)

150. *Personnel Literature.* Washington, D.C.: U. S. Civil Service Commission. (Published bi-monthly.)

*151. Peters, Herman J., Riccio, Anthony C., and Quaranta, Joseph J. *Guidance in the Elementary School.* New York: The Macmillan Company, 1963. Pp. 329, $3.50.

152. Peters, Herman J., and Shertzer, Bruce. *Guidance: Program Development and Management.* Englewood Cliffs, N.J.: Charles E. Merrill, Inc., 1963. Pp. 592, $7.50.

153. Porter, E. H., Jr. *An Introduction to Therapeutic Counseling.* Boston: Houghton Mifflin Company, 1950. Pp. 224. (Out of print.)

154. Prescott, Daniel A. *The Child in the Educative Process.* New York: McGraw-Hill Book Company, Inc., 1957. Pp. 502, $7.50.

*155. *Psychological Abstracts.* Sections on Personality and Abilities, Therapy and Guidance, and Educational Psychology. Washington, D.C. American Psychological Association. (Published bi-monthly.)

156. Redl, Fritz, and Wattenberg, William W. *Mental Hygiene in Teaching,* 2nd ed. New York: Harcourt, Brace & World, Inc., 1959. Pp. 562, $6.50.

*157. Remmers, H. H., Gage, N. L., and Rummel, J. Francis. *A Practical Introduction to Measurement and Evaluation.* New York: Harper & Row, Publishers, 1960. Pp. 370, $4.75.

158. Robinson, Francis P. *Principles and Procedures in Student Counseling.* New York: Harper & Row, Publishers, 1950. Pp. 321, $3.75.

159. Robison, Sophia M. *Juvenile Delinquency: Its Nature and Control.* New York: Holt, Rinehart and Winston, Inc., 1960. Pp. 559, $6.75.

160. Roe, Anne. *The Psychology of Occupations.* New York: John Wiley & Sons, Inc., 1956. Pp. 340, $6.75.

161. Roeber, Edward C., Smith, Glenn E., and Erickson, Clifford E. *Organization and Administration of Guidance Services,* 2nd ed. New York: McGraw-Hill Book Company, Inc., 1955. Pp. 294, $6.95.

162. Rogers, Carl R. *Counseling and Psychotherapy.* Boston: Houghton Mifflin Company, 1942. Pp. 450, $6.00.

*163. Rogers, Carl R. *Client-centered Therapy: Its Current Practice, Implications, and Theory.* Boston: Houghton Mifflin Company, 1951. Pp. 560, $6.75.

164. Rogers, Carl R., and Dymond, Rosalind F. (eds.). *Psychotherapy and Personality Change.* Chicago: The University of Chicago Press, 1954. Pp. 496, $8.50.

165. Rosecrance, Francis C., and Hayden, Velma D. *School Guidance and Personnel Services.* Englewood Cliffs, N.J.: Allyn and Bacon, Inc., 1960. Pp. 373, $6.00.

166. Ross, Vivian. *Handbook for Homeroom Guidance.* New York: The Macmillan Company, 1954. Pp. 134, $4.00.

167. Rothney, John W. M. *The High School Student: A Book of Cases.* New York: Holt, Rinehart and Winston, Inc., 1953. Pp. 286, $3.25.

168. Rothney, John W. M., and Roens, Bert A. *Guidance of American Youth.* Cambridge, Mass.: Harvard University Press, 1950. Pp. 270. (Out of print.)

169. Sanderson, Herbert. *Basic Concepts in Vocational Guidance.* New York: McGraw-Hill Book Company, Inc., 1954. Pp. 338. (Out of print.)

170. Schneiders, Alexander A. *Personal Adjustment and Mental Health.* New York: Holt, Rinehart and Winston, Inc., 1955. Pp. 587, $6.50.

171. *Secondary School-College Cooperation: An Obligation to Youth.* (Clyde Vroman, chairman, Editorial Committee) Ann Arbor, Michigan: American Association of Collegiate Registrars and Admission officers, 1955. Pp. 130.

172. Shaffer, Laurence Frederick, and Shoben, Edward Joseph, Jr., *The Psychology of Adjustment,* 2nd ed. Boston: Houghton Mifflin Company, 1956. Pp. 672; $7.25.

173. Shane, Harold G., and McSwain, E. T. *Evaluation and the Elementary Curriculum,* rev. ed. New York: Holt, Rinehart, and Winston, Inc., 1958. Pp. 436, $5.25.

*174. Shartle, Carroll L. *Occupational Information: Its Development and Application,* 3rd ed. Englewood Cliffs, N.J.: Prentice-Hall, Inc., 1959. Pp. 384, $9.00.

175. Shertzer, Bruce, and Knowles, Richard T. *Teacher's Guide to Group Vocational Guidance.* Cambridge, Mass.: Bellman Publishing Co., 1964. Pp. 94, $4.00.

176. Shostrom, Everett L., and Brammer, Lawrence M. *The Dynamics of the Counseling Process.* New York: McGraw-Hill Book Company, Inc., 1952. Pp. 213, $5.50.

177. Sifferd, Calvin. *Selecting An Occupation,* 3rd ed. Bloomington, Ill.: McKnight & McKnight Publishing Company, 1962. Pp. 244, $3.50.

178. Slavson, S. R. *Child Psychotherapy.* New York: Columbia University Press, 1952. Pp. 332. (Out of print.)

179. Smith, Eugene R., and Tyler, Ralph W. *Appraising and Recording Student Progress.* New York: McGraw-

Hill Book Company, Inc., 1942. Pp. 550. (Out of print.)

180. Smith, Glenn E. *Counseling in the Secondary School.* New York: The Macmillan Company, 1955. Pp. 365, $5.50.

181. Smith, Henry P. *Psychology in Teaching,* 2nd ed. Englewood Cliffs, N.J.: Prentice-Hall, Inc., 1962. Pp. 498, $7.95.

182. Splaver, Sarah. *Your College Education—How To Pay For It.* New York: Julian Messner, Publishers, Inc., 1964. Pp. 288, $4.95.

183. Stacey, Chalmers L., and DeMartino, Manfred F. (eds.). *Counseling and Psychotherapy with the Mentally Retarded.* Glencoe, N.Y.: The Free Press, 1957. Pp. 478, $7.95.

*184. Stanley, Julian C., and Ross C. C. *Measurement in Today's Schools,* 4th ed. Englewood Cliffs, N.J.: Prentice-Hall, Inc., 1964. Pp. 512, $7.50.

*185. Stefflre, Buford (ed.). *Theories of Counseling.* New York: McGraw-Hill Book Company, Inc., 1965. Pp. 350, $6.95.

186. Stevenson, Harold W. (ed.). *Child Psychology.* Sixty-second Yearbook of the National Society for the Study of Education, Part I. Chicago: The University of Chicago Press, 1963. Pp. 550, $6.50.

187. Stoops, Emery (ed.). *Guidance Services.* New York: McGraw-Hill Book Company, Inc., 1959. Pp. 302, $6.50.

188. Stoops, Emery, and Wahlquist, Gunnar. *Principles and Practices in Guidance.* New York: McGraw-Hill Book Company, Inc., 1958. Pp. 369, $6.50.

189. Strang, Ruth, *The Role of the Teacher in Personnel Work,* 4th ed. New York: Bureau of Publications, Teachers College, Columbia University, 1953. Pp. 491, $4.00.

*190. Strang, Ruth. *The Adolescent Views Himself.* New York: McGraw-Hill Book Company, Inc., 1957. Pp. 581, $10.50.

*191. Strang, Ruth. *An Introduction to Child Study,* 4th ed. New York: The Macmillan Company, 1959. Pp. 543, $6.95.

192. Strong, Edward K., Jr. *Vocational Interests of Men and Women.* Stanford, Calif.: Stanford University Press, 1943. Pp. 746.

193. Sulkin, Sidney. *Complete Planning for College.* New York: McGraw-Hill Book Company, Inc., 1962. Pp. 320, $5.50.

*194. Super, Donald E. *The Psychology of Careers.* New York: Harper & Row, Publishers, 1957. Pp. 362, $5.75.

*195. Super, Donald E., and Crites, John C. *Appraising Vocational Fitness by Means of Psychological Tests,* rev. ed. New York: Harper & Row, Publishers, 1962. Pp. 688, $8.75.

196. Super, Donald E.; Starishevsky, Reuben; Matlin, Norman; and Jordaan, Jean Pierre. *Career Development: Self-Concept Theory.* New York: College Entrance Examination Board, 1963. Pp. 100, $2.50.

197. Tappan, Paul. *Juvenile Delinquency.* New York: McGraw-Hill Book Company, Inc., 1949. Pp. 615, $8.50.

198. *Testing Guide for Teachers.* New York: Educational Records Bureau, 1961. Pp. 43, $1.00.

199. *The Yearbook of Education, 1955: Guidance and Counseling* (ed. by Robert King Hall and J. A. Lauwerys). London, England: Evans Brothers, Ltd., 1955. Pp. 644. (New York: Harcourt, Brace & World, Inc.; out of print.)

200. Thomas, R. Murray. *Judging Student Progress,* 2nd ed. New York: David McKay Company, Inc., 1960. Pp. 516, $5.50.

201. Thompson, Ronald B. *The Impending Tidal Wave of Students.* American Association of Collegiate Registrars and Admission Officers, 1954. Pp. 48.

202. Thorndike, Robert L., and Hagen, Elizabeth. *10,000 Careers.* New York: John Wiley & Sons, Inc., 1959. Pp. 346, $8.95.

*203. Thorndike, Robert L., and Hagen, Elizabeth. *Measurement and Evaluation in Psychology and Education,* 2nd ed. New York: John Wiley & Sons, Inc., 1961. Pp. 602, $7.75.

204. Thorne, Frederick C. *Principles of Personality Counseling.* Brandon, Vt.: Journal of Clinical Psychology, 1950. Pp. 471.

205. Tiedeman, David V., and O'Hara, Robert P. *Career Development: Choice and Adjustment.* New York: College Entrance Examination Board, 1963. Pp. 115, $2.50.

206. Torgerson, Theodore L., and Adams, Georgia Sachs. *Measurement and Evaluation for the Elementary School Teacher.* New York: Holt, Rinehart and Winston, Inc., 1954. Pp. 489, $7.25.

207. Townsend, Agatha. *College Freshmen Speak Out.* New York: Harper & Row, Publishers, 1956. Pp. 136. (Out of print.)

208. Travers, Robert M. W. *An Introduction to Educational Measurement,* 2nd ed. New York: The Macmillan Company, 1964. Pp. 512, $6.95.

209. Traxler, Arthur E. (ed.). *Guidance in Public Secondary Schools.* Educational Records Bulletin No. 28. New York: Educational Records Bureau, 1939. Pp. 330, $2.00.

210. Traxler, Arthur E., and Townsend, Agatha (eds.). *Improving Transition from School to College.* New York: Harper & Row, Publishers, 1953. Pp. 166, $2.75.

211. Tyler, Leona E. *The Work of the Counselor,* 2nd ed. New York: Appleton-Century-Crofts, Inc., 1961. Pp. 352, $4.75.

212. Tyler, Leona E. *Tests and Measurements.* Englewood Cliffs, N.J.: Prentice-Hall, Inc., 1963. Pp. 116, $3.95.

*213. Venn, Grant. *Man, Education and Work: Postseconddary and Technical Education.* Washington, D.C.: American Council on Education, 1964. Pp. 184, $1.50.

*214. *Vocational Guidance Quarterly.* Washington, D.C.:

National Vocational Guidance Association. (Four issues annually.)

215. Wallin, J. E. Wallace. *Education of Mentally Handicapped Children.* New York: Harper & Row, Publishers, 1955. Pp. 486, $6.00.

216. Warburton, Amber A. *Stimulating Guidance in Rural Schools.* Washington, D.C.: American Personnel and Guidance Association, 1964. Pp. 131, $2.00.

217. Warters, Jane. *Techniques of Counseling,* 2nd ed. New York: McGraw-Hill Book Company, Inc., 1964. Pp. 478, $7.95.

218. Willey, Roy DeVerl. *Guidance in Elementary Education,* rev. ed. New York: Harper & Row, Publishers, 1960. Pp. 462, $6.50.

*219. Williamson, E. G. *Student Personnel Services in Colleges and Universities.* New York: McGraw-Hill Book Company, Inc., 1961. Pp. 474, $7.50.

220. Williamson, E. G., Layton, W. L., and Snoke, M. L. *A Study of Participation in College Activities.* Minnesota Studies in Student Personnel Work No. 5. Minneapolis: The University of Minnesota Press, 1954. Pp. 99.

221. Willis, Benjamin G., and others. *Education for a Changing World of Work.* Washington, D.C.: Superintendent of Documents, 1963. Pp. 296, $1.25.

222. Wolfle, Dael (director). *America's Resources of Specialized Talent.* New York: Harper & Row, Publishers, 1954. Pp. 333. (Out of print.)

*223. Womer, Frank B., and Frick, Willard B. *Personalizing Test Use: A Counselor's Casebook.* Ann Arbor, Mich.: Bureau of School Services, University of Michigan, 1964. Pp. 102, $1.00.

224. Woolf, Maurice D., and Woolf, Jeanne A. *The Student Personnel Program: Its Development and Integration in the High School and College.* New York: McGraw-Hill Book Company, Inc., 1953. Pp. 416. (Out of print.)

225. Wrenn, C. Gilbert. *Student Personnel Work in College.* New York: The Ronald Press Company, 1951. Pp. 590.

*226. Wrenn, C. Gilbert. *The Counselor in a Changing World.* Washington, D.C.: American Personnel and Guidance Association, 1962. Pp. 195, $2.50.

227. Wrenn, C. Gilbert, and Dugan, Willis E. *Guidance Procedures in High School.* Minneapolis: The University of Minnesota Press, 1950. Pp. 71.

228. Wrenn, C. Gilbert, Hein, Reinhard G., and Schwarzrock, Shirley P. *Planned Group Guidance.* Minneapolis: American Guidance Service, Inc., 1961. Pp. 82, $2.50.

229. Wrightstone, J. Wayne, Justman, Joseph, and Robbins, Irving. *Evaluation in Modern Education.* New York: American Book Company, 1956. Pp. 482, $7.00.

*230. Zeran, Franklin R., and Riccio, Anthony C. *Organization and Administration of Guidance Services.* Chicago: Rand, McNally & Company, 1962. Pp. 302, $6.00.

GUIDANCE FILMS

Many guidance films are either rental free or eligible for acquisition under the expanded National Defense Education Act of 1964.

REFERENCES

*231. *Films: Instructional Films for Junior/Senior High School and College,* pp. 69–72. New York: McGraw-Hill Book Company, Inc., 1964.

*232. Horkheimer, Mary F., and Diffor, John W. *Educators Guide to Free Films,* 24th ed. Randolph, Wisc.: Educators Progress Service, 1964. Pp. 631, $9.00.

233. Reid, Seerley, Grubbs, Eloyse, and Clugston, Katherine W. *U.S. Government Films for Educational Use—1963.* Washington, D.C.: Superintendent of Documents, 1963. Pp. 532, $2.75.

FILMS AND FILM STRIPS

234. *The Big Question—Choosing Your Career.* New York: Association Films, Inc. 28 minutes, 16mm. Sound. Black and white.

235. *Build a Better Boy.* Albion, Mich.: Starr Commonwealth for Boys, 1965. 27 minutes, 16mm. Color.

236. *College Perspectives.* New York: College Entrance Examination Board, 1963. 28½ minutes, 16mm. Sound. Color.

237. *Counseling Adolescents.* New York: McGraw-Hill Book Company, Inc., 1954. Black and white. Sound. Three films with follow-up film strips: *A Counselor's Day,* 12 minutes; *Using Analytical Tools,* 15 minutes; *Diagnosing and Planning Adjustments in Counseling,* 18 minutes.

238. *Drop Out.* New York: McGraw-Hill Book Company, Inc., 1963. 27 minutes. Black and white.

239. *Getting Along with Parents.* Wilmette, Ill.: Encyclopaedia Britannica Films, Inc., 1954. 14 minutes. Sound. Black and white or color.

240. *Helping Teachers to Understand Children,* Parts I and II. Washington, D.C.: U.S. Office of Education, 1954. 21 and 25 minutes, 16mm. Sound. Black and white.

241. *Jobs in Atomic Energy.* Washington, D.C.: United States Atomic Energy Commission, Division of Public Information. 12½ minutes, 16mm. Sound. Black and white.

242. *Junior High School—A Time of Change.* New York: McGraw-Hill Book Company, Inc., 1964. 11 minutes. Sound. Black and white or color.

243. *Learning To Study.* Wilmette, Ill.: Encyclopaedia Britannica Films, Inc., 1954. 14 minutes. Sound. Black and white.

244. *Manage Your Career: The U.S. Army Civilian Management Program.* Washington, D.C.: U.S. Department of the Army, 1960. 30 minutes, 16mm. Sound. Black and white.

245. *Mastery of the Law*. Ann Arbor, Mich.: University of Michigan, 1960. 28 minutes, 16 mm. Sound. Color.

246. *Meeting the Needs of Adolescents*. New York: McGraw-Hill Book Company, Inc., 1953. 16 minutes. Sound. Black and white.

247. *Nature of a Job*. Detroit: Wayne University, 1953. Film Strip. 50 frames. Silent. Black and white.

248. *Next Year is Now*. Boston: John Hancock Mutual Life Insurance Co., 1962. 27½ minutes, 16mm. Sound. Black and white.

249. *Personality and Emotions*. Wilmette, Ill.: Encyclopaedia Britannica Films, Inc., 1954. 16 minutes. Sound. Black and white.

250. *Planning Your Career*. Wilmette, Ill.: Encyclopaedia Britannica Films, Inc., 1954. 16 minutes. Sound. Black and white.

251. *Prepare Through Education*. Washington, D.C.: U.S. Department of the Army, 1955. 16 minutes, 16 mm. Sound. Black and white.

252. *Thinking Collegewise*. Saxtons River, Vt.: Guidance Information Center, 1961. 20 minutes, 16 mm. Sound. Color.

253. *Three for Tomorrow*. New York: American Petroleum Institute, 1958. 28 minutes, 16mm. Sound. Color.

254. *Toward Emotional Maturity*. New York: McGraw-Hill Book Company, Inc., 1954. 11 minutes. Sound. Black and white.

255. *A University is a Teacher*. Saxtons River, Vt.: Guidance Information Center, 1961. 30 minutes. Sound. Black and white.

CHAPTER XXII

The Status and Future of Guidance in Elementary and Secondary Schools

A CAPSULE REVIEW OF THE BACKGROUND

FIFTY YEARS AGO, ONLY THE CREATIVE DREAMERS envisioned planned school guidance programs, and these only to provide better advisement to prepare young people for vocations. There were no school counselors, and such advice as was given was handled by administrative personnel and teachers.

Forty years ago in this country, a few venturesome and experimentally inclined schools, mainly in certain large cities, were beginning to make tentative explorations with programs of guidance for pupils at the secondary school level. The term "counselor" was still so rare that there was no standardization of even the spelling of the word in educational literature.

Thirty years ago, many more school people were talking about guidance and trying to do something about it; organizations of persons interested in guidance were beginning to appear.

Twenty years ago, "a guidance program" was a common term in the vocabulary of school administrators, for it had great public relations value. Some of the more modern schools had in truth developed first-rate programs of guidance. Rogers had publicly enunciated his theory of "nondirective guidance" which inspired both staunch support and raucous unbelief. "Testing-and-guidance" was frequently used as though the term were one indivisible word. There was some discussion of the need for formation of a strong national organization through a merger of the then-existing guidance and personnel associations, but the American Personnel and Guidance Association was still some years in the future.

Ten years ago, many specialists representing various schools of thought in education, psychology, sociology, and medicine were turning their attention to the guidance field. The proponents of "directive" and "nondirective" counseling were carrying on a lively debate. Professional guidance and counseling personnel was finding a basis of orientation in the APGA and its several departments. Many secondary schools and some elementary schools had introduced organized guidance programs under the direction of professional personnel, and personnel work at the college level was receiving increased attention. The administration of scholastic aptitude and achievement tests and the keeping of cumulative records were widely established in schools throughout the country. Although there was greater stress on vocational than educational guidance, the term "college counseling" was being used with increasing frequency. Mounting guidance costs were a bothersome problem in the less affluent communities.

The past decade has seen major progress in guidance and counseling at all educational levels. Elementary school guidance is now a widely-accepted concept, and one that is being applied in the schools of numerous communities. Much of the progress in guidance services may be attributed to Title V of the NDEA, which is helping many schools to meet the financial problem of improved guidance. Current guidance literature may, however, give an impression of somewhat greater professionalization of guidance than actually exists in the schools. Many articles and symposia by guidance leaders are concerned almost exclusively with client-centered theory and practice, while systematic measurement and the use of the results in counseling tend to be frowned upon. More down-to-earth articles by *school* guidance personnel frequently reveal an eclectic point of view, along with a conviction that an educational measurement program is essential, and an

351

awareness of an insistent need for increasing the efficiency of maintaining cumulative records.

A SURVEY OF CURRENT GUIDANCE PRACTICE

A brief survey carried on in the spring of 1965 among member schools of the Educational Records Bureau provides some information concerning the status of guidance in public and nonpublic schools. At the time of the survey, the Bureau's membership of some 950 institutions included, among others, 95 public schools and public

from that in the independent schools. There were, in addition, several public school systems in small- and medium-size cities, and school systems in three large cities. The Bureau member public schools may be regarded as a sampling of superior public school education in the United States. A number of public schools that have long held national renown for the quality of their educational and guidance services are included in the group.

The independent schools likewise are known for high-quality education. With only a fraction of the enrollment of the public schools in the nation, they train a large proportion of the future leaders. In view of the comparatively small size of these schools, their guidance services

---

Name of school _____ City _____

Grades included _____ Enrollment _____

Do you have an organized guidance program in secondary school? _____
elementary school? _____

Full-time guidance director? Yes _____ No _____ Part-time? Yes _____ No _____
Do your teachers perform guidance functions? Yes _____ No _____

How many full-time trained counselors? _____ Part-time? _____

Do you have a regular, comprehensive testing program? Yes _____ No _____

Maintain cumulative record cards? Yes _____ By hand? _____ By machine? _____
No _____

Are your counseling services based on any particular theory of counseling such as "client centered," "directive," "eclectic," etc.? If so, what one? _____

---

school systems and 780 independent schools within the United States. There were, in addition, 26 member colleges, 12 educational and psychological clinics and remedial education centers, and approximately 40 independent schools located in other countries.

A postal-card questionnaire was sent in April, 1965 to the 780 independent school members and the 95 public school members within the United States. The independent schools included boarding and day schools; boys', girls', and coeducational schools; elementary schools, secondary schools, and schools covering the entire K-12 grade range; schools with pupil enrollments of less than 25 to more than 800; and both church-related schools and nonsectarian private schools.

The majority of the public school members were schools in suburban communities where the ability, as well as the educational goals, of the pupils was not greatly different

naturally tend to be somewhat more informal than those of the public schools, but these services should be of general interest because of the importance of independent school education in our national life.

THE QUESTIONNAIRE AND THE RESPONSE

The brief questionnaire submitted to the independent and public schools is shown above.

Of the 780 independent schools receiving the postal-card questionnaire, replies were received from 576, or slightly more than 75 percent, in time to be used in the study. Of the 95 public schools, 70 schools, or 74 percent, replied. Response from the entire group of public and independent schools was 75 percent. The high percentage of response may be attributed to the fact that the questionnaire was short enough to be answered quickly and easily, and, further, that all schools receiving the questionnaire were members of the organization submitting it.

INFORMATION YIELDED BY THE QUESTIONNAIRE

In order to present a view of the status of guidance in Bureau member schools without becoming too detailed, it was necessary to combine a number of grade ranges. Schools including Grades K–6, K–8, 1–7, 3–8, and so forth, were grouped together as elementary schools. Similarly, schools covering Grades 7–12, 8–12, 9–12, and 10–12 were classified as one group of secondary schools— although separate computations were first made in order to determine whether any noteworthy differences existed. The group designated as K–12 included some schools with a lesser grade range, such as 1–12, 3–12, 1–10, but the majority extended from kindergarten through Grade 12.

Responses to all questions submitted to the schools, except one, are summarized in Table 9. Replies to the remaining question will be treated separately.

Of the schools responding, it will be noted that more than four fifths of the independent schools and all the public schools have organized programs of guidance at the secondary school level, while at the elementary school level only about 30 or 40 percent have introduced guidance in an organized way. At both levels, the proportion of the public schools reporting organized guidance services somewhat surpasses that of the independent schools.

As of the spring of 1965, only a little more than one fourth of the independent secondary schools and schools including Grades K–12 have a full-time guidance director, while more than half of these schools have a part-time director of guidance. Nearly eight ninths of the public secondary schools, and two thirds of the K–12 schools employ a guidance director full time. Among the elementary schools, the proportion having a guidance director either full time or part time is relatively small for both independent schools and public schools.

The high proportion of schools that say their teachers perform guidance functions may be somewhat surprising to leaders in the guidance profession. More than 90 percent of the independent secondary schools and schools including both elementary and secondary grades report that guidance functions are performed by their teachers; this is also true of more than 80 percent of the independent elementary schools. The percentage of public schools

TABLE 9. Percentage of Affirmative Replies to Certain Questions Concerning Guidance

Question	Secondary Schools Percentage		Elementary Schools Percentage		Grades K-12 Percentage	
	I.S. N=213	P.S. N=38	I.S. N=150	P.S. N=7	I.S. N=222	P.S. N=25
Organized guidance program?	84	100	29	38	81[a]	100[a]
Full-time guidance director?	29	87	8	43	27	68
Part-time guidance director?	57	8	21	4	52	20
Teachers perform guidance functions?	91	50	82	71	93	76
Regular comprehensive testing program?	94	100	97	100	98	100
Maintain cumulative records?	98	100	95	100	95	100
By hand?[b]	94	95	97	100	95	90
By machine?[b]	6	13	1	0	4	20
Particular guidance theory?	33	66	25	29	23	72
Client-centered?[c]	44	48	54	50	35	60
Directive?[c]	10	8	3	0	18	11
Eclectic?[c]	34	44	30	50	43	33
Other?[c]	12	0	13	0	4	0

[a] These percentages pertain to the secondary school grades.
[b] Percents shown are percentages of schools that do keep cumulative records.
[c] Percents shown are percentages of schools that say they have a particular theory of guidance.

that say their teachers perform guidance functions is smaller; but, even so, half of the secondary schools, and close to three fourths of the K–12 school systems report that their teachers participate in guidance.

Anyone who believes that systematic testing has no place in guidance programs may find cause for concern in the responses to the questionnaire. From 94 to 98 percent of the independent schools and 100 percent of the public schools state that they carry on a regular, comprehensive testing program. It must be noted, however, that these are responses of member schools of an organization whose main business is test service. It seems improbable that so large a percentage of affirmative replies would be received from a completely random sampling of independent and public schools.

The proportion of Bureau member schools maintaining cumulative records is equally high. From 95 to 98 percent of the independent schools and all of the public schools report that they keep cumulative records. Again, however, the percentages should be higher for ERB member schools than for schools in general, since the Bureau has always stressed the importance of cumulative records in both instruction and guidance.

For the great majority (from 90 to 100 percent) of the schools cooperating in this survey, both public and independent, the making of entries on the record is still a hand operation. (A few schools did not answer this question.) The percentage of independent schools using machine methods in maintaining records is negligible, but a number of the public schools have changed, or are in the process of changing, to data processing equipment. Because they are in a transition stage, a few public schools indicated that they were using both hand and machine methods for processing their cumulative records.

One of the most interesting parts of this survey is the question concerning guidance theory. As mentioned earlier, much of the current professional literature reads as though there were only one theory of guidance, with all counseling oriented around a client-centered theory. Yet, of the schools replying to the questionnaire, only from one fourth to one third of the independent schools indicated that they had any theory of guidance. The proportion of public schools is higher, but even among these schools, from about one third to one fourth indicated that they had no particular theory.

The schools that do adhere to some one theory tend by a rather narrow margin to favor the client-centered theory over an eclectic approach. Small percentages of both independent and public schools say that their guidance services are directive, and a few of the independent schools mention other theories. All together, only about half of the public schools and less than half of the independent

schools that admit to a guidance theory adhere to the client-centered theory.

A question in the survey asked for the number of full-time and part-time counselors in the school. The replies indicated that the median for the independent schools was one full-time counselor or two part-time counselors, although a few of the larger schools had as many as five full-time counselors or ten part-time counselors. For the public schools, the median number of full-time counselors was four or five, depending on the type of school. Because of great differences in size among the public school systems, the range in number of full-time counselors was very wide, extending, in the case of one large city school system, up to 62. The number of part-time counselors in the public schools was negligible.

For the public schools, the number of students per counselor is a more meaningful figure: however, this would be less useful information for the independent schools because so much of the counseling in those schools is done by part-time counselors. For the 68 public schools, the range is from less than 50 to more than 2500 students per counselor. The distribution is greatly skewed in a positive direction. The median number of students per counselor is 400. The Q_3 is 725 and the Q_1 is 263. The median, 400, is somewhat high in relation to what is desirable. The first quartile, 263, is within the range 250–300, the ratio of students to counselors recommended by Conant[1] as desirable for public secondary schools. Thus, only about one fourth of even such high-quality public schools as are represented in the ERB membership equal or surpass a widely publicized standard for the ratio of students to counselors.

To recapitulate the results of a questionnaire on guidance services submitted to member schools of the Educational Records Bureau:

1. The great majority of the secondary schools and a substantial minority of the elementary schools have organized guidance programs.

2. A minority of the independent schools employ a full-time guidance director, but the majority of the others have a part-time director. The majority of the public schools have a full-time guidance director at the high school level, while, as one might expect, the services of such directors are less frequent at the elementary school level.

3. Teachers perform some guidance functions in the great majority of Bureau member schools. The percentage is higher in independent schools than in public schools.

4. A regular, comprehensive testing program is uni-

[1] James B. Conant. *The American High School Today,* p. 44. New York: McGraw-Hill Book Company, Inc., 1958. Pp. v + 140.

versal in the public schools cooperating in the survey, and approaches universality in the independent schools.

5. Cumulative records are maintained by all the co-operating public schools and by nearly all the independent schools. The cumulative records in more than 90 percent of the schools are maintained by hand. A small percentage of the public schools and a negligible proportion of the independent schools have changed or are changing to data processing for keeping the records up to date. This transition may be expected to increase in the future.

6. Somewhat less than one third of the independent schools, and somewhat more than two thirds of the public schools state that they adhere to a particular theory of guidance. The client-centered theory and the eclectic viewpoint are about equally favored, with the client-centered theory receiving the slightly greater emphasis. A small proportion of both independent and public schools admit to being directive in their approach to counseling.

If one may assume that schools which say they have no particular guidance theory are, in reality, eclectic in their guidance services, a reasonable assumption, then eclecticism (freedom to choose the procedure or the combination of procedures believed to fit the child and the situation) and not necessarily client-centeredness or nondirectiveness, plays a dominant role in guidance as currently practiced in Bureau member schools.

7. The independent schools, with their comparatively small enrollments and their low pupil-teacher ratios, find less need for full-time counselors than do the public schools. Depending on their size, they tend to have from one to four full-time counselors or from two to ten part-time counselors. In most instances, the part-time counselors presumably devote the rest of their time to teaching.

The suburban public schools in the Bureau membership typically employ four or five full-time counselors. For the entire group of public schools taking part in the survey, the median pupil-counselor ratio is 400 to 1, with less than one fourth of the schools having a pupil-counselor ratio of 250 to 1 or less. With more funds for guidance and counseling available through the revised and expanded NDEA, this is a situation that seems likely to improve in the near future.

A LOOK TOWARD THE FUTURE OF GUIDANCE

The only way to estimate, with some dependability, the future in any area of education is through an assessment of past and present trends considered against the general background of present, and probable future, national and international conditions and developments.

Guidance seems to be reaching an age of maturity as a profession. There is ample room in it for both generalists, such as well-trained classroom teachers, and specialists, such as school psychologists, psychometrists, and college-admissions specialists. The need for abundant, up-to-date information about emerging vocational and educational opportunities is increasing rapidly; counselors must be equipped, willing, and ready to transmit this information to their counselees. To this extent, counselors have to be "directive"; yet they should not lose sight of the merits of the empathetic approach that has been developed through the client-centered technique.

That the United States is now in the midst of a quiet revolution in science and industry, and is going through a major social upheaval, is vividly portrayed by Paradis, in a book that high school counselors might well recommend for student reading in connection with educational and vocational guidance. In *You and the Next Decade* (5), Paradis projects current developments to 1975, citing the probable consequences in education and vocations of the imminent population explosion, the civil rights movement, electronic automation, cybernation, programed instruction, lifelong education, space exploration, supersonic jet travel, synthetic food, atomic energy, solar energy, laser beams, and cyrogenics. In connection with his discussion of each of these, Paradis lists the types of trained personnel that will probably be needed, describes the type of work likely to be involved, and gives sources of information for relevant occupational literature.

Some current trends in testing and the implications for the next decade, as seen by nine test specialists, were discussed by Bauernfeind (3). One of these specialists, Stanley R. Ostrum, Director of Test Development of the California Test Bureau, observed that the instructional program in American education is being revitalized, and he predicted that "elaborately standardized tests designed to be effective for five to ten years may be replaced by tests that will be revised and restandardized more often, but on a much more modest scale" (3:298). Arthur E. Smith, Director of Educational Services of the National Merit Scholarship Corporation, made this comment:

Today the same test is usually given to all students in one grade level. For how many students in, say, the seventh grade would the same aptitude, achievement, or interest test be completely appropriate? For how many in the same group might another test be more appropriate? Within a few years, perhaps with the aid of testing machines, it should be possible to administer the most appropriate tests to an individual at the optimum points of his development. Once there are sequential testing programs based on significant individual differences which relate to the objectives of the school, the expenditure of time and money for testing will make sense to the student, his teachers, and his parents (3:308).

Bauernfeind drew the following inferences from the ideas submitted by the nine test specialists:

Judging from these nine writings, it appears likely that ten years from now there will be (1) a greater diversity of measuring instruments; (2) a much greater emphasis on specific subject-matter achievement testing; (3) a relative de-emphasis of group mental ability or IQ testing; (4) test programs that are much better engineered in terms of publication, administration, scoring, and reporting; (5) progress toward either a master set of national norms for all tests, or equivalence tables for cross-relating sets of national norms that have been independently developed; and (6) progress toward eliminating unnecessary duplication of measurement in school testing programs (3:319).

The central trend in testing seems to be toward clarifying the traits being measured, tailoring the tests for specific individual needs, and making provisions for the prompt use of the results in helping the individual to learn and to move forward successfully toward his goals. The speed of reporting and analyzing test results will probably be increased in the years to come; and more efficient ways to use cumulative record data will probably be developed.

In fairly recent years, testing and counseling have been subjected to public criticism by a few journalists and free-lance writers. As Barclay points out, some of these critics show personal bias and faulty logic, but some of their charges do represent "deficiencies in present professional conduct and training programs" (2:16). As remedies, Barclay recommends "membership in professional organizations, a clearer understanding of the use of testing, some new considerations in counselor-training, and a systematic program to inform the public."

In the first part of this chapter, we noted some facts about guidance services in a sampling of "good" public and private schools. These facts and the other conditions cited above, when looked at in the light of what we know about guidance in the past, enable us to offer these tentative suggestions concerning the future:

1. A discernable guidance profession is evolving and is developing a concept of itself; a concept which includes elements of education, psychology, measurement, social case work, group dynamics, and cybernetics, and yet is fusing these to create a new thing. The professionalization of guidance will continue because the times demand more and better trained counselors, and because

the NDEA makes increased funds available for this training.

2. At the same time, guidance will not, in the foreseeable future, become the sole prerogative of professional counselors in the sense that medicine is the domain of M.D.s, legal matters of lawyers, and accounting of C.P.A.s. There are three main reasons for this statement. First, the number of professional counselors is still far from large enough to meet guidance needs. Second, school administrators and the public generally do not clearly differentiate the abilities, procedures, and techniques of counselors and counseling, from those of teachers and teaching. And, third, there is virtually no convincing research that, in the practical school situation, guidance by professional counselors is more helpful to individual pupils than guidance provided by other functionaries. This is not to say that such evidence could not be obtained, but it is to say that any evidence presently available on the matter is too fragmentary to be convincing.

3. The trend toward a full-time professional guidance director in each school or school system will continue. While there may always be some small schools whose size and financial condition do not make this feasible, it seems likely that nearly all schools will eventually have on their faculty a professionally trained person to assume leadership in the school's guidance responsibilities. This person will be conversant with developments in counseling, educational and vocational opportunities, measurement, and record keeping.

4. At the counselor-counselee level, however, the situation is less clear. The number of full-time counselors will almost certainly increase. All schools that can afford it will wish to have, as a minimum, one full-time college counselor and one full-time vocational counselor. The ideal ratio of students to counselor will probably be reduced from the present 250–300:1 to 200:1. But in many schools, much of the counseling will necessarily be done by persons who are part-time counselors and part-time teachers. The gap between the attitudes, approaches, and techniques of counselors and teachers will narrow, as teachers learn more and more to concentrate their efforts on the individual student and his needs, and as counselors come to understand their counseling function as a learning process.

5. In the future, the greatest growth in professional guidance will take place at the elementary school level. This is because until recently elementary schools have depended almost entirely upon their teachers to perform guidance functions. Hence, there is more room for growth in professional counseling in these schools than in higher units of the educational system. Teachers will continue to be the main counseling functionaries for

elementary school children, but the tendency already under way to utilize professional guidance leadership will continue and will grow.

6. Secondary schools and colleges, and elementary schools as well, are already pretty largely saturated with the philosophy and techniques of educational and psychological measurement and the maintenance of cumulative records. Sporadic attacks upon testing in the public press and in lay books will continue, although in diminished number as the novelty of this type of attack wears off. Notwithstanding these occasional statements against testing, the amount of measurement and record keeping will continue to increase, for these instruments meet administrative and educational needs and are, moreover, encouraged by public funds made available by government agencies.

7. To an increasing degree, high-speed electronic computers and data-processing equipment will become handmaidens of guidance. These will be used by large and medium-size school systems, by colleges and universities, and by state departments of education to produce rapid, low-cost test records, and summaries of social histories, anecdotal material, counseling interviews. Complete individual pupil cumulative records will eventually be produced in this way, speedily and at a cost of a few pennies per pupil. But herein lies not only a benefit but a danger as well. For, in order to take advantage of these marvelous developments, schools must sacrifice their initiative and freedom to experiment with new and different recording procedures. They must stay within the limits of a code and be content with coded information intelligible only to one who has the key. The development of this equipment will no doubt be a necessity because of the huge numbers of students to be educated and guided; but it should be recognized for what it is— a concession to necessity and not a step forward in the excellence of individual pupil records.

8. Community psychological and remedial agencies, and boards of cooperative educational services for larger units than local school systems, will, to an increasing degree, furnish specialized personnel, and serve as referral agencies for resolving those difficulties of individual pupils that the schools themselves are not prepared to handle.

9. During the decades ahead, counselors will probably give more attention to helping girls and women make better use of their abilities and talents in educational and vocational pursuits. In the 1963 report of the President's Commission on the Status of Women, this challenge to counselors was made:

Because of differences in life patterns of women as contrasted with men, the counseling of girls and women is a specialized form of the counseling profession. From infancy,

roles held up to girls deflect talents into narrow channels. Among women of all levels of skill there is need for encouragement to develop broader ranges of aptitudes and carry them into higher education. Imaginative counseling can lift aspirations beyond stubbornly persistent assumptions about "women's roles" and "women's interests" and result in choices that have inner authenticity for their makers.

Individuals should be helped to find out what alternatives exist, aided to reach judgments about them, and encouraged to make plans and take appropriate steps to execute them.

Lack of parental stimulation often conditions grade school youngsters from low-income families to settle for less education than their abilities warrant even before they reach high school. Daughters of families that are well able to pay for higher education too often see no reason for going as far as they could. In both cases, counselors can supply missing motivation (1:13–14).

10. A theory of counseling, something which is indistinct or nonexistent in the majority of schools, will emerge. It will reflect the Rogerian client-centered influence, but will be essentially eclectic as applied to counseling in the schools. Guidance will center upon the individual student and his needs, but guidance officers will freely use cumulative history data in gaining as full an understanding of the individual as possible. They will expect the student to take the lead in decision making pertinent to his own future, and will even thrust this role upon him; but they will not regard the word "directive" as inherently bad, and they will not hesitate to make limited use of directive procedures when, in their judgment, the occasion and the counselee's bewilderment require action and not vacillation. They will be mature enough to accept, when necessary, a degree of positive responsibility for the decisions of their counselees, regardless of the shibboleths of any particular point of view. Then will guidance have arrived at a professional status comparable to medicine or law.

11. For students who have idealistic tendencies and who are willing to put their abilities to work, service in the Peace Corps will probably continue to offer special opportunities. Counselors should be aware of the objectives of the Peace Corps as defined by Congress in 1961, namely "to promote world peace and friendship by making available to interested countries Americans who will: (1) help the people of these countries meet their needs for trained manpower; (2) help promote a better understanding of the American people on the part of the peoples served; and (3) help promote a better understanding of other peoples on the part of the American people." The Director of the Peace Corps, Sargent Shriver, states: "Thousand of volunteers are today doing important jobs in developing nations around the world. As they do their jobs, they present a new concept of America to their co-workers and those who live

around them. And they are participating in a continuing education experience that will be meaningful to them for the rest of their lives" (6:3).

In the words of John F. Kennedy, "We are at the beginning of an era when the inroads of poverty, hunger, and disease will be lessened and when men and women everywhere will have it within their power to develop their potential to the maximum."[2] Counselors of tomorrow will have much to do with the realization of this power.

REFERENCES

1. *American Women.* Report of the President's Commission on the Status of Women. Washington, D.C.: U.S. Government Printing Office, 1963. Pp. v + 86.

2. Barclay, James R. "The Attack on Testing and Counseling," *Personnel and Guidance Journal,* XLIII (September 1964), 6–16.

3. Bauernfeind, Robert H. *Building a School Testing Program.* Boston: Houghton Mifflin Company, 1963. Pp. xvii + 343.

4. Johnson, Walter F., Jr. "Our Impact on Tomorrow," *Personnel and Guidance Journal,* XXXVIII (September 1959), 15–18.

5. Paradis, Adrian A. *You and the Next Decade.* New York: David McKay Company, Inc., 1965. Pp. ix + 179.

6. Public Affairs Staff. *Opportunities in the Peace Corps: A Fact Booklet* (S. Norman Feingold, ed.). Washington, D.C.: B'nai B'rith Vocational Service, 1963.

7. Traxler, Arthur E. "Guidance in E.R.B. Member Schools: A Survey," *1965 Achievement Testing Program in Independent Schools and Supplementary Studies,* pp. 71–75. Educational Records Bulletin No. 88. New York: Educational Records Bureau, 1965. Pp. xii + 75.

[2] President Kennedy's speech at Denver, Colorado, October 14, 1960.

Indexes

Index of Names

Abbott, Winona, 145
Adams, Georgia Sachs, 327, 329, 338, 339, 342, 348
Afflerbach, Janet, 80
Ainsworth, Mary D., 117, 122
Alcorn, Marvin D., 325, 328
Allen, Frederick H., 309, 317
Allen, Richard D., 9, 11, 203, 291, 294, 300
Allen, Robert M., 120
Alley, Otis E., 88
Allport, Floyd H., 101, 109, 111
Allport, Gordon W., 101, 109, 110, 111, 120, 123
Ames, Louise Bates, 117, 120, 126, 146, 344
Anastasi, Anne, 331, 338, 342
Anderson, Kenneth E., 88, 325, 327
Anderson, L. Dewey, 67
Anderson, Rose G., 61, 62, 71
Anderson, Roy N., 70
Anderson, Scarvia, 12, 154, 342
Andrew, Dean C., 17, 333, 343
Andrew, Dorothy M., 68, 70
Angers, William P., 307
Apostal, Robert, 32
Appell, M. L., 307
Arbuckle, Dugald S., 29, 289, 314, 317, 333, 343
Arnold, Dwight L., 318
Aron, Betty, 116, 120
Arthur Philip, Brother, 289
Ashbaugh, E. J., 239, 267
Ashcraft, Kenneth, 289
Attwell, Arthur A., 327
Aumack, Gordon D., 295, 300
Axelrad, Sidney, 337, 344
Ayer, Fred C., 185

Babcock, Virginia F., 88
Baer, Max F., 27, 29, 300, 324, 328, 337, 343
Baker, Harry J., 67, 110
Baker, John Q., 307
Baker, Robert L., 269, 283, 289
Baldwin, Alfred L., 145, 307, 331, 343
Ball, Rachel S., 146
Ball, W. N., 300
Baller, Warren R., 269, 307
Banks, Waldo R., 29
Barahal, George D., 293, 300
Barbe, W., 283
Barclay, James R., 179, 356, 358

Bardon, Jack I., 290
Barlow, Melvin L., 337, 343
Baron, Denis, 94, 289, 332, 346
Barr, A. S., 145
Barrett, Dorothy M., 69, 70
Barrett, E. R., 83
Baruch, Dorothy W., 337
Bauernfeind, Robert H., 94, 154, 355, 356, 358
Beall, John V., 29
Beals, Lester, 29
Bear, Robert M., 90, 91
Bechtold, Mary Lee, 17
Beck, Samuel J., 99, 117, 120
Becker, Elsa, 185
Beckman, R. O., 101, 120
Bedell, Ralph, 90
Beers, Lester D., 88
Beery, John R., 301
Bell, Hugh M., 29, 101, 110, 120
Bellak, Leopold, 116
Beloff, Halla, 111
Bennett, George K., 29, 57, 58, 59, 60, 67, 69, 70, 274, 283, 339, 343
Bennett, Margaret E., 327, 328, 336, 343
Bennett, Marjorie G., 57, 58
Bennett, Richard E., 87
Benton, Arthur L., 67, 70
Berdie, Ralph F., 12, 29, 111, 179, 300, 317, 338, 342, 343
Berg, Irwin A., 327
Bergstein, Harry B., 317
Bernard, Harold W., 94, 289, 332, 343
Bernreuter, Robert G., 101, 111, 120
Beymer, L., 328
Bickel, Charles L., 88
Bicker, H., 145
Billett, Roy O., 111
Bingham, Walter V., 37, 42, 339
Birnbaum, Max, 29, 343
Bixler, Harold H., 80
Blackmer, Alan R., 344
Blade, Mary F., 70
Blake, Walter S., Jr., 28, 33
Blanchard, Howard L., 333, 343
Blatz, William E., 127, 145
Bloom, Benjamin S., 70, 83, 94
Blyth, M. Isobel, 87
Bodel, John K., Jr., 88
Bolmeier, E. C., 241, 243, 244, 267
Bonan, Frederic, 86
Bonney, Merl E., 142, 144, 145
Bonney, Warren C., 145, 322, 326, 328

Bonsall, Marcella Ryser, 108, 118
Bordin, Edward S., 307, 333, 343
Borow, Henry, 321, 329, 337, 343
Bott, E. A., 127, 145
Bowes, Fern H., 145
Bowman, Douglas J., 17
Bowman, Fred Q., 334, 345
Bowman, Howard A., 81, 234
Boyd, Gertrude A., 289
Bradfield, James M., 94
Bradford, Jeanne M., 78
Bradford, Leland P., 328
Brainard, P. P., 111
Brainard, R. T., 111
Brammer, L. M., 293, 300, 347
Branan, John M., 312, 317
Branom, M. E., 79
Brant, Richard M., 317
Brantley, G. D., 238, 242, 267
Breese, Fay Huffman, 145
Brewer, John M., 274, 283, 337, 343
Brewster, Royce E., 17, 294, 300
Brickman, Leonard, 12
Brieland, Donald, 142, 145
Brinkman, Albert R., 335, 344
Bristow, A. B., 185
Britton, Ralph D., 153
Broedel, John, 328
Brooks, Nelson, 84, 85
Brown, B. Frank, 154
Brown, D. F., 301
Brown, Fern G., 292, 300
Brown, Frederick G., 78, 94
Brown, James I., 83
Brown, Marion, 126, 133, 145
Brown, W. Gordon, 88
Brown, William F., 119, 121
Brownstein, Samuel C., 27, 29
Bruce, Harold W., 68
Brueckner, L. J., 79
Brundage, Erven, 29
Bryan, Miriam, 80
Bryan, Roy C., 267
Bucher, Charles A., 28, 33
Budd, G. F., 145
Buckham, Kenneth, 318
Buonanno, Bernard J., 203, 291
Burack, Marvin, 328
Burke, Paul J., 78, 79
Burnham, Paul S., 70
Buros, Oscar, 56, 57, 58, 59, 60, 61, 62, 63, 64, 65, 66, 67, 68, 70, 78, 79, 80, 81, 82, 85, 88, 91, 93, 94, 97, 99, 100,

361

Index of Subjects

List of Publishers

Allyn and Bacon, Inc.
Englewood Cliffs, N.J.

American Association of Advertising Agencies
200 Park Ave.
New York, N.Y.

American Association of Junior Colleges
1777 Massachusetts Ave., NW
Washington, D.C. 20006

American Book Company
55 Fifth Ave.
New York, N.Y. 10003

American College Testing Program
Box 168
Iowa City, Iowa 52240

American Council on Education
1785 Massachusetts Ave., NW
Washington, D.C. 20006

American Educational Research Association
1201 16th St., NW
Washington, D.C. 20006

American Guidance Services, Inc.
720 Washington Ave., SE
Minneapolis, Minn.

American Institute of C.P.A.s
666 Fifth Ave.
New York, N.Y. 10019

American Institute of Mining and
  Metallurgical Engineers
345 East 47th St.
New York, N.Y.

American Personnel and Guidance Association
1605 New Hampshire Ave., NW
Washington, D.C. 20009

American Petroleum Institute
Committee on Public Affairs
1271 Avenue of the Americas
New York, N.Y

American Psychological Association
1333 16th St., NW
Washington, D.C. 20006

American Statistical Association
810 18th St., NW
Washington, D.C. 20006

Appleton-Century-Crofts, Inc.
440 Park Ave So.
New York, N.Y. 10016

Barron's Educational Series, Inc.
113 Crossways Park Drive
Woodbury, N.Y. 11797

Beacon House Press
Box 311
Beacon, N.Y.

Bellman Publishing Company
Cambridge, Mass.

B'nai B'rith Vocational Service
1640 Rhode Island Ave., NW
Washington, D.C. 20006

The Bobbs-Merrill Company, Inc.
4300 W. 62nd St.
Indianapolis 6, Ind.

William C. Brown Co.
Dubuque, Iowa

Bureau of Educational Measurements
Kansas State Teachers College
Emporia, Kan. 66801

373

Bureau of Educational Research
School of Education
University of Oregon
Eugene, Ore.

Bureau of Educational Research and
   Service
State University of Iowa
Iowa City, Iowa

Bureau of Occupational Information and
   Guidance
California State Department of Education
721 Capitol Ave.
Sacramento 14, Calif.

Bureau of Publications (Teachers College Press)
Teachers College
Columbia University
New York, N.Y. 10027

Bureau of School Services
University of Michigan
Ann Arbor, Mich. 48104

California Test Bureau
Del Monte Research Park
Monterey, Calif.

University of California Press
Berkeley, Calif.

The Catholic University of American Press
620 Michigan Ave., NE
Washington, D.C. 20017

Center for Psychological Service
George Washington University
Washington, D.C.

Chamber of Commerce of the United States
1615 H St., NW
Washington, D.C. 20006

Channel Press
400 Community Drive
Manhasset, N.Y.

The University of Chicago Press
5750 Ellis Ave.
Chicago, Ill. 60637

College Entrance Examination Board
475 Riverside Drive
New York, N.Y. 10027

Columbia University Press
2960 Broadway
New York, N.Y. 10027

Committee on Diagnostic Reading Tests, Inc.
Mountain Home, N.C.

Consulting Psychologists Press, Inc.
270 Town and Country Village
Palo Alto, Calif.

Copley Productions
434 Downer Place
Aurora, Ill.

Cornell University Press
124 Roberts Place
Ithaca, N.Y

Coronet Films
Coronet Building
Chicago, Ill. 60601

Crowell-Collier Publishing Co.,
640 Fifth Ave.
New York, N.Y.

Division of Educational Reference
Purdue University
Lafayette, Ind.

Division of Research and Field
   Service
Indiana University
Bloomington, Ind.

Doubleday & Co.
Garden City, N.Y.

Educational Records Bureau
21 Audubon Ave.
New York, N.Y. 10032

Educational Test Bureau
720 Washington Ave., SE
Minneapolis 14, Minn.

Educational Testing Service
Princeton, N.J. 08540

Educators' Progress Service
Randolph, Wisc.

Educators' Tests & Services Associates
120 Detzel Place
Cincinnati 19, Ohio

Encyclopaedia Brittannica Films, Inc.
Wilmette, Ill.

Foster and Stewart
Henry Stewart, Inc.
210 Elliott St.
Buffalo, N.Y.

The Free Press
60 Fifth Ave.
New York, N.Y. 10011

The Fund for the Advancement of
   Education

477 Madison Ave.
New York, N.Y. 10022

General Motors Corporation
Department of Public Relations
Detroit, Mich.

Ginn and Company
72 Fifth Ave.
New York, N.Y. 10011

Government Printing Office
Washington, D.C. 20025

Grune & Stratton, Inc.
381 Park Ave. So.
New York, N.Y. 10016

The Gryphon Press
220 Montgomery St.
Highland Park, N.J.

Guidance Information Center
Academy Ave.
Saxtons River, Vt.

Harcourt, Brace & World, Inc.
757 Third Ave.
New York, N.Y. 10017

Harper & Row, Publishers
49 E. 33rd St.
New York, N.Y. 10016

Harvard University Press
44 Francis Ave.
Cambridge 38, Mass.

D. C. Heath and Company
285 Columbus Ave.
Boston 16, Mass.

Holt, Rinehart and Winston, Inc.
383 Madison Ave.
New York, N.Y. 10017

Houghton Mifflin Company
2 Park St.
Boston 7, Mass.

Inor Publishing Company
205 Lexington Ave.
Sweet Springs, Mo.

Institute for Personality and
   Ability Testing
1608 Coronado Drive
Champaign, Ill.

International Business Machines Corp.
Armonk, N.Y.

International Textbook Company
1001 Wyoming Ave.
Scranton 9, Pa.

International Universities Press, Inc.
227 W. 13th St.
New York, N.Y

Interstate Printers and Publishers, Inc.
Danville, Ill.

John Hancock Mutual Life Insurance Co.
Public Relations Department
200 Berkeley St.
Boston 7, Mass.

Journal of Clinical Psychology
Brandon, Vt.

The Julian Press
80 E. 11th St.
New York, N.Y. 10003

J. B. Lippincott Company
East Washington Square
Philadelphia 5, Pa.

McGraw-Hill Book Company, Inc.
330 W. 42nd St.
New York, N.Y. 10036

David McKay Company, Inc.
750 Fifth Ave.
New York, N.Y. 10017

McKnight & McKnight Publishing Company
Towanda Ave.
Bloomington, Ill.

The Macmillan Company
60 Fifth Ave.
New York, N.Y. 10011

Charles E. Merrill Books, Inc.
Englewood Cliffs, N.J.

Julian Messner, Publishers, Inc.
8 W. 40th St.
New York, N.Y.

Methods & Materials Press
Springfield, N.J.

University of Michigan
Audio-Visual Education Center
720 E. Huron St.
Ann Arbor, Mich. 48104

The University of Michigan Press
Ann Arbor, Mich. 48104

The University of Minnesota Press
2029 University Ave., SE
Minneapolis 14, Minn.

National Association of Independent
   Schools
4 Liberty Square
Boston 9, Mass.

National Association of Secondary-School
  Principals
1201 16th St., NW
Washington, D.C. 20036

National Education Association
1201 16th St., NW
Washington, D.C. 20036

New American Library of World Literature, Inc.
501 Madison Ave.
New York, N.Y.

W. W. Norton & Company, Inc.
55 Fifth Ave.
New York, N.Y. 10003

The Odyssey Press, Inc.
55 Fifth Ave.
New York, N.Y. 10003

Office of Education
Department of Health, Education, and
  Welfare
Washington 25, D.C.

Oxford University Press
Fairlawn, N.J.

The Personnel Press, Inc.
20 Nassau St.
Princeton, N.J. 08540

Philosophical Library, Inc.
15 E. 40th St.
New York, N.Y.

Porter Sargent
11 Beacon St.
Boston 8, Mass.

Prentice-Hall, Inc.
Englewood Cliffs, N.J.

Project TALENT Office
University of Pittsburgh
Pittsburgh, Pa.

The Psychological Corporation
304 E. 45th St.
New York, N.Y. 10017

Psychometric Affiliates
1743 Monterey
Chicago, Ill. 60643

Public Affairs Press
Washington, D.C.

G. P. Putnam's Sons
200 Madison Ave.
New York, N.Y.

Rand McNally & Company
Chicago, Ill.

RCA Institutes, Inc.
350 W. 4th St.
New York, N.Y. 10014

The Ronald Press Company
15 E. 26th St.
New York, N.Y. 10010

Russell Sage Foundation
230 Park Ave.
New York, N.Y.

Rutgers University Press
New Brunswick, N.J.

Scholastic Book Services
50 W. 44th St.
New York, N.Y.

Science Research Associates, Inc.
259 E. Erie St.
Chicago, Ill. 60611

Sheridan Supply Company
P.O. Box 837
Beverly Hills, Calif.

Signet Books, New American Library of
  World Literature
501 Madison Ave.
New York, N.Y.

Simon and Schuster, Inc.
630 Fifth Ave.
New York, N.Y.

South-Western Publishing Company
Cincinnati, Ohio

Stanford University Press
Stanford, Calif.

Starr Commonwealth for Boys
Albion, Mich.

The Steck Co.
P.O. Box 2028
Austin, Texas 78767

State University of Iowa
Iowa City, Iowa

C. H. Stoelting Co.
424 N. Homan Ave.
Chicago, Ill. 60624

Superintendent of Documents
Washington 25, D.C.

Syracuse University Press
Syracuse 10, N.Y.

Taconic Foundation
666 Fifth Ave.
New York, N.Y.

U.S. Atomic Energy Commission
Division of Public Information
Washington, D.C. 20045

U.S. Department of the Army
Washington 25, D.C.

D. Van Nostrand Company, Inc.
24 W. 40th St.
New York, N.Y.

Vocational Advisory Service
23 E. 26th St.
New York, N.Y.

Vocational Guidance Center
371 Bloor St., W.
Toronto 5, Canada

Wadsworth Publishing Co.
Belmont, Calif.

Wayne University Press
Detroit, Mich.

Western Psychological Services
10655 Santa Monica Boulevard
Los Angeles 25, Calif.

David White Co.
60 E. 55th St.
New York, N.Y.

John Wiley & Sons, Inc.
605 Third Ave.
New York, N.Y. 10016

The H. W. Wilson Company
950 University Ave.
New York, N.Y. 10052

Yale University Press
New Haven 7, Conn.